A HISTORY OF
ENGLISH DRAMA
1660–1900

A HISTORY OF
ENGLISH DRAMA
1660-1900

BY

ALLARDYCE NICOLL

VOLUME II
EARLY EIGHTEENTH
CENTURY DRAMA

THIRD EDITION

CAMBRIDGE
AT THE UNIVERSITY PRESS
1961

PUBLISHED BY
THE SYNDICS OF THE CAMBRIDGE UNIVERSITY PRESS

Bentley House, 200 Euston Road, London, N.W.1
American Branch: 32 East 57th Street, New York 22, N.Y.
West African Office: P.O. Box 33, Ibadan, Nigeria

First Edition   1925
Second Edition 1929
Third Edition   1952

Issued as Volume II of
A History of English Drama 1660–1900

Reprinted   1955
                  1961

First printed in Great Britain at the University Press, Cambridge
Reprinted at Whitefriars Press, Tonbridge

PREFACE

IN preparing this volume I have allowed as much as possible of the original text (published in 1925) to stand. Some portions have been rewritten and corrections have been made throughout, but for the most part new material and references to the many recent studies devoted to special aspects of the subject have been placed in the supplementary sections to the various chapters, which appear together after page 407.

Although the register of performances is fuller than the corresponding registers in other volumes in this series, I have allowed the lists to stand, chiefly because the information they present is at present unobtainable elsewhere. It should, however, be emphasised that this Hand-list must be used in close conjunction with the supplementary notes, since the facts given in these notes expand and occasionally correct the information printed in the main text.

A. N.

ABBREVIATIONS

Drury Lane (D.L.)
Lincoln's Inn Fields Theatre, old building (L.¹)
Lincoln's Inn Fields Theatre, new building (L.²)
King's Theatre (Opera House) in the Haymarket (H.¹)
Little Theatre (French House) in the Haymarket (H.²)
Goodman's Fields Theatre (G.F.)
Covent Garden Theatre (C.G.)
New Wells, Clerkenwell (N.W.)
Bartholomew and Southwark Fairs (B.F. and S.F. with name of owner of booth)
May Fair (May F. with name of owner of booth)

CONTENTS

Chapter One
THE THEATRE

PAGE

I. Introductory 1

II. The Audience 8

III. The Theatre 25

IV. The Actors and Actresses 39

Chapter Two
TRAGEDY

I. Introductory: The Tendencies of the Age . . 51

II. Elizabethan, Restoration and Foreign Models . . 66

III. Heroic Dramas: 1700–1750 74

IV. Pseudo-Classic Tragedies 85

V. Augustan Tragedies 96

VI. Domestic Tragedies, and Plays of Private Woe . . 114

Chapter Three
COMEDY

I. Types of Augustan Comedy 125

II. Elizabethan, Restoration and Foreign Models . . 139

III. Comedies of Manners 147

IV. Comedies of Intrigue 165

V. Comedies of Humours 174

VI. Comedies of Sensibility 179

VII. Farces 208

CONTENTS

Chapter Four

MISCELLANEOUS FORMS OF DRAMA

PAGE

I. Introductory 218

II. Tragi-Comedies and Pastorals 220

III. Italian and English Operas 225

IV. Ballad-Operas 237

V. Pantomimes 251

VI. Masques and Political Plays 258

VII. Burlesques and Rehearsals 262

Appendix A

THE THEATRES: 1700–1750 271

Appendix B

SELECT DOCUMENTS ILLUSTRATING THE HISTORY OF THE
  STAGE 274

Appendix C

HAND-LIST OF PLAYS: 1700–1750:

  i. English Plays and Operas 294

  ii. Italian Operas, Oratorios and Serenatas . . 387

  iii. Repertoire of the French and Italian Comedians. 400

Supplementary to Chapter One 408

Supplementary to Chapter Two 415

Supplementary to Chapter Three 418

Supplementary to Chapter Four 424

Supplementary to Appendix A 429

Supplementary to Appendix C 430

INDEX 453

CHAPTER I

THE THEATRE

I. *Introductory*

IF, in dealing with the drama of the Restoration period, it was noted that that subject, when compared with Elizabethan theatrical productivity, had been comparatively neglected, it may be said that the drama of the years which followed, from 1700 onwards to the middle of the nineteenth century, had been almost entirely forgotten by scholars and critics. Sir A. W. Ward, progressing further than most, brought his dramatic history to a close with the year 1714; Nettleton has hurried rapidly over these years of "decay" and of "disintegration"; Genest has presented a selection of dramatic performances from 1660 to 1830; a few individual writers have touched upon minor aspects of the theatre of the time; but no one has ever attempted to analyse in anything like fullness the whole dramatic productivity of the age, from *Cato* and *The Conscious Lovers* to the flimsiest of pantomimes and the silliest of Italian operas.

A period of decay and disintegration it was in many ways. Sentimentalism, during the first half of the eighteenth century, was steadily gathering way and banishing laughter from the stage. Classicism, imported from France, was slowly driving out the more natural expression of true emotion. Pantomime was usurping the attention of the play-goers and vitiating their taste for higher forms of comedy and of tragedy. Italian opera succeeded in breaking down the desire for more legitimate drama. In no wise can it be denied that, as we watch the drama progressing from 1610 to the end of the eighteenth century, we see in general only a retrograde movement, arrested at moments, in the early years by men such as Ford and Shirley, in the later by others such as Dryden and Otway and Congreve and Steele, but moving nevertheless relentlessly along the one inevitable path. The study of an art form in its decay is not a pleasant thing; and if this were all perhaps the greater oblivion that could fall on the dramatic productivity of those years the better.

The more we come to analyse this period of the drama, however, the more we come to realise that the retrograde movement so apparent on the surface was countered by a series of forward developments, never carried to artistic fulfilment in those years, but of boundless significance when we carry our gaze onwards to our own times. The drama certainly has seen a remarkable rebirth in the last years of the nineteenth century, but that rebirth is to be understood aright only when it is associated historically with the dramatic work of the preceding two centuries. Sentimentalism thus may have killed the comedy of Congreve for a time, but out of that sentimentalism grew the larger humanitarianism which followed, out of it too came an entirely new dramatic type, the *drame*. Classicism may have succeeded in stifling to a certain extent the freer expression of tragic passion, but in the very midst of the classical movement developed and flourished that strange species of tragedy, which was destined to pass over to France and later to Germany, influencing Diderot and Lessing and Kotzebue and Schiller, ultimately travelling to the north and giving rise there to Ibsen and Björnson and Strindberg. Fundamentally, Ibsen, the master of our present-day English dramatists, is the descendant of George Lillo, forgotten playwright of 1730. If, therefore, we do not find any startling masterpieces in this age, we discover many forms of dramatic art which show that the creative spirit was still alive in the theatre. *The Conscious Lovers* was in reality a new form of drama; and so was *The London Merchant*. Italian opera was a novelty in England, and the Italian *Commedia dell'arte* gave rise now to native English pantomime. *The Beggar's Opera* was a new discovery, how charming and how fascinating yet, may be realised by those who have had the pleasure of witnessing one or another of the recent thousand odd performances at the Lyric Theatre, Hammersmith.

Still a further note may be made concerning the study of drama in these years. Not only was the theatre then as always a sure index of public taste and of almost intangible literary and intellectual movements, but it was intimately in touch with nearly all the great men of letters of the time. It is true that Pope, disgusted with the reception of his one and only play, abandoned the playhouse, and that Swift remained purely the pamphleteer, the poet and the novelist, but apart from those the drama was eagerly patronised by almost all the men famous now for their poetry and their prose. Steele was the great populariser of the sentimental comedy; Addison with his *Cato* set up a landmark in the history of tragedy; Fielding was a prolific playwright before ever he even thought of *Joseph Andrews* or of *Tom Jones*; Thomson and Young both wrote tragedies for the stage. Even those men of letters of the time who did not actually pen plays were keenly interested in the playhouses. It was Swift who, according to rumour, gave Gay his idea for *The Beggar's Opera*. Only through a study of the stage of these years can we gain a true impression of the literary development and ideals of the early eighteenth century; even particular works, such as Pope's *The Dunciad*, cannot properly be appreciated until we enter into the mysteries of the daily repertoire of Drury Lane and of Lincoln's Inn Fields and of the Haymarket.

Such a study can in no wise be dissociated from the actual history of the theatres themselves. In this respect, we note in this half century many changes which serve to mark it out from the period of the Restoration. The interest in drama now became more wide-spread. A new trading class had arisen and was taking its place alongside the older aristocracy. The Court no longer formed the entire focus of public attention, and with this fundamental alteration from Stuart days, numerous changes are to be witnessed in the theatre and in the plays written for the theatre. The whole of sentimentalism and of the bourgeois tragedy is, of course, to be associated with this rise of the middle classes, but the movement must be traced in greater detail if we are to

appreciate it aright. New theatres, independent of the old
patent houses, were springing up to accommodate the larger
audience—the Queen's Theatre in the Haymarket, the French
House in the Haymarket, the Little Theatre in Lincoln's Inn
Fields, the Theatre Royal in Covent Garden, the two playhouses in Goodman's Fields[1]—and outside of London
interest in the drama was penetrating rapidly. Tentatively
provincial theatres began to emerge, being utilised by
regular stock companies as well as by the touring players
and the lesser strollers with their "drolls[2]." Bath had its
theatre now, for which Mrs Centlivre wrote one of her
comedies[3], as had Tunbridge Wells, where was presented by
the Duke of Richmond's Servants about 1712 *Pastora: or, The
Coy Shepherdess*, Norwich, Richmond[4] and a number of other
towns. Dublin, too, had its well-established theatre, vying
with the playhouses in London, providing for those playhouses, sometimes actors[5], sometimes dramas[6]. Interest in

---

[1] For notes on the theatres and the dramatic companies see Appendix A.

[2] That these drolls were still played, both in the provinces and in
the theatrical booths at the London Fairs, is proved by the advertisements in the newspapers and by the collection of dramatic pieces called
The Stroler's Pacquet Open'd (1742). The old strolling companies still
persisted, and new ones were springing into being. An interesting account
of one of these is to be found in Mrs Charlotte Charke's own *Narrative*
of her life in which she describes her "various and surprizing vicissitudes
of fortune, during nine years peregrination" (1755). That the older companies still were in being is proved by an advertisement for S. July 4,
1724, when a band of comedians travelling under a licence granted
by Charles II promised to perform *The Recruiting Officer* at Epsom
Wells.

[3] *Love at a Venture* (New Theatre, Bath, acted by the Duke of Grafton's
Servants, and printed in 1706).

[4] There seem to have been two or three theatres at Richmond. One
was in existence in the early years of the eighteenth century. Another
was built by Pinkethman in 1718. It was described in the *St James's
Evening Post* for T. June 3 of that year. In 1730 another playhouse
was erected higher up the hill than Pinkethman's and was occupied
for a time at least by the L.I.F. players (see *The Daily Journal*, W. June 3,
1730).

[5] For a number of those actors and actresses who started their theatrical
careers in Ireland see W. R. Chetwood's *A General History of the Stage*
(Dublin 1749).

[6] Coffey's *The Beggar's Wedding*, for example, seems first to have been
acted in Dublin, and was later brought over to the Haymarket and Drury
Lane.

the theatre penetrated even into Puritan Scotland; there, too, we find theatres arising and companies performing. Our sphere of study, therefore, is considerably wider than it could have been in the whole of the period from 1660 to 1700, and that enlarged sphere of study is due chiefly to the break away of drama from the Court atmosphere and the inclusion in the playhouse of other elements driven away from the drama in the days of Charles II. It is certainly true that for the first years of the period we hear the old complaints concerning the bad way of the playhouses and the paucity of spectators. We know in what a state the Drury Lane company was about 1700 through the secession of the Lincoln's Inn Fields actors. "About this Time," we are told, "the *English* Theatre was not only pestered with Tumblers, and Rope-Dancers from *France*, but likewise Dancing-Masters, and Dancing-Dogs; shoals of *Italian* Squallers were daily imported; and the *Drury-Lane* Company almost broke[1]." The same complaint is made in the preface to Cibber's *The Lady's Last Stake* (H.[1] 1707), and in *Farewel Folly* (D.L. 1705) we are informed that theatrical matters were "very grave at one House; and not very merry at the other[2]." The regular actors evidently suffered heavily in face of other counter-attractions, so that we are not surprised when we find that some of the People of Quality in 1707 felt themselves obliged to open a subscription to encourage the drama[3]. The Lincoln's Inn Fields theatre seems to have suffered in the early years of the century, and later in the twenties. In the verse satire entitled *The Players turn'd Academicks: or, A Description (in Merry Metre) Of their Translation from the Theatre in Little Lincolns-Inn-Fields, to the Tennis-Court in Oxford* (1703), an anonymous writer provides us with the information that "*never was such wretched Acting seen by those who go under the Name of* Her Majesty's Servants." This probably explains the notes in

---

[1] Curll, E., *The Life of That Eminent Comedian Robert Wilks, Esq;* (1733), p. 8.
[2] See for the alleged reason, *infra*, p. 38.
[3] An account of this subscription is given in Cibber's *Apology* (ed. Lowe, ii. 4–5). The prologue written especially for this occasion by Dennis and supposed to be spoken by the spirit of Shakespeare is printed in *The Muses Mercury* for Jan. 1706–7.

The Daily Courant advertisements for *The Libertine* (May 1, 1704) and *Don Quixote* (August 9, 1704): "not to dismiss tho' the Audience should be small" and "we shall not dismiss, let the Audience be what it will." The miserable straits into which this playhouse had fallen about 1719 is testified by many authors. The preface to Theobald's *The Tragedy of King Richard the II* (L.² 1719) and that to Sewell's *The Tragedy of Sir Walter Raleigh* (L.² 1719) show that the actors of this house were being neglected; in the same year a subscription was opened to enable them to carry on[1]. That this subscription was necessary is proved by the remark of "Corinna" in her *Critical Remarks on the Four Taking Plays Of this Season* (1719) that *Sir Walter Raleigh* was acted at a playhouse which was the contempt of the town. As Gabriel Rennel in his *Tragi-Comical Reflections of a Moral and Political Tendency, occasioned By the Present State of the two Rival Theatres in Drury-Lane and Lincolns-Inn-Fields* (1725) puts it: "A Winter or two ago the *Theatre* in *Lincolns-Inn-Fields*, commonly called the *New-House*, was ready to expire under the severest Frowns of Fortune and the Town. The *Actors* were reduced to a more hungry and ragged Condition than a *Company* of *Country-Strolers*. They were *miserable* in more than one Sense, and were now almost as generally pitied as they once had been despised....In short, every Body fled from a Set of People who looked like *real Ghosts*, and who *appeared* in such *frightful Shapes* as scared even *Parsons* and *Undertakers* from their House[2]." Some sort of a recovery seems to have been made[3],

[1] The dedication to Lord Brooke of Leigh's *Kensington-Gardens* (L.² 1719) speaks of "the noble Example you have shewn, in being the first Subscriber towards the Support of our Theatre." Settle's *The Lady's Triumph* (L.² 1718) was dedicated to these subscribers. For some details concerning the takings at this house see B.M. Egerton MS. 2321–2322.

[2] pp. 7–8.

[3] Whincop (p. 231) attributes this turn of affairs to the production of Fenton's *Mariamne* in 1723. "And very happy," he says, "it was for that House that this Play was brought thither, it giving a new Turn to its Affairs; for till *Mariamne* was performed there, the Stage at *Lincolns-Inn-Fields* had been so neglected, and the Actors in so little Esteem, that, except upon some extraordinary Occasions, they hardly received half Money enough to defray their Expences, nay, oftentimes acted to Audiences of five or six Pounds."

so that we find Fielding in *The Historical Register, For the Year 1736* (H.² 1737) commenting on the success of Lincoln's Inn Fields and attributing that success to the presence of mirrors there¹. Later still, however, towards the end of this period, Theophilus Cibber testifies in the preface to his adaptation of *Romeo and Juliet* (H.² 1744) to the popularity of the Haymarket theatre and the consequent decline of the rest. He calls to mind especially "one filthy, foggy, dismal, dreary Night...when one of the Theatres-Royal debated, till very late, whether they should play or no, to a most scanty Company; and the other Theatre-Royal forbore to light the Candles, which the thin Appearance they had would hardly enable them to pay for, and so courteously dismissed the very few who through foul weather had come to see them²." These complaints appear again and again during the fifty years, but they are complaints which are, after all, eternal and hardly confined to one half-century. The fact remains that two and sometimes three theatres were running constantly in London, in place of the one and occasional two of Restoration times. No doubt the author of *A Proposal For the better Regulation of the Stage* (1732) was nearer the truth when he declared "'Tis very visible that this great *Metropolis* can support two Theatres, beside the *Opera*, in all the Elegancy, and Expence of Entertainment³."

The tradesmen, moreover, who aided in the success of more theatres than the days of Charles II had known, did not confine themselves to being merely spectators. Coming into the theatres, they, like the courtiers of a former reign, started to write plays. These efforts of theirs, naturally, were both for the bad and for the good. Lillo brought a new world into the playhouse, but not all had the talents of Lillo. There are at least two outspoken prefaces of the period in which the respective authors declare that they had but scanty knowledge of the art which they were attempting. No doubt these two were but a couple representative of many less brave than they. In the Restoration age the bulk of the plays produced were written by a dozen men—Dryden, Shadwell,

¹ 1.   ² p. 78.   ³ p. 43.

Settle, D'Urfey, Otway, Southerne, Tate, Congreve, Etherege and Wycherley are the chief. In the early eighteenth century we are startled at the number of one-play writers. There are, certainly, Fielding and Mrs Centlivre and Cibber who were prolific playwrights, but fully half of the dramas produced during this time were penned by men unassociated with literature and uneager for literary glory. There are twice as many individual dramatists in the one period as in the other, and more than four times the number of anonymous plays. Undoubtedly many of these unliterary authors aided at once in destroying the brilliance of the comedy of manners, and in introducing new motives and new themes destined to provide the basis for the modern stage.

II. *The Audience*

It must not be presumed, of course, that the audience, suddenly and in a few years, changed entirely its character, or that even in the last portion of this period the atmosphere of the theatres was middle class rather than aristocratic. If anything, the air of eighteenth century London was more "fashionable" than it had been before; and only too many of the richer middle class aped the manners and the vices of the People of Quality. All that can be said is that the body of spectators was larger than it had been, that the middle classes were growing in importance and power, and that the close connection between Court and theatre was for ever shattered.

There are, in this connection, two exceedingly interesting contemporary pronouncements, interesting not only because they show us the character of the audience, but because they reveal a consciousness in the minds of some critics at least of the change which had come over the theatres in the early years of the century. The first is in Dennis' *The Comical Gallant* (D.L. 1702), where he contrasts the audience of Charles II's time with that of his own day. The former spectators, he believes, were more intelligent; they were capable of judging for themselves on the merits of plays; now there were too many counter-attractions and too much business to be done to leave their minds free. What those counter-attractions and that business were is explained to us by Steele in *The Tatler*.

"The Place," he says, "is very much altered since Mr. *Dryden* frequented it; where you used to see *Songs*, *Epigrams*, and *Satyrs*, in the Hands of every Man you met, you have now only a Pack of Cards; and instead of the Cavils about the Turn of the Expression, the Elegance of the Style, and the like, the Learned now dispute only about the Truth of the Game[1]."

The extent to which this passion for cards drew audiences away from the theatres is emphasised in the epilogue to Mrs Centlivre's *The Gamester* (L.[1] 1705):

> *In vain we Labour to divert your Care,* ⎫
> *No Song, nor Dance can Bribe your Presence here,* ⎬
> *You fly this Place like an Infectious Air.* ⎭
> *To yonder happy Quarter of the Town,*
> *You Croud; and your own Fav'rite Stage disown.*

The audience, agreed all, had degenerated, and Steele was but voicing a general opinion when he indulged in bitter irony: "The Play of *The* London *Cuckolds* was acted this Evening before a suitable Audience, who were extremely well diverted with that Heap of Vice and Absurdity[2]."

These words show us fairly clearly the true state of things during the first years of the century. The audience was as dilettante, as little serious, as the audience of Dryden; it was at the same time more frivolous and not by any means so intelligent. Its mind was fluttered by trivial things, and the gaming tables, so satirised by Mrs Centlivre and by Colley Cibber, and only too much frequented by the latter, formed the centre of their thoughts. Still, the theatre was a meeting-place, a fashionable amusement rather than a place of art. Any outside thing could divert the attention of the spectators. Charles Shadwell considered himself lucky because his *The Fair Quaker of Deal* (D.L. 1710) was a success, "notwithstanding the Tryal in *Westminster Hall*, and the Rehearsal of the new Opera[3]." Even gossip about new plays could destroy

---

[1] *The Tatler*, No. 1, April 8, 1709.
[2] *Id*. No. 8, April 26, 1709.
[3] Preface.

enthusiasm for others. Welsted's *The Dissembled Wanton*
(L.[2] 1726), we are told by Whincop[1], "came out at the Time
when the Town was big with Expectation of Mr. *Moor
Smyth*'s Play; but I believe, had Mr. *Welsted*'s Comedy not
appeared till after *The Rival Modes*, it would have had better
Success." We know how in the last years of the seventeenth
century, Farquhar's *A Trip to the Jubilee* (D.L. 1699) destroyed the career of other new plays; and as late as 1728 we
find Fielding complaining that his *Love in Several Masques*
(D.L. 1728) came out when *The Provok'd Husband* was playing
and "contemporary with an Entertainment which engrosses
the whole Talk and Admiration of the Town[2]." Many a
writer felt the evils of this fashionable and would-be-
fashionable audience, and not only one echoes the words of
Chaves in *The Cares of Love* (L.[1] 1705):

> *What foolish Frenzy does our Bard possess?*
> *To write a Play, yet hope from you success?*
> *To bring old Customs on our Modern Stage,*
> *When nought but Farce and Song can please the Age?*

Good plays, thought this writer, might go down with a rough
audience, as in Shakespeare's time, but now,

> *The homely Treat of Nature ne'er will hit;* ⎫
> *That's too Mechanic, and too obsolete* ⎬
> *To please Our finer Taste of Box and Pit...* ⎭
> *Old Shakespear's Genius Now is laid aside,*
> *And Johnson's Artful Scenes in vain are try'd;*
> *Otway and Wycherley, tho' Bards Divine,*
> *Whose Nervous Passion, Wit and Humour shine,*
> *To empty Benches to Our Cost we Play.*

The fashionable vices, the fashionable dilettanteism, and the
fashionable thoughtlessness were largely responsible for that
"ridiculous *Corruption* of our *Theatrical Entertainments*[3],"
for "our present *Polite Taste*, when nothing will go down
but BALLAD-*Operas* and Mr. LUN's Buffoonery[4]." Steele's

---

[1] p. 301.

[2] Preface. The entertainment probably was Gay's *The Beggar's Opera*,
which had been produced nearly a fortnight previously.

[3] Curll, E., *The Life of That Eminent Comedian Robert Wilks, Esq;* (1733),
preface, p. vii.

[4] *Id.* p. 11.

reference to "the present Taste of Theatrical Representations[1]," although more vague, points to the same corruption of appreciation. The theatre was midway between two extremes. It was not universal as in Shakespeare's time, and it was not aristocratic as in the time of the Restoration; it was merely fashionable.

Nor was the playhouse cured by any means of that licence which distinguished it in the days of Dryden. Steele could not refrain from taking notice in *The Tatler*[2] of a "Young Nobleman, who," in the midst of a performance of *The Country Wife* at Drury Lane, "came fluster'd into the Box" and created confusion among a group of ladies attended by their cavaliers. Drunkenness in the theatres was still a common thing; the aristocrats still regarded the playhouse as something of their own. "As infamous a Fellow as ever broke the Head of a Box-Keeper," is a chance remark of Sir Friendly in Cibber's *The Lady's Last Stake* (H.[1] 1707) and it is suggestive of much. In 1700 Sir Andrew Stanning was mortally wounded as he came out of a theatre[3]. On Monday, Dec. 14, 1702 we are informed in *The Daily Courant* a duel took place on the stage between a Mr Fielding and a Mr Goodyer[4]. Powell's riotous misdemeanours are chronicled by Fitzgerald[5], and the forcible entry into Drury Lane on Nov. 22, 1709 is well known[6]. There was a disturbance at the theatre in 1717[7], and a duel took place at Lincoln's Inn Fields during a performance of *The Modish Citizen* the following year[8]. A bill of 1720 for the same theatre mentions the riots occasioned by gentlemen coming behind the scenes[9], and on Wednesday,

[1] Preface to 1722 edition of Addison's *The Drummer*.
[2] No. 3, April 14, 1709.
[3] Fitzgerald, P., *A New History of the English Stage*, i. 231.
[4] See also E. Curll's *The Life of Mrs Oldfield*, and Fitzgerald, *op. cit.* i. 232.
[5] *Op. cit.* i. 264–5.
[6] See *infra*, Appendix A.
[7] Fitzgerald, *op. cit.* ii. 13–4.
[8] Fitzgerald, *op. cit.* ii. 12–3.
[9] Fitzgerald, *op. cit.* ii. 8; January 19, "Whereas the Liberty of the Scenes has been lately abus'd by Rioting, and disturbing the Audiences, None for the future will be admitted but who shall take Tickets at the Stage-Door." See also bill for January 26, 1719/20.

Feb. 1, 1720/1 an assault was made on the actors of that
house[1]. In May 1735 the actor Macklin succeeded in murdering
his companion Hallam by thrusting his stick into the other's
eye[2]. On Saturday, Feb. 19, 1737 occurred at Covent Garden
a riot caused by unruly footmen[3], and a few months later
there broke out the notorious riot over the French performers
licensed to play in the metropolis[4]. Barely two years
had passed by when another riot broke out at Drury Lane
consequent on Fleetwood's advertisement regarding Madame
Chateauneuf[5]. A fierce struggle burst forth at Drury Lane
during a performance of *The Rehearsal* on Tuesday, Dec. 6,
1743, organised by the friends of Macklin[6]; Saturday, Nov.
17, 1744 witnessed a riot because of the raised prices at
Drury Lane[7]; and the last year of the period, 1749, introduces
us to the riot arising out of the "Bottle Conjurer" hoax at
the Haymarket[8].

When we trace these continual disturbances, these riots and
these duels, stretching from the opening of the eighteenth
century to the close of the fifty years, we realise that the
theatre was truly in much the same position in which it had
been in 1680.

There was, besides this, an ever-growing abuse which fell

[1] Fitzgerald, *op. cit.* ii. 8.

[2] Fitzgerald, *op. cit.* ii. 112–4; there is a full account of the episode in
E. A. Parry's *Charles Macklin* (1891), pp. 26–30. For Quin's similar
behaviour see Fitzgerald, *op. cit.* ii. 120–1.

[3] See particularly *The Daily Journal*, Tuesday, Feb. 22 and *The Daily
Gazetteer*, Wednesday, Feb. 23.

[4] This was at the Little Theatre in the Haymarket, Monday, Oct. 9,
1738. See *The London Daily Post* for Tuesday the 10th and for Saturday
the 21st. An appeal of the managers of the French company was inserted
in *The London Daily Post* for November 8. Fitzgerald summarises the
episode, *op. cit.* ii. 105–7.

[5] Wednesday, Jan. 23, 1739/40. See Genest, iii. 606. *The London Daily
Post* has an account of the riot in the number for Tuesday 29th.

[6] Genest, iv. 53. See also *The London Daily Post* for Friday 9th.

[7] The riot was continued on Monday 19th. For the struggles of the
actors against the managers, especially on the particular battle waged by
Macklin, and the cause of the riot of 1743, see the pamphlets cited by
R. W. Lowe in his *Bibliographical Account of English Theatrical Literature*
(1888), pp. 95–6.

[8] Fitzgerald, *op. cit.* ii. 154–5. See *A Letter to the Town, Concerning
the Man and the Bottle* (1749) and *A Modest Apology for the Man in the
Bottle. By Himself* (1749).

heavily on many unfortunate authors. This was the disturbance caused by bodies of young men who seemed to fancy that they were privileged, on every first night, to indulge in as much noise and tumult as they cared. Reference to these rowdies is common, but possibly a few quotations here will serve to show the prevalence of the custom from the first years to the last. Miller, among all the dramatists, was the most seriously affected. In his "dramatic piece," *The Coffee-House* (D.L. 1738), we are told that he introduced scenes which some Templars believed reflected on a pet coffee-house of their own. There was a row, but it was quelled, only to break out again when it was discovered that inadvertently the engraver of the frontispiece to the printed play had chosen this very coffee-house as his model. Poor Miller's plays thereafter had but a sorry time of it. His *Art and Nature* (D.L. 1738) was thoroughly damned by his opponents, and as for *An Hospital for Fools* (D.L. 1739), it was "damn'd at the Theatre Royal...not one Word of it being heard, from the Disturbance that was in the House the only Night it was acted[1]." It was "a Time when it was the Fashion to condemn them all, right or wrong, without being heard; and when Parties were made to go to new Plays to make Uproars, which they called by the odious Name of *The Funn of the first Night*. And on the very Night I am speaking of, at the End of the Play, was acted for the first Time a new Farce, called, *An Hospital for Fools*, of which one single Word was not heard that the Actors spoke, the Noise of these First-Night Gentlemen was so great; however the Actors went thro' it, and the Spectators might see their Mouths wag, and that was all[2]." Popple in his preface to *The Lady's Revenge* (C.G. 1734) had to complain that some eight or ten young fellows came to damn his play, and, although they were ousted, the unhappy piece was withdrawn. West's *Hecuba* (D.L. 1726) "was not heard. A rout of Vandals in the Galleries intimidated the young Actresses, disturbed the Audience, and prevented all Attention[3]." In the 1761 edition of Gay, Pope and Arbuthnot's *Three Hours after Marriage*

[1] Whincop, p. 261. [2] *Id.* p. 183. [3] Preface.

(D.L. 1717) there is printed a letter, "Written by a Person of Distinction in London, To his Friend in the County of *Cornwal*," which describes the second performance of that play. After the prologue was spoken, "the storm began, and the criticks musick of cat-calls join'd in the chorus.—The play was acted like a ship tost in a tempest." In the first act of the anonymous satire called *The Contre Temps* (1727) we are presented with a "*Chorus of D...k...s, L...d...s, and Tupees rang'd on each Side the Stage, according to their Factions; Cat-calls in their Hands, and Whistles*," while Boadens in Act IV of *The Modish Couple* (D.L. 1732) draws for us what was no doubt a true picture of the times:

"I will wager you now five hundred Pounds," says Grinly, "that half a Score of us shall quite demolish the best Piece that can come on any Stage.... Very well, Sir; but now comes our time, for the third Act being begun; the first piece of Wit that is utter'd, *Hiss* cry two or three of us—In a little time after, a stroke of Humour comes out, *hoh, hoh, hoh*, cry others. Then perhaps a serious Scene comes in Play, *Yaw* say the rest, and so on, till the Play is pretty well over. And for the last two or three Scenes, where the silly Rogue thinks he has shewn his Judgment the most, and on which the whole Business of the Piece depends, we strike up such a Chorus of *Cat-calls, Whistles, Hisses, Hoops,* and *Horse-laughs,* that not one of the Audience can hear a Syllable, and therefore charitably conclude it to be very sad Stuff.—The Epilogue's spoke, the Curtain falls, and so the poor Rascal is sent to the Devil."

The terror which these fine gentlemen aroused in the breasts of author and of actor is to be seen reflected in the introduction to Fielding's *Don Quixote in England* (H.² 1734), where the Player enters all trembling to announce that "there are two or three of the loudest Cat-calls in the Gallery that ever were heard."

As is evident from the above references, faction, personal and political, often influenced deeply the minds and actions of the "first-nighters." Colley Cibber, when he had advanced in fame and importance, had an experience somewhat similar to that encountered by Miller. His *The Non-Juror* appeared in 1717, and was met with a chorus of praise from the anti-Catholic party; it raised up for its author, however, enemies

enough among the Jacobites[1]. His next play, *The Refusal*
(D.L. 1721), had nothing to do with political or religious
controversy, but his "Enemies shew'd themselves very
warmly at" its "Representation...they began to hiss it before
they had heard it, and I remember" (it is Whincop who is
writing) "I remember very well, began their Uproar, on the
first Night, as soon as he appeared to speak the Prologue.
However it went on for six Nights, not without Disturbances
[at] every one of them[2]." *Cæsar in Ægypt* (D.L. 1724),
evidently, was passed over with silent contempt, but when
the actor-author brought forward *The Provok'd Husband*
(D.L. 1728), a comedy altered from an unfinished piece by
Vanbrugh, the tumult broke out again. "Such is the Power
of Prejudice," remarks the author of *A Companion to the
Play-House* (1764), "and Personal Pique in biassing the
judgment that Mr. *Cibber*'s Enemies, ignorant of what Share
he had in the writing of the Piece, bestowed the highest
Applause on the Part which related to Lord *Townly*'s Pro-
vocations from his Wife, which was mostly *Cibber*'s, at the
same Time that they condemned and opposed the *Journey to
London* Part, which was almost entirely *Vanbrugh*'s, for no
other apparent Reason but because they imagined it to be
Mr. *Cibber*'s." The following year was produced the pastoral
ballad-opera, *Love in a Riddle* (D.L. 1729), and once more
on "the first Night there was a great Disturbance in every
Part of the Performance, but when Miss *Raftor* [Mrs. *Clive*
that now is] sung; for this was the first Night of her Appearing,
and she was received with much Applause....On the second
Night was a greater Disturbance than on the first, and the
Actors would not have been suffered to go on, notwithstanding his Royal Highness the Prince of *Wales* was there,
being too, I think, the first Time he had been at the Theatre
since his Arrival in *England*, if Mr. *Cibber* had not come upon
the Stage, and assured the Audience, that if they would
permit them to go thro' the Play that Night quietly, in Respect
to the Royal Presence, he would not insist upon its being

---

[1] For the pamphlets directed against this drama see *infra*, p. 190.
[2] Whincop, p. 197.

acted the next Night for his Benefit....Yet out of this Piece, thus damned, was taken...DAMON *and* PHILLIDA, a Ballad Farce, which not coming out as a new Piece, nor Known by every Body to be *Cibber*'s, was much applauded, and has continued to be frequently acted to this Day. Which shews to what Lengths Party-Prejudice was carried against this Author[1]." Cibber's last work was *Papal Tyranny in the Reign of King John* (C.G. 1745) and this, as Whincop informs us[2], "was rehearsed privately, and brought out, on a sudden, before there was a Time to form a Party against it, and so met with Applause." In the words of Bullock, "The Rage of Party is so predominant, that ev'n publick Diversion is interrupted[3]"; a fuller account of false judgment may be found in the long address to the reader in Cibber's *Ximena* (D.L. 1712). Many a writer must have wished with Havard that "*his dismal Story*" might be "*without Offence to* Whig *or* Tory![4]" and only too many in laying their futile works before the eyes of a patron echoed Charles Johnson's words: "I humbly desire Your Protection for the following Scenes from the Rage of a Despairing Faction[5]." Early in the century Dennis in putting forward his *Gibraltar* (D.L. 1705) found many "Calamities which attended the Rehearsal" and had the mortification to experience a common fate; on the first day it was "not suffer'd to be heard[6]." The storm on this occasion seems, however, to have been greater than usual, for the author of *A Critical Specimen* (1715) suggests as the heading for a chapter in Dennis' life: "Of the Bombardment of Gibraltar, and how several Chiefs engaged in that dreadful enterprise were, contrary to the laws of Arms, almost pelted to Death with Apples and Orange-Peel[7]." Little consideration seems to have been paid as to whether a particular author deserved such a reception. Just after the Licensing Act of 1737, Jacob had performed at Covent Garden three little playlets collected together under the title, *The Nest of*

---

[1] Whincop, p. 197; cf. also Cibber's *Apology*, ed. Lowe, i. 244–5.
[2] Whincop, p. 198.   [3] *Woman is a Riddle* (L.[2] 1716), I. i.
[4] *King Charles the First* (L.[2] 1737).
[5] *The Country Lasses* (D.L. 1715), Dedication.
[6] Preface.   [7] p. 12.

Plays, but " *The first Representation of the*...Performance *was interrupted, e'er it well began, in the Presence of a numerous and polite* Audience, *by some People, who, it seems, were determined, as they themselves declared, to silence without any Distinction, the* first Fruits *of that* Act *of* Parliament *which was thought necessary for the Regulation of the* Stage[1]*."* It was not for nothing that it had long

> *been the Clamour of the Age,*
> *That Party-Feuds have rent both State and Stage*[2].

The obvious remedy for all this was to pack the audience, and that, we have good reason to believe, was done whenever possible. There were some authors too proud to accept this assistance, such as Havard, who in his *Scanderbeg* (G.F. 1733) disdainfully wrote in his prologue:

> *I ask not any to espouse my Cause,*
> *For I shou'd blush at Party-made Applause,*

but the majority had no such scruples. Dennis, in his *Remarks on a Play*, call'd *The Conscious Lovers* (1723), attacks Steele for "*the scandalous Artifices that were practis'd to secure Success*[3]," and Steele himself openly confesses that for his friend's *Cato* (D.L. 1713) he brought "together so just an Audience on the first Days of it, it should be impossible for the Vulgar to put its Success or due Applause to any Hazard[4]." It was perfectly true that, as the prologue to this play declares, the ears of the audience had long

> been filled with tragic parts,
> Blood and blank-verse have hardened all your Hearts;
> If e'er you smile, 'tis at some party strokes,
> Round-heads and wooden shoes are standing jokes!

but the remedy seems somewhat dubious. The methods which Steele and Addison adopted are excellently, if satirically, described by Dennis in *The Character and Conduct of Sir John Edgar, Call'd by Himself Sole Monarch of the Stage in Drury-Lane* (1720):

---

[1] Preface.
[2] Mrs Haywood's *The Fair Captive* (L.[2] 1721), Prologue.
[3] Preface.   [4] Preface to the 1722 edition of *The Drummer*.

So, Sir *John*, if you will pardon a little Digression, I will felicitate you upon those dextrous Politicks, by which you have so much refin'd upon his; [i.e. "your Elder Brother of *Brentford*"] and by which, when you bring any Thing upon the Stage, you secure Success to your Works. For old *Bays* was contented with the Printing a Hundred Sheets, in order to insinuate his Play into the Boxes; But you, Sir *John*, upon the like Occasion, have, by way of Lucubration and Speculation, printed a Hundred Thousand Sheets. He, poor Wretch, was satisfy'd with placing a Dozen or two of his Friends in the Pit, who were instructed to do their Duty: But you, Sir *John*, upon such an Occasion, have order'd a Thirty Pound Dinner to be got ready at the *Rose*....In short, you have almost fill'd the Pit and Galleries with your Creatures; who have been order'd, at some certain Signals, to clap, huzza, to clatter their Canes and their Heels to such a degree, that the Hissing of a Hundred Snakes could no more be heard, than in the Uproar and Din of a Battel[1].

Other dramatists before Steele, however, had tried the same game, as, indeed, Dennis acknowledges. In point of fact, the author of *The Life of Mr. John Dennis The Renowned Critick* (1734) declares that when this writer's *Iphigenia* came to be played in 1699 "His intimate Friend, Colonel *Codrington*," took "a great deal of Pains to support his Interest, at the Representation, not only by writing the *Epilogue* to it, but by engaging all his Friends to take Tickets for the Poet's Night[2]." "*Party-Claps*," no doubt instigated by the poet and his friends, predominated at the performance of Rowe's *Lady Jane Gray* in 1715[3], and Killigrew secured a patron in the Duke of Argyll "whose Interest was so powerfully supported, that it was said the Profits of his Play amounted to above a Thousand Pounds[4]." In Fielding's *Eurydice Hiss'd* (H.² 1737) may be found a satirical portrait of a poet making up a party for the first night, and there is in this connection an interesting, and in a way entertaining, dialogue in the introduction to *The Humours of the Court* (1732):

[1] p. 21.

[2] p. 21. There is, of course, a distinction between first-night and third-night support.

[3] According to the testimony of the author of *Remarks on the Tragedy of the Lady Jane Gray; in a Letter to Mr. Rowe* (1715).

[4] Whincop, p. 255. The play was *Chit-Chat* (D.L. 1719).

Player. Why as Times go any thing will go down that is dull
and out of the way, provided you have good Seconds;
but if you have not good Seconds, nothing will go down
be it ever so good.

Poet. Seconds, Sir! what are they? I never heard of them
before.

Player. Why 'tis a new Way to make a Play run, tho' 'tis never
so lame; a sort of arbitrary Government lately introduced
into the Theatre with pretty good Success.... 'Tis but
getting a little Army of Friends into the Pit, with good
oaken Towels, and long Swords, to make them look
terrible, and let them clap you lustily, and no-body will
dare hiss, for fear of being knocked down.

Besides the indignity of the practice, however, there was one
other disadvantage. Too obvious cramming of audiences
seems to have been looked on askance by people of the time.
Steele may have been successful in his efforts, but of Moore
Smythe's *The Rival Modes* (D.L. 1727) the poet Young wrote
to Tickell on Feb. 21, 1726/7: "Mr Moore's play is a bad
one, yet met, through his indiscretion, a worse reception than
as a first performance it deserved. His circumstances are
very bad, and too great an eagerness to mend them by the
profits of his play made him too pressing in the methods he
took to do it effectually, and it disgusted the town." Truly
were the authors between a Scylla and a Charybdis; no one
knew which was the lesser evil of the two.

The whole age, of course, is shot through and through
with politics. We can no more understand the stage without
a fairly intimate knowledge of the Whig and Tory contro-
versies than we can appreciate the works of Swift and of
Addison without such a knowledge. The period is not only
stacked with dozens of unacted political pieces, from ballad-
operas and farces to regular five-act tragedies, but in play
after play, apparently innocent of ulterior motives, we may
read and read rightly between the lines. Rowe's *Tamerlane*
(L.[1] 1701), which extolled William III and presented
Louis XIV as a monster of villainy, may be taken as a
typical example. How far this injured the particular dramas
depended largely on the strength of the author's convictions.

This political element was a tradition carried on from
earlier days, but alongside of the older party quarrels
there is to be discerned a note which is something of a
novelty. The only playwright of the late seventeenth century
who deliberately enunciated patriotic, as distinct from party,
sentiments, was Roger Boyle, Earl of Orrery; in the early
eighteenth century we find dramatist after dramatist em-
phasising in prologue, epilogue and body of play the glory
of England. "This Day I am of Age," cries the heroine of
Mrs Centlivre's *The Gotham Election* (1715), "and I chuse you
for my Guardian,—and if you can bring me unquestionable
Proofs of your being an Honest Man;—that you have always
been a Lover of your Country...and that you'd spend every
Shilling of my Portion, in Defence of Liberty and Property...
I'll sign, seal, and deliver myself into your Hands the next
Hour[1]." What damsel of the age of the Merry Monarch
would have thought of that? There is a note of superiority
in the speeches of the characters that sometimes amazes us.
"My Lord," declares a character in the same authoress' *The
Wonder* (D.L. 1714), "My Lord, the *English* are by nature,
what the ancient *Romans* were by discipline—courageous,
bold, hardy, and in love with Liberty[2]." Even Pyrrhus in
Dr Trapp's *Abra-Mule* (L.[1] 1704) can decide that the fair
Eastern maid

excels
Ev'n *English* Beauties[3].

Many of the heroes are filled with a boundless, or apparently
boundless, love of their own land. Sir Harry Wildair in the
play of Farquhar's to which he gives the title, abandons his
fopperies; "Look ye, Captain," says he, "give me thy hand;
once I was a Friend to *France*; but henceforth I promise to
sacrifice my Fashions, Coaches, Wigs, and Vanity, to Horses,
Arms, and Equipage, to serve my King in *propria persona*, to
promote a vigorous War, if there be occasion[4]." Similar
expressions in the prologues to Dennis' *Appius and Virginia*
(D.L. 1709), to Sewell's *Sir Walter Raleigh* (L.[2] 1719), to

---

[1] iii.   [2] i. i.   [3] ii. i.   [4] v. iv.

Havard's *King Charles the First* (L.[2] 1737), and to Frowde's *The Fall of Saguntum* (L.[2] 1727) may be taken as typical of sentiments everywhere enunciated. Some of the more intelligent authors may have seen through, and in some instances certainly did see through, the veneer of hypocrisy in all this. Amidst the numerous cries of Liberty and England Farquhar could not resist his *bon mot*—"I am a free-born *Englishman*, and will be a Slave in my own way[1]," but this is perhaps too much of a witticism to be taken seriously. Charles Johnson, however, assuredly saw through the cheat. The prologue to his *The Gentleman-Cully* (L.[1] 1701) is directed against "The Modern Patriot,"

> *a Creature*
> *Of a strange spightful Heterogeneous Nature.*
> *Love for his Country does his Breast inspire,*
> *And warms it with a mercenary Fire.*

Still later, Fielding in *The Author's Farce* (H.[2] 1730) displayed his consciousness that patriotic appeal and handkerchiefs were employed in tragedies almost entirely for effect:

> *But Handkerchiefs and* Britain *laid aside,*
> *To Night we mean to laugh, and not to chide*[2].

It is natural that in this atmosphere of party politics and of real or assumed patriotic sentiment, the censorship should have been busy. The Licensing Act of 1737 is well known, with its effects upon the theatres and upon entirely innocent dramas; a detailed account of it may therefore be omitted in this book. For the moment it may be sufficient to glance at some of the more pronounced and more peculiar aspects of the exercise of the Lord Chamberlain's privilege. The main point to be noted is that the censoring of plays was not always a question of party politics; it was most often due to the personal desire of particular politicians, and even sometimes of individuals wholly or largely unconnected with the Whig and Tory machines. Baker, for example, penned a comedy called *An Act at Oxford* in 1704, and this was suppressed because it gave offence to the authorities of the

---

[1] *The Recruiting Officer* (D.L. 1706), III. ii.
[2] Prologue.

University city. The author overcame the difficulty by renaming the *dramatis personæ* and by shifting the scene. In its altered form *Hampstead-Heath* was presented at Drury Lane in 1705. D'Urfey was within his rights in ridiculing the "conjuring" by which Baker had brought "Oxford *upon* Hampsted-heath[1]," but it was the Lord Chamberlain, not Baker, who should have been blamed. The same year Macswiny made an adaptation of Molière's *L'Amour Médecin*, styling it *The Quacks*, but it "was to be stiffled, because the other House were to Act one upon the same Subject[2]." Permission came at last, but the performance, which had been intended earlier, was deferred for some time[3]. The other play was without a doubt *The Consultation*, an unprinted comedy, presented at the Queen's Theatre, Haymarket, on April 24, 1705[4]. Vanbrugh's interest was strong enough to gain the temporary suppression of a rival work. Only two years before this date Gildon had been in similar trouble, in his case, however, for more political reasons. He had been attracted by the theme of Lee's *Lucius Junius Brutus*, and had written a tragedy on the same subject, and, presumably, with the same title. Unfortunately, Lee's drama had been, in the seventeenth century, suppressed[5], and the censor came down heavily on Gildon's effort. It was banned, and the restriction was taken off only when Gildon had restyled it *The Patriot*, changed its scene from Rome to Florence and made its hero Cosimo de' Medici. Mrs Centlivre had a prologue for her *The Perplex'd Lovers* (D.L. 1712) condemned, for what reason is not now known, and the story of Gay's *Polly* is notorious. From all accounts the office of the censor was not worked on any set plan, or even with fair play. Walter Aston in the

---

[1] *The Modern Prophets* (D.L. 1709), Preface.
[2] Preface.
[3] It was advertised for March 22, but seems not to have come out until the 29th.
[4] Jacob, p. 299, and Whincop, p. 291, both assert that *The Quacks* was acted at Haymarket. Their mistake aids in confirming *The Consultation* as the rival production. On the banning of this play see Cibber's *Apology*, ed. Lowe, i. 247, and F. Fowell and F. Palmer's *Censorship in England*, p. 120.
[5] See vol. I (1660–1700), p. 10.

dedication to his *The Restauration of King Charles II* (1732) tells us that Potter, the manager of the Haymarket theatre, on accepting the drama, warned the author it would have to go before the Lord Chamberlain or his representative. The play was given to some official, and Aston received word it might be played. He distributed the parts and had the piece put in rehearsal when, suddenly, without warning and at the last moment, came a peremptory order that it was not to be staged. The reason here no doubt was political; but there was nothing of political cause in the suppression of Mrs Charke's *The Art of Management* (York buildings, 1735). This lady had been dismissed by Fleetwood, the manager of the Theatre Royal, and wrote her play as a satire on him. It was produced at York buildings, but she too received sudden word that she "*was to suffer from Civil Power*," this time "*for exhibiting a Satyr on the Managers of* Drury Lane[1]." After the Licensing Act of 1737, of course, the number of plays suppressed increased markedly, and the number of ludicrous situations increased likewise. Brooke's *Gustavus Vasa* (1739) was banned possibly with some show of justice[2]; but there does not seem to have been such justice in the treatment of the poet Thomson, whose *Edward and Eleonora* was banned the same year[3]. As for Paterson—the suppression of his play becomes almost a joke. That author, at least according to the *Biographia Dramatica*, had been a friend of Thomson's and had unluckily copied out for him his above-mentioned tragedy. It was this copy which was sent to the Lord Chamberlain's office, and when his own *Arminius* (1740) came along, the handwriting was at once recognised. A licence was promptly and firmly refused. Kelly's *The Levee* (1741) was banned because it showed up the political patron and his notorious promises, and Fielding's *Miss Lucy in Town* (D.L. 1742), after it had been acted "some Nights with good

---

[1] Preface.

[2] See the preface to the printed copy, and also Johnson's ironical *A Compleat Vindication of the Licensers of the Stage from the Malicious and Scandalous Aspersions of Mr. Brooke, author of Gustavus Vasa. With a Proposal for making the Office of Licenser more extensive and effectual* (1739).

[3] See Fowell, F. and Palmer, F., *op. cit.* pp. 148–9, and *infra*, p. 93.

Applause" was "forbad to be played any more, by an Order from the Lord Chamberlain[1]." It was said that a nobleman had complained of a satirical portrait of himself in the farce. Even Shakespeare (when popular) was not exempt. In September 1744, Theophilus Cibber altered and staged at the Little Theatre, Haymarket, *Romeo and Juliet*. It promised to be a glorious success, and Fleetwood, manager of the Drury Lane house, became so alarmed that he sought for and found protection in the Lord Chamberlain. The playing of *Romeo and Juliet* was given over.

These details concerning the audience, their tastes and dislikes, and concerning the external forces operating upon the drama are all necessary for an understanding of the plays of the time. To these largely was due the strange heterogeneity of contemporary tragedy and of contemporary comedy. Many minds and many tastes had to be satisfied. Pseudo-classicism in tragedy was for the critics of the Dennis type, but the critics did not form by any means the whole of the audience. There was still demanded from many the heroic bombast of the older Restoration tragedy, while the ladies delighted in tears and pathetic situations. In *Vertue Betray'd*, says Jacob[2], "and the *Earl of Essex* the Author has had the good Fortune to please the Fair Sex," and of the latter play he adds, "whenever it is represented, the Fair Sex have some Difficulty to refrain from Tears." The "She-tragedies" popularised by this writer, Banks, and by Rowe may have been written for the same section of the audience. At any rate, Swift, in his *Thoughts on Various Subjects*, declared that "it is observable that the ladies frequent tragedies more than comedy." The reason is no doubt to be found in the explanation given above rather than in Swift's own suggestion "that in tragedy their sex is deified and adored, in comedy exposed and ridiculed." Even if we include the critics, the gallants with still some Restoration

---

[1] Whincop, pp. 235–6. As Genest notes, the prohibition must have been temporary only, as this comedy, after being acted for the first time in May 1742, was put on again the following October.

[2] p. 10.

sympathies and the lady-folks of both, we have not summed up the audience of the time. The middle classes, as we have seen, were come to the theatre, and for them was penned the bourgeois tragedy and the comedy of sentiment. Sentimental comedy, on the other hand, would hardly appeal to the several old courtiers of Charles who survived with Betterton to recall ancient days. Hence the preservation of the comedies of manners and the many dubious situations and risky amours. For everyone political plays, and for those who desired merely to be amused or have their senses tickled, the pantomime and the ballad-farce and the opera. From whatever angle we look at it we find the drama of the early eighteenth century, as the drama of all centuries, more fully explained by a reference to the audience than by a reference to any other thing.

III. *The Theatre*

Other influences also have, naturally, to be taken into account, but they are all subservient to this. Of the theatre itself not so much, perhaps, need be said as of the theatre of the Restoration because, with that peculiar conservatism so characteristic of the stage, the theatres of 1750 were employing much the same effects, and were utilising the same "machines" and conventions, as were employed in the theatres of 1670.

Fundamentally, the interiors of the playhouses remained unchanged. There were still the rows of boxes, still the slightly immoral galleries[1], still the apron stage, still the proscenium doors, still the little-used curtain. It would seem to be undeniable that the greater part of the business of each piece went on in the same way towards the front of the stage, notwithstanding the alteration in the Drury Lane house chronicled by Cibber[2]. Again and again we find the old

---

[1] See Gay, Pope and Arbuthnot's *Three Hours after Marriage* (D.L. 1717), IV.

[2] *Apology*, ed. Lowe, ii. 84–7. Rich, in order to gain extra room in the theatre, cut off part of the apron stage, removing two of the entrance doors which stood on each side. This problem of the proscenium doors is a complicated one. Restoration stage practice is discussed briefly in vol. i (1660–1700), pp. 51–3. It has generally been assumed that in the

stage-directions bidding characters to "come forward," especially after any sort of "discovery" towards the back of the stage. "SCENE *draws and discovers the* High-Court" runs a direction in Havard's *King Charles the First* (L.² 1737) and later, "*The King is brought forward; the Scene closes*[1]." In Lillo's *The Christian Hero* (D.L. 1735) Hellena is discovered "*on a Sofa in a Melancholy Posture.*" A song is sung and she "*rises and comes forward*[2]." So in Phillips' *Hibernia Freed* (L.² 1722) O'Brien and Eugenius "*come forward*" after having entered towards the back of the stage[3], as do Lucinda and Qarma after a song in Oldmixon's *The Governour of Cyprus* (L.¹ 1703)[4]. The scene in Gataker's *The Jealous Clown* (G.F. 1730) "*opens and discovers* Leonora *reading; she shuts the Book and advances*[5]." In Mrs Haywood's *The Fair Captive* (L.² 1721) we find "*The Grand Visier discovered on a Couch, in a melancholy Posture: Soft Musick, which ended, he comes forward*" and "*The* Visier's *Chamber, he sleeping on a Couch, rises and comes forward*[6]." Hewitt's *Fatal Falshood* (D.L. 1734) has "Louisa *discover'd in a Chair...soft Musick plays, then...she rises, and goes forward*[7]," while in Hurst's *The Roman Maid* (L.² 1724) occurs the direction "*Soft* MUSICK. DIOCLESIAN *alone at a Table in a melancholy Posture: After the Musick he rises and comes forward*[8]."

As will be seen from the first of the above examples, the ancient custom of scene-shutting or of scene-closing was in usage, and it remained in usage throughout the whole of the period. It was a simple method whereby with a minimum of trouble the playwright was able to shift his characters to a new locality without their ever leaving the stage[9].

eighteenth century only two doors were in operation, but several years ago W. J. Lawrence informed me that a prompt text dated 1714 in the Bodleian has clear references not only to upper and lower doors of entrance but also to middle doors. Unfortunately I have not been able to locate this copy.

[1] IV. (ii).   [2] I. i.   [3] I. i.   [4] I. i.
[5] Scene iv.   [6] II and v. (ii).   [7] I. iii.
[8] IV. v. It will be noted that this "melancholy Posture" and "soft Musick" was a favourite seventeenth century theatrical device for arousing pathos and sentimental feelings.
[9] Odell notes particularly flagrant examples of this change of locality in Young's *Busiris* (D.L. 1719), I. i and IV. i. (*Shakespeare from Betterton to Irving*, i. 265-6.)

G. C. D. Odell has discovered in some *Critical Remarks* (1719) by one "Corinna" a peculiar contemporary criticism of such devices, but, as he observes, "Corinna" was far ahead of her time in theatrical judgment[1]. What we do notice in this period is the rapid increase in the number of "discoveries" revealed by this means. "*The* SCENE *opening, discovers Lord* George *and Lady* Gentle *rising from Play*," "*The* SCENE *drawing, discovers Mrs.* Conquest *in an Arm'd-Chair*," occur in Cibber's *The Lady's Last Stake* (H.[1] 1707)[2]. In the same author's *Perolla and Izadora* (D.L. 1705) we have "*The* SCENE *drawing Discovers* Pacuvius" and "*The* SCENE *Opening, Discovers a Scaffold for the Execution of* Blacius[3]." The "SCENE *opens, and discovers*" several characters in Burnaby's *Love Betray'd* (L.[1] 1703)[4]. "*The flat Scene opens, and discovers*" others in Crauford's *Courtship A-la-mode* (D.L. 1700)[5]. In Addison's *The Drummer* (D.L. 1716) we find a series of such, employed to reveal the supposed ghost and Vellum's office. One of the most peculiar and the most interesting of the uses to which this scene-drawing was put was the revelation of some murdered man or scene of torture. The various methods by which the pseudo-classic dramatists endeavoured to compromise between the French rule of no death on the stage and the English love of exciting incident must be left till a later portion of this book[6], but here may be noted one of the commonest and handiest of their devices, one which had analogies on the Greek stage itself[7]. In Mallet's *Mustapha* (D.L. 1739) the "*Back Scene opening discovers the mutes and soldiers in attitudes of grief round the body of* MUSTAPHA[8]." Thomson in his *Agamemnon* (D.L. 1738) employed just such a device: "*The Back-Scene opening discovers at a distance*, Agamemnon's *Body*[9]," as does Beckingham in *The Tragedy of King Henry IV. of France*

---

[1] *Op. cit.* i. 266–7: "But we have no Notion of opening and shutting Scenes, that is, removing of Walls and Partitions, meerly to show us that the Author's ill Contrivance can find no other Ways to do."
[2] v. (ii) and v. (v).
[3] I. (ii) and v. (ii).   [4] II.   [5] IV. ii.
[6] See *infra*, pp. 54–5.
[7] See Flickinger, R. C., *The Greek Theater* (1918), p. 241.
[8] v. ix.   [9] v.

(L.² 1719): "*The Scene changes, and discovers* Charlotta *dead*[1]."
In Rowe's *The Royal Convert* (H.¹ 1707) the scene draws to
reveal instruments of torture[2].

It is strange that, with all this apparent sense of the value
of scene-drawing "discoveries," the playwrights did not
realise to what uses they might put the curtain. No doubt
the curtain was employed on some occasions, as in Restoration
times, but the scantiness of reference to its use makes us
believe that, when it was so employed, it was for very special
and ornate effects. Peculiarly enough, there seem to be even
fewer early eighteenth century stage-directions in regard to
the use of the curtain than are discoverable in the texts of
Restoration dramas. Of the employment of the curtain at
the very beginning of plays there are a few records. One is
in Crauford's *Courtship A-la-mode* (D.L. 1700): "*The Curtain
drawn.*" Gildon uses it similarly for effect in *Love's Victim*
(L.¹ 1701). The scene here is "*the Inside of a Magnificent
Temple....The Curtain rises with terrible Claps of Thunder.*"
In Theophilus Cibber's pantomime *The Harlot's Progress*
(D.L. 1733): "After the Overture, the Curtain rises." An
exactly similar stage-direction occurs in Theobald's *Dramatick
Entertainment, call'd Harlequin a Sorcerer* (L.² 1724)[3]. So,
too, we find mention of the curtain at the end of dramas. The
"*Curtain falls*" at the close of Frowde's *The Fall of Saguntum*
(L.² 1727), but extant evidence leaves us uncertain whether
the normal usage was to have the curtain falling at the end
of the play or after the epilogue. Taking Frowde's play along
with a pronouncement in Fielding's *The Miser* (D.L. 1733)
it would seem that both were in practice. The fact remains
that, except for a very few dramatists, there was no consciousness that the curtain could be used either at the close of acts
or at the close of the play. That there was such a consciousness in respect to the opening scene, when the curtain,

---

[1] v. (ii). [2] v. iii.
[3] The curtain is used to present a tableau also in v. i. of Mrs Manley's
Lucius, The First Christian King of Britain (D.L. 1717). On Fielding's
occasional use of the curtain see Odell, *op. cit.* i. 275–6. W. J. Lawrence
refers to the employment of the curtain in an article contributed to
The Stage (June 9, 1921).

according to the testimony of Gay's *The Captives* (D.L. 1724)[1], normally rose after the prologue was spoken, may possibly be capable of proof, but towards the conclusion of every act we discover the same frantic eagerness to get the characters safely off the stage, the dramatists providing for them, where necessary, suitable tags. Tags were usual in nearly all eighteenth century plays, from the first years to the last. The rumour that they disappeared about 1736 has but slender foundation on fact[2]. Sometimes they were metaphorical and poetic, as in Frowde's *The Fall of Saguntum* (L.[2] 1727)[3]—so poetic that they were often printed in italics, as in the same author's *Philotas* (L.[2] 1731)[4]. At other times they were proverbial and introduced with an effort after naturalness. Says a character in Steele's *The Conscious Lovers* (D.L. 1722): "I remember a Verse to the Purpose.

> They may be false who Languish and Complain,
> But they who part with Money never feign[5]."

How necessary they were esteemed in those days may be realised by the fact that Clinket in Gay, Pope and Arbuthnot's *Three Hours after Marriage* (D.L. 1717) was bemoaning as the greatest of all her losses—"the tag of the acts of a new comedy![6]"

The scenes employed on this stage must have been, as in Restoration days, of several kinds. There was the ordinary flat used for an apron scene As in earlier days, the normal scenic system was a simple one of flats and wings, but supplemented now by the use in spectacular productions of "cloths" and set-pieces[7]. Without doubt, the old incoherence remained. The fire-scene in *The Island Princess*[8] shows us the strange anomaly of stationary figures presumably

---

[1] Prologue: "*Yet judge him not before the curtain draws.*"
[2] See Odell, *op. cit.* i. 280.   [3] Especially in I., II. and IV.
[4] End of II.   [5] I. i.   [6] II.
[7] There can hardly be any doubt but that lateral side scenes were in use alongside of back-cloth and wings. Odell (*op. cit.* i. 398) cites happily a letter of Aaron Hill to Garrick, dated July 11, 1749, in which he speaks of "columns, standing separate from the slanting scenes."
[8] It occurs in the 1711 Beaumont and Fletcher; and has been reproduced by G. C. D. Odell, *op. cit.* i. 294.

fleeing from the conflagration with real actors dashing about
the stage. Ambitious effects enough were attempted in the
operas of the day, with verisimilitude down to sparrows and
tomtits, but these, as G. C. D. Odell with justice shows, were
not usual in ordinary legitimate drama. The fact that special
efforts were not made to deck out these ordinary plays seems
proved by the emphasis which contemporaries laid on the
special scenery of *Cato*, bought with the benefit money which
Addison grandiloquently refused, and that of *King Henry the
Fifth* (D.L. 1723) for which Hill provided the actors with
£200. On the other hand, while we realise that special
scenery would not be painted for every new farce, not even
for every new tragedy, it is but reasonable to suppose that
rich effects once employed for the operas would be utilised
once more, when done with, for more ordinary productions.
This supposition is strengthened when we find that, in spite
of attempts at novelty, the scenes presented have about them
a strange conservatism. Beyond the commonplace chambers
and streets and views of London, the scenes we find referred
to again and again in our reading of early eighteenth century
drama are the very scenes which appeared in one Restoration
heroic tragedy after another. They come into tragedy and
tragi-comedy and ballad-opera and farce with a monotonous
frequency, so that we are led to believe that the actual
painted scenes were utilised over and over again, and maybe
written up to by far-sighted dramatists. In Steele's inventory
of "the Moveables of *Ch...r R...ch* Esq;" given in the 42nd
Tatler[1], we are told that there are "Groves, Woods, Forrests,
Fountains, and Country Seats, with very pleasant Prospects
on all Sides of them," and groves, forests, woods and fountains we know were common enough in the seventeenth
century. The grove in this period occurs at the old Lincoln's
Inn Fields in Gildon's *Love's Victim* (1701)[2], in Oldmixon's
The Governour of Cyprus (1703)[3], and at the new Lincoln's
Inn Fields in Carey's *Teraminta* (1732)[4]. At Drury Lane it

---

[1] This list is given again with a few additions as an appendix to *The
Life of That Eminent Comedian Robert Wilks, Esq;* (1733).
[2] II. i.: "The Grove before the Temple."
[3] I. i.   [4] I. iii.

appears in Theobald's *The Persian Princess* (1708)[1] and in Settle's *The City Ramble* (1711)[2]. Woods are common, and a grotto occurs in III. i. of Addison's *Rosamond* (D.L. 1707)[3]. Besides these, temples, often temples of the sun, were much favoured as in olden times. One occurs in Gildon's *Love's Victim* (L.[1] 1701)[4], another in Theobald's *The Persian Princess* (D.L. 1708)[5], another in Rowe's *The Royal Convert* (H.[1] 1707)[6], another in Mrs Pix' *The Double Distress* (L.[1] 1701)[7], others in Frowde's *The Fall of Saguntum* (L.[2] 1727)[8], Hurst's *The Roman Maid* (L.[2] 1724)[9], Jeffreys' *Merope* (L.[2] 1731)[10] and Gay's *The Captives* (D.L. 1724)[11]. Prison scenes were quite as usual as they had been in the days of Charles; such scenes appear in Cibber's *Perolla and Izadora* (D.L. 1705)[12], in Martyn's *Timoleon* (D.L. 1730)[13], in Carey's *Teraminta* (L.[2] 1732)[14] and *Amelia* (H.[2] 1732)[15], in Dennis' *Appius and Virginia* (D.L. 1709)[16], in Mrs Manley's *Lucius the First Christian King of Britain* (D.L. 1717)[17], in Theobald's *The Persian Princess* (D.L. 1708)[18], in Gay's *The Captives* (D.L. 1724)[19] and in Mrs Haywood's *The Fair Captive* (L.[2] 1721)[20]. The list could be continued almost indefinitely. Familiar scenes, likewise, were the palaces and pavilions, which appear in Frowde's *The Fall of Saguntum* (L.[2] 1727)[21], in Hurst's *The Roman Maid* (L.[2] 1724)[22], in Griffin's *Injur'd Virtue* (Richmond? 1715)[23], in Martyn's *Timoleon* (D.L. 1730)[24], in Mrs Haywood's *The Fair Captive* (L.[2] 1721)[25], in Carey's *Amelia* (H.[2] 1732)[26] and *Teraminta* (L.[2] 1732)[27], and in Gay's *The*

---

[1] III. i.: "A Night Scene of a thick Grove." [2] v. (i).

[3] A "Grotto that changes to Country House" occurs in the 1744 inventory given in Wyndham, H. S., *Annals of Covent Garden Theatre*. A garden and "Harvey's palace" are also noticeable items there.

[4] I. i.: "The Inside of a Magnificent Temple."

[5] II. ii.: a "Temple of the Sun." [6] IV. i.

[7] III.: a "Temple of the Sun."

[8] I. i.; IV. (i); v. (i).

[9] III. i: "*The Temple* of Vesta *with an Altar*."

[10] v. i.   [11] v. i.   [12] v. (i).   [13] III. i. and IV. ii.

[14] II. iii.   [15] III. viii.   [16] v.

[17] v. (ii).   [18] III. ii.   [19] IV. i.

[20] IV. (i).   [21] II. ii.   [22] I. i.

[23] II. iii.

[24] IV. iii.: "*An Apartment in the Palace of* Timoleon, *Darken'd*."

[25] IV. (ii)   [26] I. vii.: "*A Pavilion*"   [27] III. iii.

Captives (D.L. 1724)[1], as well as the open spaces or landscapes which we find in D'Urfey's *Ariadne* (1721)[2] and in Carey's *Amelia* (H.[2] 1732)[3]. There are besides a few "Delightful Wildernesses" as in Dennis' *Rinaldo and Armida* (L.[1] 1699)[4], relics of old-time stagery.

In discovering all these scenes of a stock character, one would naturally seek in the Italian operas of the time for the appearance of similar sets. The search is not a vain one. The supposition advanced above that the actual painted scenes presented in tragedy after tragedy were the same stock pieces which had originally done service in the more ornate productions of the opera houses seems to be almost proved by a comparison of the stage directions already quoted with the stage directions preserved in the texts of the operas. The first scene of *Camilla* (D.L. 1706) is "*A Champian Country with Plains and easie Hills, the End of a Wood on one Side, and Prospect of a City at Distance*"; scene iv. of the first act moves to "*A Chamber in the Royal Palace*"; and I. vii. and III. i. are "*The Palace*" itself. "*A Wood*" appears in II. x. Similar appearances of familiar panoramas occur in one after another of these productions. In *L'Idaspe Fedele* (H.[1] 1710) I. i. is "*A Field Opening to the Walls of* Susa, *in which is a Breach made: The Camp of the* Medes *and* Persians, *who are lying before it*"; II. i. is "*A Pleasant Grove near the Palace*"; II. ix. and III. vi. "*A Prison.*" In *Etearco* (H.[1] 1711) we find "*A Wood, and a tempestuous Sea*[5]," "*a Garden (Giardino di Fiori)*[6]," "*A pleasant Prospect of Fountains*, &c. (*Delitiosa, con fonti, e Ruscelli presso le Mura d' vn Antico Palasso*)[7]," "*a dark Prison* (Priggione con picciol' Lume)[8]," and "*a Court*[9]," besides chambers and other unimportant scenes. "*A Prison*" in *Ernelinda* (H.[1] 1713) is described in Italian as a "Prigione orribile[10]," and in this play appears the regular "*Palace* (Pallazzo Reale)[11]," "*A Garden*[12]," and a "*Gran Sala*[13]." The palace is altered in *L'Odio e L'Amore* (H.[1] 1721) into "A

---

[1] I. i.
[2] I. i.: "a pleasant champion Country."
[3] I. i.: "*A spacious Country.*"
[4] I. i.
[5] I. i.
[6] I. viii.
[7] II. iv.
[8] III. i.
[9] III. vi.
[10] III. i.
[11] I. i. and III. viii.
[12] II. i. and III. v.
[13] I. vii. and II. iv.

Royal Pavillion[1]," and here occurs "The Temple of Revenge
illuminated, and her Statue, with a naked Sword in its Hand,
and the *Persian* Standard on one Side of it. An Altar kindled,
and at the Foot of it a Vessel full of Blood, with the Head of
CYRUS the General within it[2]," Later "the Temple appears
darken'd." Dark rooms seem to have been fairly popular, in
opera and in tragedy. Examples have been given above.
Finally, we may note in *Il Muzio Scevola* (H.[1] 1721) the
occurrence of "A Royal Pavilion[3]," "A shady Bank of the
Tiber. HORATIO, and afterwards IRENE in a Boat[4]," and "A
Forest[5]."

These scenes, then, which occur with such monotonous
frequency, and which were ridiculed in Carey's *The Dragon
of Wantley* (C.G. 1737)[6] and earlier in Mrs Aubert's *Harlequin-
Hydaspes* (L.[2] 1719)[7], would seem to have been originally
produced for such Italian musical productions and utilised
in later prose and blank verse drama. That this supposition
is not merely a fanciful one is proved by the fact that on
S. Oct. 19, 1717, the D.L. company advertised a performance
of *Cato* with a new set of scenes "taken from the Opera."
We may go even further, and say that there is evidence that
actual scenes which had been originally painted in the reign of
Charles II were being utilised in the days of Queen Anne. When
Settle's *The Empress of Morocco* was revived at Drury Lane
on Aug. 2, 1704, it was advertised in *The Daily Courant* "as
it was perform'd several times at Court, by Persons of Great
Quality, before his late Majesty King Charles II. with all the
Scenes which were originally represented in it when acted at
the Theatre, particularly the Fleet of Ships, and the Hell
Scene." Nothing could seem to be plainer; the old successes
of 1673 had been carefully stored away at the Dorset Garden
house to be disinterred thirty years later.

---

[1] I. i.   [2] II. i.   [3] I. i. and viii.; II. i. and vi.; and III. i.
[4] II. v.   [5] II. viii.

[6] That the ridicule was intended seems proved by the introduction
of just such stage directions as have been cited above: cf. I. i. "*A Rural
Prospect*," II. i. "*A Garden*." So in *The Dragoness*, I. i. "*A Magnificent
Temple*," ii. "*A Desart*," III. ii. "*A Prison*."

[7] For I. i. "*The Stage represents a Garden*," and for II. i. "*The Stage
represents a Prison*."

For the original scenic work done in the eighteenth century itself, foreign artists seem largely to have been employed. We know, certainly, of a Mr Harvey and of a Mr Lambert who, in 1732, were engaged at the Covent Garden theatre, and the name of another English playhouse artist, Hayman, has been filched by Professor Odell from the ruins of time[1]; but most of our references are to Italian or other Continental painters. It was a foreigner whom Fielding ridiculed in *Tumble-Down Dick* (H.[2] 1736). Divoto was working at Drury Lane in the earlier years of the century, and Servandoni was employed by Rich to paint decorations for *Alceste*. Still another name might be added to this list. The printed text of *L'Idaspe Fedele* (H.[1] 1710) contains a note at the beginning: "*The Musick Compos'd by Signor* Francesco Mancini. *The Scenes Painted by Signor* Marco Rizzi *of* Venice." This is the first instance I know of the mention of a scenic artist in bill or in text of play.

The influence of all this scenery was gradually making itself felt in the actual work of the dramatists, and this influence was probably intensified by the pseudo-classic unities. We still find plays in which easy change of scene was possible, as in Mrs Centlivre's *Love's Contrivance* (D.L. 1703), and even yet scenes could be shown for less than a dozen of lines. v. iv. of Cibber's *The Careless Husband* (D.L. 1704) extends to barely seven lines, and in Mrs Centlivre's *A Wife well manag'd* (D.L. 1715) occurs a scene of twelve lines[2]. At the same time there was an attempt on the part of the dramatists to avoid needless alterations of scenery. We discover only six separate sets in Steele's *The Conscious Lovers* (D.L. 1722) and there are only two or three (including "*A Royal Pavilion*") in Frowde's *Philotas* (L.[2] 1731). The audience, however, constantly demanded show, and if pseudo-classicists, urged forward by pecuniary arguments on the part of the managers, were cutting down their scenic effects, they made up for it by fairly rich costume and by other external

---

[1] *Op. cit.* i. 316–7. The references are to *The Daily Journal*, Sept. 18, 1732 and *An Essay on the Theatres* (1745).
[2] Scene iv.

aids. Steele sums it all up pithily enough in his prologue to
Vanbrugh's *The Mistake* (H.¹ 1705):

> *The first Dramatick Rule is, have good Cloaths,*
> *To charm the gay Spectator's gentle Breast,*
> *In Lace and Feather Tragedy's express'd,*
> *And Heroes die unpity'd, if ill-dress'd...*
> *If 'tis a Comedy, you ask—Who dance?*
> *For oh! what dire Convulsions have of late*
> *Torn and distracted each Dramatick State,*
> *On this great Question, which House first should sell*
> *The new* French *Steps, imported by* Ruel?[1]

Machines were still in fashion, so that the same author could
cry out in the prologue to his own play of *The Funeral* (D.L.
1701) that

> *Nature's Deserted and Dramatick Art,*
> *To Dazle now the Eye, has left the Heart;*
> *Gay Lights, and Dresses, long extended Scenes,*
> *Dæmons and Angels moving in Machines,*
> *All that can now or please or fright the Fair*
> *May be perform'd without a writer's Care,*
> *And is the Skill of Carpenter, not Player.*

Cibber's *Xerxes* (L.¹ 1699) has its stage portents in I. i. and
a "Magician's *Cave*" in IV. ii. In Rowe's *Ulysses* (H.¹ 1705)
Pallas makes her appearance in the clouds[2]. A typical
machine of this type will be found depicted in the frontispiece
to Lediard's *Britannia* (H.² 1732). In addition to these there
were the extra effects. In *The Tatler* "inventory" of Rich's
"moveables" already mentioned[3], there is "A Sea, consisting
of a Dozen large Waves, the Tenth bigger than ordinary,
and a little damaged," which might be compared with the
tempestuous sea in *Etearco* (H.¹ 1711)[4]; it no doubt came in
handy also for *The Tempest*. There are besides "A Dozen and
a half of Clouds, trimm'd with Black, and well conditioned
...A Rainbow a little faded...A Set of Clouds after the *French*
Mode, streaked with Lightning, and furbelow'd...A New-

---

[1] Du Ruel and his wife were among the chief attractions of the Drury
Lane house in the early years of the century.
[2] III.   [3] *Supra*, p. 30.   [4] *Supra*, p. 32.

Moon, something decay'd...A Setting-Sun, a Pennyworth.'' In addition there is enumerated "A Mustard-Bowl to make Thunder with[1]," and (a cruel cut at Dennis) "Another of a bigger Sort, by Mr. *D——is*'s Directions, little used," "Spirits of Right *Nants* Brandy, for Lambent Flame and Apparitions," "Three Bottles and a half of Lightning," "One Shower of Snow in the whitest *French* Paper" and "Two Showers of a browner Sort." From Steele's satirical essay we are enabled to form some sort of an idea of a performance in Queen Anne's days.

Amid all these sights and sounds moved the actors, and by their side frequently sat spectators. The evil habit of having the audience on the stage was apparently suppressed in the days of Charles, only to grow up again in the last years of the seventeenth century[2]. It was destined to endure on into the times of Garrick. Not only were amphitheatres arranged for special performances, such as benefits, but evidently seats were occupied at fixed prices on regular acting days. The former practice is attested to in bill after bill from the earliest days to the latest[3], and references to the latter are not infrequent in the texts of plays. At Betterton's famous benefit on April 7, 1709, Steele tells us there had "not been known so great a Concourse of Persons of Distinction...The Stage it self was covered with Gentlemen and Ladies, and when the Curtain was drawn, it discovered even there a very splendid Audience[4]." Only occasionally was the stage banned to the spectators. "It is humbly desir'd," runs the close of *The Daily Courant* advertisement for Cibber's *She Wou'd and She Wou'd Not* (D.L. 1702), "that no Gentleman may Interrupt the Action by standing on the Stage the First day."

---

[1] "A Quart of bottled Light'ning" and a thunder bowl are also included in Webster's poem, *The Stage* (1713). See likewise *The Spectator*, No. 502, Sept. 10, 1714.

[2] See vol. i (1660–1700), pp. 11–12.

[3] The amphitheatre was often arranged at the first performance of operas (cf. *The Daily Courant* notice of the first production of *Arsinoe*), and was an almost invariable accompaniment of benefits. The bill for *Measure for Measure*, April 12, 1738, might also be consulted, as well as Hogarth's engraving of *The Beggar's Opera*.

[4] *The Tatler*, No. 1, April 8, 1709.

Similar announcements are to be discovered here and there, spasmodically, throughout those fifty years. G. C. D. Odell quotes from the playbill of Dalton's *Comus* (D.L. 1738): "N.B. To prevent any Interruption in the Musick, Dancing, Machinery, or other Parts of the Performance, 'tis hoped no Gentleman will take it ill, that he cannot be admitted behind the Scenes, or into the Orchestra"—and this, with its apologetic tone, is as typical as any[1].

The advertisement for Griffin's *Whig and Tory* (L.[2] 1720) states that tickets for admission to the "scenes" could be had at the stage door, price half a guinea each[2]. Quite naturally, such a habit must have given rise to many abuses. Steele in *The Spectator*[3] speaks of that part "of the Audience who shall set up for Actors, and interrupt the Play on the Stage," while in *Sir Giddy Whim* (1703) Alderman Sharp converses thus with Captain Smart: "You get your first load of Claret by Seven—then to the Play-house, where you reel about the Stage, disturb the Actors, and expose your self to all the World at once."

It is to be suspected that the reference given above as to payment for entry to the stage actually applies to admission to the "scenes." Gallants would be willing to pay a little extra to get into conversation with the actresses; but perhaps the payment included a stance upon the stage as well. The wording of the advertisement for Pinkethman's benefit on Monday, Oct. 26, 1702 (the play was Cibber's *Love makes a Man*) seems quite explicit: "All Persons that come behind the Scenes, are desired to pay their Money to none but Mr.

---

[1] Odell, *op. cit.* i. 283. The orchestra, or, as it was sometimes called, "the Musick Room," seems to have been a favourite spot for more privileged auditors. Along with the notice of *Comus* might be taken those of *The Fatal Marriage* at D.L. on T. Feb. 2, 1711/12, of *The Emperour of the Moon* at L.I.F.[2] on T. Jan. 19, 1719/20, of *The Way of the World* at D.L. on M. March 5, 1721/2, of *Alexander* at the opera house on T. June 7, 1726 ("By His Majesty's Command, no Persons whatsoever to be admitted behind the Scenes"), and of *The Recruiting Officer* at G.F. on F. Oct. 31, 1729 ("No Money returned after the Curtain is drawn up or Persons admitted behind the Scenes").

[2] At D.L. on M. March 5, 1721/2 no persons were to be "admitted into the Boxes or behind the Scenes but by Sealed Tickets."

[3] No. 502, October 6, 1712.

Pinkethman." In Cibber's *The Lady's Last Stake* (H.[1] 1707)
Lord George offers to take Mrs Conquest, who is dressed as,
and is mistaken by him for, a man, "behind the Scenes, and
there are Ladies of all sorts, Coquets, Prudes, and Virgins
(they say) serious and Comical, Vocal,—and Instrumental[1]."
Mrs Bullock, in speaking the epilogue to Beckingham's
Scipio Africanus (L.[2] 1718) refers to the "pert and noisy
Sparks" who "stand peeping here"—"[*Pointing to the
Scenes*" runs the stage direction. Evidently some attempt
was made by royal warrant to limit the abuse, so that Motteux
found matters in a bad way at the playhouses in 1705: "now
no body comes behind the Scenes[2]," but, as is evident from
the other references quoted, the habit was by no means
completely suppressed till many years after that date[3].

The costumes utilised by the actors appear to have been
of a miscellaneous character. Contemporary comedy required
nothing, of course, save the clothes "*à la mode*" as well as
a few rustic garments; but in tragedy a certain attempt as in
Restoration times was made to secure at least a semblance
of historical accuracy. Again Steele's inventory gives us a
glimpse of customary properties. "An Imperial Mantle,
made for *Cyrus the Great* and worn by *Julius Caesar*, *Bajazet*,
King *Harry* the Eighth, and Signior *Valentini*...*Roxana's*
Night-Gown...The Imperial Robes of *Xerxes*, never worn
but once...The Whiskers of a *Turkish* Bassa...The Complexion
of a Murderer in a Band-box; consisting of a large Piece of
burnt Cork, and a Cole-black Peruke...A Suit of Clothes for
a Ghost, *viz.* a bloody Shirt, a Doublet curiously pink'd, and
a Coat with Three great Eyelet-Holes upon the Breast"—
again we must remember that the list is satirically conceived,
but possibly not very far from the truth for all that. Turning
from it to illustrations prefixed to dramas of the age we can
see just such sets of costumes and disguisings. There is a
certain attention paid to Roman costuming in the frontispiece to Beckingham's *Scipio Africanus* (L.[2] 1718) but such

---

[1] v. i.
[2] *Farewel Folly* (D.L. 1705), I. i.; *supra*, p. 5.
[3] On the grenadiers on the stage see Odell, *op. cit.* i. 285–7

attention is by way of being somewhat exceptional[1]. For Barford's *The Virgin Queen* (L.[2] 1728) and for Charles Johnson's *The Victim* (D.L. 1714) the heroes and heroines are all more or less in eighteenth century garments. Peculiarly enough more attention seems to have been paid to male characters than to female; we hardly ever come across a picture of an actress in anything but the eighteenth century hoop, but of actors we have many portraits with at least a semblance of Roman, Eastern or historical English clothes. As typical an illustration as any is to be found in the 1713 duodecimo edition of Addison's *Cato* (D.L. 1713), where the two sexes are thus clearly distinguished. In one respect, however, the men retained an old traditional piece of property, irrespective of whatever century they were supposed to be in. "A Plume of Feathers, never used but by *Oedipus* and the Earl of *Essex*" is an entry in Steele's inventory. It may be seen adorning an Egyptian hero in the frontispiece to Marsh's *Amasis* (C.G. 1738)[2].

With difficulty, then, and constant travail, the theatre was moving forward, clinging almost frenziedly to the ancient customs which had been in vogue not only in the time of Charles II but even in that of Charles I. We are certainly now in an atmosphere nearer to modern times, but never, all through the eighteenth century, were the traditional elements entirely cast off.

IV. *The Actors and Actresses*

It has been said again and again, by those who have more or less tentatively touched upon this period of our drama, that the eighteenth century was an age, not of the author, but of the actor; and this statement, as a general proposition, may be regarded as fundamentally true. It was not that the actors

---

[1] An interesting plea for historical costuming was made by Aaron Hill in a letter to Wilks, October 28, 1731, quoted by Odell, i. 326, but the general poverty of the costumes is well attested to by *Mist's Weekly Journal*, Feb. 2, 1722/3, and *The Prompter*, Jan. 24, 1734/5 (cf. *id.* i. 324–5).

[2] See *The Spectator*, No. 42, Wednesday, April 18, 1711: "The ordinary Method of making a Hero, is to clap a huge Plume of Feathers upon his Head"; and Ralph's *Taste of the Town* (1731).

were entirely or even directly responsible for the decay in tragedy and in comedy, but undoubtedly they aided in furthering that decay, consciously and unconsciously. From the accounts of eye-witnesses the theatre seems to have been rich then in masters and mistresses of the dramatic art. Cibber, Booth, Doggett, Wilks, Quin, Barry, Macklin, Garrick, Mrs Bracegirdle, Mrs Oldfield, Kitty Clive—these and a host of others have been remembered down to the present time, and we cannot but suppose that they were technically brilliant and emotionally inspiring. It is certainly true that some of these encouraged dramatists to pen for them plays, which, if not masterpieces, were often well-constructed and witty or poetical; but undoubtedly the fact that they could pass off on an audience poor and trivial works led towards the fabrication of a mass of dull and uninteresting tragedies, comedies and farces.

In view of the fact that there are so many theatrical memoirs of this age, from Cibber's *Apology* down to the flimsiest of biographical sketches and the bitterest of controversial pamphlets[1], it were here mere waste of time to rechronicle the virtues and the parts of various actors and actresses. What may be profitable, however, will be to indicate some of the tendencies of those actors and actresses in so far as these have a bearing upon the dramatic productivity of the period.

It would appear incontrovertible that, up to the time of Macklin and Garrick, the general trend of acting was, for tragic pieces, heavy and bombastic, for comedies, either purely farcical or "genteel." The heavy classic-heroic tragedy was, therefore, well suited for those who were to interpret it; and the farces and farcical comedies, along with the "genteel" comedy which arose out of the comedy of manners, toned in with the style of Bullock and of Mrs Oldfield and of Wilks. Thus Cibber wrote many of his principal parts deliberately for the last-named actress[2]; O'Bryan tells us that Farquhar

---

[1] An almost complete list will be found in R. W. Lowe's bibliography of English theatrical literature. The Garrick pamphlets should be noted particularly.

[2] See his preface to *The Provok'd Husband* (D.L. 1728).

drew Sir Harry Wildair in *A Trip to the Jubilee* "on purpose for" Wilks[1]; Lillo's *Elmerick* (D.L. 1740) was so well fitted for Quin that we must suppose the play was written for that actor; and Steele leaves his testimony that many authors wrote their farcical quarrels for Bullock and Pinkethman[2]. Again, as in the period of the Restoration, we must attribute the popularity of many plays, and the reappearance in play after play of similar types of character, to the influence of particular actors; just as we must attribute to their influence the gradually growing dominance of action over dialogue. "The Dialogue" of Farquhar's *A Trip to the Jubilee*, comments Steele, "in it self has something too low to bear a Criticism upon it: But Mr. *Wilks* enters into the Part with so much Skill, that the Gallantry, the Youth, and Gaiety of a young Man of plentiful Fortune, is looked upon with as much Indulgence on the Stage, as in real Life, without any of those Intermixtures of Wit and Humour, which usually prepossess us in Favour of such Characters in other Plays[3]," while of *The Recruiting Officer* (D.L. 1706) he informs us that it is "Mr. *Estcourt*'s proper Sense and Observation" which "supports the Play. There is not, in my humble Opinion, the Humour hit in *Sergeant Kite*; but it is admirably supply'd by his Action[4]." Fielding in *The Author's Farce* (H.[2] 1730) has an interesting commentary on this. Bookweight speaks of "your acting Plays and your reading Plays," and proceeds to explain: "Why, Sir, your acting Play is entirely supported by the Merit of the Actor; in which case it signifies very little whether there be any Sense in it or no. Now your reading Play is of a different stamp, and must have wit and meaning in it."

More and more attention was being placed upon the actor. There were evidences of gagging in Restoration times, but never did the practice seem to become so habitual as in the early eighteenth century. "You are never to perplex the

---

[1] *Authentic Memoirs, or, the Life and Character of that most Celebrated Comedian, Mr. Robert Wilks* (1733).
[2] *The Tatler*, No. 7, April 25, 1709.
[3] *Id.* No. 19, May 23, 1709.   [4] *Id.* No. 20, May 25, 1709.

drama with speeches extempore," advises Clinket in Gay, Pope and Arbuthnot's *Three Hours after Marriage* (D.L. 1717), to which Plotwell's reply is instructive. "Madam," he says, "'tis what the top players often do[1]." It was a "gag" of Cibber's in *The Rehearsal* concerning this very play which led to his enmity with Pope. Once more Steele provides us with little items of information. "The Actors," he remarks of a performance of *Love for Love*, "were careful of their Carriage, and no one was guilty of the Affectation to insert Witticisms of his own[2]," while of Cave Underhill he confesses that "he has not the Merit of some ingenious Persons now on the Stage, of adding to his Authors; for the Actors were so dull in the last Age, that many of them have gone out of the World, without having ever spoke one Word of their own in the Theatre[3]." Provision for this gagging, however, was still sometimes made by lazy dramatists themselves. In ii. ii. of Carey's *Hanging and Marriage* (L.² 1722) Mother Stubble enters crying "Aw law! what shall I do? what shall I do, &c." and the stage direction follows "*A great deal more of this Stuff.*" Undoubtedly for the increase of this practice the *commedia dell' arte* is largely to be blamed. Here the English players saw their Italian fellow-artists indulging in whole acts of improvised dialogue; and their own restraint must have fallen the heavier upon them. The belief in the sanctity of the written, well-meditated word was passing away[4].

One other influence of the actor must be taken note of in this period, an influence that even more directly concerns the production of dramatic works. Again and again we find complaints that the actor-managers who governed the playhouses were self-seeking in their aims, contemptuous of the dramatists, insolent in their manners. Cibber and Steele, it must be thought with some justice, were those chiefly attacked. Charles Shadwell in presenting *The Fair Quaker of Deal* (D.L. 1710) to the public mentions the "famous Comedian" (Cibber) who "took care to beat it down," and

[1] i. [2] *The Tatler*, No. 1, April 8, 1709. [3] *Id.* No. 22, May 30, 1709.
[4] On this whole subject see an interesting study by S. T. Graves entitled *Some Aspects of Extemporal Acting* (*Studies in Philology*, xix. 4, October 1922).

in his dedication to *The Invader of his Country* (D.L. 1719)
Dennis has a violent attack against "two or three Insolent
Players" (one of whom was Cibber) who, he asserts, laid
aside his play through mere envy. The same year Sewell in
penning his preface to *The Tragedy of Sir Walter Raleigh*
(L.² 1719) saw fit to remark upon the rudeness with which
the same actor habitually treated aspiring authors. With
needless insolence, at least according to the dramatist, Cibber
refused Fenton's *Mariamne* (L.² 1723); it was taken to the
other house and proved a gorgeous success. *A Proposal For
the better Regulation of the Stage* (1732) speaks of "the
Tyranny of the Players," the impertinence of Cibber and the
ill-treatment of the poets[1]. Dennis in his *Remarks on a Play,
call'd The Conscious Lovers* (1723) has a bitter attack upon
Steele and his actor companion. Looking back, Henry Carey,
in complaining of the new government of Drury Lane,
reflected that

> Ev'n *Cibber*, Terror to the Scribbling Crew!
> Would oft Sollicit me for something New[2].

When the triumvirate disappeared in the thirties of the
century, the complaints by no means ceased. "Now,"
continues Carey,

> Now, Younger Rulers Younger Authors take,
> Not for their Merit, but for Cheapness sake.

This poem of Carey's was written because of the treatment
of his own *The Honest Yorkshire-Man* (H.² 1735), a treat-
ment which, in his opinion, was "a Manifestation of the bad
Taste and monstrous Partiality of the Great *Mogul* of the
Hundreds of *Drury*, who, after having had the Copy Nine
Months in his Hands, continually feeding me with fresh
Promises of bringing it on the Stage, return'd it at last in a
very ungenerous Manner, at the end of the Season[3]." A more

---

[1] The author of *The Laureat* (p. 49) repeats the same criticism.
[2] *Of Stage Tyrants* (1735).
[3] Preface to Gilliver and Clarke's octavo edition of 1736; this preface
is not in Cook's octavo edition of the same year, which was probably
pirated. The author remarks on a specially bold piece of underhand
publishing in connection with his play

elaborate complaint was made in the preface to Hawling's *The Impertinent Lovers: or, A Coquet at her Wit's End…With a Preface, and Remarks upon its Usage. Submitted to Sir Richard Steel, and the three Gentlemen concerned with him as Patentees* (D.L. 1723). According to this, the play was given to Chetwood about the end of April. The parts were cast, and August 2 was suggested as the first night. On July 24, however, the actors informed the author that they would not risk its production unless he engaged to shoulder the responsibility for the charges of the 2nd and 3rd performances, a total of £70. An agreement was come to by which it was to be given on August 20, the author paying down £12 in cash. An order came prohibiting any playing after the 16th of the month, and it was decided that the comedy should be given on the 13th. On the 12th, however, the actors declared it would be deferred. It was definitely fixed for the following Thursday; but on Wednesday came another postponement till Friday. It was then badly acted with the by that time "stale" masque of *Acis and Galatea*; and was never repeated. The story, coloured as it may be by prejudice, has at any rate some sort of sincerity about it; and, as has been seen, does not lack corroborative evidence of a similar sort. Whether it was usual or not, this is the first mention of which I know concerning a money demand from the managers for the production of a drama. Ayres takes up the lament in the preface to his *Sancho at Court* (1742); there he accuses Fleetwood of envy, carelessness and malice. "*As Things are now circumstanced*," he says, "viz. *the Approbation of the Players, the Licencing-Office and the ill-natur'd Critic, not to say any thing of the Publick, an Author has but a small Chance of succeeding.*" Dower similarly complains that he waited on the proprietor of the theatre "every Day, or every other Day" from Oct. 23, 1726 to the 23rd of Dec., and had his comedy, *The Salopian Esquire* (1739), rejected in the end. It is very difficult now to make up our minds concerning the exact truth of these indictments. It is almost certain that the playwrights had indeed to suffer from the carelessness and perhaps from the insolence of the actors and the managers; but there are still several things to be taken into account. While Cibber, Steele, and, later, Fleetwood were the central butts for the complaining crew, others were attacked alongside of them. *The Lunatick*, an anonymous and unacted comedy of 1705, is "Dedicated to the Three Ruling B—S at the New House in L.—I.—F." (Betterton, Mrs Barry and Mrs Bracegirdle), who are referred to as that "most Arbitrary and Most Hermophrodite (sic) Conjunction." The chagrin of petty poetasters is responsible, probably, for many of the complaints, and of these poetasters there were, as we have seen, only too many. It is perfectly true that the actors, in giving the public what it wanted in the shape of pantomime and of show, were aiding in the debasement of the stage, but they had to keep a heavy check on the playwriting propensities of the age. Even in *Farewel Folly* (D.L. 1705) we hear of the mass of new dramas—"more than ever will be launch'd[1]," and Charles Johnson, writing in the preface to *The Successful Pyrate* (D.L. 1712), declares that there were so many new plays being written that "you wou'd think the whole Town were turn'd Playwrights." The mass of anonymous dramas produced between 1730 and 1740 tells its own tale; the insolence of the players was possibly merited. We must, therefore, endeavour to appreciate this aspect, as other aspects, of the age from no extreme angle. Undoubtedly the actors were pestered by nuisances; on the other hand, there were many good authors who found their way unduly hard, and Fielding in *Pasquin* (H.[2] 1736) was drawing a probably not over-coloured picture of their trials and difficulties when he put his satirical speech into the mouth of Fustian:

These little things, Mr. *Sneerwell*, will sometimes happen. Indeed a Poet undergoes a great deal before he comes to his Third Night; first with the Muses, who are humorous Ladies, and must be attended; for if they take it into their Head at any time to go abroad and leave you, you will pump your Brain in vain: Then, Sir, with the Master of a *Play-house* to get it acted, whom you generally follow a quarter of a Year before you know whether he will receive it or no; and then perhaps he tells you it won't do, and returns it you again, reserving the Subject, and

[1] I. i.

perhaps the Name, which he brings out in his next *Pantomime*; but if he should receive the Play, then you must attend again to get it writ out in Parts, and Rehears'd. Well, Sir, at last the Rehearsals begin; then, Sir, begins another Scene of Trouble with the Actors, some of whom don't like their Parts, and all are continually plaguing you with Alterations: At length, after having waded thro' all these Difficulties, his Play appears on the Stage, where one Man hisses out of Resentment to the Author; a Second out of Dislike to the House; a Third out of Dislike to the Actor; a Fourth out of Dislike to the Play; a Fifth for the Joke sake; a Sixth to keep all the rest in Company. Enemies abuse him, Friends give him up, the Play is damn'd, and the Author goes to the Devil, so ends the Farce[1].

Indirectly connected with this relationship between the actor-manager and the author, and likewise bearing upon the dramatic productivity of the time, must be taken another marked aspect of eighteenth century theatrical life, the rivalry between the playhouses. Such rivalry, of course, exists in all times and in all countries. It is to be seen reflected in *Hamlet*, and was decidedly marked in those years when the Duke's actors produced their spectacular operas and the King's men replied with *The Mock Tempest* and with *Psyche Debauch'd*; but in the eighteenth century this rivalry seemed to develop along intense lines of its own. If one house scored a success in any direction, another attempted to outdo it in its own *métier*. Already has been quoted a significant passage from Vanbrugh's *The Mistake* (H.[1] 1705)[2], a passage which can be proved from an examination of the extant play bills by no means an exaggeration. In the early years of the century we can see the two houses battling with each other in the introduction of *entr'acte* amusements. At first it is merely a case of a few dancers, an instrumentalist, a singer; within a few years all sorts of trivialities are introduced into the theatres. The Haymarket company announce Dryden's *All for Love* on Wednesday, Dec. 12, 1705 with dancing "especially the *Grand Dance*" performed by M. L'Abbe, M. de Barques, M. Davencourt, M. Legard, Mrs Elford and Mdlle Noisy. The following Monday (the 17th)

---

[1] IV. i.   [2] *Supra*, p. 35.

the advertisements of Drury Lane cap the announcement with
another; they are to play Crowne's *Sir Courtly Nice* with
various violin sonatas by Signior Gasperini and M. Paisible,
singing by Mr Ramondon and "the Boy," and several "*petit
Dances*" making, so they tell us, if put together, "a Grand
One," performed by M. Cherrier, M. Laforest, M. Laving,
M. Cottin, Mr Claxton, Mr Pinkethman, Mrs Lucas and
Madam Quiet. On Friday, June 18, 1703 the Drury Lane
company produced Cibber's *Love's Last Shift* with entertainments by the "famous Mr. *Clynch* of *Barnet*" who gave an
"imitation of an *Organ* with 3 Voices, the *Double Curtel*, and
the *Bells*, the *Huntsman* with his *Horn* and *Pack of Dogs*; All
which he performs with his Mouth on the open Stage." A
month or two before the same band of players had announced
as an additional attraction to a performance of Southerne's
Oroonoko (Tuesday, April 27, 1703) entertainments by the
famous Mr Evans, a vaulter, from Vienna, and at Dorset
Garden theatre on Friday, April 30, two French rope-dancing
girls along with their father as Harlequin (all come straight
from the Soldan's court at Constantinople) took their places
alongside of Mr Evans. The later years show precisely the
same feverish rush to engage entertainers, and two famous
French female rope-dancers accordingly appeared at Lincoln's
Inn Fields on Thursday, Oct. 11, 1705 in the midst of a
performance of Crowne's *The City Politiques.* Nor was this
rivalry confined to *entr'acte* shows. In 1707 the news that
Cibber was producing *The Double Gallant* seems to have
leaked out. This was performed at the Haymarket on Saturday, Nov. 1, 1707. The day before the Drury Lane company
revived Burnaby's *The Reform'd Wife* (D.L. 1700), on which
Cibber's comedy was largely based. The same year both
houses played Howard's *The Committee* against one another[1].
Evidently there was rivalry in prologues and epilogues as well.
On Friday, Dec. 26, 1707, the Drury Lane company, per-
forming Brome's *The Northern Lass*, announced "an Equi-
Vocal Epilogue after the old English manner, Compiled and
Spoken by the famous Singer Signior Pinkethmano, upon an

[1] On T. Oct. 10, 1707

Ass that never appear'd but twice on either Stage," while the Haymarket players, giving Banks' *The Unhappy Favourite*, advertised "the last new vocal Epilogue, Compos'd and Perform'd by the famous Signior Cibberini, after the newest English, French, Dutch, and Italian Manner." A particularly noticeable instance of this rivalry is to be seen in the twin productions of *The Cobler of Preston* a year later. Apparently, early in January 1715/6, Charles Johnson decided to make a farce out of Shakespeare's *The Taming of the Shrew*, introducing in it a trifle of political reference to the '15 Rebellion. Somehow or other information of this came to the Lincoln's Inn Fields house, and Christopher Bullock, in his own words, "*thought it might be of as goood Service to our* Stage, *as the other*." So he "*set to work on* Friday *Morning the 20th of* January, *finished it on the* Saturday *following, and it was acted on the* Tuesday *after*[1]." Johnson's piece was thus cut out, and was not produced till February 3, when it proved not very successful owing to the previous appearance of Bullock's piece. If we pass on still further in the century we discover precisely the same conditions operating. On Wednesday, Nov. 11, 1719 Dennis' *The Invader of his Country* was produced at Drury Lane; the Saturday following the Lincoln's Inn Fields actors revived the Restoration adaptation of *Coriolanus* by Tate. Eight years later, the Lincoln's Inn Fields players are found introducing "a new Song, being a Burlesque on the Ceremonial Coronation of Anne Bullen as perform'd at the Theatre in Drury Lane," and doing all in their power to ridicule the popular show of the rival house. Instances such as these, which are to be taken merely as typical of countless others, show that in our estimate of the repertoires and dramatic productivity of the time, due allowance must be made for the rivalry of the houses. The whole pantomime furore is connected with this, as may be seen from the list preserved by Weaver[2]. One such success was promptly capped by a similar production at the other theatre. As Molloy expresses it in his epilogue to Jeffreys' *Edwin* (L.[2] 1724):

[1] Preface to the play.   [2] *Infra*, p. 252.

Yon Rival Theatre, by Success made great,
Plotting Destruction to our sinking State,
Turn'd our own Arms upon us,—and—woe be to us,
They needs must raise the Devil to undo us!
Strait our Enchanter gave his Spirits Wing,
And conjur'd all the Town within this Ring.

The references are to the *Harlequin Doctor Faustus* of Drury Lane and *The Necromancer; or Harlequin Doctor Faustus* of Lincoln's Inn Fields.

As a final note to this brief glance at eighteenth century theatrical conditions, a word may be said concerning the actresses. The influence of women like Mrs Oldfield has already been noted[1]; but attention may be drawn to one theatrical convention for which the women were directly responsible. The old-standing tradition of presenting women-characters in the dress of men, established on the Elizabethan stage, and still popular in the Restoration, seemed to receive a new lease of life in this century. The reason undoubtedly was two-fold. The study of comedy during this time shows that, while an external chastening allied to sentimentalism is to be traced everywhere, the age was as immoral as, if not more immoral than, before. It could not always have the "luscious dialogue" it secretly craved for, and it made up for that in various ways, of which this was one. That the habit of dressing women as men was not indulged in purely for dramatic purposes is proved by the fact that there are numerous epilogues of the time spoken by actresses, often young actresses, dressed as beaux. That to Moore's *Mangora* (L.[2] 1717) was given by Mrs Spiller "in Man's-Cloaths," and it is sufficiently free and suggestive. Mrs Bradshaw was called in to recite the epilogue to Charles Johnson's *The Generous Husband* (D.L. 1711) and Miss Robinson, clad in similar wise, pronounced those to Breval's *The Strolers* (D.L. 1723) and to Mallet's *Eurydice* (D.L. 1731). The attraction which these had for the audience is shown by the fact that they were specially advertised. On Wednesday, March 27, 1706, for example, the Drury Lane management, in billing

---

[1] *Supra*, p. 40.

Banks' *Vertue Betray'd*, put among the notices detailing the
various entertainments of singing and dancing that of the new
epilogue spoken by the child who acted the Princess Elizabeth[1].
The second reason is to be discovered in the actresses themselves. While many of their men companions were heavy
and sedate, a large number of these women seem to have
been light, airy and saucy in their manners. Boys' parts
suited them to perfection. They probably demanded them,
and the playwrights were not slow to suit their tastes and
the tastes of the audience[2]. No one seems to have looked with
critical eyes on the absurdities which arose from the convention. In Hill's *The Fatal Vision* (L.[2] 1716), for example,
the Empress of China, Caimantha, lives for years with her
husband, unknown, as Selim, his favourite eunuch. The
follies of such a situation are evident to us now, but Hill's
play seems to have had some sort of success. The audience
asked as few questions as did the audience of Restoration
times.

---

[1] A Miss Younger.
[2] It is impossible to present a full list of such parts in contemporary
tragedy and comedy, but a selection may be permitted. In Cibber's
The Lady's Last Stake (H.[1] 1707) Mrs Oldfield played the part of
Mrs Conquest in boy's garments. Burnaby has women as men in three
plays: *The Modish Husband* (D.L. 1702), *The Ladies Visiting-Day*
(L.[1] 1701) and *Love Betray'd* (L.[1] 1703). In the first, Camilla is taken by
Mrs Oldfield; in the second Fulvia by Mrs Bracegirdle. Marina (acted by
Mrs Oldfield) in *Farewel Folly* (D.L. 1705) "personates a Young Rake."
Elvira appears as a man in Manning's *All for the Better* (D.L. 1702) and
Olivia in the same author's *The Generous Choice* (L.[1] 1700) is similarly
garbed. A girl as a man occurs in Mrs Manley's *Lucius, The First Christian
King of Britain* (D.L. 1717) and Rowe introduces Cleone as a man in
The Ambitious Step-Mother (L.[1] 1700). Mrs Pix utilised the same device
in *The Adventures in Madrid* (H.[1] 1706). Charles Johnson was particularly
fond of it. Women as men appear in *Injur'd Love* (D.L. 1711), in *The
General Cashier'd* (1712) and in *The Apparition* (D.L. 1713). The practice
endured long. We find it in Mrs Haywood's *A Wife to be Lett* (D.L. 1723),
in Lillo's *The Christian Hero* (D.L. 1735), in Kelly's *The Levee* (1741)
and in Cunningham's *Love in a Mist* (Dublin, 1747).

CHAPTER II

TRAGEDY

I. *Introductory: The Tendencies of the Age*

B EFORE we can deal adequately with any one type of
dramatic productivity of this time, we must to some
extent analyse the general movements of the age as they
affected tragedy and comedy in common. Already has been
noted the political element, which was, undoubtedly, of
prime importance in the shaping of particular dramatic
situations and characters. Noted, too, has been the disintegrating influence of pantomime, opera and farce. For our
purpose, however, probably the most important movement
of the time was that to which has been given the name of
pseudo-classical, and which found noble dramatic champions
in John Dennis, Joseph Addison and Charles Gildon. It was
this century which saw the crystallisation of that body of
"rules" so ridiculously enunciated by Rymer some twenty
years before. It was this century, too, which witnessed, in
Cato, the triumph of the classical tragedy. It cannot be
denied that the classical theories put forward by Dennis and
Gildon bore fruit in this time, or that they deeply influenced
the tragic productivity of the stage. The critics declared for
Aristotle's rules as interpreted by France, and to a certain
extent they imposed their authority. There were only one or
two writers bold enough to hazard even a hint that the terrible
Unities were not fundamentally essential. Farquhar did so
temerariously in his *Essay on Comedy*; Johnson in the prologue to *The Female Fortune-Teller* (L.² 1726) openly boasted
he had neglected them all; Rowe in *The Tragedy of Jane
Shore* (D.L. 1714) silently, but none the less deliberately,
violated them; Cibber in his prologue to *Ximena* (D.L. 1712)

cast some gentle satire on the stricter rules; Carey indulged
in a little ridicule when he solemnly declared in his *Hanging
and Marriage* (L.[2] 1722):

> The Time. *Exactly even with the Action.*
> The Place. *A Little Country Village.*
> The Action. *As follows.*

These, however, were but stray voices. For the most part
hardly anyone thought of going counter to the precepts of
ancient and modern. With Mrs Centlivre they believed, or
professed to believe, that the Unities were "the greatest
Beauties of a Dramatick Poem[1]"; and the typical form of
criticism is to be found in Jacob's commentary upon Beckingham's *Scipio Africanus* (L.[2] 1718):

> He hath hit the Diction of the Stage very well; his Expressions
> are all very proper, and his Sentiments just. His Plot is founded
> on Truth, as delivered to us by History, and is indeed very well
> suited for a Dramatick Performance. The Action is one and entire;
> the Episodes very judiciously interwoven, so that they conduce
> and seem to belong to the main Design. The Characters are well
> drawn, and the Unities of the Stage preserv'd: In short, it is
> an excellent Tragedy, conformable to the Rules of the Drama,
> and the Precepts of our Modern Criticks[2].

Again, however, there is the necessity to guard against any
extreme judgment of the period. In spite of the fact that the
"rules" were everywhere worshipped in theory, in practice
a very considerable amount of latitude was permitted. The
place of action need not necessarily be one definite spot; it
might include a town, so that several portions of that town
could be shown upon the stage in the course of a drama.
There are hardly more than two or three plays of this time,
apart from one-act farces, where the scene remains one and
entire from opening to close; on the other hand, we can find
no play where the action repeatedly shifts, as in Shakespeare,
from one end of the world to the other. Once more is
discoverable the compromise of the eighteenth century
between the tastes of the audience and the precepts of the

---

[1] *Love's Contrivance* (D.L. 1703), preface.
[2] *The Poetical Register: or, The Lives and Characters of the English
Dramatick Poets. With an Account of their Writings* (1719), p. 281

critics. As regards the Unity of Time, an amount of argument on various sides had failed to fix a definite limit. There are plays, like Jacob's *The Fatal Constancy* (D.L. 1723), in which the " *Time of the* Action *is no longer than that of the* Representation[1]," but usually the playwrights indulged in longer periods. Five hours is the fictional duration of Charles Shadwell's *The Fair Quaker of Deal* (D.L. 1710), six hours that of his *The Humours of the Army* (D.L. 1713). Leigh in *Kensington Gardens* (L.[2] 1719) allowed himself twelve, and Charles Johnson in *The Cobler of Preston* (D.L. 1716) and the anonymous author of *The Apparition* (D.L. 1713) permitted themselves thirteen. The domination of the Unities, it will be observed, penetrated even into the realm of farce. In Action, again, some trifling licences were allowed, subplots of a minor kind being indulged in by all but the ultraclassical dramatists. So, too, with the number of characters on the stage, there is to be discovered little unanimity. Some playwrights did strive to secure decorum by limiting the speaking persons in their plays. Mitchell has but four in *The Fatal Extravagance* (L.[2] 1721), Oldmixon six in *The Governour of Cyprus* (L.[1] 1703), Savage in *Sir Thomas Overbury* (D.L. 1723) and Johnson in *The Sultaness* (D.L. 1717) seven, Cibber eight in *Xerxes* (L.[1] 1699); but not all held to such strict limits. We can say only that there was a general tendency, noticeable from Elizabethan days on to the eighteenth century, to limit the changing of scene, the duration of action, the introduction of sub-plot and the number of characters; but that the more prescribed classical formulæ are rarer even in the eighteenth century than approaches towards Elizabethan freedom.

In none of these points, however, do we touch the real centre of controversy. Regarding the "beauty" of the Unities all in theory and with minor reservations might agree; but on the question of death upon the stage there was a sharp break not only between the pseudo-classicists and those we

---

[1] Another tragedy with a limit of two and a half hours is Hill's *Elfrid* (D.L. 1710), and Arthur's ballad-opera *The Lucky Discovery* (C.G. 1738) is no longer.

may call Shakespearians, but between the general tastes of the audience and the tastes of those who endeavoured to follow France in her dignified but chilly way. We find, therefore, in this period a striking variety of devices for finishing off tragedies. In some plays, and they are the fewest of all, nothing indecorous is permitted to take place on the stage. Deaths are duly relegated behind the scenes, to be dully narrated to a bored and yawning audience. There are, on the other hand, many dramas of the time full of bustle and fighting and murder *coram populo*; where no attempt is made to follow the dismal injunctions of the French. It is fairly obvious, from even a most cursory glance at the repertoires of the time, that the latter had the greatest success. Only the most fanatic of the pseudo-classicists kept the rigid path of theatrical chastity and railed at the audience for its vulgar tastes. Between these two schools we come across a number of compromisers; men with pseudo-classic ideals who were yet not prepared to let a single stab or two stand between them and immediate success, or who, and this is the more interesting for our purpose, devised other methods of pleasing both the one side and the other. Ambrose Philips is as good an example of this class as any. In *The Briton* (D.L. 1722) he allowed Cartismand to stab Gwendolen in full view of the audience. Whether this struck him as rather revolutionary or not, in his next play, *Humfrey, Duke of Gloucester* (D.L. 1723), he permitted Gloucester to be smothered off the stage—but placed Beaufort before the audience so that he might look through the proscenium door to report on the progress of the smothering. More thrilling than the classical after-the-event narration it must have been, but pale when compared with the devices of heroic dramatists of the time. One other method of circumventing the pseudo-classical rules and itself as old as the Greek theatre has been noted above. Many playwrights found ways of escape by these scene-drawings which revealed to the spectators the result of violence, if not violence itself[1].

A correct appreciation of the real scope of pseudo-classicism

[1] *Supra*, p. 27.

in eighteenth century drama is a thing exceedingly difficult
to obtain. On the one hand, there is everywhere traceable
the power of French precepts; but that power was in many
ways a kind of tyranny. Pseudo-classical plays were extolled
by the critics; a few, like Addison's *Cato* (D.L. 1713), were
popular successes[1]; yet on the whole pseudo-classicism was
not deeply welcomed by the audiences of the age. An
analysis of several typical years of dramatic endeavour will
display this more clearly than anything else. Full, or comparatively full, records of dramatic performances do not start
till the years 1703–4, when we find the managements of
Drury Lane and of Lincoln's Inn Fields advertising fairly
regularly in the pages of *The Daily Courant*. Selections from
these advertisements have been given by Genest, but never
have they been reproduced completely. In 1703, the Drury
Lane company, after playing at Bath, opened their London
season on Wednesday, October 6; they continued acting until
August 23, 1704. During this time they performed, with
occasional interruptions, six days a week, the total number
of productions amounting to 190. The first thing we note
in the lists of their repertoire is the fact that tragedy holds a
very subordinate place, there being barely 65 nights given to
serious drama altogether. The only other earlier lists with
which we could compare these are those given in *Henslowe's
Diary*, a brief examination of which proves that tragic or
serious plays held then a much more important place in the
repertoires of the companies. Of the 65 nights given to
tragedy in the season 1703–4, Shakespeare occupied 20[2]
(*Lear* 3, *Hamlet* 4, *Macbeth* in the operatic version 6, *Timon
of Athens* in Shadwell's version 2, *Caius Marius* of Otway 3,
Richard III of Cibber 1, *Titus Andronicus* of Ravenscroft 1).
Besides the Shakespeare dramas, we find represented plays
of Banks (*Vertue Betray'd* 1, *The Albion Queens* 8, *The
Unhappy Favourite* 4); Southerne (*The Fatal Marriage* 4,
Oroonoko 5); Otway (*Venice Preserv'd* 3, *The Orphan* 1);

---

[1] Although the success of *Cato* was largely due to political enthusiasm.
[2] The numbers after the titles of the plays indicate the number of
performances during the season.

Lee (*The Rival Queens* 1); Shadwell (*Don John* 3); Settle (*Ibrahim* 2, *The Empress of Morocco* 2, *The Heir of Morocco* 1); and Dryden (*The Conquest of Granada* 1). It is perfectly obvious from this that what, in tragedy, appealed to the audiences of 1703–4 were Shakespearian, pathetic and "domestic" plays, and after those the heroic dramas. There is not a single pre-1700 classical tragedy included in the list. The season 1704–5 carries on the same tradition. Drury Lane opened on Sept. 11, 1704 and closed on July 27, 1705, some 193 performances being given. Of these, 146 evenings were devoted to comedy and 15 more to new operas. Tragedy is represented only 28 times. Of these 28 times, Shakespeare took up 13 (*Titus Andronicus* 1, *Hamlet* 4, *Lear* 2, *Timon of Athens* 2, *Macbeth* 4). There were also 4 performances of Restoration heroic dramas (Dryden's *Œdipus* 2, Settle's *The Empress of Morocco* 1, Lee's *Mithridates* 1); the rest were of pathetic plays (Banks' *The Unhappy Favourite* 3, *The Albion Queens* 1; Southerne's *Oroonoko* 2; Otway's *Venice Preserv'd* 1). From this brief examination of the repertoires of the opening years of the century, it may be profitable to pass to an analysis of the plays produced in a certain series of years throughout the period; for this purpose the end of every decade may be selected. In the season of 1708–9, the Drury Lane company performed for about 181 nights, during which time they devoted 38 to tragedy. Again Shakespeare comes first on the list, with *Hamlet* 4, *Macbeth* 4, *Othello* 2, *Lear* 2 and *Henry VIII* 1. The heroic tragedy is represented by Lee (*Sophonisba* 1, *The Rival Queens* 3), Dryden (*Œdipus* 1, *The Indian Emperour* 3, *The Conquest of Granada* 1, *Aureng Zebe* 1) and Settle (*The Heir of Morocco* 1). Besides these Dryden's *All for Love* and *Troilus and Cressida*, Southerne's *The Fatal Marriage* and *Oroonoko*, Shadwell's *Don John* and Otway's *Venice Preserv'd* were all given once. A new tragedy appeared in Dennis' *Appius and Virginia* 4. Once more a repertoire composed of Shakespearian, heroic and pathetic tragedies.

Ten years later 72 nights out of 176 (almost one-third the total repertoire) were given to tragedy, a sign possibly of a slightly changing popular taste. Among these serious dramas presented appear 7 of Shakespeare's, *Julius Cæsar* 3, *Lear* 1, *Othello* 2, *Macbeth* 4, *Hamlet* 1, *Richard III* 1 and *Henry VIII* 2. The tragedies of an heroic cast are represented by Dryden's *The Indian Emperour* 1 and Lee's *Cæsar Borgia* 2, and other Restoration types occur in Otway's *Venice Preserv'd* 2 and *The Orphan* 3, Southerne's *Oroonoko* 3 and *The Fatal Marriage* 1, Dryden's *All for Love* 10, Banks' *The Unhappy Favourite* 1, Congreve's *The Mourning Bride* 6 and Shadwell's *Don John* 1. A new play, Young's *Busiris*, occupied 9 nights, Rowe's *Jane Shore* 2 and his *Tamerlane* 5. Pseudo-classicism appears only in Addison's *Cato* 4, Cibber's *Ximena* 3 and Philips' *The Distrest Mother* 2—a total of 9 out of 72 performances.

During the season 1728–9 three theatres were running, Drury Lane, Haymarket and Lincoln's Inn Fields. The first gave 173 performances in all, 61 of which were of tragedies. Pseudo-classicism here is represented by Philips (*The Distrest Mother* 6) and Addison (*Cato* 2), but the vast majority of the dramas acted were of the types most popular in the foregoing years. Shakespeare occupied 17 evenings (*Hamlet* 2, *Henry VIII* 6, *Othello* 3, *Richard III* 2, *Macbeth* 2, *Lear* 1, *Timon of Athens* 1). Beaumont and Fletcher's *The Maid's Tragedy* was presented once. Heroic in tendency are Lee's *Theodosius* 4 and *Mithridates* 1; pathetic are Congreve's *The Mourning Bride* 2, Otway's *The Orphan* 3, Southerne's *The Fatal Marriage* 3 and Banks' *Vertue Betray'd* 1 and *The Albion Queens* 1. In addition to these Shadwell's *Don John* 4 was performed, along with Dryden's *All for Love* 3, Rowe's *Tamerlane* 5 (slightly heroic) and *The Fair Penitent* 4 (definitely pathetic) and Theobald's *Double Falshood* 1 (an adaptation of an early Caroline play). At Lincoln's Inn Fields during the same season tragedy secured only 31 out of 153 acting nights; Shakespeare occupied 12 of the 31 with *Lear* 1, *Othello* 3, *Hamlet* 3, *Julius Cæsar* 1, and *Macbeth* 4. Dryden's *Œdipus*, Banks' *The Unhappy Favourite*, Otway's *Venice Preserv'd* and Rowe's *Tamerlane* were given once each. The remaining 15 nights were devoted to new dramas, Barford's

The Virgin Queen 3, Madden's *Themistocles* 9 and Mrs Haywood's *Frederick* 3. The operas of *Thomyris* and *Camilla* were given twice each. The Haymarket company during the same months were occupied mainly with the popular *Hurlothrumbo*, but they too succeeded in putting on *The Unhappy Favourite, The Orphan, Don Carlos, Venice Preserv'd* and *Oroonoko*.

The season 1738–9 shows a slightly smaller proportion of tragedies at Drury Lane, 58 out of 190. Shakespeare once more is well represented in *Hamlet* 5, *Julius Cæsar* 4, *Othello* 2, *Richard III* 2, *Macbeth* 2, *Henry VIII* 5 and *Lear* 1. One performance each was given to Otway's *Venice Preserv'd*, Banks' *The Unhappy Favourite*, Southerne's *Oroonoko* and Banks' *The Albion Queens*. *The Orphan* secured a representation of 2 nights. Rowe's *Tamerlane* ran 3 times, *Lady Jane Gray* 4, *Jane Shore* 1, Addison's *Cato* 6 and *The Siege of Damascus* 2. Mallet's *Mustapha*, a new play, ran for 14 nights. Here still Shakespearian and pathetic elements seem to retain their favour. At Covent Garden the same season more tragedies were performed, no less than 60 out of a total of 176. We note here a larger infusion of Restoration pieces, Lee's *Theodosius* 3, *The Rival Queens* 3 and *Mithridates* 3 appearing alongside of Southerne's *Oroonoko* 2, Otway's *Venice Preserv'd* 3 and *The Orphan* 1, Dryden's *All for Love* 3 and *Œdipus* 1, Congreve's *The Mourning Bride* 2 and Banks' *The Albion Queens* 2. Rowe, too, seems to have been fairly popular; *Jane Shore* 2, *Tamerlane* 2, *The Fair Penitent* 2 and *The Royal Convert* 5 were all presented on the boards. Shakespeare proved moderately fashionable with *Macbeth* 4, *Hamlet* 3, *Lear* 2, *King John* 2, *Richard II* 4 and *Henry V* 4[1]. Marsh's *Amasis* appeared once, Philips' *The Distrest Mother* twice, Addison's *Cato* once, and Fenton's *Marianne* twice. Shirley's *The Parricide* 1 is a solitary new play, damned on its first appearance.

With the Drury Lane repertoire of 1748–9 we come upon a changed set of circumstances. Tragedy here occupies 86 out

---

[1] I include the last-mentioned play among the tragedies because of its serious tone.

of 180 nights, and, in place of the moderate percentage of Shakespearian plays noted in the foregoing years, we discover that over half of those 86 nights (44 in all) were devoted to Shakespeare. *Hamlet* ran 6 times, *Richard III* 4, *Othello* 4, *Lear* 4, *Henry V* 1, *Macbeth* 5 and *Romeo* no less than 20. This increase in popularity we must attribute to Garrick's endeavours, which were, of course, based on the enthusiasm for the "bard of Avon" observable in all the seasons from 1734–5 onwards. Restoration plays this season appear only in Otway's *The Orphan* 4 and *Venice Preserv'd* 1. Rowe's *The Fair Penitent* was given 5 times, *Jane Shore* 3 and *Tamerlane* 2, Thomson's *Tancred and Sigismunda* once, Philips' *The Distrest Mother* once and Lillo's *The London Merchant* once. Dr Johnson's *Irene* had a successful run of 13 nights and Hill's *Merope* of 11. At Covent Garden during the same season tragedy was granted only 57 nights out of a total of 148, and of these 57 Thomson's *Coriolanus* occupied 10. Only 6 were given to Shakespeare (*Lear* 2, *Othello* 1, *Julius Cæsar* 3), but Restoration drama is more fully represented than at Drury Lane, in Lee's *Theodosius* 2 and *The Rival Queens* 1, Otway's *The Orphan* 1 and *Venice Preserv'd* 1, Southerne's *Oroonoko* 6 and Dryden's *Don Sebastian* 2. Rowe was still popular in *The Fair Penitent* 3, *Jane Shore* 7 and *Tamerlane* 2. Addison's *Cato* ran 5 times, Young's *The Revenge* twice and Philips' *The Distrest Mother* 8 times; Hughes' *The Siege of Damascus* appeared but once.

To sum up the results presented by an examination of these lists is fairly easy.

1. Tragedy as a whole is clearly subordinate in the repertoires, in the early years to comedy, later to opera and comedy, and, towards the middle and end of the period, to opera, comedy and pantomime. In spite of Swift's declaration already quoted[1], it would seem that tragedy proved very much less paying than other forms of theatrical entertainment, and this may be the explanation of the fact that there is practically no writer of these fifty years who is definitely a tragic dramatist, no writer who did not stoop from the more serious realms to produce an opera or a farce.

[1] *Supra*, p. 24.

Let others be with Tragick Lawrel's Crown'd,
Where undisturb'd the Heroe struts around,
And Empty Boxes Eccho to the Sound,

says Baker in his prologue to *Tunbridge-Walks* (D.L. 1703), and Hillaria in the same comedy declares that, when she goes to the play-house, "if 'tis a Tragedy," she turns "and talks to the Beaus behind[1]."

2. Undoubtedly, the most popular tragic dramatist was Shakespeare. Long before Garrick's birth his plays were successful on the stage, and, even though the audiences were not prepared to witness all his dramas in an unaltered form, he never lost his hold upon the hearts of his countrymen. This was true of the time when the more progressive men were trying to make thoroughly fashionable the heroic drama; it was true when their successors were endeavouring to establish the stricter forms of pseudo-classic tragedy on the English stage.

3. Pathos was next in favour, Banks, Southerne and Otway, with Rowe in the later years, being specially successful.

4. Next to that comes the heroic drama, with works by Dryden, Settle and Lee as regular stock-plays.

When we turn from these repertoire lists to new productions for the theatre, we find that there is a decided correspondence between the groups of new and old dramas. There are far fewer tragedies in proportion to the total number of plays, for example, in the handlist to this volume than in the handlist covering dramatic activity from 1660 to 1700 or in Sir Walter Greg's *Handlist of Plays* up to 1642. Moreover, purely classical dramas are both rare and generally unsuccessful. The prime motive forces in the tragic creation of these fifty years are pathos and heroics, modified by Shakespearian influence and sometimes by classical precept. Pseudo-classicism, then, is found to be rather an external force in the age, and uncreative at that. Only in one respect, as will be

---

[1] IV. i. Cibber also speaks of the grumbling at L.I.F. when Betterton proposed to put on a tragedy (ed. Lowe, i. 229). At the same time, the taste of the age seems to have been reverting again to the tragic type after the early thirties of the century.

seen later[1], did that movement exercise a truly great and beneficial influence.

The typical tragic form all through these years is not, therefore, the classical form, but a peculiar amalgam of diverse forces. The classicists declared an historical theme advisable if not absolutely necessary, and accordingly we get the innumerable *Gustavus Vasas* and *Sir Walter Raleighs* and *Jane Shores* of the time. The heroic drama was still popular and so the treatment of many of these themes betrays the influence of Dryden and Lee. Pathos taken from Otway and Southerne is plentifully introduced and reminiscences of Shakespeare are everywhere. This conglomerate type is generally false in character-delineation and conscious of its own defects. To it may be given the name of Augustan tragedy.

Alongside of this and of the purely classical plays must be numbered the pathetic tragedy, often dealing with domestic themes, and leading ultimately to Lillo's *The London Merchant* (D.L. 1731), as well as the pure heroic drama taken over from the period of the Restoration. The trouble in the age was lack of orientation. No single tragic dramatist, save Lillo and to a lesser extent Moore, knew precisely at what he would aim. The passion which had been retained in Restoration days was almost gone, and everyone felt the want of spirit in the tragedy of the time. Here becomes evident an interesting difference between the mood of the late seventeenth century and the mood of the eighteenth century. Whereas overweening self-confidence had been a characteristic of the former period, modesty and bashfulness formed the characteristic of this.

> *If in a well-work'd Story they aspire,*
> *To imitate old* Rome's *or* Athen's *Fire,*
> *It will not do, for strait the Cry shall be,*
> *'Tis a forc'd heavy piece of Bombastry,*

says the prologue to Mrs Centlivre's *The Beau's Duel* (L.[1] 1702). The only language that could be used in the theatre was this forced rhetoric; and yet the age was conscious

[1] *Infra*, p. 63.

of its weaknesses. The compiler of *The Companion to the Play-House* (1764) has well noted the lack of plainness and simplicity which characterised the eighteenth century drama, attributing it partly to the disuse of blank verse as a medium for comedy:

> Whether the refined Stile of *Addison*'s *Cato*, and the flowing Versification of *Rowe* first occasioned this Departure from antient Simplicity it is difficult to determine: but it is too true, that *Southerne* was the last of our Dramatick Writers, who was, in any Degree, possest of that magnificent Plainness, which is the genuine Dress of Nature; though indeed the Plays even of *Rowe* are more simple in their Stile, than those which have been produced by his Successors[1].

With this inflated diction and lack of orientation, it is but natural that almost everyone should have felt the weakness of contemporary tragic drama. Hardly any dared to try unknown paths. "I won't pretend to give you an Account of the Plot," says Steele of an imaginary tragedy, "it being the same Design upon which all Tragedies have been writ for several Years last past; and from the beginning of the First Scene, the Frequenters of the House may know, as well as the Author, when the Battle is to be fought, the Lady to yield, and the Hero proceed to his Wedding and Coronation[2]." The fact was realised by all, and Theobald was but voicing a universal thought when in the prologue to Jeffreys' *Edwin* (L.[2] 1724) he declared:

> *Oft have you mourn'd, in this degenerate Age,*
> *How low is sunk the noble Tragic Rage.*

Concerning the weaknesses of this Augustan drama much was written by contemporaries, and many efforts were made to suggest means whereby it might be verified. The classical critics were without a shadow of doubt right in saying that love had ruined the spirit of tragedy.

> *The Hero and the Lover long have been*
> *The pleasing Bus'ness of the Tragick Scene,*

announced the prologue to Mountfort's *Zelmane* (L.[1] 1704). That love had come over from Restoration days. It appeared

---

[1] I. xxxix.　　　[2] *The Tatler*, No. 22, May 30, 1709.

in a weakened form in the pathetic dramas, and the Caroline
formula of "Love and Honour" was but slightly altered to
"Love and Liberty" in the more heroic dramas of the age of
Anne. Love and liberty form the main motive force in Duncombe's *Junius Brutus* (D.L. 1734); they give the title to
Charles Johnson's *Love and Liberty* (1709); the hero of
Martyn's *Timoleon* (D.L. 1730) "burns with Liberty, and
Love[1]"; love we find in Charles Johnson's *The Victim* (D.L.
1714) is still "Tyrannic[2]." It is to the credit of the classical
dramatists and critics that they diagnosed aright this failure in
the tragedies of their own time. Probably the most important
pronouncement of this realisation of theirs is to be found in
Jacob's account of Dennis (obviously inspired by the playwright himself):

When he first began to write Tragedy, he saw, with Concern,
that Love had got the entire possession of the Tragick Stage,
contrary to the Nature and Design of Tragedy, the Practice
of *Sophocles*, *Euripides*, and our Countryman *Shakespear*. As his
Intentions were more to get Reputation than Money, and to gain
the Approbation of the Judicious and Knowing (which he look'd
upon as a certain Earnest of future Fame) rather than a Crowd
of ignorant Spectators and Readers; he resolv'd to deviate a little
from the reigning Practice of the Stage; and not to make his
Heroes whining Slaves in their Amours; which not only debases
the Majesty of Tragedy, but confounds most of its principal
Characters, by making that Passion the predominant Quality in
all; and which must for ever make the present and succeeding
Writers unable to attain to the Excellency of the Ancients: But
he did not think it adviseable at once to shew his principal
Characters wholly exempt from it, apprehending that so great
and sudden an Alteration might prove disagreeable; he rather
chose to steer a middle Course, and to make Love appear violent,
but at the same time to give way to the force of Reason, or to the
influence of some other more noble Passion; as in *Rinaldo*, it
gives place to Glory; in *Iphigenia*, to Friendship; and in *Liberty
Asserted*, to the publick Good. He thought by these means an
Audience might be entertain'd and prepar'd for greater Alterations,
whereby the Dignity of Tragedy might be supported, and its
principal Characters justly distinguish'd[3].

---

[1] Prologue. [2] II. i.
[3] p. 69.

This is but Tickell's couplet prefixed to Addison's *Cato*
(D.L. 1713),

> *Too long hath Love engross'd* Britannia's *Stage,*
> *And sunk to Softness all our Tragic Rage,*

elaborated in critical prose. The diagnosis was due not to
Dennis alone, but to the body of pseudo-classic opinion.

The pseudo-classicists, however, could not give to tragedy
that which in reality it wanted. They could not draw
interesting studies of character; they could not introduce
passion because they disdained "enthusiasm"; and they
could not supply that particular atmosphere of overwhelming
supermundane existence which has been a marked characteristic of all great drama. The feeling of fate and the
presence of passion seem necessary elements in tragedy; and
these were hardly seen in the eighteenth century until Lillo
came forward with *Fatal Curiosity* (H.² 1736). It was the
domestic dramatists who, in reality, were destined to give
the only live force to the serious drama of the age.

That the period, as it advanced, was endeavouring more
and more to recapture some of the tragic spirit is seen,
I believe, in the reaction to the comic epilogue which was
for many years regarded as a necessary appendix to every
tragedy. This comic epilogue, witty, cynical and genteel, was,
as it were, a kind of well-bred protest against any sort of
enthusiastic sentiment; but by the twenties of the century
there were arising men who felt that a genuine tragic atmosphere could not subsist alongside of this cynical after-speech.
The first protest against the habit of which I know appears
in the epilogue to W. Phillips' *Belisarius* (L.² 1724), but his
cry was not repeated until many years had passed. That
there were silent complaints abroad can perhaps be shown
by the almost apologetic epilogue to Lewis' *Philip of Macedon*
(L.² 1727). An actress enters on the stage:

> *'Tis mighty well!—that anxious Pomp is o'er,*
> *That stiff uneasy Grandeur of an Hour!*
> *Nor Queen nor Princess (thank my Stars!) am I;*
> *Were you, O Ladys, were you but to try*
> *What Pleasure 'tis—the laying Greatness by!...*

And happy rest the Bards, who brought in Vogue
With Tragic Scenes the Comic Epilogue.
What! let our courteous Audience bear away,
In pensive Mood, th' Impression of the Play!—
No; that, be sure, we're careful to destroy,
And close each deep Catastrophe with Joy...
This House would be the emptiest Place on Earth,
Did we not tagg our Tragedies with Mirth.

By 1731 Aaron Hill had again enunciated the protest in his unspoken epilogue to Jeffreys' *Merope* (L.² 1731), and capped that by another in his own *Alzira* (L.² 1736). A shamefaced complaint occurs in Miller's *The Universal Passion* (D.L. 1737), and both Brooke and Mallet fought against the practice in 1739. The epilogue to the latter's *Mustapha* (D.L. 1739) was spoken by Quin and directed against the "wanton jokes" presented at tragedies; that to *Gustavus Vasa* (1739) recalls the days of Nell Gwynn and speaks of later more judicious tastes. About the same time, other writers proceeded to inveigh against the follies of the habit. Says Fielding in satiric wise,

> *The Play once done, the* Epilogue, *by Rule,*
> *Should come and turn it all to Ridicule;*
> *Should tell the Ladies that the Tragic-Bards,*
> *Who prate of Virtue and her vast Rewards,*
> *Are all in Jest, and only Fools should heed 'em;*
> *For all* wise Women *flock to* Mother Needham[1],

and Thomson, in the epilogue to *Agamemnon* (D.L. 1738), declares himself "*to modern Epilogue a Foe*" and "*Thinks such mean Mirth but deadens generous woe.*" That the practice was not killed by these protests is made clear by the fact that Thomson found it necessary seven years later to repeat his warning and to conjure the audience to preserve the feeling for tragedy:

> *O keep the dear Impression in your Breast,*
> *Nor idly lose it for a wretched Jest*[2].

[1] *Pasquin* (H.² 1736), Epilogue.
[2] *Tancred and Sigismunda* (D.L. 1745), Epilogue.

The year before Miller had seen fit to enter his similar plea[1], and it was the same year that Cibber took up the cry in *Papal Tyranny in the Reign of King John* (C.G. 1745):

> *Now, after Tragedy, you know, the Way*
> *Is to come forward, with an Air so gay,*
> *Not to support,—no, no,—to ridicule the Play.*
> *With flirting Fan, and pointed Wit, so jolly,*
> *Crack Jokes on Virtue, as an unbred Folly.*
> *How oft has the* Grecian *Dame, distress'd,*
> *Been dismal Company—till made a Jest?*

The aged actor manager recalls the words of what no doubt was a typical beau who would exclaim:

> After all
> That Epilogue was dev'lish comical!
> Better, by half, than all their hum-drum Sorrow!
> I'cod I'll come and hear't again to-morrow!

Even although a certain section of the audience refused to give up their "wanton jokes," the fact that there were men with a higher sense of harmony and a true regard for the spirit of tragedy shows the conscious and meritorious efforts which were being made during this half-century towards a revitalisation of tragedy. The reaction to the comic epilogue is not important in itself; but it is characteristic of the time.

II. *Elizabethan, Restoration and Foreign Models*

As with Restoration tragedy, so with Augustan, it must be emphasised that the fundamental basis of all dramatic endeavour lay in the English drama of the past. The Restoration types were simply carried on, and renewed interest in and appreciation of Shakespeare encouraged imitations and alterations of earlier tragedies. When we look at the dramatic repertoires briefly sketched above, it is true, we are struck by the comparative lack of pre-Commonwealth dramas represented apart from those of Shakespeare; and it is to be confessed that of the contemporaries of Shakespeare the early eighteenth century audiences knew but little. On the other hand, it must ever be remembered that the substratum of

---

[1] Epilogue to *Mahomet, the Impostor* (D.L. 1744).

Restoration tragedy was itself Elizabethan, and the Restoration heroic drama was fully appreciated in the Georgian theatre.

That Shakespeare was fully appreciated in the period 1700–1750 requires little proof. The critics looked up to him; Pope and Theobald vied with each other in editing his works. Not a season passed but some half a dozen of his plays appeared on the boards of the theatre. The age teems with reminiscences of his characters, his themes and his language. The only writer of the time who placed him not in the very first rank seems to have been Gildon who, in his preface to *Love's Victim* (L.[1] 1701), declared that though he "drew *Othello*...finely" he yet "made a scurvy piece of *Desdemona*" and that "*Otway* alone seemed to promise a Master in every Kind." Otherwise, Shakespeare was taken by all as the representative of true dramatic genius. His ghost is supposed to speak the epilogue to Gildon's *Measure for Measure* (L.[1] 1700); the same ghost along with that of Dryden appears among the *dramatis personæ* of Mrs Boyd's *Don Sancho* (1739); and once more this spirit is called forth in the epilogue to Mrs Hoper's *Queen Tragedy Restor'd* (H.[2] 1749). Many are the exhortations of authors to follow him. One such occurs in Charles Johnson's *The Wife's Relief* (D.L. 1711)[1] and another in "Timothy Fribble's" *Tittle Tattle* (1749), where the epilogue cries:

> *Rouze*, Britons, *rouze, this* modish Taste *despise*,
> *And let* Good Sense *to its* Old Standard *rise;*
> *Frequent your* luscious Pantomimes *no more*,
> *But* SHAKESPEARE, *like your* Ancestors *adore.*

The last reference points to a state of affairs which in the thirties and the forties dramatists never ceased to deplore. Says a dancer in Fielding's *Pasquin* (H.[2] 1736), which, be it remembered, is "A Dramatick Satire on the Times":

Hang his Play, and all Plays; the Dancers are the only People that support the House; if it were not for us they might act their *Shakespeare* to empty Benches[2].

---

[1] Prologue.
[2] III. Cp. *Tumble-Down Dick* (H.[2] 1736), Introduction; and *infra*, p. 255.

In 1723, Moses Browne, writing in the prologue to *Polidus*, bemoaned the tastes of the spectators:

> When Otho *and* Astartus *win the Prize,*
> *And* Hamlet, *and* Othello *you despise,*

a cry of despair which was echoed a few years later:

> *To strike the Soul with Horror, and Surprize,*
> *Our Barns we burn, our fiery Dragon flies:*
> *With Gods and Goddesses we fill the Scene,*
> *Who dance—at the Command of* Harlequin.
> *And if these fail a crouded House to bring,*
> *Our Heroines warble, and our Heroes sing.*
> Cæsar, Othello, Brutus, *and* Macbeth
> *Shrink at the Names of* Hunter, *and* Mackheath[1].

That this does not entirely represent the true state of affairs is proved by the repertoire lists, and there were many signs of encouragement. Apparently some ladies of fashion actually raised a subscription to aid the actors in staging Shakespeare —"Shakespeare's Ladies," they were called. In the season 1737–8 these gentlewomen evidently (if we are to judge by the theatre advertisements) persuaded Rich to produce a number of Shakespeare's plays at his house. Concerning these G. C. D. Odell[2] quotes from Ralph's *The Case of our Present Theatrical Disputes fairly Stated* (1783) a passage to the effect that "the Ladies of the *Shakespear* Club" had given a very noble instance of their desire to encourage the reviving of old plays, no doubt a reference to this. At least three other references to these "Shakespearian" ladies, apparently unknown to Odell, are to be found in contemporary literature. Fielding in his *The Historical Register, For the Year 1736* (H.[2] 1737) speaks of "*Shakespear*'s Ladies, or *Beaumont* and *Fletcher*'s Ladies[3]," the latter evidently an otherwise unknown circle, and the prologue to Lynch's *The Independent Patriot* (L.[2] 1737) has the lines:

> *By a late Instance they* (i.e. the ladies) *seem well inclin'd,*
> *To make the Ear the Passage to the Mind.*

---

[1] Martyn's *Timoleon* (D.L. 1730), Prologue "by a friend."
[2] *Op. cit.* i. 260.   [3] III.

A note to the word "late" leaves us in no doubt as to what Lynch was referring to: "Alluding," he says, "to the Ladies Subscription, this Winter, for the Revival of *Shakespeare*'s Plays." It is possible that another subscription was raised later, for "Timothy Fribble" in the prologue to *Tittle Tattle* (1749) declares that "the Ladies are reconcil'd to Sense; and *Shakespear* is now become their Favourite."

That this effort of the ladies of quality was not without effect is shown by the surprising number of revivals of little known or totally unknown Shakespearian plays in the thirties and forties of the century. *Henry V* came out at Goodman's Fields on Thursday, Feb. 5, 1736, and at Covent Garden on Thursday, Feb. 23, 1738. *King John* was revived at the latter theatre on Saturday, Feb. 26, 1737, and *Richard II*, in its unaltered form, on Monday, Feb. 6, 1738. *Romeo and Juliet*, in Theophilus Cibber's adaptation, was given at the Haymarket on Tuesday, Sept. 9, 1744, and proved later, in its original form, a popular success at Covent Garden. Shakespeare's tragedies, however, had at no period of the seventeenth and eighteenth centuries been quite forgotten, and the remarkable enthusiasm of those years will be more apparent when we glance later at the numerous performances of the long-forgotten romantic comedies and tragi-comedies[1]. One instance of this enthusiasm might, in passing, be noted here. On Friday, April 28, 1738 the Drury Lane company performed *Julius Cæsar*, always a fairly popular play, in aid of a fund for erecting a monument to Shakespeare. *The London Daily Post* announced a few weeks later that the proceeds amounted to £170 with an additional £30 still to be gathered for tickets[2]. Rich at Covent Garden, evidently feeling that something of the same nature would be expected of him, advertised[3] that, as the season was late, he would defer a similar performance at his theatre till the autumn. This performance actually took place on Tuesday, April 10, 1739, *Hamlet* being the play selected and the money gathered amounting to £82. 16*s*.

---

[1] *Infra*, p. 138.
[2] Monday, June 5, 1738.
[3] Tuesday, July 25, 1738.

Apart from this interest in Shakespeare taken by the spectators, an interest which culminated happily in the restoring of a more or less original text of the Elizabethan plays, we can trace the influence of Shakespeare on the dramatists themselves. Adaptations may here be left out of account, but Rowe's *The Tragedy of Jane Shore* (D.L. 1714), Havard's *King Charles the First* (L.[2] 1737) and Shirley's *Edward the Black Prince* (D.L. 1750) are all worthy of notice as being "Written in Shakespeare's Style." Cibber took the idea of his *Papal Tyranny in the Reign of King John* (C.G. 1745) from Shakespeare's historical tragedy; Lillo's *Marina* (C.G. 1738) is a reworking of *Pericles*; Young's *The Revenge* (D.L. 1721) seems to owe something to *Othello*; and Mitchell's (or Hill's) *The Fatal Extravagance* (L.[2] 1721) is confessedly based on the pseudo-Shakespearian *Yorkshire Tragedy*.

Besides Shakespeare, other Elizabethan dramatists furnished their suggestions to the playwrights of the time. D'Avenant's *The Unfortunate Lovers* gave Bellers the suggestion for his *Injur'd Innocence* (D.L. 1732); Massinger's *The Fatal Dowry* is the basis of Rowe's *The Fair Penitent* (L.[1] 1702); Charles Johnson's *Love and Liberty* (1709) shows its debt to Fletcher's *The Double Marriage*, just as Cibber's *Cæsar in Ægypt* (D.L. 1724) displays its debt to *The False One*; Rowley's *All's Lost by Lust*, a play acted in Restoration times, provided Mrs Pix with ideas for *The Conquest of Spain* (H.[1] 1705); and Dekker and Massinger's *The Virgin Martyr* gave to Griffin material for his adaptation, *Injured Virtue: or, The Virgin Martyr* (Richmond, Duke of Southampton and Cleaveland's men, 1714). Still more potent, probably, was the influence of the heroic and pathetic dramatists of the time of Charles II. The atmosphere of Dryden's *All for Love* is to be traced in Cibber's *Cæsar in Ægypt* (D.L. 1724) and in Frowde's *Philotas* (L.[2] 1731), while Cibber was obviously remembering Maximin when he wrote his *Xerxes* (L.[1] 1699). Roger Boyle, Earl of Orrery, because he was near to the classic temper of later times, likewise laid his impress on the early eighteenth century dramatists. Mallet's *Mustapha* (D.L.

1739) is indebted to him, as is Shirley's *Edward the Black Prince* (D.L. 1750). Crowne's work was used by Havard for his *Regulus* (D.L. 1744), and Lee's *Lucius Junius Brutus* by Gildon for *The Patriot* (D.L. 1703) and by Duncombe for his *Junius Brutus* of 1734. D'Avenant's *The Law against Lovers* was taken over by Gildon (along with Shakespeare's original) for his *Measure for Measure* (L.¹ 1700). Otway's influence is, of course, writ large over the whole period, and alongside of him stands Southerne. Marsh's *Amasis* (C.G. 1738), the anonymous *The Rival Brothers* (L.¹ 1704), Young's *The Revenge* (D.L. 1721) and Theobald's *The Perfidious Brother* (L.² 1716) all show the influence of *The Orphan*. Wandesford's *Fatal Love* (H.² 1730) was similarly suggested by Southerne's *The Fatal Marriage*.

We have, therefore, in this period to note the old heroic element taken over from Dryden and Orrery, the pathetic note of Southerne and Otway, and the Shakespearian style, the last sometimes altered out of all recognition. Later, too, we shall have occasion to note the influence of the domestic dramas of Elizabethan and of later times. We must never forget that Lillo himself wrote a play on the theme of *Arden of Feversham* (D.L. 1759)¹.

While this indebtedness of the early eighteenth century theatre to past English models is incontrovertible, there must be taken into account also the growing influence of French tragedy. Here was the prime source of the pseudo-classicism of the time. There was the growing power of Racine to conjure with, and Voltaire in the middle of our period was becoming an international force. With their lack of self-confidence, the dramatists more and more turned to Paris. Cibber adapted Corneille's *Le Cid* (1636) in his *Ximena* (D.L 1712)², and probably had memories of *Pompée* when he was penning *Cæsar in Ægypt* (D.L. 1724). *Cinna's Conspiracy* (D.L. 1713), attributed to the same author, is an altered

---

¹ *Arden of Feversham*, altered, according to the bills, by Mrs Haywood, was performed earlier at the Haymarket on Wednesday, Jan. 21, 1736.
² It was translated also by Ozell in 1714.

translation of *Cinna* (1640). *Horace* (1640) obviously influenced Whitehead in *The Roman Father* (D.L. 1750)[1]. Edmund Smith's *Phædra and Hippolitus* (H.[1] 1707) is taken mostly from Racine's *Phèdre* (1677) and Ambrose Philips' *The Distrest Mother* (D.L. 1712) is but a free adaptation of the *Andromaque* (1667), already utilised by Crowne. Boyer's *Achilles* (D.L. 1699) is taken from *Iphigénie* (1674), Johnson's *The Sultaness* (D.L. 1717) from *Bajazet* (1672), and the same author's *The Victim* (D.L. 1714) is a sort of combination of *Iphigénie* and Euripides' *Iphigenia in Aulis*. Voltaire it is, however, who most influenced the theatre at this time. He himself was nearer the English temper than any of his predecessors. In *Brutus* (1730) he deliberately imitated the English stage; in *Ériphyle* (1732) he introduced an Hamletian ghost; while in *Zaïre* (1732) he rose to a direct reworking of *Othello*. "C'est au théâtre anglais," he says in the *Epître dédicatoire* to the last-mentioned work, "que je dois la hardiesse que j'ai eue de mettre sur la scène les noms de nos rois et des anciennes familles du royaume. Il me paraît que cette nouveauté pourrait être la source d'un genre de tragédie qui nous est inconnu jusqu'ici, et dont nous avons besoin. Il se trouvera sans doute des génies heureux qui perfectionneront cette idée, dont *Zaïre* n'est qu'une faible ébauche." He was wrong in his assumption; as de Julleville shows, there were a score and a half of tragedies before him dealing with French annals, from *La Pucelle de Domrémy* (1580) of P. Fronton du Duc to other works in the late seventeenth century; yet Voltaire none the less stands forward as the populariser at least of the new style, the style of England. In this country his works were eagerly seized upon by several enthusiasts, even if they never became widely popular. *Brutus* (1730) was taken over by Duncombe in his *Junius Brutus* (D.L. 1734). *Zaïre* (1732) became the *Zara* (D.L. 1736) of Hill, and *Alzire* (1736) was adapted by the same English author as *Alzira* (L.[2] 1736). *Mahomet* (1741), that play cynically dedicated to Pope Benoît XIV, was altered by Miller as *Mahomet*

---

[1] Thomas Corneille's *Persée et Démétrius* provided Young with something more than the groundwork of *The Brothers* (D.L. 1753).

the Impostor (D.L. 1744). *Mérope* (1743) gave Hill's adaptation at Drury Lane in 1749. It is in the year 1743 that we find a marked break in Voltaire's dramatic productivity; his *L'Orphelin de la Chine* did not appear till 1755, and hence the story of subsequent adaptations concerns the dramatic history, not of the first, but of the second half of the century[1].

Whether Voltaire's fame was greatest in England before 1744, as T. R. Lounsbury avers, or whether it rose to a height only after that date (the thesis of H. L. Bruce), the fact remains that Voltaire was a most potent force in the development of English tragedy for fifty or more years after 1730. He not only brought England still more into touch with France; he not only exercised a considerable influence on the many writers with whom he came personally into contact; he provided a model of tragic drama which, while classically conceived, yet formed a compromise between Racine and the plays of more "English" character. He pointed, too, the way towards the *drame* of later years both in France and in England. No one ever could make much of Racine in England; his style was too much his own and his tension too restricted for the London stage. Voltaire, on the other hand, without much alteration, could be performed as satisfactorily in London as in Paris.

The influence of France among the continental nations was all predominant at this time, but Italy, even apart from comedy and the opera, played its slight part in the development of English tragic drama. Addison's *Cato* (D.L. 1713), it has been suggested, was inspired by an Italian *Catone d'Utica*. The only Italian tragedy thoroughly represented on the English stage, however, seems to have been Maffei's *Merope* (1713) which was twice rendered, once by Jeffreys (L.² 1731) and once by Ayre (1740). Maffei's tragedy was thoroughly classical, and seemed designed to suit the moods and tastes of the Augustan critics, but none other of the

---

[1] For the influence of Voltaire see Lounsbury, T. R., *Shakespeare and Voltaire* (1902), Ballantyne, A., *Voltaire's Visit to England, 1726–9* (1893), Collins, J. C., *Montesquieu and Rousseau in England* (1908), and Bruce, H. L., *The Period of Greatest Popularity of Voltaire's Plays on the English Stage* (*Mod. Lang. Notes*, 1918, pp. 20–3).

plays of his contemporaries found their way into English. Tasso[1] and Boccaccio[2] might still exercise their charm, but Italian opera took away men's minds in general from the chaster productions of the Italian tragic muse.

III. *The Heroic Dramas*

Elsewhere have been explained the characteristics which rank tragedies among the class named heroic[3]. It is perfectly true that there were but few recurrences to rime as a dramatic medium in the eighteenth century, save of course in opera and in pastoral, but what, it would seem, has been never sufficiently stressed, is that the elements of the Drydenesque tragedy, often in the crudest of forms, endured over the borders of the two centuries and still continued to exercise their influence even after 1750. Not only so, even the trappings of the heroic tragedy remained. Already has been noted the fact that the scenes which had come to be associated with the Dryden tragedy and tragi-comedy continued to be used with due frequency—palaces, prisons and temples carrying on the tradition of *The Indian Queen*, *The Conquest of Granada* and *The Empress of Morocco*. So, too, the old heroic exclamations beloved of Settle and Lee continued in the mouths of many heroes and monarchs of the eighteenth century. "Furies and Hell!" is a cry in Cibber's *Xerxes* (L.[1] 1699)[4]; "Hell and Confusion!" occurs in Rowe's *Ulysses* (H.[1] 1705)[5]; "Hell and Confusion, Horror and Despair!" as well as "Hell and Furies!" appear in Havard's *Scanderbeg* (G.F. 1733)[6]; Mrs Haywood's *Frederick, Duke of Brunswick-Lunenburgh* (L.[2] 1729) has "Death and Confusion![7]", and Hurst's *The Roman Maid* (L.[2] 1724) "Damnation! Hell and Furies! Flames and Tortures!" as well as "Furies! Confusion! Horror![8]"; "Tortures and Death!" appears in Mrs Pix' *The Double Distress* (L.[1] 1701)[9], "Rocks, Poison, Daggers!"

---

[1] Cf. Dennis' *Rinaldo and Armida* (L.[1] 1699).
[2] Cf. Mrs Centlivre's *The Cruel Gift* (D.L. 1716).
[3] See vol. i (1660–1700), pp. 100–1 and 168–9.
[4] I. i.   [5] IV.   [6] III. vii. and IV. ii.
[7] II. i.   [8] II. ii. and IV. viii.   [9] III.

in Frowde's *Philotas* (L.² 1731)[1], "Confusion! Hell!" in
Barford's *The Virgin Queen* (L.² 1728)[2], "Confusion, Death
and Hell!" in Lillo's *The Christian Hero* (D.L. 1735)[3].
Ranting and bombast still endured. Passages such as the
following:

> Hark! how Fate thunders to the wondring World;
> The *Sultan* strikes—the Universe falls down,
> And at one Blow I end the human Race[4],

might have come from a work by Dryden or Settle or Lee.
How far, too, even the external features of the older heroic
drama were retained may be realised by an examination of
the last act of Boyer's *Achilles* (D.L. 1699). The play is an
adaptation from Racine, yet the author has indulged in a
variety of showy incidents highly reminiscent of his predecessor, Dryden. "*The Sun is Eclips'd; Shrieks in the Air;
Subterranean Groans and Howlings; Thunder*," "*Clashing of
Swords within*," "*Thunder and Lightning; The Altar is lighted;
The flat Scene opens, and discovers a Heaven at a distance;*
Diana, *in a Machine, crosses the Stage*," "*The Winds and Sea
roar; Shoutings*"—all of these might have come out of a
drama of 1670.

It has already been pointed out that, of the comparatively
few tragedies written between 1700 and 1750, the great
majority were of the type which can be called only by the
name of Augustan. Among the others, however, the pure
heroic species holds an important place, there being decidedly
more of these than plays of the classic type. It is difficult,
naturally, to categorise exactly; but we may with fair authority
mass together here a number of dramas which in general aim
recall Dryden rather than Shakespeare or Racine. They may
still be styled heroic even though there is evident in them a
few characteristics of the classic or pathetic nature. One of
the peculiar things apparent in this section of dramatic
endeavour is that even the classical writers often veered over
to the side of the Restoration in their efforts. Charles Gildon

---

[1] III. i.   [2] v.   [3] IV. ii.
[4] Havard's *Scanderbeg* (G.F. 1733), v. viii.

was thus one of the high-priests of pseudo-classicism, yet two of his dramas can be called by no other name than heroic. In *Love's Victim: or, The Queen of Wales* (L.[1] April 1701) he certainly acknowledges Otway as his master[1]. It is equally true that he condemns the ordinary heroic writers for making all their manners and persons English, irrespective of whether "the Scene was in *Rome*, in *Madrid*, in *Africa* or the *Indies*[2]," that he acknowledges a debt to Alcestis and Andromache, that he

> makes a bold Essay
> To show Domestic Virtue here to day[3],

introducing an ancient Britain scene. On the other hand, as soon as we read the stage direction to 1. i. we know where we are: "*The Inside of a Magnificent Temple...The Curtain rises with terrible Claps of Thunder*"—we are in the world of heroic grandeur. Rhesus is a typical hero of olden times, and Guinoenda is as typical a heroine. In spite of the fact that the former can bring sentimentally inclined words of tenderness to his lips:

> O! *Druid*! she was the tenderest Wife!
> So good! so soft! so loving! Gods! Oh! Gods!
> Yet she is dead! by hellish Treachery dead!
> The best of Women slain by the most Wicked!

we feel that he is by nature more akin to Almanzor than to Cato or Jaffier.

Following up his first effort, in *The Patriot, or The Italian Conspiracy* (D.L. 1703), Gildon went direct to Lee for a model[4]. Here again we come upon a play which has characteristics of the heroic type, even while the author in the preface utters some of his most severely classical dicta.

Gildon's companion, John Dennis, penned more of the pseudo-classic type of tragedy, but even he, in the last year of the seventeenth century, wrote his *Rinaldo and Armida* (L.[1] 1699), a kind of compromise between serious dramatic opera

---

[1] Cp. *supra*, p. 67.   [2] Preface.   [3] Prologue.
[4] *Supra*, pp. 22 and 71.

and tragedy. Based on Tasso, but with variations[1], and in spite of several attempts at careful delineation of character in the figures of Rinaldo and of Armida, the play presents features which show clearly the influence of Dryden.

A similar union of heroic and other forces is to be seen in Colley Cibber's *Xerxes* (L.[1] *c.* Feb. 1698/9), wherein the central figure, who gives his name to the play, seems almost a direct copy of Dryden's Maximin. While Artabamus is not a typical hero of the older mould and while a vast amount of pathos is introduced in the person of Tamira, we feel in the external trappings of the play and in the characterisation alike the impress of the heroic. The following scene truly must be accorded those qualities:

Xerxes. How now! What, would your grave devotion startle me?
Away, draw out an able band of archers,
Mount 'em on the battlements of yon lofty tower,
And let 'em shoot a thousand arrows 'gainst the sun.
   2 *Magi*. O blasphemy!
   Xerxes. As many chains be thrown into the sea,
And bind the blue-hair'd *Neptune* to a rock!
Prepare a hundred bars of vast hot glaring iron,
Then plunge them hissing down
Into the burning bowels of the deep;
And while his scalding billows boil and foam
With raging torture;
There let him rave, and dash his batter'd limbs,
Like a despairing slave for ever....
                                          [*Thunder*.
By *Jove* they're there! Ha! what means this rising storm?
By all my power unshaken, my foes above are startl'd
At my daring fury; I'll stand and view
The god-like war? See! how the fleet winds   [*Louder*.
Are posted to the sun, with tidings of
Impending danger! Hark! the dreadful news
Is told, in peals of bursting thunder! ha!
By arms the noble charge is given!   [*The stage is darken'd*.
For see! th' alarm'd god retires!

---

[1] The author in his preface states that the "Manners of *Rinaldo* in *Tasso*" are "unequal." He was "therefore at Liberty to form a Character from *Tasso*'s Hint that was more agreeable" to his subject.

There is one thing to be observed concerning this development of pure heroics in the early eighteenth century, and that is that no single writer wholly indulged in heroics throughout all his life, the majority of these dramas having been written either by men who, like Gildon and Dennis and Cibber, approached the type at definite periods in their careers or by the "one-play" writers of the time. One of the latter was Alexander Fyfe who in 1705 came forward with what he styled an "opera," entitled *The Royal Martyr, K. Charles I* (unacted), a regular heroic tragedy of the worst sort.

> Your Name with Mortals sets you out at odds,

says Prince Rupert to the King,

> Then for Diversion combat with the Gods[1],

and the Queen assures Charles of the mob,

> They'd all be Gods like us, this is the draught;
> The people with that gilded Bait are caught.

Even Settle never wrote so disastrously as that. Lewis Theobald is an example of the other type of writer. He, too, started his dramatic career with an heroic play, *The Persian Princess: or, The Royal Villain* (D.L. May 1708)[2], written and acted when he was but eighteen years of age. Artaban here is a hero of the old style, chastened only a trifle by the spirit of the new age.

> But in this Cause for my *Amestris* fought,

he explains to his friend,

> (O think me not a vain and idle Boaster;)
> Had *Hercules* himself attack'd my Life;
> I could with Ease have warded all his Strokes,
> As I did *Mirvan*'s.

William Mountfort, if he indeed be the author of the play[3], wrote a more popular piece in *Zelmane: or, The Corinthian Queen* (L.[1] 1704)[4]. Again in this play we discover the typical figures of the Restoration drama. Zelmane, the

---

[1] I. i.   [2] It was evidently unsuccessful (Whincop, p. 293).
[3] The dedication states that "the following Poem was a piece left unfinished by Mr. M——t." If so, it must, of course, have been written before 1692; but it is almost certain that most of the dialogue at least is of eighteenth century workmanship.
[4] See the dedication.

heroine, loves the hero, Amphialus; Arbaces is the regular ambitious prince, and Pirotto the time-honoured villain.

William Taverner's one tragedy, *The Faithful Bride of Granada* (D.L. *c.* March 1704), was of the same type, ending, like Theobald's drama, on a happy note. The villain here is Oliman, but he differs in no essential characteristics save his name from the Pirotto of the former tragedy. Zelinda is the usual distressed heroine and Abinomin the distressed but valorous hero.

About the same time, Mrs Manley in *Almyna: or, The Arabian Vow* (H.[1] Dec. 1706) and later in *Lucius, The First Christian King of Britain* (D.L. May 1717) provided the stage with dramas of a similar cast. The first was unsuccessful, being produced unfortunately "between *Devotion* and *Camilla* (the Eunuch having then never Sung but once)[1]." It owed "something of a Hint from the *Arabian* Nights Entertainments"—the first English drama, apparently, taken directly from that collection of tales. The elements of heroic action in it are perfectly traceable. In *Lucius*, the scene is early Britain, but the characters are the same. There is once more the heroic love, the typical villain, the unrequited maiden, the storm and stress of the Drydenesque tragedy. Particularly interesting in this play are the stage directions, especially one in the fifth act where we are presented with "*The Outer-part of the Temple of* Jupiter" and where later we are told that "*The Curtain drawn up, discovers an Altar to* Jupiter"—a puzzling reference unless "curtain" here signifies "drop-scene."

Abra-Mule: Or, Love and Empire (L.[1] Jan. 1703/4), by Dr Joseph Trapp, was a much more successful play[2], and an earlier, than those of Mrs Manley. The prologue, certainly, emphasises its lack of sensations:

> Few Actors are to fall, no Ghosts to rise; ⎫
> No Fustian roars, nor mimick Lightning flies; ⎬
> No Thunder from his Heroes, or the Skies. ⎭

---

[1] It was given out on M. 16 Dec. and on W. 18, the prices being raised because of the "extraordinary Charge for Habits." The reference to "*Devotion*" may be to Christmas. *Camilla* was acted on S. Dec. 14 and on T. Dec. 17.

[2] Jacob, p. 260.

but in spite of this, there is the same love-passion, the same traitors and tyrant and murders on the stage, the same traditional revolution—all that goes to make up a true heroic drama. How close this play is to those of Dryden or of Settle may be shown by a brief summary of the plot. Abra-Mule is wooed by Pyrrhus. She is bought by Mahomet, who falls in love with her. She also afflicts the heart, and reason, of Solyman. Mahomet discovers her talking to Pyrrhus and condemns both of them to the rack. After a welter of wild and conflicting emotions they are rescued and happily married, Solyman magnanimously abandoning his claims. It is a sort of *Almanzor and Almahide* over again.

Nor is Edmund Smith's *Phædra and Hippolitus* (H.[1] April 1707)[1] much different. Here we have an example of the classicised heroic play. Taken from Racine, it has about it all the atmosphere of the older type. Hippolitus (acted by Booth) is the familiar hero; Ismena (acted by Mrs Oldfield) is the no less familiar heroine. The whole drama advances on heroic lines, and the variations from the French tend all in the one direction. It is interesting to note that this was a play heavily patronised by the pseudo-classicists of the age[2].

Like Dennis' *Rinaldo and Armida*, *Irene; or, The Fair Greek* (D.L. Feb. 1707/8) by Charles Goring was intended for a dramatic opera, but coming out just when the Haymarket theatre had been given over to opera, the author was "sensible ...that" it "appear'd to the greatest Disadvantage on the Stage, strip'd of Her Ornaments of Musick by a Superior Order[3]." Once more there is to be seen a strongly heroic plot, with a scheming Sultana Valide, the queen-mother, a hero in Aratus and a heroine, although she is set in a somewhat unusual situation, in Irene.

The heroic drama was by no means stifled in the later decades of the century. Mrs Centlivre's *The Cruel Gift*

---

[1] The exact date of production is unknown. On April 21 it had been acted four times; it was repeated on the 22nd, the 25th and 26th.

[2] See particularly *The Spectator*, No. 18, March 21, 1711.

[3] Dedication. It was acted only on M. 9, Tu. 10 and W. 11 Feb., 1707/8.

(D.L. Dec. 1716)[1] is of a mixed romantic-heroic cast with its scene in Verona. In it, the King of Lombardy is moved by Antenor to seize Lorenzo who has married secretly the Princess Leonora. Learchus, Antenor's son, circumvents the villainies of his father, and preserves Lorenzo. In the end the hero turns out to be the Duke of Milan's son. Why his birth has been concealed the authoress does not deign to explain to us, one of the characters at the end merely remarking that at "another Time" he would tell all. The play is a poor one and deserves little notice[2].

An adaptation of Racine's *Bajazet* with heroic elements is Charles Johnson's *The Sultaness* presented at D.L. in Feb. 1716/7. Bajazet is something of a type character, and Roxana is of the class made popular by Dryden. While the plot adheres fairly closely to the French model, the atmosphere has been changed in the direction of Drawcansir drama. The hero of Benjamin Martyn's *Timoleon* (D.L. Jan. 1729/30) burned, as we have already seen, "*with Liberty, and Love*[3]." Timoleon and Eunesia are thoroughly heroic characters, and the fighting, tumult and scenic effects show the indebtedness to Dryden. The play was a fair success[4], but, if contemporaries are to be credited, not without the assistance of a fair amount of factional applause[5]. Even more heroic than any of these is James Darcy's *Love and Ambition* (T.R. Dublin, 1731)[6] with its scene "Arabia the Happy," its ambitious villain Reseck, in love with the heroine Alzeyda, its hero Cosmez, its slighted love-lorn damsel Leiza. In reading a play such as this we begin to realise more fully the historic importance of Dryden in the history of later English drama.

Of Aaron Hill's *The Fatal Vision: or, The Fall of Siam* (L.[2] Feb. 1715/6) one hardly knows what to say. At first

---

[1] The running title is *The Cruel Gift: or, The Royal Resentment*.
[2] Jacob, p. 34, traces the source to "*Sigismondo* and *Guicarda*, a Novel of *Boccacce*." Whincop, p. 191, asserts that Rowe gave some finishing touches to the piece.
[3] *Supra*, p. 63.   [4] Whincop, p. 260.
[5] See *Remarks on the Tragedy of Timoleon* (1730).
[6] It was produced under Thomas Elrington who was in command of Smock Alley from 1720 to 1732. *A Companion to the Play-House* (1764) says it was acted with "some Success."

sight it might be regarded as a burlesque, with its ironical
dedication to Gildon and Dennis, but it seems to have been
intended seriously by its author. In it, he declares, he had
"*endeavoured to observe the* rules, *with all the necessary*
strictness. *And yet, at the same time, indulge the common
taste for* fulness *of* design." It was a "*new essay to reconcile
the* ancient, *and the* modern *plans of Tragedy, the first endeavour of the kind*" in the opinion of the author. The plot
of this drama is a mass of wild complications, involving the
hero Orontes, the unknown son of Caimantha the empress
of China, who has lived for years with her emperor disguised
as Selim, his favourite eunuch. If the whole thing be not a
practical joke, we must realise how near we are to Settle in
the following short dialogue, displaying the boundless confidence of the tyrant king and the sophistries of the heroic
type:

> *Uncham.* Selim! I would not die. Methinks, 'tis poor,
> And sets me on a level with my slaves,
> To know, that death has wider pow'r than I...
> *Selim.* When Princes, full of years, and glories, die,
> They not *lose* being, but *begin* to *be*;
> For those we now call *Gods*, were *Men*, like *You*;
> But *dyed* to *live*, as you, now, *live* to *dye*.

The *Biographia Dramatica* declares this thing was produced
with success.

Another writer, who, without any suspicion of burlesque,
inclined towards the heroic school, was David Mallet. His
two tragedies produced before 1750, *Eurydice* (D.L. Feb.
1730/1) and *Mustapha* (D.L. Feb. 1738/9), are definitely of
this type. The first, based on the same plot as Tracy's
Periander (L.² Jan. 1730/1), was produced in rivalry to that
drama. The plot is developed along the time-honoured lines,
and Periander on the brink of death recalls Maximin. At his
end he sees

> hated PROCLES,
> The cause of all my ruins!—Traitor, yes,
> I come, I fly, to plunge thee deeper still
> In this red sea of tortures.

The tragedy was a great success[1], and set many mouths a-wagging concerning supposed political references in it[2]. *Mustapha*, as has been noted above[3], owes considerably to Orrery's Restoration work. In both plays Solyman is roused to suspicion of Mustapha by Roxalana, who is in league with Rustan. Too late he discovers his error; and by that time Zanger has committed suicide in fulfilment of a vow given to his brother. Zanger's character is almost certainly an elaborated portrait of his prototype in Orrery's play.

William Havard, likewise, touched the heroic type in two tragedies, *Scanderbeg* (G.F. March 1732/3) and *Regulus* (D.L. Feb. 1743/4). The first, which was a failure[4], is a classical heroic tragi-comedy with a typical boastful hero in Amurat, and two pairs of distressed lovers in Scanderbeg and Deamira and in Lysander and Zaida. The rant of the piece may be exemplified by three lines from the fifth act, lines which recall a notorious passage in a play of Lee's:

> Hark! how Fate thunders to the wondring World;
> The *Sultan* strikes—the Universe falls down,
> And at one Blow I end the human Race.

Regulus is of the same type, with not quite so marked heroic features as has *Scanderbeg*. Regulus, however, as in Crowne's play, is definitely conceived as a "hero[5]," and Corvus as a "villain."

There are several other works produced about this time which manifest the same or similar features. *The Fair Captive* (L.² March 1720/1) was "originally writ by Capt. *Hurst*, and by him deliver'd to Mr. *Rich*, to be acted soon

---

[1] Whincop, p. 259.

[2] See *Remarks on the Tragedy of Eurydice. In which It is endeavoured to prove the said Tragedy is wrote in favour of the Pretender, and is a scurrilous Libel against the present Establishment* (1731).

[3] *Supra*, p. 70. Herbert W. Starr ("Sources of David Mallet's 'Mustapha, A Tragedy'," *NQ*, clxxxi. 1941, 285–7) shows that, while the author was influenced by earlier dramatic versions, his main source was Knolles' *Generall Historie of the Turkes*.

[4] The editors of the *Biographia Dramatica* suggest this was due to the fact that the audience suspected Havard of having stolen his plot from Whincop's play. The same suggestion of theft is made concerning Lillo's drama on the same theme (see *infra*, p. 84).

[5] Garrick took this part, and, according to a contemporary, succeeded in giving warmth to the drama.

after the Opening of the New House" and reworked by
Mrs Haywood, who, according to her own "advertisement,"
left not more than twenty lines of the original. The plot is
thoroughly heroic. Alphonso comes seeking for his love
Isabella whom Mustapha holds in bondage. He is captured,
but after a thrilling series of excitements he manages to save
his love. There is a little quivering of jealousy, but the play
ends in reconcilement and marriage. It seems to have been
a failure on the stage[1]. Capt. Robert Hurst himself gave one
similar drama to the theatre in *The Roman Maid* (L.[2] Aug.
1724), a dull play, with a usual boasting emperor in Dioclesian, a hero in Galerius Cæsar and a Christian heroine in
Paulina. Moses Browne's *Polidus: or, Distress'd Love* (private
theatre in St Alban's street, 1723?) may with as much ease be
dismissed. Its only interesting points are the small comic
underplot and the infusion of pathetic motives. Fettiplace
Bellers' *Injur'd Innocence* (D.L. Feb. 1731/2) is as poor a
production, but is possibly hardly as heroic as the other.
Based on D'Avenant's *The Unfortunate Lovers*, it recalls a
number of amorphous Restoration dramas where heroic
elements met with others taken over from Elizabethan plays.
The one tragedy which truly calls for special attention here
is Lillo's *The Christian Hero* (D.L. Jan. 1734/5), the theme
of which, according to the preface to *Scanderbeg* (1747), was
stolen from Whincop[2]. Scanderbeg in Lillo's play is mag-
nified into a hero, and Althea into a heroine. Hellena is the
love-lorn maiden who dies after saving the life of the hero.
The only variation from the Restoration norm lies in the
introduction of an extra amount of pathos, which removes
the play in spirit just a trifle from Dryden and Settle.

The heroic note, as is evident, was being weakened in this

---

[1] Whincop, p. 239.
[2] The preface dismisses Havard's play as unhistorical. The direct
accusation of fraud is enunciated clearly: "*This very modest Gentleman*
(i.e. Lillo) *having seen the Piece before us, and knowing too that the Author's
Widow had a great Dependence upon it, soon after brought out a Tragedy
founded on the same Story, and called it* THE CHRISTIAN HERO." At
Edinburgh in 1735 was published *The Life of George Castriot, King of
Epirus and Albania, commonly called Scanderbeg; On which is founded
the Tragedy of The Christian Hero*.

century by the introduction of pathetic situations and of pseudo-classical dialogue, but to the end it retained its force. More important still, it formed an integral part of the typical "Augustan" tragedy, and its power is hence to be gauged correctly not merely from a study of the comparatively few pure specimens of the type, but from an analysis of the component elements of that larger group.

IV. *The Pseudo-Classic Tragedies*

The pseudo-classical school in drama did not achieve success before the production of *Cato* in 1713, and never, as has been already noted, secured full meed of approbation from the average body of spectators. Purely classical plays appeared spasmodically all through these fifty years, but they were often unsuccessful and hardly any save *Cato* was paid the compliment of even occasional revival.

Abel Boyer's *Achilles: or, Iphigenia in Aulis*[1] (D.L. *c.* Dec. 1699) is one of the earliest we meet with. It was a failure on the stage; this the author, with characteristic literary immodesty, attributed to the fact that it came out immediately after Dennis' play on the same theme at Lincoln's Inn Fields and contemporaneously with Farquhar's *A Trip to the Jubilee.* As has been noted, this classic drama breaks away into heroic ecstasies towards the close[2].

Among the other pseudo-classic writers John Dennis stands prime in importance. He had started with comedy during the last decade of the seventeenth century and passed from that to the operatic and heroic *Rinaldo and Armida* of 1699. The same year saw the production of his first truly classic work, *Iphigenia* (L.[1] Dec. 1699), taken from Euripides' *Iphigenia in Tauris.* Like Boyer's play, it was unsuccessful, answering not, according to Downes, "the Expences they were at in Cloathing it[3]." Even the efforts of his friends could

---

[1] The title was altered to *The Victim; or Achilles and Iphigenia in Aulis* in the edition of 1714, after the appearance of Charles Johnson's *The Victim,* presumably to display the similarity of plot and treatment.
[2] *Supra,* p. 75.
[3] p. 45. See also Whincop, p. 215. It was apparently never revived.

not make it pass muster[1]. From this play Dennis passed to a more patriotic theme in *Liberty Asserted* (L.[1] Feb. 1703/4), a tragedy devised to catch the temper of the hour, with statements that

> The *English* always were a Gallant Nation,
> And Foes to Force, and Friends to Liberty.

It is a poor production, but, because of its sentiments, was hailed "with very great Applause[2]." If contemporaries are to be believed, the applause almost turned the poor poet's brains[3]. Noticeable in the production are the heroic elements visible in the hero Ulamar and his love Irene.

With *Appius and Virginia* (D.L. Feb. 1708/9) Dennis returned to more purely classical themes, although here too can be traced the patriotic enthusiasm aroused by Marlborough's victories. It was unsuccessful, running only for four nights[4], and won for its author ridicule because of his newly invented thunder[5]. As a drama, it is almost entirely negligible. *The Invader of his Country; or, The Fatal Resentment* followed at Drury Lane, after a long interval, in November 1719. It carried on Dennis' classic and patriotic proclivities, the piece being designed as an historical parallel, with Coriolanus figuring forth as the Old Pretender. From the point of view of pseudo-classicism, this definite attempt of Dennis to "unify" Shakespeare deserves to be noted[6].

Apart from Dennis and Gildon, undoubtedly the most important of the early pseudo-classicists was Ambrose Philips, who in March 1711/12 brought out his *The Distrest Mother* at Drury Lane, a play based on Racine with the usual change in the fifth act. The tragedy as a whole is a good one; the characters of Andromache and Pyrrhus are well drawn,

---

[1] *Supra*, p. 18.   [2] Jacob, p. 68.

[3] Whincop (p. 214) tells two stories regarding the ridiculous self-esteem of the author.

[4] See Whincop, p. 215.

[5] See *supra*, p. 36. The story is told in Charles Dibdin's *A Complete History of the English Stage*, iv. 357; Pope's *Essay on Criticism*, i. 584 contains a reference to it.

[6] For an analysis of the two plays see Genest, iii. 4–5 and Odell, i. 239–41. Dennis' work was unsuccessful (cf. Whincop, p. 215), being acted only three times.

making up for a certain stiffness in those of Hermione and
Orestes. The applause meted out to it was fairly extensive[1],
a fact which is of importance when we remember that it was
produced the year before *Cato* was placed on the stage and
that Addison is said to have written the highly successful
epilogue[2]. The cast was brilliant; and the drama to the
Queen Anne audience must have come as a peerless masterpiece. The prologue by Steele spoken by Wilks deserves
notice alongside of the epilogue as it displays clearly the
consciousness of weakness in the age and the factors that were
leading towards the intensification of pseudo-classic rules:

> *Since Fancy of it self is loose and vain,*
> *The Wise by Rules, that airy Power restrain...*
> *But* Shakespear's *self transgress'd; and shall each Elf,*
> *Each Pigmy Genius, quote Great* Shakespear's *self!*
> *What Critick dares prescribe what's just and fit,*
> *Or mark out Limits for such boundless Wit!...*
> *Our Author does his feeble Force confess,*
> *Nor dares pretend such Merit to transgress;*
> *Does not such shining Gifts of Genius share,*
> *And therefore makes Propriety his Care.*
> *Your Treat with study'd Decensy he serves;*
> *Not only Rules of Time and Place preserves,*
> *But strives to keep his Characters intire,*
> *With* French *Correctness and with* British *Fire.*

It was possibly the success of *The Distrest Mother* that led
Addison to let the players produce his *Cato* in April 1713.
Cato must have been long on the stocks before that date;
indeed there is some slight evidence to make us believe that,
as a rough draft at any rate, it was originally penned before
1700. Cibber avers he had seen four acts of it in 1703, the
reason for its being held back from the theatre having been
the advice of Pope. It was eventually sent to the players
through the insistence of Hughes[3]. At once it was hailed

---

[1] Jacob, p. 203; *Spectator*, No. 614, Nov. 1, 1714. It seems, however, that
the first audience was packed. Spence tells us that "an audience was laid
for the Distressed Mother; and when they found it would do, it was prac-
tised again, yet more successfully for Cato" (*Anecdotes*, 1830, p. 46).

[2] It is printed as "by Mr. *Budgell*" but current gossip gave it to Addison.

[3] See the Bohn *Addison*, vi. 715–8, which collects some scattered
authorities.

with applause, being "acted with the greatest Approbation of any that has been represented on the Theatre, in this or any preceding Age[1]." The political parties shouted themselves hoarse in an endeavour to show that they and they alone respected liberty. Voltaire gave it his praise[2]; it was patronised by royalty[3]; contemporaries from Dennis to Young showered encomia upon it[4]. It produced a shower of pamphlets such as no other play had done, writers scrambling one over another to say something of this fresh phenomenon[5]. It was translated into Italian, French, German, and probably did more than any other single drama to raise the esteem of England on the continent in the early eighteenth century[6]. It is difficult now to estimate aright the enthusiasm evoked by this play. The dialogue to readers of the twentieth century seems dull and passionless. The love element in the adoration of Marcia by Juba and of Lucia by Portius and Marcus is artificial. Sempronius and Syphax are but conventional villains. Even contemporaries noted that the plot was one not well suited for dramatic treatment. A certain amount of the English praise must assuredly be credited to

[1] Jacob, p. 3.
[2] See his *Discours sur la tragédie* forming the preface to *Brutus* (1730).
[3] Bohn *Addison*, vi. 720.   [4] *Id.* 723-4.
[5] See particularly: Dennis, J., *Remarks upon Cato* (1713) and *Letters upon the Sentiments of the two first Acts of Cato* (dated Jan. 1717) in *Original Letters* (1721, pp. 303-57); anonymous, *The Life and Character ...of...Cato* (1713); *Cato Examin'd* (1713); *Mr. Addison turn'd Tory* (1713); *The Unfortunate General* (1713); Sewell, W., *A Vindication of the English Stage* (1716); anonymous, *A Parallel betwixt the Tragedy of Cato and the Cato of Utica of Mr. Des Champs* (1719).
[6] In Italian *Il Catone* of A. M. Salvini appeared in 1715 (reprinted 1725) and *Il Catone in Utica* by Gaetano Golt in 1776. Dubost translated a few scenes into French in *Nouvelles Littéraires* (Hague, Oct. 1716, viii. 285); *Caton* appeared in vol. viii of *Le Théâtre anglois* (1746); G. Guillemard's *Caton d'Utique* was issued in 1767 and the translations of the Vicomte A. H. de Dampmartin (*La Mort de Caton*) and of Chéron de la Bruère (*Caton d'Utique*) appeared in 1789. L. A. V. Gottsched adapted it as *Cato, ein Trauerspiel* in 1735; another anonymous German rendering was published in 1763. Even before those dates J. C. Gottsched had used Addison's last act for his *Der sterbende Cato* (1731) taken from Deschamps' *Caton d'Utique* (1715). In Polish *Cato* appeared as *Katon ....wierszem przerobił Aleks. Chodkiewicz* (Wilno, 1809; 2nd edition, 1817). See A. G. Hegnauer's essay on *Der Einfluss von Addisons Cato auf die dramatische Literatur Englands und des Continents in der 1. Hälfte der 18. Jahrhunderts* (1912).

political associations; a certain amount of the foreign to the
realisation that England had at least one thoroughly classic
dramatist; but that cannot be all. There remains the fact
that in Cato, the philosopher, Addison was able to paint a type
such as his age could paint. For the Augustans the realisation
of passion was difficult if not impossible; but reason was
theirs, and the realm of thought. There is not any great
depth in Addison's presentation of the Roman orator, but
there is sincerity; and it was sincerity which the eighteenth
century, in its drama at least, normally lacked. It is the
atmosphere of truth, the feeling of purpose, which is in *Cato*
that led to the full appreciation of that drama. Dennis had
blundered along in a semi-heroic way, striving at passion with
a passionless pen; Addison wrote a tragedy which, save for
its love scenes, obviously an afterthought, completely ruled
out passion from its province. It is hard to conceive that any
truly great tragedy could be written without emotion, but
what might be done in this way Addison has done. This is
the reason that *Cato* is a landmark in the tracing of eighteenth
century tragic development.

Charles Johnson's *The Victim* (D.L. Jan. 1713/4), based on
Racine's *Iphigénie*, but by no means a mere translation, is
the next tragedy in point of date which can be styled classical.
It is not a noteworthy drama, and had but little influence on
the progress of the type. Johnson's only other classical play
is *Medea* (D.L. Dec. 1730), an adaptation of Euripides and
Seneca. Its plot is fairly well-worked out, but, like *The
Victim*, it hardly merits detailed attention. Much more
important are his heroic *The Sultaness* (D.L. 1717) already
mentioned, and the domestic *Cælia* (D.L. 1732).

Charles Beckingham's *Scipio Africanus* (L.² Feb. 1717/8)
has more intrinsic and historic value. Apparently it is taken
from no previous play, the subject-matter being derived
directly from Livy. In style it approaches more nearly to
the heroic than any of the other plays dealt with above.
Scipio is conceived somewhat in the Almanzor strain. There
is, too, a certain amount of pathos; the sub-plot dealing with
Semanthe, Trebellius and Lucilius has evidently been intro-

7   N E D II

duced in order to provide that distressful element without which, the epilogue informs us, no play would take. It was acted with applause; possibly contemporaries felt about it as Jacob did: "The Characters are well drawn, and the Unities of the Stage preserv'd: In short, it is an excellent Tragedy, conformable to the Rules of the Drama, and the Precepts of our Modern Criticks[1]."

Beckingham's other play, *The Tragedy of King Henry IV. of France* (L.[2] Nov. 1719), is somewhat colder than his first. It is a drama less in the heroic strain, dealing as it does with the love of Henry for Charlotta, wife of the Prince of Condé. It presents an amount of anti-Catholic sentiment, the king being slain in the end by Ravilliac, "an Enthusiastick Desperate Youth, employ'd by the Priests to murder" him; but in spite of that would not appear to have been as successful.

In the twenties of the century pseudo-classicism in tragedy seems to have become a trifle more popular. In 1722 John Sturmy came forward with his *Love and Duty: or, The Distress'd Bride* (L.[2] Jan. 1721/2). The title "doth heroically sound," but the conduct of the piece is decidedly chill, and the plot is to be associated with *The Suppliants* of Æschylus. The prologue presents as a merit in the play that the words of the heroine "rarely do...with Sense make War," but even the nonsense of Fyfe is preferable to the dullness of Sturmy's blank verse.

Sesostris: or, Royalty in Disguise, Sturmy's only other tragedy, appeared at the same theatre in January 1727/8. This play is as cold as the other, but its plot, dealing with the murder by Omar of the King of Egypt, the saving of Sesostris, the Pharaoh's son, by Phanes, the murdering by him of Omar's son, and the loves of Sesostris and Ariaspe, the daughter of Phanes, has a certain historical importance because of the apparent use made of it by Voltaire in *Mérope* and by Browne in *Barbarossa*.

Richard West's one play, *Hecuba* (D.L. Feb. 1725/6)[2], had an unfortunate reception[3]. An adaptation from the Greek, it

---

[1] p. 281. The author was only 19 when he wrote the play.
[2] It is attributed to West by Whincop, p. 309.
[3] See *supra*, p. 13.

is noticeable for its freshness and for the fine passages of blank verse which occasionally sparkle through its dialogue:

> There on the Desart Mountains let him howl,
> Howl to the Winds; or with the prowling Wolf,
> Bay the cold Moon, smote with Despair and Hunger;
> There, undeplor'd, among the Savage Race,
> A Savage more forlorn and curs'd than they:
> There, amid lasting Tortures let him waste
> A wretched Life[1].

There were few writers of the early eighteenth century who could capture a melody such as moves in these and similar lines.

A much poorer drama is Sir Hildebrand Jacob's *The Fatal Constancy* (D.L. April 1723), a tragedy of love and treachery. The constancy of Hesione, daughter of Zimon, for Omphales is sometimes affecting, and the villainy of Ammon is fairly well motived, but the drama as a whole is chill and uninteresting.

David Lewis' *Philip of Macedon* (L.[2] April 1727) mingles a certain heroic element with a classical atmosphere. In it, Perses, son of Philip, plots against his father and against his brother, Demetrius. The latter, loving Isteria, a Gaulish princess, does not suspect his villainy; he is accused of friendship to Rome and commits suicide by his father's order. A slight infusion of happiness is introduced in the sub-plot, which concerns the forbidden love of Olympias, Philip's daughter, for Antigonus. After the death of his son the King abdicates and presents the latter with his kingdom. The plot, as will be evident, is interesting as showing the eighteenth century treatment of what might well be an heroic theme.

Distinct traces of heroic sentiments are observable also in the otherwise classical drama of Richard Barford, *The Virgin Queen* (L.[2] Dec. 1728). The play is uninteresting, and evidently the author felt no call to pen further for the stage[2].

---

[1] v.

[2] Pope has an allusion to it in *An Epistle to Dr. Arbuthnot*, l. 55:
> "Bless me! a packet—'tis a stranger sues,
> A *Virgin Tragedy*, an Orphan Muse."

Philip Frowde's *The Fall of Saguntum* (L.[2] Jan. 1726/7) is likewise a classical constructed drama of love and honour. Fabius here loves Timandra and is beloved by the Amazon captive, Candace. The conflict of crude and violent emotions is as in Restoration plays; Fabius is mortally wounded, Candace is ravished[1] and slays herself, and Timandra runs heroically mad.

Of a very similar character is *Philotas* (L.[2] Feb. 1730/1) by the same author. Philotas, a general of Alexander, appears before us wrapt in Persian luxury. He is enamoured of Antigona, the betrothed of Arsaces, who lives disguised as his slave. Cleora, the wife of Philotas, appears on the scene and, with the aid of Clitus, calls him back to duty. Craterus, the typical villain, has meanwhile slandered Philotas to Alexander; Philotas is tried, and Arsaces, seeking for revenge, urges Antigona to add her voice to those of his accusers. Philotas is condemned to torture; at the last moment the schemes of Craterus are laid bare and Antigona dies alongside her lover. Quite evidently *All for Love* has been before the author in his treatment of Cleora and Antigona; the influence of Dryden, indeed, is writ large upon this classical play.

Classicism, within a few years of the date of production of Frowde's dramas, was approached more satisfactorily by James Thomson, famous now as the author of *The Seasons*, but noted in his own time as author of five tragedies. *Sophonisba*, the first of these, appeared at Drury Lane in February 1729/30 and seems to have met with success[2]. It is interesting to compare this play with Lee's work on the same theme. Sophonisba is no longer a lover; she is almost wholly a patriot and her alliances with Syphax and with Masinissa are dictated purely by her desire to save Carthage. It is certainly true that this conception of her character enables Thomson to avoid many of the weaknesses evident in Lee's work; but his

---

[1] For a cynical criticism on this part of the plot, see Genest, iii. 192.

[2] Whincop, p. 294. On this play were issued in 1730, *A Criticism on the New Sophonisba, a Tragedy* and *A Defence of the New Sophonisba... In answer to a Criticism on that Play. By a Friend of the Author's.*

play has about it a chill which even contemporary audiences seem to have felt[1].

Agamemnon (D.L. April 1738), his second drama, is an excellent tragedy of the heavier sort, but, in spite of the fact that it had a powerful cast, Quin acting Agamemnon, Milward Egisthus, Cibber Melisander, Mrs Porter Clytemnestra and Mrs Cibber Cassandra, it does not appear to have been successful[2]. Thomson's models here seem to have been Æschylus and Seneca, although the manner in which the theme is developed speaks highly for the originality of the author. Like all the classical tragedies, *Agamemnon* can hardly be styled a masterpiece, but for dramatic effect and for delineation of character, within its own class it is a noteworthy production.

Edward and Eleonora followed; but this play was banned by the censor in 1739. The pathetic elements here are more pronounced than in any of Thomson's other works, although the treatment is thoroughly classical. It has a certain interest in that the theme chosen is one that normally would have been counted romantic. The atmosphere of the Holy Land, the stabbing of Edward with a poisoned dagger, the sucking of the wound by Eleonora, the high chivalry of the disguised Selim—all these recall memories of *The Talisman*[3].

In *Tancred and Sigismunda* (D.L. March 1744/5) Thomson succeeded in penning a fine, affecting, though at times heavy, dramatic poem. This tragedy again has a certain romantic colouring. Tancred, the unknown son of Manfred of Sicily, loves Sigismunda. He is elevated to the throne, and Sigismunda's father, Siffredi, endeavours to trick him into a marriage with the princess Constantina. Sigismunda believes

---

[1] Cf. the account in the *Biographia Dramatica*. On Thomson's dramatic work see Léon Morel, *James Thomson: sa vie et ses œuvres* (1895), pp. 541–604. In connection with the comment *supra*, p. 23, on the banning of *Edward and Eleonora*, Jean B. Kern "The Fate of James Thomson's *Edward and Eleonora*", (*Modern Language Notes*, lii. 1937, 500–2) suggests that a valid reason for the censor's action may be found in the author's apparent reflection of political events in his presentation of a quarrel between a king and his heir.   [2] Whincop, p. 295.

[3] In 1739 was published *The History of the Life and Reign of the Valiant Prince Edward,...and his Princess Eleonora. On which History, is founded a Play...call'd, Edward and Eleonora; now in Rehearsal at the Theatre in Convent-Garden.*

he has been faithless, and consents to marry Osmond. The last-mentioned noble grows jealous and slays his newly-married wife, and in his turn is slain by Tancred. The plot, which seems to owe its being to *Gil Blas*, is well carried out, and the play is thoroughly dramatic save for the improbability of the blank signed parchment on which Siffredi writes Tancred's promise to wed Constantina. While the treatment is classical to a degree, the theme shows clearly Thomson's move from the duller realms of pseudo-classicism to the spacier realms of romantic enthusiasm. *Tancred and Sigismunda* was accepted by contemporaries as a masterpiece[1]; and was, like Addison's *Cato*, translated into French and German[2].

Unfortunately, Thomson was not to continue long in the service of the stage. *Coriolanus* (C.G. Jan. 1748/9), a classical retreatment of Shakespeare's story, was his last, and un-doubtedly his poorest play. It failed to attract any notice on the stage, in spite of Quin's endeavours to make it a success[3].

No other classical author succeeded in reaching to the heights attained by Thomson. In 1734 William Duncombe gave a fair *Junius Brutus* (D.L. Nov. 1734) to the stage, but it deserves in no wise to be compared with Thomson's works. A confessed adaptation of Voltaire, the play has some merit in the last scenes, where the author has departed some-what from the French original. The struggles in the minds of Titus (love and patriotism) and of Brutus (dignity as a senator and affection as a father) are well-managed and developed.

Another attempt at giving to the stage a tragedy formed on the best-approved plan of the pseudo-classicists, Dr Samuel Johnson's *Irene* (D.L. Feb. 1748/9)[4], would assuredly have been long forgotten had it not been for the name of the author. *Irene* is strictly regular; the scene is unchanged from first scene to last, the time is only a few hours, the action is

---

[1] It was acted "with some Applause" according to Whincop, p. 295.

[2] *Tancrède et Sigismonde* by Brugière de Barante appeared in *Chefs-d'œuvre des théâtres étrangers*, vol. iv in 1822; *Blanche et Guiscard* of B.-J. Saurin, an adaptation, was published in 1763 and reprinted in 1772. J. H. Schlegel issued his rendering, *Tankred und Sigismunda*, along with *Eduard und Eleonora* in 1764.

[3] See Odell, i. 354-5.

[4] Acted under the title of *Mahomet and Irene*.

one and entire. Everything is according to the true pseudo-classical pattern; all that is lacking is tragic spirit and fire. Declamation dominates *Irene*, sometimes declamation which rises to the height of a grand rhetoric, but declamation will not make a play, so that we remain cold alike at the patriotism of Demetrius and Leontius, the villainy of Cali, the agony of Irene. A frigid chill enwraps the whole work.

Chill in tone, likewise, is William Whitehead's *The Roman Father* (D.L. Feb. 1749/50), the plot of which is confessedly based on Corneille's *Horace*. Beyond a touch of pathos in some of the scenes, Whitehead professes that he has discarded rigidly all the trappings that might have made his tragedy please[1]. The best scenes in the play are those in which Horatia inveighs against patriotism; but these after all tend to destroy the unity of the play, which at the close extols the hero who thinks only of his fatherland[2].

As a close to this section might be noted one or two plays which for various reasons fall somewhat outside the regular account of the pseudo-classic tragedy. Of these, Robert Gould's *Innocence Distress'd: or, The Royal Penitents* (published in 1737 but written much earlier), derives interest from its classically inspired treatment of that plot which had already given *The Fatal Discovery* and was to provide Walpole with material for *The Mysterious Mother*. The marriage of Theodorus to his own daughter and sister is here told in accordance with the best classic rules. The two renderings of Maffei's *Merope* (that by George Jeffreys, L.[2] Feb. 1730/1, and that by William Ayre, unacted 1740) deserve mention. The second is a more or less dull translation; but the former introduces some attempt at novelties[3]. Finally, William Hatchett's *The Rival Father: or, The Death of Achilles* (H.[2] April 1730), confessedly based on Corneille's *Mort d'Achille* and Racine's *Andromaque*, and thus dealing with a theme

---

[1] See the prologue.

[2] On this play see *The Story on which the New Tragedy, call'd, The Roman Father, is founded; Remarks on the New Tragedy, call'd, The Roman Father*, and *A Comparison between the Horace of Corneille and the Roman Father of Mr. Whitehead* (all 1750).

[3] It was a failure; the audience, however, was not dismissed the second night as the *Biographia Dramatica* states (see Appendix C).

similar to that of *The Distrest Mother* (D.L. 1712), requires notice for its endeavour to preserve strict decorum while presenting material intended to secure success on the stage.

Even such a brief survey as this must have displayed fully enough the miserable paucity and poverty of the pseudo-classic type of tragedy. Beyond Addison's one play and the few of Thomson there is none on which we should care to linger. Continually, too, these pseudo-classical productions had to break down, giving way to pathos or to heroics. Whatever it was in the realm of pure poetry, pseudo-classicism on the stage was by way of being a forced effort; its successes were rather *tours de force* than naturally written dramas. The fact seems to have been that while classicism spread its influence far and wide over the theatre, it never succeeded in gripping the attentions of the auditors or in itself producing anything brilliant or noteworthy.

V. *The Augustan Tragedies*

It has already been pointed out that the typical form of eighteenth century tragic drama, to which has been given the name of Augustan, was an amalgam of diverse forces—pseudo-classicism influencing it externally, pathos entering in to colour certain scenes and characters, Shakespearian style directing occasionally dialogue and theme, and heroics flickering luridly if spasmodically over the whole production. Quite naturally, this type presents no very decided and characteristic elements; it is to be regarded as a blundering attempt on the part of men who knew not what they desired to furnish actable plays for the theatre. They could give nothing definite to the stage; their plays are amorphous, chaotic in plot and undistinguished in character-drawing, yet such as they are they form the typical dramatic productions of the period.

Mrs Pix, possibly, is the first to call for attention. Her tragi-comedy, *The False Friend, Or, The Fate of Disobedience*, after her two tragedies, her farce and her two comedies of 1696–8, appeared at Lincoln's Inn Fields in the spring of 1699.

This play, which seems to have been almost universally neglected by those who have written of her works[1], is symptomatic of her later efforts. Already she had tried heroics in *Ibrahim* and in *Queen Catherine*; now she attempted an essay in a slightly domestic theme with a "moral" plot. The play is not valuable unless when considered in relation to her other works. From this date (1699) to 1705 Mrs Pix furnished the stage with three tragedies, all presenting mixed characteristics of classicism, heroics and pathos. *The Double Distress* came out at Lincoln's Inn Fields about March 1701, an unsuccessful production. Interesting in it are the many passages in rimed verse. *The Czar of Muscovy* (L.[1] c. March 1701) was produced at the same theatre a few months later. It is more classical than any of her other dramas, although in this tragedy of Dmitri the Pretender there are many features of a sentimental cast. Particularly noticeable are the touches of nature love, such as Marina's moralisations in v. iii.; "How happy is the humble Cottager, who never knows the Madness of Ambition?" is a sentence premonitory of many sentimentalisings in the years to come. Mrs Pix' last serious drama was *The Conquest of Spain* (H.[1] c. May 1705)[2], a play founded on Rowley's *All's Lost by Lust*. There are elements of romantic treatment in it; there are features of the heroic tragedy; there is the loyalty adored by the Stuart writers[3]; there are the same touches of nature love[4]. Even from this necessarily brief account, it will be evident that Mrs Pix gave nothing new to the theatre. Her plays have interest solely because they provide early examples of that union of the separate dramatic forces which was to dominate tragedy for well over fifty years.

Of far greater intrinsic importance is Nicholas Rowe, the true link that binds Otway with Lillo. Rowe's tragedies number

---

[1] It is not mentioned in Jacob, Whincop, Ward or the *Cambridge History of English Literature*. Genest includes it in his account, but makes the mistake of calling the heroine's name Louisa instead of Lovisa (ii. 172).

[2] Downes, p. 48, says it was the first new play at the Haymarket and that it ran six days. Its ascription to Mrs Pix is due to him.

[3] Cf. the lines quoted by Genest (ii. 332).

[4] Particularly Margaretta's speeches in I. i.

seven in all, dating from 1701 to 1715. Many are well-written; nearly all were successful. For these reasons, Rowe is a dramatist whose works must fully be mastered before any true appreciation of eighteenth century tragic development can be possible. *The Ambitious Step-Mother*, which came out at Lincoln's Inn Fields about December 1700, was, according to Downes[1], "well *Acted*...the Play answer'd the Companies expectation." The preface to this drama displays at once the tendencies of the author and the reasons for his success. It abounds in praise of Otway; the pathos of the writer of *The Orphan* has for him such a charm as is exercised by no other thing. "Moving *Otway*," as the prologue declares, is the master of the poet. To follow Otway and present a scene of tenderness meant in this case the breaking of the pseudo-classical rule of Poetic Justice, and the fact that this play was successful, even while it offended several critics because of such violation, shows the comparative powerlessness of the stricter pseudo-classic party. "If therefore," remarks Rowe, "I had sav'd *Artaxerxes* and *Amestris*, I believe...I had destroy'd the greatest occasion for Compassion in the whole play." Pathos, however, by no means completely dominates *The Ambitious Step-Mother*. The plot is obviously reminiscent of Orrery's *Mustapha* and is conducted along good old heroic lines, with Artaxerxes as hero, Amestris as heroine, Artemisa as plotting queen, Mirza as villain, Memnon as noble general. How far the sentiments of the characters correspond with those of the Settle school may be gauged from Artaxerxes words in Act II.:

> Seek for thy Father in that plotting Fellow,
> The Hero's race disclaims thee.

Truly Sir A. W. Ward is not far wrong in styling this drama "one of those Oriental palace-intrigues of which heroic tragedy was so fond[2]." With *Tamerlane* (L.[1] *c*. Dec. 1701) Rowe, like Gildon, moved to more political realms, creating in Tamerlane a figure of all virtue (William III) and in Bajazet a monster of all vice (Louis XIV). In spite of the self-esteem which Rowe appears to have felt in it, this

---

[1] p. 45.   [2] iii. 314.

tragedy must be regarded as immeasurably weaker than his
first drama. The love scenes of Axalla and Selima are insipid,
and those of the unhappy Arpasia and Moneses unreal. They
are interesting only as revealing the passage of the author
from an atmosphere of heroics to a more pathetic sphere[1].

The Fair Penitent followed at the same theatre in May 1703,
and of a sudden we find ourselves moved into a new atmosphere, where Rowe seems to be speaking the true language
of his heart. The dialogue is more poetic than in the two
former plays, rising indeed to pitches of excellence as in the
speech of Calista in Act II.:

> Away, I think not of him. My sad Soul
> Has form'd a dismal melancholy Scene,
> Such a Retreat as I wou'd wish to find;
> An unfrequented Vale, o'er-grown with Trees
> Mossie and old, within whose lonesom Shade,
> Ravens, and Birds ill-omen'd, only dwell;
> No Sound to break the Silence, but a Brook
> That bubling winds among the Weeds; no Mark
> Of any Human Shape that had been there,
> Unless a Skeleton of some poor Wretch,
> Who had long since, like me, by Love undone,
> Sought that sad Place out to despair and die in.

The plot is an old one, taken from Massinger's *The Fatal
Dowry*, but it is developed in a manner fresh and interesting.
Altamont has married Sciolto's daughter, Calista, who had
already had a liaison with Lothario, her faithless lover. She
still adores him, and Horatio, Altamont's friend, discovers her
secret. She and Sciolto commit suicide. The theme, as will
be seen, is in a way domestic, a fact duly noted in the prologue;
what is even more important is that it is the first of Rowe's
"she-tragedies," a type of drama inaugurated by Banks in the
seventeenth century, and destined to be so common in the
following years. *The Fair Penitent* was a brilliant success in
its own time. It may be that some of the applause was due
to the then entrancing figure of Lothario, a Lovelace of the

---

[1] The *Biographia Dramatica* says that it was acted for many years
at Dublin on November 4, King William's birthday, and occasionally
on November 5. A reference to Appendix C will make it plain that this
custom prevailed in the London theatres till 1750.

reign of Anne, who, according to Mrs Inchbald at the
beginning of the nineteenth century, could no longer appeal,
women then having "learnt to spell" (whatever that had to
do with it) and having "made other short steps in the path
of literature[1]." It may be, too, that the brilliant cast had its
influence in the successful launching of the drama, for Powell
was Lothario, Betterton Horatio, Verbruggen Altamont, Mrs
Barry Calista and Mrs Bracegirdle Lavinia. Above all,
however, it must have been the play itself which appealed
to the audience. Already men and women were feeling the
call towards the bourgeois tragedy[2].

After a brief excursion into comedy, Rowe returned to
tragedy with *Ulysses* (H.[1] Nov. 1705). Downes tells us that
it "being all new Cloath'd, and Excellently well perform'd
had a Successful run[3]." For some reason, this drama is
again heroic in character. One wonders whether it may not
have been penned about the same time as *Tamerlane* and
deferred until now. There are in it portents and heroic love
and disguisings and rant, all in the olden style, with only a
touch of pathetic sentiment. In *The Royal Convert* (H.[1] Nov.
1707), on the other hand, we are out of this atmosphere.
There are still elements of heroic action, but the scene is
ancient Britain and the plot has about it a domestic air. On the
whole, however, this play does little to advance Rowe's fame.

Rowe's last two dramas surpass by far this, or any other
of his works; they are indeed by way of being masterpieces.
A gap of half a dozen years separates *The Royal Convert* from
The Tragedy of Jane Shore (D.L. Feb. 1713/4) and we note
that this latter play is deliberately stated on the title-page to
be "Written in Imitation of Shakespear's Style." It may have
been that Rowe was meditating on the Elizabethan during
those six years; but only too often the eighteenth century

---

[1] *The British Theatre*, 1808, vol. x, pp. 3–5.
[2] This tragedy was adapted into French as *Caliste ou la Belle Pénitente*
...*imitée de l'anglois* (by the Marquis de Mauprié), 1750 (later reprinted
at Hague, 1753). As *La Belle Pénitente* it appears in *Le Théâtre anglois*
(1746, vol. v).
[3] p. 48. See *Critical Remarks on Mr. Rowe's Last Play, call'd Ulysses*
(1706).

authors when they said Shakespeare meant Dryden or another, and in this case Rowe seems to have meant Banks. Banks it was who before him dealt with tragic themes from English history, setting a woman figure in the centre of the action. Heywood, of course, had been even earlier in the field with semi-domestic drama of the same kind, but Heywood no one remembered in those years. The theme of *Jane Shore* has certain features in common with that of *Tamerlane*, particularly the presentation of a maiden who sacrifices all for a faithless lover; but the tone of the play is far different from the tone of the earlier work. On careful examination it seems to be largely a compromise between the classic tragedy of royal types and the domestic tragedy of humbler characters. Assuredly the surroundings of the chief figures are noble and even royal, but the most important and the most touching scenes in the play are those in which Jane Shore, starving and destitute, is rescued by her husband. *The Tragedy of Jane Shore* proved a success, then and later[1]; and its fame passed over Europe in its French adaptations[2].

The Tragedy of Lady Jane Gray (D.L. April 1715) approaches even nearer to Banks, for the author has gone so far as to treat a theme already dramatised by the Restoration writer. Here once more we approach both classic-heroic and domestic sentiments. Lady Jane, loved by Guilford and Pembroke, marries the latter and is persuaded to take the crown. Guilford saves Pembroke's life and he and Lady Jane are cast into prison. Pembroke obtains a reprieve but is thwarted by the Bishop of Winchester. Such is the bare plot of this tragedy, one excellently suited for dramatic develop-

---

[1] Several pamphlets appeared on this play: *Memoirs of the Lives of King Edward and Jane Shore* (1714); *Life and Character of Jane Shore* (1714); and *A New Rehearsal, or Bays the Younger. Containing an Examen of The Ambitious Stepmother, Tamerlane, The Biter, Fair Penitent, Royal Convert, Ulysses, and Jane Shore* (1714; written by Charles Gildon; a second edition in 1715 included an examen of *Lady Jane Gray*).

[2] *Jeanne Shore, ou le Triomphe de la Fidélité, à la patrie et à la roiauté* (by L. D. C. V. G. D. N.; Londres 1797); *Jane Shore* (by F. G. J. S. Andrieux in *Chefs-d'œuvre des Théâtres étrangers*, 1822, vol. ii). Note may be taken also of Lemercier's *Richard III. et Jeanne Shore, drame historique...imité de Shakespeare et de Rowe* (1824). P. C. Liadières has a play on the same subject, also influenced by Rowe, published the same year.

ment. It is difficult to estimate precisely how far Rowe has succeeded in giving life to it. Lady Jane seems but a statue and Guilford is an unreal figure. In Pembroke, however, we have one of the few well-drawn types of eighteenth century drama and his presence saves the play from failure. This last tragedy of Rowe's was welcomed on the stage[1], the applause meted out to it probably being intensified by the patriotism and anti-Popery so painfully evident in even the most striking scenes.

Rowe's work in tragedy is seen, from this brief account, to have been somewhat purposeless. He was a talented man; he had a genius for the theatre; he had pity and he had emotion; but he failed to stamp any personality into his works, either because of a lack of dominant will-power, or because of that particular chaos into which all the realm of Melpomene seemed then to have been flung and which reacted so grievously upon the subjects of that muse.

Besides Rowe there was hardly any other single "Augustan" dramatist of the age whose works rose to genuine heights of dramatic power. Compared with those who had made glorious the age of Elizabeth, Rowe is a poor writer; compared with those who followed, he is seen to have a talent lamentably lacking during the whole fifty years.

Colley Cibber's work in tragedy hardly deserves any very minute consideration. *Perolla and Izadora* (D.L. Dec. 1705), which was, save for his adaptation of *Richard III*, his first work in tragic realms, is a mixture of classic treatment and heroic atmosphere. The theme is taken from Orrery's *Parthenissa*, and turns on the hates of Blacius and Pacuvius, running counter to the loves of Izadora[2], Blacius' daughter, and Pacuvius' son, Perolla. The play is full of follies, a mass of nonsense evidently inherited by Cibber from Restoration drama. Typical of the psychological unreality of the work are Blacius' words in Act III. when he hears the sentence on his life:

---

[1] Whincop, p. 280. See *Remarks on the Tragedy of Lady Jane Gray* (1715).
[2] Not Izidora, as Sir A. W. Ward gives it (iii. 486).

> O fatal Chance! *Rome* then and *Blacius* are no more!
> Tell my Daughter what has happened.

In spite of a good cast, this tragedy was not a success, running
to barely six consecutive performances and being repeated
once on Jan. 2, 1705/6[1].

In *Ximena: or, The Heroick Daughter* (D.L. Nov. 1712)
Cibber essayed another "Augustan" drama, taking for
adaptation Corneille's *Le Cid*. There are classical elements
in this tragi-comedy of his, although the prologue shows
dissatisfaction with stricter canons:

> *not confin'd to Rules,*
> *Those* Prudes, *the Criticks call them, Feasts for Fools.*

The main influence in the work is that of the heroic play.
A fairly happy conclusion is devised by which Gormaz is
saved and Ximena marries Carlos. Many of the characters
are depicted in the old English manner, and Corneille's
drama, itself a trifle "romantic," is rendered still more so
in its newer dress. Beyond a few telling lines[2], however,
Ximena may be comfortably reburied in that oblivion which
ordinarily it has occupied and from which it need hardly be
disinterred.

A tragedy with a happy ending is, likewise, *Cæsar in Ægypt*
(D.L. Dec. 1724), a drama which is obviously a kind of
prologue to *All for Love* and betrays many features of the
heroic type. It opens with the defeat of Pompey by Cæsar.
The latter falls in love with Cleopatra. Ptolemy, who has
murdered Pompey, plans treachery and is himself slain, while
Antony complicates the plot by loving Cleopatra when his
duty is to plead for Cæsar. As is evident, there is a great
similarity between Cibber's play and Fletcher's *The False
One* and Pierre Corneille's *Pompée*. It is probable that Cibber
had read both; but his model was Dryden, and he thought,
too, of the critics who imposed the classical rules.

---

[1] In the preface to *Ximena*, Cibber declares that the third night of
Perolla and Izadora did not give him £5. No doubt it was kept running
a few evenings more because of the actor's influence.

[2] Cf. the speech in v. i.:

> "Has Nature lost its privilege to weep,
> When all that's valuable in life is gone?"

Papal Tyranny in the Reign of King John (C.G. Feb. 1744/5), the last fruit of Cibber's skill, is a pitiful piece of work. Based on a poor play of Shakespeare's, it seems to have been designed purely as a party work directed against the Catholics. It ran for twelve nights, undeservedly[1].

Among the dramatists who produced such plays of a mixed sort in the early years of the century, three of the women writers must be noted, Mrs Wiseman, Mrs Catharine Trotter and Mrs Eliza Haywood, figures to be set alongside of the more heroic Mrs Manley and Mrs Pix. The first has but one tragedy to her credit, *Antiochus the Great: or, The Fatal Relapse* (L.[1] 1702), a very dull albeit bloody play, with a strange admixture of Elizabethan, heroic and classic elements. Whincop declares that it was acted with applause[2]. Mrs Trotter had already started her career in the seventeenth century, producing then *Agnes de Castro* and *The Fatal Friendship*. Her later work is not distinguished by any very high merits. *The Unhappy Penitent* (D.L. *c.* July 1701) is a dull drama, and *The Revolution of Sweden* (H.[1] Feb. 1705/6), in Downes' words, "wanting the just Decorum of Plays, expir'd the Sixth Day[3]." The latter is a poor piece of work, with a strained and chaotic plot, and passions atrophied and chill. Its only interest lies in its classic treatment of otherwise heroic subject-matter. Much finer is Mrs Haywood's *Frederick, Duke of Brunswick-Lunenburgh* (L.[2] March 1728/9), which has well-developed characters in Frederick and in Adelaid, a maiden whose passion is aroused by the neglect she supposes has been cast on her.

Among the early writers likewise must be noted the strange figure of Charles Johnson, whom we have already dealt with

---

[1] It is to be observed that Cibber seems to have made his alteration as early as 1736. Cibber himself mentions it in a letter to *The London Daily Post* (M. 7. ii. 1737) and it was ridiculed in *The Daily Journal*. Fielding alludes to it also in *The Historical Register* (H.[2] 1737). On Feb. 20, 1744/5 the Drury Lane management performed the original *King John*, declaring that it had not been acted at that theatre for fifty years, which seems to point to a theatrical tradition that it had been revived in the late seventeenth century. The revival of Feb. 20 was deferred apparently until Cibber's benefit was over (see *The London Daily Post*, F. 15. ii. 1745). *King John* had been revived previously at C.G. in 1737.

[2] p. 302.   [3] p. 49.

as producing an heroic tragedy and a couple of classic dramas. We shall find later that this man, thoroughly representative of his age, contributed to the theatre not only two "Augustan" tragedies, but a number of farces and ballad-operas and domestic tragedies and sentimental comedies as well. *Love and Liberty* (1709), based on Fletcher's *The Double Marriage*, is noticeable for its union of heroic sentiments and pathos. The sentimental tendency of the author is apparent in the love of nature expressed (a trifle conventionally) by several of the characters. "Let us to some sweet Solitude repair," says Castruchio, to which Dardania:

> The Lark shall wake us with harmonious Songs,
> And Nightingales conclude the Ev'nings Consort,
> There uncorrupted Nature ev'ry where,
> Will give us a kind Taste of Paradice[1].

The reason for the union of pathos and heroic atmosphere in this play is to be found in the assertion given in the prologue to *The Force of Friendship* (H.[1] April 1710) that Otway was his master. The plot of this latter tragedy is more "domestic" than that of the other. Anselmo abandons Julia and makes love through Lothario to Aspatia. The two last-mentioned themselves fall in love. Obviously Johnson has here been striving to reproduce the atmosphere of *The Orphan*; but he had not yet moved out of the conventional realm of stock character-drawing. *Cælia* was still to come.

Round about the same years other writers were providing the theatres with similar plays. In 1702 or 1703, John Oldmixon brought forward *The Governour of Cyprus* at Lincoln's Inn Fields, a fairly good specimen of its class. The plot has relationships with various Restoration non-heroic dramas, and deserves attention on account of its careful treatment. Issamenea's husband is thought to be dead, and she marries Phorsano, who soon abandons her for Lucinda. The husband Iopano returns disguised as a Moor, and Issamenea, after a series of entanglements, stabs him. On discovering his identity, she poisons herself. Many of the complications are improbable, but the theme is treated in a

---

[1] IV. iii.

way that shows Oldmixon to have had a special talent for the stage.

One of the many single play dramatists is Sir Thomas Moore, who brought out at Lincoln's Inn Fields in December 1717 *Mangora, King of the Timbusians. Or, The Faithful Couple*, a tragedy spoken of modestly by the author as a "Trifle[1]." The scene is Paraguay in the Indies and the characters are mostly Spaniards or Indians. While not wholly "contemptible" as Whincop styles it[2], *Mangora* hardly deserves praise for any great intrinsic merits. Its heroic atmosphere, however, its spirits, its rant and its typical ending all entitle it to consideration in the tracing of dramatic development.

The Tragedy of Sir Walter Raleigh (L.[2] Jan. 1718/9) by Dr George Sewell returns for subject-matter to an English theme, mingling that with political hatred of Spain. The plot is complicated by the unhistoric love of young Raleigh for Olympia, daughter of Salisbury, who, along with Gundamor, plots the hero's ruin.

In the twenties of the century this particular tragic type was indulged in most satisfactorily by Ambrose Philips, whose *The Distrest Mother* (D.L. 1712) has already been noted as a classic production[3]. In *The Briton* (D.L. Feb. 1721/2) he turned to an English theme, and at the same time departed a trifle from the classic model he had at first espoused. The characters are drawn more on the heroic plan, and there is an amount of action on the stage which shows that the author had passed into the service of other ideals. It may be noted that this tragedy was a success[4]. *Humfrey, Duke of Gloucester* (D.L. Feb. 1722/3), likewise scened in England, although at a more historical period, was also fairly popular[5]. The ultimate source is confessedly 2 *Henry VI*, from which some thirty lines are directly borrowed, but the play as a whole is almost entirely new[6]. It possibly indicates that admiration of Shakespeare was responsible for the change

---

[1] Dedication.   [2] p. 262.   [3] *Supra*, p. 86.
[4] Whincop, p. 276.   [5] *Id*. p. 276.
[6] For an analysis of the two plots see Odell, *op. cit*. i. 248–50.

from ultra-classicism to the modified form of it displayed in *The Briton*.

Two dramas of a somewhat kindred species by Philips' name-sake, Captain William Phillips, may be considered here. *Hibernia Freed* appeared at Lincoln's Inn Fields in February 1721/2[1]. This is a semi-historical piece presenting to us a picture of Ireland under the Danes. O'Niell is depicted as a hero, and Sabina as a distressed heroine saved in the end by her lover. In *Belisarius* (L.[2] April 1724) the scene is carried to Byzantium, but once more we get the centre of the drama in the love-passages. It is true that there are decided evidences of the influence of classicism in this drama, but there is a certain strength and emotion present which seems a relic of Restoration times. The scene where Almira discovers Belisarius blinded rises to a height rare in the early eighteenth century[2].

Distinguished by praise from no less an authority than Gibbon[3], John Hughes' *The Siege of Damascus* (D.L. Feb. 1719/20) evidently merits some special notice. Not only has the historical spirit of the age been well preserved, but there is a decided attempt to depict a hero who shall have an almost Shakespearian flaw in his character. The plot is well conceived. Phocyas loves Eudocia, the daughter of Eumenes, who plans her for Herbis. The lover defeats the Saracens, but on his return is spurned by Eumenes. He tries to flee from the besieged city with Eudocia but is captured. Meanwhile Caled has promised, on the advice of the magnanimous Abudah, to let the citizens of the town have leave to depart. A piece of treachery is planned and Phocyas is slain by an arrow. On his death Eudocia decides to enter a nunnery. It is said that originally Phocyas was made by Hughes to give

---

[1] It is attributed to Phillips by Whincop (p. 276) and does not appear in Jacob.

[2] This play is also attributed to Phillips by Whincop (p. 306). It is not certain whether this William Phillips is the same as the author of *The Revengeful Queen* (D.L. 1698) noted in vol. i (1660–1700), p. 423.

[3] *Decline and Fall of the Roman Empire* (ed. J. B. Bury, 1908), v. 426 note.

up his religion for the sake of the city; but that this was altered to suit the tastes of the time[1].

An important writer who rose to fame about this time, but whose work cannot be confined to any single decade of the period, is Aaron Hill, who commenced his activity as a playwright in 1710 and whose last dramas were not published until 1760. Famous as a translator and adapter of Voltaire, this man, who wrote farce, domestic tragedy, classical tragedy, heroic tragedy and opera, claims remembrance not only for his certain skill but for his independent judgment in theatrical matters and for his whole-hearted attempts to raise the status of the stage and all connected therewith.

Elfrid: or The Fair Inconstant, which came out at Drury Lane in Jan. 1709/10, is but a poor production, and was not over successful. It has, however, touches in it which betoken a certain potential talent, later to be developed. Hill, in his after-life, was somewhat contemptuous of this early work of his and rewrote it as *Athelwold* (D.L. Dec. 1731). The alterations made in the conduct of the second drama are exceedingly instructive. In the first play, Athelwold is wholly blameless, an innocent hero brought to destruction by his wife; in the second, the same character brings ruin on himself by his having forsaken Ethelinda. In *Elfrid* the heroine is false to her husband through her desire for queenship; in *Athelwold* she holds her trust. The former tragedy presents the king as a slave to his passions, mean and immoral; the latter shows him as a magnanimous prince with an inner royalty of spirit that places him above his subjects. What an advance Hill had made in dramatic conception and technique may be seen in the dialogue and in the particularly fine scene of the hero's death in the second play.

---

[1] That these tastes were hypocritical is seen by the epilogue:

> "Well, Sirs; you've seen, his Passion to approve,
> A desperate Lover give up all for Love,
> All but his Faith.—Methinks now I can spy,
> Among you airy Sparks, some who wou'd cry
> Phoo, Pox—for that—what need of such a Pother?
> For one Faith left, he wou'd have got another."

Hughes himself died on the evening of the first performance of his play (Feb. 17, 1719/20).

Hill's next tragedy after *Elfrid* was *The Fatal Vision* (L.²
1716) already noted as an heroic tragedy, or, just possibly,
as a burlesque on that species. With Mitchell, a trifle later,
he seems to have collaborated in a bourgeois drama, *The
Fatal Extravagance* (L.² 1721), and then progressed, like so
many of his contemporaries, to admiration of Shakespeare.
*King Henry the Fifth: or, The Conquest of France, By the
English* (D.L. Dec. 1723) is a reworking of the Elizabethan
play, with the comic parts omitted and an addition in the
form of a sub-plot dealing with Harriet, daughter of Lord
Scrope, seduced by the King and disguised as a boy. This
drama was intended, evidently, for the Little Theatre in the
Haymarket[1], but was handed over to Drury Lane. For it the
author provided £200 that it might be suitably mounted[2].

With *Alzira: or, Spanish Insult Repented* (L.² June 1736),
which came out after *Athelwold* (D.L. 1731), Hill turned to
Voltaire, with whom he had become personally acquainted
when the French author was a visitant in England. *Alzire, ou
Les Americains* was first produced in Paris on Jan. 27, 1735/6,
and Hill was quick to realise that this was a play which might
make an appeal on the English stage, partly for political
reasons, partly because in it Voltaire had broken away from
the Racine tradition and was moving towards a new form of
art. In his adaptation Hill has made several changes, giving
new names to Don Gusman (now Don Carlos) and to Montèze
(now Ezmont), but in the main his tragedy moves along the
lines marked out by that writer who became truly the friend
and the terror of Europe.

Hill's success in *Alzira* led him to follow up his translation
with another of *Zaïre*, a tragedy which had been originally
produced in Paris on August 13, 1732. *The Tragedy of Zara*
(D.L. Jan. 1735/6)[3] preserves again the main features of the
French play, but there are a few changes calculated to suit
English taste. The independence of the translator in the
matter of stage-craft may be seen in his preface where he

---

[1] Cf. Whincop, p. 248.
[2] Victor, *The History of the Theatres* (1761). For an analysis of the
plays see Odell, *op. cit.* i. 252–3   [3] See Appendix C.

pronounces against the artificial style of acting and declares that as an experiment he gave the parts of the hero and heroine to two unknown performers. It was in this play, owing to Hill's activities, that Mrs Cibber won her first great success. A third adaptation followed in *Meropé* (D.L. April 1749)[1], an alteration of *Mérope* (Paris, Feb. 20, 1743), a rendering that requires little individual attention. With this drama of *Meropé*, Hill's work in the first half of the eighteenth century was done. One later play of his however, *The Roman Revenge* (Bath, 1753?) may be considered here in brief wise. The importance of this tragedy is the evident influence in it of Voltaire's style, classicism being united with pathos in a manner very similar to that employed by the French writer. It presents, too, an interesting poetic licence in that Brutus is discovered to be the natural son of the man he murders, none other than Julius Cæsar.

With the *Mariamne* (L.[2] Feb. 1722/3) of Elijah Fenton we move back once more to Eastern realms. This play was an immense success[2], and in some ways deserved to be applauded. The characters, it is true, are thoroughly stock in conception, and there is a considerable amount of mawkish sentimentalism towards the close, but the treatment of the plot is good and the author undoubtedly felt for many of his *dramatis personæ*. The emotional nature of the play it is which singles it out for special notice in those years of passionless theorising.

From about this time, for what reason it is difficult to tell, there seems to have been a little recrudescence of interest in Asiatic themes. Mottley's *The Imperial Captives* appeared at Lincoln's Inn Fields in February 1719/20. It is confessedly based on a French work, and mingles once more pathetic scenes with classic atmosphere. In the final reunion of Thrasimond and Eudosia there is presented in it something of a happy ending. The same author's *Antiochus* (L.[2] April 1721) is another undistinguished tragedy with kindred characteristics.

---

[1] The second accented *e* is in the original title page.

[2] Whincop, p. 231. Connected with the appearance of this play are two pamphlets, *The History of Herod and Mariamne* and *The Unhappy Loves of Herod and Mariamne*, both designed as introductory to the play (1723).

John Gay's one tragedy, *The Captives* (D.L. Jan. 1723/4), has a scene of the same type. It is concerned with plots and revolutions and a hero released by a beautiful slave. It was acted successfully, evidently under the title of *The Fair Captive*[1].

The *Periander* (L.[2] Jan. 1730/1) of John Tracy is set in Corinth and seems indebted for its theme to French romance[2]. Execrable in construction, it shows peculiarly enough a certain freshness in its dialogue, and a fair skill in the presentation of inner conflict in the mind of Hypsenor.

Charles Marsh, before passing to adaptations of Shakespearian dramas, seems to have been swayed by the twin forces of pathos and Eastern heroics. In his *Amasis, King of Egypt* (C.G. Aug. 1738) he has presented a tragedy which in theme is simply a variant of *The Orphan* and in atmosphere a reproduction of many another Asiatic tragedy. Psammenitus is the hero here, and Miriana, to whom he is secretly married, the heroine. Amasis is the equivalent of Polydore in Otway's play and his action is the same. The verses prefixed to the tragedy and addressed to Southerne, with their praise of Otway and of Rowe, show clearly the tendencies of the author.

Among the Eastern dramas may be numbered also *Mahomet the Impostor* (D.L. April 1744) of James Miller, the one tragedy of a writer prolific in sentimental comedy. The plot is based on Voltaire's drama, *Le Fanatisme, ou Mahomet le Prophète*, first acted on Aug. 9, 1742, but there are many variations in the development of the action. The bigotry that is evident in every line of Mahomet's utterance destroys any opportunity for the arousing of true tragic spirit in the play as a whole.

For the scene to his *Elmerick: or, Justice Triumphant* (D.L. Feb. 1739/40) George Lillo, departing from his bourgeois themes, passed to Buda. The plot of the play, in spite of a considerable number of touching and sentimental passages, is heroically conceived. Elmerick is left governor of Buda. His wife, Ismena, is ravished by Conrad, whose sister, the Queen, adores himself. He causes the Queen to

---

[1] Whincop, p. 239.   [2] Genest, iii. 308.

be strangled; Ismena dies; and Conrad stabs himself. In
the midst of this general massacre, the King returns and
Elmerick tells to him his mournful tale[1].

Still farther East went Dr Michael Clancy for the subject-
matter of his *Hermon Prince of Chorœa, or, The Extravagant
Zealot* (Dublin, 1740)[2]. The scene of this tragedy is Pekin
and the play is of the numerous classic-heroic type of the
age. The blank verse deserves notice, but all dramatic sense
in the tragedy is lacking.

A peculiar drama of a slightly earlier time is *Arminius* (1740)
by William Paterson. This tragedy deals with the battles of
the Romans and has interest because of its anti-war sentiments. "What Woes," we are told,

> attend on War! when the dire God
> Rides forth in red Array! around him rage
> Despair and Ruin; at his iron Wheels
> Captivity is dragg'd; and in his Train
> Come rav'ning Famine and devouring Plague[3].

The structure is again classically heroic; but the emotions
differ in many places from the typical heroic passions of past
times.

Before passing from the more Eastern works, slight mention might be made of William Hatchett's *The Chinese Orphan*
(1741), which is described as "An Historical Tragedy.
Alter'd from a Specimen of the Chinese Tragedy, in Du
Halde's History of China. Interspers'd with Songs, after the
Chinese Manner." This work has special importance, notwithstanding the dull rhetoric of its blank verse, in that an
obvious endeavour is made by the author to secure an almost
romantic, oriental effect. Hatchett's other play, *The Rival
Father* (H.[2] 1730), is, peculiarly enough, classical in treatment.

This rapid résumé of the progress of the "Augustan" type
of tragedy may be finally closed with a slight examination of
one or two of the later historical dramas. Henry Brooke's
Gustavus Vasa (1739) has won a certain amount of notoriety

---

[1] See Whincop, p. 258, who says it was acted in 1735 (cp. Victor,
op. cit. ii. 115).
[2] See Hughes, S. C., *The Pre-Victorian Drama in Dublin* (1904), p. 61.
[3] II. iii.; quoted also in Genest, iii. 613.

because of the action of the Lord Chamberlain in suppressing it, and to a certain extent it is worthy of remembrance as a well-constructed and well-written dramatic work. The conception of Gustavus and of Cristiern is especially good. William Havard has already been noted for his work in the heroic style. His *King Charles the First* (L.[2] March 1736/7), written, we are told, "in Imitation of Shakespeare," belongs rather to this section. The usual darkening of Cromwell's figure is indulged in and Fairfax is heavily whitewashed. In order "to heighten the Distress in the last Act[1]," history is falsified to enable the dramatist to introduce a pathetic scene which shows Charles parting from his Queen[2]. Edward Young, long ere he planned his *Night Thoughts*, brought out two tragedies, *Busiris* (D.L. March 1718/9) and *The Revenge* (D.L. April 1721), the latter of which is, like *King Charles the First*, decidedly reminiscent of Shakespeare. Both show the influence of the Restoration heroic tragedy, particularly the former, but the Moor Zanga in *The Revenge* undoubtedly recalls Iago and perhaps also the Abdelazer of Mrs Behn. Young's plays, while they exhibit strength of purpose and a certain powerfulness of utterance, do not mark themselves out as being in any way exceptional in their age[3]. William Shirley's *Edward the Black Prince: or, The Battle of Poictiers* (D.L. Jan. 1749/50) is another drama "Attempted after the Manner of Shakespear." The production is not a notable one, the blank verse being poor and the construction stilted. The only really fine parts of the play are those which concern the fatally vacillating Arnold and the fair captive Mariana, scenes which seem to recall *The Black Prince* of Orrery. In spite of a fine cast (Garrick played Prince Edward) the play "met with very indifferent success[4]." The historical

---

[1] Preface.

[2] This is illustrated in the frontispiece. The play was moderately successful.

[3] *The Brothers* (1753), as was noted in *The London Magazine* (xxv. 433), is largely an adaptation of Thomas Corneille's *Persée et Démétrius*. On this see the thesis on Young by W. Thomas (1901), pp. 299–303. It is strange that Young made no confession of his indebtedness to the French piece.

[4] *Biographia Dramatica*. In 1750 there was issued *An Examen of the Historical Play of Edward the Black Prince; or, The Battle of Poictiers. In*

"Augustan" type was treated, in a less satisfactory manner, by Tobias Smollett in *The Regicide: or, James the First of Scotland* (1749), written when the author was but 18 years of age. The preface attacks in no measured terms the evils of Patrons and Patentees, but the play itself hardly deserved representation on the stage. It is hopelessly rhetorical and, like so many of these plays, full of impossible sentiments.

With Smollett's effort we may close this survey. It is evident that this Augustan tragedy was that which most truly expressed the general tendencies of the age, precisely because there was no informing purpose in that age. The admixture of classicism, heroics and pathos was what pleased it best. It is clear, also, that while the heroic atmosphere, often set in oriental realms, was ever dominant, even in writers whose inclinations were strictly classical, the influence of Shakespeare and of Otway was operating, not only on individual authors, but upon the whole age, to reduce the violence of the heroics and bring in a surer, steadier note. These Shakespearian dramas were most commonly historical in subject-matter and so met the stream of influence which came from Rowe and his "she-tragedies." At the same time, other men, often largely untouched by Shakespeare's charm, had been going back to early Britain, and they, too, helped towards the break-down of the oriental school. The historical plays modelled upon Shakespeare, the "she-tragedies" popularised by Rowe and these pre-historic British plays all helped to prepare the ground for the domestic drama, which stands unique in this age, apart from classicism and from heroicism alike.

VI. *Domestic Tragedies, and Plays of Private Woe*

This domestic drama, we may say, constitutes the one vital and creative force in the whole of the tragic productivity of the years 1700 to 1750. Classicism had brought but little to the theatre; heroics had but perpetuated a type of play which

which the Merits and Defects of that Dramatick Essay, are candidly considered, and impartially pointed out. With A Critical Review of Mr. Barry, in the Character of Ribemont.

had run its true course decades before; the typical Augustan drama was aimless and chaotic, a mixture of heterogeneous elements inharmoniously fused together. All of these, in one way or another, depended on tradition; their themes were the same, their characters typically conceived, their language stilted and unnatural. The bourgeois tragedy on the other hand was progressive and revolutionary. An outcome of the sentimental movement which was sweeping over Europe, it sought for new expression of tragic facts; it pitted its strength against the forces of unreality and classicism in an endeavour to find a new field of tragic emotion.

The history of this species of drama has been well traced by Ernest Bernbaum in *The Drama of Sensibility*, a book of subtle theory and careful research; but there are several aspects of the subject which seem to have been neglected in that work[1]. Seven tragedies only are dealt with in this general survey as presenting features of sentimentalised bourgeois drama—the anonymous *The Rival Brothers* (L.[1] 1704), Mitchell's or Hill's *The Fatal Extravagance* (L.[2] 1721), Lillo's *The London Merchant* (D.L. 1731) and *Fatal Curiosity* (H.[2] 1736), Charles Johnson's *Cælia* (D.L. 1732), Hewitt's *Fatal Falshood* (D.L. 1734) and Cooke's *Love the Cause and Cure of Grief* (D.L. 1743). The first three of these are dealt with as being "revolutionary" in scope and aim. The Elizabethan and Restoration bourgeois drama is for the most part dismissed; and the tendencies towards domestic tragedy in the eighteenth century, apart from those in the plays mentioned, are more or less neglected.

It is certainly true that in the earlier periods there was little of that peculiar conception of pity which Ernest Bernbaum has noted in the sentimental drama[2], but the deliberate breakaway of domestic plays from the old "royal" conception of tragedy cannot be dissociated from the efforts of Lillo and Hill. Otway on every hand is hailed by the eighteenth-century

---

[1] An important study also is that of Singer, H. W., *Das bürgerliche Trauerspiel in England* (1891); the introduction by Sir A. W. Ward to the *Belles Lettres* edition of Lillo's *The London Merchant and Fatal Curiosity* (1906) is likewise valuable.

[2] *Op. cit.* p. 36.

revolutionaries as a master, and *The Rival Brothers* of 1704 is nothing but a reworking of *The Orphan* theme. The fount of the domestic sentimentalised tragedy as expressed in the works of Lillo is to be found in *Arden of Feversham*, in Heywood's *The English Traveller* and *A Woman Killed with Kindness*, and in *The Yorkshire Tragedy*. These Elizabethan or Jacobean attempts in this style were taken over in the period of the Restoration by Otway in *The Orphan* and by Southerne in *The Fatal Marriage*, and so passed on to those who were to elaborate the style still more in the early part of the eighteenth century. The treatment of humble, contemporary, middle-class themes, and the tendency towards the substitution of prose for blank-verse, would seem to be of more consequence than that conception of character which Bernbaum in his study makes the almost final test.

The various movements toward the introduction of domestic themes in the eighteenth century itself, briefly hinted at above, have likewise never been sufficiently noted. The pathos and sentimentalism which appear in some otherwise heroic or classic plays of the age—notably in those of Rowe and of Charles Johnson—proved one method of approach. Indeed, one play of the latter, *The Force of Friendship* (H.[1] 1710), confessedly influenced by Otway, has already been noted as an almost domestic tragedy[1]. Another wholly tentative movement is, as we have seen, to be traced in the introduction of early British scenes and scenes taken from later English history. The fifty years with which we are dealing literally teems with these. Gildon's *Love's Victim* (L.[1] 1701), a play of the pathetic-heroic class, is set in primitive Britain, as are Rowe's *The Royal Convert* (H.[1] 1707), Mrs Manley's *Lucius, The First Christian King of Britain* (D.L. 1717), Philips' *The Briton* (D.L. 1722), Jeffreys' *Edwin* (L.[2] 1724) and Hill's *Athelwold* (D.L. 1731). Innumerable are the *Charles I's*, *Sir Walter Raleighs*, *Sir Thomas Overburys* and *Jane Shores*, all ultimately springing from the example of John Banks in the seventeenth century. In those plays, which are mostly pathetic, we discover a mean as it were between the classical or Eastern settings and those of the

---

[1] *Supra*, p. 105.

domestic drama. The age was growing a trifle tired of its
heroics and pined for something more poignant to stir its
emotions; and in this way numbers of the traditionally inclined dramatists strove to please the two conflicting parties.
As a testimony how far this desire for "private woe" operated
on the minds of the audience nothing could be more instructive than the prologue to Charles Johnson's *The Sultaness*
(D.L. 1717), a play based on Racine:

> The Tragic Muse has with unweary'd Toil,
> Thro' ev'ry Age, and every distant Soil,
> Search'd after Heroes; ransack'd *Greece* and *Rome*
> And rais'd our *British* Monarchs from the Tomb...
> This Night, two Lovers of our Age we show,
> A sad, true Tale, a Modern Scene of Woe;
> Yet, that our Herœ may affect you more,
> We bring him from the distant *Turkish* Shore:
> Then, think not that the Theme too fresh appears;
> A thousand Leagues, are like a thousand Years.

Johnson's words show well the feelings of the time. Classic
rule bade a foreign scene or distant place; but contemporary
taste preferred "A sad, true Tale, a Modern Scene of Woe."

The true source of the eighteenth century domestic
tragedy is, then, obviously Rowe, and Rowe is the link between
Otway, Banks and Southerne and those who succeeded him.
Rowe's plays are not, however, thoroughly bourgeois; the
merit of being first in the field in this direction belongs to an
anonymous writer who in 1704 brought out at Lincoln's Inn
Fields a drama entitled *The Rival Brothers*[1], a play clearly
inspired by *The Orphan*. Alithea here is the mother of
Theodor and Horatio, both of whom love Victoria, the
daughter of Lord Honorius, half-brother of Alithea. Victoria
loves Theodor alone, but is pursued as well by Lord Belmont,
who had come to propose marriage to Alithea. The love
affairs are complicated also by the presence of Belinda, Lord
Belmont's daughter, who loves Horatio. The main plot is
worked out as in Otway, although Horatio's motives are not
the same as Polydore's, and in the end Theodor stabs himself
and Victoria dies. The play is a good one, although it lacks

---

[1] The running title is *A Fatal Secret or The Rival Brothers*.

the unity of the Restoration tragedy. Particularly noticeable in it is the sense of fate, a marked feature of the seventeenth century bourgeois tragedy and one that influenced the German writers of later *Schicksalstragödie*. The motto may well be found in Act IV.:

> Our Life is all a Journey in the dark,
> Where ev'ry step we take is on the Brink
> Of some most horrid dreadful Precipice.
> And now we Pass on safe, and now we fall,
> We know not how, All Chance, at least in us.

Between the production of this play and the appearance in 1721 of *The Fatal Extravagance*, Bernbaum finds no development of domestic tragedy, but there is one play which comes close at least to that species—Lewis Theobald's *The Perfidious Brother*, produced at Lincoln's Inn Fields in February 1715/6. Quite clearly the writer intended his drama to be of the bourgeois type. "*In This, if Ought,*" he declares in the prologue,

> our Author hopes he may
> Assume some little Merit from his Play.
> Since, stripp'd of Regal Pomp, and glaring Show
> His Muse reports a Tale of Private Woe.
> Works up Distress from Common Scenes in Life
> A Treach'rous Brother, and an Injur'd Wife.

The plot is a hackneyed one, taken from Filmer's *The Unnatural Brother* (L.[1] 1699), possibly through the intermediate hands of one Mestayer[1]. Sebastian is married to Luciana. His younger brother Roderick tries to ruin him, and endeavours to seduce Luciana into sinning with his uncle Gonsalvo. While he fails in some of his evil practice, he succeeds in poisoning Sebastian's mind. Beaufort is the typical misunderstood friend of earlier tragedy, and his marriage to Selinda at the close of the play provides a moderately happy ending for at least part of the plot. The drama as a whole is a fine one, and, while not in any way suggesting the element of fate, deserves to be remembered as a well-constructed work modelled on the lines laid down by Otway[2].

---

[1] In 1716 the latter published a drama of his on the same theme in order to prove plagiarism. Theobald in his preface denies the theft.

[2] Jacob p. 258, says it was written on the plan of *The Orphan*.

Concerning the authorship of the next definite attempt at domestic tragedy, *The Fatal Extravagance* (L.[2] April 1721), considerable doubt has prevailed. The play as originally performed was in one act, and later was expanded into two and more. It was published under the name of Mitchell, but seems actually to have been the work of Hill. Whincop[1] says merely that the former "was said to be greatly obliged to Mr. *Aaron Hill*" in its composition, but Victor[2] declares it was almost entirely by the latter, and it was reprinted (in one act) in the 1760 collected edition of Hill's dramatic efforts. The source is *The Yorkshire Tragedy*, but the development of character and of plot is altered to accord with the sentimental ideals of the time[3]. The "*private sorrows*" and the "*Domestic fears*" dealt with are duly emphasised in Hill's prologue. Only four characters in all are introduced: Bellmour, sunk in debt, who kills Bargrave in order to save Woodly; Courtney his friend; and Louisa his wife. Here for the first time in the eighteenth century the sense of fate is used to full effect, the whole of the actions of the *dramatis personæ* being warped and changed by some superior power. Here, too, appears for the first time in this age a true bourgeois drama, set in England and without the least attempt at heroicising. Undoubtedly Hill deserves the credit, normally given to Lillo, of having been the first to introduce to his age the tragedy of contemporary English types and to provide the definite basis for the popular *Schicksalstragödie* of later years.

George Lillo's *The London Merchant* was not produced till ten more years had elapsed, but a few months before the appearance of that play was acted at the Haymarket another bourgeois drama, *Fatal Love, Or, The Degenerate Brother* (H.[2] Jan. 1730), by Osborne Sydney Wandesford. This tragedy, which is not mentioned in Bernbaum's study, is a play of "private life." "The Plot," we are told in the prologue, "tho' Foreign, might have happened here." It is not, like *The Fatal Extravagance*, revolutionary in its aims,

---

[1] p. 261.   [2] *Op. cit.* ii. 123.
[3] Cf. Bernbaum, *op. cit.* pp. 129–31.

but it must be taken into account with the other domestic plays of the period. Genest has styled it merely a plagiarised performance[1], declaring it simply a reworking of Southerne's *The Fatal Marriage*, but the plot is conducted along lines different from those of the Restoration tragedy and the characterisation is of a more sentimental cast.

None of the dramas so far mentioned were very popular, although the applause given to *The Fatal Extravagance* both at its initial presentation and at later revivals may be taken as registering the tastes of the audience. The way had been well prepared for the appearance at Drury Lane in June 1731 of George Lillo's *The London Merchant: or, The History of George Barnwell*. The town came somewhat dubiously to it, sneering at "the presumption of the author, in hoping to make them sympathise in the sorrows of any man beneath the rank of an emperor, king or statesman[2]," but a few days showed that its success was assured. Queen Caroline read it; English men of letters, even Pope himself, gave it their support; Rousseau patronised it in France; Diderot compared it with plays of Sophocles and of Euripides; Marmontel with those of Racine; Lessing imitated it in *Miss Sara Sampson*; Goethe and Schiller acknowledged its power[3]. Reading it now, we cannot divine at first what precisely it was which so affected contemporary writers and writers of the succeeding half century; but a glance at later tragic endeavour will show us that Lillo is the true father of Ibsen and of those who in our modern days have returned to domestic scenes for the terror and awe of tragic emotion. Otway and his followers had been too pathetic to secure the true tension of tragedy;

---

[1] iii. 282.

[2] *Biographia Dramatica*. Sir A. W. Ward's introduction, already cited, is illuminating, and there is an interesting study by W. D. Hudson in *A Quiet Corner in a Library* (1915). Cf. also Bernbaum, *op. cit.* pp. 150–3. L. Hoffman's inaugural dissertation on *George Lillo* (Marburg, 1888) does not contain quite so much of value.

[3] A French translation as *Le Marchand de Londres* by P. Clément was published in Paris in 1748 and a second edition was issued in London in 1751. At Hamburg in 1772 (reprinted 1781) appeared a rendering in German by H. A. B. Bassewitz as *Der Kaufmann von London*; and in the *Spectatoriaale Schouwburg*, vol. viii (1775) was given a Dutch translation as *De Koopman van Londen*.

Hill had merely taken an old Elizabethan play and reworked it. Lillo deliberately sought for a hitherto undramatised plot, and, without an undue infusion of pathetic sentiments, wrought it out into a telling story of real life. *The London Merchant* is not a masterpiece. It lacks artistic unity; its characters are moulded too much on a kind of morality tradition; there is not sufficient of that feeling of fate which marked out *The Fatal Extravagance*. Notwithstanding this, it is a landmark in the history, not only of English drama, but of European drama. It is the first conscious deliberate effort in the new style.

Fatal Curiosity: A True Tragedy of Three Acts followed at the Haymarket in May 1736. "*No fustian Hero rages here to Night*," cried Fielding in the prologue,

> *No Armies fall, to fix a Tyrant's Right:*
> *From lower Life we draw our Scene's Distress:—*
> *—Let not your Equals move your Pity less!*
> *Virtue distrest in humble State support;*
> *Nor think, she never lives without the Court!*

The story is a telling one. Old Wilmot and Agnes his wife are sunk in poverty. They deem their son, who had gone to India, dead. Young Wilmot unexpectedly returns and reveals himself to his sweetheart, Charlotte; but, wishing to refine on his joy, he decides to go disguised to his parents' house. There he gives his mother a casket of jewels to keep for him. The old couple meditate over the riches and finally murder him. Just as the fell deed is accomplished, friends arrive and all joy is turned to sorrow. Old Wilmot kills his wife and then commits suicide. The sense of fate here, so admirably developed, is the source of that element so evident in continental plays of a later time[1]. Here, too, is the first presentment of that peculiar sentimental emotion seen at its full in the works of Laurence Sterne, where refinement upon joy or sorrow is indulged in luxuriously. *Fatal Curiosity* is

---

[1] See Jakob Minor's *Die Schicksalstragödie in ihren Hauptvertretern* (1883). *Fatal Curiosity* was translated by W. H. Brömel as *Stolz und Verzweiflung* in 1785 (reprinted in *Deutsche Schaubühne*, vol. xxxi. 1788). The theme was adapted in Zacharias Werner's *Der Vierundzwanzigste Februar*, in Gertrude Robins' *The Home-Coming* and in Rupert Brooke's *Lithuania*.

a much greater play than *The London Merchant*, and stamps Lillo as being a genius of no common rank.

In spite of the popularity of *The London Merchant*, which in Bernbaum's opinion was somewhat artificial[1], Lillo had no direct successors till a number of years had elapsed. Charles Johnson's *Cælia: Or, The Perjur'd Lover* (D.L. Dec. 1732) seems hardly to have been influenced by his example. Much closer is Johnson to the spirit of Richardson than to that of his fellow-dramatist. This drama, however, belongs to the same tradition, an advertisement to the 1733 edition of *Achilles* informing us that *Cælia* "is founded on a True Tragical Story in Common Life, and the Incidents very Natural and Moving." We are presented here with characters destined to become typical; Wronglove, a kind of Lovelace; Bellamy, the virtuous man friend; and Cælia, a species of Clarissa Harlowe, the afflicted heroine. It is noticeable that *Cælia* was unsuccessful, because, it is said, of the too great realism of the Mrs Lupine scenes[2]. The age was becoming fastidious in its moral tastes.

Two years later appeared John Hewitt's *Fatal Falshood: or Distress'd Innocence. A Tragedy In Three Acts* (D.L. Feb. 1733/4), patronised by Aaron Hill[3]. The plot again, like the plots of most of these bourgeois plays, presents several features of interest. Belladine has been forced to marry Louisa. His father dies, and, the restraint being removed, he marries once more, this time his old sweetheart Maria, who is ignorant of his initial matrimonial bond. Rainford, Louisa's brother, aims at vengeance and succeeds in murdering Belladine after the latter has slain Louisa in her disguise as a man. There is in this drama a queer mixture of classicism (the Unity of Action is strictly preserved), of romantic situation (as in the disguising of Louisa), of attempts at realism, and at the same time of the preservation of tragic decorum (the medium is blank-verse). Once more, we cannot claim Hewitt for a genius; but his play has originality and some sparks of power.

---

[1] *Op. cit.* p. 158.
[2] See the Advertisement to the Reader.
[3] Who wrote the epilogue.

A few more years elapsed, and then Thomas Cooke carried on the tradition in *The Mournful Nuptials, or Love the Cure of all Woes* (1739), later acted and republished as *Love the Cause and Cure of Grief, or The Innocent Murderer* (D.L. Dec. 1743)[1]. The play seems to be more influenced by *The Fatal Extravagance* than by *Fatal Curiosity*, although Bernbaum feels certain that in the latter play is to be discovered its immediate inspiration. Freeman is a "farmer," Weldon "a neighbouring gentleman" of Kent. The former loves Charlotte, daughter of Briar, who is discovered lying dead. Freeman is accused of the murder, but Weldon at the end confesses that he was the assassin. The play is of that serious kind of *drame* which introduces a tragic atmosphere but finally brings the whole plot to a conclusion not unhappy. In this way *Love the Cause and Cure of Grief* anticipates the problem play of later years, and is distinctly premonitory of Ibsen and of Björnson to come. Noticeable is the appeal in the prologue to the practice of the Greek stage, when

> *The tragic Muse cast not her Eye so low,*
> *Or view'd regardless Scenes of humble Woe.*

The bourgeois dramatists were by this time carrying the war into the territory of their enemies.

This was the last true bourgeois tragedy of the half century, but one kindred drama, Anthony Brown's *The Fatal Retirement*, acted once in November 1739 at Drury Lane, must be noted as a further attempt in the manner of Otway. Quin styled it "the *very worst Play* he had read in his Life[2]"—an exaggeration which sufficed to damn it on its solitary evening's production. The epilogue insists that it is a scene "of Private Woe," but the characters are given continental names, and there is no attempt to secure the atmosphere that Hill, Lillo and Cooke had conjured into being. The greatest interest of the play arises from the fact that it is almost a detective drama, the plot being based on the tracing down of the villain Pravamor who has deflowered Leonora.

---

[1] Bernbaum does not seem to be aware of the earlier edition and title. He quotes only the second (pp. 178–9).

[2] Whincop, p. 182.

Throughout the fifty years of this survey, it will be seen that domestic drama as such had not a very successful career; the efforts were tentative rather than final. Moreover, within the number of domestic plays we can distinguish three clearly marked types; the tragedies based on the example of *The Orphan*, the tragedies of fate, and the realistic tragedies such as Johnson's *Cælia* or Lillo's *The London Merchant*. All three pointed forward to more noble developments in the future; but, except for *Fatal Curiosity*, the first half of the eighteenth century gave no masterpiece, even in this its most creative sphere, to the theatre[1].

[1] As a final note, it may be mentioned that the domestic tragedy of the more extreme sort seems to have been heavily patronised by Fielding. He supported Lillo; and a glance at the repertoires in Appendix C will show how often domestic tragedies were acted at the Haymarket during the time of his direction of that theatre.

CHAPTER III

COMEDY

I. *Types of Augustan Comedy*

IT has already been noted that comedy, during the fifty years from 1700 to 1750, was more patronised by the play-goers than tragedy. All through this time three or four comedies were produced to one tragedy; in certain years the proportion was even higher than that; it never sunk below. This, however, presents in itself nothing extraordinary, tragedy in all ages being less welcomed by work-weary or war-weary or dilettante spectators than the brighter and, in a way, less exacting forms of drama. What is of excessive interest for our study is to note what particular forms of comedy were the most popular, in an attempt to gauge the precise tendencies of the age.

Before coming to the actual repertoires, it may be well to indicate briefly the main types of comic development in the reigns of Anne and of the Georges. The last years of the seventeenth century had handed on to the era of Cibber a series of very definite comic traditions. The comedy of manners was in the full flush of its highest bloom in Congreve when the year 1700 came. *The Way of the World* appeared in the first year of the new century, and even Jeremy Collier's outburst seemed to have done little as yet towards chastening the irresponsible gaiety which characterised the type. Beside this stood the comedy of humours, less potent since Shadwell's death, but dominant still in critical and popular esteem. There was not "much of Comedy known," thought Gildon, "before the learned *Ben Johnson*, for no Man can allow any of *Shakespear's* Comedies, except the *Merry Wives of* Windsor[1]," and Ben Jonson was for others besides Gildon the English master *par excellence* of the comic muse. There was, too,

---

[1] *The Life of Mr. Thomas Betterton* (1710), p. 173.

the comedy of intrigue, inherited from Fletcher by Mrs Behn, and yet patronised, although only too often degenerating into farce. Farce, as has been noted[1], in the last years of the century was assuming more and more of a dominant position, usurping in the minds of the public the position held before by more regular dramas. Finally, in the last years of the seventeenth century, there has been observed the growing power of sentimentalism, the encroaching of emotion into the intellectualism of pure comedy, without that romantic flavour which gave to Shakespeare his exquisite humour. Cibber's *Love's Last Shift* was one of the final triumphs of the age.

These five types of comic development were taken over by the dramatists of the eighteenth century. Farquhar and Vanbrugh, Burnaby and Fielding carried on the manners tradition. The comedy of humours was patronised by Charles Shadwell and Miller, by Charles Johnson and Baker. Intrigue gained a new vitality in the hands of Mrs Centlivre and of Taverner. Farce was popular all through the period in the plays of Bullock and Gay and Cibber and Fielding. The sentimental comedy, as is well known, developed rapidly in this time under Steele and Cibber, Miller and Kelly. Beyond these, however, several new types emerge, types not always capable of being placed in distinct categories by themselves. Out of the comedy of manners grew the "genteel" comedy of the eighteenth century, where social folly ruled and affectation reigned. The comedies of manners, too, united with the sentimental and gave rise to a peculiar moral-immoral drama, where the atmosphere was of Congreve and the aim was of Cibber. After 1728 came the popularity of the ballad-opera, separately to be considered. Burlesques were numerous, all springing ultimately from Buckingham's *The Rehearsal* of 1671; and "satires," political and other, appear year after year in the repertoires of the companies and in the booksellers' lists. Thus, even if we leave out for the moment a large class of miscellaneous dramas such as Fielding's *The Historical Register, For the Year 1736* (H.[2]

[1] See vol. i (1660–1700), pp. 247–60.

1737) and the tragi-comi-pastoral farces of the age, as well as the ballad-operas and pantomimes, we find no less than eight clearly-marked species of comedies each calling for special attention.

It must not, of course, be presumed that this age any more than those of Elizabeth or of Charles II had classes of comedies self-enclosed and independent. More than half of the plays of the time cannot in any wise be esteemed purely of one kind or another. Manners, humours, burlesque, sentimentalism—all often enter into the make-up of one single comedy. All we may do is to note the prevailing moods and the separate "ideas" of the types, and, for purposes of convenience, classify the individual plays under separate headings according as these plays manifest more of one quality or another.

Undoubtedly, in the later years especially, all of the higher species of comedy were being driven from their places by farce, ballad-opera, pantomime and opera. There is obvious justification in the many contemporary complaints regarding the taste of the times. The rapid increase of burlesques after 1710 keeps pace with the degenerating appreciation of the audience. While noting this gradual making way on the part of comedy as a whole for the slighter species of drama and of opera, we may attempt in some wise to estimate the relative popularity within the bounds of comedy itself of the main types already mentioned. It is, in the first place, not at all the truth that sentimentalism in its pure form ruled the period. Whether we look at new productions or at regular repertoires, we find that sentimentalism plays but a small part in the daily fare of the playhouses. Among the new plays, comedies of manners, of humours and of intrigue are most numerous. There are a few "genteel" comedies and a certain number of the moral-immoral class. Of pure sentimental dramas there are not many. Ernest Bernbaum in his study numbers barely twenty produced during the fifty years. On the other hand, of plays with greater or less sentimental tendencies there are considerable numbers. Sentimentalism, indeed, holds in relation to comedy much the same position that classicism does to tragedy. Few authors wrote purely classical dramas, few classical tragedies were successful, yet classicism colours nearly all the works of the age. So it is with the sentimental movement. Almost every writer was infected more or less by its spirit, yet pure sentimentalism was not popular and the number of perfectly unadulterated sentimental comedies hardly exceeds half a score.

An examination of several typical repertoires will serve to illustrate the foregoing statements, and for our purpose we may take again those seasons selected to exemplify the equivalent movements in the sphere of tragedy. In that of 1703–4 at Drury Lane, comedy, as has been shown, was by far in excess of tragedy[1]. Of these comedies, the type of humours was undoubtedly the most patronised. Jonson's own *Epicœne* was played 3 times, *Volpone* 4 times and *Bartholomew Fair* twice; Shadwell's *The Squire of Alsatia* tops the list with 13 performances; *The Lancashire Witches* secured 6 nights and *The Miser* 2. Howard's *The Committee* (2) may be taken as of the same class, as well as Ravenscroft's *The London Cuckolds* (1) and Dryden's *Sir Martin Mar-all* (1). Among the Elizabethan plays revived, Beaumont and Fletcher are represented by *The Pilgrim* (as an opera, 6), *Rule a Wife and Have a Wife* (2) and *The Chances* (in Buckingham's version, 1). The tragi-comedy, *A King and No King*, was given once; while Brome's *The Jovial Crew* secured 3 performances. Of the Restoration dramatists, a number of the farcical and manners writers are well patronised; Congreve in *The Old Batchelour* (2), Wycherley in *The Plain Dealer* (2), Etherege in *The Comical Revenge* (1), Mrs Behn in *The Rover* (3) and *The Emperor of the Moon* (as an opera, 7), Crowne in *Sir Courtly Nice* (1), Dryden in *The Spanish Fryar* (2) and *Secret Love* (1), Vanbrugh in *The Relapse* (2) and *Æsop* (2), Mountfort in *Greenwich Park* (2), D'Urfey in *The Fond Husband* (2) and *The Marriage-Hater Match'd* (1). Shakespeare is hardly represented at all, *The Taming of the Shrew*

---

[1] *Supra*, p. 55. It may be noted here that in the following analysis of repertoires I have included among the sentimental plays a few dramas which are not strictly of that type, but which present in one or two scenes a few sentimental features.

being given once, and *The Tempest* as an opera once. Of later dramas we find Cibber's *Love's Last Shift* (4), *The School-Boy* (2) and *Love Makes a Man* (5), Mrs Centlivre's *Love's Contrivance* (5), Steele's *The Funeral* (2) and Baker's *Tunbridge-Walks* (6). Steele's *The Lying Lover* was produced for the first time during the season and ran for 6 nights. It is obvious here that sentimental works were not at all among the most popular pieces, and that the tastes of the spectators were by no means squeamish. *The London Cuckolds* and *The Relapse* are sufficiently vulgar and representative of the "manners" of the Restoration age.

The season 1704–5 shows just such a run of stock-plays. Beaumont and Fletcher again appear with *The Pilgrim* (1), *The Chances* (1) and *The Beggar's Bush* (3), Jonson with *Bartholomew Fair* (2), *Epicœne* (1) and *Volpone* (2), Brome with *The Jovial Crew* (3) and *The Northern Lass* (9), Shakespeare with *The Taming of the Shrew* (1) and *Henry IV* (3). Restoration comedies are easily the most numerous, with Dryden (*Secret Love* 6, *Sir Martin Mar-all* 2, *The Spanish Fryar* 6, *An Evening's Love* 2, *Amphitryon* 2), Congreve (*The Old Batchelour* 3), Mrs Behn (*The Emperor of the Moon* 4, *The Rover* 3), Howard (*The Committee* 7), Villiers (*The Rehearsal* 5), Ravenscroft (*The London Cuckolds* 1), Mountfort (*Greenwich Park* 1), Farquhar (*The Constant Couple* 2), Etherege (*The Comical Revenge* 5, *She Wou'd if She Cou'd* 3), Rawlins (*Tunbridge Wells* 1), Otway (*The Souldier's Fortune* 2), Crowne (*Sir Courtly Nice* 3), Wycherley (*The Plain Dealer* 3) and Vanbrugh (*The Relapse* 3, *Æsop* 1). Of later dramas we find Cibber's *Love's Last Shift* (1), *The School-Boy* (3), *Love Makes a Man* (2) and Baker's *Tunbridge-Walks* (3). Cibber's *The Careless Husband* was a new production (16), as were Steele's *The Tender Husband* (7), Motteux' *Farewel Folly* (6), Dennis' *Gibraltar* (2) and MacSwiny's *The Quacks* (5). In spite of the number of performances of Cibber's play, the same proportion is to be seen as in the former year; the Restoration drama, and by no means the most moral specimens of it, seemed to prove the most popular.

Passing on to 1708–9 we find much the same order of plays.

At Drury Lane in this season Jonson is again represented in *Volpone* (2), *The Alchemist* (7), *Bartholomew Fair* (2) and *Epicœne* (3); Beaumont and Fletcher in *Rule a Wife and Have a Wife* (1), *The Chances* (2), *The Scornful Lady* (1) and *The Humorous Lieutenant* (1); Brome in *The Jovial Crew* (1) and *The Northern Lass* (2); Shakespeare in *Henry IV* (3). It is Restoration comedy, however, which provides most of the dramatic fare. Presented during the year there are to be found Ravenscroft's *The London Cuckolds* (3), Mrs Behn's *Emperor of the Moon* (2) and *The Rover* (4), Shadwell's *The Lancashire Witches* (1), *The Squire of Alsatia* (2), *Epsom Wells* (7) and *Bury Fair* (2), Dryden's *Amphitryon* (3) and *The Spanish Fryar* (2)[1], Crowne's *Sir Courtly Nice* (2) and *The Country Wit* (2), Congreve's *Love for Love* (3) and *The Old Batchelour* (2), Howard's *The Committee* (3), Mountfort's *Greenwich Park* (2), Vanbrugh's *The Relapse* (2), Wycherley's *The Country Wife* (2), Otway's *The Souldier's Fortune* (1), Buckingham's *The Rehearsal* (1), Etherege's *The Comical Revenge* (1) and *The Man of Mode* (1), D'Urfey's *A Fond Husband* (1) and *The Marriage-Hater Match'd* (1) and Farquhar's *The Constant Couple* (2). Eighteenth century non-sentimental plays also took up some considerable space in the repertoire, Farquhar's *The Recruiting Officer* being given 7 times, *The Beaux Stratagem* 5 times, and *The Stage Coach* once (as an after-piece). The only old plays that could be accorded the title of sentimental are Cibber's *Love's Last Shift* (1), *Love Makes a Man* (3) and *The Careless Husband* (1), Mrs Centlivre's *The Gamester* (3), and Steele's *The Tender Husband* (1) and *The Funeral* (1). This last section secures, as will be seen, only ten performances out of a total of upwards of two hundred. Nor were any of the new plays given sentimental in tone; Baker's *The Fine Lady's Airs* (4), Cibber's *The Rival Fools* (4), D'Urfey's *The Modern Prophets* (3) and Mrs Centlivre's *The Busie Body* (7) being all either "genteel" or satirical in atmosphere.

During the same season the Haymarket theatre put on just such a set of comedies. *Volpone* (1) is there, and *The Al-*

---

[1] The Cibber adaptation of *Marriage a la Mode* was given once.

chemist (2), *Epicœne* (3), *Rule a Wife and Have a Wife* (2), *The Scornful Lady* (3), *The Chances* (4), *Wit without Money* (1) and *The Jovial Crew* (2) are all represented. *The Mayor of Quinborough* (1) is by way of being an innovation. Restoration plays, as in the other house, are by far the most numerous. Here we get Congreve's *Love for Love* (5) and *The Old Batchelour* (2), Betterton's *The Amorous Widow* (6), Dryden's *Marriage a la Mode* (2), *The Spanish Fryar* (1) and *Amphitryon* (1), Crowne's *Sir Courtly Nice* (2), Ravenscroft's *The London Cuckolds* (1), Buckingham's *The Rehearsal* (1), Shadwell's *Epsom Wells* (3), Dogget's *The Country Wake* (1), Carlisle's *The Fortune Hunters* (1), D'Urfey's *Don Quixote I* (1) and *A Fond Husband* (1), Mrs Behn's *The Rover* (4), Howard's *The Committee* (1), Farquhar's *The Constant Couple* (3), Etherege's *She Wou'd if She Cou'd* (1) and *The Man of Mode* (1). The eighteenth century plays performed during the season are nearly all of the older types: Farquhar's *The Beaux Stratagem* (3) and *The Recruiting Officer* (5), Farquhar's *The Stage Coach* (as an after-piece, 5) and Mrs Centlivre's *The Busie Body* (4). The only sentimentally inclined dramas are Cibber's *Love's Last Shift* (2), *Love Makes a Man* (5) and *The Careless Husband* (2) along with Steele's *The Funeral* (2) and *The Tender Husband* (2). Among the new plays appear only two comedies, and these are farcical: Mrs Centlivre's *The Man's Bewitch'd* (3) and Charles Johnson's *Love in a Chest* (as an after-piece, 1). In the whole season the Haymarket audiences were thus permitted to view scenes even approaching towards sentimentalism only some 13 times.

Out of 104 nights given to comedy during the season 1718–9 at Drury Lane only 6 were devoted to Shakespearian plays, 3 to *Henry IV* and 3 to *The Tempest* (still in the operatic form). Early seventeenth century comic endeavour is still fairly well represented by Beaumont and Fletcher (*Rule a Wife and Have a Wife* 3, *The Chances* 2, *The Humorous Lieutenant* 2, *The Pilgrim* 1), Jonson (*Volpone* 1, *Epicœne* 1, *Bartholomew Fair* 2) and Brome (*The Jovial Crew* 1, *The Northern Lass* 2). Once more, however, it is among the ranks of the Restoration

dramatists that we find the greatest popularity. Here are
Congreve's *Love for Love* (4), *The Old Batchelour* (3) and
The Way of the World (3), Wycherley's *The Country Wife* (2),
Etherege's *She Wou'd if She Cou'd* (1) and *The Man of Mode*
(2), Vanbrugh's *Relapse* (4) and *Æsop* (1), Crowne's *Sir Courtly
Nice* (3) and *The Country Wit* (1), Dryden's *The Spanish
Fryar* (3), *Sir Martin Mar-all* (1) and *Amphitryon* (1),
D'Urfey's *Love for Money* (2), Mountfort's *Greenwich Park*
(1), Shadwell's *Lancashire Witches* (1), Farquhar's *The Con-
stant Couple* (4), Buckingham's *The Rehearsal* (1), Howard's
The Committee (5) and Betterton's *The Amorous Widow* (1).
The Restoration style, too, is continued in Farquhar's *The
Beaux Stratagem* (3) and *The Recruiting Officer* (2), Cibber's
She Wou'd and She Wou'd Not (1), Shadwell's *Fair Quaker of
Deal* (1) and Mrs Centlivre's *The Busie Body* (1). Senti-
mentalism of a kind occurs only with one or two plays,
Cibber's *Love's Last Shift* (3), *Love Makes a Man* (1), *The
Careless Husband* (3) and *The Non-Juror* (1), along with
Steele's *The Tender Husband* (4). Two new plays produced
during the season, Johnson's *The Masquerade* (7) and Killigrew's *Chit-Chat* (11), have little of the serious note in them.
Sentimentalism, it is clear, is as yet unpopular with the
spectators. The after-pieces given at this theatre introduce
merely farcical and pantomimic features, if we except the
peculiar play of Gay's, *The What D'Ye Call It* (5). *Orpheus
and Eurydice* (1), *Harlequin turn'd Judge* (3), *The Shipwreck* (1),
Mars and Venus (5) and *The Dumb Farce* (10) present the
latter; *Hob* (3) and *The Stage Coach* (1) the former. At Lincoln's Inn Fields this season conditions appear much the
same as at Drury Lane, with the sole difference that more
attempts seem to have been made at this theatre to introduce
opera of an English sort, *The Prophetess* being given twice,
The Island Princess 4 times and *The Pilgrim* once. Shakespeare gains 6 out of 90 nights devoted to comedy (*Henry IV*
2, *Cymbeline* 3, *The Jew of Venice* 1), while Norris' *The Royal
Merchant* was shown twice. Dryden appears in *The Spanish
Fryar* (3), Congreve in *The Double Dealer* (4), *Love for Love*
(2) and *The Old Batchelour* (1), Vanbrugh in *The Provok'd*

Wife (4), Howard in *The Committee* (6), Betterton in *The Amorous Widow* (2), Mrs Behn in *The Emperor of the Moon* (5), D'Urfey in *Don Quixote* (Part II, 1), Jevon in *The Devil of a Wife* (2), Dr D'Avenant in *Circe* (operatic, 7), Shadwell in *The Squire of Alsatia* (2). Farquhar's *The Recruiting Officer* (1) and *The Twin Rivals* (1), Vanbrugh's *The Confederacy* (1), Shadwell's *The Fair Quaker of Deal* (4), Estcourt's *The Fair Example* (1), Bullock's *Woman's Revenge* (4) and *Woman's a Riddle* (4), and Mrs Centlivre's *The Busie Body* (5) are all in the older style. The slightest hints of sentimentalism only are apparent in Cibber's *Love Makes a Man* (3) and in Mrs Centlivre's *The Gamester* (2). The anonymous *Younger Brother* (3), and Taverner's *'Tis Well if it Takes* (5), both new plays, are modelled on non-sentimental masters, while *Harlequin Hydaspes* (1) is a pure burlesque. Pantomime, among the after-pieces, is represented in *Pan and Syrinx* (2), *Amadis* (5) and *The Jealous Doctor* (1); *The Passion of Sappho* (1) and *Venus and Adonis* (10) are musical pieces; and *Hob* (6), *The Cobler of Preston* (5), *The Hypocondriack* (1), *The Walking Statue* (1) and *The Stage Coach* (1) are farces.

At Drury Lane during the season 1728–9, 112 comedies were given out of a total of 173 performances. Shakespeare barely makes an appearance with *Henry IV* (Part I 3, Part II 5) and *The Tempest* (in the Shadwell version as an opera 5). Beaumont and Fletcher as well as Jonson are fairly well represented in *The Humorous Lieutenant* (1), *The Chances* (1), *Rule a Wife and Have a Wife* (4), *Wit without Money* (2), *The Scornful Lady* (3), *The Alchemist* (2), *Epicœne* (1) and *Volpone* (1). Restoration comedies, however, again fill up the majority of the nights: Congreve (*Love for Love* 4, *The Old Batchelour* 4, *The Way of the World* 4), Howard (*The Committee* 5), Vanbrugh (*The Relapse* 4, *The Provok'd Wife* 4, *Æsop* 1), Buckingham (*The Rehearsal* 2), Dryden (*The Spanish Fryar* 1, *Amphitryon* 1), Farquhar (*The Constant Couple* 3), Bettērton (*The Amorous Widow* 2), Crowne (*Sir Courtly Nice* 2), Etherege (*The Man of Mode* 3), Mrs Behn (*The Rover* 3) and Wycherley (*The Country Wife* 2) all being well patronised. Cibber's *The Double Gallant* (3) and *She Wou'd and She Wou'd Not* (1), as well as Farquhar's *The Beaux Stratagem* (4) and *The Recruiting Officer* (3) are all in the older style. Of comedies approaching towards sentimentalism we find only Steele's *The Funeral* (3) and *The Tender Husband* (4), and Cibber's *Lady's Last Stake* (3), *The Careless Husband* (3), *Love Makes a Man* (1) and *The Provok'd Husband* (8)—occupying 22 nights in all. An analysis of the repertoire of this season, however, would not be complete without a mention of three new ballad operas, *Love in a Riddle* (2), *The Village Opera* (5) and *The Lover's Opera* (1, as an after-piece), in addition to the regular after-pieces in the form of "entertainments" or farces. *Harlequin Dr Faustus* was given 7 times, *Perseus and Andromeda* 38, *Harlequin Happy* 8, *The Devil upon Two Sticks* 8, and *The Cheats of Harlequin* once, while at different times there are to be noted Gay's *The What D'Ye Call It* (14), Breval's *The Strollers* (6), Farquhar's *The Stage Coach* (1), Cibber's *The School-Boy* (1) and Dogget's *The Country Wake* (1). The performances at Lincoln's Inn Fields have a very similar character, with the exception that 43 of the 122 nights given to comedy were devoted to the popular *Beggar's Opera*, which had been produced only a few months before the beginning of the season. Shakespeare is better represented here in *The Merry Wives of Windsor* (5), *Henry IV* (2), *Measure for Measure* (in Gildon's adaptation, 3) and *The Jew of Venice* (Granville's reworking of *The Merchant*, 1). Norris' *The Royal Merchant*, an alteration of *The Beggar's Bush*, was given twice, the operatic *Prophetess* thrice, *The Island Princess* twice and *The Pilgrim* twice. *Volpone* also saw two performances. Most favoured, however, are the Restoration playwrights, including Dryden (*The Spanish Fryar* 2), Wycherley (*The Country Wife* 5), Vanbrugh (*The Provok'd Wife* 3), Mrs Behn (*The Rover* 3, *The Emperor of the Moon* 4), Ravenscroft (*The London Cuckolds* 2), Congreve (*The Old Batchelour* 2, *The Double Dealer* 3), Carlisle (*The Fortune Hunters* 3), Betterton (*The Amorous Widow* 1), Otway (*The Cheats of Scapin* 1), and D'Urfey (*The Fond Husband* 1). Eighteenth

century plays in the older style appear in Farquhar's *The
Beaux Stratagem* (5) and *The Recruiting Officer* (2), Bullock's
Woman's Revenge (3), Mrs Centlivre's *The Busie Body* (3)
and *A Bold Stroke for a Wife* (1), Vanbrugh's *The Mistake*
(3), *The Confederacy* (3) and *The False Friend* (4), and Baker's
Tunbridge-Walks (1). Only Cibber's *Love's Last Shift* (1)
and Addison's *The Drummer* (1) are sentimental. The after-
pieces given at this house include six pantomimes, *The Necro-
mancer* (10), *Harlequin a Sorcerer* (4), *Apollo and Daphne* (8),
The Rape of Proserpine (10), *The Humours of Bedlam* (2) and
The Cheats (2); as well as five farces and ballad operas, *The
Country House* (5), *The Cobler's Opera* (4), *The What D'Ye
Call It* (4), *Hob's Opera* (1) and *Flora* (15).

The season 1738–9 introduces us to hardly anything that
is startlingly different. The first part of *Henry IV* was given
4 times and the second part twice; Beaumont and Fletcher's
Rule a Wife and Have a Wife ran 3 nights and *The Pilgrim* 6;
Jonson's *Epicœne* secured one performance and *The Alchemist*
two. Restoration comedies are by far the most numerous,
with Vanbrugh's *The Relapse* (3), *The Provok'd Wife* (4) and
Æsop (3), Farquhar's *The Constant Couple* (1), Congreve's
The Double Dealer (4), *The Old Batchelour* (2), *Love for Love*
(5) and *The Way of the World* (1), Dryden's *The Spanish
Fryar* (4) and *Amphitryon* (4), Howard's *The Committee* (5),
Etherege's *The Man of Mode* (3), Wycherley's *The Plain
Dealer* (4) and Betterton's *The Amorous Widow* (1). Of the
earlier style, too, are Farquhar's *The Beaux Stratagem* (4),
The Twin Rivals (6) and *The Inconstant* (2), Vanbrugh's
The Confederacy (3), Cibber's *She Wou'd and She Wou'd Not*
(5) and *The Double Gallant* (3), Mrs Centlivre's *The Busie Body*
(4) and *A Bold Stroke for a Wife* (5), Fielding's *The Miser* (7)
and Baker's *Tunbridge-Walks* (3). Sentimentally inclined are
Cibber's *The Careless Husband* (2), *Love's Last Shift* (2),
Love Makes a Man (3) and *The Provok'd Husband* (3),
Addison's *The Drummer* (3), Miller's *The Man of Taste* (1)
and *The Mother in Law* (1), and Steele's *The Tender Husband*
(3) and *The Conscious Lovers* (3). Gay's *The Beggar's Opera*,
besides, secured a run of 7 nights. Among the after-pieces,

pantomime is represented in *Colombine Courtezan* (20), *The Harlot's Progress* (14), *Harlequin Grand Volgi* (4), *Harlequin Restor'd* (4), *Robin Goodfellow* (34), *The Burgo-Master Trick'd* (2), *The Fall of Phaeton* (4), *Harlequin Shipwreck'd* (12) and *Mars and Venus* (1), while farce or ballad opera makes its appearance in *An Old Man taught Wisdom* (13), *The Devil to Pay* (18), *The Intriguing Chambermaid* (8), *The Mock Doctor* (13), *Damon and Phillida* (3), *Flora* (1) and *The Beggar's Wedding* (1). Perhaps *The What D'Ye Call It* (1) may be counted sentimental, and *The King and the Miller of Mansfield* (14) is certainly so. At Covent Garden, Shakespeare appeared, during the same season, with *Henry IV* (Part I 2, Part II 1), *The Jew of Venice* (1), *The Merry Wives of Windsor* (1) and *Much Ado About Nothing* (1). Beaumont and Fletcher are represented by *Rule a Wife and Have a Wife* (4), *Wit without Money* (3) and *The Royal Merchant* (4); Jonson's *Volpone*, besides, was given twice. The remaining nights were given fairly evenly to late seventeenth and to eighteenth century pieces. Of the former we note Farquhar's *Love and a Bottle* (1), Dryden's *The Spanish Fryar* (4), Ravenscroft's *The London Cuckolds* (2), Congreve's *The Way of the World* (3), *The Old Batchelour* (2) and *The Double Dealer* (3), Vanbrugh's *The Relapse* (3) and *The Provok'd Wife* (2), Mrs Behn's *The Rover* (2) and *The Emperor of the Moon* (4), Betterton's *The Amorous Widow* (2), Wycherley's *The Country Wife* (1), Howard's *The Committee* (2), Shadwell's *The Squire of Alsatia* (1) and D'Urfey's *Don Quixote* (1). The eighteenth century comedies presented are not by any means all of the sentimental kind. Among them appear Shadwell's *The Fair Quaker of Deal* (6), Farquhar's *The Recruiting Officer* (3), *The Beaux Stratagem* (4) and *The Twin Rivals* (2), Cibber's *The Double Gallant* (4) and *She Wou'd and She Wou'd Not* (1), Vanbrugh's *The Mistake* (3) and *The False Friend* (2), Mrs Centlivre's *The Busie Body* (3), Gay's *The Beggar's Opera* (2) and Johnson's *The Country Lasses* (4). The sentimental or sentimentally inclined plays include Cibber's *Love's Last Shift* (5) and *Love Makes a Man* (6), and Steele's *The Conscious Lovers* (4), *The Tender Husband* (5) and *The*

Funeral (3). The after-pieces are very similar to those given at Drury Lane; pantomimes, *The Necromancer* (15), *The Royal Chace* (35), *The Rape of Proserpine* (22), *Perseus and Andromeda* (24) and *The Jealous Farmer* (1); farces and ballad operas, *The Honest Yorkshireman* (4), *The Devil to Pay* (3), *The Dragon of Wantley* (17), *Margery* (19), *The Lucky Discovery* (5), *The Mock Lawyer* (2), *Flora* (2), *The Cheats of Scapin* (6), *The Country Wedding* (1), *Damon and Phillida* (3), *The Stage Coach* (6), *The Beggar's Wedding* (1), *The Cobler's Opera* (2), *The Country House* (3) and *The School-Boy* (1) with the sentimental-satiric *The What D'Ye Call It* (3) and the moralising *Toy-Shop* (2).

The season 1748–9 at Drury Lane shows an appreciable increase in the performance of Shakespearian comedy. *The Merchant of Venice* ran 3 nights, *Twelfth Night* 2, *Much Ado About Nothing* 16 and *Measure for Measure* was given once. Massinger's *A New Way to Pay Old Debts* secured 4 performances and Jonson's *The Alchemist* 2. The number of Restoration plays produced is correspondingly smaller, although there still appeared Vanbrugh's *The Relapse* (3) and *The Provok'd Wife* (4), Etherege's *She Wou'd if She Cou'd* (1), Congreve's *Love for Love* (4) and *The Double Dealer* (2), Ravenscroft's *The London Cuckolds* (1), Wycherley's *The Country Wife* (1) and Shadwell's *The Squire of Alsatia* (1). Among the eighteenth century non-sentimental plays may be numbered Mrs Centlivre's *The Busie Body* (5) and *A Bold Stroke for a Wife* (5), Vanbrugh's *The Confederacy* (1), Cibber's *She Wou'd and She Wou'd Not* (1), Farquhar's *The Recruiting Officer* (1) and *The Beaux Stratagem* (4), Gay's *The Beggar's Opera* (4), and Fielding's *The Miser* (3). Sentimental comedies this season, however, secure a larger proportion of the entire number of acting nights than they had done in the previous years. Cibber's *Love Makes a Man* saw 2 nights, and *The Provok'd Husband* 5, Hoadly's *The Suspicious Husband* 7, Steele's *The Conscious Lovers* 5 and *The Funeral* 3, Moore's *The Foundling* 3. Sentimentalism, too, appears among the after-pieces in *The King and the Miller of Mansfield* (8). These after-pieces, however, are on the whole mainly pantomimical or farcical, including *Vertumnus and Pomona* (9), *The Triumph of Peace* (11), *Apollo and Daphne* (1), *Don Jumpedo* (1), *The Lottery* (7), *The Lying Valet* (11), *The Anatomist* (19), *The Devil to Pay* (13), *The Intriguing Chambermaid* (19), *The School-Boy* (4), *Miss in her Teens* (10), *Tom Thumb* (1), *The Mock Doctor* (4), *An Old Man taught Wisdom* (10), *The Emperor of the Moon* (4), *Lethe* (17), *Tit for Tat* (7) and *The Hen-Peck'd Captain* (1). The decrease in the number of pantomimes is very noticeable here. At Covent Garden during the same months Shakespeare's *Henry IV* was given 12 times, *The Merry Wives of Windsor* 7, *As You Like It* once and *Measure for Measure* thrice. *The Royal Merchant* and *Volpone* appeared twice each. Restoration comic endeavour is represented in Vanbrugh's *The Provok'd Wife* (4) and *The Relapse* (3), Dryden's *The Spanish Fryar* (3), Congreve's *The Old Batchelour* (3), *The Double Dealer* (1) and *The Way of the World* (2), Ravenscroft's *The London Cuckolds* (1), Mrs Behn's *The Rover* (1) and *The Emperor of the Moon* (1), Howard's *The Committee* (2), Etherege's *The Man of Mode* (2) and Crowne's *Sir Courtley Nice* (1); later plays in the same or similar strains occur in Farquhar's *The Constant Couple* (3), *The Recruiting Officer* (2) and *The Beaux Stratagem* (3), Gay's *The Beggar's Opera* (12), Mrs Centlivre's *The Busie Body* (2), and Cibber's *The Double Gallant* (1). Sentimentalism is apparent only in Cibber's *The Provok'd Husband* (5), *The Careless Husband* (3), *Love Makes a Man* (2) and *Love's Last Shift* (1), and Steele's *The Conscious Lovers* (2). Dalton's *Comus*, a musical piece, was performed 5 times. Pantomime is more largely represented among the after-pieces of this house in *Apollo and Daphne* (56), *The Royal Chace* (16) and *Don Jumpedo* (10). Farce and ballad opera occur in *The Mock Doctor* (4), *The Lying Valet* (3), *The Devil to Pay* (5), *The Lottery* (2), *Damon and Phillida* (11), *Flora* (3), *The Muses' Looking Glass* (1), *The Gentleman Gardener* (3) and *Miss in her Teens* (1). *The King and the Miller of Mansfield* ran 4 nights, and *Henry and Emma* was performed once.

As with the repertoires of tragic works, so with these of

comedies and farces it is not difficult to analyse the results obtained from an examination of these lists. Sentimentalism obviously is the least popular of all the comic types, Etherege, Wycherley, Congreve, Farquhar, Vanbrugh, Dryden and the rest maintaining their place in the theatres all through the 50 years. The Shakespearian comedy does not make much appeal until after 1735, when the romantic comedies once more take their position upon the boards of the playhouses in a comparatively unaltered form. The tendency towards the introduction of after-pieces may be traced from the early years of the century until it reaches a culmination in the thirties and forties, when hardly any but a new play or an operatic piece was performed without these appendages. It is observable also that the Lincoln's Inn Fields and Covent Garden theatres seemed to rely more on operatic and pantomimic after-pieces while Drury Lane preferred farces and farcical ballad-operas. Such an analysis as this must form the only sure basis for any enquiry into the theatrical tastes and endeavour of the period. It must be supplemented, however, by a further enquiry into the borrowings from Elizabethan, Restoration and foreign sources, an enquiry which, it will be realised, must be taken hand in hand with the other.

II. *Elizabethan, Restoration and Foreign Models*

The direct indebtedness of the age to Elizabethan and to Restoration comedy is even greater than its indebtedness to the tragedy of those periods, nor can this indebtedness in any wise be indicated by a mere list of ascertained borrowings. The influence of Fletcher and of Etherege is on many a play the plot of which is original and the characters new. Any list of adaptations and of imitations, therefore, must be regarded as indicative only of a vast number of other unchronicled borrowings. Fletcher and his companions freely were pilfered from during the Anne and Georgian eras. *Wit at Several Weapons* gave Cibber the theme for *The Rival Fools* (D.L. 1709); Johnson used *The Custom of the Country* along with Middleton's *A Mad World, My Masters* for *The Country*

Lasses (D.L. 1715); and the latter Elizabethan play was utilised by Bullock for his rival farce, *The Slip* (L.² 1715). *The Knight of the Burning Pestle* may have suggested to Steele the coffin scene in *The Funeral* (D.L. 1702), and *The Wild Goose Chase* gave to Farquhar the plot for *The Inconstant* (D.L. 1702). Griffin's *Whig and Tory* (L.² 1720) was certainly suggested by *The Maid in the Mill*, and Manning's *All for the Better* (D.L. 1702) by *The Spanish Gipsy*. A certain number of the earlier comedies were, moreover, reduced to farces in the thirties and forties of the century, generally by anonymous writers. Thus *The Sham Pilgrims*, produced on Thursday, January 31, 1734, was announced in the bills as from Beaumont and Fletcher. Ralph's *The Lawyer's Feast* (D.L. 1743) is from *The Spanish Curate*, which furnished another farce, acted at Drury Lane in 1749. The same year a farce taken from *The Little French Lawyer* was acted at this theatre. Beyond these, we find a great number of types and of single situations taken over in more or less disguised forms. The influence of Shakespeare's comedy, until near the end of the half century, is less constant. It has to be remembered that the Restoration period had cut out of the acting list the entirety of the romantic comedies. *The Merry Wives of Windsor* and *The Taming of the Shrew* were, accordingly, almost the only plays regularly seen upon the stage during the first years of the eighteenth century. The latter play was utilised by Charles Johnson and by Bullock for their rival farces, each called *The Cobler of Preston* (D.L. and L.² 1716). Dennis reworked *The Merry Wives of Windsor* into *The Comical Gallant* (D.L. 1702) and Taverner *The Comedy of Errors* into *Every Body Mistaken* (L.² 1716). It would appear that *The Comedy of Errors* likewise formed the basis of two anonymous farces, *See if you Like It* (from Plautus and Shakespeare, according to the bills) and *The Ephesian Duke*. It is in the beginning of the eighteenth century, however, that we first find adaptations of the romantic comedies. Granville's *The Jew of Venice* (L.¹ 1701) is the first of these, but it was to be followed up by Burnaby's *Love Betray'd* (L.¹ 1703) from *Twelfth Night*, Charles Johnson's *Love in a Forest*

(D.L. 1723) from *As You Like It* and *A Midsummer Night's Dream*, Miller's *The Universal Passion* (D.L. 1737) from *Much Ado About Nothing*, and Lillo's *Marina* (C.G. 1738) from *Pericles*. Leveridge's *Pyramus and Thisbe* (L.[2] 1716) and a play of the same title with music by Lampe (C.G. 1745) are in the older strain of comical humours. This period, more-over, did not stay at adaptations, as the records of the revivals of the years 1737–1749 demonstrate fully. *Much Ado About Nothing* came out at Covent Garden on Wednesday, Nov. 2, 1737, a slightly revised *Cymbeline* on Monday, March 20, 1738, *As You Like It* at Drury Lane on Saturday, December 20, 1740, *Twelfth Night* at the same theatre on January 15, 1741, *A Winter's Tale* at Goodman's Fields on the same day, *The Merchant of Venice* at Drury Lane on Saturday, February 14, *All's Well that Ends Well* at Goodman's Fields on Saturday, March 7 and *The Comedy of Errors* at Drury Lane on Wednesday, November 11, 1741. Nearly all of these proved to be popular successes, and did much towards the development of a new tone in the comic productivity after 1740[1].

Various other early seventeenth century writers were eagerly ransacked. Ben Jonson's influence, of course, is cast over the whole period. Randolph's *The Conceited Pedlar* gave Dodsley the idea for *The Toy-Shop* (C.G. 1735)[2]; the same author's *Amyntas* provided material for the anonymous *The Fickle Shepherdess* (L.[1] 1703); Marston's *The Dutch Courtesan*, or Betterton's adaptation of it, *The Revenge*, was utilised by Bullock for *The Woman's Revenge* (L.[2] 1715). Corey's *The Metamorphosis* (L.[1] 1704)[3] was based on the old *Albumazar*, as was *The Fashionable Lover* (D.L. 1706) on Nabbe's *The Bride*. Shirley's *The Lady of Pleasure* suggested parts of Taverner's *The Maid the Mistress* (D.L. 1708), and additional hints seem to have been gained for this play from *No Wit No Help like a Woman's*[4]. *The Gamester* gave Charles

---

[1] The revival of the original *Henry IV* at Covent Garden in 1738 is also noticeable in this connection.

[2] It is interesting to note that *The Muses Looking Glass* was revived at Covent Garden on Monday, March 14, 1748.

[3] It is said on the title-page to have been "Written Originally by the Famous Moliere"; but there is no play of Molière's at all resembling it.

[4] Or from the adaptation, *The Counterfeit Bridegroom*.

Johnson's *The Wife's Relief* (D.L. 1711), and *Hide Park*
influenced Cooper's *The Rival Widows* (C.G. 1735). Charles
Johnson's *The Masquerade* (D.L. 1719) possibly owes some-
thing to *The Lady of Pleasure*, and Molloy's *The Half-Pay
Officers* (L.² 1720) has borrowed a trifle from *The Wedding*
as well as from *Henry IV*, *Much Ado About Nothing* and
Love and Honour. Brome's *The Jovial Crew* was ballad-
operatised at Drury Lane in 1731 and Carlell's *Arviragus and
Philitia* reworked by Charles Johnson as *The Successful Pyrate*
(D.L. 1712).

Restoration comedies were equally sought after for suggestions and hints. Dryden's *Secret Love* and *Marriage a la Mode*
were wrought into *The Comical Lovers* (H.¹ 1707) by Cibber,
and *Sir Martin Mar-all*, along with Jonson's *The Devill is an
Asse*, provided Mrs Centlivre with the plot of *The Busie
Body* (D.L. 1709). *Secret Love* might also appear to have
suggested *Love at a Venture* (Bath 1706?) by the same
authoress. Wycherley's *The Country Wife* certainly inspired
Burnaby's *The Ladies Visiting Day* (L.¹ 1701) and Jevon's
The Devil of a Wife was made into a ballad-opera by Coffey
as *The Devil to Pay* (D.L. 1731). The same writer turned
D'Urfey's *Love for Money* into *The Boarding-School* (D.L.
1733). Digby's *Elvira* gave part of Mrs Centlivre's *The
Wonder* (D.L. 1714). Cokain's *Trappolin creduto Principe*
was worked into a farce by Drury as *The Devil of a Duke*
(D.L. 1732); the comic parts of Southerne's *The Fatal
Marriage* were abstracted by Griffin for *The Humours of
Purgatory* (L.² 1716); Ravenscroft's *Dame Dobson* gave
assistance to Charles Johnson for *The Female Fortune Teller*
(L.² 1726); and Shadwell's *The Woman Captain* provided
Odell with *The Prodigal* (H.² 1744).

It is noticeable in this list that, of all the dramatists of the
manners school, only one was filched from openly. The
reason for this is obvious. The comedies of manners were
well known in their original form to the audiences of the
day, and any direct borrowing would have been at once
noted and commented upon. Nor did the spectators feel
that they required their comedies of manners in any altered

dress. Etherege, Wycherley and Congreve appeared on the boards of the theatres approximately as they had done in 1670 and in 1700[1].

During the early part of the eighteenth century far greater attention seems to have been paid to Greek and Roman comedy than in the period 1660–1700. Dennis and others knew their Aristophanes fairly well, and not only one dramatist passed directly to Terence and Plautus. Steele's *The Conscious Lovers* (D.L. 1722) is, as is well known, based upon the *Andria* of the former, and Bellamy used the same Latin comedy for *The Perjur'd Devotee* (1741). Cooke took his *The Eunuch* (D.L. 1737) directly from Terence, and Fielding seems to have been aware of Plautus' drama when he borrowed from Molière for *The Miser* (D.L. 1733).

The field of classical comedy, however, was too small for any great amount of direct adaptation. It is still in the realm of the French theatre that we find the largest continental influence on the playwrights. Again and again went the dramatists to Molière; again and again they sought among the contemporary writers of Paris themes for their plays. If anything, translation and adaptation reached a higher level in this time than in the preceding periods. As early as 1703 a writer of some verses prefixed to Baker's *Tunbridge-Walks* (D.L. 1703) was giving expression to the complaint, common in later years, that nothing save French dramas were to be discovered on the stage:

> Then we may hope there will agen appear,
> Humour and Wit on th' *English* Theatre,
> Unborrow'd from the *French:* For to our Shame,
> Our Comedy of late from *Gallia* came:
> Our Heroes learnt from theirs the Art of fighting[2],
> Our Poets too have mimick'd theirs in Writing;
> And by Translation strove to build their Fame,
> Barren of Mother-Wit, and of Invention Lame.

---

[1] While a certain amount of Bowdlerising undoubtedly was indulged in, we cannot assume that a play like *The Country Wife* could have been very much tampered with.

[2] The reference is, of course, to the actual wars; not to the heroes of tragedy.

Whoever was the author of the prologue to *Three Hours after Marriage* (D.L. 1717)—Gay, Pope or Arbuthnot—put the same idea in a still stronger manner:

> *How shall our Author hope a gentle Fate,*
> *Who dares most impudently—not translate*[1].

The year following, Mrs Centlivre in the prologue to *A Bold Stroke for a Wife* (L.[2] 1718) gave utterance to the same cry:

> *To-Night we come upon a bold Design,*
> *To try to please without one borrow'd Line:*
> *Our Plot is new, and regularly clear,*
> *And not one single Tittle from* Moliere.

As late as 1735 we find Popple in the epilogue to *The Double Deceit* (C.G. 1735) raising once more the outcry against translations from the French.

Molière was, evidently, still much in demand. Miller utilised *La Princesse d'Élide* along with *Much Ado About Nothing* for *The Universal Passion* (D.L. 1737). Cibber's *The Refusal* (D.L. 1721) is taken partly from *Les Femmes Savantes*. Fielding used *L'Avare* for *The Miser* (D.L. 1733) and Hughes translated literally one act of the same play. *Le Médecin malgré Lui* was employed by Mrs Centlivre for *Love's Contrivance* (D.L. 1703) and by Fielding for *The Mock Doctor* (D.L. 1732). *La Malade Imaginaire* was filched from by Miller for *The Mother-in-Law* (H.[2] 1734). *Monsieur de Pourceaugnac* was directly translated or adapted by Vanbrugh and Congreve as *Squire Trelooby* (L.[1] 1704), by an anonymous author (perhaps Ozell) the same year, and by Sheridan in *The Brave Irishman* (Dublin, 1737). MacSwiny's *The Quacks* (D.L. 1705) is but an alteration of *L'Amour médecin*, and there seems to have been another translation of the same play, possibly by Vanbrugh, but unprinted[2]. Steele used *Le Sicilien* for *The Tender Husband* (D.L. 1705). *L'École des Maris* and *Les Précieuses Ridicules* gave to Miller *The Man of Taste* (D.L. 1735). Charles Johnson seems to have used *Don Garcia* for *The Masquerade* (D.L. 1719) and Vanbrugh

---

[1] Although the basis of this play itself seems borrowed from a farce contained in the collection called *Le Théâtre Italien*.

[2] See *supra*, p. 22.

Le Dépit Amoureux for *The Mistake* (H.[1] 1705). Molloy took
Le Cocu imaginaire for *The Perplex'd Couple* (L.[2] 1715) and
Miller borrowed from the same play in *The Picture* (D.L.
1745). An anonymous *George Dandin* appeared at Drury Lane
in 1747. So far did the demand for translation go that Corey,
as we have seen, actually printed *The Metamorphosis* (L.[1] 1704),
an original play, as "Written Originally by the Famous
Moliere."

Other French authors, too, came to play their part in the
development of English drama. Dancourt's *Les Bourgeoises
à la Mode* provided Estcourt with the plot of *The Fair Example*
(D.L. 1703) and Vanbrugh with that of *The Confederacy*
(H.[1] 1705). Charles Shadwell's *The Humours of the Army*
(D.L. 1713) borrows from the same author's *Les Curieux de
Compiègne*, and Vanbrugh translated directly his *La Maison
de Campagne* (D.L. 1698). Thomas Corneille's *Le Deuil*[1] was
utilised by Mrs Centlivre for *The Man's Bewitch'd* (H[1]. 1709).
Regnard's *Le Joueur* was taken over by the same authoress
for *The Gamester* (L.[1] 1705). Fielding also employed Reg-
nard's *Le Retour Imprévu* in *The Intriguing Chambermaid*
(D.L. 1734). Cibber's *The Double Gallant* (H.[1] 1707) and
Mrs Centlivre's *Love at a Venture* (Bath 1706?) are both
taken from Thomas Corneille's *Le Galand Doublé*. La Chapelle's *Les Carosses d'Orléans* became in English Farquhar's
popular after-piece, *The Stage Coach* (L.[1] 1704), and Fuzelier's
Momus fabuliste the anonymous *Momus turn'd Fabulist*
(L.[2] 1729). It would seem, too, that Miller had used the
title and part of the plot of Vadé's *L'Hôpital des Foux* for
An Hospital for Fools (D.L. 1739). Even more interesting is
it to chronicle the first appearance of the French *drame*
in an English dress. To Kelly belongs all the merit arising
from this innovation, his *The Married Philosopher* (L.[2] 1732),
adapted from Destouches' *Le Philosophe marié*, being the
initial attempt on the part of a London dramatist to give to
his stage a representation of the more revolutionary forms of
Parisian dramatic art. This effort Kelly continued in *Timon
in Love* (D.L. 1733), a slight alteration of Delisle's *Timon le*

---

[1] Published under the name of Hauteroche.

Misanthrope. Others soon followed his example. Rousseau's *Le Caffé* became Miller's *The Coffee-House* (D.L. 1738) and the same French writer's *Le Flatteur* was used by Miller, along with Delisle's *Arlequin Sauvage*, for *Art and Nature* (D.L. 1738). The title to this play was probably inspired by Chollet's *L'Art et la Nature*, a one act piece first performed the same year in Paris. The way was being truly well prepared for the full influx of *drames* which flooded England in the second half of the century.

Along with the influence of French literary works, must be taken into consideration also the influence of the French and Italian comedians who, year after year, came over and performed in London. Their greatest influence was in the direction of pantomime, but we can trace even in the realms of the regular drama the impress made by them. Their repertoires of comedies and farces taught the English dramatists many a stage trick, stage character and stage situation[1].

While French and, to a certain extent, Italian still continued to play their part in urging forward the eighteenth century comic stage, it is observable that that vast enthusiasm for things Spanish which had swayed the minds of the Caroline courtiers had, in this period, largely disappeared. Almost the only direct influence which is to be traced in these fifty years is that of *La Dama Duende* upon Bullock's *Woman is a Riddle* (L.[2] 1716). A few writers, such as Mrs Centlivre, may have taken hints from Spanish dramatists, but nowhere can we discover the wholesale adaptation noticeable in the period of the Restoration. Cervantes, certainly, still played his part; Fielding wrote *Don Quixote in England* (H.[2] 1734) under his spell. Charles Johnson's *The Generous Husband* (D.L. 1711), Molloy's *The Coquet* (L.[2] 1718), Gay's *Dione* (1720) and the same author's *The Rehearsal at Goatham* (1754) are all from well-worn themes in the Spanish novelist's works; but the Spanish drama for the English playwrights was dead. Its influence had passed away with the departure of Charles II.

---

[1] See Appendix A. A brief list of their repertoire is given in Appendix C.

II. *The Comedies of Manners*

The eighteenth century, as we have already seen, opened with the full flower of the Congrevian comedy. *The Way of the World* (D.L. 1700) was, assuredly, not a success; but its failure is perhaps to be attributed rather to the accidental circumstances connected with its first production than to the marked change in taste in the audience. Maybe its wit is almost too refined for the theatre, but it did gain its place in the repertory. At the same time, the Restoration mood was beginning to fade away, and by 1700 Congreve's work in comedy was done. He was yet to write his masque, *The Judgment of Paris* (D.G. 1701) and take an undetermined share in the translation of *Monsieur de Pourceaugnac*, but these are dramas that can hardly in any serious manner add to his fame as a playwright.

Congreve was, however, by no means the last of the dramatists of the school of manners. Many of the best works of George Farquhar and of Sir John Vanbrugh were yet to be penned, and these men were followed by not only one other dramatist who strove to reproduce in slightly altered forms the spirit of the Congrevian comedy. Farquhar's work had started in the last years of the seventeenth century. *Love and a Bottle* and *The Constant Couple* had appeared at Drury Lane in 1699, and in these two plays he showed the tendencies of his art. *The Constant Couple* had evidently been a brilliant success, and it is not surprising to find that its author speedily planned for it a sequel, *Sir Harry Wildair: Being the Sequel of the Trip to the Jubilee* (D.L. *c.* April 1701). This, unlike most sequels, was a success on its first production[1], but we, reading it in the light of other dramas of the time, can trace in it elements of disintegration. The pure spirit of the comedy of manners is still present in it, but foreign tones are entering in to spoil the brilliance of its wit. The passage already quoted from the fifth act[2], and the final tag,

> So, spite of Satyr 'gainst a marry'd Life,
> A Man is truly blest with such a Wife,

show clearly the traces in it of incipient sentimentalism. In the midst of its greatest gaiety intrudes an element of thought.

---

[1] Jacob, p. 98; Whincop, p. 230.   [2] *Supra*, p. 20.

The Inconstant: or, The Way to Win Him followed at Drury Lane about February 1702. This comedy, based on Fletcher's *The Wild-Goose Chase*, itself an early type of a comedy of manners, has less of the sentimental note, but that note appears nevertheless in those scenes where Oriana, dressing as a boy, follows her wayward lover to the house of the courtesan Lamorce and saves him there from an ignominious death. A comparison with the original Fletcherian play will show how much the spirit of the original has been altered[1].

The Twin-Rivals (D.L. Dec. 1702) was likewise a failure, for what reason does not seem perfectly clear. The influence of the newer school is here once more to be seen in the preface with its long comments on Jeremy Collier and its profession of moral aim accomplished by means of a true poetic justice. This profession is probably cynical and satiric, for *The Twin Rivals* is not a comedy of which the author of *A Short View* would have approved, and there is more than a touch of sarcasm in the words of the Elder Wouldbee at the close: "And now I hope all Parties have receiv'd their due Rewards and Punishments." Whether these words are scornful and satiric or not, however, we can easily see how the influence of Collier and the kindred influence of the sentimental drama were operating on the minds of playwrights such as Farquhar to destroy the unity of their work.

It was probably the uncertainty concerning their aims, or the confusion between the spirit in which they had been reared and the newer atmosphere of the time that led both Farquhar and Vanbrugh, and, along with them, Congreve, to turn to farce. Farquhar's next work, in any case, was but an expansion of La Chapelle's *Les Carosses d'Orléans* as *The Stage Coach* (L.[1] *c.* Jan. 1703/4)[2]. Although this piece has but three acts[3], Farquhar appears to have called in the

---

[1] Farquhar in his preface mentions the failure of this play, a failure which he attributes to the presence of French dancers at the other house. Whincop, p. 230, no doubt mistakenly, speaks of its "good Success"; he was thinking, possibly, of later revivals.

[2] It is possible that Motteux' reference to "*slender Stage-Coach Fare*" (*The Inconstant*, prologue) may indicate a still earlier production of this farce.

[3] Not one as Genest states (ii. 305), although it seems to have been later reduced in length.

assistance of Motteux to aid him in the rendering[1]. There is little brilliance in the farce, but it was long popular as an after-piece.

In *The Recruiting Officer* (D.L. April 1706), a brilliantly successful comedy, Farquhar returned to pure comedy. This play is full of an exuberance of wit, and succeeds in recapturing not a little of that Restoration spirit which the eighteenth century authors seemed to be losing. At the same time, even in it there are signs of change. The atmosphere is no longer the atmosphere of the town. We are out in the countryside, and, if the principal characters are city characters, we may still feel the alteration in spirit from the politer drama of Congreve. There is, too, to be noted the greater realism of this comedy, in marked contradistinction to the element of artificiality traceable in the best plays of the preceding half-century. The immorality, which before had been often graceful and debonair, has here developed into a coarse licentiousness, and that callousness which will be marked as a characteristic of eighteenth century dramatic art is to be seen only too clearly in the abandonment of poor Rose, who, because of the reality of the play, seizes upon our sympathies. Even though she disappears amid the rioting of drunken laughter, we cannot forget her in her night of tears. That the audience felt no abhorrence at the crudity of the sentiments may be realised in a moment by a reference to the repertoires of 1706 and the succeeding years.

With *The Beaux Stratagem* (H.[1] March 1706/7) we reach the end of Farquhar's career as a dramatist. As with an effort he has turned back to the spirit of his masters, and has produced a comedy more purely of manners than even his first seventeenth century works. Brilliance is in this comedy, and artificiality once more takes the place of realism. The mutual parting of Mr and Mrs Sullen, to which Mrs Oldfield, no doubt thinking of current hypocrisy and Societies for the Reformation of Manners, objected strongly, is quite in the Restoration style. Farquhar's life closed with his greatest literary triumph[2].

[1] Whincop, p. 231.   [2] He died in the midst of its initial run.

As a dramatist, Farquhar falls far short of Congreve, nor has he the strange virulence and strength of Wycherley. He is airier, more foppish, more, it may be said, of the newer age of Anne than of the Restoration. He is in a way a link between these two periods, standing between Congreve and Cibber, just as Cibber stands between the period of Anne and that of the early Georges.

Of Sir John Vanbrugh, Farquhar's chief companion in the early eighteenth century, much has been said, both laudatory and condemnatory. He stands, like Farquhar, much below Congreve, lacking wit and finesse; but, at the same time, he has other qualities, lower perhaps in degree, which stamp him as a true son of the theatre. "His best jokes are practical devices," says Hazlitt in his fourth lecture on *The English Comic Writers*, "not epigrammatic conceits....He has more nature than art: what he does best, he does because he cannot help it." It is this "nature" which, as Palmer has noted, renders his work more vulgar and immoral than the work of many Restoration playwrights[1]. His adulteries are no longer comic and airy; they are passionate. Truly "he killed the comedy of sex for the English theatre."

Vanbrugh's first three plays, *The Relapse*, *The Provok'd Wife* and *Æsop* all appeared in the last decade of the seventeenth century. Save for an adaptation of Fletcher, *The Pilgrim*, acted at Drury Lane about March 1699/1700, his first production in the later period was *The False Friend* (D.L. *c.* Feb. 1701/2). This comedy was unsuccessful, possibly but not certainly for the reason suggested in the prologue, which is directed against Collier and shows, if not his power, at any rate the fear he had infused into the breasts of the playwrights:

> *You Dread Reformers of an Impious Age,*
> *You awful Catta-nine-Tailes, to the Stage,*
> *This once be Just, and in our Cause engage.*
> *To gain your Favour, we your Rules Obey,*
> *And Treat you with a Moral Piece to Day;*
> *So Moral, we're afraid 'twill Damn the Play.*

[1] *The Comedy of Manners* (1913), pp. 201–3 and 224.

Whether Vanbrugh was serious or not we cannot tell. The play is certainly peculiar for its semi-tragic conduct of the story, but the main plot is that of a good old intrigue comedy. Guzman loves Leonora who is pursued by Don John. She is, however, the wife of Don Pedro, Don John's friend. Don John is stabbed at the close after confessing that he had attempted to wrong the husband; but the end of the play leaves us quite uncertain as to whether Guzman may not succeed to Leonora's favours. "You to your self alone, shall owe your smart," says the wife, "For where I've given my hand, I'll give my heart"; and the ambiguity of her words is emphasised in the epilogue:

What say you, Sirs, d'ye think my Lady'll 'scape?

Whatever sincerity is to be found in Vanbrugh's protestation, therefore, we can see in this play, as in those of Farquhar, the disturbing influence of the "Reformation of the Stage."

The Confederacy (H.[1] Oct. 1705) is more of a pure comedy, but again lacks the sparkle of the older writers. This lack of brilliance is made up for by the magnificently developed plot and by the forceful, if somewhat rough, outlines of some of the figures. Derived from Dancourt's Les Bourgeoises à la Mode, it develops its theme in a vigorous manner, so that characters such as Gripe and Moneytrap, Dick Amlet and his mother, stand out with a certainty shared by but few figures in contemporary drama. The end of the play is morally successful, but as Flippanta remarks, "we have been more lucky than wise"; the atmosphere is the atmosphere of old.

In December 1705 was next performed at the Haymarket The Mistake, somewhat more of an original play than the editors of the Biographia Dramatica make out[1]. As if the farcical spirit were impressing itself more and more upon him, Vanbrugh has made of this comedy a series of endless confusions. The plot is not so finely managed as that of The Confederacy, and stage business still more than in that drama takes the place of wit and characterisation.

[1] It is partly derived from Molière's Le Dépit Amoureux, or, more probably, from Dryden's An Evening's Love (note the names of Jacintha and Lopez).

Practically all of Vanbrugh's later work is thus seen to be adaptation of previously written comedies. *Squire Trelooby* (L.[1] March 1704), in which he collaborated with Congreve and Walsh, seems to have been a still deeper descent into direct adaptation. It is a poor enough work, and in spite of "the great Names concern'd in...it[1]," would not appear to have been very successful. Another adaptation of the same French play as *Monsieur de Pourceaugnac, or, 'Squire Trelooby* appeared the same year. According to the preface, this translation, which has been attributed to John Ozell, was "design'd for the English Stage," but was prevented by the other rendering. The editors of the *Biographia Dramatica* have no authority for stating that it was foisted on the public and that efforts were made to induce readers to believe they were buying the work of Vanbrugh, Congreve and Walsh.

The Country House (D.L. Jan. 1698), another rendering from Dancourt and just such another production, although long held to be one of Vanbrugh's eighteenth century efforts, has now been proved to belong to the last years of the century preceding. While it won not a little success as an afterpiece, it obviously cost its author but small pains and does not deserve overmuch critical attention.

Finally, may be noted among Vanbrugh's works the fragment called *A Journey to London*, published by Cibber in 1728 in order to show precisely the scope of his indebtedness for *The Provok'd Husband*. It is a fair piece of rough farce, but has nothing of sterling merit in it. On the whole, Vanbrugh's work may thus be held disappointing. Most of it is based on French comedy, and only too often it degenerates into the realm of farce. Both he and Farquhar, therefore, display the comedy of manners in a stage of decay, with the weakening of the wit of previous writers into sentimentalism and farcical situation. It is possible that both these playwrights are a trifle over-rated; a true reader of eighteenth century comedy must sometimes feel that their works fade

---

[1] John C. Hodges has an interesting article on "The Authorship of *Squire Trelooby*" (*Review of English Studies*, 1928, iv. 404–13), in which he disentangles the confused history of this piece and the mixed claims of Vanbrugh, Congreve, Walsh, Ozell and Ralph. See also *infra* under these authors in Appendix C.

in importance when put alongside the scattered works of some other less well-known writers.

Among these less well-known dramatists first in time and intrinsic merit must be numbered "Mr William Burnaby[1]," to whom have been atrributed four plays, only one of which, *Love Betray'd* (L.[1] 1703), falls outside the scope of this section of our enquiry. *The Reform'd Wife* appeared at Drury Lane in the spring of 1700, with what success we do not know. In spite of a certain "reforming" touch emphasised in the title, the atmosphere of this comedy breathes the spirit of the Restoration, not only the cynical spirit of that time but the air of wit which transfused all the dramas of Congreve. The scene in which Careless tells Sir Solomon Empty of his assignation with Astrea is decidedly fine, and the character of Lady Dainty, while it breathes the new artificiality of a "genteel" age, is well drawn. Why Genest, who, of course, as a critic can never be trusted, was so severe on the comedy[2], and why in general this, as others of Burnaby's works, has been so completely forgotten by students of the stage, is a question which can hardly be answered.

The Ladies Visiting-Day (L.[1] *c.* Jan. 1700/1) is equally fine, and again reproduces the atmosphere of Restoration cynicism and wit[3]. The plot is excellent, the dialogue skilful and the characters successfully delineated. That part of the action appears to be borrowed from Wycherley's *The Country Wife* shows clearly the school to which Burnaby belonged[4].

Burnaby's third effort in the manners style, *The Modish Husband*, was produced at Drury Lane about January 1701/2. Once more the older atmosphere is reproduced, Sir Lively Cringe, "One that is not so wicked as to believe ill of Women," is a character of true Restoration stamp, and the Lady

---

[1] For a biographical and critical study see F. E. Budd, *The Dramatic Works of William Burnaby* (1931). Paul P. Kies has an interesting note on "Lessing and Burnaby" (*Modern Language Notes*, 1935, l. 225–30).

[2] iii. 192–3.

[3] It is not, however, so cynical as the writer of the article on Burnaby in the *Dictionary of National Biography* makes out. The Polidore scenes are not very immoral, and the love of that character for Fulvia is pure.

[4] Cibber in his turn borrowed from these first two plays of Burnaby for *The Double Gallant*.

Cringe-Camilla scenes recall similar episodes in Etherege and in Wycherley.

These three dramas, well worthy of being recalled from an unmerited oblivion, are valuable both historically and intrinsically. They show the still dominant power of the manners type in its purer form during the early years of the century, and in many ways are superior in technique and in dialogue to the more belauded comedies of better-known authors. In them so far the conflict between sentimental and "reforming" aims and the manners style was having no deleterious effects.

Burnaby was by no means alone in thus following Congreve. The early years of the century are full of comedies which contain marked elements of the aims and methods of the manners school. With a slight infusion of sentimentalism, such is *As You Find It* (L.[1] April 1703), the one comedy of Charles Boyle, later the Earl of Orrery. The new spirit of the age can certainly be traced in the soliloquy of Hartley concerning his wife[1], but the main plot, especially that portion of it which deals with Chloris and Jack, is precisely in the older strain. The play is decidedly finer than Genest will admit[2]. The prologue has interest as showing the same elements common in the eighteenth century as in the age of Charles II:

> *We Know 'tis hard for Comedy t' escape,*
> *Without a Dance, a Duel, or a Rape.*

The moralising sentimentalism of Steele had yet to come.

A poorer example of the same school is to be found in David Crauford's *Love at First Sight* (L.[1] March 1704). The address to the reader declares that it had been written in 1699, and assuredly its tone is of the seventeenth century. The lack of wit in it, however, and its chaotic structure hardly permit any detailed analysis of its characteristics. Here might likewise be noted the same author's previously produced play, *Courtship A-la-mode* (D.L. July 1700), with its more than usually free prologue by Farquhar, although this

---

[1] v.   [2] ii. 292-3.

comedy can hardly be styled manners in tendency. It is rather a rough boisterous drama of no very decided character, veering close to the realms of farce. Its main point of interest lies in the strange epilogue written for Pinkethman, with its variant couplets for two contingencies—"If they Hiss" and "If they don't Hiss." Presumably the former were employed.

John Corey, Cory or Corye, an actor, to be distinguished from the Restoration author of the same name, brought out slightly earlier a comedy somewhat of the Congreve style, *A Cure for Jealousie* (L.[1] *c.* Dec. 1699)[1]. It is not a brilliant work, meeting "with no Success[2]" and hardly deserving any. Its interest lies in the attempt made by the author to catch again something of the wit of the older comedy.

The Different Widows: Or, Intrigue All-A-Mode, an anonymous play, probably written by Mrs Pix, was produced at Lincoln's Inn Fields apparently about November 1703.[3] There is much of intrigue in this work—intrigue of a not always salubrious character—and there is an attempt at least to display fine wit in the dialogue. The comedy was possibly an actor's production. In I. i is mentioned the new fine imposed on stage oaths, and the epilogue jests sarcastically at the moral tendencies of the time. "Virtue's, then our only Theme to day," it states, pointing mockingly to the poetic justice of the close and the conversion of the *dramatis personæ*; "This we cou'd wish *Collier* him self cou'd hear."

For a few years after 1704, it is true, Farquhar and Vanbrugh almost alone upheld the style of manners. We have already seen that the repertoires of the companies did not change seriously, but the sentimentalism of Cibber and of Steele, allied to the work of the Society for the Reformation of Manners, was probably having its effect on the dramatists. Towards the close of the second decade, however, there appears to have been a certain reawakening of interest in the type. Mrs Centlivre, who had been since 1700 the chief

---

[1] This was printed in 1701, but the preface declares it appeared during the run of Farquhar's *The Constant Couple*.

[2] *A Companion to the Play-House*, where the date is given wrongly as 1704. Whincop, p. 206, dates it 1705.

[3] Genest, ii. 291.

upholder of the comedy of intrigue, seemed to turn towards the style of Congreve in her last plays. *A Bold Stroke for a Wife* (L.[2] Feb. 1717/8), in which she seems to have been assisted by Mottley[1], was a great success. While this comedy is not so cynical as is the work of Burnaby, and while the plot, which deals with the outwitting of her four "humorous" guardians by Ann Lovely, is largely in the intrigue style, the influence of the comedy of wit is evident in many scenes. *A Bold Stroke for a Wife* is an excellent play, and well deserved its contemporary and subsequent success.

Four years elapsed between this and Mrs Centlivre's final comedy, *The Artifice* (D.L. Oct. 1722). That part of the plot which treats of Ned Careless, engaged to Olivia but ruining and deserting a Dutch girl, Louisa, and intriguing with Mrs Watchit, is thoroughly Restoration in character. The whole play has not, of course, the sparkle and the brilliance of Congreve, but it is easy to see in it how Mrs Centlivre moved from her initial intrigue and farce to the higher types of humours and manners.

About the same time, in the later teens and early twenties, other writers followed Mrs Centlivre's example. Charles Johnson, who has already been noted as one of the most prolific and diversified dramatists of the time, after passing through a series of experiments in various types of tragedy and of tragi-comedy, came in 1719 to essay a drama in the manners style. *The Masquerade* (D.L. Jan. 1718/9) seems very much indebted for its general tone to the work of Mrs Centlivre. There is a certain borrowing from Shirley's *The Lady of Pleasure* and from Molière's *Don Garcia de Navarre*, but the model of the writer has obviously been the masters of the intrigue and manners schools. The plot is a conventional one of love, jealousy and trickery. Sir George's jealous love for Sophronia is duly ridiculed and the viciousness of the age appears in the Smart-Coelia episodes. Only one slight note of sentimentalism is allowed to enter into those scenes where Mr Ombre is presented as discharging his wife's gambling debts. For some reason this drama came

[1] Whincop, p. 191.

in for several attacks from the critics[1]; but on the stage it proved a success.

After an excursion into Shakespeare adaptation (*Love in a Forest*, D.L. Jan. 1722/3), Johnson again attempted the manners atmosphere in *The Female Fortune-Teller* (L.[2] Jan. 1725/6)[2]. This is a reworking of Ravenscroft's *Dame Dobson*, but the changes made throughout warrant the inclusion of the comedy, not among those of the followers of Jonson, but among those of the followers of Congreve.

Plays of the intrigue-manners school were also produced about these years by Charles Molloy. *The Perplex'd Couple: Or, Mistake upon Mistake* (L.[2] Feb. 1714/5), of which "The Incident of the Picture in the Third Act, something in the Fourth, and one Hint in the last Act[3]" are from Molière's *Le Cocu Imaginaire*, is almost a pure comedy of intrigue, and not very successful at that[4]; but *The Coquet: Or, The English Chevalier* (L.[2] April 1718) is nearer the Etheregian model. Although Bellamy in the end is conquered by Julia's virtue, the whole comedy is in the gay, innuendo-loving, anti-matrimonial style of the Restoration. The dialogue is good, with a decided brilliance scintillating from it. *The Coquet*, however, when produced, failed to please[5].

With "but indifferent Success[6]," likewise, was performed *The Wife of Bath* (D.L. May 1713) by John Gay, a comedy which, in spite of its Chaucerian inspiration, owes more to

[1] See a letter of Dennis "To Mr George Sewel March 10 1718/9 " in *Original Letters* (1721), pp. 122–5, and "Corinna's" *Critical Remarks on the Four Taking Plays Of the Season; viz. Sir Walter Raleigh, The Masquerade, Chit-Chat, and Busiris King of Egypt. Dedicated to the Wits of Button's Coffee-House. By Corinna, a Country Parson's Wife* (1719). The latter accuses Johnson of having stolen scenes from Steele's *The Tender Husband*, from Mrs Centlivre's *The Gamester* and from Taverner's *The Artful Husband*.

[2] The play is not certainly by Charles Johnson; but is regularly attributed to him.

[3] Preface.

[4] Whincop (p. 262) in attributing this play to Molloy, states that it was produced with little success.

[5] Whincop, p. 262.

[6] Jacob, p. 115; he suggests that part of the plot is from Farquhar's *The Recruiting Officer*. Whincop (p. 238) says it was damned even at the later revival at Lincoln's Inn Fields.

the dramas of the time of Charles II than to any others. Chaucer is represented much as a witty gallant of that period, gaining the hand of Myrtilla only after working on her superstitions. While offensive to true lovers of the fourteenth century poet, *The Wife of Bath* must be accounted a good comedy, and it is difficult to explain its lack of success.

Unquestionably the finest plays of the later years of the period which show the influence of the manners style are those of Fielding, but Fielding was often too farcical to allow of the free expression of the spirit of the comedy of manners. Even his best plays show the power of diverse schools—manners, intrigue, humours and sentiment meeting in one. His first comedy, *Love in Several Masques* (D.L. Feb. 1727/8) is of such a nature. There is a plentiful infusion of humours here—Sir Positive Trap and Formal and Rattle and (the first of Fielding's typical maidservants) Catchit—but in the scenes of Merital and Hellena there is abundant evidence of the influence on Fielding of the Restoration comedy. This play, which was unsuccessful, owing, according to the author, to the fact that it appeared immediately after the lauded Cibber success, *The Provok'd Husband*, and "contemporary with an Entertainment which engrosses the whole Talk and Admiration of the Town[1]," shows well Fielding's boisterous comic spirit at its best.

His immediately following plays were all either sentimental or farcical, but with *The Old Debauchees* (D.L. June 1732), a three act piece founded on the story of Father Girard and Miss Cadiere, he made a return to a comedy somewhat in the style of Dryden. It lacks, nevertheless, the brilliance of the author of *Secret Love* or that of his companion, Etherege. The same weakness may be traced likewise in *The Miser... Taken from Plautus and Moliere* (D.L. Feb. 1732/3), one of Fielding's most popular pieces. Formed in the style of the manners comedy[2], it just fails to capture that full grace and

---

[1] See *supra*, p. 10. On the general history of Fielding's pieces *The History of Henry Fielding* by W. L. Cross should be consulted. This contains an elaborate analysis of practically all available information on the inception and circumstances and production of his plays.

[2] Except that the Harriet-Cleremont portion savours of the sentimental.

refinement which was Congreve's. Fielding never quite succeeded in raising himself out of the rut of farce. The fact that, in a study such as this, his plays cannot be considered together, shows the lack of aim in his art. At one moment we find him an ardent follower of Jonson; at another he is imitating Congreve; at another Buckingham; at another Cibber and Steele. He has good plots and witty dialogue, but this lack of purpose in his comedies renders his work as a dramatist far inferior to his work as a novelist.

After those of Fielding, there are but few comedies written in this manners style. There are a certain number, such as Conolly's *The Connoisseur: or, Every Man in his Folly* (D.L. Feb. 1735/6)[1], which unite something of the manners tone with humours or sentimentalism; but, like *The Connoisseur*, they are usually unimportant intrinsically and had but dubious receptions on the stage. The latter fact is interesting when we compare these new works with the repertoires of the theatres. The two seem mutually contradictory; but an explanation of the difficulty exists. The age, as is perfectly evident, still delighted in scenes such as had been displayed by Etherege and by Wycherley. Obviously there was but little definite change in the morals of the people at large. There was a consciousness in the hearts of all, save the most fanatic, that all the Societies for the Reformation of Manners were but hypocrisy writ large. The poets, remarks "Mr B—[2]" in the epilogue to Mrs Centlivre's *The Perjur'd Husband* (D.L. (1700),

> *now plead Guilty: And confess the Stage*
> *Has been immoral, and debauch'd the Age.*
> *Nay, They will mend—But wish that in their station,*
> *All Men were pleas'd to forward Reformation.*

The gallants and the beaux, in pit and boxes, they knew, had not altered. Cynicism in this connection appears repeatedly in the dramas of the time. Mrs Lovejoy in Baker's *The Fine Lady's Airs* (D.L. 1708), on being pressed by

---

[1] Attributed to Conolly by Whincop (p. 203) and other chroniclers of the stage.

[2] Probably Burnaby.

Sir Harry, gives utterance to thoughts that must have been in the minds of many: "Was ever any thing so impudent? he's a charming Fellow tho', and two hundred a year is a charming Allowance too.—But Virtue! Virtue!—oh! that I had liv'd in good King Some-body's Days." In 1716 Bullock was speaking of the "Viciousness of the Age[1]," conscious that only external change had come, and in 1736 Mrs Clive was giving the following advice to poets:

> Next of our Author's Humour, Wit and Plot,
> Style—Chaste Expression, and—I know not what.
> I saw how 'twas—and, faith,—I ask'd him plainly
> If he propos'd Success, from being cleanly?
> I bad him, here and there, throw in a Scene
> (But pray, says I—take care it's wrapt up clean)
> Of something....Psha!....You all Know what I mean[2].

Cynicism, callousness, external veneer of morality and inner viciousness all aided in making the plays of Wycherley and his companions popular on the stage. The free epilogues spoken by girls hardly in their teens—a habit begun in the last decade of the previous century—continued unabashed. Miss Robinson was given one by Fielding in *Love in Several Masques* (D.L. 1728). Miss Porter spoke the epilogues to Mrs Pix' *The Double Distress* (L.[1] 1701) and to Oldmixon's *The Governour of Cyprus* (L.[1] 1703); Miss Jones that to *The Female Rake* (H.[2] 1736). A particularly obnoxious epilogue was recited by Miss Stone at the end of Mottley's *The Imperial Captives* (L.[2] 1720) and another by Miss Jenny Cibber at the end of Odell's *The Prodigal* (H.[2] 1744). The loose "dialogues," too, were just as popular as they had been in preceding years, and boy and girl, woman and man, sang their dubious duets in 1730 as they had done in 1690. Mrs Wiseman's *Antiochus* (L.[1] 1702) has such "dialogues," as have Manning's *All for the Better* (D.L. 1702), Oldmixon's *The Governour of Cyprus* (L.[1] 1703) and Mrs Pix' *The Adventures in Madrid* (H.[1] 1706). Fielding's *The Mock Doctor* (D.L. 1732) carries on the tradition. Even bedroom scenes,

---

[1] *Woman is a Riddle* (L.[2] 1716), I. i.
[2] Conolly, *The Connoisseur* (D.L. 1736), epilogue.

of a nature somewhat similar to those of the Restoration, could be presented before the public, as in Odell's *The Patron* (H.² 1729).

At the same time, the influence of Jeremy Collier, along with the influence of the sentimental comedy, created a certain spirit antagonistic to the production of the fine comedy of the previous age. The old plays could be performed successfully in the theatre, but their style could not be reproduced by the playwrights. In the Restoration there was little of extraneous interest to disturb the minds of the dramatists. These dramatists were purely intellectual, purely cynical, purely circumscribed within their own narrow circle. In the eighteenth century wars and patriotism came to give men other thoughts. Emotion was creeping into the world of the intellect—Luvah usurping the place of Urizen, as William Blake would have said. The gallants were meeting with the citizens and acquiring new ideas. While the immorality was there as of old, the free untrammelled cynicism had disappeared. There was no dominant tradition, no all-consuming purpose, to guide the steps of the dramatists in one direction. The comedy of manners, therefore, slowly died away as a creative element in dramatic productivity, even at the very time when Congreve and Wycherley were most popular in the theatre. Once more, contraries may be proved true.

There was one development of the comedy of manners, however, which for a time promised to assume larger proportions, as a type of comedy well fitted to mirror the tendencies of the first half of the eighteenth century. The "genteel" comedy which arose in the reign of Queen Anne or a trifle earlier and flourished for a number of years seemed for a time to be developing along novel lines and about to win a success denied to the stricter imitations of Restoration licence. This type of comedy, which is an adaptation of the comedy of manners to the more artificial, more effeminate age, was started by Cibber about the end of the first half dozen years of the century, and, because of the acting of Mrs Oldfield and others, won a triumph in its time. The first true hint of it appears in *The Double Gallant: or, The Sick Lady's Cure* (H.[1] Nov. 1707). Based on Mrs Centlivre's *Love at a Venture* (Bath, 1706?), Burnaby's *The Ladies Visiting-Day* (L.[1] 1701) and the same author's *The Reform'd Wife* (D.L. 1700), with title and suggestions from Thomas Corneille's *Le Galand Doublé*, this comedy presents perfectly the atmosphere of the artificial social life which flourished in the period. Lady Dainty, acted by Mrs Oldfield, is a perfect study, as is Careless, her lover. The exploits of Atall (acted by Cibber himself) in his wooing of Clarinda and Sylvia and in his associations with the amorous Lady Sad-life are excellently managed. There are quite a number of witty touches in the comedy, as in that transformation of the after-the-murder scene in *Macbeth*. "She has an Intrigue," declares Sir Solomon. "An Intrigue!" cries Lady Sadlife, "Heaven's, in our Family![1]" "How civilly we Women hate one another![2]" might have come from Congreve. In spite of flashes like these, however, the weakness of the genteel species is evident in this comedy. The play does not depend ultimately on wit for its being, but on the artificial manners of the time, and the vanishing of these manners leaves us not the basis on which we could judge its merits aright.

The Rival Fools (D.L. Jan. 1708/9), filched from Fletcher's *Wit at Several Weapons*, but not so successful as the former play[3], carries on the same tradition. Its prologue declares quite openly against any sentimental purpose:

> *No Set-dress Morals form'd in't to affright you,*
> *From the dear modish Follies that delight you...*
> *No, faith! All sorts of Men and Manners may*
> *From these last Scenes go unreprov'd away.*
> *From late Experience taught[4], we slight th'old Rule*
> *Of Profit with Delight: This Play's—All Fool!*

Throughout the conduct of the comedy many are the hits directed at those whom Cibber, in his own way, had before been assisting. "Nay, that's not the thing neither," remarks

---

[1] III. (iii).   [2] II. i.
[3] Jacob, p. 39.
[4] The reference is probably to *The Lady's Last Stake* (Hay.[1] 1707) which does not seem to have been successful; cf. *infra*, p. 185.

Young Outwit in IV. i, "for a man may be a perfect rogue, if he has but industry and assurance enough to go thro' with it; if you were but clerk to some *suburb* Justice of Peace now —or informer to the Society—or—it's a mighty matter to have the protection of the law—," to all of which Sir Gregory makes reply—"Ay, so it is, indeed, cousin; I believe they'd find me for their purpose; for tho' I say it I am a man of very reform'd principles." Hardly anything could be a better comment on the age. In this play appears much of the same sort of witty satire as in that conversation in V. i concerning the payment of the musicians. Sir Oliver Outwit demurs at the bill:

> *Y. Out.* Death! sir, they are all *Italians*.
> *Sir Ol.* Why, what then, sir, mayn't an *Italian* be a Scoundrel, as well as an *Englishman*?
> *Y. Out.* Lord! sir, I wou'd not have this heard for the universe. Does not the whole nation adore 'em, sir? Is any man allowed common sense, among the better sort, that is not ravish'd with their musick? And is any thing a more fashionable mark of a gentleman, than to pay an extravagant price for't?

Yet the play, as before, does not depend on wit; its manners are the foolish manners of the time, and usurp all attention.

The only other play of Cibber's which at all comes within this category is *The Refusal; or, The Ladies Philosophy* (D.L. Feb. 1720/1). Borrowing slightly from Molière's *Les Femmes Savantes* and utilising the excitement caused by the South Sea stock for a theme, Cibber has succeeded here in making a comedy of excellent structure and characterisation. The atmosphere is the atmosphere of a sophisticated artificial society. Granger wins Sophronia by pretending in himself an exalted idealism, and Witling's folly is the folly of his time. The comedy possibly would have been successful had it not been for the feeling raised against the author by his notorious *The Non-Juror* (D.L. 1717)[1].

In 1716 Mrs Mary Davys produced a comedy of similar qualities in *The Northern Heiress: Or, The Humours of York* (L.² April 1716). In this play the conduct of a portion of

---

[1] *Supra*, p. 15.

the main plot is interesting. A favourite situation in sentimental comedy was the presentation of a pair of lovers one
of whom becomes suddenly rich, and the other of whom
abandons his or her claim of marriage. A sudden break in
fortune reverses their positions and it is the one who abandoned the claim who now renews the protestations and the
other who demurs. In Mrs Davys' comedy Isabella, to test
Gamont, pretends she has lost her fortune. There is no
doubt but that the lover would have ceased to pay her his
addresses; only—he has discovered the trick. He professes
to adore her, fortune or no fortune, and so marries her in the
end. The fundamental assumption, it is to be noted, of the
"genteel" comedy is that woman, artificial, affected, vain,
is a thing to be sought after and won by sheer brute strength
or else by trick, the lover playing up to her nonsensical ideals,
as with Lady Dainty and Sophronia, or by sheer deceit, as
here. In this it is as distinct from the comedy of manners as
from the sentimental comedy. In both of these women meet
men on equal terms, in the one for a conflict of sex and wit,
in the other for a self-abnegating battle of altruistic idealism.
Only here, in the comedy of "genteel" characteristics, do we
find this attitude of masculine superiority and feminine
foible.

This same attitude towards women is to be seen also in the
"much expected" play of James Moore Smythe, *The Rival
Modes* (D.L. Jan. 1726/7)[1]. The giddy Amoret and the
serious Melissa are there treated by Sagely and Bellamine
precisely as Sophronia is treated by her lover. The wit is not
so fine as in Cibber's comedy already mentioned, but it is
sufficient not to warrant Genest's severe condemnation[2].
Noticeable are the two characters of Late-Airs and Toupet,
symbolising the qualities of beaux of the seventeenth and the
eighteenth century respectively, and acted by Colley Cibber
and his son Theophilus.

James Miller's *The Man of Taste*[3] (D.L. March 1734/5),
nearly a decade later, carried on the same style. Based on

[1] *Supra*, p. 19.   [2] iii. 157.
[3] The running title is *The Man of Taste: or, The Guardians.*

Molière's *L'École des Maris* and *Les Précieuses Ridicules*, it endeavours to capture some of that fine air which Fielding's unknown friend declaimed against in a prologue to *The Miser* (D.L. 1733):

> *Too long the slighted Comic Muse has mourn'd,*
> *Her face quite alter'd, and her Art o'erturn'd;*
> *That Force of Nature now no more she sees,*
> *With which so well her Johnson knew to please...*
> *Our Modern Bards, who to Assemblies stray,* ⎫
> *Frequent the Park, the Visit or the Play,* ⎬
> *Regard not what Fools do, but what Wits say,* ⎭

so that comedy was become but "*A dull Collection of insipid Jokes.*" *The Man of Taste* was a success[1], no doubt because of its skilful mirroring the polite life of the age.

Dr J. Baillie's *The Married Coquet* (1746)[2] might be noted as one of the later representatives of this school. A certain amount of sentimentalising is apparent here, but the whole comedy is set in the midst of a dubious but genteel society, the substratum of which is the society of the Restoration.

So flickered out the genuine comedy of manners in the early eighteenth century. Although Congreve and Wycherley lived still in the theatre, their successors had lost all power. The genteel comedy has not the strength and the intellectual wit of that drama which made glorious the last years of the Restoration period.

IV. *The Comedies of Intrigue*

The spirit of the manners style is, of course, frequently to be traced in comedies not wholly of the Congrevian cast, and in none more than in the comedies of Spanish intrigue imitated through the works of Mrs Behn and others from the similar dramas produced by Fletcher and his companions in the early seventeenth century. These comedies of intrigue present no features different from the elements already noted in the type during preceding years. Then, as now, there was a distinct tendency on the part of those dramatists who indulged in intrigue to descend to farce.

[1] Whincop (p. 261) who attributes it to Miller.
[2] It was published posthumously for the benefit of his widow.

Unquestionably, of all the writers of this particular school, Mrs Susannah Centlivre is the most important, both for the intrinsic merit of her works and for the influence which she exerted. The career of this authoress is to be compared with that of Mrs Behn, many of whose most characteristic qualities she seems to have inherited. After a trial at tragedy with *The Perjur'd Husband* (D.L. 1700), she essayed her first attempt at comedy in *The Beau's Duel, or, A Soldier for the Ladies* (L.¹ *c.* June 1702)[1], a strictly moral play although abounding in all that trickery and deception so dear to the lovers of intrigue.

The Stolen Heiress or the Salamanca Doctor Outplotted appeared at the same theatre in December 1702. Partly farcical, it deals with its theme in a capable manner. The two plots, one revolving around the elopement of Palante and Lucasia and the other treating of Don Sancho and his fiancée Lavinia, are excellently developed, so that, in spite of a mass of stage business, the whole seems not too heavily involved.

With *Love's Contrivance, or, Le Medecin Malgre Lui* (D.L. June 1703), Mrs Centlivre turned to execute an intrigue-farcical adaptation of Molière. Part of the plot is original: Selfwill desires to marry Lucinda to Sir Toby Doubtful, but Bellmie succeeds in the end in winning her by the aid of Octavio and Martin, the mock doctor. Perhaps Martin has more of the *vis comica* in him than either his predecessor in Lacy's play or his successor in Fielding's. *Love's Contrivance*, possibly because of its semi-farcical nature, was a great success, and parts of it in later years were frequently employed as after-pieces.

After a few excursions into other but related kinds of comic productivity, Mrs Centlivre again essayed intrigue in *The Platonick Lady* (H.¹ Nov. 1706). This comedy, however, in spite of its brilliant setting forth[2], hardly deserves more

---

[1] The exact date of production is not known. On W. Oct. 21, 1702, it was acted "*with the Addition of a New Scene, and a new Prologue and Epilogue, with a Whimsical Song sung by Mr Pack*" (*Daily Courant*).

[2] The prologue was written by Farquhar, and the cast was a rich one. Betterton played Sir Thomas Beaumont, Booth Sir Charles Richly, Wilks

than brief mention. *The Busie Body* (D.L. May 1709) is a much finer play, one of the masterpieces, indeed, of this type. In it Sir Jealous Traffic, a merchant who adores Spanish ways and who plans his daughter, Isabinda, for a Spanish husband, is a well-drawn character. The plot develops around the loves of Isabinda and Charles, son of the miserly Sir Francis Gripe, and those of Sir Francis' daughter, Miranda, and George Airy. The chief figure in the whole play, however, is Marplot, an honest meddler, possibly suggested to the authoress by a reading of Dryden's *Sir Martin Mar-all*. It is said that this comedy was almost rejected by the actors, yet it won such a success that two houses played it against one another in the year 1710[1]. *Mar-Plot, or, The Second Part of the Busie Body* (D.L. Dec. 1710) was the direct result of this success. The blundering Marplot continues in the sequel his series of blundering errors; Charles indulges in some doubtful amours with Donna Perriera; and a new theme is introduced with the characters of Colonel Ravelin and Mdlle Joneton. On the whole, however, the sequel is not so good as the original play, and we are made to feel the brutality of the age in the casting off of poor Marton, Joneton's sister. A similar callousness, it is peculiar, may be noted in Mrs Behn's sequel to *The Rover*.

Previous to the production of *Mar-Plot*, Mrs Centlivre had given another intrigue comedy to the age in *The Man's Bewitch'd: or, The Devil to Do about Her* (H.[1] Dec. 1709), an adaptation, apparently, of *Le Deuil*, a play presumably penned by Thomas Corneille[2]. The figures are mainly conventional—Captain Constant with his testy father, Laura the heiress, and Sir David Watchum, her guardian. The merit of the play lies entirely in the situations and in the clever tricks of the *dramatis personæ*[3].

Captain Beaumont, Cibber Sharper, Mrs Bracegirdle Lucinda and Mrs Oldfield Isabella. In spite of this it does not seem to have been popular. Produced on M. Nov. 25, 1707, it ran only for the succeedin' three nights.

[1] Whincop, pp. 189–90; Jacob, p. 33.

[2] This indebtedness is noted in the *Biographia Dramatica*.

[3] It was well cast with Wilks as Faithful, Doggett as Num, Cibber as Manage and Mrs Oldfield as Belinda.

A descent into farce, *A Bickerstaff's Burying* (D.L. 1710), followed, and then, with *The Perplex'd Lovers* (D.L. Jan. 1711/12), Mrs Centlivre again returned to what may be regarded as her first love. Taken confessedly from a Spanish play, which so far has not been traced[1], it is not so witty and entertaining as the preceding works. This is the last but one of Mrs Centlivre's plays of this kind. The end comes in *The Wonder: A Woman Keeps a Secret* (D.L. April 1714), but this play is truly a triumph. Owing its contemporary success partly to the magnificent acting of Mrs Oldfield as Violante[2], it was yet so excellently constructed and so full of buoyant grace that it held the boards until well on into the nineteenth century[3]. The plot is a complicated one. Felix adores Violante, daughter of Don Pedro, who has designed her for a nunnery. She befriends Isabella, daughter of Don Lopez, who has planned for her an unhappy marriage. Felix, believing Violante has a man concealed in her room, grows furiously jealous, but the secret is faithfully kept till the end of the play disentangles the plot.

As has already been seen, Mrs Centlivre, after this, tended towards the production of comedies after the manners style, but even in these a fair infusion of intrigue elements is to be traced. While Mrs Centlivre is the chief upholder of this particular type in the whole of the early years of the eighteenth century, she was however surrounded by a number of others, few of whom wrote in this style so consistently as she, but who, taken together, aided in making intrigue one of the dominant species of comic productivity of the time. This prevalence of intrigue elements is somewhat peculiar when we consider the dying away of the school in the late years of the seventeenth century[4].

In *Love Makes a Man* (D.L. Dec. 1700) Colley Cibber, taking his theme from Fletcher's *The Custom of the Country* and *The Elder Brother*, produced a comedy of a mixed intrigue

[1] Preface.   [2] Preface.
[3] A translation into Polish as *Kobieta dotrzymuiąca sekretu* by W. Bogusławski appeared in 1820 (in his *Dzieła dramatyczne*, tom. iii).
[4] For Mrs Centlivre's work in general see *Die Komödien der Mrs Centlivre* by Robert Seibt (*Anglia*, xxxii and xxxiii, 1909–10).

and Jonsonian sort. In it Carlos, a pedant awakened to life by love, flies in a boat with Angelina, who has been destined by her father for the sprightly puppy Clodio. They are captured, and Louisa becomes deeply enamoured of Carlos. The supposed murder and the revenge motive are carried out almost precisely as in the early seventeenth century play. The adaptation is a good one, and proved a popular success for many years. *She Wou'd and She Wou'd Not; or, the Kind Impostor* (D.L. Nov. 1702) was an equally successful production, the plot of which is to be traced to a Spanish source. The theme, which deals mainly with the exploits of Hypolita in her disguise as a man, is well worked out, and there are some truly excellent scenes scattered throughout the five acts of the drama. Before he turned to the genteel comedy and to sentiment, intrigue was well served by Cibber, and his example may have done somewhat to add to the popularity of the type.

About December 1701 Charles Johnson, if he indeed be the author[1], presented the Lincoln's Inn Fields with *The Gentleman-Cully*, a play acted by the "Young Company" during vacation. Without wit, and without the least infusion of sentimental motives, it carries on in a fairly unoriginal manner the old elements of this style. Only once more was Johnson to touch this type of comedy again, in *The Generous Husband: or, The Coffee House Politician* (D.L. Jan. 1710/11), a London-scened play full of the best Spanish tricks and disguises. *The Generous Husband*, however, is not so pure an example of this school as is the former drama. Humours enter into it, in Postscript "A Coffee House Politician" and in Dypthong "A Critick," and the influence of Congreve is apparent in the Veramant-Fictitia-Lucy episodes, wherein the first, loving Fictitia, engages in an intrigue with Lucy, just "to exercise" his "Teeth[2]."

Francis Manning, likewise, provided early specimens of

---

[1] Jacob, p. 313, marks the play as anonymous, as does Whincop, p. 309. It is attributed by Coxeter.

[2] The play was evidently ill-received (cf. Dedication). Genest (ii. 475) traces part of the plot to Cervantes' tale, *The Jealous Estremaduran.*

this species of dramatic effort. *The Generous Choice* made its appearance at Lincoln's Inn Fields in Lent, 1700. Slightly influenced by sentimentalism, it is largely intrigue in character, and seems suggested either by *The Comedy of Errors* or, as Genest suggests, by a Franco-Italian piece, *The Two Harlequins*[1].

All for the Better: Or, The Infallible Cure (D.L. 1702) came out three years later, with a prologue by Farquhar. It is based partly on Middleton and Rowley's *The Spanish Gipsy*, and shows its indebtedness to the earlier Jacobean intrigue school, in spite of the fact that sentimental motives are stressed in the elaboration of the Alphonso-Isabella portion taken from the earlier play[2].

The anonymous *The Portsmouth Heiress: or, The Generous Refusal* (1704), we are informed in the preface, was written during the time of stage reform and consequently was not acted. Dramatic poets have ever an entertaining way of discovering new reasons for their lack of success, and this no doubt is one of them. The play is not witty, and seems to owe something to Dryden's wild-gallant types. L'Bell is the heiress, who, "disguis'd by the Name of *Selinda*," is pursued by Rainer. As Lucia, her maid, poses as the mistress, the complications that ensue may well be imagined. Perhaps underneath the plot lies some reference to contemporary social gossip.

William Taverner's *The Maid the Mistress* (D.L. June 1708) is worked out on similar lines, but has a more complicated series of interwoven themes. The title to the play comes from the device of Charlot, who, cheated of her estate by Sir David Fancy, acts the maid in his house and eventually captures her adored one, Gaylove. With this are mingled two other themes, one in which Beauford secures Harriot, destined by Sir David for Squire Empty, and another in which Lady Fancy, confined by Sir David, pretends to assign an intrigue with

---

[1] ii. 224. *Les Deux Arlequins* was in the repertoire of the French comedians in 1718; its original production seems later than 1700.

[2] Noticeable is the rather pleasant roistering song in II. i, "Come, let us be jolly," set by Daniel Purcell.

Gaylove. The play is excellently constructed and hardly deserved its ill-success. Another intrigue play of the same author's is *The Artful Husband* (L.² Feb. 1716/7), a fair comedy of trickery. The main plot concerns Belinda, who, dressing as a man, goes through a ceremony of marriage with Lady Upstart, and eventually consents to give her hand to Sir Harry Freelove. This portion of the theme has a close similarity to that of Middleton's *No Wit No Help like a Woman's*, already utilised by Mrs Behn in *The Counterfeit Bridegroom*. From Shirley's *The Lady of Pleasure*, too, Taverner has drawn the theme of the reclaiming of Winwife's spouse.

A. Chaves' single drama, *The Cares of Love, or, A Night's Adventure* (L.¹ Aug. 1705), is a much poorer comedy. It mingles Spanish intrigue (the scene is Toledo) with a sentimental motive in the relations of Florencio and Lisena, and with plentiful satire of Italian opera.

Richard Wilkinson's *Vice Reclaim'd; or, The Passionate Mistress* (D.L. June 1703), later reworked as *The Quaker's Wedding* (L.² 1719), is a rollicking intrigue comedy of no very special merits, reminding one forcibly of *The Different Widows*, a play already noted as having been produced at Lincoln's Inn Fields about November 1703.[1] Although there is no external proof, it might be suggested that the two comedies were by the same author.

Marry, or Do Worse (L.¹ Nov. 1703), by William Walker, was a failure[2], although it is a fair comedy in the older strain. Snap is quite an excellent fool-wit of a servant and, while the whole is not very licentious, the "Restoration" spirit aids in keeping the atmosphere of the play harmonious.

Among the early writers may be noted also Mrs Pix (Mary Griffith), who in the last decade of the seventeenth century had produced an intrigue play in *The Spanish Wives*. *The Beau Defeated: Or The Lucky Younger Brother* (L.¹ c. March, 1700) is confessedly based on a French comedy[3]. This is a

---

[1] On the authorship see also *supra*, p. 155.
[2] Preface. There is only one record of performance, M. Nov. 1.
[3] Dedication. This French work has not been traced. Jacob, p. 11, gives the play wrongly to one Barker.

good comedy of intrigue opening vivaciously with the conversation of Mrs Rich and Betty, and fairly well developed in the later scenes. *The Adventures in Madrid* (H.[1] summer, 1706) is a three act piece of no particular merit introducing stock characters of a rather monotonous type. Obviously Mrs Pix has here been endeavouring to emulate Mrs Centlivre, but she lamentably lacks the flair for the theatre which the latter possesses in so marked a degree.

Slightly later in the century a number of other writers aided in keeping up the popularity of the species. In December, 1716, Christopher Bullock came forward with *Woman is a Riddle* (L.[2]), an interesting comedy-farce derived from *La Dama Duende*. The main features of the Spanish play have been preserved, with, of course, a number of variations in treatment. Miranda is made to cheat Manly by means of a secret door leading from her house to his, and at the same time to deceive Sir Amorous Vain-Wit. In the end she succeeds in capturing Manly for herself, in marrying off Clarinda to Sir Amorous, and in promoting a marriage between her brother Courtwell and Lady Outside. *Woman is a Riddle* cannot be considered apart from the unfortunate Richard Savage's *Love in a Veil* (D.L. June 1718). Whincop tells the story of the two plays from the point of view of the latter. *Woman is a Riddle*, he says, "was brought to him (Bullock), while a Manager of the Theatre, by Mr *Richard Savage*...and when he had made a few Alterations in it, he brought it on the Stage as his own; a Practice, that they say, has been used by more Play-houses than one[1]." The author of *A Companion to the Play-House*, on the other hand, while noting the quarrel between the two authors, declares that the original translation from the Spanish was made by neither, but by a Mrs Price, who gave three MS copies away, one each going to Bullock and Savage respectively. These authors at once set to work on the literal rendering, and of the two Bullock was first in the field. It may be noted here that *Woman is a Riddle* was reduced to a farce as *The Litigious Suitor Defeated: or, a New Trick to get a Wife* in *The Stroler's Pacquet* of 1742.

[1] Pp. 183-4.

By a gentleman of "Christ's College," Oxford, was penned *The Apparition: or, The Sham Wedding* (D.L. Nov. 1713), another comedy of trickery that descends perilously near to farce. In it the Restoration atmosphere is preserved almost unaltered. More of a sentimental note is traceable in Leonard Welsted's *The Dissembled Wanton; or, My Son Get Money* (L.² Dec. 1726), a play the ill-success of which has been noted[1]. The intrigue here depends upon the character of Charlotte, who has been sent by her father, Lord Severne, to France, and who returns disguised as Sir Harry Truelove, cheating thus even her lover, Beaufort, and her brother, Colonel Severne. The latter, who loves Emilia, is jealous of Sir Harry, and tragedy is almost in the air when Emilia makes an assignation with the pretended gallant[2].

Charles Molloy's *The Perplex'd Couple: Or, Mistake upon Mistake* (L.² 1715) has already been dealt with as a kind of intrigue-comedy; and the same author's *The Coquet: Or, The English Chevalier* (L.² 1718), while it obviously betrays the influence of Etherege, has in it many elements of the intrigue style. Francis Hawling's *The Impertinent Lovers: or, A Coquet at her Wit's End* (D.L. Aug. 1723)[3] is a very similar play, probably borrowed from some Spanish comedy or novel. The characters are of a stock type, but some of the situations are novel and the dialogue is fresh and interesting.

Typical of intrigue as it appeared still later in the period is Fielding's *The Temple Beau* (G.F. Jan. 1729/30), a good comedy revolving around the Temple rake, Wilding, and his libertine courses. By 1730, however, intrigue was dying away as a popular type of drama. The decay was no doubt hastened by the arising in those years of ballad-opera; but possibly the most direct cause was the fact that no single author took up the style consistently after Mrs Centlivre. It will be noticed that the majority of the intrigue plays mentioned above were written either by men who wrote

[1] *Supra*, p. 10.
[2] The central idea of the play seems taken from Southerne's *Sir Anthony Love.*
[3] The attribution to Hawling is by no means certain; see *Biographia Dramatica.*

only one comedy or by men who, like Taverner, Johnson and Fielding, turned for one brief moment to this world of trickery and deception. Intrigue, of course, goes ill with sentimentalism, and the intrigue of the later years tends to be banished out of the realm of comedy proper and to appear only in the slighter regions of farce.

V. *The Comedies of Humours*

In *The Dissembled Wanton*, intrigue play though that be, Welsted, after tracing the "grand tour" of the Comic Muse from Greece to Rome, and from Rome to France, Spain and England, rested on the names of Jonson and of Shadwell as masters of their craft. Jonson, according to him, is the true leader, while

> Shadwell, *at Distance, the great Model Views,*
> *And with unequal Steps his Sire pursues;*
> *But few beside the happy Mark have hit.*

The words indicate the tremendous enthusiasm felt by the age for the works of the masters of the comedy of humours. Jonson was a classical scholar, and as such appealed to the Augustans, and his "laborious art" possibly endeared itself more to a period essentially uncreative in the free romantic manner than did the fine careless imaginative powers of Shakespeare. Jonson's comedy, too, being based fundamentally on satire, made a powerful appeal to the age of Pope, so that not only can we find during this time many "humours" plays modelled entirely on the Jonsonian plan but "humours" qualities in comedies of quite different schools. The one thing that retarded the fuller development of the type in those fifty years was the lack of any Shadwell in the age to devote himself rigidly to that style. The comedy of humours, therefore, shows some of that waning popularity which marked the fortunes of the comedy of intrigue after Mrs Centlivre had deserted it.

In the very first years of the century it seemed as if the true successor of Shadwell had been found in Thomas Baker, but this author, after giving four plays to the stage, disappeared in 1708 or 1709. *The Humour of the Age* (D.L.

c. Feb. 1700/1)[1] is described in the modest dedication as "the first Essay of a young Author, that has but just reach'd the Twenty First Year." The comedy shows evidences of youthful workmanship, but is a fair specimen of the Shadwellian style of drama.

Tunbridge-Walks: Or, The Yeoman of Kent (D.L. Jan. 1702/3), an exceedingly popular play, was a decided improvement on his first attempt. There are many good "humours" in it, among them Maiden, Squib, Woodcock and Mrs Goodfellow, the last "A lady that loves her Bottle." The first character mentioned was, as the editor of *A Companion to the Play-House* notes, the prototype of a long line of effeminate "*Fribbles*, Beau *Mizens*, &c. that have been drawn since," and is possibly a portrait of the author's own person in his youth. The play deserved well the success it achieved, although probably it was the fine acting of Mrs Verbruggen as Hillaria to which it owed a good deal of its contemporary popularity[2].

With *An Act at Oxford* Baker was less fortunate. The play, evidently owing to its having given offence to the University, was banned. The dialogue is good and the construction fair. Evidently the author himself thought it was too good to leave, for at Drury Lane on October 30, 1705 there appeared a comedy of another name, *Hampstead-Heath* —but no more than a reworking of the forbidden drama[3].

After this Baker produced only one other comedy, *The Fine Lady's Airs: Or, An Equipage of Lovers* (D.L. Dec. 1708)[4],

---

[1] This and the other three plays, though issued anonymously, are credited to Baker by Jacob, p. 8, and are advertised under his name in the list of dramas at the beginning of Johnson's *The Masquerade* (1719). Whincop, p. 166, gives some details of his career.

[2] See Tony Aston, *A Brief Supplement to Colley Cibber, Esq.; His Lives of the late Famous Actors and Actresses* (1748), p. 19. "The Part of *Hillaria*," he thinks, "cou'd not be said to be Acted by any one but" Mrs Verbruggen.

[3] *Supra*, p. 21.

[4] In *The Daily Courant* for F. Dec. 10, 1709, appears an advertisement: "To be speedily published The Fine Ladies Airs or the Equipage of Lovers as acted at Drury Lane, by the author of the Yeoman of Kent." A trifle later the public were informed "that at present the Author is in his Airs and designs to sell his Copy once more," and later still "All

and it is hardly so Jonsonian in style, betraying marked features of the manners school. This no doubt signifies that Baker, as others, would have shown himself a follower of Congreve rather than of Shadwell had he continued his dramatic career.

Shadwell's son, Charles Shadwell, on setting up as a dramatist, quite naturally embraced the Jonsonian style. By no means possessed of the talents of his father, he yet gave two quite fair comedies to the age. The first of these is *The Fair Quaker of Deal, or, The Humours of the Navy*, produced at Drury Lane in February 1710. A thoroughly realistic piece, with Jenny Privates and Jiltups, it displays clearly the influence exercised by the elder Shadwell on his descendant. The success of this play seems to have led the young author to pen a companion piece, *The Humours of the Army* (D.L. Jan. 1712/3), with a bevy of national types, Col. Hyland (Scots), Major Cadwalader (Welsh), Major Outside (Irish) and Capt. Mathematicks (French). Its ultimate source seems to have been Dancourt's *Les Curieux de Compiègne*; but the development is new[1].

Other writers besides these two, however, engaged in the humours style in the first decade or decades of the century. Captain William Phillips, who may have been that William Phillips who wrote *The Revengeful Queen*, penned amidst his tragedies one comedy, *St. Stephen's Green Or The Generous Lovers* (T.R. Dublin, 1700), which, with its Sir Francis Feignyouth, Wormwood, Vanity and Trickwell, is purely of the Shadwellian school[2]. Mrs Trotter's *Love at a Loss; or, Most Votes Carry It* (D.L. *c.* Nov. 1700), as a background to a manners plot revolving round Beaumine "a Gay Roving

differences between the Author and Bookseller are amicably accomodated." Whincop (p. 167) notes that with this play "the House opened, after having been shut up six weeks, on account of the Death of Prince *George* of *Denmark*; it had good Success on the Stage." D'Urfey, however, in the preface to *The Modern Prophets* declares it was an "Abuse of the fair Sex...and deservedly hist."

[1] It appears to have met with fair success although Whincop (p. 285) marks it as a failure.

[2] Apparently this play is not in Whincop or Genest; both Mears and Chetwood attribute it to Phillips.

Spark" and a slight sentimental element in the figure of
Lesbia, employs many of Jonson's devices. The anonymous
writer of *Sir Giddy Whim, or, The Lucky Amour*[1] (1703)
likewise employs the same atmosphere. This play is a good
one, in spite of the declaration in the prologue that

> *Plot and good Manners was his least concern,*
> *He Knows you come to laugh, and not to learn.*

The character of Sir Giddy Whim is a new one, and is well
drawn. Another anonymous play of humours written about
the same time is *The Fashionable Lover: or Wit in Necessity*
(D.L. *c* April 1706), borrowed to a certain extent from Nabbes'
The Bride. It has one excellent scene where Viletta wanders
alone and in fear.

For some reason the Jonsonian comedy on the stage waned
in popularity from 1710 to about 1730. Almost the only
pure comedy of this type produced during these years is
John Leigh's *Kensington-Gardens; Or, The Pretenders* (L.[2]
Nov. 1719)[2]. We are presented here with the gay Lucinda
surrounded by her various lovers, Sir Vanity Half-Wit,
Sir Politick Noodle, Captain Hackit, Grogram and Varnish,
all offering admirable opportunities for the displayal of a
kind of rough Shadwellian wit.

About 1730 the style seemed once more to come into
fashion. In January of that year James Miller produced at
Drury Lane *The Humours of Oxford*[3], his first drama. The
long descriptions of the *dramatis personæ* and the presence of
such figures as that of Lady Science, a "great Pretender to
Learning and Philosophy," indicate at once the influence of
Shadwell. In the same year Fielding indulged in much the
same atmosphere. *Rape upon Rape; or, The Justice Caught in
his Own Trap* (H.[2] June 1730)[4] is a good comedy, but obviously
modelled on old lines; Politick and Squeezum are stock
characters and the rough realism allied to satire at once
recall Jonson's plays. By no means all of Fielding's comedies

---

[1] Apparently not in Whincop or Genest.
[2] Acted under the sub-title.
[3] The title-page gives the play as by a gentleman of Wadham College.
It is attributed to Miller by Whincop (p. 261).
[4] Acted later as *The Coffee-House Politician;* see Appendix C.

are of the humours kind, but this effort of 1730 he followed with that of *The Miser* (D.L. Feb. 1732/3), a comedy in which he mingles wit with the Jonsonian style. The classical or Gallic types here are exaggerated just as Jonson exaggerated them, Lovegold, Lappet and Ramilie all being more pronounced than the similar figures in the original comedies of Plautus and of Molière. *The Miser* was an immense success, and proves the best of all the adaptations of the earlier plays. *The Wedding-Day* (D.L. Feb. 1742/3) is equally Jonsonian in spirit. It is an interesting play, not only intrinsically, but historically as showing the taste of the age. Millamour is presented as loved by Clarinda. The latter, because of his neglect, marries Stedfast, who in the end turns out to be her own long-lost father. Millamour, meanwhile, has debauched Lucina, who, at the close of the play, is dispatched to a nunnery. He is adored also by Charlotte, but she contents herself finally with his friend Heartfort. Needless to say, Millamour and Clarinda are united in the last act. The dialogue in places is sparkling, but no amount of sparkling dialogue can take away the feeling of brutality and lack of sympathy conveyed to us by the comedy as a whole. Fielding, following in Jonson's footsteps, has here lost the artificiality of the Congreve style.

Among the plays of a date either immediately before or immediately after those of Miller and Fielding might be mentioned John Sturmy's *The Compromise: or, Faults on both Sides* (L.² Dec. 1722). This comedy, which is one of the few partly Jonsonian plays produced between 1710 and 1730, mingles Shadwellian types such as Sir Lewis Despotick and Sir Clement Harpye, with others imitated from the intrigue plays of Mrs Behn and of Mrs Centlivre. So Gabriel Odingsells' *The Bath Unmask'd* (L.² Feb. 1724/5) can hardly be described as a pure comedy of humours, although Jonson's influence is evident in many a scene. Decidedly Shadwellian, on the other hand, is Richard Gwinnet's *The Country 'Squire: or, A Christmas Gambol* (private performance, 1731?), a poor work of three acts which descends at times to the level of farce. Matthew Draper's *The Spend-Thrift* (H.² Jan. 1731), which owes something to *The London Prodigal*, has likewise borrowed considerably at the Jonsonian fount. This brief list might be closed with a mention—and more than a mention it deserves not—of Thomas Odell's *The Prodigal: Or, Recruits for the Queen of Hungary* (H.[2] Oct. 1744), itself a free adaptation of Shadwell's *The Woman Captain*.

A summary of the development of this type during the fifty years from 1700 to 1750, therefore, shows us that, after a period of popularity from 1700 to 1710, there came a lull in the appreciation of Jonson's methods, a lull which was broken in 1730 by Miller and Fielding. The total number of comedies of humours is seen to be exceedingly small, although we recognise that Jonsonian characters may be traced in countless comedies of the intrigue or sentimental class, and that Jonson's own comedies, as well as those of Shadwell, still held the boards of the theatre.

VI. *The Comedies of Sensibility*

A consideration of the growth and progress of the sentimental drama in this period possibly presents the greatest number of difficulties. Sentimentalism itself is so elusive a movement and sentimental motives so constantly appear in comedies of a quite unsentimental type that the exact tracing of that tendency which reached a height in the novels of Richardson and of Sterne is indeed a task hard and tortuous.

The whole account of sentimentalism in any age and in any form of literary activity must depend, obviously, on the definition given to the mood or philosophical theory from which it takes its rise. On this subject something has been said in the previous volume of this *History*[1] where it was stated that while "pity" and "a certain confidence in the goodness of human nature" are undoubtedly the basis of later sentimental novels, dramas and poems, the origins of the mood are to be sought for in simpler channels. Sympathy, not with the characters on the stage but as exemplified in their own actions; the relating of art to life; the return to a highly artificial love of natural scenery and rural landscape; and the

[1] Pp. 263-4.

deliberate enunciation of a moral or social problem—these appear the commonest features of the sentimental comedy in the early years. Sentimentalism of this type is a distinctly English development. It arose in the early seventeenth century, and, after being lost for a time, was revived by the Restoration writers after 1680. From these Restoration writers it was taken over by the dramatists of the reign of Anne and was by them brought several stages forward. French playwrights, seeking for novelty, seized upon Steele and Cibber, and, from imitations of English sentimental dramas, came to elaborate a still more philosophic, tearful, pathetic comedy—the *comédie larmoyante*—which in its turn crossed the channel to influence deeply the dramatic writers of the later eighteenth century. It is the first stages in this development which it is our business here to trace.

Before coming to the actual plays in which these elements can, in greater or less degree, be discerned, a few words may be said concerning the more particular manifestations of these features in the first half of the eighteenth century and concerning the attitude taken towards sentimentalism in general by the writers of that time. Especially may be noted in the interesting prologue to Whitehead's *The Roman Father* (D.L. 1750) a reference to current ideas which goes a certain distance towards defining the meaning of the word sentimental at the middle of the century. A "*Moral*, Sentimental, *Stroke*," for Whitehead was the utterance of the poet *in propria persona*, not part of dramatic dialogue, and this explains to a certain extent the numbers of "sentimental sentences" which abound in the drama of this time. It explains also the weakness of many of these sentimental plays, the true sense of character-drawing being lost in the enthusiasm of the poet for his own particular ideals of right and of wrong. These sentimental sentences are of various kinds. Sometimes they are merely sententiously pedantic and priggish as in Cibber's *The Careless Husband* (D.L. 1704). "Why truly," says Lady Easy, "I'm half angry to see a Woman of your Sense, so warmly concern'd in the Care of her Outside; for when we have taken our best Pains about it, 'tis

the Beauty of the Mind alone that gives us lasting Value[1]."
Sometimes they are satirically democratic as in Fielding's
Don Quixote in England (H.[2] 1734) where we are informed that
"Gaols in all Countries are only Habitations for the Poor,
not for Men of Quality. If a poor Fellow robs a Man of
Fashion of Five Shillings, to Gaol with him: But the Man of
Fashion may plunder a thousand Poor, and stay in his own
House[2]." This question of democratic sentiment is a difficult
one. The whole sentimental movement, of course, is fundamentally opposed to the cynical aristocratic existence of former
times. From its inception the middle classes were intimately
associated with the development of the type; but that does
not mean that the writers were in any way revolutionary.
Dodsley might show that a King after all was naught but
a man, and he and Fielding might be accused of attempts to
overthrow the ministry[3], Miller might raise his voice in
defence of tradesmen[4], but very few of the playwrights before
1750 were even as revolutionary as these. Most contented
themselves with purely moral maxims that had no reference
to political or social conditions. In two ways, however, even
the least revolutionary showed their dissatisfaction with the
life of their time. Nearly all turned from the city to nature.
It may have been nature artificialised, nature not far from
Arcady, but still it was nature. This nature love is to be
found, of course, in dramas not otherwise sentimentally
inclined. "How happy is the humble Cottager, who never
knows the Madness of Ambition?" cries Marina in Mrs Pix'
The Czar of Muscovy (L.[1] 1701)[5], and Margaretta in the same
authoress' *The Conquest of Spain* (H.[1] 1705) cries for

> the Feast of Nature,
> The downy Peace of a retir'd Life[6].

Even Baker in *The Humour of the Age* (D.L. 1701) could make
Tremila proclaim on the happiness of

> the Nymphs, that tread the peaceful woods,
> Where Nature in her best Perfection shines,
> Beyond the faint pretending Power of Art[7].

---

[1] II. i.   [2] I. ii.
[3] See preface to *The Historical Register, for the Year* 1736 (H.[2] 1737).
[4] See *The Coffee-House* (D.L. 1738) and *infra*, p. 203.
[5] v. iii.   [6] I. i.   [7] III. i.

In spite of the appearance of these and of similar pronouncements in plays entirely unsentimental, this reversion
to nature worship may be intimately associated with that
genre which rose under Cibber and Steele and Dodsley. A
further development of this is the cult of the "noble savage,"
immortalised later by Jean-Jacques Rousseau. Gay's *Polly*
(1729) possesses a few of these high-souled primitive men,
and Miller uses Julio in his *Art and Nature* (D.L. 1738) in
order to satirise the follies and vices of civilised society. The
great characteristic of the sentimental play, however, is the
problem, directly stated or implied. It occurs in nearly all
of Cibber's works in this style; it appears in the comedies of
Steele and Addison and Miller. This problem usually takes
for granted the presence of some latent good in human nature;
but it may exist in and for itself with characters wholly
unrelieved by any virtue or humane sense of justice.

The sentimental movement was not allowed to pass by
without comment. Many men seem to have been aware of
the ridiculous situations presented in the comedies of the
time. The satire, on the other hand, is not so deeply marked
as one might have expected, when we consider the tendencies
of Pope and of Swift and of their many followers in verse
and in prose. The first appearance of adverse criticism came
in the form of an anonymous play, *The Roving Husband Reclaim'd...Writ by a Club of Ladies, in Vindication of Virtuous
Plays* (1706)[1]. This skit, on the few occasions when it has
been noticed by stage-chroniclers, has been taken literally,
according to its title, but the exceedingly vulgar opening and
the ridiculous reconciliation and conversion at the close show
it for what it was, the good humoured attack of some anti-
sentimentalist at those artificial fifth-act-repentance dramas
of Cibber and of his companions. In 1723 Dennis, no doubt
largely because of his personal anger against Steele, took up
the attack. "When Sir *Richard* says, that any thing that
has its Foundation in Happiness and Success must be the
Subject of Comedy," he declares, "he confounds Comedy

[1] Ernest Bernbaum quotes the title of this piece from the British
Museum Catalogue, and conjectures that it was a sentimental drama.

with that Species of Tragedy which has a happy Catastrophe. When he says, that 'tis an Improvement of Comedy to introduce a Joy too exquisite for Laughter, he takes all the Care that he can to shew, that he knows nothing of the Nature of Comedy[1]." Others followed Dennis in their criticism, and a good deal of contemporary ridicule may be found expressed in the comic epilogue to Dance's *Pamela* (G.F. 1741), where the situations of the play are amusingly discussed:

> Unhappy *Belvile*, what a Wife, protect her,
> No doubt he'd often have a Curtain Lecture.

While we note the numbers of sentimental comedies written and produced, therefore, we must always bear in mind two things; that there was ever an undercurrent of amused cynicism in regard to these sentimental plays as well as a certain amount of quite definite opposition, and that the repertoire-lists of the theatres show that sentimental dramas by no means formed the bulk of the playhouse fare.

The inclusion of the various elements discussed above into the make-up of the sentimental species naturally widens to a considerable extent the scope of this subject, and many more plays will be included here than are given, for example, in Ernest Bernbaum's excellent work on *The Drama of Sensibility*[2]. For purposes of comparison, it may be well to enumerate those comedies which are admitted into his study. Between 1700 and 1704 Bernbaum finds no more than four sentimental dramas, Estcourt's *The Fair Example*, Steele's *The Funeral* and *The Lying Lover*, and Cibber's *The Careless Husband*; from 1704 to 1709, another four, Mrs Centlivre's *The Gamester*, Farquhar's *The Beaux Stratagem*, Steele's *The Tender Husband*, and Cibber's *The Lady's Last Stake*; from 1710 to 1728, five, Addison's *The Drummer*, Charles Johnson's *The Masquerade*, Shadwell's *Irish Hospitality*, Steele's *The Conscious Lovers*, and Cibber's and Vanbrugh's *The Provok'd Husband*; from 1729 to 1732, three, George

---

[1] *Remarks on a Play, Call'd, The Conscious Lovers, A Comedy* (1722), p. 6.
[2] On the sentimental drama should also be consulted O. Waterhouse's essay in *Anglia* (xxx. 1907), *The Development of English Sentimental Comedy in the 18th century*.

Lillo's *Silvia*, Theophilus Cibber's *The Lover*, and Kelly's *The Married Philosopher*; from 1732 to 1750, four, Popple's *The Lady's Revenge*, Jacob's *The Prodigal Reform'd*, Dance's *Pamela*, and Moore's *The Foundling*. There are several things which must here be carefully considered. First, two or three of these plays might easily be apportioned to other spheres of dramatic activity; Farquhar's *The Beaux Stratagem*, for example, has been dealt with above as exhibiting the last features of the manners style. Its sentimental elements seem to be subordinate to others inherited from Congreve. Second, within the separate periods mentioned by Bernbaum, not only are there many other comedies of a distinctly sentimental class (taking sentimentalism according to his definition), but there are also numerous others which seem to display sentimental motives of the nature indicated above. Without including the many plays which exhibit sporadically sentimental situations or motives, there will be found included in this section over forty dramas, twice as many as the twenty enumerated in Bernbaum's study. Third, the repertoires must ever be borne in mind if we are to judge the spirit of the age aright and to trace truly the development of the sentimental motives in these fifty years. Fourth, alongside of Cibber's *The Careless Husband* and *The Lady's Last Stake* there stand a number of what can be styled only by the name of moral-immoral comedies, which aim at catching, if not the best, at least something, of both worlds; introducing themes repugnant or *risqué*, but preserving the sentimental note by some occasional moralisations or unnatural conversions at the close.

This last aspect of the subject may perhaps most satisfactorily be dealt with first, actual examples showing the general tendencies and scope of the type. Cibber's *The Careless Husband* (D.L. Dec. 1704) is not in essence a truly sentimental drama. The aim, of course, is a moral one, in theory at least. "The best Criticks," announces the author in his dedication, "have long, and justly complain'd, that the coarseness of most Characters in our late Comedies have been unfit Entertainments for People of Quality, especially the Ladies: And therefore I was long in hopes that some able Pen...wou'd generously attempt to reform the Town into a better Taste, than the World generally allows 'em." There are many moralisations scattered throughout the body of this play[1], and there is the usual reconciliation at the end. All these, however, do not take from the fact that the general atmosphere of the comedy is immoral, the situations frequently reminding one of similar situations in Restoration dramas. The first portion of the plot deals with Sir Charles Easy's long deception of his wife. He has been unfaithful both with Edging, her maid, and with Lady Graveairs. The famous scene when Lady Easy, finding her husband and Edging asleep on two chairs, lays her "Steinkirk" on his head lest he catch cold, leads to his final conversion. Alongside of this plot appears another, in which Lady Betty Modish, adored by Lord Morelove, amuses herself with Lord Foppington, a coarse ignorant *roué*. The atmosphere of the play as a whole is the atmosphere of the genteel drama; the moral aim is largely extraneous and seems to us to-day unnaturally forced. *The Careless Husband*, it is to be observed, was a brilliant success in its own time, mostly because of the character of Lady Betty Modish, written for and acted by Mrs Oldfield[2].

Moral in aim, likewise, is *The Lady's Last Stake, or, The Wife's Resentment* (H.[1] Dec. 1707). "A Play," declares Cibber in the dedication, "without a just Moral, is a poor and mercenary Undertaking." Again we get the intrigue and the gallantries of the Restoration drama alongside of the usual sentimental sentences and the unnatural close. Lord Wronglove here is the sinner, and his wife, unlike Lady Easy, is jealous. A divorce is prevented only through the offices of a *deus ex machina* in the shape of Sir Friendly Moral, who causes a reconciliation. Beside this theme appears the gayer

---

[1] Such as that already quoted, *supra*, p. 180.

[2] Jacob, p. 39, notes that it "was acted with very great Applause" and adds that "'tis reported that he had some Assistance in it from his Patron"—the Duke of Argyll—"and Mr *Manwayring*." It was translated into German as *Der sorglose Ehemann, ein Lustspiel...aus dem Englischen ...übersetzt* (Göttingen, 1750).

one in which Lord George aims at Lady Gentle, but fails, Mrs Conquest (another Oldfield part) securing him in the end. Decidedly weaker than *The Careless Husband*, and less successful, this comedy practically exists for Mrs Conquest. She it is who provides almost all the interest in the piece.

Cibber, however, is only one of those who produced comedies of a cast similar to this, some seriously sincere, some hypocritical. Mrs Centlivre gave one to the theatre in *Love at a Venture* (Bath, Grafton's men, 1706?), a play taken from *Le Galand Double*, but possibly owing its initial inspiration to Dryden's *Secret Love*. The plot is an easy one of intrigue. Belair, a wild spark, falls in love with Camilla, intrigues with Beliza, who, unknown to him, is Sir William Freelove's fiancée, and attempts also Sir William's sister, Lady Cautious. There appear, however, in the midst of this, sentences of just such a nature as are to be found in Cibber's work, and Belair's "Oh, Transport, oh, unexpected Happiness![1]" when he is united to Camilla strikes the same note of artificial hypocrisy.

A comedy of kindred nature is the anonymous *Injur'd Love; or, The Lady's Satisfaction* (D.L. April 1711)—a "plain told Tale, and home-spun Moral wrought[2]." Here, Rashlove has cast off Fidelia, his wife, along with Lucie, and marooned them on a desert island. They dress as men, and, with Thrivemore, a shipwrecked mariner, are rescued by Captain Cruize. Thrivemore loves Annabella, who had become Widow Richlove during his absence and is contemplating marriage with Rashlove. Captain Cruize also falls into the throes of love, adoring Charmilla, daughter of Rashlove and Fidelia, and by a trick puts off Young Scrape, who had been intended for her. As minor features of interest there are Sir Bookish Outside, a virtuoso, Lady Outside, Fidelia's sister, who makes love to the latter in her disguise as Ogle, and Snuffle, "an ignorant, Canting, Hypocritical Pedant." Situations such as those in III. iii carry us back directly to the Restoration; but the social problems involved in the development of the play and the moralisations scattered

[1] v. i.   [2] Prologue.

freely through the five acts make the comedy a true specimen
of the moral-immoral type, veering to sentimentalism.

The same year appeared Charles Johnson's *The Wife's
Relief: or, The Husband's Cure* (D.L. Nov. 1711), another
drama centering on a matrimonial problem. The main plot
may be summarised as follows. Riot, married to Cynthia,
tries to seduce Arabella. The two women plan together and
Arabella agrees to an assignation. Meanwhile Riot tells
Volatil, who is in love with Arabella, of his success; the two
men gamble for the assignation and Volatil wins. Cynthia
informs Riot that she took Arabella's place and he is so affected
with horror that he repents of all his evil ways. At the end of
the play we are made to believe that Volatil had been met
by the two women and himself been made ashamed of the
part he was playing. A still more serious underplot is presented
beside this. Horatio adores Aurelia; he is imprisoned for
supposedly killing Valentine, who loves Teraminta. This
tragi-comical portion is resolved happily, but with difficulty.
Humour is provided in the figures of Sir Tristram Cash,
"a humorous old Fellow," in Young Cash, "a lewd young
Fellow, endeavouring to be a Rake," and in Spitfire. There
is no question here but that the aim of the author was sentimental. In the prologue he praises as the finest writer he who

> *Is* always every thing *he represents,*
> *And* Feels *the very Characters he Paints,*

but the methods by which he secures his effect are, to say the
least, dubious. For over four acts the play might be taken for
a Restoration comedy[1].

Sentimental purpose of a like kind occurs in Thomas
Killigrew's *Chit-Chat* (D.L. Feb. 1718/9), where once more a
plot of flagrant immorality is used as a means of forcing a
moral conclusion. The theme is different, but the inter-
mingling of immorality and of moralisation is the same.
Marlove has in this play induced Moderna, who loved
Alamode, to marry Worthy. Bellamar adores Florinda,

---

[1] A great deal of the action is, of course, obviously borrowed from
Shirley's *The Gamester*. For an analysis of the relationship between the
two plays, see Genest, ii. 490–3.

Worthy's sister, but Marlove, seeking to get him for herself, tries, with the aid of Lurcher, to hinder the match. Meanwhile Bellamar discovers the Alamode-Moderna amour; and Marlove, in order to work out her own ends, causes Worthy to believe that it is Bellamar himself who is intriguing with his wife. He watches her, and discovers her in an arbour with Alamode, whereupon he casts her off and gives Florinda to Bellamar. It is noticeable that this play, like Cibber's *The Careless Husband*, was patronised by the Earl of Argyll, who by his interest caused the profits to rise above £1000[1].

Mrs Haywood's *A Wife to be Lett* (D.L. Aug. 1723) again varies the theme of forced marriages. Her Marilla has promised her father on his death bed to marry in accordance with Fairman's wishes. He settles on Toywell, a mercenary fool. In similar manner Celemena is to be married to Sneaksby, a drunken lout. Courtly and Gaylove by tricks beat off both their rivals, and the pairs of lovers are happily united. The title-plot of the play, however, is more serious. Sir Harry Beaumont loves Mrs Graspall, whom her husband sells for £2000[2]. Just at the critical moment the lover is confronted by Amadea, his former fiancée, and repentance follows. A third theme deals with the winning of the widow Stately by Jonathan Shamble, but it is purely comic. Here again aim and method seem at variance. The interest of the play lies mainly in the intrigue and assignation scenes; yet a moral sentimental conclusion is duly presented to us.

Finally, as a later example of this species of comedy, might be taken John Mottley's *The Widow Bewitch'd* (G.F. June 1730). The plot of this is even more immoral than that of any of the above-mentioned plays. Colonel Courtly loves Arabella. He had previously slighted Matilda, but begs her to aid him in his new amour. She persuades him to pay his addresses to Lady Languish, whose husband is thought dead. Arabella meanwhile feignedly gives ear to Stanza, and Free-

---

[1] Whincop, p. 255. See the attack on this play by Corinna cited above, p. 6.

[2] This portion of the plot seems taken from *Love the Leveller* (D.L. 1704).

love also pays his addresses to Lady Languish. In the end all comes right; Courtly and Arabella marry; the former, disguised as a parson, pretends to unite Stanza to Mimick and Matilda to Cocade just "to give" them "some little Taste of the Effect of that Artifice by which" they "really intended to impose upon" him; and Lady Languish discovers her long-lost husband. The sentimental and moralising note is, perhaps, not so much in evidence here as in the other dramas, but it is apparent in many scenes and is deeply stressed at the close.

The still more definitely sentimental comedies present features much the same as those visible in the plays already discussed, with the callousness and the hypocritical morality often unduly pronounced. It is here possibly unprofitable to discuss these plays according to decades or set periods as Ernest Bernbaum, for the exigencies of his particular thesis, was compelled to do. Sufficient be it to note that in each section of his survey there is to be discovered a far larger proportion of purely or mainly sentimental plays than he would allow.

Colley Cibber and Sir Richard Steele obviously call for first mention. Already in 1696 the former had succeeded in popularising the species with his *Love's Last Shift*. With *The Careless Husband* and *The Lady's Last Stake*, as we have seen, he pursued something of the same course, and in *The Non-Juror* and *The Provok'd Husband* he provided the theatre with two excellent comedies of the same type. *The Non-Juror* (D.L. Dec. 1717) is, like many of the eighteenth century semi-sentimental dramas, largely political in tone, being directed against the English and Roman Catholics. The basis, obviously, is the *Tartuffe* of Molière, taken, probably, through the adaptation of Medbourne. The plot is simple. Sir John is hoodwinked by Wolf, who has designs on Maria, though he also makes proposals to Lady Woodvil. Many attempts are made to disabuse the Knight's mind, but all efforts fail until the close of the play. The lighter side of the comedy is provided by the sprightly and affected Maria (one could easily guess, without being informed, that the character was performed by Mrs Oldfield), who is adored both by Heartly, and, in a forlorn sentimental way, by Charles. *The Non-Juror* won an immediate popularity, for, while it succeeded in estranging the Jacobite faction[1], it was welcomed hilariously by their opponents. Pamphlets for and against it rushed from the press[2], and the advertisement all meant money and fame for the author.

The Provok'd Husband; or, A Journey to London (D.L. Jan. 1727/8) has nothing of this political atmosphere, "The Design of" it "being chiefly to expose, and reform the licentious Irregularities that too often break in upon the Peace and Happiness of the married State[3]." The basis is Vanbrugh's unfinished *Journey to London*, which Cibber later printed in order to show how much of *The Provok'd Husband* was his own; but practically all the sentimental portion owes nothing to the elder writer. This sentimental portion deals with the pleasure-loving propensities of Lady Townly (acted by Mrs Oldfield). Her husband loves her, but, acting on Manly's advice, threatens a divorce. Manly himself adores Lady Grace, Lord Townly's more sober sister; and eventually among them all a happy conclusion is arrived at. The "Journey to London" part concerns the visit to the metropolis of Sir Francis Wronghead and his cheating by Count Basset. There is nothing very mawkish in the development of either theme; and the moderate

---

[1] See *Apology*, ii. 185–9.

[2] *The Theatre-Royal Turn'd into a Mountebank's Stage. In some Remarks upon Mr Cibber's Quack-Dramatical Performance, called the Non-Juror...By a Non-Juror* (1718); *A Lash for the Laureat: or an Address by Way of Satyr; Most Humbly Inscrib'd to the Unparallel'd Mr Rowe, On Occasion of a late Insolent Prologue to the Non-Juror* (1718); Joseph Gay, *A Compleat Key to the Non-Juror. Explaining the Characters in that Play, with Observations thereon* (1718); H. S. *Some Cursory Remarks on the Play Call'd The Non-Juror* (1718). Bullock's *The Per-Juror* (L.[2] 1717) was evidently designed to catch the tide of popular favour; and there is a hit at the play in Sewell's *Sir Walter Raleigh* (L.[2] 1719). *A Clue to the Comedy of the Non-Juror* (1718; re-issued the same year as *The Plot Discover'd*) is an attack on Bishop Hoadly. See also *The Comedy call'd the Non-Juror...With Remarks and a Key* (1718) and consult Miles, D. H., *The Original of the Non Juror* (*Proceed. M. L. A. Amer.* 1914).

[3] Dedication. See also *Reflections on the principal Characters in the Provoked Husband* (1728).

success of the play seems well deserved. While Cibber's moral tendency is rather oppressive in the whole of the Townly scenes, the cleverness and skill of the production makes this one of the best of early eighteenth century comedies[1].

Steele had an equally serious turn of mind. His attitude to life, indeed, his inveighing against vices to which he himself was only too grievously addicted, shows that he had the same careless mentality as that possessed by the foppish actor. In *The Funeral; Or, Grief A-la-mode* (D.L. c. Dec. 1701)[2], without indulging in the full expression of that moralisation which he was later to help in popularising, he showed the main tendencies of his art. *The Funeral* is a fair play, but it is by no means brilliant. Lady Harriot is a well-drawn figure, and Trusty, "the earliest example of a type which became familiar to the stage[3]," a novelty. The main fault of the play is that it mingles, sometimes a trifle inharmoniously, elements of the comedies of manners, of humours and of sentiment. The wit of many scenes comes from the first; the satire directed at the undertakers and at the lawyers comes from the second; and the honesty of Trusty, the true love of Lord Hardy for Lady Sharlot and that of Campley for Lady Harriot are decidedly derived from the third. The main atmosphere of the comedy, however, is not sentimental; Steele's moralising power would seem not to have wakened as yet into its full activity.

The Lying Lover: Or, The Ladies Friendship (D.L. Dec. 1703) has as its design "to banish out of Conversation all Entertainment which does not proceed from Simplicity of Mind, Good-nature, Friendship, and Honour[4]." Thus the hero, in Steele's own words, "*makes false Love, gets drunk, and kills his Man; but in the fifth Act awakes from his Debauch,*

---

[1] For an account of its performance see *supra*, p. 15. A German translation appeared as *Der erzürnde Ehemann...Aus dem Englischen übersetzt* in 1753.

[2] It was printed between Dec. 18 and Dec. 20; the music to the songs was issued between the 16th and 18th of the month. Cibber says it was acted "with more than expected Success" (*Apology*, i. 263).

[3] Ward, iii. 494. Adam in *As You Like It* and other trusty servants of the Jacobean period must not, of course, be forgotten.

[4] Dedication.

with...Compunction and Remorse[1]." While we notice here the old confusion between immoral themes and fifth act repentances, we find that in conception Steele has moved far beyond Cibber. The "*mutual Sorrow between an only Child, and a tender Father in...Distress*," he thinks, may be "*an Injury to the Rules of Comedy*[2]," but all through, this distress, and the accompanying emotional sympathy, helps to remove the play from the realms of Congreve's art.

> *That Touch within, which Nature gave*
> *For Man to Man, e'er Fortune made a Slave,*

is emphasised in the epilogue and in many sentimental scenes of the drama. Basing his work on Thomas Corneille's *Le Menteur*, the author completely transforms many of the situations of that comedy, and, as in the fifth act, moves into a sphere that is nearer tragedy than comedy proper. *The Lying Lover*, he declares, "was damn'd for its Piety[3]," although Jacob says it "met with Success[4]." It was no doubt too revolutionary for its time.

In *The Tender Husband: or, The Accomplish'd Fools* (D.L. April 1705) Steele continued on his sentimental career. Save for some older type of satire in the presentation of Bridget, the whole conduct of the plot is in this moralising style, a moralising style, however, which permits of such callousness as is apparent in the Fainlove episode. Although an infinitely duller and weaker comedy, this play was much more successful than *The Lying Lover*[5]. It would appear that Addison, besides penning the epilogue, aided Steele somewhat in the composition of the drama[6].

Steele's last play, *The Conscious Lovers*, did not come out until November 1722, at Drury Lane. It is an adaptation of Terence's *Andria*, sentimentalised out of all recognition. The favourite *bêtes noires* of the newer school are here duly attacked—the marriages of convenience, duels and the evils of the law. Love in the comedy is tender and pure; the air

---

[1] Preface.   [2] Preface.
[3] *Mr Steele's Apology for Himself and his Writings* (1714), p. 48.
[4] p. 249.   [5] Whincop, p. 290, notes its "great Success."
[6] See *Spectator*, No. 555, Sat. Dec. 6, 1712.

is positively thick with sympathy and pity and emotion; the mood of *The Lying Lover* appears again, intensified a thousand-fold. Mrs Inchbald is wrong in saying that *The Conscious Lovers* was the first play that taught an audience to think and feel at a comedy[1], but certainly it was one of the most pronounced of the early sentimental dramas. Its success, when contrasted with the comparative failure of *The Lying Lover*, may be taken as symbolising the changing tone of the age. Nor was its fame confined to England. It was translated into French by Vasse as *Les amans généreux* in 1784 and anonymously as *Les amans réservés* in 1778. A German rendering had already been published in 1752. Around it, too, revolved a wide and at times fierce pamphlet controversy. Apparently it was heavily advertised before production, and Dennis saw fit on November 2 to issue *A Defense of Sir Fopling Flutter... In which Defense is shewn, that Sir Fopling...was rightly compos'd by the Knight his Father... and that he has been barbarously and scurrilously attack'd by the Knight his Brother, in the 65th Spectator. By which it appears that the latter Knight knows nothing of the Nature of Comedy*[2]. On November 29 Benjamin Victor came to Steele's aid, and attacked an adverse notice of the play in *The Freeholders' Journal*, with *An Epistle to Sir Richard Steele, On his Play, call'd, The Conscious Lovers*. A second edition of this work followed immediately with the addition of an epilogue spoken by Mrs Oldfield and not printed with the play. About January 24, 1722/3 was issued *Remarks on a Play, call'd The Conscious Lovers, a Comedy*, written by Dennis[3], shortly after the appearance of a tract entitled *Sir Richard Steele and his New Comedy, call'd the Conscious Lovers, vindicated from the malicious Aspersions of Mr John Dennis*. As a final blast came an anonymous pamphlet entitled *The Censor Censured: or, the Conscious Lovers Examin'd...Into which Mr Dennis is introduced by way of Postscript; with some Observations on his late Remarks.*

[1] *The British Theatre*, vol. xii.
[2] On this and other pamphlets see H. G. Paul's study of *John Dennis* (1911), pp. 81 ff., and G. A. Aitken's *The Life of Richard Steele*, ii. 284.
[3] It was advertised in *The Daily Journal* for Jan. 24, in *The British Journal* for Jan. 19, and in *The Post Boy* for Jan. 26.

Sentimentalism, not quite so deeply marked it is true, is to be found in a play produced even before those of Cibber and of Steele, *The Bath, or, The Western Lass* (D.L. *c.* July 1701), written by Thomas D'Urfey, a dramatist more famed for his seventeenth century writings[1]. The main plot deals with the hopeless marriage of Sophronia and Lord Love-chace. She adores Transport, and he intrigues with Lydia, the wife of Sir Oliver Oldgame. The solution of the problems at the end, and the lie which Colonel Philip tells in order to shield his sister, Sophronia, both show that D'Urfey was continuing the sentimental strain which he had helped to introduce on to the English stage over a dozen years previously. Touches of sentimentalism, too, appear in *The Modern Prophets: Or, New Wit for a Husband* (D.L. May 1709), a play "the Theme" of which, according to the author, "was altogether a Novelty," and "Morally intended[2]." This moral aim is emphasised again in the prologue which declares that

> *We truckle with profound Humility,*
> *Presenting now a moral Comedy.*
> *And dedicate to grave religious Rulers,*
> *A piece that ridicules their Ridiculers*[3].

Of the several other sentimental plays produced within the first decade of the century, Richard Estcourt's *The Fair Example* (D.L. April 1703) holds an important place. Derived from Dancourt's *Les Bourgeoises à la Mode*, it modifies its French original quite as much as Steele did his. Part of the plot, that dealing with Mrs Fancy and Sir Charles, is obviously modelled on Congreve, but Lucia, the "fair example," and Springlove are conceived quite in the sentimental

---

[1] Whincop (p. 227) seems to be wrong in stating that this play had been acted in 1697.

[2] Epistle Dedicatory.

[3] The same author's *The Old Mode & the New, or, Country Miss with her Furbeloe* (D.L. March 1702/3) is in the older farcical Jonsonian style. Sir Fumbler Old-Mode is the only fairly well-drawn character. It may be noted that the date, 1709, given by Ebbsworth in the *Dict. of Nat. Biog.* is evidently wrong. The play has no date on the title-page; but it was printed most probably in 1704.

fashion. Estcourt's play, according to Jacob, was a success[1], possibly because of the non-sentimental portion.

Peculiarly enough, one of the chief writers of the manners school, William Burnaby, turned this same year to produce a play distinctly sentimental in conception. *Love Betray'd; or, The Agreable Disapointment* (L.[1] Feb. 1703) is an adaptation of *Twelfth Night*, borrowing some fifty lines direct from Shakespeare. The alteration is a bad one, but is interesting as proving the relationship which undoubtedly exists between the revival of attention paid to Shakespeare's romantic comedies, with their atmosphere of humour and emotion, and the development of the sentimental drama of the eighteenth century[2].

A year or two after this Mrs Centlivre took up the tale in a still more deliberate manner with *The Gamester* (L.[1] *c*. Jan. 1704/5), adopting as her field the drama of purpose, precisely as her predecessor Mrs Behn had done. In technique she obviously owes much to the work of Congreve, but her tone is the tone of Cibber and of Steele. The evils of the gambling tables are presented to us in the misfortunes which befall Valere. Angelica promises to wed him if he abandons his cards, and as an earnest presents him with her picture. Dressing as a man, she wins it from him, and his shame leads to what we are to believe is a real repentance. More than the mere plot, the language shows the moralising tendency. "You may cheat Widows," declares Hector in II. ii. "Orphans, Tradesmen, without a Blush—but a debt of Honour, Sir, must be paid." The moral feeling of the citizen class was being aroused, and, even if hypocritical, was making its presence felt in the theatre. The basis of Mrs Centlivre's drama is French, Regnard's *Le Joueur*, but the tones of the two comedies differ entirely. The outlooks of the authors are entirely at variance[3].

[1] p. 94, "acted with Applause." There are only two records of performance, S. April 10 and F. Nov. 26.
[2] For an analysis of the plays see Odell, *op. cit*. i. 81–3.
[3] See Grober, Fritz, *Das Verhältnis von Susannah Centlivres "The Gamester" zu Regnards "Le Joueur"* (1900) and Bernbaum, *op. cit.* pp. 98–9.

A drama of similar tendencies by the same author, not noted by Ernest Bernbaum, is *The Bassett-Table* (D.L. Nov. 1705). In this the atmosphere of Jonson is combined with a definite social problem. Lady Reveller is presented as a coquettish gamester beloved by the serious Lord Worthy; Sir James Courtly is the good-humoured careless gambler; Mrs Sago the merchant's wife who apes the vices of those more highly born. The contrast to the "amiable diversions" of the gamblers is shown in the rather "sober" and "religious" Lady Lucy, who, like similar characters in Cibber's plays, serves to point the moral. That *The Bassett-Table* was regarded by contemporaries as a kind of companion play to *The Gamester* becomes evident when we find the Haymarket company putting on the latter comedy evidently as a counter-attraction to the former[1].

Peculiarly enough, as is noted in Bernbaum's study, the years from 1710 to 1728 display a strange lack of purely sentimental comedies. *The Conscious Lovers* in this time assuredly carried on the style with all thoroughness, but we find fewer dramas of the type during these eighteen years than we might have expected. At the same time, it must be remembered that sentimental motives appear in fully half of the plays produced within this period and that practically all types of legitimate drama were depressed owing to the rapidly developing interest paid to pantomime and Italian opera.

Charles Johnson's *The Country Lasses, or, The Custom of the Manor* (D.L. Feb. 1714/5) is one of the important plays which Bernbaum has inadvertently omitted. "I hate London"; says Modely in I. i, "where their Pleasures, like their *Hyde-Park* Circle, move always in one Round; where Yesterday, To-day, and To-morrow, are eternally the same." The plot harmonises well with sentiments such as these. Heartwell and Modely arrive in the country and fall in love with Flora and Aura, the former a supposed daughter and the latter the real daughter of Freehold. Modely tries to rape Aura; Freehold rescues her, and she, dressing as a man, comes to fight her

---

[1] *The Gamester* was given on M. Nov. 19 at H.[1], the day before the appearance of *The Bassett-Table*.

lover in a duel, allowing Modely to fancy he has killed her.
Reappearing at the end, she puts him on probation, promising
to marry him at the close of two years. As a more comic
subplot, the devices of Lurcher, nephew to Sir John English,
are introduced. Part of the plot is clearly based on Mrs Behn's
The City Heiress, or from the source of that comedy, Middleton's *A Mad World my Masters*, but the general atmosphere
is the atmosphere of the eighteenth century.

The Artful Wife (L.[2] Dec. 1717) of William Taverner has
also a sentimental substratum. The typical "sentimental
sentences" abound here in profusion. The comedy opens
with Lord Absent's soliloquy, "How unnecessary is Thought!
What Confusion has it occasion'd! What Animosities has it
rais'd in the World![1]" passes through Lady Absent's medita-
tions, "How delightful is the Matrimonial State, when two
Minds have but one Desire!...Methinks there should be but
few bad Women, Virtue is so delightful![2]" and ends with her
husband's moralisation, "A *Title* may be bought, but Honour
must be in *Nature*, and born with a Man." The plot, too, is
interesting. Sir Francis Courtal, after having seduced Ruth,
makes attempts to secure the favours of Lady Absent and of
Lady Harriet. The former of the two ladies finds herself
neglected by her husband, not through any evil in him but
through sheer indolence on his part. Lord Absent comes across
a letter which his wife has left for Sir Francis, but is assured
by her that he shall hear all that passes between them.
Through this device the libertine is exposed, and forced to
marry Ruth. Lord Absent, for his part, realises his mistakes
and is reconciled to his wife. Obviously inspired by Cibber's
efforts, *The Artful Wife* is a fair comedy, but was not successful on the stage[3].

Two years previously had been produced a peculiar play of
John Gay's entitled *The What D'Ye Call It, A Tragi-Comi-
Pastoral Farce* (D.L. Feb. 1714/5), which may perhaps be
considered here. It is, certainly, satirical, being of an "allegorical" sort for the purpose of exposing "several of our

[1] I. i.   [2] I. ii.
[3] Jacob, p. 257.

eminent Poets[1]," and possibly ridiculing certain tendencies in
contemporary tragedy[2]. The preface likewise is satirical, but
possibly beneath the satire lies an occasional touch of seriousness. The author there undertakes to answer certain critical
objections. He defends the mingling of high and low characters
by adducing the example of Sophocles. In regard to the "*meanness of the Sentiments*," he declares "*that the Sentiments of
Princes and Clowns have not in reality that Difference which they
seem to have: their Thoughts are almost the same, and they only
differ as the same Thought is attended with a Meanness or Pomp
of Diction.*" These remarks, it would seem, have more than
a grain of seriousness in them, just as the marriage of Squire
Thomas and Kitty, the leading away of Peascod as a deserter and
the appearance before the Justices of the ghosts of slain soldiers
are not all meant to be ludicrous. In *The What D' Ye Call It*
we appear to have a counterpart to Swift's satires, folly and
wisdom, buffoonery and depth of passion, meeting in the one
work. From this point of view, Gay's fantasy may well take its
place alongside the other sentimental comedies of the age.

A posthumous comedy by the same author, *The Distress'd
Wife*, produced at Covent Garden in March 1733/4, but not
printed till 1743, presents a somewhat similar conflict of
diverse forces. The scene (III. viii) between Pert and Fetch
is thoroughly of the older immoral style; but the bundling
off of the extravagant Lady Willit and the presentment of
Uncle Barter are decidedly sentimental. The comedy as a
whole, however, has hardly sufficiently marked features to
warrant its being classed in one group or another.

Griffin's *Whig and Tory* (L.[2] Jan. 1719/20) similarly unites
in its scenes a variety of different atmospheres. Ned Indolent
and Maria, the latter of whom turns out to be the daughter
of Sir Rowland, form centres of sentimental interest, but the

---

[1] Jacob, p. 115.

[2] See *A Complete Key to the last new Farce The What D' Ye Call It.
To which is Prefix'd a Hypercritical Preface on the Nature of Burlesque, and
the Poets Design* (1715). The author of this pamphlet finds satire of *Othello,
Julius Caesar, The Distrest Mother*, several of Dryden's plays, *Venice
Preserv'd, Jane Shore, The Earl of Essex, Alcibiades* and *Cato*. It is attri-
buted to Griffin and Theophilus Cibber in the *Biographia Dramatica*.

other portion of the plot belongs by no means to the older school. Heartfree and Aminta plan to marry. For various reasons Reynard and Charlotte wish to prevent their uniting. Each of the latter pair plots to circumvent the lovers, and both end by marrying one another[1].

During this period one of the most noticeable plays has so far remained unchronicled. This is *The Drummer, or, The Haunted House* (D.L. March 1715/6) of Joseph Addison, published anonymously in 1716 and later reissued, with a long preface by Steele, in 1722. The play is a good one, although it met with but poor success in its own time[3], and that, too, in spite of the fact that Steele had praised it in *Town Talk*[4], and had gathered together a judicious audience for the first night[5]. *The Drummer* has universally been accredited one of the chief works of the sentimental school[6], and was freely translated or adapted in French and German during the eighteenth century[7]. The later appreciation of this drama and the lack of immediate contemporary success seem to prove that sentimentalism of the sincerer kind had not by any means established itself in England by 1716. A play by a well-known author, even if it had decidedly sentimental features, might succeed, but a drama by an unknown writer, presenting a wife faithful to a husband she supposes dead and a highly moralising hero, was almost bound to fail.

During the thirties of the century, on the other hand, sentimentalism in comedy seemed to gain a new lease of life.

---

[1] This theme is taken from Fletcher's *The Maid in the Mill*. W. M. Peterson (*Notes and Queries*, Jan. 1957) draws attention to the fact that Griffin's manuscript diary (British Museum, Egerton 2320) records performances which do not agree with theatrical advertisements in the newspapers.

[2] Steele's preface   [3] No. 9, Feb. 13, 1715/6.   [4] *Supra*, p. 17.

[5] Ward, iii. 439; Bernbaum, p. 123; Aitken, G. A., *The Life of Richard Steele* (1889), ii. 91–2, 270–2. See also Axon, W. E. A., *The Literary History of the Drummer* (1895).

[6] By Destouches as "*Le Tambour Nocturne*" in *Nouveau Recueil Choisi* (1733, vol. v, not acted till 1762) and Descazeaux Desgranges as *Le Prétendue Veuve ou L'Epoux Magicien* (1736); J. C. Gottsched as *Das Gespenst mit der Trummel* (in *Die deutsche Schaubühne*, 1742, vol. ii) and L. A. V. Gottsched under the same title "*Ein Lustspiel des Herrn Addisons nach dem Französischen des Herrn Destouches übersetzt*" (in *Neue Sammlung von Schauspielen*, 1764, vol. v).

Between 1721 and 1731 there is a lull in the attention paid
to the species, but from 1732 to 1738 we have a whole series
of dramas almost purely of the sentimental pattern. In point
of date Theophilus Cibber's *The Lover* (D.L. Jan. 1730/1)
is the first to call for attention. Granger is the well-known
figure of the hypocritical Puritan. He has debauched and
robbed his ward Laetitia and at the same time makes
addresses to Inanthe, the beloved of Eustace. Inanthe pretends
that she has lost all her money; Granger offers to take her into
keeping, a proposal she indignantly refuses, while Eustace,
who has been afraid to speak to her before, offers her his
hand. In the same way Eugenio, loving Harriet, departs to
a foreign land in order that he may make his fortune equal
hers. Thus were the sentimental heroes unduly sensitive
in matters of matrimonial finance. In the end all is well, and
Granger thoroughly exposed. While the hypocrite is by no
means a new character in the sentimental drama, the situations of Eugenio and Eustace seem to be the first of a series
of such repeated well on into the nineteenth century.

Ernest Bernbaum finds in this play a certain influence
of Fielding's *The Temple Beau* (G.F. 1730[1]), and certainly
more than one drama by the latter author betrays features
of the sentimental style. *The Modern Husband* (D.L. Feb.
1731/2), for example, in spite of its somewhat odious theme
and immoral situations, is full of the new spirit in the relations
between Mr and Mrs Bellamant, and the prologue strikes
a note that might have been uttered by a Cibber or a Steele:

> Tho' no loud Laugh applaud the serious Page,
> Restore the sinking Honour of the Stage!
> The Stage which was not for low Farce design'd,
> But to divert, instruct, and mend Mankind.

Along with this play of Fielding's might be numbered two
comedies of William Popple, *The Lady's Revenge: Or, The
Rover Reclaim'd* (C.G. Jan. 1733/4) and *The Double Deceit,
Or, A Cure for Jealousy* (C.G. April 1735), dramas of the
Cibber type of moral-immoral sentimental comedy. The
prologue to *The Lady's Revenge* emphasises that that play

[1] p. 145.

was intended to be of a "serious" cast. The comedy opens characteristically with a soliloquy on the "Lovely Morn" by Sir Harry Lovejoy. This does not, however, prevent the plot being presented with a freedom rarely to be found outside the Restoration period. This moralising Sir Harry has seduced Lucia and got her married off to Sir Peregrine Traffick. After her marriage he has attempted to renew his intrigue with her, but failed. Sir Peregrine, unfortunately, dies, and Lucia again succumbs to Sir Harry's charm. The libertine lover of Lucia, however, adores Angelina, has an intrigue with Betty, Angelina's maid, and succeeds in seducing Maria. Towards the end of the comedy Lady Traffick absolves him from any vow given to her; Maria is married off to Sir Lively Brainless; Betty is given to Tom, who gets a farm for taking her; and Angelina, without a word of reproach, marries Sir Harry. *The Double Deceit*, while not so immoral, presents a plot of almost equal interest. This play has a double plot. The first concerns Sir William Courtlove, who wishes his son, Young Courtlove, and his nephew, Gaylife, to marry Harriet and Fanny Richly respectively. The two young men dress as Jerry and Frank, their servants, and make the latter pose as their masters. The girls learn of the plan and change places with their maids. The two sets fall mutually in love and are married. The second plot deals with the jealousy of Bellair and Violetta's endeavour to cure him. The play is decidedly sentimental, but, be it noted, the two masters disguised as servants will not marry the maidens disguised as maids until they learn their real identity; Frank and Jerry are thoroughly cheated and believe they are securing for themselves two heiresses. Democracy was arising in these years; middle class drama was being produced; but the old class standards of the Restoration were too severe and too firmly implanted in the natures of the populace for any too revolutionary sentiments to be introduced.

Still another of the sentimental dramas of the thirties is Charles Boadens' *The Modish Couple* (D.L. Jan. 1731/2), a good comedy with a well-constructed plot, worthy of esteem in spite of Genest's epithet "dull" and Fielding's attack on it in *Pasquin* (H.[2] 1736). It would appear to have been a failure on the stage[1]. Here domestic problems form the chief interest. Lord and Lady Modely quarrel with one another, not from "any strong Passion to Pleasure, or real Aversion to one another; but a wild Affectation only of being fashionably vicious[2]." Claremont, secretly married to Clarissa, makes love to Lady Modely, and his wife does likewise to Lord Modely. The husband and wife change places at the assignations and are accordingly reconciled. The plot and characters are not new[3], but the treatment is good and the dialogue well above the average of the age.

The same year which saw the production of *The Modish Couple* witnessed the appearance of the first translation into English of a French *drame*. Destouches' *Le Mari honteux de l'être, ou, Le Philosophe marié*, produced in 1727, was one of the most important works of the Gallic sentimental movement, and John Kelly[4] did well to start with it. While he has made certain changes in minor details, the main features of the French plot are allowed to stand unaltered. Old Bellefleur has lost his money through standing surety for a friend. His son has been brought up by Odway and has secretly married Melissa. Odway, not knowing of this, plans to unite his young charge and his step-daughter. Melissa is annoyed by the addresses of Sir Harry Sprightly, and Odway cannot understand young Bellefleur's manner and actions. Reconciliation accompanies the explanation in the fifth act. *The Married Philosopher*, thus produced at Lincoln's Inn Fields in March 1732, was destined to be the forerunner of a whole series of French-inspired sentimental dramas, which eventually were to drive the cruder and more tentative type of sentimental play from the stage. The era of the *drame* may truly be said to have begun.

Kelly's effort was taken up, a few years later, by a writer of

[1] Whincop, p. 178.　　　　　　　　　　[2] II. ii.
[3] Bernbaum (p. 149) finds indebtedness in this play to Cibber's *The Careless Husband* (D.L. 1704).
[4] The translation is anonymous, but Whincop (p. 254) attributes the work to Kelly. A later rendering is to be found in Mrs Inchbald's *The Married Man* (Hay. 1789).

some importance, the Rev. James Miller. Miller had started his dramatic career with *The Humours of Oxford* (D.L. 1730), a quite unsentimental comedy, and had passed from that to an adaptation of Molière's *La Malade Imaginaire* as *The Mother-in-Law: Or, The Doctor the Disease*, a highly success- ful play acted at the Haymarket in February 1733/4. In this comedy the future tendencies of his work are to be traced in the declaration that the play contained "not...one indecent Expression, not one immoral Thought[1]," a declaration which, we must confess, was thoroughly honest and sincere. *The Man of Taste* (D.L. 1735), with its condemnation of ordinary stage fare, another adaptation from Molière, has already been noted[2], and the general moral tone of his art is intensified still more in *The Universal Passion* (D.L. Feb. 1736/7), a not very brilliant fusing of *Much Ado About Nothing* and Molière's *La Princesse d'Élide*. Here again a "strict Regard" is paid "to Decency and good Manners," the author believing that "People may be very well diverted with Exhibitions of this kind without the least Violation being offered to Virtue, Truth or Humanity, and that the world is at present happily inclin'd to support what is produced with that Intention[3]." Miller's general tendencies, therefore, led him naturally to the production of *The Coffee House* (D.L. Jan. 1737/8), an adaptation of *Le Caffé* of Rousseau. The comedy depends for its merriment on a series of "humours" not ill drawn, the coffee house scenes, with the Poet writing verses and Puzzle refusing to stay because a common player is expected, being excellently depicted. Beyond this, however, runs a vein of democratic sentiment. "If a great many Gentlemen had not marry'd Tradesmen's Daughters," declares a character in the first act, "They must have been glad to have turn'd Tradesmen themselves for a Living—provided they had Capacity enough, I mean."

Art and Nature followed at Drury Lane the next month (Feb. 1737/8). The theme seems taken mainly from Rousseau's *Le Flatteur* with suggestions from the *Arlequin Sauvage* of

---

[1] Dedication.   [2] *Supra*, p. 165.
[3] Dedication.

Delisle. Peculiarly enough, the title is the same as that of Chollet's contemporaneous *L'Art et la Nature*, a one-act piece acted in 1738. The plot is a strictly sentimental one. Truemore loves Flaminia, daughter of Sir Simon Dupe. He leaves for the Indies and introduces Courtly to Sir Simon before his departure. Courtly proves an unfaithful friend and endeavours to get Flaminia for himself. Julio is the savage of the play, and he, by his honesty and uprightness, wins the affections of Violetta. "Bless me," he cries on one occasion[1], "what a Country am I got into? What shameless Animals am I brought amongst?"—the sentiments of not only one other primitive native brought on the stages of England and the Continent during the eighteenth century.

Besides Miller, Robert Dodsley is probably the most important of the sentimentalists of the thirties[2]. After a couple of "Entertainments" printed in *A Muse in Livery*, this interesting valet, bookseller and poet produced at Covent Garden in February 1734/5 a daring little "dramatic satire" entitled *The Toy-Shop*, borrowed in conception maybe from Randolph's *The Conceited Pedlar*. The Master of the Toy-shop is the central figure, a philosophic and quixotic merchant who moralises over his goods and the prices he charges for them. The play is slight, certainly, but it has a novelty of conception and a certain broader method of looking at the world, two qualities which show the individuality of the author.

The King and the Miller of Mansfield (D.L. Jan. 1736/7) carries us even more definitely into the sphere of democratic sensibility. There is no special merit in the plot, which narrates how the King, losing his companions in a forest, is entertained incognito by the plain Miller and succeeds in making amends for the evil practices of one of his courtiers, Lord Lurewell. The value of the play lies in its evident sincerity and in the more daring of its sentiments. "Of what advantage is it now to be a King?" asks the monarch as he traverses the unknown ways of the wood. "Night shows me

---

[1] iv. iii.
[2] On this writer see the monograph by R. Straus, *Robert Dodsley, Poet, Publisher and Playwright* (1910).

no respect: I cannot see better, nor walk so well, as another man. What is a king? Is he wiser than another man?" These queries remind us of other similar queries being put then and afterwards in France, fated to be answered in deeds some half a century later. The sequel to this little play, *Sir John Cockle at Court* (D.L. Feb. 1737/8) as well as *The Blind Beggar of Bethnal Green* (D.L. April 1741) are cast in the form of ballad-operas and may fitly be left for discussion in a later chapter. The sentimental note in both is even more pronounced than in the two preceding dramatic pieces.

While not so revolutionary, a similarly marked sentimental note is to be found in Sir Hildebrand Jacob's peculiar little collection, *The Nest of Plays* (C.G. Jan. 1737/8), consisting of three short pieces, *The Prodigal Reform'd*, *The Happy Constancy* and *The Tryal of Conjugal Love*. All are deeply tinged with sensibility. In the first Old Severn succeeds by a trick in rescuing his son from licentious ways, and in the last we find an interesting variation of the often utilised theme of the *curioso impertinente*. Sir Jasper is a whimsical old man married to a young wife. He sends Belair to test her. She falls and rejoices in the consequent divorce. The treatment of the theme shows that Jacob had considered in a fairly careful and thoughtful manner a problem of married life.

In addition to the plays enumerated above, there are a few others which show elements of a definitely sentimental character. Francis Lynch's *The Independent Patriot: or, Musical Folly* (L.² Feb. 1736/7) mingles a situation of an undoubted sentimental character with satire of the Italian opera, but the dialogue is so poor that the comedy deserves no more than bare mention. More important intrinsically is Mrs Cooper's *The Rival Widows: or, Fair Libertine* (C.G. Feb. 1734/5), a play which unites rather doubtful intrigue with decidedly moral features. Here, Sir William Freelove, who gives his son a small annuity, is praised in comparison with Modern, who indulges his son in everything. The main action of the comedy concerns young Freelove's chase of Lady Bellair, a frolicsome widow with a good heart but much affectation. The last act seems based on Shirley's *Hide Park*, and the editors of the *Biographia Dramatica* hint that the idea of the whole was borrowed from St Foix. It might be suggested that Shadwell's *The Squire of Alsatia* likewise gave some inspiration to the authoress.

Peculiarly enough, when we consider the growing power of sentimentalism in the fields of prose fiction and of poetry, the forties of the century show far fewer purely sentimental comedies than do the preceding ten years. We have to remember, however, that there were many counter-attractions in the theatrical world and that sentimental motives, as has been noted above, appear in dramas of quite different categories.

In the year 1740 one Dorman published a two act play entitled *Sir Roger de Coverly: or, The Merry Christmas*[1]. This comedy is quite worthless but must be placed alongside the works of Dodsley as showing the development of the more humanitarian type of sentimental drama.

Dance's *Pamela* came out at Goodman's Fields in November of the following year[2]. This play, like some of the other sentimental dramas already noted, starts a new tradition, for it is the first dramatisation in English of a regular novel, testifying to the enormous contemporary popularity of Richardson's work. The main theme is preserved practically unaltered, but, as with most adaptations of novels on the stage, the dialogue is stilted and all the charm of the original seems to have vanished.

Between the *Pamela* of 1741 and the year 1750, there appeared only one other definitely sentimental play, a play, however, of the utmost importance, none other than Edward Moore's *The Foundling* (D.L. Feb. 1747/8)[3]. The power of sentimentalism by this date is well emphasised in the prologue written by Brooke:

[1] It is said by Whincop (p. 218) to have been acted with success at D.L. in 1746. There is record of only one performance that year.

[2] There is a puzzle concerning the authorship of two dramatic versions of *Pamela* which appeared in 1741–2: on these see the supplementary notes to Appendix C. It now seems most probable that Giffard was responsible for the play acted at Goodman's Fields.

[3] Hoadly's *The Suspicious Husband* (C.G. 1747) is not so distinctly sentimental, but will be considered in this section as exemplifying the union of sentimental and other elements.

He, like all Authors, a conforming Race!
Writes to the Taste, and Genius of the Place;
Intent to fix, and emulous to please
The Happy Sense of these politer Days,
He forms a Model of a virtuous Sort,
And gives you more of Moral than of Sport;
He rather aims to draw the melting Sigh,
Or steal the pitying Tear from Beauty's Eye;
To touch the Strings, that humanize our Kind,
Man's sweetest Strain, the Musick of the Mind.

The plot, dealing with the familiar false parentage theme, acts up well to the prologue. Fidelia is Sir Charles' daughter, but she does not know it. Her virtue in the end conquers quite the libertinism of Belmont—"And now *Fidelia*," he cries, "What you have made me, take me—a Convert to Honour! I have at last learnt, that Custom can be no authority for Vice; and however the mistaken World may judge, He who sollicits Pleasure, at the Expence of Innocence, is the Vilest of Betrayers." *The Foundling* owes its brightest parts, such as those of Rosetta and Colonel Raymond, to the inspiration of early non-sentimental comedy, but its general tone is the tone of the French *drame*. It may fitly be taken as the connecting link between the sentimentalism of the early and the sentimentalism of the late eighteenth century. It aids in bridging the gap from the times of Cibber and of Steele to those of Cumberland and of Mrs Inchbald.

Finally might be noted here Dr Benjamin Hoadly's *The Suspicious Husband* (C.G. Feb. 1746/7), a play which succeeded, partly because of its own merits, partly because of Garrick's inimitable acting of the part of Ranger. This comedy, which apparently excited a considerable amount of contemporary interest[1], has a certain sentimental tone about it, but the presentation of the character of Ranger, borrowed, it is said, from Fielding's *The Temple Beau* (G.F. 1730), is

[1] Two pamphlets appeared on it: Foote's *The Roman and English Comedy Consider'd and Compar'd. With Remarks on the Suspicious Husband* (1747) and *An Examen of the New Comedy, call'd, The Suspicious Husband ...To which is added, A Word of Advice to Mr. G--r--ck; and a Piece of Secret History* (1747). In March 1746/7 the Drury Lane company produced a farce by Charles Macklin styled *The Suspicious Husband Criticized or The Plague of Envy.*

sufficiently free. In *The Suspicious Husband* Hoadly succeeded in penning a diverting piece, full of intrigue and comic action, but read apart from the stage it appears insipid and lacking in wit. It shows the weakening of the genteel comedy inaugurated by Cibber when that genteel comedy had become transfused with sentimental emotions.

VII. *Farces*

It is a descent perilous from the attempted sublimity of the sentimental dramas to the unaffected abandon of the farcical school; but the two went together in that age and must be considered together now. Everything conspired to make this weakest form of comedy popular. The Italian operas often called for afterpieces; pantomime had to be rivalled with equal absurdity. The true wit of the comedy of manners having vanished, action came to take its place. The frequent dullness of the sentimental comedy and the excessive chill of all the Augustan tragedy cried out for something that should be thoughtless and absurd and risible.

A few of the earlier farces have already been noted, particularly those of Sir John Vanbrugh. Vanbrugh's works, indeed, are as interesting as any, for they show the descent from the wit of the comedy of manners to the trivial incident of the other school exemplified in the work of one man. During the first years of the century others besides this master of comedy attempted the type. John Corey's *The Metamorphosis: Or, The Old Lover Out-witted* (L.[1] Sept. 1704) is interesting as being announced as "Written Originally by the Famous Moliere," without a whit of borrowing from the French. Part at least of the plot, however, seems derived from Tomkis' *Albumazar*, as Whincop and Genest noted[1]. It is a fairly satisfactory farce and deserved more recognition than it actually received.

Owen Macswiny's *The Quacks, or, Love's the Physician* (D.L. March 1704/5)[2] is a similar farcical play, this time

---

[1] p. 206 and ii. 326.
[2] Genest (ii. 320) gives March 18 as the date of first acting. It was advertised for Th. 22, but seems to have been deferred. Actually, it was produced on Th. March 29. According to the title-page it was twice banned; see *supra*, p. 22.

really borrowed from a play of Molière's, *L'Amour Médecin*.
A fairly free translation, with the doctors Medley, Caudle,
Tickle, Pulse, Novice and Refugee all new, it is a laughable
and creditable production.

T. Walker's *The Wit of a Woman* was first produced at
Lincoln's Inn Fields in June of the preceding year[1]. It, too,
is well-written, with an amount of somewhat boisterous fun.
Several other similar pieces, besides the farcical works of Vanbrugh and of Farquhar, are traceable in these early years.
Cibber produced one in *The School-Boy: or, The Comical
Rivals*, a work not printed till several years later, but certainly
performed by the winter of 1702. This play is not of much
intrinsic importance, introducing as it does the well-worn
figure of a Jesuit priest and the habitual moneyless son and
stingy father of regular comedy. Rowe's *The Biter* (L.[1]
c. Nov. 1704)[2] is almost equally worthless, in spite of Genest's
praise[3]. Save for the characters of Sir Timothy Tallapoy,
"An *East-India* Merchant, very Rich...a great Affecter of
the *Chinese* Customs," and Mariana (acted respectively by
Betterton and Mrs Bracegirdle), it rises little above commonplace levels. Rowe's genius lay hardly in the realm of
farce.

Considerable uncertainty would seem to surround two
plays, *Farewel Folly: or, The Younger the Wiser...With A
Musical Interlude, call'd The Mountebank: or, The Humours
of the Fair* (1707) and *The Amorous Miser: or, The Younger
the Wiser* (1705). Genest has assumed that the play of 1707
is but a reworking by Motteux of an earlier farce of his,
acted as *Farewel Folly* but printed as *The Amorous Miser*[4].
As a matter of fact the two plays have hardly anything in
common. *The Amorous Miser* runs on the theme of the old
Pedro's desire to marry his son's fiancée and of Diego's

---

[1] It is attributed to Walker at the end of *The Cares of Love* (L.[1] 1705).
There are only two records of performance, S. June 24 and Th.
Aug. 17.
[2] It was the "last new Farce" on M. Dec. 4; Downes (p. 46) says it
ran for six nights. It was published on Dec. 5, 1704.
[3] ii. 327. Ward (iii. 433[3]) condemns.
[4] ii. 318. This follows the article in the *Biographia Dramatica*.

attempts to hoodwink him. In *Farewel Folly* the same central situation occurs—Old Holdfast and Young Holdfast being both in love with Isabella. The other characters, however, are entirely different, and there is no appearance in the earlier play of the important figure of Mimick the actor. If we may trust an advertisement in the newspapers for Tuesday, February 6, 1704/5, we may assume that *The Amorous Miser* has nothing whatever to do with Motteux[1].

Dennis is another serious writer who attempted the farcical strain in these years. In *Gibraltar: Or, The Spanish Adventure* (D.L. Feb. 1704/5) he essayed the evidently popular type, with such marked lack of success that he omitted the play from the list of his productions supplied to Jacob for *The Poetical Register*[2]. It would appear that a party was made against it. In the preface Dennis speaks of "the Calamities which attended the Rehearsal"; on the first day, he adds, it was "not suffer'd to be heard[3]."

As displaying the more burlesque elements of the farcical type there may be mentioned here the anonymous play, *The Lunatick...Dedicated to the Three Ruling B—S at the New House in L.—I.—F.* (1705), a bitter attack upon Betterton, Mrs Barry and Mrs Bracegirdle[4].

The second decade of the century took up farce with an equal enthusiasm, Mrs Centlivre proving a stalwart supporter of this species of drama as of the comedy of intrigue. *A Bickerstaff's Burying, or, Work for the Upholders* (D.L. March, 1709/10)[5] turns on the idea of an island where the spouse is buried with her husband. It has little of merit save a slight infusion of theatrical wit.

Rough farcical satire at the Tories was presented by this

---

[1] "The last new Play, call'd, Farewel Folly...is in the Press, and will be speedily publish'd. And whereas there is an Advertisement, that on Tuesday, February 6. will be publish'd, the last new Comedy, Entitul'd, The Amorous Miser...This is certifie (*sic*), That no such Comedy has ever been Acted." But see supplementary notes to Appendix C.

[2] See Jacob, p. 286. Whincop (p. 214) notes its failure.

[3] See *supra*, p. 16.

[4] *Supra*, p. 45. It was later altered as *The Female Advocates* (D.L. 1713).

[5] Whincop and the *Biographia Dramatica* give 1717 as the date of acting. It was revived at D.L. in 1715 as *The Custom of the Country*.

authoress a few years later in her unacted *The Gotham Election*
(1715)[1], a trivial play of absolutely no value whatsoever.
More important is *A Wife well Manag'd* (D.L. 1715), a one-
act farce, in which Lady Pisalto falls in love with the inevitable
Catholic priest, Father Bernardo. Don Pisalto, discovering
the intrigue, disguises himself as the Father and soundly
thrashes his wife. She in her turn makes an attack upon the
real Father[2].

Other writers, too, between 1710 and 1720 flocked to give
the theatre their similar wares, making those years truly the
years of farce in the history of the stage. Christopher Bullock,
the comedian, furbished up from suggestions in Middleton's
A Mad World my Masters a one-act play entitled *The Slip*
(L.[2] Feb. 1714/5), performed the day before Charles Johnson's
The Country Lasses, which was taken from the same Elizabethan comedy, appeared at Drury Lane[3]. It was a great
success[4], and may be credited with a fair amount of genuine
merit.

Woman's Revenge: Or, A Match in Newgate (L.[2] Oct. 1715),
taken from Betterton's *The Revenge: or, a Match in Newgate*,
itself an adaptation of Marston's *The Dutch Courtesan*, and
interesting as a kind of predecessor of *The Beggar's Opera*[5],
is a blend of pure comedy and farce, but was soon reduced
to a mere droll in *The Stroler's Pacquet* (1742).

Following this, Bullock wrote two pure farces for the
theatre, a worthless piece called *The Adventures of Half an
Hour* (L.[2] March 1715/6) and *The Cobler of Preston* (L.[2] Jan.
1715/6), the latter an adaptation of the Induction to *The
Taming of the Shrew*[6]. Once more, in this piece, Bullock was
brought into rivalry with Charles Johnson, and succeeded
where Johnson did not[7]. Possibly the latter author may have

---

[1] Later reprinted in 1737 as *The Humours of Elections.*
[2] Whincop (p. 185) gives this farce wrongly to Carey.
[3] *Supra*, p. 196.
[4] Both Jacob (p. 285) and Whincop (p. 184) note the applause given to it.
[5] See the account in *A Compleat Key to the Beggar's Opera, By Peter
Padwell of Paddington, Esq.*; printed as an appendix to the second (1728)
edition of *Woman's Revenge.*
[6] For an analysis of the plays see Odell, i. 229–30.
[7] *Supra*, p. 48.

been led into adding to his own farce after the production of the rival play; in any case, his *Cobler of Preston* is marred by a double instead of a single deception and introduces a quite unnecessary political element connected with the recent Jacobite rising.

Woman is a Riddle (L.[2] 1716), Bullock's next play, is a pure comedy of intrigue, but he was too eager for rough success to remain even at those not over-chilly heights. *The Per-Juror* (L.[2] Dec. 1717) is merely a slight skit, "performed," says Whincop[1], "in Opposition to *Cibber's The Nonjuror*." It is largely satirical and lets its lash fall heavily on the mercenary J.P.s of the time. Apparently it aroused some slight flutter of interest in its own days, for not only was it frequently reprinted, reaching a fourth edition even by 1718, but it awakened, as did so many plays then, a little newspaper controversy of its own.

Charles Johnson, whom we have thus found in rivalry with Bullock, and who was one of the most diversified of all the dramatists of the period, contributed, besides *The Cobler of Preston*, another farce in *Love in a Chest* (H.[1] May 1710), a rather trivial after-piece. Johnson's work was in the main too serious to allow him to succeed well in the lighter domains of the illegitimate sister of the Comic Muse.

Almost all of Benjamin Griffin's work, on the other hand, is farcical. *Love in a Sack* appeared at Lincoln's Inn Fields in June 1715, *The Humours of Purgatory* in April 1716, *The Masquerade: or, An Evening's Intrigue* in May 1717. The second of these is unquestionably the most interesting. The plot is based on an episode in D'Urfey's *Don Quixote*, and the character of the hypochondriac is as well worked out as the farcical form of the drama permits. The last-mentioned play too contains good types in Reveller "An humorous old Gentleman of the Town" and Ogle "An old ridiculous Lover."

Another successful writer of these flimsier dramas is Captain John Breval, who gave between 1717 and 1733

[1] p. 184.

three farces and a mock opera to the stage. *The Confederates*, issued under the pseudonym of Joseph Gay and apparently never acted, was printed in 1717[1]. Designed as a satire on *Three Hours after Marriage* (D.L. 1717), and presenting Gay, Pope, Arbuthnot, Cibber, Lintot (the publisher), Mrs Oldfield and Mrs Bicknell under their own names[2], it earned for its author dubious fame among the heroes of *The Dunciad*. The farce has little intrinsic merit, but presents interesting sidelights on the social life of the time and on the lives of the principal characters.

The Play is the Plot (D.L. Feb. 1717/8), although styled a comedy, is really a pure farce, perhaps, as Jacobs suggests[3], from a French play. The theme is a stock one—the efforts of Captain Carbine to win Fidelia from the clutches of her father, Sir Barnaby Bindover—but its real merit lies in the mock tragedy introduced into the fifth act. From the last two acts the author or another later formed a farce, *The Strolers* (D.L. July 1723), and the original play was utilised also for *The Mock Countess* (D.L. April 1733).

Three Hours after Marriage (D.L. Jan. 1716/7), which, as has been noted above, gave rise to the satirical farce of *The Confederates*, was apparently the joint venture of Arbuthnot, Pope and Gay, although printed under the name of the last-mentioned only. To the ill-success of this piece attention has been drawn already[4]. Judged fairly, it is seen to have not a little merit, but its coarseness is certainly unworthy of the hands of the three *littérateurs* who brought it into being; one might have expected more from such a mighty triumvirate. What offended the age most was, no doubt, the personal satire. Fossile is evidently Dr Woodward, Professor of

---

[1] Whincop (p. 182) attributes it to Breval, as does the list appended to Cibber's *Apology* (1750). Jacob (p. 289) marks it as anonymous.

[2] The frontispiece shows Arbuthnot in Highland dress, Pope as an insignificant little man, and Gay with a fool's cap.

[3] p. 284.

[4] *Supra*, p. 14. See also Jacob, p. 115, and Whincop, p. 238, who both note its immorality. In 1717 there appeared *A Letter to Mr. John Gay, concerning his late Farce, entituled, A Comedy* and *A Complete Key to the New Farce, call'd Three Hours after Marriage*. The first is subscribed "Sir Timothy Drub" and the second "E. Parker, Philomath."

Gresham College[1], Clinket as evidently the Countess of Winchelsea. The Countess of Hippo Kekoana is the Duchess of Monmouth, and Sir Tremendous is, of course, John Dennis. The fathering of Clinket's play by Plotwell is said to be a hit at Cibber[2]. With this piece the way towards *The Dunciad* was being opened.

Previous to this, Gay alone had written *The Mohocks. A Tragi-Comical Farce* (1712)[3], another satirical piece dedicated "to Mr. D***" (Dennis), because the "Subject of it is *Horrid* and *Tremendous*." It seems to attack definitely *Appius and Virginia* (D.L. 1709). Again its interest lies rather in its pictures of the time than in intrinsic value. The peculiar *The What D'Ye Call It* (D.L. 1715) has been noted among the sentimental plays; but here might be mentioned *The Rehearsal at Goatham* (1754), taken from the story of Gines de Passamonte in Cervantes and designed with an aim similar to that of Mrs Centlivre's play.

While farce always remained popular on the stage, the actual penning of new pieces seems to have fallen off in the twenties of the century, partly because of other attractions, chief among which, at any rate after 1728, must be accounted the ballad-opera. W. R. Chetwood thus started with farcical works, *The Stock-Jobbers* (1720) and *South-Sea; or, The Biters Bit* (1720), the latter a satirical picture of a year famous in English financial history, and passed on in 1729 to produce operas modelled on Gay's plan.

Charles Molloy's *The Half-Pay Officers* (L.[2] Jan. 1719/20) should be noted here. Presenting a peculiar fusion of episodes, characters and speeches from *Henry V*, *Much Ado About Nothing* and *Love and Honour*, it yet develops its theme in a fairly interesting manner. The author's object seems to have been to provide a play for Mrs Fryar, who, when she acted Widow Rich in it, was upwards of 85 years of age[4].

---

[1] For this and other identifications see *A Complete Key* mentioned in the note above. There Fossile is given as "Dr. W—d—d" which a MS. note in the British Museum copy elucidates.

[2] See also the letter already noted (*supra*, p. 14).

[3] The dedication is signed W. B. The attribution to Gay appears in Whincop, p. 239.   [4] See preface and Genest, iii. 37.

Intrigue of a sort enters into Moses Browne's *All Bedevil'd:
or, The House in a Hurry* (private performance, 1723), a one-
act farce presenting the typical lovers in Faithful and Clara,
the typical rival in Sir Humphry Grub, and the typical rascal
in Dick Grub—a work calling for hardly any detailed attention. So, too, Thomas Odell's *The Smugglers* (H.[2] May 1729),
a farcical comedy, depending for its effect mainly on oddities
of dialect and national behaviour, may be readily dismissed.

With Fielding's *The Letter-Writers: Or, a New Way to
Keep A Wife at Home* (H.[2] March 1731), it might have
appeared that a new era of farce was opening up in the
theatres. But *The Letter-Writers* stands almost alone in
Fielding's dramatic productivity. He has many other plays
which he styles by the name of farces, but these are either
ballad-operas or burlesques The pure farce, as here, he was
not again to indulge in. Of all eighteenth century farces,
Fielding's is perhaps the best; the idea of the threatening
letters is a clever one, and Commons and Rakel are vigorously
drawn types.

Much poorer is Philip Bennet's *The Beau's Adventures*
(1733), a play that depends for its merriment on the fact that
Whimsical, who loves Lucy, takes upon himself the name of
No-body and gives great confusion to honest and worthy-
minded people thereby. Thomas Cooke's *The Eunuch, or,
The Darby Captain* (D.L. May 1737) is more interestingly
written. It is, as the title shows, an adaptation of Terence's
Eunuchus, with a few suggestions from the *Miles Gloriosus* of
Plautus. Poor rough rustic farce of a kindred quality may be
discovered likewise in E. Dower's *The Salopian Esquire*
(1739).

After the decay of ballad-opera in the late thirties of the
century farce again seems to have revived a trifle. John Kelly's
The Levee (1741)[1] is a quite fair two act satire of a nobleman's
patronage, and the anonymous "moral drama," *Bickerstaff's
Unburied Dead* (L.[2] Jan. 1742/3) presents an interesting scene
in act II with the figure of Virtuoso. Thomas Sheridan's
The Brave Irishman: or, Captain O'Blunder (G.F. Jan.

---

[1] It was attributed to Kelly by Whincop (p. 254).

1745/6)[1], taken mainly from *Monsieur de Pourceaugnac*, won likewise a success on the stage and has fair merits. Like this originally Irish in origin, we find John Cunningham's *Love in a Mist* (Dublin, 1747), with a hackneyed plot of a girl's attempts to capture a wayward lover. More interest attaches to John Stevens' *The Modern Wife; or, The Virgin her own Rival* (G.F. April, 1745)[2], which reminds us of the Restoration productions of Ravenscroft and of Tate.

Lethe (D.L. April 1740) and *Miss in her Teens* (C.G. Jan. 1746/7) were David Garrick's two contributions to this type of dramatic literature before 1750. The first is an entertaining satire which introduces a number of contemporary characters each of whom explains to Æsop his special idiosyncrasies[3]. *Miss in her Teens* is a still more brilliant piece, the basis of which is to be found in Dancourt's *La Parisienne*[4]. The characters presented have more vitality than is commonly apparent in farcical figures, and the dialogue, although without the depth of true wit, has a sparkle and verve which speaks highly of Garrick's genius.

Finally, in this section might be noted the drolls contained in *The Stroler's Pacquet Open'd* (1742), typical pieces performed at Bartholomew Fair and by strolling companies in provincial towns. The importance of the stages at the Fairs is well known; even the best comedians played there, and the influence of the droll tradition is certainly to be traced in the productions of men like Bullock and Griffin.

This section of our study, then, has been a section of descent. Farce we find helping to drive legitimate comedy from the stage, partly by usurping the place of that legitimate comedy, partly by turning the minds of the dramatists to the producing of popular, profitable, if slight and trivial, after-

---

[1] This work was originally produced in Dublin in 1737.

[2] Whincop (p. 291) is wrong in saying this was unacted.

[3] On the versions of this piece see Appendix C. Garrick expanded the farce in 1777 when he was asked to read a play before the King. In this version the character of a Jew is introduced for the first time; it has so far remained unprinted. The manuscript was formerly in the possession of the late Sir Israel Gollancz.

[4] For Garrick's indebtedness to Baker's *Tunbridge-Walks* (D.L. 1703) see *supra*, p. 175.

pieces. This farce, as has been evident, was fed from two
sources, from a debasing of the comedy of intrigue and the
comedy of Molière and from the "droll" tradition. Through
theatrical exigencies it was made necessary in order that one-
act after-pieces might be provided for opera and for tragedy.
The combination of causes led towards the enthronement of
farce instead of comedy, just as similar causes led towards
the debasing of tragedy and the cultivation of dramatic forms
which in themselves betrayed clear signs of degeneration and
decay.

CHAPTER IV

MISCELLANEOUS FORMS OF DRAMA

I. *Introductory*

THE preliminary study of tragedy and of comedy, and particularly the final glance at the arising and flourishing of farce, prepares the way for a consideration of those hybrid forms of dramatic productivity which filled the eighteenth century stage. Farce and sentiment, allied to the influence of the opera, inevitably gave rise to the ballad-opera of Gay and his successors. The desire for show and for spectacle, combined with the still prevalent love of artificialised heroic elements, produced the furore for the Italian opera. Some of the same tendencies, combined with the influence of the *commedia dell' arte*, aided in popularising pantomime. The frequent disgust felt by contemporaries at one or another of these forms, or at the dullness of the Augustan tragedy, gave rise to the many "rehearsals" and burlesques, which connect the original *Rehearsal* of Buckingham with *The Critic* of Sheridan.

It would have been impossible to deal satisfactorily with these various types of drama in the chapters devoted to tragedy and to comedy proper; a more adequate treatment seems obtainable only by banishing the motley crew to a chapter of its own. At the same time, it is to be observed that there are among these harlequinade elements not a few productions of sterling value, and that there are included here types of drama which in themselves are in no wise to be despised. Opera represents probably one of the highest forms of dramatic art, where the powers of music, painting, poetry, dancing and interpretation meet on one common ground. Through this very fact, however, that opera is so high a form, the pitiful operas of the eighteenth century seem the more debased. The sight of Hydaspes struggling sonorously with the lion, or that of the effeminate heroes tearing their passion into soprano shreds, could hardly awaken in us overmuch enthusiasm. It is to be noted, too, that in this chapter has been treated a series of quite normal dramatic types. Tragi-comedy and pastoral have thus been segregated from the positions they might otherwise have held, because they also in a way exhibit features which have something in common rather with the degenerating tendencies of the time than with the normal progress of tragedy or of comedy.

In dealing with all of these, and particularly in speaking of the degeneration of the age, that process of degeneration must carefully be distinguished from the decadent movement visible in the drama from 1610 to 1642. Then, the decay lay in the presentation of tragic themes, in the obsession on the part of the dramatists in unnatural sex relationships, in the debased social and moral ideals of the time. None, or little, of this is to be traced in the degeneracy of the drama from 1700 to 1750. The decay lay rather in the reaction to classical chill as expressed in burlesque and farce, and in the confusion between sentimental and other motives in comedy It lay, that is to say, in the lack of a dominant purpose and faith in any form of drama. England, like the rest of Europe, was passing through a chaos of conflicting ideals; it was between the throes of the death of the world that had been and the throes of the birth of the world that was to be. Lillo and Steele point forward to the future, but other dramatists can only vaguely remember the past. The degeneration, therefore, is not the degeneration of a great period falling into the sere and yellow leaf, but the degeneration of taste due to a complexity of standards and of aims. There is nothing decadent about the early eighteenth century drama, as there had been about the drama in the first half of the seventeenth century. In spite of the weakness in actual fulfilment, the age is full of motives and ideals which were later to be perfected by dramatists of the nineteenth and twentieth centuries.

II. *Tragi-Comedies and Pastorals*

Concerning tragi-comedy, English criticism was peculiarly inconsistent. Fundamentally, of course, the strict application of the pseudo-Aristotelian unity of action opposed it entirely, condemning it as a monstrosity. There were many men, however, who, with Dryden, preferred to make an appeal to nature and recognised the type as permissible, if not distinctly to be recommended, and there were others who, noticing the success of older tragi-comedies on the stage, were prepared to sacrifice neo-classic dignity to popular taste. The special type of tragi-comedy which is exemplified in many heroic dramas of the period 1663 to 1679 did not seize upon the pathos-loving or classical playwrights with any great strength; but sporadic attempts were made by a number of men to form plays which united comic with tragic elements—rarely, be it confessed, with any sort of success. Later, the impress of the sentimental school gave rise to a number of "comedies" so serious that they can hardly be classed among the productions of the laughing Muse. In all, there are barely a dozen of both types all told, and the weakness of most of them warrants no more than cursory treatment here.

The year 1700 saw the production of at least two, Gildon's *Measure for Measure: Or, Beauty the Best Advocate* (L.[1] *c*. Feb. 1699/1700) and Mrs Centlivre's *The Perjur'd Husband, or, The Adventures of Venice* (D.L. *c*. Oct. 1700). The first is, as the title indicates, merely a reworking of Shakespeare's play, with a few additional elements taken from D'Avenant's *The Law against Lovers*[1]. It is a fantastic production, including a series of "Entertainments of Musick," introducing, too, caves and witches and wizards and sailors and Tritons and Nereids and shepherds and shepherdesses and nymphs. The whole concludes satisfactorily enough with "*The Grand Dance.*" *The Perjur'd Husband* is slightly more interesting as being an attempt to reproduce something of the older style of tragi-comedy in an original manner. There is a

---

[1] For an analysis of the play see Genest iii. 221–3 and Odell i. 72–5.

definitely tragic plot here run alongside one that is of almost equal importance and as definitely comic. The first is not well motived and the climax is too sudden. Up to the last act, in spite of Bassino's treachery to Placentia, it is not evident that an unhappy conclusion is approaching. The second portion deals mainly with Lady Pizalto, who makes assignations with Ludovico. The latter dresses as Lucy and is discovered. Lucy herself is bribed by Pizalto, but, after obtaining from him a thousand pistoles, cheats him in the end. The play fails because of an ill-conceived union of diverse elements.

Vanbrugh's *The False Friend* (D.L. 1702), a play which might be included among the tragi-comedies, has already been noticed[1]. At about the same date appeared a similar play, *Love the Leveller: or, The Pretty Purchase* (D.L. Jan. 1703/4), written by one who signs himself G.B., and apparently a success[2]. Noticeable here is the low-comedy element of Count Festolin, Dewcraft and Sordico, the last-mentioned an interestingly novel character, which runs parallel with a more serious portion. Apart from the figure of Sordico the play is worthless and ridiculous. Genest has well censured the foolish anachronism of placing chocolate-houses, as well as persons such as Sir Thomas and Lord Pickerup, in ancient Egyptian realms[3]. It might be observed that in the comic part of this play there is a decided infusion of sentimentalism, Dewcraft being thoroughly converted by the virtue of Sordico's wife.

Save for a purely religious "Dramatick Entertainment" styled *The Pilgrims* (1701), an entirely negligible piece, no serious dramas or definite unions of tragic and comic elements appeared for some years after 1704. In 1712, however, Charles Johnson, ever seeking for new dramatic media, produced *The Successful Pyrate* (D.L. Nov. 1712), a "Play" as he styled it, following the practice of Southerne. The scene is Madagascar, and there we are introduced to Zaida, daughter of Aureng-Zebe, and the pirate king Arviragus, a character

---

[1] *Supra*, p. 150. [2] *To the Reader*.
[3] ii. 298.

taken from the real figure of Captain Avery and obviously suggested by Carlell's *Arviragus and Philicia*. The surroundings of these persons are, as might be surmised, thoroughly heroic, the pirate king making his rapine sound "heroically great"; but again there is to be found alongside of them a "Mobb," consisting of Herring, Porpoise, Shark and Codshead, a group who provide for the play a considerable comic element. The tendencies of this work seem to have given some offence to various worthies of the latter part of the reign of Anne, and Dennis went so far as to pen a letter " *To the Master of the Revels. Writ upon the first acting of a Play call'd, The Successful Pyrate*[1]," in which he inveighed against the author's "making a Tarpawlin and a Swabber...the Hero of a Tragedy."

Likewise styled " A Play," *Double Falshood: or, The Distrest Lovers* (D.L. Dec. 1727) is interesting, because it was printed as "written Originally by W. Shakespeare; And now Revised and Adapted to the Stage By Mr. Theobald." There is no question now about its Shakespearian associations; even in its own time scholars were quick to see that Shakespeare's hand was nowhere apparent, but there is no reason to doubt that Theobald, as he states, had come into possession of a manuscript of an early seventeenth century drama, written, conjectures Farmer, by Shirley, or by Massinger, according to the conception of Malone. In the preface to the play Theobald informs us that there were extant in his time no less than three manuscripts, one being a copy in the handwriting of Downes and once the property of Betterton. The statement is valuable as showing the strength of the playhouse traditions in the early eighteenth century. This tragi-comedy was successful on the stage, not only in its own time, but in later years as well.

Three years later appeared Thomas Walker's *The Fate of Villany* (G.F. Feb. 1729/30), a poor and unconvincing drama. The plot is an exceedingly improbable one. Ramirez is a villain. Sebastian marries Victoria secretly, but the king of Arragon falls in love with her. Sebastian is banished and

---

[1] *Original Letters* (1721), pp. 194–6.

Ramirez brings word of his death. Victoria is then forced to marry the king. Rinaldo, a prisoner, turns out to be the father of Sebastian and of Carlos, who is really Bellamante dressed as a man. In the end the king relinquishes Victoria and espouses Bellamante instead. The influence of the Beaumont and Fletcher plays is here evident.

Thomas Cooke's *The Triumphs of Love and Honour* (D.L. Aug. 1731) has something of the same romantic atmosphere, the theme again one of love and resignation. It hardly deserves more than a brief mention[1]. Written, like this, in three acts is also Lillo's *Marina...Taken from Pericles Prince of Tyre* (C.G. Aug. 1738)[2], a reworking of the Shakespearian play. It is to be observed that the brothel scenes are retained here in almost their full entirety. The sentimental dramatists of the time were not over squeamish in their tastes.

From those plays which have been noted, it is obvious that the Beaumont and Fletcher romance, as well as the commoner union of tragic and comic elements in drama, was attracting the minds of several men in this age, in spite of all neo-classical strictures. Quite possibly, these " plays " are to be connected with the rising of the serious sentimental comedy and of the bourgeois tragedy.

Along with these plays, too, go a few others, either of a more pastoral character or of a more poetic form. Thus Croxall, "a Gentleman-Commoner of Oxford," produced in 1720 what evidently proved a highly popular closet-drama, *The Fair Circassian*, wrought out of the Song of Solomon, and Thomas Delamayne in 1742 similarly made from Virgil's *Æneid* "A Dramatick Poem" entitled *Love and Honour*. Neither of these, obviously, was intended for the stage. Most of the pastoral plays, on the other hand, were written for production in the theatre, and took a quite definite place in the development of the drama[3]. Translations of the

---

[1] Noticeable, however, are the *Considerations on the Stage* appended to the play. These deal mainly with *Lear*, *The Squire of Alsatia* and *Rosamond*.

[2] For an analysis of the play see Genest iii. 562–7 and Odell i. 257–9.

[3] For a full survey of this type in the eighteenth century see Marks, Jeanette, *English Pastoral Drama* (1908).

regular Italian plays and original productions are plentifully scattered throughout the fifty years. In 1726 P. B. Du Bois issued a rather lame prose rendering of Tasso as *L'Aminta, Di Torquato Tasso, Favola Boscherecchia Tasso's Aminta, A Pastoral Comedy, In Italian and English*. William Ayre's more delicate verse translation followed in 1737. *Il Pastor Fido* was turned into an opera by Rossi and performed at the Haymarket in 1712. Daniel Bellamy's few *Pastoral Dialogues* (1722) from the same source may be neglected, but the re-rendering of Fanshawe's *The Faithful Shepherd* of 1736 must take its place in the history of pastoralism in English drama. Other translations from the Italian operas will be noted hereafter.

The rendering of these Italian pastorals moves parallel with the composition of more original plays and operas. To the same tradition belong many of the numerous "masques" of this period, which, however, must be considered by themselves. In the spring of 1703 was produced at Lincoln's Inn Fields *The Fickle Shepherdess*, an anonymous reworking of Randolph's *Amyntas*, "play'd all by Women." It is noticeable for hardly anything save the Mad Song sung in act II by Mrs Bracegirdle:

> Hast, give me Wings and let me fly,
> That I may mount the starry Sky,
> And there, of all the Gods enquire
> How I may squench my fierce Desire:
> See where the charming Nymph does lie,
> Oh! Give her to me, or I die.
> I'll mount above and Rescue my Sire,
> And I'll tumble the Tyrant down,
> He shall not dare to Embrace my Fair,
> Tho' grac'd with th' Imperial Crown.
> See! See! *Neptune* with his watry Train,
> Come, come, ye Tritons, come all around,
> Come plunge me in the watery Main,
> And all my Flames Confound—

a poem which seems a far-off echo of Blake's more famous verses.

A few years later was issued Tony Aston's *The Coy Shep-*

herdess (T.R. Dublin, *c.* 1709), later revised and presented at Tunbridge Wells about 1712 as *Pastora: or, The Coy Shepherdess*. Written in fairly smooth verse, the play is interesting as having been conceived in Ireland and later acted by a band of provincial players. Beyond noting Gay's *Dione* (1720), a fair piece taken from the Marcella tale in *Don Quixote*, there is probably no need to burden this account with further details of the pastoral convention in the later years of the period. While the popularity of the type is testified in regular dramas, in operas and in masques, it is to be confessed that the general level of workmanship in the pastoral form is undoubtedly poorer and weaker than is that even in contemporary tragedy and comedy.

III. *Italian and English Operas*

Even more important for a study of the stage between 1700 and 1750 is the opera, of the Italian, English or English-Italian species. Opera, as has been noted, was growing in popularity in the last years of the Restoration age. Purcell had succeeded in popularising his own type of "dramatic opera" with prose or blank verse dialogue breaking into song; but even in the late seventeenth century had been witnessed a regular French production, with recitative and aria, the *Ariane ou le Mariage de Bacchus* performed by the Royal Academy of Music. The hint suggested by this piece, however, was not to be taken up until the early years of the eighteenth century. The way had to be gradually prepared for the fuller development of the opera in England, first by the increasing number of songs permitted into regular tragedy and comedy, secondly by the growing popularity of English dramatic opera, and thirdly, in the late nineties of the seventeenth century, by the introduction on the concert platform or on the stage of French and Italian singers who gave excerpts from musical productions in their own tongues[1].

[1] The literature of the opera is fairly large. The following is a selection of works specially devoted to the history of the species in the years 1700–1750: Burney, Dr C., *A General History of Music, from the Earliest Ages to the Present Period* (1789, vol. iv); Hawkins, Sir John, *The General History of the Science and Practice of Music* (1776); Myers, C. L., *Opera in*

The story of the actual introduction of the Italian type of opera on the English stage is one at once glorious and inglorious. All through the years 1700 to 1704 it was obvious from the "Singing and Dancing" given before and after and in the midst of almost every play, as well as from the repeated performances of the operatic *Macbeth* and *Tempest* and *The Prophetess*, that the time was ripe for the introduction of something new. We are quite prepared, therefore, for the production of *Arsinoe, Queen of Cyprus*, a joint work of Pierre Antoine Motteux, Thomas Clayton, Nicolino Haym and Charles Dieupart, on January 16, 1704/5 at Drury Lane. For his source Motteux, who was mainly concerned with the preparation of the libretto, chose Tomaso Stanzani's *Arsinoe. Drama per Musica*, originally set by Petronio Franceschini and produced at the Teatro Formagliari at Bologna in 1677. Sung entirely in English, it was an immediate success, for, in spite of the fact that the author of *A Comparison of the French and Italian Musick and Operas* (1709)[1] thought it "little deserved the Name of an Opera" and had "nothing in it but a few Sketches of antiquated *Italian* Airs," it ran no less than fourteen times during the first season, beat even that record by seventeen performances during 1705–6, and continued its popularity for many years in face of countless rival attractions.

This tentative experiment of *Arsinoe* soon led the way to further developments. On April 9, 1705 Vanbrugh and Congreve opened their new house in the Haymarket, producing there within a short time a pastoral opera composed, according to the author of *A Comparison*[2], "by *Gia - - - o Gr - - - r* (i.e.

England, 1656–1728 (1908); Fassini, Sesto, *Gli Albori del Melodramma Italiano a Londra* (*Giornale Storico*, vol. lx, p. 340 ff.; published as a separate thesis 1914); Nicoll, A., *Italian Opera in England. The First Five Years* (*Anglia*, xxxiv). Noticeable, also, are two MSS. in the British Museum, one compiled by F. Colman and covering the years 1712 to 1728 (Add. MS. 11,258) and another, a list of *Dramas of Italian Opera* (Burn. 521 B). On the foreign singers, see Burney, *op. cit*. iv. 195. He notes the presence of an Italian lady at York Buildings on Jan. 10, 1692/3, of Signor Tosti at Charles-street, Covent Garden on April 3, 1693, and at York Buildings on Oct. 26, 1693, and for several weeks thereafter. In 1698 there was a special concert of Italian music.

[1] p. 65.   [2] p. 66.

Giacomo Greber), a *German*," and, according to Downes[1], "perform'd by a new Set of Singers, Arriv'd from *Italy:* (the worst that e'er came from thence) for it lasted but 5 Days, and they being lik'd but indifferently by the Gentry; they in a little time marcht back to their own Country." To this opera Cibber gives the title *The Triumphs of Love*[2], but it seems to have been performed on Tuesday, April 24, 1705 as "The Loves of Argasto" and the title-page to the printed text reads *The Loves of Ergasto. A Pastoral. Represented at the Opening of the Queen's Theatre.*

By this time there were many discussions concerning the new species, discussions which gave point to Dennis' *An Essay on the Opera's After the Italian Manner, which are about to be Establish'd on the English Stage: With some Reflections on the Damage which they may bring to the Publick* (1706), a tract in which the author strives to defend the Purcell type of opera against the Italian. Not any amount of critical stricture, however, could stifle the novelty. On Thursday, March 7, 1706 at the Haymarket Theatre "was perform'd, an Opera, call'd *The Temple of Love*; consisting of Singing and Dancing: The Singing Compos'd by Monsieur *Sidgeon*: The Version into *English*, by Monsieur *Moteux* from the *Italian*[3]." Downes' attempt at spelling the composer's name is obviously a phonetic one, the music being by Gioseppe Saggione, whose wife, Maria Gallia, took a principal part in the production. The Italian source of this work has remained untraced; it was evidently not a success[4].

Meanwhile, the Drury Lane company, feeling the necessity for some attractions to counteract the novelties at the Haymarket, produced *Camilla*, a faithful rendering of *Il Trionfo di Camilla, Regina de' Volsci. Drama per Musica*, a *melodramma* by Silvio Stampiglia published at Naples in 1696. The music of Marcantonio Buononcini was, on the testimony of the author of *A Comparison*[5], "prepared for the *English*

---

[1] p. 48.   [2] Which Burney confuses with Motteux' later work.
[3] Downes, p. 48.
[4] Downes says it ran for six days. The only record apart from the one given above is for S. March 16.
[5] p. 66.

Stage by *N - - - o Ha - - - m*" (i.e. Nicolino Haym). From the agreement printed later in this volume[1], the libretto is seen to be due to one Northman and to Motteux. The epilogue emphasises the attempt on the part of the actors to provide counter attractions for the public. Referring to the abortive attempt to unite the two playhouses, it declares that the reigning monarch

> Left 'em free,....New Theatres to Build.
> And see what Fruits from Our Divisions spring,
> Both Houses now Italian Musick sing...
> But this We know, had that dire Union been,
> You ne'er in England had Camilla seen.
> They wou'd some Masque have shewn, or Country Farce:
> Paris's Judgment, or the Loves of Mars....
> To please this Audience, we'll no Charges spare,
> But chearfully maintain a Vig'rous War.

In their effort they seem to have been successful. *Camilla* was performed nine times before the actors left for Dorset Garden and twice at the latter theatre. During the following season (1706–7) it was performed no less than twenty-one times in all, and was promptly revived in November 1707, when the theatres reopened.

In the meantime, Addison, fired with thoughts of patriotism and gain, essayed to pen a purely English opera "after the Italian Manner," styling his result *Rosamond* (D.L. March 1706/7) and securing the services of Clayton as composer. *Rosamond* was a dismal failure; barely it "struggled through, and mounted the Stage, on purpose to frighten all *Englana* with its abominable Musick[2]." We may, it seems, assume that this music was the chief reason of its non-success, for Jacob has a note to the same effect—"Being very ill set to Musick, it had not the Success due to its Merit[3]."

More successful was *Thomyris, Queen of Scythia* (D.L. April 1707), the production of Motteux, apparently original[4], set to airs of Scarlatti and Buononcini by Pepusch and Agos-

---

[1] See Appendix B.
[2] *A Comparison*, p. 68.   [3] p. 3.
[4] The *Tomiri* published at Venice in 1680 has nothing to do with Motteux' libretto.

tino Steffani[1]. This opera, which likewise received the condemnation of the author of *A Comparison*, ran for six nights
in the first season, and was given eleven times during that of
1707–8.

Within the next few months several other attempts were
made to establish the *genre* even more firmly on English soil.
Motteux was responsible once more for *Love's Triumph*
(H.[1] Feb. 1707/8), a translation of *La Pastorella* by
Cardinal Ottoboni, with music by Cesarini Giovannini del
Violone and Francisco Gasparini. According to the author
of *A Comparison*, the idea of translating it came first from
"Signior *Val - - - no's* (i.e. Valentino Urbani) Head[2]." It was
not quite so successful as the former production. Macswiny
next took up the tale with *Pyrrhus and Demetrius* (H.[1] Dec.
1708), largely adapted from Adriano Morselli's *Pirro e
Demetrio* (Venice, 1690), a fairly popular production. By
this time a movement was being made towards the introduction of opera entirely sung in Italian. Even now some of
the singers took their parts in that language and were answered
by others in English[3]. After the appearance of *Clotilda*
(H.[1] March 1708/9), "prepared," says the author of *A Comparison*[4], "by the same *Swiss* Count that had the Management
of *Thomyris*[5]," there was produced at the Haymarket the
first completely Italian opera, *Almahide* (Jan. 1709/10) with
music composed probably by Buononcini. It proved a
success, and at once established the Italian form on the
English stage. It were needless to carry the history of this
type much further. *Hydaspes*, with music by Francesco
Mancini, appeared formally on Thursday, March 23,
1709/10[6], and *Etearco*, composed by Buononcini, followed

---

[1] See *Harmonicon* (1832), p. 123.   [2] p. 72.
[3] See *The Spectator*, No. 18, Wednesday, March 21, 1710/11.
[4] p. 79.
[5] This piece seems a hash from many composers. The author of the
libretto is unknown. It has been suggested that this *Clotilda* may be
derived from a similarly named *dramma per musica* by G. B. Neri, mentioned
in Salvioli's *Bibl. univers. del teatro italiano* (1894), p. 793. The "*Swiss*
Count" was John James Heidegger, who had lately arrived in England.

[6] There were semi-public rehearsals on Th. March 2 and M. 6. The
opera was advertised first for March 14, but was deferred till the 16th,
and then to the 23rd. It had a fair success.

on Wednesday, January 10, 1710/11. Within a month Händel was destined to flutter English theatre-goers with the production of *Rinaldo* (H.[1] Feb. 1710/11) and thereafter the progress of the Italian opera lay largely in his hands. All the aristocratic society of London flocked to the fashionable divertisement, so that when "The Queen being lately return'd to S. James's from Windsor, and recover'd from her late dangerous illnesse, had a withdrawing Room on Tuesdays ...ye opera dayes" were "alter'd to Thursday There being no Opera Wednesday nor Fridays in Lent[1]." Only serious political disturbance could shake their devotion to this "darling folly." Thus there was "No Opera performed since ye 23 July" 1715 to October 31, "ye Rebellion of ye Tories and Papists being ye cause—ye King and Court not liking to go into such Crowds these troublesome times[2]."

There is no need to stress the importance of this Italian opera for a true appreciation of eighteenth century stage history. Not only was the opera one of the favourite amusements of the better-class spectators, but its influence is to be traced in many ways on the ordinary dramatic literature of the time. The regular dramatists and the regular actors were, quite naturally, jealous of its success, and satire of the Italian singers with their nonsense rimes and their tremendous salaries, as well as satire of the French terpsichoreans who accompanied them on the stage, literally appears everywhere in Augustan literature from *The Spectator* and *The Dunciad*[3] to the full-fledged farcical burlesques performed in the playhouses. To present here even the dramatic satire would be wholly impossible, but a selection of the comments of contemporaries may not be out of place as revealing at once the weaknesses of this form in the eighteenth century and the impression it made upon the men and women of the time. Steele presents a very early criticism of the recitative and aria when he makes Trim sing his money out of Campley in II. i of *The Funeral* (D.L. 1701). This, it will be noted,

---

[1] B.M. Add. MS. 11,258, folio 23 recto, under date 1713/4.
[2] *Id.* folio 27 verso.
[3] See particularly iv. 45-9.

ante-dates the production of opera "in the Italian manner" upon the English stage. With the actual appearance of *Arsinoe* and of *Camilla*, naturally, the satire becomes almost universal. The author of the epilogue to Steele's *The Tender Husband* (D.L. 1705) indulged in a little patriotic appeal,

> *Britons*, who constant War, with factious Rage, ⎫
> For Liberty against each other wage,   ⎬
> From Foreign Insult save the *English* Stage. ⎭
> No more th' *Italian* squaling Tribe admit,
> In Tongues unknown; 'tis Popery in Wit.

This satire of the "Tongues unknown" is a common one. "And pray, what are your Town Diversions?" asks Baker in *Tunbridge-Walks*[1], "To hear a Parcel of *Italian* Eunuchs, like so many Cats, squawll out somewhat you don't understand." "What hear you now?" inquires Nickum in Corey's *The Metamorphosis* (L.[1] 1704), and Sir Credulous telling him that it is "A Squawl somewhat like Singing" he exclaims "That's an *Italian* Singer, mightily in Vogue at a Consort in *York-Buildings*[2]." Cibber, too, was mightily contemptuous. His references to the Italians in *The Rival Fools* (D.L. 1709) have been quoted above[3]; and his epilogue to *The Careless Husband* (D.L. 1704) shows well the uneasiness felt in the breasts of English actors:

> *We're still in Fears (as you of late from* France)
> *Of the Despotick Power of Song, and Dance:*
> *For while Subscription, like a Tyrant Reigns,* ⎫
> *Nature's Neglected, and the* Stage *in Chains,* ⎬
> *And* English *Actors Slaves to swell the* Frenchmans *Gains.* ⎭

His contempt is still further expressed in the epilogue to *The Double Gallant* (H.[1] 1707) where he declares that

> *His Groveling Sense*, Italian *Air, shall Crown,*
> *And then, he's sure, ev'n Nonsense will go down.*

The references to "song" and "France" and "dance"— which by the way were found as good rimes for couplets as they had been in the Restoration period—abound in the first decade. We find them in the epilogue to Charles Boyle's

---

[1] I. i.   [2] I. i.   [3] *Supra*, p. 163.

As You Find It (L.[1] 1703) and in a modified form in Addison's prologue to Smith's *Phaedra and Hippolitus* (H.[1] 1707):

> Long has a Race of Heroes fill'd the Stage,
> That rant by Note, and through the Gamut rage;
> In Songs and Airs express their martial Fire,
> Combate in Trills, and in a Feuge expire;
> While lull'd by Sound, and undisturb'd by **Wit**,
> Calm and Serene you indolently sit;
> And from the dull Fatigue of Thinking free,
> Hear the facetious Fiddles Repartie:
> Our Home-spun Authors must forsake the Field,
> And Shakespear to the soft Scarlatti yield.

Many were the writers who found that they could not please the audience

> Without Song or Dance,
> Without Italian Airs, or Steps from France[1].

Nor did the satire cease after the opera had fully established itself. The prologue to Havard's *King Charles the First* (L.[2] 1737) declares that

> Our Bard, as then, despises Song and Dance,
> The Notes of Italy, and Jigs of France.

Moore Smythe proclaims that "the Composers of our Opera's scorn to call in the Assistance of good Poetry, that they may show how the Science of Musick can shine by it self[2]"; Fielding hits at the Italian singers in *Pasquin* (H.[2] 1736) and the same author makes Goddess Nonsense choose Signior Opera for her own in *The Author's Farce* (H.[2] 1730). The chorus is universal: the author to please, according to one,

> ought to have a song or dance,
> The tune from Italy, the caper France[3];

another gives advice,

> Let your Sounds have Sense,
> Old England will with English Throats dispense,
> And take what's well design'd, for Excellence...
> Ev'n France in That her Liberty maintains;
> Her Songs, at least, are free from Foreign Chains,
> And Peers and Peasants sing their Native Strains[4];

[1] Taverner's *The Maid the Mistress* (D.L. 1708), prologue.
[2] *The Rival Modes* (D.L. 1727), I. i.
[3] Dodsley's *The Toy-Shop* (C.G. 1735), epilogue.
[4] Cibber, *Love in a Riddle* (D.L. 1729), prologue.

All were agreed that nonsense lived in this form of drama[1].

Satire, however, was by no means the only method whereby the authors of the time strove to ruin the Italians. All through the fifty years there were sporadic attempts made, first to revive an interest in English "dramatic opera" after the Purcell model, and secondly, to pen purely English operas "after the Italian manner." An early example of the second class has already been noted in Addison's *Rosamond* (D.L. 1707).

The older type of dramatic opera never quite died away, but it never succeeded in attracting audiences accustomed to the recitative and aria of the Italian type. Oldmixon produced one at Drury Lane about February 1699/1700, *The Grove, or, Love's Paradice*, with music by Daniel Purcell. It seems to have been originally designed as a pastoral but "in the three last Acts, the Dignity of the Characters rais'd it into the form of a Tragedy[2]." It is a fairly good specimen of its class. Thomas D'Urfey's *Wonders in the Sun: or, The Kingdom of the Birds* (H.[1] April 1706)[3] is an interesting effort at a type of comic opera, the music to which was composed by Draghi, Eccles and Lully. The action of the Daemon of Socrates and the two visitors reminds one strongly of Virgil in Dante's epic, and there are suggestions in it which take us close to Swift's *Gulliver's Travels* of later years[4]. In spite of its novelty it was a dismal failure on the stage[5]. Another seventeenth century writer, Elkanah Settle, tried his hand at opera during the early years of this period. *The Virgin*

[1] In addition to the above, the following satirical remarks all contain some matter of interest: Cibber's *The Lady's Last Stake* (H.[1] 1707), III. i; Miller's *The Universal Passion* (D.L. 1737), epilogue; Addison's *Rosamond* (D.L. 1707), verses by Tickell; the same author's *Cato* (D.L. 1713), prologue by Pope; the anonymous *Contre temps* (1727); Gay's *Polly* (1729), introduction; Martyn's *Timoleon* (D.L. 1730), prologue; Ayres' *Sancho at Court* (1742), III; Miller's *The Coffee-House* (D.L. 1738), I. ii; Welsted's *The Dissembled Wanton* (L.[2] 1726), I. i; and Lynch's *The Independent Patriot* (L.[2] 1737). Satire of Mdlle de l'Epine will be found in Wilkinson's *Vice Reclaim'd* (D.L. 1703), prologue, and in *The Amorous Miser* (D.L. 1705). Farinelli's salary is attacked in Carey's *The Honest Yorkshire-Man* (G.F. 1735).   [2] Preface.
[3] Not 1710 as Whincop (p. 127) gives it.
[4] Particularly the High-Flyers and the Low-Flyers.
[5] Downes (p. 50) says that it did not cover half of the expenses.

Prophetess: or, The Fate of Troy appeared at Drury Lane in
May 1701, at a time when its author was in a state of high
unpopularity. It is a highly scenical piece, which seems to
have met with no success[1]. In *The Lady's Triumph. A Comi-
Dramatic Opera* (L.[2] March 1717/18) Settle made an attempt
to follow the tradition started by D'Urfey, but with little
success. The hey-day of his prime was long over. He had
been reduced to writing for the booths at Bartholomew Fair
and acting in them, and "shared the misfortune of several
other gentlemen to survive" all his "numerous poetical
issue[2]." The anonymous *Alarbas* (1709), written "By a
Gentleman of Quality" is of the same type. Its preface, in
which we find the complaint that the "Opera-Theatre" is
"wholly taken up with *Italian* Airs, and the other totally
excluding the Musical Part," shows clearly that this was
designed in opposition to the *Arsinoes* and the *Camillas* of the
time. Although there are attempts at emotion and at the
delineation of character in it, this work must on the whole be
accounted a failure. The triumph of this form of opera in the
age, a form which needs little comment, is *The British Enchanters; or, No Magick like Love* (H.[1] Feb. 1705/6) by
George Granville, Lord Lansdowne. The preface declaims
against recitative and declares that the non-aria portion of
an opera should be "pronounced," not sung. Granville has
obviously remembered here his seventeenth century work in
the heroic school, and his opera has about it some of the
strength which occasionally clings to the heroic tragedy.
Particularly noticeable in the play are the stage directions,
which display well the love of swift action and scenic effect.
In II. i, for example, we get the following:

Fight again, Arcalaus *still retreating 'till off the Stage. Instruments of Horrour are heard under Ground, and in the Air. Monsters
and Daemons rise from under the Stage, whilst others fly down
from above, crossing to and fro in Confusion: Clashing of Swords
behind the Scenes: Thunder and Lightning, during which Time the
Stage is darken'd. On the sudden a Flourish of all the Musick
succeeds, the Sky clears, and the Scene changes to a pleasant Prospect.*

[1] The later droll, acted as late as 1747, was taken from this work.
[2] *The Briton*, Feb. 19, 1723/4

In such wise did the upholders of English dramatic opera attempt to win away men's fancies from the Italian type.

More numerous are the operas "after the Italian Manner," many authors endeavouring, and usually with equal failure, to follow Addison's attempt. The preface to *Rosamond* is directed against the opera in Italian, and most of the other authors of English opera proclaim with him their desire to purge the stage of inanity and nonsense. Hughes, in putting forward his *Calypso and Telemachus* (H.[1] May 1712) prefaced it with a note declaring that his work was "*an Essay for the Improvement of Theatrical Musick in the* English *Language, after the Model of the* Italians." The author recognises willingly enough the merit of Italian music but sees equal beauty in the English tongue and determines that both might be welded together. Some of the lyrics in this opera are good, but as a whole the work does not deserve overmuch praise. A similar preface is prefixed to Lewis Theobald's *The Rape of Proserpine* (L.[1] 1727), a kind of union between opera after the Italian manner and pantomime. The dedication decides that there are "many essential Requisites still wanting" in the Italian type. The author inveighs against the foreign tongue and against the high salaries paid to the performers, high salaries which forbad the managers to provide adequate scenic effects. Daniel Bellamy, too, made an attempt in this style, in his production at a private school of *Love Triumphant: or, The Rival Goddesses* (Easter, 1722), described as a pastoral opera and largely inspired by Congreve's *The Judgment of Paris* (D.G. 1701). As *The Rape of Proserpine* lay between the pantomime and the opera, so this lies between the opera and the masque.

Probably the most important contributions to this type are the two operas of Henry Carey. *Amelia. A New English Opera...After the Italian Manner* appeared at the Haymarket in March 1732[1]. This is a sort of adaptation of Beaumont and Fletcher romantic tragi-comedy to the realm of opera and is on the whole a fairly successful piece of work. *Tera-*

---

[1] The music was composed by J. F. Lampe. The libretto is attributed to Carey by Whincop (p. 184).

minta came out at Lincoln's Inn Fields in November of the same year. Again the influence of the Beaumont and Fletcher school is apparent, although the tone is more pastoral than was that of *Amelia*.

Others followed along the same lines. John Gay attempted the species in *Acis and Galatea* (L.[2] March 1731), adopting a story from Ovid's *Metamorphoses* and securing Händel to compose the music. This is undoubtedly one of the best of these productions and was met with a certain amount of applause in the theatre[1]. Less important intrinsically is the anonymous *Apollo and Daphne* (1734), a pitiful production as a whole although containing some rather pleasant lyrics. The same criticism might be passed on D'Urfey's earlier work, *Ariadne: or, The Triumph of Bacchus* published in his collection of *New Opera's, with Comical Stories, and Poems* (1721). Lediard's *Britannia* (H.[2] Nov. 1732) shows the English opera, again "after the Italian Manner," adapted to patriotic motives, the object of the work being to show in allegorical wise "the Glory and the Happiness of *Great Britain*[2]." J. Lockman's *Rosalinda* (Hickford's Room, Jan. 1739/40), with music by J. C. Smith, is more after the style of Carey's *Amelia* and *Teraminta* but possesses not even the occasional beauty of verse apparent in these operas. Of a kindred character is Dr Arne's *Don Saverio* (1750) with its distinctly romantic theme.

As a whole those who attempted to provide for the theatre something which might take the place of Italian opera failed dismally in their efforts. To have been successful, a fine free lyric power would have been necessary, and that the age lamentably lacked. There was no Metastasio among them to reveal the true beauty of the English tongue, and the Italian opera proceeded on its path of glory almost unchecked. There were others, however, who essayed consciously and unconsciously the task of defeating the Italians by providing

---

[1] Gay included in it verses by Dryden, Pope and Hughes. The popularity of the work is attested by Lockman in his preface to *Rosalinda* (Hickford's Room, 1740).

[2] The music was composed by J. F. Lampe.

a counter-attraction of a different kind, and herein there lay a certain amount of success. What the English serious opera "after the Italian Manner" could not do, the ballad-opera did.

IV. *The Ballad-Operas*

It is but a step from this serious opera to that peculiarly eighteenth century production, the ballad-opera or ballad-farce or comic opera, call it what we will[1]. This form of drama did not spring into popularity until after the extraordinary triumph of Gay's *The Beggar's Opera* in 1728. Its period of greatest success was between 1729 and 1738, during which time it almost ousted the regular comedies and tragedies from the stage. Written usually in one, two or at most three acts, these ballad-operas, ordinarily composed of airs accompanied by prose, blank verse or rime[2], adopted nearly all the species of comic invention from farce to sentimentalism and Arcadian refinement. In a way, this ballad-

---

[1] The type received a considerable variety of names in its own day; "Opera" (Coffey's *The Devil to Pay*, D.L. 1731, *The Female Parson*, H.[2] 1730 and *The Boarding-School*, D.L. 1733, the anonymous *Momus turn'd Fabulist*, L.[2] 1729, Chetwood's *The Lover's Opera*, D.L. 1729, the anonymous *Flora*, L.[2] 1729, Gay's *Achilles*, C.G. 1733, Lillo's *Silvia*, L.[2] 1730, and Gataker's *The Jealous Clown*, G.F. 1730), "Comic Opera" (the anonymous *The Jovial Crew*, D.L. 1731), "Opera-Comedy" (Ayres' *Sancho at Court*, 1742), "Farcical Opera" (Coffey's *The Merry Cobler*, D.L. 1735), "Ballad-Opera" (Colley Cibber's *Damon and Phillida*, H.[2] 1729, and Freeman's *The Downfal of Bribery*, 1733), "Burlesque Opera" (Carey's *The Dragon of Wantley*, C.G. 1737), "Tragi-Comi-Farcical Ballad-Opera" (Chetwood's *The Generous Free-Mason*, H.[2] 1730), "Tragi-Comi-Operatic Pastoral Farce" (Drury's *The Rival Milliners*, H.[2] 1736), "Tragi-Comi-Pastoral Farcical Opera" (Hawker's *The Wedding*, L.[2] 1729), "Histori-Tragi-Comi-Ballad-Opera" (Aston's *The Restauration of King Charles II*, 1732), "Comic Masque" (*Roger and Joan*, C.G. 1739), "Comedy" (Fielding's *The Mock Doctor*, D.L. 1732), "Farce" (Fielding's *The Lottery*, D.L. 1732), "Interlude" (Carey's *Nancy*, C.G. 1739), "Dramatic Piece" (Miller's *The Coffee-House*, D.L. 1738), "Musical Entertainment" (Mendez' *The Chaplet*, D.L. 1749), and "Dramatic Fable" (Miller's *An Hospital for Fools*, D.L. 1739). Whincop commonly styles them all merely Comedies or Farces; Genest prefers the term Ballad Farce.

[2] Blank verse and rime appear only in pastorals or burlesques. Thus the former is the medium of Theophilus Cibber's *Damon and Phillida* (D.L. 1732) and of Carey's *Nancy* (C.G. 1739); rime that of Mendez' *The Chaplet* (D.L. 1749), Drury's *The Rival Milliners* (H.[2] 1736) and Kelly's *The Plot* (D.L. 1735).

opera harmonised with the contemporary musical *drames* and *comédies à ariettes* of France, although pure farce dominated over the English species far more than it did in the similar productions of Paris[1]. A few plays, such as those of Dodsley and of Arthur, might retain a high sentimental atmosphere, and a very few French musical comedies might be translated into English, but such facts cannot be stretched to imply that the ballad-opera as a whole had any decided tendency, one way or another. If it was anything at all, it was satirical and burlesque in tone, Breval, Gay, Carey, Drury and Fielding all employing the species to ridicule various forms of tragedy and of serious opera, and countless authors from the time of Gay onwards having their satiric hits at the follies of people of quality and of statesmen in power.

The ballad-opera in itself is a perfectly normal development of previous English drama. It has already been seen how airs and songs were being introduced into regular comedy and tragedy, so that

> *Shakespear's* sublime in vain entic'd the Throng,
> Without the Charm of *Purcel's* Syren Song[2].

The Restoration period had come very near to discovering the ballad-opera in *The Triumphant Widow* of the Duke of Newcastle[3], but just failed to catch that essential form which charmed the audiences of 1730. The popularity of the species in the eighteenth century is to be explained by the facts that serious opera had thoroughly accustomed men's minds to the musical drama, and that both this serious opera and the pseudo-classical tragedy presented many features eminently ridiculous and fit for satirical treatment. Comedy, too, had by that time degenerated considerably from the heights it had held when Etherege and Congreve wrote. Disintegrating elements everywhere were at work; so that we may explain the development of the ballad-opera as a perfectly regular development of those comedies and farces which had intro-

---

[1] On the French *drame* and its relationship with the English types, see Gaiffe, F., *Le Drame en France au xviii⁴ Siècle* (Paris, 1910).

[2] Granville's *The Jew of Venice* (L.[1] 1701), epilogue.

[3] See vol. i (1660–1700), p. 215.

duced songs into the midst of the dialogue, fostered by the decay of the true comic spirit, by the desire to emulate the success of the Italian opera and by the prevalence of burlesque and satirical motives.

The entire ballad-opera activity may conveniently be divided into a series of species or groups. There are satirical ballad-operas; there are pure burlesques; there are farces; there are sentimental dramas; and there are pastorals. That is to say, the ballad-opera, while it provided a new technical form, a new medium, for the writers, did not at the same time provide a fresh atmosphere distinct from the ordinary tones of regular comedy and farce. It is evident, therefore, that in any consideration of the respective popularity of the various types of Jonsonian, Congrevian and sentimental drama, the musical ballad-opera must be taken into account. As is obvious, the initial impetus given to the species was in the satiric strain. Gay's *The Beggar's Opera* (L.² Jan. 1728) was recognised by contemporaries at once as an attack, veiled in farcical forms, at the Walpole government. The managers of Drury Lane, with what some said was characteristic stupidity, had refused it as a worthless piece of work, but John Rich, evidently a more far-sighted individual, divined its merit and put it on the stage. Its success was nothing less than triumphant. Particularly since the revival of this work at the Lyric Theatre, Hammersmith (1919–1923), the story of its original inception and of its first magnificent run has become well-known. The witty airs, the frank realism added to fantastic settings, the obvious political hits, all contributed towards making it a glorious success. The gallant Don Juanism in Macheath, the slightly sentimental note in Polly, the jealous motives in Lucy, the rough humours in Peachum and his wife were realised even then as being masterpieces. While we may recognise that the ballad-opera is not one of the highest forms of dramatic art, we must admit that *The Beggar's Opera* is an almost perfect specimen of its type, with nothing inharmonious in the whole production. This "Newgate pastoral," possibly suggested to the author by Swift, is perfectly consistent with itself, and the author has conjured

the audience into that "willing suspension of disbelief" no
less than Coleridge has done for his tales of diablerie. Not
so much perhaps can be said for Gay's later production. It
has been pointed out already how, in *The Mohocks* (1712)
and *The What D'Ye Call It* (D.L. 1715), he had been moving
towards the elaboration of this peculiar operatic form, but
once it was achieved he seems to have been incapable of
carrying on his own creation. *Polly: An Opera. Being the
Second Part of the Beggar's Opera* appeared in print in 1729.
Its composition would seem to have been started immediately
after *The Beggar's Opera* had proved itself on the Lincoln's
Inn Fields stage, but Walpole, burning under the light but
stinging lash of the earlier play, saw fit to have it banned.
It was printed by subscription and brought to the author
exactly double the amount he had received for his first opera[1].
It is readily recognisable that *Polly* has nothing of the charm
that lies in *The Beggar's Opera*. The characters have changed,
and, with them, the entire atmosphere of the work. Macheath,
disguised as a negro, is no longer the gallant scapegrace he
was in London. He is cowardly and mean. Polly, too, is
less interesting, and the introduction of the "noble savage"
in Cawwawkee seems artificial and forced. In place of a
witty, coarse satire with plenty of personal reference, we are
confronted with a more general satire which does not ring
so true. In place of a frank "Newgate pastoral," we have

---

[1] £800 seems to have been the sum (*Notes and Queries*, 1st series,
i. 178). Spence (ed. Singer, 1858, p. 162) appears to have been exaggerating
when he stated that the amount received was £1100 or £1200. The
story of the Duchess of Queensberry's ardent soliciting of subscriptions
is told in Hervey's *Memoirs* i. 120–1. A very readable and compact outline
of the history of this work is given by Oswald Doughty in his edition
of the play (1922). On both ballad-operas *The Life of Mr. John Gay,
author of the Beggar's Opera, &c.* (1733) might be consulted. See also
Schulz, W. E., *Gay's Beggar's Opera: Its context, history, and influence*
(1923). On *The Beggar's Opera* and its airs, *John Gay's Singspiele mit
Einleitung und Anmerkungen. Neu herausgegeben von G. Sarrazin* (Weimar,
1898); *Zwei Opera-Burlesken aus der Rokokozeit. Zum ersten Mal mit der
Musik neu herausgegeben...von Georgy Calmus* (Berlin, 1912); and
A. E. H. Swaen's *The Airs and Tunes of John Gay's Beggar's Opera*
(*Anglia* xliii. 1919) might be consulted. D. H. Stevens has an interesting
essay on the after-effects of this ballad opera in *The Manly Anniversary
Studies*.

before us a confusion between a realistic drama and an artificial sentimental comedy. *Polly* is manifestly an afterthought.

Gay's only other attempt in the type of drama which he had thus popularised was a kind of burlesque, *Achilles* (C.G. Feb. 1732/3). In it Achilles is taken into the household of Lycomedes and reveals to Deidamia that he is a man. Lycomedes falls in love with him as a woman, and in the end he is discovered by Ulysses. This work seems partly a burlesque of classical story, partly a satire of political and personal application[1].

Immediately after the success of *The Beggar's Opera*, a number of writers hurried to pen plays of a similar tendency, most of them being either plain comic situations reworked in the new style, or else satiric burlesques of one kind or another. Thus Henry Carey, who had written and published a farce called *The Contrivances* in 1715, hurried to refurbish up his older work, and so succeeded in getting it acted as a ballad-opera in 1729. It is an ordinary farcical production, and as such is well done, but it hardly deserves lengthy mention. This first hurried effort of Carey's was destined to bear later fruit in the burlesque *Chrononhotonthologos* (H.[2] 1734) and in the sentimental *Nancy* (C.G. 1739).

Other dramatists were equally wide awake to the possibilities of the type. W. R. Chetwood's *The Lover's Opera* appeared at Drury Lane in May 1729. Based on the threadbare theme of severe parents and intriguing children, it obviously owes its direct inspiration to Gay's work[2]. The most noticeable element in it is the satire of the Quakers in the person of Aminadab Prim, an element which, it has been suggested, Chetwood took from Mrs Centlivre's *A Bold Stroke for a Wife* (L.[2] 1718). This ballad-opera Chetwood followed with *The Generous Free-Mason: Or, The Constant Lady. With the Humours of Squire Noodle, and his Man*

---

[1] See *Achilles Dissected: Being a Compleat Key of the Political Characters in that new Ballad Opera, written by the late Mr. Gay. An Account of the Plan upon which it was founded. With Remarks upon the Whole. By Mr. Burnet* (1733). This is said to have been written by Guthry.

[2] See the Preface.

Doodle (H.[2] Dec. 1730)[1], again a work of farcical tendencies, written in a mixture of blank verse, rime and prose. The plot is a fantastic one. Sebastian, a free-mason, runs away with Maria, but is captured by Mirza. The King of Tunis falls in love with Maria and his Queen with Sebastian. As Mirza is a free-mason he contrives the escape of the lovers. Alongside of this runs a low comedy theme wherein Old Moody attempts to marry his daughter Cœlia to Squire Noodle. She eventually succeeds in uniting herself to her sweetheart Cleremont[2]. Altogether this is one of the best ballad-operas of these years.

In May 1729, at Lincoln's Inn Fields likewise, appeared Essex Hawker's *The Wedding....With an Hudibrastick Skimmington*, the overture and incidental music to which were provided by Pepusch. Purely farcical, with its characters of Rako, Pear-tree and Razoir, "a *French* Barber," it warrants little commendation, but fits in its place in the farcical development of this type.

More important is *The Village Opera* (D.L. Feb. 1728/9) of Charles Johnson. Johnson was ever ready to take advantage of current fashions in the theatrical world, and as soon as any he seems to have appreciated to the full the opportunities presented by the success of Gay's triumph. Again a theme of dominating parents is employed. Rosella is destined for Freeman, but he, loving Betty her maid (who turns out to be the daughter of a wealthy Mr Bloom), contrives to get her married to her beloved, Heartwell. The plot is given a slight turn of originality in that Brush counterfeits to be Freeman and the real Freeman is consequently treated as an impostor. The whole play, although farcical, has decided sentimental features. It proved a great success, both in its original form and in the alteration by Bickerstaff as *Love in a Village* (C.G. 1762). Peculiarly enough, Johnson made no other efforts in this species of dramatic composition.

[1] Whincop (p. 192) states that it was given only at Bartholomew Fair: it was originally produced there in Aug. 1730 but was soon taken over into the regular theatres.

[2] The influence of the Beaumont and Fletcher romantic tragi-comedy is evident in this play. The name Doodle is probably taken from the earlier Pompey Doodle.

Thomas Odell's *The Patron: Or, The Statesman's Opera* (H.[2] May 1729) is more satirical in tone. Here Betty, pretending to be the wife of Merit, goes to the house of Lord Falcon, "a Minister of State" and secures for Merit, who is "a Gentleman outdone by depending on Lord *Falcon*," a patent for £400 a year. Fairly coarse, and in its coarseness recalling Restoration licence, it evidently is nearer in spirit to *The Beggar's Opera* than any of the other works noted above. Its success, however, does not appear to have been what the author would have wished[1].

More prolific in this type of drama proved Charles Coffey. *The Beggar's Wedding. A New Opera. As it is Acted at the Theatre in Dublin, with great Applause* was issued in 1729 and later, as cut down to one act and performed at Drury Lane in July 1729, under the title of *Phebe; or, The Beggars Wedding*. It was also played the same year at the Little Theatre in the Haymarket[2]. The theme of mistaken offspring is in this the central motive. Phebe is considered to be the daughter of Quorum and Hunter the son of Chaunter. The errors consequent on this double mistake, all complicated by the actions of Chaunter, who is king of the beggars, fill out a not too well-developed plot.

The Female Parson: or, Beau in the Sudds (H.[2]) appeared in April 1730, but saw only a couple of performances[3]. A strange admixture of vulgarity and sentimentalism, it tells how Lady Quibus, married to Sir Quibble Quibus, loves Captain Noble, who in the end is transformed as in the Cibberian comedy to an honest and pure young man, causing the lady to cry in the usual artificial strain "Ha! what do I hear! so sudden and so blest a Reformation![4]"

The Devil to Pay; or, The Wives Metamorphos'd (D.L. Aug. 1731), taken from Jevon's *The Devil of a Wife*, and evidently due partly to the activities of Mottley, proved more popular. Whincop[5] says the author's benefit was not till

---

[1] See *Biographia Dramatica*.
[2] See Genest iii. 236; and lists in Appendix C.
[3] See the *Biographia Dramatica* and Appendix C.
[4] II. iii.
[5] p. 199.

the thirty-third night, but that then he cleared fully £700. It was "oftener acted than any one Piece on the Stage," he thought. In 1732, because of some offence given to the Nonconformists, it was cut down from three acts to one by Theophilus Cibber, and continued on its career with a new lease of life. Davenport Adams chronicles an adaptation of it performed at Niblo's Garden, New York, as *The Basket-Maker's Wife*, as late as December 1852.

From D'Urfey's *Love for Money: or, The Boarding School*, Coffey next took *The Boarding-School: Or, The Sham Captain* (D.L. Jan. 1732/3), billed by the actors as *The Boarding School Romps*, but this proved less successful, even although Miss Raftor was applauded as Jenny.

The Merry Cobler: or, The Second Part of The Devil to Pay (D.L. May 1735) was obviously an endeavour to recatch popular favour. Here Sir John is presented as attempting an intrigue with Nell, and Jobson retaliating on Lady Loverule. Possibly the theme was repugnant to an audience filled with ideas of the rights of Quality, for it was "acted...one Night, in the Year 1735, with no Applause[1]."

This, save for an unimportant play, *The Devil upon Two Sticks: Or, The Country Beau* (D.L. April 1729), closed Coffey's career. His record is a peculiar one of success and failure; possibly it may be taken as indicative of the difficulties presented by the ballad-opera as a type. Here, as in regular comedy and tragedy, more than mere journeyman-work was required to ensure permanent success.

Meanwhile others of various calibre had attempted works in the same style. T. Walker, the original actor of Macheath, seems to have been the author of *The Quaker's Opera* given at Southwark Fair in 1728, a poor adaptation of a farce of 1725 styled *The Prison-Breaker*. The author of *Momus turn'd Fabulist: or, Vulcan's Wedding* (L.[2] Dec. 1729) has been conjectured to be one Ebeneezer Forrest. This ballad-opera is confessedly based on "a *French* Farce," which is to be identified as *Momus, Fabuliste, ou Les Noces de Vulcain*, a one-act piece by Fuzelier, acted with immense success in

---

[1] Whincop, p. 200.

1719. The English adaptation appears to have been equally popular[1].

In December 1730, Thomas Gataker's *The Jealous Clown: or, The Lucky Mistake* appeared at Goodman's Fields. It is but a poor farce on a threadbare theme which introduces such stock characters as Sir Timothy Gripe, a usurer; Love-well, a gallant hero; Leonora, the miser's daughter, and a theatrical clown.

With these years, however, other more important writers had taken up the writing of ballad-operas. Of these un-doubtedly the most talented was Henry Fielding, who had already made for himself a name as an author of comedies and of burlesques. His work in *The Beggar's Opera* style began with *The Welsh Opera: or, The Grey Mare the Better Horse* (H.[2] April 1731)[2], a farcical piece concentrating upon the loves of Robin and Sweetissa, who nearly are separated because of the forged letters left by Squire Owen. *The Lottery* (D.L. Jan. 1731/2) is probably even better. The character of Cloe, who comes to town proud in the possession of the £10,000 which, she feels sure, will be hers through her lottery-ticket, is one well-drawn and developed. Deservedly *The Lottery* was a great contemporary success. *The Mock Doctor. Or The Dumb Lady Cur'd* (D.L. June, 1732), adapted from Molière, was equally popular, and again the characterisa-tion of one of the figures, Gregory, rises above the usual level of such performances. In this play Miss Raftor acted the part of Dorcas with her usual vivacity and spirit. *The Intriguing Chambermaid* followed at Drury Lane in January 1733/4. Regnard's *Le Retour Imprévu* (1700) was here the source of the play, and the witty treatment of the theme makes Fielding's play gayer and more sprightly than the French original. *The Intriguing Chambermaid* scored another

---

[1] See *Biographia Dramatica*.

[2] This was "revised" for the performance on May 26. On Saturday, June 5, 1731, it was advertised that the whole was being lengthened into *The Grub-Street Opera*. Two editions of this came out in the summer and autumn of 1731. As *The Grub-Street Opera* the piece seems to have been acted in July. For this and other questions concerning Fielding's dramatic work see the excellent study by W. L. Cross, *The History of Henry Fielding*.

success for its author. With *Don Quixote in England* (H.[1] c. April 1734) Fielding turned to the realms of satire and of incipient sentimentalism. It would appear that this work was originally penned before 1728 and subsequently revised, like Carey's *The Contrivances*, to accord with the prevailing fashion. Difficult as it is to imitate the inimitable Cervantes, Fielding has in this slight piece secured something of that particular tone which made *Don Quixote* so popular. *An Old Man Taught Wisdom: Or, The Virgin Unmask'd* (D.L. Jan. 1734/5) shows a certain deepening of the sentimental strain. The marriage of Lucy to the reflective footman is precisely in the mood of the Richardsonian type of literature, although Fielding modifies its effect by introducing a series of humours such as Goodwill, Blister, Coupee, Quaver and Wormwood. That this admixture of two elements caught the taste of the age is proved by the tremendous popularity of this work. This popularity forced Fielding to pen a sequel under the title of *Miss Lucy in Town* (D.L. May 1742), in which Lucy finds herself in a house of ill-fame favoured with the attentions of Lord Bauble. Apparently this latter character was taken as a portrait of a particular nobleman and the play suffered in consequence at the hands of the Lord Chamberlain[1].

Miss Lucy in Town was to be Fielding's last effort in this strain. By 1742 the furore for the ballad-opera was dying away, and the future novelist, like Charles Johnson, ever looking to the public, had turned again to farce, burlesque and comedy.

The remaining farcical ballad-operas, or at least such of their number as deserve individual mention, may easily be dismissed. Tony Aston's *The Fool's Opera; or, The Taste of the Age* (Oxford, 1731) seems to be a one-act satire on Gay's work, this satire being intensified by "A Ballad, Call'd, A Dissertation on the Beggar's Opera." Mrs Elizabeth Boyd's *Don Sancho: or, The Students Whim, A Ballad Opera*

---

[1] See Whincop, pp. 235–6, and *Biographia Dramatica*. The suppression as is evident was not of long duration. There is a contemporary pamphlet referring to the scandal—*A Letter to a Noble Lord, To whom alone it Belongs. Occasioned by a Representation at the Theatre Royal in Drury-Lane, of a Farce, called Miss Lucy in Town* (1742).

of Two Acts, with Minerva's Triumph, A Masque (1739) never saw production on the stage, but is interesting for the fact that among the *dramatis personae* are "Shakespear and Dryden's Ghosts," which are conjured up by Don Sancho. Daniel Bellamy's *The Rival Priests: or, the Female Politician* (1739) presents a kind of intrigue variant of the usual farcical ballad-opera. This play introduces a Don Antonio who seems nothing more than a replica of the similarly named character in Otway's *Venice Preserv'd*. In Walter Aston's *The Restauration of King Charles II. or, The Life and Death of Oliver Cromwell* (1732) we discover yet another kind of this species. It is a poor production of an anti-Puritan cast, but is valuable for its semi-serious, semi-humorous treatment of history. Along with Fielding's *Don Quixote in England* (H.² 1734) might be considered James Ayres' *Sancho at Court: or The Mock-Governor* (1742), which presents Sancho as a governor, with at his levee, amid the Spanish types, the figures of Lord Sparkish, Never Out, Colonel At Wit and Lord Smart. Ballad-operas introducing low humour of a somewhat similar tone were produced in the thirties of the century by Robert Drury, whose work might well be compared with that of Coffey. This author's *The Devil of a Duke: or, Trapolin's Vagaries* (D.L. Aug. 1732) is but a poor alteration of Cokain's play as adapted by Tate. *The Mad Captain* (G.F. March 1732/3), on the other hand, seems to have an original plot, but it deserves little attention, as does *The Rival Milliners: or, The Humours of Covent-Garden* (H.² Jan. 1735/6), with its mixture of pastoral and farcical scenes. Drury's work has only an historical value; his plays have no merit in themselves, but possess an interest when they are considered in relation to the works of other writers of the time. Not many others are of even such historical importance. The anonymous *The Jovial Crew* (D.L. Feb. 1730/1) proved a popular, but undistinguished, adaptation of Brome's comedy *The Female Rake; or, Modern Fine Lady* (H.² April 1736) has a somewhat original plot in which Celia learns of the return of her long absent fiancé after her own secret marriage, but the dialogue is lacking in vital spirit. E. Phillips' *The Livery Rake and*

Country Lass (D.L. May 1733) is a poor farcical specimen of the type[1], as is Miller's *The Picture: or, The Cuckold in Conceit* (D.L. Feb. 1744/5), based on Molière's *Le Cocu Imaginaire*, with music composed by Arne.

Besides these farcical ballad-operas, there are, as has been noted above, three special types which found fair popularity during the period. The sentimental, pastoral and "political" ballad-operas all have features which separate them off from the more farcical of their kind. Henry Carey's *Nancy: or, The Parting Lovers* (C.G. Dec. 1739) may be treated as typical of the first. "The Subject of this *Interlude*," we learn from the preface, "is taken from Nature itself, and discovers the Force of *Love in Low Life*." The theme of a man pressed for the navy and leaving his weeping sweetheart is conducted purely in the sentimental strain, and proved popular in its original form as an "Interlude" and later in its more decided ballad-opera structure as *The Press Gang: or, Love in Low Life* (1755) and, towards the end of the century, as *True-Blue* (Royalty, 1787)[2]. In Lillo's *Silvia; or, The Country Burial* (L.² Nov. 1730) a union of immoral and sentimental motives is apparent. The plot of this work presents a number of decidedly interesting features. Sir John desires Silvia to live with him, but he succeeds in securing Lettice in her place. This theme of intrigue runs parallel with another wherein Timothy Stick watches in mourning by his wife's grave. The first part is evidently perilous in the extreme, but the treatment is as sentimental as could be desired from the author of *The London Merchant*. Probably because of the union of the two forces, however, *Silvia* was not successful upon the stage[3].

An even more thoroughly sentimental piece is J. Arthur's *The Lucky Discovery: or, The Tanner of York* (C.G. April 1738) which also utilises a situation somewhat *risqué*. Modish in this piece is a typical gallant, making love to Mrs Bark.

---

[1] This piece was acted first as *The Livery Rake or the Intriguing Servant* and later (at the Haymarket) under the title of *The Livery Rake Trapped or the Disappointed Country Lass*.

[2] On this play see Appendix C.

[3] Whincop, p. 258.

The latter agrees to an assignation with him, but arranges that Mrs Modish shall take her place. Modish at the last moment grows afraid of his intrigue and sends Bark in his stead. There is a "lucky discovery" before any harm is done. The theme is an old one[1], but some skill is shown in its development here. With these sentimental dramas might be numbered *Timon in Love: or, The Innocent Theft* (D.L. Dec. 1733), a fantastic piece by John Kelly, the author mainly responsible for the acclimatisation of the French *drame* in England. This ballad-opera is itself taken from Delisle's *Timon le Misanthrope*, and mingles a pretty tale of Timon, Jupiter and Mercury, with another in which characters of the *commedia dell' arte* make their appearance. In spite of its novelty, it does not seem to have met with that success which in reality it deserved. Most typical of all in extreme sentimental motives, however, are the ballad-operas of Robert Dodsley, whose revolutionary plays, *The Toy-Shop* (C.G. 1735) and *The King and the Miller of Mansfield* (D.L. 1737) with the sequel to the latter, *Sir John Cockle at Court* (D.L. 1738)[2] have already been dealt with[3]. *The Blind Beggar of Bethnal Green* (D.L. April 1741), without being any less sentimental than these, is cast in the regular mould of *The Beggar's Opera*. It has no great literary value, but is interesting because of its enunciation of new social codes. "Wants," says the Beggar, "real or imaginary, reach all states; and as some beg in rags, there are some not asham'd to beg even in velvet. All men are beggars in some shape or other; those only are scandalous ones, who beg by impudence what they should earn by merit."

Beyond these sentimental ballad-operas, there are the pastorals, sometimes fantastically conceived, sometimes crudely comic and realistic. Colley Cibber is probably the most interesting dramatist who attempted this type. Early in his career he had produced a "pastoral interlude" called *Myrtillo* (D.L. Nov. 1715), a poor thing which had moderate

---

[1] The direct source of the plot is evidently Charles Johnson's *The Wife's Relief* (D.L. 1711); *supra*, p. 187.
[2] The last mentioned play is formed on the lines of the ballad-opera.
[3] *Supra*, p. 204.

success as an after-piece, as well as an alteration of Dogget's *The Country Wake* as *Hob, or the Country Wake* (D.L. Oct. 1711). Naturally neither of these is in *The Beggar's Opera* style, but the latter at least was reworked into a regular ballad farce. The person responsible for this adaptation of an adaptation seems to have been John Hippisley, whose *Flora; An Opera....Being the Farce of the Country-Wake, alter'd after the Manner of the Beggar's Opera* appeared at Lincoln's Inn Fields in April 1729. This was followed by *A Sequel to the Opera of Flora* (L.[2] March 1731/2). Both appear to have been moderately successful. Cibber himself, soon after the production of Gay's work, came forward with *Love in a Riddle* (D.L. Jan. 1728/9), a tale of the transplanted children of Arcas (Amyntas and Ianthe) and those of Ægon (Iphis and Pastora) with their mutual loves. This piece was damned the first night for political reasons[1], and Cibber apparently reduced it to one act as *Damon and Phillida*, which, being produced anonymously, proved a success. Still later, Cibber's son Theophilus reworked the alteration and got it issued as *Damon and Phillida: or, The Rover Reclaim'd*[2]. Theophilus Cibber was likewise responsible for an operatic version of Allan Ramsay's *The Gentle Shepherd* (1725) as *Patie and Peggy; or, The Fair Foundling* (D.L. Nov. 1730), in which he reduced the action of the original to one act and changed the dialect from Scots to English. It has no value; whatsoever is good in it is the work of Ramsay.

Besides this effort of Theophilus Cibber's, there were one or two other attempts to make money out of the Scots ballads. The most important of these was Joseph Mitchell's *The Highland Fair; or, Union of the Clans* (D.L. March 1730/1), a poor piece of work but of value because of its endeavour to exploit the lowland airs and to arouse interest in the romance of Scottish history. "It is not the Dialect," we are informed in the preface, "but the Musick, Manners and Dresses of the Country, from which it takes its Title." Mitchell, unfortunately, had but little *flair* for the theatre, and his work, while of some importance historically, has practically no intrinsic value.

---

[1] *Supra,* p. 15.   [2] See Appendix C.

As a final note to this brief outline of the development of the ballad-opera in the years immediately following the appearance of Gay's work, it may be observed that the type was largely utilised for the expression of satire stronger than any introduced by the author of *The Beggar's Opera* himself. Thus Mark Freeman's *The Downfal of Bribery: or, The Honest Men of Taunton. A New Ballad Opera Of Three Acts. As it was lately perform'd by a Company of Players at a certain noted Inn at Taunton in Somersetshire* (1733) is a purely topical piece written from direct political motives, and the anonymous *The Humours of the Court: or, Modern Gallantry* (1732) has, as its sole object, the revealing of some open "secrets" of the thirties of the century. Such pieces, of course, while of some interest as showing the popularity of the type, do not have any theatrical connections.

It is evident that the ballad-opera, which thus usurped so much of public attention in the period 1728–1733, died a natural death in the later thirties. The older ballad-operas after that date still continued to be revived in the theatres, of the provinces as of the metropolis, but the creative element had disappeared. Sporadic attempts may be traced in the later years of the century to reproduce the success of Gay's experiment; comedy and farce for decades to come displayed clearly the impress of the ballad-opera form; but the later examples are to be regarded rather as survivals than as regular developments in the history of the species. The comic opera is in reality a separate type of dramatic art.

V. *Pantomimes*

Of that other symptomatic theatrical innovation of the eighteenth century, the pantomime, not much can be said here, but the popularity of this kind of drama must also be carefully marked if we are to estimate the early eighteenth century theatres aright. Of the success of this type there cannot be the slightest doubt. Prices were raised for pantomimes, and the actors sometimes succeeded in gaining double the amount from a show of this sort than they did from an ordinary comedy or tragedy[1]. Satire of the pantomime is to be found from Pope's *Dunciad*[2] to the epigram possibly by Theophilus Cibber,

> Shakespeare, Rowe, Johnson, *now are quite undone*,
> *These are thy Triumphs, thy Exploits*, O LUN![3]

Concerning the origin of the pantomime there seems to be a certain amount of doubt. John Rich, or "Lun," is usually credited with the origination of the form, but John Weaver, a dancing master employed at Drury Lane, claimed for himself, and was supported by Cibber in his claim[4], that he was truly the innovator. Certainly *The History of the Mimes and Pantomimes* (1728) by this Weaver is the clearest account we possess of the development of the type up to the end of the first quarter of the century, and this work may serve as an outline for the present section of our analysis. Included in it is a list of pantomimic performances, stretching from *The Tavern Bilkers* (D.L. 1702), designed on the "Italian model" to Lun's *The Rape of Proserpine* (L.[2] 1726). Of these pieces Weaver was responsible for the first, and for *The Loves of Mars and Venus* (D.L. 1717)[5], *Perseus and Andromeda* (D.L. 1716), *Orpheus and Eurydice* (D.L. 1718), *Harlequin turn'd Judge* (D.L. 1717) and *Cupid and Bacchus* (D.L. 1719)[6].

---

[1] See Genest iii. 158; and Theophilus Cibber, *The Lives and Characters of the most Eminent Actors and Actresses of Great Britain and Ireland* (1753), p. 67.

[2] iii. 253 ff.

[3] *Theophilus Cibber, to David Garrick, Esq.; with Dissertations on Theatrical Subjects* (1759). The same epigram appears in Van der Gucht's engraving of Harlequin and Punch kicking out Horace (B.M. 1838, dated conjecturally 1729). Other satirical prints may be noted: that given as the frontispiece to *Harlequin-Horace. Or, The Art of Modern Poetry* (1731), *The Stage's Glory* (B.M. 1869, dated April 1731), *Rich's Glory or his Triumphant Entry into Covent-Garden* (B.M. 1899, by Hogarth, dated Dec. 18, 1732), *Risum Teneatis Amici?* (B.M. 1833, dated 1729). A formal criticism of pantomime appears in Carey's *Of Stage Tyrants* (1735). See also *infra*, p. 268.   [4] *Apology*, ii. 179–80.

[5] Which Cibber regards as the first of the type (*op. cit.* ii. 180).

[6] It is exceedingly difficult to determine precisely the "authorship" of these early pantomimes or to disentangle one from another. Titles tended to be similar, and frequently it is impossible to say definitely that two pieces of the same name, or nearly of the same name, were identical or represented entirely independent treatments of a general theme. For the pantomimes listed by Weaver see the separate titles in the Hand-list.

Lun created *Harlequin Executed* (L.² 1716), *The Jealous Doctor* (L.² 1717), *Amadis* (L.² 1718), *The South-Sea Director* (L.² 1720), *Jupiter and Europa* (L.² 1721), *The Necromancer: or, Harlequin Doctor Faustus* (L.² 1723), *The Sorcerer: or, The Loves of Pluto and Proserpine* (L.² 1724), *Daphne and Apollo: or, The Burgomaster Trick'd* (L.² 1726) and *The Rape of Proserpine* (L.² 1726). Thurmond was responsible for *The Dumb Farce* (D.L. 1719), *A Duke and No Duke* (D.L. 1720), *Harlequin Doctor Faustus* (D.L. 1723), *Harlequin Sheppard* (D.L. 1724), *Apollo and Daphne* (D.L. 1723) and *Wagner and Abericot* (D.L. 1726).

As is evident, four distinct strains can be traced in these titles. The influence of classic myth, that of the Italian *commedia dell' arte*, that of previous English farce, and that of contemporary satire are all represented. The novelty of the eighteenth century pantomime consisted in the elaborating of the unspoken devices of Harlequin and Columbine into a regular story told by "heel" instead of "head," but the pantomime has many points of relationship with opera and farce of the time. Most commonly, indeed, these silent antics of the pantomime characters were combined with dialogue recited or sung by other figures moving alongside of the dancers and acrobats.

Of the descriptions of the pantomimes which have come down to us, only one or two need be mentioned. *Harlequin Incendiary: or, Columbine Cameron. A Musical Pantomime* (D.L. March 1745/6), with airs composed by Arne, may be taken as typical of the mingling of pantomimic, satirical and operatic elements. It is largely political in character, the Pope appearing in person and uttering thoroughly melodramatic sentiments:

> This Day we appear on a mighty Design,
> And to make it succeed, all Hell must combine;
> Old *England*, once more, we have hope to subdue,
> If our Friends are but firm, and the Devil prove true.

Intermingled with this religious and political satire flit in and out the figures of the *commedia dell' arte*.

One of Lun's productions has been preserved as *A Dramatick*

Entertainment, call'd Harlequin a Sorcerer: With the Loves of Pluto and Proserpine (L.² Jan. 1724/5; printed 1725). Here again is a mingling of spoken and unspoken action. The former portion, which has been attributed to Lewis Theobald, contains some fair verses, sung by a series of concert artists including Leveridge and Mrs Barbier, but obviously this was not what the audience most looked to. They were impressed by the scenic effects, as that of the first act where

After the Overture, the Curtain rises, and discovers dark rocky Caverns, by the Side of a Wood, illumin'd by the Moon; Birds of Omen promiscuously flying, Flashes of Lightning faintly striking.

They were impressed, too, by the antics of Harlequin. The original *Perseus and Andromeda* of 1716 has apparently not been printed, but there is extant a *Perseus and Andromeda* of 1730, likewise attributed partly to Theobald. The serious part is thoroughly operatic in style, but there are mingled with it comic parts after the model of the *commedia dell' arte*, including "A *Spanish* Merchant, Father to *Columbine*, A *Petit-Maitre*, in Love with *Columbine*, *Harlequin*, a Wizard, also in Love with *Columbine*, *Columbine*, Daughter to the *Spanish* Merchant, a *Valet de Chambre*" and "a *Spaniard*." To Theobald also have been attributed the words given in *The Rape of Proserpine* (L.² 1726), another operatic-pantomimic entertainment, introducing a union of similar elements.

Among the other pieces of this kind which have been printed, one of the most interesting is Theophilus Cibber's *The Harlot's Progress; or, The Ridotto al' Fresco: A Grotesque Pantomime Entertainment* (D.L. March 1733), a work which introduces in a series of moving tableaux the characters of Hogarth's prints, along with the inevitable figures of Italian farce. Alongside of this might be noted as the work of a capable writer *Merlin in Love: or, Youth against Magic. A Pantomime Opera* (printed 1760 but written earlier). Hill, the author, evidently knew well what the spectators of the time desired, and a stage direction from act III of this work may be taken as typical of the general action of all these pieces:

*After the air, she directs him to the easy chair; into which he leaps,
antickly, up, and reclines himself, in a lolling, extravagant posture.*

On a sudden, the head of the chair sneezes; and Harlequin
*beginning to move, as in surprize, is caught fast, by an arm of the
chair, about his waist; at which, twisting his face round, with great
agony and distortion, the other arm of the chair is rais'd above his
head, which is grasp'd violently by the hand of it.*

Harlequin *roars out, and struggles to get loose.* Columbine,
behind, starts up, and leans, trembling, against the side of the cave.

*At length, he breaks free.... The easy chair rises, slowly, into
figure of a man (the back part falling down, to form the tail of his
robe) and appears to be* Merlin.

As has been noted above, satire of this type soon came
into being, and not the least interesting of these satires are
those which are themselves cast in the form of pantomimes
and entertainments. "Monsieur *Pantomime*" is one of the
claimants for the laurel at the court of Nonsense in Fielding's
The Author's Farce (H.² 1730) and Witmore, in the course of
that satirical piece, gives utterance to the dramatist's own
sentiments when he cries,

But now, when Party and Prejudice carry all before them,
when Learning is decried, Wit not understood, when the Theatres
are Puppet-Shows, and the Comedians Ballad-Singers: When
Fools lead the Town, wou'd a Man think to thrive by his Wit?—
If you must write, write Nonsense, write Opera's, write Entertainments, write *Hurlo-thrumbos.*

Fielding turned again to ridicule the species in *Tumble-Down
Dick: or, Phaeton in the Suds. A Dramatick Entertainment of
Walking, in Serious and Foolish Characters: Interlarded with
Burlesque, Grotesque, Comick Interludes, call'd, Harlequin
a Pick-Pocket....Being ('tis hop'd) the last Entertainment that
will ever be exhibited on any Stage. Invented by the Ingenious
Monsieur Sans Esprit. The Musick compos'd by the Harmonious
Signior Warblerini. And the Scenes painted by the Prodigious
Mynheer Van Bottom-Flat* (H.² April 1736). This satire,
directed principally at *The Fall of Phaeton*, which had been
given at Drury Lane in March 1736, is dedicated "To
Mr. *John Lun*, Vulgarly call'd *Esquire*," to whom, in the

words of the author, "we owe (if not the Invention) at least the bringing into a Fashion, that sort of Writing which you have pleased to distinguish by the Name of Entertainment." While attacking one particular work, it passes beyond mere ridicule of a single pantomime. The Introduction, with the characters of Machine, the composer, Fustian, the author, and Sneerwell, a critic, is a direct satire of the species as a whole. Machine's pantomime, we learn, is to be produced along with *Othello*, of which the composer wishes acts I and IV cut out:

> *Fustian*. Death and the Devil!...Shall *Shakespear* be mangled to introduce thir Trumpery?
> *Prompter*. Sir, the Gentleman brings more Money to the House, than all the Poets put together.

Besides *The Fall of Phaeton*, the popular entertainments of *Harlequin Doctor Faustus* and *Pluto and Proserpine* are glanced at, and there is delicious ridicule of theatrical effects in the introduction of "two or three Girls carrying Farthing Candles." Fielding's satire, however, comprehensive as it was, does not seem to have done more than the other satires to kill the popularity of the pantomime.

Among those other satires, five deserve independent mention, *The Plot* (D.L. Jan. 1734/5) attributed to Kelly, *The British Stage* (1724), *The English Stage Italianiz'd* (1727), *Harlequin Student* (G.F. March 1740/1), and *Harlequin-Horace* (1731). The first of these is a one-act piece in rime and airs, with "Tradgetitive" dialogue, introducing an English and a French Harlequin as well as "A Troop of *French* Comedians" among the *dramatis personae*. The satire in this is directed mainly against continental innovations of the pantomimic kind. *The British Stage; or, The Exploits of Harlequin: A Farce. As it is Performed by a Company of Wonderful Comedians at both Theatres, with Universal Applause; With all its Original Songs, Scenes, and Machines. Design'd as an After-Entertainment for the Audiences of Harlequin Doctor Faustus, and the Necromancer* (1724) is interesting largely for the comments in the stage directions, which call before us the spectators of the theatres:

Enter the Dragon, *spitting Fire....(The whole Audience hollow with Applause, and shake the very Theatre.* [An ass] *endeavours to mount the* Dragon, *falls down, the* Dragon *is drawn up in the Air by Wires.*
(*The Audience ring with Applause.*
Enter Windmill.
Harl[equin]. Advance, Mr. *Windmill,* and give some Entertainment to this great Assembly.—
(*The Audience hollow and huzza, and are ready to break down the House with Applause.*
They dance with the Ghosts, Devils, and Harlequin.
(*The Audience clap prodigiously.*

The trivial methods by which the approbation of the spectators was secured by Lun seem to take shape before us in this piece. Three years later appeared *The English Stage Italianiz'd, In a New Dramatic Entertainment, called Dido and Æneas: or, Harlequin, A Butler, a Pimp, a Minister of State, Generalissimo, and Lord High Admiral, dead and alive again, and at last crown'd King of Carthage, by Dido. A Tragi-Comedy, after the Italian Manner; by way of Essay, or first Step towards the farther Improvement of the English Stage* (1727)[1]. While this is directed mainly against the continental type of pantomime, it may be taken here as showing the general trend of satirical opinion against the *commedia dell' arte* tradition. Its object is for ever to "banish from the Stage, *Shakespear, Johnson, Dryden, Otway, Wycherley, Congreve, Rowe, Addison,* and all those formal fellows[2]," and to do so by uniting pantomime with the opera. A final advertisement declares that "For the Benefit of the *English* Quality and others who have forgot their Mother-Tongue, This Play is translating into *Italian* by an able Hand: and will be sold by the Orange-Women and Door-Keepers, at Six

---

[1] On the title-page this is given as by D'Urfey, who had died in 1723. At the end is an affidavit dated 14 Nov. 1726 which declares that that author was still alive. D'Urfey, however, had come in the eighteenth century to occupy the place Flecknoe held in the period of the Restoration; and the explanation seems to be that his name was taken as representative of dullness in literature generally. Forsythe, in his monograph on D'Urfey (i. 176) rather too seriously argues from internal evidence that the piece is spurious.
[2] Preface.

Pence each, during the Time of its Performance." *Harlequin Student: or The Fall of Pantomime, with the Restoration of the Drama; An Entertainment As it is now performing, with great Applause, by Persons for their Diversion, between the two Parts of the Concert, At the late Theatre in Goodman's Fields* (G.F. March 1740/1) is not so bitterly satiric, but has a decided interest in that it has "A Description of the Scenes and Machines painted by Mr. *Devoto*, particularly of *Shakespear's* Monument As lately erected in Westminster Abbey." Finally, we reach the non-dramatic *Harlequin-Horace: or, The Art of Modern Poetry* (1731), dedicated to "*J---n R---H*, Esq;" This is a fairly capable survey of the degenerating tastes of the time, and informs us how

> Long labour'd *Rich*, by Tragick Verse to gain
> The Town's Applause—but labour'd long in vain;
> At length he wisely to his Aid call'd in,
> The *active Mime*, and *checker'd Harlequin.*

Pantomime, Italian opera and ballad-opera must all be taken as displaying in marked form the disintegrating elements in the eighteenth century theatre. The satires considered above show quite clearly the directions in which popular taste was moving. The old had been killed, and the new was but barely born. Everything conspired towards a weakening of the drama. Sentimentalism had worn out comedy; the elements making for true tragic productivity were absent; song had come from Italy and dancing from France; the spectators were artificial and affected, seeking always after novelty. Pantomime, ballad-operas, "Hurlothrumbos" exactly suited their tastes.

VI. *Masques and Political Plays*

The various types of irregular drama dealt with in the preceding sections do not by any means exhaust the various kinds of drama produced during the eighteenth century which can be classed only in categories by themselves. One of these, the masque, has, I believe, never been even noted by any of the few historians of this particular period in the development of the English theatre. The musical masque or interlude was the result of the demand made by the managers for after-pieces, which in the Restoration period had been in the main short one or two act farces. Late in the seventeenth century, however, Motteux had produced a successful specimen of the masque in *The Loves of Mars and Venus* in which Mrs Brace-girdle, according to the testimony of Tony Aston, "sung very agreeably[1]," and which was revived frequently in the early years of the following century. This was followed about 1701 by another little drama of the same character, *Acis and Galatea*, evidently produced with *The Mad Lover*. It, too, proved fairly popular. The musical tendency which led towards the introduction of the Italian opera, and the desire on the part of English writers to compete with the Italians, naturally led to a rapid development of the masque in the first half of the eighteenth century. Colley Cibber, always wide-awake and ready to supply current theatrical requirements, soon turned out his *Venus and Adonis* (D.L. March 1714/5), which, the preface declares, was an attempt to introduce to the town "*a little good music in a language they understand.*" The music may have been good, but his verses assuredly are not. Not untypical is the last air of Venus,

> O! pleasing horror!
> O! melodious yell!
> Hark! Hark!
> All nature rings with sorrow!
> Poor *Adonis'* Knell.

The majority of these masques are just such as Cibber's, poor endeavours to rival the opera made so popular by the Valentini and the Senesini brought over from Rome and Florence. They are invariably either mythological or pastoral—like the Italian operas—and differ from them only in that their dialogue is English and their actions limited to one or two acts. Barton Booth produced one in *The Death of Dido* (D.L. April 1716) written in fairly smooth verse, and evidently popular[2]; Theobald wrote another in *Decius and*

---

[1] *A Brief Supplement to Colley Cibber, Esq.; His Lives Of the late Famous Actors and Actresses* (1740), p. 4.
[2] Jacob, p. 282, under the title *Dido and Æneas*. Its music was composed by Pepusch.

Paulina (L.² 1718), likewise a success¹. Thomas Cooke's *Albion; or, The Court of Neptune* (1724) hardly merits serious attention, and Thomas Broughton's *Hercules* (Oxford, 1745) is equally poor². Among the early specimens of the type might be mentioned an anonymous *Presumptuous Love* (L.² March 1715/6), which was introduced into an unprinted comedy called *Every Body Mistaken*, an alteration of *The Comedy of Errors*³, as well as Hughes' *Apollo and Daphne* (D.L. Jan. 1715/6) with music by Pepusch. The hey-day of the masque is to be found, however, rather in the years after 1730 than in those before. Some passages in Mendez' *The Chaplet* (D.L. Dec. 1749) are pretty⁴, and *The Chaplet* may be taken as introducing us to the pastoral type of masque. Dr Dalton's *Comus* (D.L. March 1737/8) was probably the most successful of all these works⁵. Milton's original has here been added to with lyrics taken from various other sources, and general alterations have been made to accommodate the work to the tastes of an eighteenth century audience. The "dramatic pastoral" of John Hoadly entitled *Love's Revenge* (1734) is one of the most successful of these Arcadian masques, and with it might be coupled the "pastoral opera" of the same author, called *Phoebe* (1748). *Robin Hood* (D.L. Dec. 1750) is noticeable for little save that "The Musick" was "compos'd by the Society of the *Temple* of *Apollo*." *Roger and Joan; or, The Country Wedding* (C.G. March 1738/9), with music by Lampe, is nothing but the comic part of Motteux' *Acis and Galatea* with a few additions⁶.

There is not much that is remarkable in this masque production of the eighteenth century, but the very presence of these masques and their popularity from early years to late prove still further evidence of the tastes of the audience, tastes which, as has been seen, were moving steadily away from regular five-act comedy and tragedy.

---

¹ The title declares it was "perform'd...in the Dramatick Opera of Circe"; Jacob, p. 258, states it was performed in *The Lady's Triumph*. See Appendix C. The music was composed by Galliard.
² Music by Händel.   ³ Music by W. Turner.
⁴ Music by Dr Boyce.   ⁵ Whincop, p. 207.
⁶ Marks, J., *Pastoral Drama in England* (1908), p. 186.

One other sign of the disintegrating elements in the theatre is to be discovered in the large numbers of completely un-classifiable dramas. It is not that these pieces gave anything startlingly new to the stage; they were rather hashes of past dramatic material, often ill-conceived and badly welded together. What, after all, are we to make of Fielding's *The Historical Register, For the Year* 1736 (H.[2] April 1737)? In its three acts we get no clear plot. There is political satire in the figure of Quidam (Walpole); there is theatrical satire in the allusions to the quarrel of Mrs Cibber and Mrs Clive over Polly as well as in the characters of Pistol (Theophilus Cibber) and Ground-Ivy (Colley Cibber)[1]. There are witty passages in it, but the whole seems nothing but a medley of confused elements not too harmoniously fused together. We can discover here nothing creatively novel, and in this the play is but typical of a large number of other dramatic works produced during these fifty years which depart altogether from the characteristics of previous comedies or tragedies, and yet fail to establish forms that are of definite character and of definite importance. Perhaps we may dismiss plays such as the three of John Blanch, *The Beaux Merchant* (1714), *Swords into Anchors* (1725) and *Hoops into Spinning Wheels* (1725), all unacted pieces and all written in the provinces. These three dramas, if we may accord them that title, seem to have been composed under the trinal inspiration of Steele, Jonson and Terence, and the admixture of sentimental motives, of English humours and of Roman types is both inartistic and confusing. An equally confused and confusing play is Mrs Charlotte Charke's *The Art of Management; or, Tragedy Expell'd* (York Buildings, Sept. 1735), an attack upon Fleetwood as manager of Drury Lane. Typical, too, is Daniel Bellamy's *The Perjur'd Devotee: or the Force of Love* (1740), in which an attempt is made, according to the author, to present "*Terentian* Humour, join'd with *Cowley*'s wit[2]." These pieces may be taken as representative of many others.

So, too, with the political and topical plays of the period

---

[1] See C. W. Nichols' note on this play in *Mod. Lang. Notes*, Nov. 1923.
[2] The plot is from *Andria* and *Naufragium Joculare*.

we find a weakening of true dramatic conception. Political plays had flourished in Restoration times[1], but the greater majority of these are clustered around the last decade of the seventeenth century and seem to lead the way towards the still greater popularity of the type in the age of Anne and later. Tom Brown's *The Stage-Beaux toss'd in a Blanket: or, Hypocrisie Alamode; Expos'd in a True Picture of Jerry - - - A Pretending Scourge to the English Stage* (1704) is one of the first of these, indulging, as its title shows, in ridicule of the reverend Jeremy Collier. *The General Cashier'd* (1712) is more purely political in tone, and may be compared with *The Earl of Mar Marr'd; With the Humours of Jockey, the Highlander* (1715), a contemptuous attack upon the Jacobites[2]. *The Inquisition* (1717), the author of which has been suggested to be Dr George Sewell, is another attack upon the Tories and High Church party, as is Robert Ashton's *The Battle of Aughrim: Or, The Fall of Monsieur St. Ruth* (1728), a riming tragedy. Chetwood's *South-Sea; or, The Biters Bit* (1720) is a satire of the notorious "Bubble"; the operatic *Callista* (1731) seems to deal with court scandal of the period; *C - - - and Country* (1735) certainly retails some contemporary gossip; and *The Humours of Whist* (1743) turns upon the popular card game of the time. So the tale goes on; the accumulation of such pieces, even although few or none of them were acted, pointing in one clear direction.

VII. *Burlesques and Rehearsals*

We come, finally, to the reaction. Already have been noted a few burlesques of particular types of drama, in especial the opera and the pantomimic entertainment; but those few mentioned in the preceding sections of this book form only an infinitesimal portion of the vast burlesque dramatic literature of the time. Nearly all of these satirical plays are cast in the form of a rehearsal, and nearly all show the direct influence of Buckingham's famous work of Restoration times.

---

[1] Vol. i (1660–1700), pp. 10–11.
[2] This is by J. Phillips.

Here undoubtedly Henry Fielding stands forward as the most important figure. His *Tumble-Down Dick* (H.[2] April 1736) has been dealt with in a previous section as a satire of pantomime, but before the production of this skit, Fielding had turned out several similar works. *The Author's Farce; And The Pleasures of the Town* had been produced at the Haymarket in March 1730, apparently with success[1]. The characters, except for the central figures, are in the main purely farcical and satirical. Dr Orator, Monsieur Pantomime, Mrs Novel, Don Tragedio and Sir Farcical Comick all show the scope of this burlesque. Cibber comes in for a good deal of abuse, as does Bookweight, the publisher, and his satellites. The same year, also at the Haymarket, appeared Fielding's more artistic and more formal satire, *The Tragedy of Tragedies; or, The Life and Death of Tom Thumb the Great. With the Annotations of H. Scriblerus Secundus*[2]. This seems to have come out originally in one act, but was enlarged to three acts when played at the Haymarket and Drury Lane in 1731. Undoubtedly one of the best of literary burlesques, it attacks both the follies of the dramatists and the follies of the critics. The *dramatis personae* are well described. King Arthur is "a passionate sort of King, husband to Queen *Dollallolla*, of whom he stands a little in fear; father to *Huncamunca*, whom he is very fond of, and in love with *Glumdalca*"; Tom Thumb himself appears as "a little Hero with a great Soul somewhat violent in his Temper, which is a little abated by his love for *Huncamunca*"; Lord Grizzle is "extremly zealous for the liberty of the Subject, very cholerick in his Temper, and in love with *Huncamunca*"; Queen Dollallolla is described as the "wife to King *Arthur*, and mother to *Huncamunca*, a woman intirely faultless, saving that she is a little given to Drink, a little too much a Virago towards her Husband, and in love with *Tom Thumb*."

---

[1] Whincop, p. 232.

[2] The original title was *Tom Thumb*; it was later altered and added to; see Appendix C. The "scholarly" notes do not appear in the earlier edition. H. S. Hughes in an article in *Modern Philology* (xx. i, Aug. 1922) demonstrates Fielding's indebtedness in this play and in his other burlesques to his friend James Ralph's satirical work, *The Touch-Stone* (1728).

Among the various "walkers-on" we find "*Courtiers, Guards, Rebels, Drums, Trumpets, Thunder* and *Lightning*." The satire in the body of the play is nothing less than brilliant, and this satire covers the tragedies not only of the eighteenth century, but also of the preceding Caroline periods[1]. Probably for us to-day the most interesting and entertaining portions in it are not these satirical references to long forgotten plays, although the famous "Oh! *Huncamunca, Huncamunca*, oh![2]" is ever a perpetual joy, but the ridicule of the ways of the commentators and critics. This was an innovation of Fielding's own, and it is to be confessed that he did his work magnificently. The line beginning "The mighty *Thomas Thumb*" is duly annotated:

Dr. B[entl]y reads, The mighty Tall-mast Thumb. Mr. D[enni]s, The mighty Thumping Thumb. Mr. T[heobal]d reads, Thundering. I think Thomas more agreeable to the great simplicity so apparent in our author.

One of the best of these annotations occurs in II. vi, and it may serve as representative of the others:

There is great dissention among the poets concerning the method of making man. One tells his mistress that the mould she was made in being lost, Heaven cannot form such another. Lucifer, in Dryden, gives a merry description of his own formation:

Whom Heaven, neglecting, made and scarce design'd,
But threw me in for number to the rest.—*State of Innocence.*

In one place the same poet supposes man to be made of metal:

I was form'd
Of that coarse metal, which, when she was made,
The Gods threw by for rubbish.—*All for Love.*

In another of dough:

When the Gods moulded up the paste of man,
Some of their clay was left upon their hands,
And so they made Egyptians.—*Cleomenes.*

---

[1] See the Temple edition, p. 81. The plays mentioned or ridiculed include Addison's *Cato*, Banks' *The Albion Queens*, *The Unfortunate Favourite*, *Cyrus*, and *Vertue Betray'd*; Dennis' *Liberty Asserted*; many of Dryden's; Eccles' *Noah's Flood*; Fenton's *Mariamne*; Fletcher's *The Bloody Brother*; Gay's *The Captives*; Johnson's *Medea* and *The Victim*; Hopkins' *The Female Warriour*; several of Lee's; Mallet's *Eurydice*; Otway's *Don Carlos* and *Caius Marius*; Rowe's *Tamerlane*; Tate's *Injur'd Love*; Theobald's *The Persian Princess*; Thomson's *Sophonisba*; and Young's *Busiris* and *The Revenge*.　　[2] II. v.

In another of clay:

> Rubbish of remaining clay.—*Sebastian*.

One makes the soul of wax:

> Her waxen soul begins to melt apace.—*Anna Bullen*.

Another of flint:

> Sure our two souls have somewhere been acquainted
> In former beings, or, struck out together,
> One spark to Africk flew, and one to Portugal.—*Sebastian*.

To omit the great quantities of iron, brazen, and leaden souls, which are so plentiful in modern authors—I cannot omit the dress of a soul as we find it in Dryden:

> Souls shirted but with air.—*King Arthur*[1].

After the success of this work, Fielding left the burlesque form alone until in June 1732 he brought forward at Drury Lane *The Covent-Garden Tragedy*, and in March 1736 at the Haymarket *Pasquin...Being the Rehearsal of Two Plays, viz. A Comedy call'd, The Election; And a Tragedy call'd, The Life and Death of Common-Sense*. The former of these makes somewhat coarse reading. Fielding evidently desired to ridicule in it the pseudo-classic drama of *The Distrest Mother* type, but his travesty of Pyrrhus as Lovegirlo and of Andromache as Kissinda is at once vulgar and inartistic. *Pasquin*, on the other hand, is a brilliant satire, well conceived, with plentiful references to the difficulties of the poets, the folly of the pantomimes and the absurdities of the Italian opera. Several passages from this work have been quoted above[2], but to realise its full force it must be read as a whole. Fielding has carried through his "Dramatick Satire on the Times" with a verve which makes it one of the most notable works of the century[3]. In *Pasquin* and in *The Tragedy of Tragedies* the author of *Joseph Andrews* fully re-established the burlesque as a regular dramatic type, and gave many suggestions to his followers.

---

[1] *The Tragedy of Tragedies* was later revised by Mrs Haywood and William Hatchett as *The Opera of Operas; or, Tom Thumb the Great* (H.² May 1733) and presented with music by Arne and Lampe.

[2] *Supra*, p. 45.

[3] *Eurydice: or, The Devil Henpeck'd* (D.L. Feb. 1736/7) is also set in rehearsal form but does not merit much serious attention. The central idea, however, is a clever one, almost Shavian in conception; it shows how Eurydice does not want to return with Orpheus and cheats him into looking back.

Both before and after his time, other writers had taken to the satirical form. Elkanah Settle has among his eighteenth century works a piece called *The City Ramble: or, A Play-House Wedding* (D.L. Aug. 1711), based on Beaumont's *The Knight of the Burning Pestle* with suggestions from *The Coxcomb*. It is a well-written play, but, because of the author's unpopularity, ran for only a few nights. A rather good little burlesque tragedy is introduced into act v of Captain J. D. Breval's *The Play is the Plot* (D.L. Feb. 1717/8). The anonymous *The Contre Temps; or, Rival Queans* (1727) takes the Italian opera singers as its butt, Faustina, Cuzzoni, Heidegger, Händel and Senesino all appearing in person[1]. Satire of the opera occurs also in Breval's *The Rape of Helen* (C.G. May 1733), a one-act piece which brings the Grecian gods down to mother earth[2]. Even earlier than this Estcourt had produced his *Prunella: An Interlude Perform'd in the Rehearsal.... The Sense and Musick collected from the most Famous Masters By Mr. Airs* (D.L. Feb. 1707/8)—a burlesque of *Arsinoe* and *Camilla*. The fashion endured for long. One of the best of the operatic type is Henry Carey's *The Dragon of Wantley* (C.G. May 1737), the music to which was supplied by J. F. Lampe. The scene is "*Wantley* in *Yorkshire*, and the adjacent Places," which, "being infested by a huge and monstrous *Dragon*, the Inhabitants, with *Margery Gubbins* at their Head, apply to *Moore* of *Moore-Hall*, a Valiant Knight, for Relief; he falls violently in Love with *Margery*, and for her Sake undertakes the Task; at which *Mauxilinda*, a Cast-off Mistress of his, is so enrag'd, that she attempts to kill *Margery*, but is prevented by *Moore*, who reconciles the contending *Rivals*, kills the *Dragon*, and has *Margery* for his Reward." This burlesque was so successful that Carey saw fit to pen a sequel, entitled *Margery: or, A Worse Plague than the Dragon* (C.G. Dec. 1738)[3] which shows the new Lady Moore a ter-

---

[1] This piece is printed as Cibber's in the 1777 collected works of that author. Its inclusion seems to have been due to the Puck-like prank of the scholar, Stevens.

[2] It is not certain that this play is by Breval, the attribution to whom seems due to the compiler of *The New Theatrical Dictionary*.

[3] It is styled *The Dragoness* in the 1743 edition of his *Works*.

magant and Moore flying for assistance and consolation to
Mauxilinda. The plot, however, "concludes happily, according to the Custom of all Operas; no matter how improbable, absurd and ridiculous." The anonymous *Pyramus and
Thisbe* (C.G. Jan. 1744/5) is of the same species, adapted, as
is obvious, from the Bottom-Quince portions of *A Midsummer-
Night's Dream*. Ralph's *The Fashionable Lady; or Harlequin's
Opera* (G.F. April 1730) includes in its satire the pantomime
and the *commedia dell' arte* as well as the opera. Mr Ballad
and Mr Drama appear among the *dramatis personae* along with
Harlequin, Scaramouch, Pierot, Punch, Pantaloon and Columbine. The same dramatic types are ridiculed also in Aaron
Hill's *The Snake in the Grass* (printed 1760). Here Tragedy
appears "*struck dumb, and buried alive.*" None of these last-
mentioned pieces has any great literary value.

The list of the burlesques could be extended almost
indefinitely, but a brief glance at one or two others may be
sufficient here. The opera is satirised once more in D'Urfey's
The Two Queens of Brentford: or, Bayes no Poetaster (1721),
which is described as "The Sequel of the Famous Rehearsal,
Written by the late Duke of Buckingham." The rehearsal
form occurs, too, in *Tittle Tattle; or, Taste A-la-Mode* (1749),
by "Timothy Fribble." This is not in reality directed fundamentally against any particular kind of dramatic entertainment, although the epilogue ends on a hortatory note[1].
The main object of the play is to ridicule the fashionable
follies of the time, and for this purpose Swift's *Polite Conversation* has largely been drawn upon. Mrs Hoper's *Queen
Tragedy Restor'd* (H.[2] Nov. 1749) is but a poor piece of work,
attacking mainly the classical tragedy and the degenerate
comedy of the period, and utilising Shakespeare's ghost to
speak the epilogue[2]. Finally we come to three pieces of a
much more fantastic kind. Henry Carey's *The Tragedy of
Chrononhotonthologos* (H.[2] Feb. 1733/4) is a fair burlesque of

---

[1] *Supra*, p. 67.
[2] The *Biographia Dramatica* says it was acted one night only at the
Haymarket, the authoress herself appearing as Queen Tragedy. The
production was a failure, the expenses of music and candles not even
being met. See, however, Appendix C.

tragic follies, although it passes rather far into the realm of the ridiculous where

> The Fiddle Faddle Numbers flow,
> Serenely dull, Elaborately low[1].

Tragedy, comedy, pantomime, opera, all are here attacked. In act I, for example, we find the following passage:

> Bid Harlequino decorate the Stage,
> With all Magnificence of Decoration:
> Giants and Giantesses, Dwarfs and Pigmies,
> Songs, Dances, Music in its amplest Order,
> Mimes, Pantomimes, and all the magic Motion
> Of Scene Deceptiovisive and Sublime.
> An Entertainment of Singing here, after the Italian
> Manner, by Signior Scacciatinello, and Signora
> Sicarina.

Here pantomime and opera are treated as one. Contemporary tragedy, however, comes in for its full share of abuse, probably the wittiest satire being that contained in the Queen's speech in I. ii:

> Day's Curtain drawn, the Morn begins to rise,
> And waking Nature rubs her sleepy Eyes.
> The pretty little fleecy bleating Flocks,
> In Ba'as harmonious warble thro' the Rocks:
> Night gathers up her Shades in sable Shrouds,
> And whispering Oziers tattle to the Clouds.
> What think you, Ladies, if an Hour we kill,
> At Basset, Ombre, Picquet or Quadrille?

a not infelicitous "taking off" of eighteenth century would-be grandeur and unconscious bathos.

The two plays of Samuel Johnson of Cheshire, Hurlothrumbo; or, The Super-Natural (H.[2] March 1729) and The Blazing Comet; The Mad Lovers; or, The Beauties of the Poets (H.[2] March 1731/2) perhaps deserve mention here. Both are wild, confused pieces, displaying to the full the insanity of the author. This insanity, however, must have been allied to a touch of genius, for these two pieces, if regarded from the point of view of satire, contain not a few piercing thrusts at contemporary dramatic follies.

---

[1] Prologue.

It is well thus to close the account of early eighteenth century theatrical endeavour with the burlesques and the satires. In many ways, these burlesques, including among them *The Beggar's Opera*, are among the best and the brightest things which the age of Anne and that of the Georges have given to us. After all, the period of Pope was a period of satire, and many must feel that quite a number of these "rehearsals" rival in actual merit the work of Buckingham. Even more important for us is the light which the satires cast upon the dramatic productivity of time. We should see the Italian opera and the pantomimic display but dimly were it not for them. In these there is mirrored the general decay of the stage. At the same time, when we read those burlesques, we must never forget the presence in the eighteenth century of the older wit, which was to flourish later in the hands of Goldsmith and Sheridan, we must never forget the low rumblings of revolution heard in the work of Lillo and of Moore, or the more permanently important features of the sentimental comedy. Alongside of the decay of the older drama, a new drama was coming tormentedly to birth. The age of Pope, in its own way, was creating the modern theatre.

APPENDIX A

The Theatres; 1700–1750

As the list of plays and performances in this volume extend to a much greater length than the list of plays presented in *A History of Restoration Drama*, I have merely indicated here the theatres open during the half-century from 1700 to 1750. For a full account of the history of the companies Fitzgerald's work should be consulted.

Drury Lane (D.L.) 1700–7 under Rich who was silenced 5/3/07. Skipwith assigned his share to Brett 6/10/07. An order was issued 31/12/07 that D.L. should act only plays, H.[1] only operas; the two houses started under this arrangement 13/1/08. Brett assigned his rights to Wilks, Estcourt and Cibber 31/3/08. The D.L. company was silenced 6/6/09. On 22/11/09 Collier burst into the theatre and started with a new company 23/11/09. On 23/11/10 Swiney with Cibber and the other actors returned. In April 1712 Collier forced Swiney back to H.[1] and joined Cibber. Steele granted a licence for D.L. 19/1/15. Cibber suspended 19/12/18; Steele's licence revoked 23/1/19; D.L. silenced 25/1/19; Wilks, Cibber and Booth given a licence 27/1/19. Break up of the old actors about 1730–3. Theophilus Cibber left the theatre 28/5/33, and returned 28/11/34. The theatre had a varied career up to the time when Garrick took over its management.

Lincoln's Inn Fields (old theatre; L.[1]). Used by Betterton and seceded actors till 1705 when the company moved to H.[1].

Dorset Garden (D.G.). Used very occasionally for performances by the D.L. company in the early years of the century. Demolished June 1709; cf. W. J. Lawrence, *The Old Duke's Theatre in Dorset Garden* (*Architectural Review*, Nov. 1919, xlvi. 276).

Haymarket (called originally the Queen's Theatre, later the Opera House and the King's Theatre; H.[1]). Built under the direction of Vanbrugh and Congreve; opened 9/4/05. Given over to Swiney 1705–6 and so used till Dec. 1707 when performances were limited to operas. In 1709–10 Swiney was joined by Cibber and other actors from D.L. and the theatre was used by them till 18/11/10. The theatre thereafter was tenanted by various opera companies, and for a few months in 1718–9 by French comedians. The theatre is associated with the activities of Händel and the Royal Academy of Music.

Lincoln's Inn Fields (new theatre; L.²). Opened 18/11/14 under John Rich; continued to be utilised by the actors till the opening of C.G. (along with the English actors occasionally appeared French comedians). Thereafter it was used by various companies, notably in the season 1736–7 by Giffard's G.F. company. After the Licensing Act musical pieces were frequently performed there.

Haymarket (the Little or French Theatre; H.²). Opened 29/12/20 with French comedians, used by various English and foreign companies, notably those of Samuel Johnson of Cheshire (1728–30) and Fielding (1735–7). Plays and musical pieces were given in it occasionally after the Licensing Act.

Goodman's Fields. For an account of the two theatres in Ayliffe-street see the supplementary notes. Although a minor playhouse, Goodman's Fields has an important place in theatrical history because of the part it played in the establishment of the Licensing Act and because its stage first welcomed David Garrick to London.

Covent Garden (C.G.). Opened 7/12/32 under Rich with old L.² actors. Continued performances of plays, and occasionally of operas, on to 1749.

MINOR THEATRES

Punch's Theatre. Used by Martin Powell 1710–12 for puppet plays and operas.

St. Martin's-lane Theatre. Described in 1712 as situate in Litchfield-street.

Punch's Theatre (on Tower Hill). Used by Harris in 1721.

Figg's New Amphitheatre (adjoining the City of Oxford Arms, Oxford Road, Marylebone Fields). Entertainments advertised 1724–5.

Punch's Theatre (at the Old Tennis Court in St. James' near the Haymarket). Under Charke (1737–8) and under Yeates (1739–40).

New Wells, Clerkenwell (N.W.). Entertainments; first mention about 1738.

New Wells, Leman-street, Goodman's Fields (N.W., G.F.). Probably the first G.F. theatre under a new name. Used for entertainments from about 1738.

Hickford's room, Haymarket. Musical pieces occasionally performed from 1739.

Crown and Anchor, Strand. Oratorios given 1739–40.

Sadler's Wells (S.W.). Entertainments from 1740.

New Theatre in James'-street, Haymarket. Used for plays occasionally from 1741.

New Theatre in Beaux-street. Used for plays in 1742.

New Theatre, Shepherd's Market. Used for plays after 1742.

Old Theatre, Southwark. Used for plays 1744–5. Probably this was a theatrical booth.

Puppet Theatre (Panton-street). Under Madame de la Nash 1745–6.

Besides these, theatres were fairly regularly used in the summer months at Richmond, Greenwich, Twickenham, Tunbridge Wells and Bath, and during May Fair, Bartholomew Fair, Tottenham Court Fair and Southwark Fair the regular actors presented entertainments comprising regular plays, drolls, ballad operas and pantomimes. Some interesting notes on provincial performances are given by T. S. Graves in an article on *Strolling Players in the Eighteenth Century* (*Notes and Queries*, July 7, 1923) which supplements various facts given by E. Colby in his *Strolling Players of the 18th Century* (*id.* 27 Aug. 1921).

APPENDIX B

Summary of documents connected with the history of the stage, 1700–1750, preserved in the Public Record Office

I. *Documents of a literary interest.*

i. L.C. 7/3. Heading "Mr Nicholini Hyams articles | wth Mr Rich relating to y^e | Performance of Camilla | Jan^{ry} 14th 1705." "Articles of Agreement Indented made & agreed upon the | ffoutheenth day of January Anno-Dñi 1705 By & Between | Nicolas Hyam gent on the one part and Christopher Rich Esqr | one of the Patentees of the Theatres in Covent Garden & Dorsett | Garden London on the other part as followeth | ffirst Whereas the said Nicolas Hyam hath a fair score of the Vocall | and Instrumentall Musick with ye words in Italian written | under the Notes being the Opera called Camilla which words | Mr Hyam hath att his' owne charge procured a Gentleman to | Translate into English prose and Mr Rich hath att his owne | charge procured one Mr Northman to putt the said prose into | English Verse as suitable to the Notes of the Score of ye Italian | Musick as he can, And Mr Haym is writing out a new Score & | incerting Mr Northmans words under the Same with some necessary | additions alterations and abbreviations as he in his Iudgement | thinks best which he promises to finish with all possible Speed | & to advise Mr Rich in casting the parts to ye Singers and | to teach up the same parts and Musick and to give his best dilligence | and assistance therein as a Master Composer in the practices of the | Vocall and Instrumentall musick & to make proper Tunes for the | Dances in Such Opera and att his owne Charge to provide two fair | Scores of such Opera with ye English words and Notes.... | Now the said Nicolas Hyam in Consideration of one hundred pounds.... | doth bargaine | and Sell unto ye Said Christopher Rich" the Italian score and two English Scores; "and Mr Hyam is not publickly to | Performe any parts of the Musick of the said Opera of Camilla as | Sett in Italian or as now new alter'd by him or as ye same shall be | Alter'd by Mr Motteux or any other person" without Rich's consent. Haym further covenants to play his own part on the bass viol during the performances of the opera. Further details regarding the performances are given, and Haym is provided with permission to accompany his scholar, Joanna Maria, at the rival theatre in the Haymarket. [For the production of *Camilla* see Appendix C under Operas. Joanna Maria was probably none other than the "Baroness" mentioned in a later document.]

ii. L.C. 5/157, p. 287. Rubric "Order for Acting | M.͏ʳ Gay's pastorall | Tragedy." "I do hereby Order and direct that M.͏ʳ Gays | Pastorall Tragedy be imediately Acted after M.͏ʳ | Hugh's." Directed to Wilks, Cibber and Booth; dated Feb. 16, 1719/20. [This evidently refers to *Dione*, which was apparently never acted; Hughes' *The Siege of Damascus* came out at D.L. on Wed. Feb. 17.]

iii. L.C. 5/160, p. 104. Letter to the theatre managers: "My Lord Chamberlain has directed | me to let you know, that it is his Grace's Orders yᵗ | you send constantly the Advertisments of the play | you intend to Act, to M.͏ʳ Edward Owen printer | of the Daily Courant, who will insert them | gratis." Dated Jan. 29, 1728/9.

II. *Licences to Various Companies.*

i. L.C. 5/154, p. 35. Rubric: "License for a New | Company of Comedians": "Whereas We have thought fitt for the better | reforming the Abuses, and Immoral[i]ty of the Stage That a New | Company of Comedians should be Establish'd for our Service, under | Stricter Goverm.͏ᵗ and Regulations than have been formerly | We therefore reposing especiall trust, and confidence in | Our Trusty and Welbeloved John Vanbrugh & Will.͏ᵐ Congreve | Esq.͏ʳˢ for the due Execution, and performance of this our Will & | Pleasure, do Give and Grant unto them the sᵈ John | Vanbrugh, and Will.͏ᵐ Congreve full power & Authority | to form, constitue, and Establish for Us, a Company of | Comedians with full and free License to Act & Represent | in any Convenient Place, during Our Pleasure all | Comedys, Tragedys Plays, Interludes Operas, and to perform | all other Theatricall and Musicall Entertainm.͏ᵗˢ whatsoev.͏ʳ | and to Settle such Rules and Orders for the good Goverm.͏ᵗ | of the said Company, as the Chamberlain of our Household | shall from time to time direct and approve of | Given at our Court at S.͏ᵗ James this 14ᵗʰ day of | December in the third Year of Our Reign. | By her Majestys Command | Kent." [Haymarket licence.]

ii. L.C. 5/155, p. 44. Rubric: "Licence for a | Company of Comed.͏ⁿˢ": "Anne R: | Whereas We have thought fit for the good Goverm.͏ᵗ | of the Stage and for the better Entertainm.͏ᵗ of the Town | and Encouragm.͏ᵗ of the Undertakers, that only one Company of | Comedians shall be hereafter allow'd and Established by | Our Royall Licence under the direction of ye Chamberlain | of Our Household for the time being | And Whereas Owen Swiney Gent. Mr Robt Wilks M^r | Colley Cybber and Mr Thom^s Dogget have been Represent^d | to Us, by reason of their long experience & other good qualifica^{ns} | as fit psons to be Undertakers & to have ye Managm^t of Our s^d | Company | We therefore reposing Especiall trust and confidence in y^e | S^d Owen Swyney Robt Wilks Colley Cybber & Thom^s Dogget | do give and grant unto them full power & Authority | to form Constitute and Establish for us a Company of | Comedians wth full and free Licence to Act..." Dated November 6, 1710. [Haymarket licence.]

iii. L.C. 5/155, p. 157. Licence to Collier, Wilks, Cibber and Doggett, dated April 17, 1712, in same terms as above. [Drury Lane licence.]

iv. L.C. 5/155, p. 158. Licence, dated April 17, 1712, to Owen Swiney for opera at the Haymarket.

v. L.C. 5/155, p. 261. Licence, dated November 11, 1713, to Collier, Wilks, Cibber, Doggett and Booth.

vi. L.C. 5/156, p. 31. Licence, dated October 18, 1714, to Steele, Wilks, Cibber, Doggett and Booth.

vii. L.C. 5/156, p. 282. Licence, dated Jan. 27, 1719/20, to Wilks, Cibber and Booth. [v. vi. and vii. are all licences for Drury Lane.]

III. *Various Documents relating to the Management of the Companies.*

i. L.C. 7/3. Heading: "Establishm^t of | ye Company | An Establishm^t for ye Company."

"Men		pr. an̂	Women			
	Betterton	150	Barry... ...	...	150	120
	more to teach ...	50	Bracegirdle ...	...	150	120
120	Verbruggen ...	150	Rogers ...	...	060	60
120	Powell	150	Bowman ...	...	070	60
120	Wilks	150	Lee	...	060	50
80	Cyber	100	Ofield ...	...	080	70
80	Booth	100	Porter ...	...	040	35
70	Bowman	080	Willis... ...	...	040	35
60	Mills	060	Prince ...	...	040	35
40	Bayly	050	Mountford ...	...	030	30
50	Griffin	050	Betterton Housekeep^r			
			& to teach to act ...		080	80
		1090			800	695

besides a guiney a time
when he acts

60	Underhill	...	...	080
100	Dogget	...	...	100
100	Johnson	...	...	100
70	Pinkerman	...	...	080
50	Bullock	...	...	060
40	Norris	...	...	050
40	Bright	...	...	040
40	Pack ...	...	...	040
30	Leigh	...	...	040
30	Trout	...	...	030

1460		620

Men ...	...	...	1090
	...	...	0620
Women	...	...	0800
Pentions & Young Actors		...	190

	[deleted]	2600
	Tot:	2700

Singers

Master to teach Leveridge		...	40
Hughes	...	...	20
Cook ...	...	...	20
Mrs Hudson ...		...	30
Lindsey	...	...	20
Mills ...	...	...	20

	150

to be allowd—each
when they sing, wch
wth ye charge of addi-
tionall singers amounts
to 200

	Tot:	350

under Officers

2 Treasurrs or office keeprs at 75 each ...		150
12 Doorkeeprs at 20 each		240
Wardrobe keepr & servt		60
4 Tiremen at 20 each ...		80
4 Tirewomen at 25 each		100
4 Scenemen yt are car- penters at 25 each ...		100

dancers

Master to compose & teach

Labbé	...	...	...	60
De Ruell	...	...	...	40
Charrier	...	...	...	30
Mrs Elford ...	...	...	40
Mrs Mayers	...	...	40
Devonshire girle	...	...	20
Miss Evans	...	...	20

	250

to be allowd besides—every
time they dance wch wth
ye charge of additionall
dancers amounts to ... 250

	Tot:	500

Musick

Master to oversee ye Musick Mr Eccles	...	...	40
Twenty musitians allowing near 20 p week to each for 40 weeks comes to		...	760

	800

House Rent	...	...	600
Candles wax, tallow & oile			600
3 Managers...	...	...	600

	1800

Totalls

Players	...	...	2700
Dancers	...	...	500
Singers	...	...	320
Under Officers	...	...	930
Rent, candles, managers	...	1800
Musick	...	...	800
Remaining for incidnts as scenes, cloaths, printing, new plays, coals & composi- tions of musick &c		...	1950

	Tot: charge	9000

2 men to look after yᵉ

Candles at 15 each ...	30
Prompter & his Clerk	60
2 Barbers	40
4 Bill carriers 10 each ...	40
3 Necessary Women at	
10 each	30
	930

Note. yᵗ gloves, ribbands, perewigs shoes &c yᵗ may be worn abroad, are not to be provided out of yᵉ publick stock, but out of their respective salarys

A Calculation of yᵉ Receipts

Supposing yᵗ for yᵉ six winter monthes or 180 | days, yᵉ House receive 50 ₰ diem, one day with | another, & yᵗ all yᵉ receipts of 100 days more wᶜʰ they | act in yᵉ year be thrown in to make up yᵉ sũm, | yᵉ receipts of yᵉ House will then amount to 90,000 [*sic!*] | wᶜʰ will be sufficient to bear yᵉ charge of yᵉ | intended establishmᵗ |

Two shillings in yᵉ pound to be stopt out of salarys | or 600 till yᵉ receipts can discharge yᵉ debt of cloaths | & scenes, after wᶜʰ to be repd. | The Directors wᵗʰ salarys to advance 200 each | towards byuying cloaths & scenes to be rep'd yᵐ at yᵉ | end of yᵉ year out of yᵉ receipts."

[In L.C. 7/3 is another document identical with above save that in the totals the singers are put down for £350 and incidentals £1920. Another document gives a list of the "Constant Charge" and the "Incident Charge" without salaries. Under the former is included "I check on yᵉ Office," and under the latter are enumerated "Trumpets Drummer Kettle Drummer...Washerwoeman Men Taylors Wœmen Taylors Feather-man" and "Painter." The date is almost certainly the late summer of 1707.]

ii. L.C. 5/155, p. 3. Rubric: "Memorandᵐ | this Ordʳ was | Sent to yᵉ Office | to be Entred ": "Whereas You have represented to me yᵗ for | the better Entertainmᵗ of the Town you have made | Agreemᵗˢ wᵗʰ the Opera ᵱformers herein after mention'd | both Vocall and Instrumeᵗ together wᵗʰ yᵉ undʳ writen | Comedians.

Singers	Instrument	Actors	Actors
Sinʳ Nicolini	Mʳ Babel Senʳ	Mʳ Betterton	Mʳˢ Barrey
Sinʳ Valentini	Mʳ Pietro	Mʳ Wilks	Mʳˢ Oldfield
Mʳ Leveridge	Mʳ Rogers	Mʳ Doggett	Mʳˢ Bicknell
Mʳ Ramondon	Mʳ Babel junʳ	Mʳ Cibber	Mʳˢ Cross
Mʳ Lawrence	Mʳ Soyan	Mʳ Eastcourt	Mʳˢ Porter
Mʳˢ Tofts	Mʳ Desabaye	Mʳ Mills	Mʳˢ Powell
Sinᵃ Margaretta	Mʳ Cadet	Mʳ Johnson	Mʳˢ Saunders

Baronesse
Mad^{ll} Girardo
Mrs Lindsey
Instrumentall
Musick
Monsr Dieupart
Sin^{r} Haym
Sig^{r} Sajony
Mr Pepush
Sig^{r} Clodio
Mr Banister
Mr Corbet
Mr Lully
Mr Paisible
Mr Aylworth
Mr Francisco
Mr Armstronge
Mr Sympson
Mr Kytes
Mr Craigg
Mr Walter
Mr Lumian [*or* Lunican]
Mr Roberts
Mr Smith
Mr Latour
Mr Davain
Dancers
Mon^{sr} Cherier
Mr Pinkethman
Mr Bullock
Mr Bowen
Mr Thurmond
Mr Husband
Mr Bowman
Mr Bullock j^{r}
Mr Thurmond j^{r}
Mr Cross
Mr Ryan
Mrs Willis
Mrs Baker
Mrs Mills
Mrs Willis ju^{r}
Mrs Granger
Mrs Robins
Miss Young

I do strictly Order and Require You the | said ꝑformers to remain under ye direction of You the | Manager or Managers of the Queens Theatre in the | Hay Market and I do hereby declare that they shall | not have leave upon any Terms whatsoever to be | Entertain'd in any other Company wthout a discharge | in writing under the hands of the S^{d} Manag^{r} or | Manag^{rs} and Approv'd by me provided their contracts | are made good by you the said Manag^{r} or Manag^{rs} | of the said Theatre" [The rules and orders issued on Dec. 24, 1709; the order is dated Jan. 9, 1709/10].

iii. L.C. 7/3. Heading: "Regulations for ye Directors of ye Playhouse": "That ye Directors, especially ye three wth salarys have | regular meeting days (two of y^{m} making a board) to | give orders for ye good goverm^{t} of ye Company....That they prepare By laws for ye better order & goverm^{t} | of ye Company, to be approv'd first by ye Honorary | directors, before they are brought to ye Ld Chamberl^{n} | to be confirm'd. | That they, together wth ye Honorary directors make a list | of all plays fit to be acted, wch they shall take care | to have revis'd, y^{t} there be nothing in y^{m} indecent. And y^{t} | they Keep in their office a fair written copy of every | new play, for their justification. | That ye board appoint plays & parts, & are impowerd to | buy in all things necessary for ye well performing | of y^{m} | That no new opera, or other expensive entertainm^{t} be | undertaken without ye consent of ye Honorary directors, | & till ye charge be first computed & allow'd by y^{m} | That there be no poets night, but y^{t} ye board agree for new | plays at certain rates <both> as well for ye printing as | ye acting; wch are after to be licensd by ye master of y^{e} | Revells, wth ye Prologues, Epilogues, & songs <deletion> & to be prin|-ted by direction of ye board | That no benefit plays be allowd, nor tickets given to | any person | One of ye directors wth salarys to be present at all

Rehear | -salls, & to see y^t ye young people are taught to dance | & sing three times a week | That ye board do at every meeting inspect ye receipts of | ye House, & give directions for paying salarys accor-|-ding to ye establishm^t once a week, & all bills & other char | -ges ye first day of every monthe. And ye Accompts of y^e | House be examin'd & allowd by ye Honorary directors every | three monthes ⟨deletion⟩ | For ye ease of ye board, & to prevent clamours, they are | not impowr'd to raise salarys, take in new players &c, or to | make any addition to ye constant charge of ye House wthout | ye approbation of ye Honorary directors, to be confirmd by | ye Ld Chamberl^n | That ye board make agreem^{ts} in writing wth every person enter-|-tain'd in ye Company, wth a penalty in case any of y^m (except | ye Instrumentall musick) perform in any other publick | place without leave. And also y^t in case ye House be com-|-manded by order from Court to for-bear acting for ye space | of six weeks or longer, during ye winter, that for y^t time | they shall be entitl'd only to halfe ⟨salarys⟩ allowance." This and the following are not dated; they belong probably to about 1710. The documents reproduced in E. Thaler, *Shakespere to Sheridan*, p. 64 and G. C. D. Odell, *Shakespeare from Betterton to Irving*, i. 324 should be compared with these. The first is dated Jan. 17, 1718 (i.e. 1718/9); the second, from internal evidence, is of Jan. 9, 1713/4.

iv. L.C. 7/3. Heading "Rules & Regulations for the Management of the Theatres": "We the Managers of her Maties Comp^y of Comedians | acting under her Maties Royall licence at the Theatre | in Drury lane Doe hereby agree for the Better | Regulation & Management of the said Company, and | for the prevention of any Disputes that may arise | among us the said Menagers in the Execution, or | Conduct of our Respective Rights or Power Granted | by the said Royal licence Doe agree, & jointly subscribe | our selves to the True, & Punctual observation of | the Following Rules, & orders viz | 1st That once a week at least, or oftner (if any | two of them require it) There shall be a meeting | of all the Menagers at the Office to consult, and | order all matters relating to the Company | 2^d That all orders shall be enter'd in a Book kept | for that use by the Treasurer, & shall not be revok'd | or Contradicted, without the Consent of all the Three | Menagers | 3^d That all orders be sign'd by all the three | Menagers And that nothing be an order, That | has not all their three hands to confirm it, | excepting any little Necessarys, that may be wanting | not exceeding the value of twenty shi‼, which any | one of the said Menagers may from time to time | direct to be bought, or Provided: And if any one | of the said Menagers shall Refuse, or neglect to be | present at the said Weekly meetings Then the other | Menagers There present shall have full Power | to order, and Direct all matters whatsoever relating | to the Company, as if such absent Menager had there | been Present | 4th That no new play be receiv'd, that is not | approv'd by all the Menagers, nor any Play Reviv'd | or the Parts of it cast without the approbation of | all the Three under their hands | 5th That no Actor, Officer, or Servant be discharg'd | taken down, or rais'd without the consents, & hands | of all the Three | 6th That all Tradesmens Bills be sign'd by all three | and Paid every week if there be mon'y enough receiv'd | & no mony shall be shar'd till all Debts, and Disburstments | be Discharg'd | 7th That the Treasurer shall not pay or refuse to | pay any mony Contrary to these orders upon Penalty | of being Discharg'd."

v. L.C. 5/155, p. 159. Rubric "Articles for regulat^g | the Opera & Comedy": "Whereas the Managers of the Opera and Comedy have | Agreed upon the foll. Articles as Necessary for their better | regulation. I do hereby Approve and confirm the Same vizt | The Undertakers and Manager of the Opera shall not be | permitted to represent any Entertainm^t upon the Stage | under his direction but Such as shall be Set to Musick | The Undertakers and Managers of the Comedy shall not | be ρmitted to represent any Musicall Entertainm^t or | to have any Dancing ρform'd but by the Actors | The Managers of ye Opera and Comedy are permitted | to ρform as often and on what days they think fitt | Wednesdays and ffrydays in Lent only excepted | That no play be Acted for the benefit of any Actor | before ye first day of March nor more than one | benefit play in one Week during the Season of | ρforming Opera | That no benefit play for an Actor or the first day | of a New play be on the same day the Opera is ρform'd | nor the third day of a New play except in the time of Lent | and during ye time of Lent there is not to be Acted | more than one New play." Dated April 17, 1712.

vi. L.C. 5/153, p. 150. Rubric "ye old Guardroom at Hampton | Court to be ffloar'd | & ye Great hall | to be fitted up for a Theatre": "These are to Pray & Require you to Floor the old Guard | Room at Hampton Court, & to Wainscoat it to ye Top | with plain Dale Wainscoat, without Mouldings, | & out of it, to make a Door into ye Great Hall, which | you are to fitt up with all Convenient speed for a Theatre." Dated Feb. 17, 1701/2.

vii. L.C. 5/153, p. 441. Rubric "direccons for | the Comedians | wⁿ they Act at | Court": "I do hereby Order that her

Majestys Comedians and | also that the Musick and Dancers appointed to performe | before her Majesty at S⁺ James on her Birth Night do | obey such orders and directions as they shall receive from | Charles Killegrew Esq Master of the Revells..." Dated Jan. 30, 1703/4.

viii. L.C. 5/153, p. 433. Order that no play, new or old, no song, prologue or epilogue be presented on the stage without being first licensed by the Master of the Revels. Dated Jan. 15, 1703/4.

ix. L.C. 5/153, p. 434. Order to the Master of the Revels to be careful in the perusing and licensing of plays. Dated Jan. 17, 1703/4.

x. L.C. 5/155, p. 125. "Anne R | Whereas We are inform'd that the Orders Wee | have already given for the reformation of the Stage, by | not pmitting any thing to be Acted contrary to Religion | or good manners have in great measure had the good | effect We propos'd and being further desirous to reform all | other indecences and disorders of the Stage, Our Will and | Pleasure therefore is, And We do hereby Strictly Command | that no pson of what quality soever presume to Stand | behind the Scenes or come upon the Stage..." Dated Nov. 13, 1711.

xi. L.C. 5/154, p. 224. Rubric "Mʳ Rich Silenc'd | from Acting": "Whereas George Powell a Player has appear'd | on the Stage and Spoke the Prologue to the Subscripcõn | Opera Yesterday on the Theatre in Drury Lane wᵗʰ out my consent & contrary | to my former Order. These are therefore strictly to require | and comãnd You not to presume to Act any Play or | Opera till further Order from me..." Dated March 5, 1706/7 [cf. p. 287].

xii. L.C. 5/154, p. 437. Rubric "Play House in Covent Garden Silenc'd": "Whereas by an order dated the 30ᵗʰ day of Aprˡˡ | last upon the Peticõn of Sevˡˡ Players &c. I did then | direct and require you to pay to the respective | Comedians who had benefit plays last winter | the full receipᵗˢ of Such Plays...And whereas I am informed yᵗ in contempt of | the Said Ordʳ yᵘ still refuse to pay and detain from | the Sᵈ Comedians yᵉ profits of yᵉ Sᵈ benefit plays I do | therefore for the Sᵈ Contempt hereby Silence you from | further Acting." Dated June 6, 1709. The original order of April 30 appears in the same volume p. 417. It forbids any deduction from the players receipts for the use of the Patent, and allows only a deduction cf £40 for the night's charges. The question of benefits caused a good deal of trouble, and later. In L.C. 5/157, p. 284 is an order to the D.L. managers not to allow any benefit before Mrs Oldfield's and Mrs Porter's (dated Feb. 2, 1719/20). The "Play House in Covent Garden" is, of course, D.L.

xiii. L.C. 5/154, p. 446. Rubric "Players to Act | at the Theatre | in the Haymark^t." This order recites the above (no. xii) and gives permission to the actors to perform at the Haymarket 4 days a week. Dated July 8, 1709.

xiv. L.C. 7/3. Endorsed "Copies of this to be | deliver'd to Cibber Wilks | & Booth, & the others | left for other Managers | or Actors. | A Copy of ye Kings Revocation | served on Cibber & Booth | & one left for Sr R. Steel. | The Lord Chamberlain's | Order for shutting up | Drury Lane Theatre | 1719." This order discharges the managers from further acting; dated Jan. 25, 1719 (i.e. 1719/20). A copy of this order is entered in L.C. 5/157, pp. 280–1. The revocation of Steele's licence appears in the same volume, p. 279 (dated Jan. 23, 1719/20). On pp. 142–3 will be found letters to the law officers regarding the scope of Steele's licence (dated Oct. 23, 1718). Wilks, Cibber and Booth were ordered to account with Steele (*id*. pp. 415–6, dated May 2, 1721). In L.C. 7/3 are preserved Steele's original petition for his licence, the Attorney-General's and the Solicitor-General's opinions on this petition (Jan. 12, 1714/5) and a copy of the grant to Steele (dated Jan. 14, 1714/5).

xv. L.C. 7/3. Heading "Mr Colliers | Memorial against Cibber | & others relative to an agreement about | his Share in the Licence of the | Theatres in the Haymarket and | Drury Lane | 6 Decr 1712." This recites that Collier, in consideration of giving up the Haymarket to Swiny, was admitted to Swiny's Share in D.L., and gives an agreement between Collier and Wilks, Doggett and Cibber by which the former covenanted to make over the lease of D.L. to the actors for a sum of £800 annually, with the deduction of £100 for Swiny (see p. 284). This agreement is dated Dec. 6, 1712. The memorial proceeds to complain that since the introduction of Booth into the management the actors refuse to give any money to Collier.

xvi. L.C. 7/3. Heading "Playhouses | 12 April 1711 | Mr Swiney." This is a letter to the Lord Chamberlain, in answer to a complaint by someone unknown. "The Person who made this Complaint agst me is made use of as a Tool by My Partners to incense My L^d against me, and thô they very well Know that w^t they alledge is a very false and Scandalous reflection upon me, yet they hope it may have some effect wth my L^d to my prejudice."

It appears from this answer that some performer had borrowed £5 from Swiny which was stopped out of his salary.

xvii. L.C. 5/160, p. 130. Entry dated April 28, 1730 silencing the Theatre in G.F. because of the complaints of the Lord Mayor and Aldermen.

IV. *Documents relating to the Management of the Opera.*

i. L.C. 7/3 and L.C. 5/155, p. 160. Rubric: "M.ʳ Swyney to receive | 100 p Ann. from | y.ᵉ Manag.ʳˢ of the | Comedy":"Whereas the Managers of her Maj.ᵗˢ Company of | Comedians have Agreed for the better Support of the | expence.ˢ of the Opera to pay to M.ʳ Owen Swyney who | by her Maj.ᵗˢ License is Appointed Manager of y.ᵉ Opera | the Sume of one hundred pounds p Ann. out of the | receipts of the Comedy the said paym.ᵗˢ to Commence from | the 1.ˢᵗ day of June 1712 after w.ᶜʰ time the money which | they paid by my Warr.ᵗ dated the 20.ᵗʰ of Nov.ʳ 1711 towards | the Rent of the Theatre in the Hay Market is to cease | and have pray'd my Warr.ᵗ there upon | I do hereby Approve and confirm the said Agreem.ᵗ | and do Order and direct the Managers of her Maj.ᵗˢ | Company of Comedians to pay to M.ʳ Owen Swyney | the Sume of One hundred pounds." Dated April 17, 1712.

ii. L.C. 7/3. Various documents connected with the above, relating to Vanbrugh's share of the costumes. *a.* Document endorsed "Sir John Vanbrugh's remonstrance against the Manager of Drury Lane house relative to the Stock of Cloaths" (dated in pencil ? Feb. 1715). This document quotes from a letter of Swiney's "in March last," in which Swiney acknowledges Vanbrugh's right in the stock of clothes, now at D.L. Quotations are also given from a letter "dated the 25ᵗʰ of October last" in which Swiney states that the £100 was paid to him in consideration of the stock of clothes left at D.L. *b.* Document endorsed "Sᵣ John Vanbrughs Case | relating to the Playhouse | Cloathes &c." This declares that in 1707 Swiney leased the Haymarket from Vanbrugh, the rent being for the clothes as well as for the house. Later Swiney took Wilks, Cibber and Doggett into partnership, and they removed to D.L. The lease, however, was retained for the sake of the clothes; £200 being allowed to Collier at the Haymarket in consideration of the rent. Still later Swiney and Collier changed houses; Collier got an order from the Lord Chamberlain that only £100 should be paid to Swiney. The actors shook off both Swiney and Collier and declared the stock theirs. Vanbrugh proceeds to give a copy of an order of the Lord Chamberlain ordering £100 to be paid to Vanbrugh at Swiney's request (dated Jan. 14, 1714/5). A copy of Colley Cibber's blunt refusal is also given (dated Jan. 22, 1714/5). *c.* Autograph letter of Vanbrugh dated Aug. 13, 1714, narrating the same facts and praying for redress. *d.* Autograph letter of Vanbrugh dated Dec. 27, 1714 again praying to have the matter settled.

iii. L.C. 5/154, p. 288. Rubric "Musitians to | pforme in yᵉ | Operas in the | Haymarkett": "I do hereby give leave to Mͬ Banister Mͬ Paisible Mͬ | Lully Mͬ La Tour Mͬ Le Sack Mͬ Elwart Mͬ Soyan | Mͬ Crouch Mͬ Babell Mͬ Francisco Mͬ Roger Mͬ | Desabeye Mͬ Cadet and Mͬ Dieupar to perform in the | Operas at the Queens Theatre in the Haymarkett." Dated Dec. 1, 1707.

iv. L.C. 5/155, p. 75. Lord Chamberlain's order to Collier. Although the receipts have been large many tradesmen's bills have not been paid. Collier is ordered not to disburse any money till he has sent a list of his receipts to the Lord Chamberlain. Dated March 5, 1710/1.

v. L.C. 7/3. Endorsed: "Directions to yᵉ Treasurᵉʳ | of the Opera in yᵉ Hay Markᵗ | 13 Febry 1712/3": "Whereas there remains in your hands the | Sume of One hundred Sixty two pounds Nineteen | Shillings being the clear receipt of the Opera Since | Mͬ Swiney left the House | I do hereby direct you to pay the said Sume of | One hundred Sixty two pounds Nineteen Shillings | to the following psons in proportion to their | Sevᵘ contracts made wᵗʰ Mͬ Swiney vizᵗ Sinͬ | Valeriano, Sinͬ Valentini Siniͬᵉ Pilotta and her | husband, Sigͬᵉ Margerita, Mͬˢ Barbier, Mͬˢ | Manio, Mͬ Hendell, Mͬ Heidegger, wᶜʰ Method | of paymᵗ You are to Observe in the clear receiptˢ | of the Opera which shall hereafter come into | your hands | But whereas Signͬ Valentini and Signrᵃ | Pillotta have already receiv'd some Money from | Mͬ Swiney in part of their contract, you are | not to pay them out of these receipts till yᵉ rest | are paid their contracts in proportion to what | they have been paid."

vi. L.C. 5/157, p. 228. Warrant for an Academy of Music; dated May 9, 1719. This appears also in duplicate in L.C. 7/3.

vii. L.C. 5/157, p. 234. Instructions to Händel. "Instructions to Mͬ Hendel. | That Mͬ Hendel either by himself or such | Correspondencᵉ as he shall think fit procure proper | Voices to Sing in the Opera. | The said Mͬ Hendel is impower'd to contract in the | Name of the Patentees with those Voices to Sing in the |

Opera for one Year and no more. | That Mʳ Hendel engage Senezino as soon as possible | to serve the said Company and for as many Years as may | be. | That in case Mʳ Hendel meet with an excellent | Voice of the first rate he is to Acquaint the Govᵗ and | Company forthwith of it and upon what Terms he or She | may be had." Dated May 14, 1719.

viii. L.C. 7/3. Various documents relating to the Academy of Music.

(a) Proposals for carrying on the Opera by means of a company.

(b) List of subscribers.

(c) Proposals for the Court of Directors, dated Nov. 27, 1719. [Dr Arbuthnot appears on this board and Pope was requested to propose a seal and motto for the academy.]

(d) Report of Attorney-General on the proposal to found an Academy of Music, dated Feb. 27, 1718/9.

ix. L.C. 5/160, p. 117. Order that no person stand on the stage at the Opera; dated Dec. 5, 1729.

V. *Documents relating to Actors and Performers.*

i. Various contracts with actors [all in L.C. 7/3]:—

(a) Mrs Oldfield "of the Pish of Sᵗ Pauls Covent-Garden Spinster" and Swiney. Agreement to act from July 1 for 13 years; salary £200 in 9 instalments with a benefit in February; 10 June to 10 Sept. to be free. Dated April 21, 1709.

(b) Mrs Mary Porter and Swiney. Agreement to act from July 1 for 5 years; salary £80 in 9 instalments; a benefit with £50 charges [all the contracts name the free dates and fix varying penalties for non-performance of the articles]. Dated May 24, 1709.

(c) Mrs Catherine Baker and Swiney. Agreement to act from date for 3 years; salary £40 in 9 instalments. Dated Sept. 9, 1709.

(d) Richard and Elizabeth Willis and Swiney. Agreement that Mrs Willis act from date for 3 years; salary £40 in 9 instalments; Mary Willis, her daughter, to receive £20. "Memo. both Eliz. and Mary to have a share in a benefit play in proportion to their Salary." In case Rich should bring a case against Mrs Willis for breach of her articles, Swiney to pay the costs. Dated Sept. 9, 1709.

(e) William Bowen and Swiney. Agreement to act from July 1 for 5 years; salary £75; one benefit in April with £50 charges. Dated June 20, 1709.

(*f*) Benjamin Husband and Swiney. Agreement to act from July 1 for 5 years; salary £65; benefit in April with £50 charges. Dated May 10, 1709.

(*g*) William Pinkethman and Swiney. Agreement to act from July 1 for 5 years; salary £100; benefit in March with £40 charges. Dated April 30, 1709.

(*h*) William Bullock and Swiney. Agreement to act from July 1 for 5 years; salary £80; benefit in April with £50 charges. Dated April 4, 1709.

(*i*) Benjamin Johnson and Swiney. Agreement to act from July 1 for 5 years; salary £100; benefit in April with £40 charges. Dated April 11, 1709.

(*j*) John Mills and Swiney. Agreement to act from July 1 for 5 years; salary £100; benefit in March with £40 charges. Dated March 30, 1709.

(*k*) Firbank and Betterton. "Feb: 12, 1701 | That Mr Firbanks son is to have 40 p^s week & a play | in March paying 30 for ye charges of ye house | That ye agreem^t is for a year certain & after y^t either | party may give six monthes notice | The salary to commence Monday next."

ii. Various documents relating to George Powell:—

(*a*) L.C. 7/3. Petition of Powell in which he states that his salary is not regularly paid. He pleads for payment or a discharge. The Lord Chamberlain has endorsed this "Mr Powell to have a discharge | when he has p^d ye debts | due to ye Company from him & to play | till 4 & 40^{li} due to Mr Smith by y^e | Young people y^e | Last Vacation be payd."

(*b*) L.C. 7/3. "7 April 1705 | Discharge to Mr Powell | Theatre Royall 7th Aprill 1705 | This is to Certifie That | Mr George Powell is at Libertie | to dispose of him selfe as he | thinks fitt. | Chr. Rich."

(*c*) L.C. 5/154, p. 119. Rubric: "Geo: Powell Comed^n | to be Apprehen^d" For refusing to obey orders, Powell is commanded to be arrested. Dated Nov. 14, 1705.

(*d*) L.C. 5/154, p. 124. Rubric: "Geo: Powell Comed^n | not to be entert^d | in the Playhouse | in Drury Lane." A command to the D.L. managers not to admit Powell because of his obduracy at the Haymarket. Dated Nov. 24, 1705 [for the consequence of this order see p. 282].

iii. Various documents relating to Thomas Doggett [all in L.C. 7/3]:—

(*a*) Autograph letter, dated Nov. 8, 1703, to the Lord Chamberlain. Doggett informs the Lord Chamberlain that some time since he agreed to act at L.I.F. for 3 years, reserving himself the liberty of ceasing from acting from May 20 to Oct. 12 each year. On May 24, 1703 he went to Bath; he received a message from Betterton and Mrs Barry, by Smith their office-keeper, desiring him to play with the company at Oxford. He promised to do so for a fee of £20 or a share. He went to Oxford the first day of the Act. When he arrived there Betterton proposed other terms and, on his refusal, gave his parts to others.

(*b*) Autograph letter to Betterton, dated "Satturday yͤ 8" [or 6; there is a pencil dating Nov. 9, 1703; if this letter is of the same period as the former the date is possibly Nov. 6, which fell on a Saturday]. "The Company has bin | so very free to tell me they thought | theire bargin with me very hard. I must | confess theire stoping part of my mony | and the trouble they have given me to gett | part is a suffecient proof they spoke theire | opinion." Doggett appeals for a discharge.

(*c*) The answer of the managers of D.L. to Doggett (dated Nov. 3, 1714). They explain that Doggett withdrew himself from the company on the introduction of Booth. They desire the Lord Chamberlain to order him back.

iv. Various documents relating to the Baroness [all in L.C. 7/3; the Baroness was a singer in the early operas]:—

(*a*) Vanbrugh's proposals: 1. either to pay the Baroness the same salary as that of Mrs Bracegirdle (£5 a week if receipts allow of it or £3 a week certain; *i.e.* £100 a year for singing twice a week); 2. if she sings with him next year she will be allowed half profits of a play in October or November. The Baroness' proposals: 1. regarding the bargain for 10 times singing (concluded the last of November 1705) she was to have 100 guineas for the performances and though she sang only 5 times she was willing to conclude the series, £57 yet remaining due on the agreement. 2. If this is paid she will sing 5 times gratis, and is willing to sing 10 times before the last of May next at 8 guineas a time.

(*b*) Letter regarding this quarrel, dated March 1, 1705 (*i.e.* 1705/6). It declares that Haym made a verbal bargain with Congreve and Vanbrugh on behalf of his scholar, the Baroness, shortly before the opening of the Haymarket, by which they were to give her 100 guineas for 10 performances before Nov. 1705.

She had only sung 5 times, and demands the liberty of singing elsewhere, and also payment of the remainder of her salary. "To shew that they did make this bargaine besides the Testimony of | Sig^{re} Nicola Haym who declares that it was made at the time above- | mentiond at the Sign of the Cock in Bow Street one afternoon | where was present also Mr Ecles, but he cannot witnes it, what | was spoken having been in a language he understands not." The letter proceeds to explain that the fact that only 5 performances were given was not due to the Baroness; "when Mr Congreve after the Acting of the | Pastoral saide to Sig^{re} Nicola that he would give his Scholler 50 Guineas for | what had been done and that they should both be at liberty | and the bargaine end, this Sig^{re} Nicola & his Scholler declard | they would agree to, but Mr Congreve with drew his ⟨words⟩ proposition."

(c) Letter from the Lord Chamberlain. "I received your letter about the Buisness | of Mr Vanbrook with the Barroness, and | think it will be very difficult for me to make | them agree who are so wide in their proposals | to each other, therefore will lett alone a little | longer ('till I come to town) in hopes they may | patch up of themselves, rather then give my | self the trouble (if I can avoid it) to make | an Agreement which very likely will please neither; But as for the former Bargain | which Mr Vanbrook does not deny, I shall | alwais think him obliged to perform & ρay | her the 50^{li} And she shall sing ye 5 times | for it, or six if he insists upon it, though the | time is Elapsed in which she was to performe it." Dated Feb. 24, 1705/6.

v. L.C. 7/3. Heading "Mr Rich his Complaint to | ye Lord Chamberlain | concerning Mrs Hooke | 9th Decr 1705." The complaint is that Vanbrugh and Congreve seduced away Mrs Mary Hooke, alias Harcourt, to the Haymarket, although she had entered into 5 years articles with Rich in October 1702. Rich includes here a copy of a letter dated Nov. 27, 1704 from Sir John Stanley forbidding him to engage any of the L.I.F. players. The complaint adds that Newman, a prompter, and Hood, a dresser, had been tempted, and that since Christmas Powell, Bowen, Doggett, Mins, Husbands, Mrs Bignall and Mrs Baker had been engaged at the Haymarket. Two notes follow: "6 Nov 1703 Upon a false surmise (?) of Mr Congreves at 3 in | the afternoon our Reviv'd Play stopt so y^t the best | part of the Audience was lost | 1705 Mr Swynys Play stopt that day it was first to be acted | altho it was for ye benefitt of Mr Johnson who was | then in prison & no Just reason for Stopping it but | kindness to Mr Vanbrugh | M^r Du Ruell & his Wife stopt." [The revived play on Nov. 6 was *Love and Danger or Mistaken Jealousie*, billed as acted but once in ten years. For Swiney's play (*The Quacks*) see p. 22.]

vi. L.C. 7/3. Heading "The Case of Catherine Tofts relating to her Agreement with Mr Rich, Shewing | the Reason why she forbears singing for him" (dated in pencil 8 Jan. 1706). Mrs Tofts declares that on Dec. 30, 1704, she agreed with Rich to sing for one year commencing Jan. 5, 1704/5. She continued with him till a dispute arose concerning £60 which the nobility gave to her; of this Rich claimed half. Everyone decided against him so that "He tooke all the Oppertunitys he could to be Revenged on her: which was in calling her to Sing oftner than She was Able to performe...Through his ill Nature he called her to sing on a Tuesday, Thursday, and Saturday in the same week, not in hopes of getting audiences (it being after Midsumer the Weather Excessive hott and the Towne very Empty) but only to shew his ill will." She found on the Tuesday after she had lost her voice. On Rich's having to pay her £100 at the end of the season he detained £20 for this failure, and would not give it to her till she had sung twice, which she did on July 10 and Oct. 29. Meanwhile she had spent much money on doctors, "And after all her Care and Expences the time being near that she was to performe again She desired him to gett Cloathes fitt for her to appear in the Opera, these that she had before being not only worne out, but were never made fitt for her, To which he answered he supposed She had a mind to improve herself that she might be in a Condition to Raise her price." After several other complaints she concludes by describing Rich as "a Man unfitt to deale with for his ill Manners & Management of them which are in his power." Her demands follow.

vii. L.C. 7/3. Heading "Proposalls delivered by Mr Dieupert on the behalfe of Mrs Tofts." 1. That Rich give her £100 and a release from all past forfeitures, she to have the jewels and he the clothes. Dieupart claimed 22 guineas "for what is past." 2. That new articles be entered into for 3 months, during which time she should sing 12 times for £200, *i.e.* £16 . 13 . 4 "each time she Sings before the Curtaine is drawn up." 3. That she provide a performer on the harpsichord. If she is sick, she will make up the missed performances at a later date. 4. That she "shall have that Roome called the Practicing Roome to Dress in," and shall be attended by two women dressers. Rich shall also "find two Bottles of Wine every time she Sings to be for her Use to dispose of them to the Gentlemen that practice with her." 5. That she shall not be obliged to sing more than twice in one day. She demands also a benefit on Tuesday Feb. 19 next. 6. That if after the articles expire she and Rich cannot agree she shall sing where she pleases. Dated Jan. 28, 1705, apparently 1705/6.

viii. L.C. 7/3. Complaint of Mrs Oldfield, dated March 4, 1708/9. The complaint is that when she acted at the Haymarket, she had an agreement for £4 a week and a benefit with £40 charges. On promise of a similar arrangement she returned to D.L., but for a benefit on March 3 Rich now detains £71 for the use of the patent.

ix. L.C. 7/3. Rich's answer. On March 20, 1703 Mrs Oldfield agreed to act at D.L. for 50/- a week, without mention of a benefit. She later deserted to the Haymarket. Since her return she had £4 a week "(altho' no woman 'till of late Years had above 50ˢ.).'' Mrs Oldfield desired *The Stratagem* to be acted for her benefit on March 3; the arrangement was that £40 should be paid for charges and she should have 2/3 of the remainder. The receipts were £134 . 3 and so her two-thirds came to £62 . 7 . 8. This is signed by Thomas Skipwith, Christopher Rich, Thomas Goodall, John Metcalfe, Richard Middlemore and William East.

x. L.C. 7/3. A letter from Owen Swiney to the Lord Chamberlain's office. He explains that he did not receive Downes into the Music because he was utterly unqualified. However, he is ready to allow Young Downes' father such a pension as the Lord Chamberlain thinks fit. The letter ends with a complaint against Rich. Dated Jan. 27, 1706/7.

xi. L.C. 7/3. Complaint of Mary Porter, dated Oct. 22, 1707. She was receiving 40/- a week when Vanbrugh let his house to Swiney. "When several of the Gentlewomen that perform'd principal Parts either neglected or were sick, she at a nights notice study'd and play'd them perfect the next night...for which she hop'd for incouragement or at least to have had such Parts given her by which she might have gain'd reputation when there was more time to study. But instead thereof generally those Parts were given to such as were below her." Her benefit play was postponed till May 2, and although half the actors were out of pay she had to provide the full £40 charges. Slightly before they began to play that winter an actress was taken in over her head. "She omits lesser matters tho absolutely necessary as Cloaths conveniency for dressing &c."

xii. L.C. 7/3. Mary Baldwin's petition for a discharge. Betterton and Mrs Barry made an agreement with her for 15/- a week. They stopped her salary and then promised her a benefit, at which, however, so many free persons were admitted that she had no profit. (Dated in pencil ? June 1703; another complaint of a like nature in the same collection is dated June 10, 1703.)

xiii. L.C. 7/3. Complaint of John Essex against Rich, undated but endorsed by Sir John Stanley Feb. 24, 1702 (*i.e.* 1702/3). The points in the complaint are 1. that Rich has stopped 32 days of Essex' salary. 2. that he has stopped him from his employment "for no Reason, but not performing a Dance when I was so lame I had not the Power to do it." He begs the favour of a discharge or payment of his salary.

xiv. L.C. 5/154, p. 115. Order, dated Nov. 2, 1705, addressed to Rich forbidding him to employ the dancer Du Ruel or his wife, who have entered into articles with the Haymarket company.

xv. L.C. 5/154, p. 126. Order, dated Nov. 29, 1705, addressed to Rich and informing him that Du Ruel has received a discharge from the Haymarket.

xvi. L.C. 7/3. Complaint of L'Abbé, the dancer, against Betterton. "Monsieur Il y a trois ans que je me suis engagé a Monsieur Batardon par mon dernier Contract; ces trois années sont expirées du vingtduexiéme Juin dernier 1703. Sans m'avoir proposé aucun autre engagement directement ni indirectement; Je Vous prie, Monsieur, de croire que J'ai toutes les raisons du monde di n'être pas content de la maniére d'agir du Sieur Batardon, à mon êgard....Je Vous supplie tres humblement d'estre persuadé, Monsieur, que si j'ai quitté le Sieur Batardon, ce n'est ni par caprice ni par mauvaise humeur ni par aucun engagement...mais c'est vniquement par vn motif d'honneur tout par, le dit Sieur Batardon m'ayant toûjours manqué de parole..."

xvii. L.C. 5/155, p. 11. Order dated June 14, 1710. "Whereas Complaint has been made to me that five of the Actors belonging to her Maj^{ts} Company of Comedians under your Managm^t vizt George Powell Barton Booth Jno Bickerstaff Thõphil^s Keen and ffranc^s Lee did not only refuse to Obey ye Orders of Mr Hill who is appointed by you to take care of the said Company, but that they did also lately in a riotous manner break open the Doors of the Play house, beating and Abusing the S^d Mr Hill and wth their Swords drawn threatning his life and have also comĩtted Sever^{ll} other [other *repeated*] insolencys and disorders These are Therefore to charge and Require you imediately to dismis and remove the s^d Powell from the Service of her Majesty's Company he having been formerly guilty of the like offences and y^t you Suspend Barton Booth Theophil^s Keen Jno Bickerstaff and ffranc^s Lee from further Acting." Addressed to Collier [see also *supra*, p. 287].

APPENDIX C

Hand-list of Plays, 1700–1750

[In the following list of plays, an endeavour has been made to include all the theatrical entertainments as well as the regular dramas produced for the first time within the first half of the eighteenth century. The titles are given from the original editions; the dates which follow in brackets are of the first performances; and the years of publication are presented thereafter. All plays printed copies of which I have been unable to see are marked with an asterisk. The majority of these were in all probability never published, but the fact that no attempt has hitherto been made to collect eighteenth century dramas or to outline the bibliography of the subject renders this a particularly difficult question. Where I have found indication of publication in the *Biographia Dramatica* or elsewhere I have inserted the particulars given in these sources. It will be recognised that the details given here are of necessity incomplete, as, apart from the fact that I have not attempted to trace the history of any play into the sixties or seventies of the eighteenth century, the lack of bibliographical research into this subject prevents a full and exhaustive summary. Following the information concerning the editions, I have given an outline of performances of each play up to the year 1750. It will be understood that this outline is also incomplete. Theatrical advertisements in newspapers did not begin until the early years of the century, and remained for a time exceedingly spasmodic. I have attempted, however, to collect here all the information that could be derived from newspaper collections in the Bodleian and the British Museum, from the Burney MSS. and from various collections of theatrical material bequeathed to the British Museum. It is manifestly impossible for the outline here presented to be without error; the enumeration of the thousands of performances could not be undertaken without a slip; but I have done all in my power to make this as accurate an account of eighteenth century theatrical activity as possible. For the sake of convenience in reference, I have subdivided this hand-list into several sections. The first contains English plays and operas; the second, Italian operas or operas translated from the Italian; the third, Italian and French pieces performed by comedians of those nationalities between the years 1718 and 1745. For pantomimes, musical entertainments, ballets, and "masques of musick" I have given only the date of first performance. A full list of dates would have seriously encumbered this appendix. Besides the abbreviations for the various theatres (see the Preface), I have employed the following contractions:

T.	Tragedy	B.O.	Ballad Opera
H.T.	Historical Tragedy	M.	Masque
C.	Comedy	Ent.	Entertainment
D.O.	Dramatic Opera	Pant.	Pantomime
O.	Opera	Past.	Pastoral
F.	Farce.	Pol.	Political Play

Where any of these abbreviations occur in brackets, the actual designation does not accord with the description on the title-page.]

I. *English Plays and Operas.*

ADAMS, GEORGE.
> The plays of Sophocles 2 vols. 8° 1729.
> ***T.** The Heathen Martyr; or, the Death of Socrates 4° 1746.

ADDISON, JOSEPH.
> O. Rosamond (D.L. March 1706/7) 4° 1707 (*bis*); 8° 1755 (Glasgow) Songs in the New Opera Call'd Rosamond...Compos'd by Mr. Tho. Clayton F. (1707).
>> 1707. D.L. T. 4/3, S. 15, S. 22. 1733. L.² W. 7/3 (with music by Arne), F. 9, W. 14, F. 16; Th. 5/4, M. 9, M. 30. 1740. D.L. S. 8/3, T. 11, S. 15, T. 18, M. 24; M. 7/4, F. 11. 1741. W. 25/2; T. 24/3. 1745. Th. 31/1; F. 1/2–S. 9, W. 13, Th. 14; T. 12/3; Th. 4/4; M. 6/5. 1747. S. 10/1, T. 13.
>
> T. Cato (D.L. April 1713) 4° 1713; 4° 1713 (2nd); 4° 1713 (3rd); 4° 1713 (4th); 4° 1713 (5th); 12° 1713 (7th); 12° 1713 (8th); 8° 1713 (Dublin); 12° 1713 (Hague); 12° 1725 (11th); 12° 1734; 12° 1735; 8° 1735; 8° 1737; 8° 1748; 12° 1750; 8° 1751 (Glasgow); 12° 1756.
>> 1713. D.L. T. 14/4–S. 18, T. 21–F. 24, T. 28–Th. 30; F. 1/5, S. 2, T. 5–S. 9; T. 20/10, Th. 29; Th. 12/11; Th. 3/12, Th. 17, T. 29. 1714. S. 16/1; M. 15/3; T. 6/4; S. 8/5; S. 2/10, S. 23; W. 10/11. 1715. F. 7/1, W. 19; Stationers' Hall T. 1/3; D.L. T. 3/5; F. 21/10; Th. 29/12. 1716. M. 6/2, T. 14; M. 19/3; F. 13/4; M. 21/5. 1717. Th. 24/1; T. 5/3; S. 19/10. 1718. S. 22/2; S. 8/3, S. 29; F. 25/4; S. 25/10; F. 26/12; L.² Th. 16/10, F. 17. 1719. D.L. Th. 5/2; T. 21/4; T. 13/10. 1720. T. 9/2; F. 13/5; T. 29/11. 1721. W. 1/2; T. 14/3; Th. 28/12. 1722. S. 31/3; Th. 11/10; W. 12/12. 1723. W. 1/5; Th. 31/10. 1724. Th. 2/1; T. 25/2; Th. 9/4; Th. 12/11. 1725. T. 9/2; S. 6/3; W. 14/4; W. 13/10. 1726. M. 7/2; M. 11/4. 1727. Th. 19/1, W. 25; Th. 13/4; F. 12/5; W. 18/10; S. 30/12. 1728. S. 14/12. 1729. S. 22/2. 1730. L.² M. 20/4; Th. 21/5; D.L. W. 6/5; Th. 1/10; T. 29/12; G.F. Th. 12/11– S. 14, M. 16; Th. 3/12. 1731. G.F. M. 15/3; T. 26/10; Th. 2/12. 1732. D.L. S. 1/1; T. 14/3; Th. 5/10; G.F. F. 18/2. 1733. D.L. S. 14/4; G.F. Th. 19/4; Th. 24/5; H.² W. 28/11. 1734. C.G. F. 18/1, S. 19; T. 12/3, T. 26; C.G. Th. 28/11, F. 29; M. 2/12, T. 3;

G.F. Th. 25/4; W. 2/10; D.L. T. 21/5; S. 14/9, T. 17; Th. 10/10;
Th. 26/12. 1735. G.F. W. 5/2; D.L. S. 1/3; S. 10/5; W. 11/6; S.
20/9; S. 13/12, W. 17. 1736. S. 6/3; S. 1/5, W. 12; W. 27/10;
F. 3/12; L.² M. 29/3; Th. 28/10, S. 30; T. 2/11, F. 5; G.F. W.
5/5. 1737. D.L. S. 19/2; W. 2/3; Th. 12/5, T. 17; Th. 8/9; T.
4/10; H.² M. 14/2; C.G. T. 31/5. 1738. D.L. M. 2/1; T. 12/9;
Th. 23/11; C.G. Th. 7/12. 1739. D.L. F. 19/1, S. 20; S. 24/3;
M. 7/5; Th. 13/9; F. 12/10; Th. 15/11. 1740. T. 8/1; Th. 6/3;
Th. 16/10; W. 12/11; C.G. M. 18/10. 1741. D.L. M. 27/4; T.
8/12. 1742. Th. 4/3; T. 4/5; C.G. Th. 25/3; M. 18/10; Th. 18/11.
1743. S. 12/2; F. 22/4; F. 28/10; F. 2/12; D.L. Th. 5/5; T. 27/9;
T. 18/10. 1744. F. 3/2; Th. 4/10; C.G. Th. 16/2; S. 10/3. 1745.
Th. 31/1; S. 30/3; D.L. S. 9/11; G.F. M. 9/12. 1746. C.G. F.
24/10; S. 20/12. 1747. G.F. Th. 22/1; C.G. S. 14/3. 1748. S.
16/4; T. 25/10; S. 12/11; W. 21/12. 1749. S. 4/2; Th. 6/4;
S. 11/11.

C.   The Drummer; or, The Haunted-House (D.L. March 1715/6) 4°
1716 (anon.); 4° 1722 (With a Preface by Sir Richard Steele, in an
Epistle Dedicatory to Mr. Congreve); 12° (Hague 1723); 8° 1749
(Glasgow); 8° 1751 (Glasgow).
     1716. D.L. S. 10/3, T. 13, S. 17. 1722. L.² F. 2/2, S. 3, M. 5,
T. 6, Th. 8, S. 10, M. 12; M. 12/3, T. 13; W. 4/4, T. 17; M.
21/5; S. 6/10; W. 21/11; S. 22/12. 1723. T. 12/2; T. 26/3; M.
14/10; F. 20/12. 1724. S. 18/1; F. 7/2, T. 18; S. 21/3; Th. 7/5;
F. 27/11; H.² M. 23/3. 1725. L.² S. 23/1; W. 19/5; W. 27/10.
1726. T. 18/1. 1727. S. 4/3; F. 13/10; W. 20/12. 1729. S. 18/1.
1730. F. 9/1; F. 30/10; G.F. M. 19/1, T. 20; Th. 19/2. 1731.
L.² F. 19/2; G.F. S. 27/2; M. 19/4; M. 22/11; W. 1/12. 1732.
L.² F. 14/1; M. 27/11; G.F. F. 4/2; Th. 2/11. 1734. C.G. M. 28/1;
G.F. W. 30/10. 1735. C.G. M. 3/2; W. 15/10. 1740. S. 22/3,
S. 29; S. 12/4; T. 6/5; F. 17/10; G.F. Th. 30/10. 1741. C.G. M.
26/10; T. 29/12. 1745. W. 23/1; D.L. M. 25/11; G.F. F. 22/11.
1747. C.G. S. 17/1. 1749. W. 27/12.

ARNE, Dr THOMAS AUGUSTINE.
Mus.D. Don Saverio...The Musick by Mr. Arne (unacted) 4° 1750.
[It is probable that the libretto as well as the music is by Arne.
For his later works see the *Biographia Dramatica*.]

ARTHUR, JOHN.
(B.O.) The Lucky Discovery: or, The Tanner of York. An Opera
(C.G. April 1738) 8° 1737 (York); 8° 1738 (anon.)
     1738. C.G. M. 24/4; M. 25/9; M. 23/10; W. 6/12. 1739. M. 19/3;
M. 28/5. 1740. W. 9/4; W. 14/5; W. 1/10, M. 6; F. 7/11, T. 11.
1741. W. 6/5; M. 21/9, W. 23. 1746. James-street M. 21/5.

ASHTON, ROBERT.
T.   The Battle of Aughrim: Or, The Fall of Monsieur St. Ruth
(unacted) 1728 (Dublin); 12° 1756 (Dublin); 8° 1771 (Dublin);
12° 1777 (Dublin); 12° (1780); 12° 1784 (Dublin); 12° 1782
(Strabane).

ASTON, ANTHONY or TONY.
*C. Love in a Hurry (Smock Alley Dublin) 1709.
Past. The Coy Shepherdess A Pastoral (T.R. Dublin) 4° 1709 (Dublin);
Pastora: or, The Coy Shepherdess. An Opera. As it was Per-

form'd By His Grace the Duke of Richmond's Servants, at
Tunbridge-Wells, In the Year 1712...The Second Edition 8° 1712.
(B.O.) The Fool's Opera; or, The Taste of the Age. Written by Mat.
Medley. And Performed by His Company in Oxford...To which
is prefix'd, A Sketch of the Author's Life, Written by Himself
8° 1731.
[R. H. Griffith ("Tony Aston's 'Fool's Opera'," *Journal of English
and Germanic Philology*, 1922, xxi. 188–9) shows that this was
published on April 1, 1731.]

ASTON, *WALTER*
(B.O.) The Restauration of King Charles II. or, The Life and Death
of Oliver Cromwell. An Histori-Tragi-Comi Ballad Opera. As it
was forbid to be Acted at the New Theatre in the Hay-Market
4° 1732. [The *Biographia Dramatica* notes only an edition of 1733;
this is probably an error. For some reason, on Th. April 27, 1732,
Aston advertised in *The Daily Post* that he had no connection with
the Haymarket company.]

AUBERT, *Mrs.*
Mock O. Harlequin-Hydaspes: or, The Greshamite (L.² May 1719)
8° 1719 (anon.) 1719. L.² W. 27/5. [This piece was advertised for
F. 22/5 but was "unfortunately prevented...by the unexpected
Arrest of the Person who was to have played the Doctor" *Daily
Courant*.]

AUBIN, *Mrs.*
*C. The Merry Masqueraders; or the Humorous Cuckold (H.² Dec.
1730) 8° 1730; 12° 1732; 8° 1734.
1730. H.² W. 9/12, F. 11.

AYRE, *WILLIAM.*
Past. Amintas (unacted) 8° (1737).
T. Merope (unacted) 8° 1740.

AYRES, *JAMES.*
(B.O.) Sancho at Court: or The Mock-Governor. An Opera-Comedy.
As it was design'd to be Acted at the Theatre-Royal in Drury-
Lane. Written by a Gentleman, Late of Trinity College, Dublin
8° 1742 (anon.).
*(B.O.) The Kiss Accepted and Returned (H.² April 1744).
1744. H.² M. 16/4, Th. 19.

BAILLIE, *Dr JOHN.*
C. The Married Coquet 8° 1746.

BAKER, *RICHARD.*
Burl. A Rehearsal of a New Ballad Opera, Burlesqued, called The
Mad-House, after the Manner of Pasquin (L.² April 1737) 8° 1737.
1737. L.² F. 22/4, M. 25.

BAKER, *THOMAS.*
C. The Humour of the Age (D.L. *c.* Feb. 1700/1) 4° 1701. See
supplementary notes; published March 22, 1700/1 (*Post Man*).
C. Tunbridge-Walks: Or, The Yeoman of Kent (D.L. Jan. 1702/3)
4° 1703 (by the author of The Humour of the Age); 12° 1714.
1703. D.L. W. 27/1; F. 12/2; W. 16/6; T. 6/7; Th. 7/10, M. 25;
M. 22/11; T. 28/12. 1704. F. 28/1; S. 26/2; F. 19/5; Th. 14/9;
M. 20/11. 1705. Th. 15/2; Th. 24/5; Th. 27/9. 1706. Th. 3/1.
1707. Th. 3/4, S. 26; Th. 23/10, F. 12/12. 1710. H.¹ M. 29/5,
W. 31; D.L. F. 22/12. 1711. Greenwich S. 25/8. 1715. L.² M.

7/3. 1718. W. 6/8; Richmond S. 16/8. 1719. L.² Th. 25/6; W. 1/7; M. 26/10. 1726. T. 5/7, F. 8, T. 12; T. 9/8. 1727. Th. 4/5; W. 14/6. 1728. T. 2/7. 1729. G.F. Th. 6/11, S. 22, S. 29; room next H.¹ S. 29/11. 1730. G.F. W. 7/1; H.² M. 16/11. 1731. G.F. M. 17/5; W. 27/10; Th. 25/11. 1732. H.² W. 8/3; L.² W. 8/11; T. 26/12. 1733. L.² M. 26/3. 1734. C.G. M. 4/2; Th. 7/11; D.L. M. 18/2, T. 19; G.F. Th. 23/5. 1735. Th. 8/5. 1736. L.² F. 17/12. 1737. M. 7/2. 1738. C.G. W. 12/7; D.L. S. 9/12, W. 13, F. 29. 1739. G.F. F. 5/12. 1746. F. 17/1. 1748. C.G. T. 8/3, Th. 10, S. 12, T. 22.

C. An Act at Oxford 4° 1704 (by the author of the Yeoman of Kent).
C. Hampstead-Heath (D.L. *Oct. 1705) 4° 1706 (by the author of the Yeoman of Kent).
    1705. D.L. T. 30/10, W. 31; Th. 1/11.
C. The Fine Lady's Airs: Or, An Equipage of Lovers (D.L. Dec. 1708) 4° (1709) (by the author of the Yeoman of Kent).
    1708. D.L. T. 14/12–F. 17. 1709. Greenwich M. 6/6. 1747. D.L. M. 20/4, W. 22.

BARFORD, RICHARD.
T. The Virgin Queen (L.² Dec. 1728) 8° 1729.
    1728. L.² S. 7/12–T. 10.

BECKINGHAM, CHARLES.
T. Scipio Africanus (L.² Feb. 1717/8) 12° 1718; 12° 1719.
    1718. L.² T. 18/2, Th. 20, F. 21, T. 25.
T. The Tragedy of King Henry IV. of France (L.² Nov. 1719) 8° 1720.
    1719. L.² S. 7/11 (acted 4 times).

BELLAMY, DANIEL, Senior and Junior.
Past. O. Love Triumphant: or, The Rival Goddesses...Perform'd on Easter-Monday, By the Young Ladies of Mrs. Bellamy's School 12° 1722.
    The Young Ladies Miscellany; or, Youth's Innocent and Rational Amusement 8° 1723. [This contains: 1. Vanquish'd Love: or the Jealous Queen; 2. Innocence Betray'd: or the Royal Impostor; 3. The Rival Nymphs: or the Merry Swain; 4. a few scenes translated from Guarini's Il Pastor Fido.]
    Dramatic Pieces, and Other Miscellaneous Works in Prose and Verse...in which are introduced, several Select Essays, never before published, by D. Bellamy, jun. 2 vols. 12° 1739–40. [These contain: 1. The Rival Priests: or, the Female Politician; 2. The Perjur'd Devotee: or the Force of Love; 3. Vanquish'd Love: or the Jealous Queen; 4. The Rival Nymphs: or the Merry Swain; 5. Innocence Betray'd or the Royal Impostor; 6. Love Triumphant: or the Rival Goddesses.]

BELLERS, FETTIPLACE.
T. Injur'd Innocence (D.L. Feb. 1731/2) 8° **1732.**
    1732. D.L. Th. 3/2–S. 5, M. 7–W. 9.

BENNET, PHILIP.
F. The Beau's Adventures 8° 1733.

BETTERTON, THOMAS.
    [For his earlier works see the Hand-list of Plays, 1660–1700.
T.C. K. Henry IV with the Humours of Sir John Falstaff (L.¹ *c.* April 1700) 4° 1700.

T.C. The Sequel of Henry the Fourth: With the Humours of Sir John Falstaffe, and Justice Shallow 8° (1720).

1707. H.¹ W. 19/11 (I). 1708. D.L. S. 24/1 (I). 1709. S. 1/1. 1710. S. 2/12. 1711. T. 8/5; T. 6/11 (I). 1712. M. 7/4 (I). 1713. M. 18/5 (I). 1714. W. 2/6 (I). 1715. S. 12/2, M. 14; L.² M. 4/4. 1716. Th. 15/3; T. 17/4; S. 20/10 (I); W. 12/12; D.L. S. 3/3; F. 11/5; T. 2/10 1717. L.² Th. 2/5 (I); D.L. T. 21/5; T. 15/10. 1718. Th. 2/1; F. 16/5; S. 27/9; L.² T. 7/1; T. 30/9. 1719. D.L. S. 10/1; Th. 7/5; Th. 22/10 (I); L.² S. 8/4; F. 2/10. 1720. F. 29/4; D.L. S. 17/9; T. 15/11 (I); S. 17/12 (II), M. 19–F. 30. 1721. T. 26/9; L.² S. 28/10 (I); F. 3/11; S. 9/12. 1722. D.L. T. 2/1; S. 5/5 (II); L.² F. 6/4; S. 29/9 (I). 1723. S. 12/1; W. 17/4; T. 21/5; Th. 24/10; Th. 5/12; D.L. S. 11/5; T. 8/10. 1724. F. 7,2; S. 3/10; L.² S. 7/3; W. 20/5; S. 7/11. 1725. T. 19/1; Th. 18/3; T. 20/4; S. 16/10; D.L. Th. 1/4; S. 18/9; T. 14/12. 1726. L.² W. 5/1; S. 29/2; W. 21/9; D.L. S. 7/5. 1727. T. 10/1; T. 21/2 (II), S. 25, M. 27; T. 14/3 (II); S. 9/9 (II); L.² M. 18/9 (I). 1728. D.L. T. 10/9 (I); F. 18/10 (II); Th. 28/11 (I); T. 3/12 (II), M. 30 (II); L.² T. 19/11 (I). 1729. D.L. T. 28/1 (I); W. 5/2 (II); W. 7/5 (II); S. 9/9 (II); L.² S. 22/3 (I); S. 29/11. 1730. D.L. Th. 12/2; T. 29/9 (II); F. 4/12 (II), F. 31 (I); L.² W. 23/4; F. 25/9 (I). 1731. D.L. M. 8/3 (I), T. 16 (II); W. 19/5 (II); Th. 14/10 (II); M. 6/12 (II); H.² M. 3/5 (I), W. 5 (I); L.² W. 29/9 (I); F. 29/10 (I); F. 31/12 (I). 1732. D.L. S. 15/1 (II); M. 17/4 (I), T. 18 (II); M. 16/10 (I), Th. 19 (II); W. 15/11 (II); G.F. S. 29/1 (I); T. 1/2 (I); Th. 30/3 (I); M. 2/10, T. 3 (I); W. 20/12 (I); L.² M. 8/5 (I); S. 25/11 (I). 1733. D.L. S. 6/1 (II); S. 3/2 (I); M. 7/5 (II); C.G. T. 10/4 (I); F. 30/11 (I); G.F. Th. 3/5 (I); T. 25/9; H.² W. 10/10 (I), F. 12 (II); M. 12/11 (I), W. 21 (I), Th. 22 (II); S. 8/12 (II). 1734. H.² W. 16/1 (I), S. 19 (II); C.G. M. 21/1 (I); Th. 21/3; Th. 14/11 (I); D.L. W. 17/4 (I), Th. 18 (II); Th. 2/5 (I), S. 4 (II), F. 17 (I); T. 24/9 (I), F. 4/10; M. 30/12; G.F. M. 29/4; W. 16/10 (I). 1735. C.G. M. 20/1; Th. 17/4; D.L. F. 11/4 (II); Th. 11/9 (I); S. 15/11 (I); G.F. T. 29/4; M. 1/11, T. 2 (I). 1736. D.L. Th. 11/3 (II); Th. 1/4 (II); M. 17/5 (I), Th. 20 (II); Th. 7/10 (I), S. 9 (II), S. 27 (I); S. 4/12 (II); L.² W. 14/4 (I); S. 20/10 (I), M. 22 (I). 1737 D.L. Th. 12/1 (I), F. 13 (II); Th. 14/9 (I), S. 16 (II); C.G. M. 13/2 (I). 1738. D.L. Th. 12/1 (I), F. 13 (II); Th. 14/9 (I), S. 16 (II); F. 13/10 (I), S. 14 (II); F. 17/11 (I); T. 19/12 (I); C.G. M 13/2 (I). 1739. D.L. T. 6/3 (I); M. 19/11 (I), T. 20 (II). 1740. F. 25/4 (I); M. 13/10 (I), T. 14 (II); G.F. 28/11 (I); Th. 18/12 (I). 1741. D.L. M. 26/1 (I), T. 27 (II); M. 6/4 (I); F. 9/10 (I); G.F. T. 27/1 (I); T. 21/4 (I). 1742. D.L. T. 27/4 (I). 1743. Th. 10/2 (I); L.² Th. 17/3 (I). 1744. D.L. F. 27/1; T. 22/5 (I). 1745. G.F. T. 26/3 (I); W. 7/4 (I); M. 2/12 (I), T. 3. 1746. D.L. F. 9/5; G.F. W. 29/10, F. 30; M. 3/11, M. 10; C.G. 6/12. 1747. G.F. F. 2/1; M. 6/4 (II); D.L. Th. 15/1 (I)– M. 19.

BIDDLE, EDWARD.
   *T. Augustus [the *Biographia Dramatica* refers to this "fragment of a play" as printed 8° 1717].

BLADEN, MARTIN.
   T.C. Solon, or, Philosophy no Defence against Love 4° 1705.

BLANCH, JOHN.
  C.   The Beaux Merchant…Written by a Clothier 4° 1714. [Attributed.]
  C.   Swords into Anchors 4° 1725 (Gloucester).
  T.C. Hoops into Spinning Wheels…By a Gentleman in Gloucestershire 8° 1725 (Gloucester). [Dedication signed J. B.]
BOADENS, Captain CHARLES.
  C.   The Modish Couple (D.L. Jan. 1731/2) 8' 1732.
       1732. D.L. M. 10/1–Th. 13. [The first date seems to have been that of original production, although the play was advertised in The Craftsman of the previous Saturday "as acted."]
BOND, WILLIAM.
  T.   The Tuscan Treaty, or Tarquin's Overthrow (C.G. Aug. 1733) 8° 1733.
       1733. C.G. M. 20/8, T. 21.
BOOTH, BARTON.
  M.   The Death of Dido…Compos'd to Musick, after the Italian Manner, by Dr. Pepusch (D.L. April 1716) 12° 1716.
       1716. D.L. T. 17/4, T. 24, W. 25; T. 15/5. 1734. H.² S. 12/1 (as Dido and Æneas, with music by Arne), M. 14, T. 15, Th. 17, S. 19, T. 22, Th. 24–S. 26, T. 29, Th. 31; Th. 7/2, F. 8, M. 11, S. 16, M. 18, T. 19.
BOYD, Mrs ELIZABETH.
  (B.O.) Don Sancho: or, The Students Whim, A Ballad Opera of Two Acts, with Minerva's Triumph, A Masque 8° 1739.
BOYER, ABEL.
  T.   Achilles: or, Iphigenia in Aulis (D.L. c. Dec. 1699) 4° 1700; The Victim; or Achilles and Iphigenia in Aulis 12° 1714.
       No records of performance; published Jan. 23, 1699/1700 (Post Boy).
BOYLE, CHARLES, Earl of ORRERY.
  C.   As You Find It (L.¹ April 1703) 4° 1703 (title page has MDCIII for MDCCIII); reprinted in Works of Roger Boyle 8° 1739.
       1703. L.¹ W. 28/4.
BOYLE, ROGER, Earl of ORRERY.
       [For his Restoration works see A History of Restoration Drama, p. 354.]
  T.   Altemira (L.¹ c. Dec. 1701; altered from The General) 4° 1702.
       No records of performance; published Dec. 20, 1701 (Post Man).
BRERETON, THOMAS.
  T.   Esther; or, Faith Triumphant 12° 1715; 12° 1719.
       [Two eighteenth century playlists mention another work of this writer—Sir John Oldcastle, a tragedy—but this seems not to have been printed.]
BREVAL, Captain JOHN DURANT.
  F.   The Confederates 8° 1717 (issued under the pseudonym of Joseph Gay).
  C.   The Play is the Plot (D.L. Feb. 1717/8) 4° 1718 (anon.).
       1718. D.L. W. 19/2–F. 21, M. 24, T. 25, Th. 27.
  F.   The Strolers…To which is added, A New Prologue and Epilogue, Spoken by Miss Robinson Jun. at the Head of her Lilliputian

Company (D.L. July 1723) 12° 1727 (two issues anon.); 12° 1729;
12° 1761; 12° 1767. [This play is taken from *The Play is the Plot;*
as Breval was alive in 1723, the alteration may be ascribed to him.
A ballad opera of the same title appeared at C.G. in May 1734.
This was no doubt the earlier farce embellished with songs.]

  1723. D.L. T. 16/7, F. 19; F. 9/8; Th. 24/10, F. 25. 1727. W.
19/4; M. 1/5, W. 3, M. 22. 1728. F. 17/5, M. 20. 1729. W. 9/4,
M. 21, F. 25; W. 7/5. 1730. M. 19/1; S. 19/9, T. 29; Th. 12/11.
1734. C.G. T. 7/5 (as a ballad opera), Th. 9, Th. 16. 1739. F. 14/9,
S. 15. 1741. D.L. T. 12/5.

Burl. O. The Rape of Helen (C.G. May 1733) 8° 1737.
  1733. C.G. S. 19/5.

T. Gustavus Vasa, The Deliverer of His Country...As it was to have
been Acted At the Theatre-Royal in Drury-Lane 8° 1739; 12° 1739
(*Dublin*).
  [Acted S.A. Dublin 3/12/1744, as *The Patriot.*]

T. The Earl of Westmoreland (Dublin, 1742, as *The Betrayer of his
Country*) 8° 1778 (in *A Collection of Plays*).
  [Acted later, in 1754, as *Injured Honour.*]

Bsq. O. Jack the Gyant Queller. An Antique History (Dublin,
27/3/1749). Songs, 8° 1749 (*Dublin*). L. 13.
  [In the author's works 8° 1778 printed as *Little John and the
Giants.*]
  [For his later works see the Hand-list of Plays, 1750–1800.]

BROWN, ANTHONY.

T. The Fatal Retirement (D.L. Nov. 1739) 8° 1739; 8° 1740.
  1739. D.L. M. 12/11.

BROWN, TOM.

(Sat.) The Stage-Beaux toss'd in a Blanket: or, Hypocrisie Alamode;
Expos'd in a True Picture of Jerry....A Pretending Scourge to
the English Stage...A Comedy. With a Prologue on Occasional
Conformity...and an Epilogue on the Reformers 4° 1704 (anon.).

BROWNE, MOSES.

T. and F. Polidus: or, Distress'd Love. A Tragedy. With a Farce
call'd, All Bedevil'd: or, The House in a Hurry 8° 1723.

BULLOCK, CHRISTOPHER.

F. The Slip (L.² Feb. 1714/5) 12° 1715.
  1715. L.² Th. 3/2, S. 5, M. 7, Th. 10, F. 11, T. 15; T. 1/3;
S. 9/4, S. 30.

C. Woman's Revenge: Or, A Match in Newgate (L.² Oct. 1715) 4°
1715; 8° 1728 (To which is added, A Compleat Key to the
Beggar's Opera, By Peter Padwell of Paddington, Esq;)
  1715. L.² M. 24/10–Th. 27; S. 12/11, Th. 24; F. 16/12, Th. 29.
1716. F. 3/2; S. 14/4; F. 19/10. 1717. W. 30/10; Th. 12/12. 1718.
Th. 6/11. 1719. F. 9/1; Th. 14/5. 1723. T. 22/10; M. 9/12. 1724.
F. 31/1; M. 25/5; T. 20/10. 1725. M. 18/1; T. 28/12. 1727. Th.
9/3; S. 8/4, S. 22; T. 23/5; W. 22/11; W. 27/12. 1728. T. 29/10;
F. 27/12. 1729. M. 19/5; S. 27/12. 1730. T. 6/1; M. 23/2; M.
30/3; T. 28/4; T. 26/5; F. 23/10; Th. 19/11; G.F. M. 5/1. 1731.
L.² F. 1/1; Th. 18/2; T. 23/3; T. 28/12. 1732. F. 2/6. 1734. C.G.
T. 5/2. 1736. W. 29/12. 1740. S. 1/3, M. 3, Th. 6, S. 15; T. 8/4.

F. The Cobler of Preston (L.² Jan. 1715/6) 12° 1716; 12° 1732; 12° 1767.

> 1716. T. 24/1–F. 27, T. 31; W. 1/2–S. 4, M. 27; Th. 1/3, S. 3; M. 2/4, Th. 5, S. 14, Th. 19; M. 21/5; F. 13/7, F. 20; W. 15/8. 1717. T. 25/6; F. 5/7; M. 28/10; T. 31/12. 1718. S. 3/5, Th. 29; T. 28/10; M. 8/12. 1719. W. 18/3; Th. 11/6. 1720. Th. 31/3. 1722. Th. 3/5. 1723. W. 8/5. 1724. F. 8/5; F. 13/11. 1726. F. 12/8, T. 16. 1730. Th. 7/5; G.F. F. 10/7, M. 13. 1731. M. 8/2, T. 9, Th. 11, F. 12; H.² W. 17/3; L.² M. 25/10. 1732. Th. 11/5. 1738. C.G. F. 7/4. 1745. G.F. M. 1/4, F. 26; Th. 2/5.

F. The Adventures of Half an Hour (L.² March 1715/6) 12° 1716.

> 1716. L.² M. 19/3. 1724. H.² Th. 20/2 (marked as new).

C. Woman is a Riddle (L.² Dec. 1716) 4° 1717; 12° 1729 (2nd); 12° 1731 (2nd; Edinburgh); 12° 1759 (3rd); 12° 1760 (Dublin).

> 1716. L.² T. 4/12–M. 10, Th. 20, W. 26. 1717. F. 4/1, F. 25; Th 21/3; T. 28/5; S. 2/11; Th. 19/12. 1718. Th. 13/3; T. 11/11; M. 8/12. 1719. T. 7/4; Th. 21/5. 1720. Th. 22/12. 1721. T. 16/5; W. 7/6. 1722. T. 9/10. 1723. M. 4/2. 1727. M. 10/4, T. 18. 1731. G.F. M. 18/10, W. 20, F. 22; W. 8/12. 1735. M. 10/3; W. 24/9, F. 26; M. 29; W. 1/10, M. 13; F. 7/11. 1737. L.² F. 21/1; W. 9/2. 1745. G.F. M. 1/4, M. 22. 1746. M. 22/12. 1748. C.G. T. 19/1, S. 23, M. 25.

F. The Per-Juror (L.² Dec. 1717) 8° 1717; 8° 1718; 8° 1718; 8° 1718 (4th); 8° 1732.

> 1717. L.² Th. 12/12, Th. 19, Th. 26, S. 28, M. 30. 1718. M. 6/1, Th. 9, T. 21; S. 22/2.

T. The Traytor (L.² Oct. 1718) 12° 1718 (anon.). [This alteration of Shirley's play is attributed to Bullock.]

> 1718. L.² S. 11/10–T. 14, M. 27. 1719. S. 21/3.

BURNABY, WILLIAM.

C. The Reform'd Wife (D.L. c. March 1699/1700) 4° 1700 (bis).

> No record of first performance; published April 2, 1700 (*Flying Post* and *London Gazette*). A second edition with an additional scene was advertised as issued in May 1700. 1707. D.L. F. 31/10; M. 3/11.

C. The Ladies Visiting-Day (L.¹ c. Jan. 1700/1) 4° 1701 (anon.).

> No records of performance; published Feb. 27, 1700/1 (*Post Boy*).

C. The Modish Husband (D.L. c. Jan. 1701/2) 4° 1702; 8° 1708 (2nd).

> No record of performance; published Feb. 5, 1701/2 (*Post Man*).

C. Love Betray'd; or, The Agreable Disapointment (L.¹ Feb. 1703) 4° 1703 (anon.).

> No record of first performance. 1705. L.¹ Th. 1/3.

CAREY, HENRY.

F. The Contrivances; or More Ways than One (D.L. Aug. 1715) 12° 1715 (anon.); 12° 1719; 8° 1729 (2nd); 12° 1731 (Dublin); 12° 1732; 12° 1743; 12° 1765 (7th); 8° (1777); 12° 1777.

> 1715. D.L. T. 9/8, F. 12, T. 16. 1716. M. 2/4; F. 25/5. 1724. H.² F. 31/1; S. 1/2–T. 4. 1729. D.L. F. 20/6, M. 30; T. 5/8, Th. 7, S. 9. 1730. S. 3/1; T. 12/5, Th. 21; T. 22/9; Th. 15/10; T. 17/11, F. 20. 1731. W. 5/5. 1732. T. 9/5; T. 31/10; G.F. M. 15/5, W. 17. 1733. D.L. F. 12/1. 1734. G.F. M. 18/3; W. 24/4; W. 1/5, W. 8, T. 14, W. 15; L.² Th. 18/4. 1735. G.F. Th. 20/3, S. 29; M. 21/4;

M. 15/9. 1736. D.L. Th. 25/3; T. 6/4, Th. 8; Th. 6/5, F. 21;
M. 25/10; C.G. T. 6/4. 1737. T. 26/4; D.L. T. 20/9, Th. 22.
1738. C.G. W. 10/5; W. 12/7. 1741. G.F. Th. 12/3, M. 16; W.
8/4, T. 14, T. 28; Th. 7/5; M. 21/9; W. 28/10; S. 7/11. 1742. M.
8/2. 1746. D.L. F. 17/1, W. 22; M. 10/2. 1747. W. 29/4.

F. Hanging and Marriage; or, The Dead-Man's Wedding...With a
Song to please every Body (L.² March 1721/2) 12° (1722).
 1722. L.² Th. 15/3.

O. Amelia. A New English Opera...After the Italian Manner (H.¹
March 1731/2) 8° 1732 (anon.).
 1732. H.² M. 13/3, W. 15, M. 20, W. 22, F. 24, W. 29; M. 17/4,
F. 21, M. 24, T. 25; S. 16/12, S. 23. 1743. Th. 24/3.

O. Teraminta (L.² Nov. 1732) 8° 1732.
 1732. L.² M. 20/11, Th. 23, Th. 30.

B.O. Betty, or The Country Bumpkins (D.L. Dec. 1732); The Songs,
as they are sung in Betty F. 1739.
 1732. D.L. F. 1/12, S. 2, W. 6–S. 9. 1733. S. 27/1.

Burl. T. The Tragedy of Chrononhotonthologos: Being the most
Tragical Tragedy, that ever was Tragediz'd by any Company of
Tragedians. Written by Benjamin Bounce, Esq; (H.² Feb. 1733/4)
8° (1734); 8° 1734 (Edinburgh); 8° 1743; 8° 1744; 8° 1753; 8°
(1760?).
 1734. H.² F. 22/2–T. 26, Th. 28; S. 2/3, T. 5, Th. 7. 1736.
M. 3/5. 1742. D.L. Th. 29/4. 1743. James-street T. 22/2. 1744.
Richmond S. 8/9. 1745. D.L. T. 30/4. 1746. G.F. S. 22/3. 1747.
D.L. S. 11/4.

(B.O.) The Honest Yorkshire-Man. A Ballad Farce. Refus'd to be
Acted at Drury-Lane Playhouse: But now Perform'd at the New
Theatre in Goodman's Fields, With great Applause (H.² July
1735) 8° 1736; pirated as A Wonder: or, An Honest Yorkshire-
Man. A Ballad Opera; As it is Perform'd at the Theatres With
Universal Applause 8° 1736; 12° 1763 (Belfast); 12° 1770 (Glasgow).
 1735. H² T. 15/7, F. 18, T. 22, F. 25, T. 29; F. 1/8, F. 8,
Th. 14, Th. 21; G.F. F. 26/9; W. 1/10, F. 3, M. 6, W. 8, F. 10,
M. 13, M. 20, W. 22, Th. 23, F. 24; M. 3/11, W. 12–W. 19,
T. 25, Th. 27–S. 29; M. 1/12, T. 2, Th. 11–T. 16. 1736. F. 6/2;
T. 30/3; M. 12/4, M. 26; W. 5/5, Th. 6; H.² M. 3/5; Richmond
M. 26/7; L.² T. 5/10, Th. 7. 1737. M. 24/1, T. 25; S. 26/3,
Th. 31; S. 2/4, M. 11, W. 13, F. 15, S. 30; M. 2/5, W. 4, Th. 5,
S. 7, T. 10. 1738. C.G. T. 14/3; S. 8/4, F. 14; F. 5/5, F. 12,
M. 15; T. 27/6; F. 7/7; T. 22/8, T. 29. 1739. M. 8/1; M. 26/3;
Th. 24/5. 1740. T. 8/1; T. 27/5; M. 10/11; Punch S. 23/2; G.F.
M. 20/10–Th. 23, W. 29, Th. 30; T. 4/11. 1741. 1741. Th. 22/1; M.
28/9; T. 3/11, W. 4, F. 6. 1742. F. 19/2; C.G. S. 6/3; S. 1/5,
M. 3, Th. 6, M. 10, F. 14; James-street M. 8/11; L.² M. 13/12,
W. 15. 1743. Th. 17/2. 1745. G.F. F. 3/5.

Burl. O. The Dragon of Wantley (H.² May 1737) 4° (1737 anon.);
8° 1738 (12th edn.); 12° 1770. [The 14th edition was published
by September 1738.]
 Songs and Duettos in the Burlesque Opera called the Dragon
of Wantley 4° 1738 (with musical score by J. F. Lampe).
 1737. C.G. W. 26/10–M. 31; T. 1/11–S. 19. 1738. M. 2/1–M.
16, W. 18–S. 28, T. 31; W. 1/2–S. 11, T. 14; Th. 2/3, T. 7, Th. 9,
S. 18, S. 25; Th. 6/4, S. 15, Th. 20, S. 22, S. 29; F. 1/9, F. 15,
M. 18, W. 20, F. 22, W. 27, F. 29; F. 6/10, F. 13, F. 20; Th. 2/11,

S. 11, Th. 16; D.L. T. 16/5; B.F. Hallam, Aug. 1739. C.G. F.
9/2; W. 16/5, Th. 17; W. 29/8; F. 7/9, M. 10, W. 12, W. 19;
T. 23/10; S. 10/11, S. 24; S. 8/12. 1740. F. 4/1, Th. 17; W. 6/2,
Th. 7; F. 19/9; F. 31/10; S. 8/11, S. 15, T. 25; F. 12/12. 1741.
Th. 16/4; S. 2/5, M. 4; W. 30/9; Th. 22/10. 1742. W. 12/5.
1743. D.L. W. 2/2, F. 4; S. 23/4, Th. 28; Th. 5/5, F. 13. 1745.
F. 15/2–T. 19; M. 4/3, T. 5. 1746. C.G. F. 18/4. 1747. D.L.
S. 7/3, M. 9, S. 14, M. 16, T. 17, Th. 19, S. 21, S. 28; Th. 2/4,
M. 6, Th. 9, W. 22; Th. 3/12, F. 11. 1748. Th. 7/1, S. 16; F. 5/2,
F. 12; S. 12/3, Th. 17; S. 16/4, T. 26, F. 29; W. 11/5.
(Burl. O.) Margery: or, A Worse Plague than the Dragon (C.G. Dec.
1738) 8° 1738 (3 edns.); called *The Dragoness* in Carey's Works 1743.
    1738. C.G. S. 9/12, T. 12–F. 22. 1739. Th. 4/1, F. 5, T. 9,
W. 10; S. 10/2, Th. 15; M. 5/3, Th. 8; S. 28/4; F. 31/8; F. 21/9.
1740. F. 11/1.
Int. Nancy: or, The Parting Lovers…Set to Music by the Author
(C.G. Dec. 1739) 8° 1739; altered as The Press Gang: or, Love
in Low Life 8° 1755 (anon.).
    1739. C.G. S. 1/12 (as The Parting Lovers), M. 3. 1740. T 15/1;
T. 18/3 (with additions by the author); W. 16/4, M. 21, M. 28;
Th. 29/5; W. 1/10 (as Nancy, or The Parting Lovers), F. 24;
Th. 20/11; F. 19/12; B.F. Hippisley and Chapman, Aug. (as The
Parting Lovers, or The Press Gang). 1741. C.G. Th. 15/1; T.
17/3; Tennis Court, Hay. T. 19/5. 1744. H.² T. 2/10 (as Love
in Low Life, or A Press Gang at Billingsgate), Th. 4, S. 6, T. 9.

CENTLIVRE, Mrs SUSANNAH (Mrs CARROLL).
T. The Perjur'd Husband, or, The Adventures of Venice (D.L.
    c. Oct., 1700) 4° 1700; 12° 1737.
        No records of performance; published October 22, 1700 (*Post
    Man*).
C. The Beau's Duel: or A Soldier for the Ladies (L.¹ *c.* June 1702)
    4° 1702; 12° 1715 (2nd corrected); 12° 1719; 8° 1727 (Dublin);
    12° 1735 (3rd); 12° 1780 (4th).
        No record of original production; published July 8, 1702 (*Post
    Boy*). 1702. L.¹ W. 21/10.
C. The Stolen Heiress or the Salamanca Doctor Outplotted (L.¹
    Dec. 1702) 4° (1703; anon.).
        1702. L.¹ Th. 31/12.
C. Love's Contrivance, or, Le Medecin Malgre Lui (D.L. June 1703)
    4° 1703. The dedication is signed R. M. but the play is certainly
    by Mrs Centlivre.
        1703. D.L. F. 4/6–M. 7, M. 14, T. 22; W. 7/7; W. 20/10. 1704.
    W. 16/2; T. 28/3; F. 28/4; W. 5/7. 1705. Th. 7/6. 1706. Th. 14/2.
    1724. L.² T. 14/7, F. 17. 1726. F. 17/6, T. 21.
C. The Gamester (L.¹ *c.* Jan. 1704/5) 4° 1705 anon.; 4° 1708 (2nd);
    12° 1714; 12° 1736 (4th); 12° 1736 (4th, a different edition); 12°
    1760 (4th, reissue of last); 12° 1756 (5th); 12° 1767 (5th).
        1705. L.¹ Th. 22/2 (with a new scene); H.¹ F. 27/4; W. 23/5;
    M. 19/11. 1706. Th. 31/10. 1709. D.L. Th. 17/3, F. 18, T. 29.
    1710. Th. 30/3; T. 23/5; Greenwich S. 29/7; M. 21/8. 1711.
    D.L. T. 29/5; F. 13/7. 1714. T. 20/7; L.² T. 21/12, W. 29. 1715.
    W. 9/2; F. 29/7. 1716. W. 11/1; M. 30/4; W. 21/11. 1717. T.
    25/6; M. 18/11. 1718. W. 29/1; S. 3/5; Richmond M. 11/8. 1719.

L.² M. 25/5; Th. 11/6. 1726. T. 2/8, F. 5. 1727. T. 17/10, F. 20;
T. 12/12. 1728. M. 13/5. 1729. G.F. Th. 20/11, Th. 27. 1730.
F. 16/1; F. 17/7; S. 24/10. 1731. L.² Th. 1/4; F. 21/5; G.F. W.
28/4. 1732. L.² M. 10/1. 1735. C.G. S. 29/3; T. 20/5; G.F. W.
9/4, S. 26; M. 22/9. 1736. Th. 26/2; L.² F. 10/12. 1737. W. 16/2.
1740. G.F. M. 29/12. 1741. S. 31/1; M. 20/4; F. 9/10; Th. 31/12;
C.G. S. 7/2, M. 9, T. 24; Th. 30/4. 1742. M. 22/2. 1743. D.L.
S. 26/11; F. 30/12. 1744. S. 6/10; T. 27/11; M. 17/12. 1745.
T. 12/3; Th. 17/10.

C.   Love at a venture (New Theatre, Bath, Duke of Grafton's men)
     4° 1706 (written by the author of The Gamester).

C.   The Bassett-Table (D.L. Nov. 1705) 4° 1706 (By the author of
     The Gamester); 12° (1706, 2nd); 12° 1735 (3rd); 12° 1736 (4th).
     1705. D.L. T. 20/11–F. 23.

C.   The Platonick Lady (H.¹ Nov. 1706) 4° 1707 (By the Author of
     The Gamester).
     1706. H.¹ M. 25/11–Th. 28.

C.   The Busie Body (D.L. May 1709) 4° (1709); 4° (1709 2nd); 12°
     1732 (5th); 12° 1746; 8° 1746 (Norwich); 8° 1753; 12° 1787 (7th).
     1709. D.L. Th. 12/5–M. 16, S. 21, S. 28; S. 4/6; S. 26/11;
     Th. 8/12, M. 26; H.¹ T. 11/10, Th. 13, S. 15; T. 1/11. 1710.
     D.L. F. 27/1; T. 16/5; T. 12/12; H.¹ S. 22/4. 1711. D.L. F. 4/5;
     F. 19/10. 1712. M. 24/11. 1713. Th. 24/9; F. 20/11. 1714. F.
     5/11; L.² W. 22/12, Th. 30. 1715. F. 14/1; M. 21/2; Th. 7/4;
     W. 28/9; D.L. M. 17/10. 1716. L.² M. 16/1; T. 12/6; F. 23/11;
     D.L. M. 20/2; F. 26/10. 1717. L.² W. 6/2; W. 22/5; Th. 28/11;
     D.L. W. 23/10. 1718. L.² S. 18/1; Th. 1/5; S. 8/11; Richmond
     M. 28/7; D.L. W. 29/10. 1719. L.² W. 4/2; F. 10/4; W. 13/5,
     T. 19; M. 5/10; D.L. M. 16/11. 1720. Th. 17/3; M. 17/10.
     1721. L.² M. 17/4; T. 6/6; W. 29/11. 1722. W. 3/1; S. 10/3;
     M. 9/4; Th. 24/5; M. 1/10; W. 5/12; D.L. S. 14/4; S.F. theatre
     actors W. 3/10. 1723. D.L. Th. 23/5; L.² M. 7/10; F. 13/12.
     1724. M. 13/1; F. 14/2; S. 9/5; F. 2/10; H.² T. 13/10. 1725.
     L.² F. 29/1; M. 22/2; T. 30/3; Th. 20/5; T. 19/10. 1726. W. 26/1;
     T. 15/3; S. 14/5; F. 16/9. 1727. Th. 2/3; F. 26/5; W. 4/10; W. 6/12.
     1728. F. 26/4; F. 8/11. 1729. S. 3/5; F. 7/11; G.F. S. 8/11. 1730.
     L.² F. 23/1; M. 16/11; G.F. M. 27/4; F. 22/5; F. 26/6; S. 31/10;
     Richmond W. 24/6; D.L. W. 28/10; M. 16/11. 1731. G.F. S. 9/1;
     T. 11/5; F. 19/11; L.² F. 29/1; M. 26/4; T. 9/11; D.L. M. 31/5;
     T. 7/12. 1732. L.² T. 11/1; S. 4/3; M. 1/5; T. 14/11; D.L. W.
     19/1; M. 8/5; S. 23/9; F. 22/12; G.F. W. 26/4; T. 10/10; S. 25/11.
     1733. C.G. S. 20/1; T. 8/5; Th. 27/9; D.L. M. 9/4; Th. 24/5;
     W. 21/11; S. 1/12; H.² F. 19/10; F. 16/11. 1734. G.F. Th. 10/1;
     S. 23/2; Th. 9/5; M. 23/9, W. 25; H.² M. 28/1; D.L. T. 5/2;
     C.G. M. 1/4; T. 7/5; M. 2/9. 1735. G.F. F. 3/1; T. 4/2; D.L.
     S. 11/1; Th. 27/2; T. 28/10; C.G. F. 17/1; M. 24/3; L.² W. 12/2;
     M. 24/3. 1736. C.G. T. 17/2; M. 29/11; D.L. S. 21/2; T. 27/4;
     T. 21/12; G.F. S. 21/2; L.² W. 5/5; F. 3/12; W. 8/12. 1737. W.
     9/3; F. 22/4; D.L. M. 16/5; T. 27/9; C.G. Th. 19/5; M. 14/11.
     1738. F. 27/1; Th. 11/5; T. 12/12; D.L. Th. 9/2; S. 23/9; W. 11/10;
     Th. 28/12. 1739. C.G. W. 31/1; Th. 10/5; W. 19/9; W. 5/12;
     D.L. Th. 31/5; W. 3/10. 1740. C.G. Th. 3/1; T. 19/2; T. 22/4;
     S. 3/5, T. 27; M. 13/10, S. 25; S. 27/12; D.L. F. 18/1; M. 26/5;
     Th. 18/9; T. 9/12; Richmond S. 16/8; G.F. F. 17/10; Th. 6/11.

1741. D.L. T. 3/2; S. 11/4; S. 12/12, F. 18; C.G. W. 6/5; W. 30/9; T. 24/11; W. 30/12; G.F. M. 4/5; M. 5/10; T. 1/12. 1742. D.L. W. 27/1; W. 10/2; F. 19/11; C.G. T. 16/2; Th. 6/5; L.² M. 29/11. 1743. D.L. T. 18/1; T. 20/9; S.F. theatrical booth F. 25/2; L.² F. 3/6; C.G. F. 21/10. 1744. S. 21/4; Th. 29/11; D.L. S. 29/9; F. 14/12; G.F. Th. 29/11; T. 4/12. 1745. S. 9/2; M. 18/11; C.G. W. 15/5; W. 13/11; Richmond W. 11/9; D.L. Th. 3/10. 1746. C.G. Th. 23/1; W. 8/10; D.L. S. 8/3; M. 4/8. 1747. C.G. W. 21/1; W. 11/11; W. 23/12. 1748. C.G. W. 3/2; M. 7/3; Th. 27/10; D.L. S. 10/9. 1749. Th. 23/2; T. 28/3; Th. 11/5; S. 16/9; Th. 23/11; F. 29/12; C.G. T. 25/4; Th. 7/12.

C. The Man's Bewitch'd: or, The Devil to Do about Her (H.¹ Dec. 1709) 4° (1710); 12° 1738.
    1709. H.¹ M. 12/12, W. 14, Th. 15. 1730. G.F. T. 28/4; W. 22/7. 1731. T. 27/4.

F. A Bickerstaff's Burying, or, Work for the Upholders (D.L. March 1710) 4° (1710); 12° 1724 (Dublin).
    1710. D.L. M. 27/3, Th. 30; Th. 11/5. 1715. Th. 5/5 (as The Custom of the Country, marked as new), T. 17; Th. 2/6. 1716. M. 14/5.

C. Mar-Plot, or, The Second Part of the Busie-Body (D.L. Dec. 1710) 4° 1711; 12° 1737.
    1710. D.L. S. 30/12. 1711. M. 1/1, T. 2, Th. 4–S. 6; Th. 24/5. 1724. H.² T. 18/2.

C. The Perplex'd Lovers (D.L. Jan. 1711/12) 4° 1712; 8° 1719 (2nd); 12° 1734 (2nd); 12° 1725 (Dublin); 12° 1736 (3rd).
    1712. D.L. S. 19/1–T. 22.

C. The Wonder: A Woman Keeps a Secret (D.L. April 1714) 12° 1714 (Written by the Author of the Gamester).
    1714. D.L. T. 27/4–Th. 29; S. 1/5, T. 4, Th. 6; Th. 16/12. 1733. G.F. W. 14/11–M. 26; M. 10/12, T. 11, Th. 20. 1734. W. 2/1, T. 8, T. 22; T. 19/2; Th. 21/3; F. 19/4; F. 17/5; S. 5/10; W. 11/12; C.G. F. 1/11. 1735. W. 1/1; G.F. T. 28/1; Th. 10/4, F. 25; W. 17/9; Th. 4/12, Th. 11. 1736. T. 2/3; Richmond W. 25/8; L.² S. 9/10. 1737. S. 1/1; S. 26/3; F. 29/4. 1741. G.F. W. 28/1; W. 29/4; M. 21/9. 1742. Th. 18/2. 1744 D.L. Th. 12/1. 1747. G.F. Th. 2/4. 1748. C.G. F. 15/4.

F. The Gotham Election 12° 1715; The Humours of Elections 12° 1737 (with running title, The Gotham Election).

F.C. A Wife well Manag'd (D.L. 1715) 12° 1715 (anon. but with portrait of Mrs Centlivre).
    No record of first performance. 1724. H.² M. 2/3.

T. The Cruel Gift (D.L. Dec. 1716) 12° 1717 (running title The Cruel Gift: or, The Royal Resentment); 12° 1734 (2nd); 12° 1736 (3rd).
    1716. D.L. M. 17/12–S. 22. 1717. F. 3/5.

C. A Bold Stroke for a Wife (L.² Feb. 1717/8) 8° 1718; 12° 1719; 12° 1724 (2nd); 12° 1728 (2nd, a reissue); 12° 1729 (3rd); 12° 1735.
    1718. L.² M. 3/2–Th. 6, S. 8, M. 10. 1728. T. 23/4; F. 12/7, T. 16. 1729. G.F. F. 14/11. 1730. Th. 8/1; M. 11/5; T. 16/6; F. 10/7; T. 20/10; Th. 17/12. 1731. S. 23/1; F. 5/2; T. 20/4; Th. 13/5; F. 29/10; W. 15/12; S.F. Fielding Th. 23/9. 1732. G.F. W. 2/2; M. 30/10; Th. 23/11; H.² Th. 23/3; T. 4/4. 1733. G.F. T. 27/3; S. 8/12. 1734. T. 26/2; M. 15/4; Th. 26/9; T. 29/10.

1735. W. 8/1; T. 11/3; H.² W. 10/12. 1736. W. 14/7. 1737.
L.² S. 5/2, Th. 10, S. 19; M. 18/4. 1738. C.G. F. 7/7. 1739.
D.L. S. 13/1, T. 16–Th. 18; W. 7/2; M. 15/10. 1740. S. 22/3;
F. 7/11; G.F. F. 24/10; S. 1/11; F. 26/12. 1741. D.L. S. 24/1;
Th. 5/3; G.F. W. 1/4; F. 16/10. 1744. M. 10/12, M. 17. 1745.
F. 25/1; M. 25/2; T. 16/4; Th. 14/11; M. 30/12. 1746. C.G. M.
28/4; S. 27/12; G.F. F. 7/11, M. 17; S. 27/12. 1747. T. 10/3.
1748. D.L. S. 24/12, M. 26, T. 27. 1749. M. 27/3; F. 5/5; Th.
28/12.

C. The Artifice (D.L. Oct. 1722) 8° 1723; 12° 1735; 12° 1736.
1722. D.L. T. 2/10–Th. 4.

CHARKE, Mrs CHARLOTTE.
*C. The Carnival or Harlequin Blunderer.
1735. L.² F. 5/9.
Sat. The Art of Management; or, Tragedy Expell'd (York Buildings
Sept. 1735) 8° 1735.
1735. York buildings W. 24/9, M. 29; W. 1/10, W. 8.
*Medley. Tit for Tat or the Comedy and Tragedy of War.
1743. James-street T. 1/2. 1749. D.L. S. 18/3, T. 28, W. 29,
F. 31; S. 8/4, T. 11, W. 26.

CHAVES, A.
C. The Cares of Love, or, A Night's Adventure (L.¹ Aug. 1705) 4°
1705.

CHETWOOD, WILLIAM RUFUS.
C. The Stock-Jobbers, or, The Humours of Exchange Alley 8° 1720.
T.C. P.F. South-Sea; or, The Biters Bit 8° 1720.
(B.O.) The Lover's Opera (D.L. May 1729) 8° 1729; 8° 1729 (2nd
with alterations); 8° 1730 (3rd edn. with alterations); 8° 1731.
1729. D.L. W. 14/5, M. 26, F. 30; M. 30/6. 1730. M. 5/1;
W. 8/4, W. 15, F. 17, W. 22; T. 19/5; T. 1/12. 1731. Th. 25/3;
W. 21/4, M. 26; G.F. F. 5/11–Th. 11, M. 15, Th. 18, F. 19,
Th. 25, M. 29; W. 1/12, Th. 2, M. 6, T. 7, Th. 16, S. 18. 1732.
M. 10/1, T. 11, Th. 13, S. 15, W. 19; F. 18/2, M. 28; S. 25/3;
T. 11/4, Th. 20; T. 2/5, M. 8, F. 19; D.L. M. 1/5. 1733. G.F.
S. 20/1, M. 22, T. 23; Th. 1/2; M. 30/4. 1734. W. 2/1, F. 25;
S. 2/2; T. 5/3; M. 6/5. 1735. Th. 13/3, M. 17. 1736. Th. 5/2;
M. 22/3; D.L. M. 22/3. 1737. L.² T. 12/4, M. 18; M. 16/5. 1738.
D.L. W. 26/4; M. 29/5. 1741. G.F. F. 10/4; D.L. T. 5/5.
T.C.F. B.O. The Generous Free-Mason: Or, The Constant Lady.
With the Humours of Squire Noodle, and his Man Doodle (B.F.
Aug. 1730; H.² Dec. 1730) 8° 1731 (by the author of The Lover's
Opera).
1730. B.F. Oates and Fielding, Aug.; S.F. Sept.; H.² M. 28/12
(with additions), W. 30. 1731. F. 1/1; D.L. M. 3/5; B.F. Yeates,
Aug. 1736. L.² W. 16/6. 1741. Tott. Court F. Lee and Woodward,
Aug.
*D.O. The Emperor of China Grand Volgi, or The Constant Couple
and Virtue Rewarded.
1731. B.F. Fielding, Hippisley and Hall, Aug.; S.F. Sept. (The
bill declares this is by the author of *The Generous Free-Mason.*)

CIBBER, COLLEY.
[For his seventeenth century works see the Hand-list of Plays,
1660–1700.]

T. The Tragical History of King Richard III (D.L. *c.* Dec. 1699/1700)
4° (1700); 12° 1719; 12° 1754; 8° 1778.

Published March 16, 1699/1700 (*Flying Post*). 1704. D.L.
T. 4/4. 1710. H.¹ S. 28/1; M. 27/3; S. 13/5. 1713. D.L. S. 14/2,
Th. 26; M. 27/4. 1714. S. 2/1; S. 27/2; S. 17/4; F. 15/10.
1715. Th. 27/1; T. 6/12. 1717. T. 1/1; S. 9/11. 1718. S. 15/3.
1719. Th. 12/2; S. 26/9. 1720. S. 13/2; Th. 19/5; S. 3/12. 1721.
L.¹ S. 11/3, M. 13, M. 27; T. 7/10; S. 16/12; D.L. T. 26/12.
1722. M. 14/5; L.² Th. 4/10; Th. 15/11. 1723. D.L. S. 9/3; L.²
F. 11/10. 1724. Th. 30/4; Th. 22/10. 1725. D.L. S. 6/2; L.² S.
1/5; T. 9/11. 1726. M. 17/10; Th. 29/12; D.L. Th. 3/11. 1727.
T. 17/1; L.² Th. 21/12. 1728. W. 3/1; D.L. Th. 23/5; W. 6/11,
W. 20; H.² M. 19/8. 1730. D.L. T. 10/11. 1731. L.² M. 15/11.
1732. G.F. M. 20/3, S. 25; Th. 11/5; D.L. S. 14/10; F. 17/11.
1733. M. 12/2; W. 17/10; F. 2/11; G.F. W. 11/4, Th. 12; C.G.
S. 15/12, W. 26. 1734. G.F. Th. 18/3; W. 8/5; F. 6/12; C.G.
Th. 16/5; Th. 26/12; D.L. S. 26/10, M. 28. 1735. T. 7/1; W. 5/2;
S. 25/10; C.G. T. 8/4. 1736. D.L. W. 26/5; S. 18/9; W. 1/12.
1737. M. 3/1; S. 1/10. 1738. M. 13/2; T. 23/5; S. 30/9. 1739.
W. 31/1; W. 17/10. 1740. M. 14/1; T. 16/9. 1741. Th. 12/2;
S. 19/12, M. 28; G.F. T. 10/2; M. 19/10–Th. 22, S. 24, M. 26,
T. 27, Th. 29, F. 30, S. 31; M. 2/11, M. 23, Th. 26; T. 15/12,
W. 23; C.G. T. 13/10, W. 14; T. 8/12. 1742. G.F. S. 6/3; W.
21/4; W. 5/5, F. 14, F. 21; D.L. F. 30/4; M. 31/5; W. 13/10,
F. 15, S. 23, Th. 28; F. 5/11, Th. 11; M. 20/12; C.G. W. 13/10,
Th. 14; M. 6/12; L.² M. 27/12. 1743. D.L. M. 3/1, T. 4, M. 10,
W. 19; M. 14/2; S. 16/3; T. 3/5; S. 17/12; L.² M. 3/1, W. 5, F. 7;
C.G. F. 28/1; M. 7/3; F. 8/4; W. 28/9; M. 14/11; S. 10/12. 1744.
M. 2/1; M. 26/3; Th. 5/4; W. 24/10; D.L. T. 3/1, S. 18; S. 7/4;
M. 7/5, Th. 31; S. 3/11; S. 15/12; H.² W. 15/1; Richmond S.
8/7; G.F. W. 5/12–S. 8, Th. 20. 1745. C.G. T. 8/1; M. 22/4;
Th. 28/11; D.L. S. 12/1; T. 12/2; T. 5/3; G.F. M. 18/3; T. 30/4;
M. 16/12; Richmond S. 6/7; Twickenham T. 13/8. 1746. D.L.
W. 8/1, Th. 9; T. 22/4, T. 29; G.F. M. 3/3; T. 11/11; W. 17/12,
F. 26, T. 30; C.G. M. 16/6; M. 20/10, F. 31. 1747. G.F. F. 6/2;
Th. 26/3; D.L. F. 6/11; C.G. M. 28/12. 1748. D.L. W. 27/1;
S. 30/4; Th. 29/9; F. 23/12; C.G. M. 29/2. 1749. D.L. S. 4/3;
Th. 6/4; Th. 16/11; C.G. M. 2/10.

C. Love Makes a Man; or, The Fop's Fortune (D.L. Dec. 1700) 4°
1701; 8° 1716; 12° 1722 (Dublin); 12° 1745; 12° 1774 (Dublin).

1700. D.L. F. 13/12. 1701. S. 7/6. 1702. M. 26/10. 1703. W.
6/10; T. 16/11; F. 17/12. 1704. W. 2/2; S. 4/3; W. 11/10; T. 19/12.
1705. F. 2/11. 1706. Th. 24/1; Th. 19/12, M. 30. 1707. M. 24/2;
S. 25/10; T. 11/11. 1708. W. 4/2; T. 12/10. 1709. F. 28/1; T.
17/5; H.¹ S. 1/10; W. 16/11. 1710. W. 4/1; Th. 16/2; M. 17/4;
M. 6/11; Greenwich Th. 15/6. 1711. D.L. Th. 1/2; M. 12/3;
F. 11/5; M. 17/12; Greenwich Th. 4/10. 1712. D.L. M. 5/5;
M. 6/10. 1713. M. 10/3; W. 18/11. 1714. T. 9/3; W. 24/11.
1715. T. 25/1; L.² Th. 21/4, S. 30; Th. 29/9; W. 2/11; T. 20/12.
1716. Th. 5/1; F. 4/5; M. 26/11; D.L. Th. 5/4; Th. 4/10. 1717.
L.² M. 4/2, M. 25; Th. 30/5; D.L. Th. 22/2; Th. 6/6; W. 9/10;
M. 11/11; M. 30/12. 1718. L.² W. 12/2; T. 6/5; M. 6/10; Th.
20/11; D.L. F. 23/5; Richmond S. 26/7. 1719. D.L. Th. 30/4;
T. 27/10; L.² F. 29/5. 1720. D.L. T. 1/3; S. 7/5, Th. 26; W. 5/10,

Th. 27; L.² T. 29/11. 1721. Th. 11/5, W. 31; T. 3/10; D.L. W.
1/11. 1722. D.L. M. 22/1; Th. 15/2; Th. 12/4, F. 27; F. 26/10;
L.² T. 27/2; F. 25/5; T. 16/10. 1723. D.L. S. 4/5; F. 15/11;
L.² F. 18/10. 1724. S. 1/2; T. 7/4; M. 18/5; M. 5/10; D.L. Th.
7/5; F. 18/12. 1725. L.² M. 3/5; T. 23/11; D.L. W. 12/5; T. 28/9.
1726. L.² M. 28/2; M. 2/5; D.L. W. 9/11. 1727. F. 13/1; W.
17/5. 1728. W. 14/2; L.² Th. 28/3; F. 3/5. 1729. D.L. M. 20/1;
G.F. M. 24/11, T. 25. 1730. M. 12/1; Th. 5/3; W. 16/9; W.
28/10; D.L. Th. 30/4; Th. 7/5; Richmond S. 18/7; L.² T. 8/12.
1731. G.F. S. 2/1; W. 17/2; T. 6/4; F. 7/5; T. 28/12; L.² S. 9/1;
F. 3/12. 1732. M. 7/2; W. 19/4; T. 7/11; G.F. S. 12/2, M. 14;
M. 24/4; T. 17/10; M. 18/12; S.F. Lee Th. 12/10; D.L. F. 1/12,
S. 2, Th. 14. 1733. S. 13/1; S. 10/3; T. 11/12, M. 31; G.F. M.
12/3; C.G. M. 7/5; M. 26/11; H.² F. 5/10. 1734. G.F. S. 19/1;
S. 6/4; M. 6/5; W. 6/11; C.G. Th. 7/2; Th. 2/5; Th. 20/9; Th.
12/12; D.L. W. 20/11. 1736. W. 18/2; Th. 27/5; F. 17/11; C.G.
S. 20/3; L.² S. 6/11; Th. 30/12. 1737. D.L. F. 4/3; F. 27/5;
S. 11/6; Th. 29/9; T. 8/11; L.² Th. 28/4. 1738. C.G. F. 7/4;
M. 9/10; M. 13/11; Th. 28/12; D.L. Th. 25/5. 1739. C.G. W.
7/2; M. 26/3; F. 18/5; W. 3/10; W. 12/12; D.L. S. 10/3, M. 19;
F. 4/5; Th. 18/10, T. 30. 1740. T. 22/1; S. 6/12; C.G. Th. 31/1;
W. 9/4; F. 16/5; M. 6/10; G.F. T. 18/11; W. 17/12. 1741. Th.
5/2; W. 22/4; W. 28/10; T. 3/11, Th. 5; S. 28/11; M. 7/12;
C.G. M. 23/2; F. 2/10; F. 4/12; D.L. Th. 7/5; T. 20/10; F. 11/12.
1742. G.F. M. 25/1, T. 26; Th. 25/2; Th. 25/3; C.G. W. 27/1;
M. 3/5; D.L. T. 2/3, Th. 25; T. 18/5; S. 16/10; W. 8/12; James-
street Th. 25/11. 1743. D.L. T. 25/1; W. 27/4; S. 24/9; T. 15/11.
1744. H.² M. 5/11; G.F. T. 18/12. 1745. C.G. F. 4/1; M. 6/5;
Th. 11/10; W. 27/11; G.F. S. 26/1; F. 26/4; T. 12/11. 1746.
C.G. M. 20/1; T. 8/4; G.F. W. 29/1; F. 28/11. 1747. C.G. T.
3/2; G.F. T. 31/3. 1748. C.G. Th. 7/1; T. 15/3; T. 19/4; D.L.
Th. 22/9. 1749. C.G. W. 12/4; F. 8/12; D.L. T. 9/5; W. 15/11.

C. She Wou'd and She Wou'd Not; or, the Kind Impostor (D.L.
Nov. 1702) 4° 1703; 12° 1719 (3rd); 8° 1725 (Dublin); 12° 1736
(4th); 12° 1748 (5th).

    1702. D.L. Th. 26/11. 1707. T. 29/4. 1714. S. 10/4, T. 13,
W. 21; M. 10/5; W. 9/6; Th. 30/9; M. 8/11. 1715. Th. 13/1;
T. 29/3; F. 20/5; M. 24/10. 1716. M. 23/1. 1717. M. 11/11.
1719. T. 31/3. 1720. F. 5/2; M. 16/5; M. 3/10; F. 25/11. 1721.
W. 17/5. 1722. T. 10/4; T. 30/10. 1723. M. 11/2. 1726. Th. 17/3.
1727. F. 5/5. 1728. T. 19/3, S. 23; F. 10/5, W. 22; Th. 7/11.
1731. L.² Th. 25/11, S. 27, M. 29, T. 30; D.L. F. 3/12; G.F.
T. 21/12. 1732. D.L. W. 5/1; L.² T. 22/2; F. 5/5; M. 23/10;
G.F. M. 10/4. 1733. C.G. M. 30/4; F. 1/6; F. 19/10; Th. 6/12.
1734. F. 22/2; T. 30/4. 1735. T. 4/2; W. 16/4; F. 24/10; M. 22/12.
1736. T. 18/5. 1737. M. 17/1; W. 12/10; H.² W. 2/3. 1738. C.G.
W. 26/4; Th. 26/10; T. 14/11–Th. 16, T. 28. 1739. D.L. F. 11/5;
F. 16/11. 1740. F. 1/2; C.G. F. 2/5. 1742. W. 3/2, S. 6; M. 22/3;
M. 17/5. 1743. W. 16/11; T. 6/12. 1744. F. 4/5; W. 3/10. 1745.
Th. 14/11. 1746. G.F. M. 6/1; C.G. W. 8/1; T. 11/2; T. 18/3;
T. 29/4; F. 10/10. 1747. Th. 15/1; W. 4/2; F. 24/4. 1748. D.L.
M. 18/1, T. 19; T. 9/2; T. 12/4; S. 17/9. 1749. F. 28/4.

F. The School-Boy: or, The Comical Rival (D.L. 1702) 4° 1707;
12° 1730; 12° 1736; 8° (1780?).

1702. D.L. S. 24/10. 1703. D.G. F. 30/4; W. 7/7. 1704. D.L.
T. 28/3; W. 4/10, F. 27; M. 4/12. 1705. S. 27/10. 1710. H.¹
M. 13/2, F. 17, M. 27; T. 2/3; D.L. M. 4/12. 1711. F. 21/12.
1712. F. 16/5; F. 5/12. 1713. W. 28/10; F. 6/11. 1715. Th. 17/3;
T. 10/5; Th. 27/10. 1716. F. 18/5; F. 14/12. 1717. F. 4/1. 1723.
H.² M. 22/4; D.L. T. 2/7, F. 26. 1724. M. 11/5, T. 19; M. 16/11;
L.² T. 20/10. 1725. D.L. T. 20/4. 1727. S. 29/4. 1728. H.² T.
5/11, W. 6. 1729. D.L. M. 12/5. 1730. L.² S. 11/4, T. 7, T. 14,
F. 17, S. 18; T. 5/5; M. 8/6; F. 18/12. 1731. Th. 25/3; W. 26/5;
W. 20/10. 1732. W. 12/4; W. 27/9; T. 14/11. 1733. C.G. M. 5/2;
M. 16/4. 1734. F. 3/5; L.² Th. 23/5. 1735. C.G. F. 17/1; F.
9/5, T. 13, F. 16, T. 27; L.² Th. 12/6 1736. C.G. Th. 13/5
1737. F. 7/1, F. 21. 1740. Th. 20/3; M. 5/5, W. 7; Th. 23/10;
S. 1/11, W. 19; D.L. S. 19/4. 1741. C.G. T. 27/10; M. 2/11;
F. 11/12. 1742. T. 16/2; M. 1/3; T. 19/11; F. 3/12; G.F. M.
22/2–F. 26; Th. 18/3; Th. 22/4; L.² W. 22/12. 1743. D.L. M.
21/3, T. 22; T. 4/10, Th. 6, S. 8, T. 25, F. 28; M. 14/11; C.G.
W. 4/5, Th. 5; F. 21/10, M. 24; Th. 24/11; T. 6/12. 1744. D.L.
M. 2/4; S. 24/11; C.G. F. 5/10. 1745. James-street W. 27/3;
C.G. T. 14/5; S. 2/11, M. 11; D.L. W. 5/6; Richmond W. 28/8.
1746. G.F. T. 4/3; W. 3/12, Th. 4, Th. 11, F. 12, Th. 18; C.G.
F. 2/5; F. 3/10; M. 3/11. 1747. G.F. T. 3/2, Th. 12, F. 13; D.L.
M. 30/3. 1748. S. 8/10, F. 26; Th. 3/11; T. 6/12, T. 20.

C. The Careless Husband (D.L. Dec. 1704) 4° 1705 (*bis*); 8° 1711:
12° 1723 (Dublin); 12° 1723 (6th); 12° 1731 (7th); 12° 1735;
12° 1752 (Dublin); 12° 1756; 12° 1760 (Dublin, 8th); 12° 1771.

1704. D.L. Th. 7/12–S. 16, Th. 21. 1705. T. 2/1, T. 9; T. 27/2;
S. 17/3; S. 2/6; S. 13/10; S. 24/11. 1706. T. 19/2; W. 3/4; H.¹
Th. 7/11, T. 12, S. 23; S. 21/12. 1707. T. 11/2; M. 10/3; S. 6/12,
T. 30. 1708. D.L. W. 21/1. 1709 S. 8/1; S. 12/11. 1710. T. 13/6.
1711. M. 19/2; F. 27/4; T. 23/10. 1712. Th. 3/1; S. 20/9; Th. 9/10.
1713. S. 7/2; S. 28/11. 1714. M. 8/3; M. 5/4; S. 13/11. 1715.
T. 11/1; Th. 31/3; T. 24/5; S. 22/10; Th. 8/12; L.² S. 19/3.
1716. D.L. S. 4/2; S. 24/3; S. 15/12. 1717. Th. 14/3; S. 23/11.
1718. S. 23/1; T. 4/3; S. 26/4; S. 15/11. 1719. S. 24/1; M. 27/4.
1720. Th. 28/1; S. 27/2; T. 26/4. 1721 T. 10/1; S. 4/2; S. 25/3;
S. 11/11. 1722. S. 13/1; Th. 15/3; S. 21/4; S. 8/9; F. 3/10. 1723.
Th. 7/3; T. 2/4; S. 2/11; Th. 12/12. 1724. M. 16/3; S. 11/4;
S. 10/10; W. 11/11. 1725. Th. 7/1; M. 8/3; W. 28/4; S. 16/11.
1726. S. 8/1; S. 26/2; M. 25/4; T. 27/9; T. 8/11. 1727. W. 19/4;
S. 14/10; S. 2/12. 1728. Th. 21/3; F. 26/4; S. 7/12. 1729. S. 1/2;
M. 14/4. 1730. G.F. Th. 12/3; D.L. S. 4/4. 1731. G.F. W. 13/1–
M. 18; M. 8/3; M. 26/4; Th. 6/5; W. 6/10; W. 3/11; T. 14/12.
1732. D.L. S. 29/1; W. 2/2; M. 6/3; Th. 13/4; G.F. F. 11/2; M. 1/5.
1733. D.L. M. 5/3; T. 17/4; G.F. T. 6/3, Th. 29; W. 23/5; H.²
S. 20/10; S. 15/12. 1734. Th. 3/1, T. 29; G.F. F. 11/1; T. 5/2,
Th. 28; T. 5/3, S. 23; M. 13/5; C.G. Th. 14/2, F. 15; F. 26/4;
D.L. M. 18/3; T. 23/4, M. 29; Th. 14/11. 1735. G.F. M. 20/1;
M. 3/2; S. 8/3; S. 12/4; W. 12/11; D.L. F. 31/1; L.² Th. 19/6;
H.² Th. 14/8. 1736. M. 16/2; D.L. Th. 29/4; M. 24/5. 1737.
L.² S. 2/4, S. 30. 1738. D.L. T. 2/5. 1739. M. 15/1; M. 9/4;
C.G. T. 21/8, W. 29; T. 2/10; W. 7/11; M. 17/12. 1740. D.L.
S. 5/1; T. 15/4; F. 16/5; S. 8/11; C.G. T. 8/1; M. 24/3; F. 25/4;
F. 19/12; G.F. Th. 27/11; W. 3/12. 1741. S. 7/2; T. 5/5; W. 7/10;

C.G. S. 18/4. 1742. G.F. M. 15/3, T. 16; M. 26/4; F. 26/11;
D.L. S. 20/3; M. 22/11; C.G. S. 1/5. 1743. L.² W. 19/1; W. 2/3;
D.L. W. 4/5. 1744. F. 11/5; H.² T. 25/9; T. 16/10; T. 11/12;
James-street M. 10/12. 1745. D.L. S. 26/1; F. 15/2; M. 6/5;
T. 8/10; C.G. S. 9/2, Th. 28; W. 1/5; T. 12/11; W. 4/12. 1746.
S. 22/2; W. 9/4; D.L. S. 1/3; W. 2/4; F. 6/6; F. 8/8; S. 25/10;
M. 22/12. 1747. G.F. T. 10/2; D.L. W. 11/2. 1749. C.G. M. 6/2,
T. 21; F. 14/4.

T. Perolla and Izadora (D.L. Dec. 1705) 4° 1706; 12° 1736.
  1705. D.L. M. 3/12–S. 8. 1706. W. 2/1.

C. The Comical Lovers (H.¹ Feb. 1706/7) 4° (1707; anon.); 12°
(Dublin? 1720); 12° 1754.
  1707. H.¹ T. 4/2, W. 5, S. 8 (as Marriage a la Mode, and so
frequently); Th. 20/11. 1708. D.L. S. 21/2; W. 19/5. 1709. S.
12/2; H.¹ Th. 29/9. 1710. M. 6/2. 1715. D.L. W. 5/1, F. 21;
F. 3/6 (as Court Gallantry, or M. a la M.). 1717. Th. 11/4. 1720.
S. 8/10–T. 11; W. 9/11. 1721. W. 12/4. 1722. F. 27/4. 1746.
M. 10/3, T. 11, S. 15; T. 1/4, Th. 24; S. 1/11. 1747. Th. 7/5.

C. The Double Gallant: or, The Sick Lady's Cure (H.¹ Nov. 1707)
4° (1707 bis); 12° 1719 (3rd); 12° 1723 (4th); 12° 1725 (Dublin);
8° (1729, 2nd); 12° 1740.
  1707. H.¹ S. 1/11, M. 3, M. 24. 1708. D.L. M. 16/2. 1712.
S. 27/12, M. 29, T. 30. 1713. S. 3/1, S. 17; M. 16/2; Th. 9/4;
M. 9/11. 1714. W. 13/1; F. 14/5; F. 22/10; T. 7/12. 1715. S. 7/5;
M. 14/11. 1716. F. 27/1. 1717. W. 27/11. 1718. M. 3/3. 1719.
F. 23/10. 1720. F. 12/2; M. 2/5. 1721. F. 13/1; M. 1/5; T. 28/11.
1722. Th. 8/2, S. 17; Th. 5/4; F. 4/5; T. 16/10; Th. 27/12. 1723.
L.² Th. 4/4; D.L. Th. 14/11. 1724. Th. 23/1; Th. 26/3; W. 14/10;
W. 2/12. 1725. S. 13/3; Th. 7/10; M. 6/12. 1726. Th. 27/1; W.
20/4; Th. 6/10. 1727. T. 7/2; M. 1/5; T. 10/10. 1728. T. 23/4;
F. 25/10. 1729. Th. 23/1; W. 30/4. 1730. T. 20/1; T. 21/4. 1731.
F. 19/2; M. 3/5; T. 28/9; T. 30/11; G.F. M. 22/3; S. 3/4, F. 23.
1732. D.L. T. 2/5; T. 24/10; F. 24/11; G.F. Th. 4/5; T. 28/11.
1733. D.L. T. 9/1; Th. 15/3; T. 1/5; G.F. W. 25/4; W. 24/10;
H.² M. 22/10; T. 13/11. 1734. Th. 10/1; G.F. T. 7/5; D.L. S.
16/11; C.G. Th. 21/11; M. 30/12. 1735. F. 14/2; M. 21/4; F.
26/9; T. 18/11; G.F. S. 15/3; D.L. S. 19/4; M. 3/11; W. 10/12.
1736. C.G. T. 10/2; M. 25/10; D.L. T. 24/2; M. 26/4. 1737.
C.G. T. 18/1; M. 18/4; F. 28/10; D.L. W. 2/2; T. 19/4; F. 11/11.
1738. C.G. S. 4/2; Th. 27/4; F. 20/10; W. 20/12. 1739. D.L.
M. 8/1, S. 27; Th. 11/10; C.G. W. 21/2; F. 11/5; S. 22/9; Th.
20/12. 1740. Th. 24/1; W. 1/10; Th. 13/11; S. 6/12; D.L. F. 8/2;
M. 24/3; Th. 6/11; G.F. M. 1/12. 1741. C.G. Th. 19/2; M. 20/4;
G.F.T. 14/4; D.L. M. 7/12. 1742. C.G. T. 19/1; S. 20/3; F. 14/5;
D.L. Th. 4/2; T. 30/3. 1743. C.G. T. 15/3; S. 16/4; M. 10/10.
1744. D.L. T. 1/5; C.G. W. 9/5; M. 17/12. 1745. D.L. M.
11/2; T. 15/10; C.G. W. 8/5; T. 10/12. 1746. M. 3/3; D.L.
W. 14/5. 1747. C.G. M. 2/2. 1748. F. 29/4. 1749. T. 11/4;
F. 17/11.

C. The Lady's Last Stake, or, The Wife's Resentment (H.¹ Dec.
1707) 4° (1708); 8° 1747; 12° 1750 (Dublin).
  1707. H.¹ S. 13/12–W. 17, F. 19. 1708. D.L. S. 28/2. 1720.
Th. 10/3. 1726. S. 22/1; M. 7/3. 1731. S. 18/12. 1732. L.² W.
26/4. 1739. D.L. T. 13/3. 1740. W. 16/4. 1741. F. 24/4. 1745.

C.G. Th. 14/3, S. 16, S. 23; F. 19/4; S. 16/11; S. 7/12, F. 20.
1746. W. 2/4; D.L. Th. 10/4; Th. 11/12. 1747. W. 21/1. **1748.**
C.G. Th. 24/3.

C.   The Rival Fools (D.L. Jan. 1708/9) 4° (1709); 12° 1753.
   1709. D.L. T. 11/1–F. 14. 1722. Th. 4/1, F. 5.

C.T.   The Rival Queans, with the Humours of Alexander the Great
   (H.¹ June 1710) 8° 1729 (Dublin).
   1710. H.¹ Th. 29/6. 1719. L.² W. 24/6 (marked as new, but
   probably the same piece), Th. 25. 1738. D.L. W. 17/5.

Int.   Hob, or the Country Wake (D.L. Oct. 1711) 12° 1715; Flora, and
   Hob in the Well 12° 1755 (Glasgow).
   1711. D.L. S. 6/10 (in all probability date of first performance)
   M. 8, S. 13, M. 15, T. 23, Th. 25; S. 3/11; Th. 13/12, S. 15,
   T. 18, Th. 27. 1712. Th. 7/2, Th. 14; Th. 13/3; S. 26/4; S. 17/5;
   Th. 9/10; W. 31/12. 1713. F. 9/1; T. 17/3; S. 11/4; T. 6/10,
   W. 21; T. 10/11, F. 20. 1715. M. 17/1, F. 28; T. 19/4, S. 30;
   M. 6/6; L.² F. 4/2, Th. 10, F. 11, T. 15; T. 1/3; Th. 7/4; Th. 2/6;
   M. 3/10, M. 17; W. 2/11; Th. 29/12. 1716. Th. 22/3; M. 9/4;
   D.L. Th. 3/5, W. 30; T. 11/12. 1717. L.² T. 8/1; T. 23/4; F.
   24/5; W. 30/10; T. 5/11; S. 21/12; D.L. M. 1/4; F. 7/6; T. 2/7;
   Th. 7/11. 1718. L.² M. 6/1; S. 15/3; T. 27/5; W. 9/7; W. 6/8;
   Th. 9/10; M. 1/12, F. 26; D.L. Th. 6/2; T. 20/5, Th. 29; F. 13/6;
   F. 25/7; F. 7/11; Richmond S. 16/8. 1719. L.² T. 31/3; Th. 14/5,
   M. 25, F. 29; D.L. M. 18/5. 1720. L.² Th. 31/3; F. 22/4; W. 4/5;
   M. 31/10; D.L. T. 19/4; S. 14/5. 1721. T. 6/6. 1722. L.² M. 9/4;
   Th. 24/5; F. 12/10; D.L. W. 2/5, M. 7, Th. 17. 1723. L.² W. 13/2;
   M. 20/5, F. 24; T. 8/10; M. 9/12; D.L. S. 30/3; T. 16/4; M. 6/5;
   S. 25; T. 2/7; F. 18/10. 1724. L.² M. 4/5, Th. 7, M. 25; W. 11/11;
   D.L. W. 21/10, S. 24. 1725. L.² M. 18/1; F. 14/5, W. 19; D.L.
   W. 19/5. 1727. Th. 4/5; F. 20/10. 1728. L.² M. 1/4, M. 22;
   F. 17/5. 1729. D.L. W. 31/12. 1730. G.F. M. 5/1. 1731. D.L.
   M. 17/5; T. 3/8; T. 28/9. 1734. F. 4/10. 1738. C.G. S. 6/5.
   1745. G.F. W. 1/5. 1749. C.G. Th. 19/10, M. 23, T. 24, S. 28;
   Th. 2/11. [See for this piece Hippisley's *Flora*. Contrary to what
   O. G. T. Sonneck says in his *Catalogue of Opera Librettos* (1914,
   i. 519) there are two separate texts of this work.]

T.   Ximena: or, The Heroick Daughter (D.L. Nov. 1712) 8° 1719;
   8° 1781.
   1712. D.L. F. 28/11, S. 29; M. 1/12–Th. 4. 1713. Th. 15/1;
   M. 2/3. 1718. F. 31/10; S. 1/11, M. 3, T. 11.

M.   Venus and Adonis (D.L. March 1714/5) 8° 1716; with Myrtillo
   8° (1720); 12° 1736 (*bis*).
   1715. D.L. S. 12/3, T. 15, T. 22, Th. 24, T. 29, Th. 31; Th.
   7/4, M. 18, Th. 28; F. 6/5, M. 23; Th. 20/10; Th. 10/11, Th. 17;
   Th. 15/12, M. 26, T. 27. 1716. F. 6/1, Th. 19; T. 3/4; W. 2/5.
   1718. L.² T. 18/11, Th. 20; M. 22/12, S. 27, W. 31. 1719. M. 5/1;
   T. 17/2; S. 7/3. 1725. F. 2/4, M. 5. 1730. M. 16/3 (evidently
   revised; advertised as "the last new inter lude"). 1748. C.G. M.
   21/3; F. 15/4.

M.   Myrtillo (D.L. Nov. 1715) 8° 1715; with Venus and Adonis 8°
   (1720); 12° 1736 (*bis*).
   1715. D.L. S. 5/11, M. 7, T. 15, T. 22, F. 25; Th. 1/12, W. 21.
   1716. W. 4/1; Th. 2/2, M. 20. 1722. L.² T. 10/4; W. 2/5; D.L.
   F. 25/5. 1728. Th. 12/9. 1730. L.² Th. 23/4.

C. The Non-Juror (D.L. Dec. 1717) 8° 1718 (5 edns.); 8° 1746; 12° 1759 (Dublin).
    1717. D.L. F. 6/12–S. 21, Th. 26, F. 27. 1718. W. 1/1, Th. 16, F. 17; F. 7/2, M. 17; M. 10/3; W. 16/4; S. 18/10; Richmond M. 18/8. 1741. Tennis Court, Hay. T. 19/5. 1743. L.² W. 9/2. Th. 10, M. 28. 1745. C.G. F. 18/10, M. 21, W. 23, F. 25, M. 28, W. 30; W. 6/11; D.L. M. 28/10–Th. 31; Th. 7/11, W. 13; W. 4/12, M. 23. 1746. C.G. W. 15/1; T. 2/12; D.L. W. 22/1; S. 15/2. 1747. C.G. M. 19/1.

C. The Refusal; or, The Ladies Philosophy (D.L. Feb. 1720/1) 8° 1721; 8° 1737 (4th); 12° 1753 (5th); 12° 1764.
    1721. D.L. T. 14/2–M. 20. 1746. F. 28/11, S. 29; M. 1/12, W. 3, S. 6, M. 8, F. 19. 1747. S. 28/2; T. 21/4; S. 19/9, T. 29; W. 28/10. 1748. S. 23/1; F. 22/4.

T. Cæsar in Ægypt (D.L. Dec. 1724) 8° 1725; 12° 1736.
    1724. D.L. W. 9/12–T. 15.

C. The Provok'd Husband; or, A Journey to London (D.L. Jan. 1727/8) 8° 1728 (3 edns.); 8° 1729; 8° 1748; 8° 1753; 12° 1753; 12° 1756 (Glasgow).
    1728. D.L. W. 10/1–M. 29, W. 31; Th. 1/2–M. 12, Th. 22, F. 23; M. 4/3, S. 16; Th. 11/4, T. 30; F. 3/5, F. 24; Th. 13/6; S. 7/9, T. 24; S. 19/10; M. 11/11. 1729. S. 18/1; Th. 20/3; T. 15/4, S. 26. 1730. G.F. M. 9/2, Th. 12, T. 17; S. 14/3, M. 16; W. 1/4; M. 6/7; W. 23/9; F. 16/10; T. 17/11; T. 15/12, S. 19; D.L. S. 14/2; M. 16/3; H.² Th. 16/7; F. 27/11. 1731. G.F. T. 12/1; W. 10/2; T. 9/3; F. 30/4; W. 13/10; T. 9/11; W. 29/12; H.² W. 10/2; F. 7/5; D.L. M. 1/11–W. 3; S. 4/12; L.² T. 2/11; W. 22/12. 1732. D.L. S. 22/1, F. 28; M. 27/3; W. 19/4; S. 7/10; G.F. Th. 17/2; M. 13/3; S. 15/4; W. 17/5; W. 25/10, S. 28; F. 10/11, W. 29; W. 27/12; L.² Th. 23/3; F. 21/4; M. 16/10. 1733. C.G. F. 19/1; S. 31/3; Th. 20/9; Th. 22/11; G.F. Th. 15/2, M. 26; M. 16/4; F. 21/9; W. 7/11; D.L. Th. 29/3; S. 7/4, F. 20; F. 25/5; H.² S. 13/10; W. 7/11; M. 19/11; T. 18/12. 1734. C.G. T. 15/1; M. 6/5; W. 16/10; T. 31/12; D.L. M. 4/3; S. 23/3; W. 22/5; M. 21/10; G.F. Th. 7/3, T. 12; W. 1/5; T. 12/11; L.² M. 1/4; T. 20/8. 1735. C.G. M. 13/1; Th. 20/3; T. 6/5; W. 17/9; M. 24/11; D.L. S. 25/1; F. 23/5; G.F. M. 17/2; S. 22/3; T. 6/5; M. 3/11; L.² W. 16/7; H.² F. 8/8. 1736. C.G. M. 5/1; S. 7/2; T. 23/3; T. 8/6; F. 17/9; M. 6/12; G.F. T. 17/2; D.L. Th. 15/4; T. 18/5; H.² T. 29/6; L.² T. 26/10. 1737. D.L. Th. 5/5; C.G. M. 9/5; M. 3/10; W. 16/11. 1738. W. 11/1; Th. 6/4; W. 27/9; W. 8/11; S. 30/12; D.L. Th. 2/2. 1739. C.G. T. 20/3; F. 14/9; W. 24/10; S. 3/11; D.L. T. 27/3; Th. 3/5, S. 26. 1740. C.G. S. 12/1; W. 16/4; M. 22/9; D.L. T. 6/5; T. 28/10; G.F. F. 31/10. 1741. C.G. S. 17/1; Th. 2/4; M. 28/9; Th. 19/11–S. 21; W. 23/12; D.L. M. 2/2, S. 7; Th. 28/5; T. 15/9; S. 31/10; G.F. Th. 23/4; F. 25/9. 1742. C.G. W. 13/1, Th. 28; S. 6/3; W. 28/4; G.F. F. 29/1; T. 20/4; D.L. M. 17/5; M. 8/11. 1743. C.G. W. 9/2; M. 21/3; Th. 21/4; F. 23/9; Th. 24/11; L.² T. 5/4. 1744. C.G. T. 31/1; T. 10/4; F. 21/9; D.L. M. 12/3, W. 28, F. 30; M. 16/4; Th. 1/11, W. 14; W. 12/12. 1745. M. 7/1; S. 16/3; Th. 18/4; W. 5/6; S. 21/9; T. 19/11; M. 16/12; G.F. M. 11/3, S. 30; Th. 25/4; M. 4/11; C.G. F. 10/5; F. 8/11. 1746. F. 10/1; S. 12/4; W. 1/10; W. 3/12; G.F. F. 10/1; T. 18/11; D.L. S. 25/1;

M. 12/5; F. 13/6. 1747. S. 3/1–T. 6, Th. 8, S. 10–T. 13, F. 23,
W. 28, F. 30, S. 31; F. 20/2, W. 25; S. 21/3; M. 6/4, S. 25;
W. 6/5; Th. 24/9; M. 26/10; M. 9/11; G.F. W. 25/2; C.G. T.
19/5. 1748. F. 15/1; T. 12/4; Th. 3/11, F. 18; W. 14/12; D.L. F.
22/1; T. 16/2, W. 17, S. 20; S. 26/3; S. 1/10; T. 18/10. 1749.
C.G. Th. 5/1; M. 17/4; F. 29/9; S. 25/11; D.L. W. 11/1; Th.
13/4; T. 10/10; F. 10/11; S. 23/12.

(B.O.) Love in a Riddle. A Pastoral (D.L. Jan. 1728/9) 8° 1729 (mis-
printed 1719); 8° 1729. 1729. D.L. T. 7/1, W. 8.

(B.O.) Damon and Phillida (H.² 1729) 12° (1729); 8° 1765; Damon
and Phillida: or, The Rover Reclaim'd (as acted at Norwich by
the Duke of Grafton's men) 8° 1730; 12° 1732 (Edinburgh);
8° 1737. [The texts of the 1729 and of the 1730 editions differ
widely.]

1729. H.² S. 16/8, T. 19; B.F. Reynolds, Aug. 1730. H.² W.
11/3, F. 20; F. 17/7, S. 18, W. 22–F. 24; F. 13/11, W. 18; L.²
M. 18/5; W. 23/9; G.F. M. 28/12–Th. 31. 1731. S. 2/1–M. 11
M. 18, F. 22; W. 10/2, S. 13; T. 2/3, Th. 4, T. 9, Th. 25; S. 3/4,
M. 5, F. 23, Th. 29; F. 7/5, W. 12, M. 17, W. 26; M. 11/10,
F. 15, W. 20, F. 22, W. 27; F. 12/11, W. 24, F. 26, S. 27, T. 30;
H.² M. 4/1, Th. 7, F. 8; W. 17/3; Tott. Court F., Yeates, Aug.;
York buildings F. 20/8; D.L. M. 7/6; F. 9/7. 1732. G.F. F. 7/1,
S. 8; S. 18/3; M. 10/4, Th. 13; M. 1/5, F. 12; L.² T. 11/4; H.²
M. 8/5; W. 29/11; D.L. M. 6/11, M. 13. 1733. G.F. S. 27/1;
Th. 19/4; Th. 3/5, M. 21; F. 28/9; M. 1/10; S. 10/11; S. 15/12,
Th. 20, F. 21; D.L. W. 2/5. 1734. G.F. F. 11/1, T. 22; W. 6/2;
Th. 18/4, F. 19; F. 10/5; C.G. W. 8/5; L.² T. 1/10; D.L. S. 5/11.
1735. G.F. M. 24/3; M. 8/12–W. 10. 1736. L.² W. 14/4; G.F.
Th. 29/4; C.G. F. 30/4; M. 20/9, W. 29; M. 13/12; D.L. Th. 26/8,
T. 31. 1737. C.G. M. 17/1; S. 26/3; T. 19/4; T. 3/5, Th. 19;
W. 21/9; W. 5/10; L.² F. 29/4; F. 22/7, T. 26; D.L. T. 11/10, S. 15.
1738. S. 18/2; M. 13/3; S. 27/5; Punch M. 13/3–Th. 16, M. 20,
T. 21, Th. 23, S. 25. 1739. D.L. S. 27/1; S. 3/2; T. 20/3; C.G.
T. 27/3; F. 25/5, W. 30. 1740. Punch M. 3/3; C.G. F. 9/5, M. 19;
G.F. S. 1/11. 1741. C.G. T. 11/5, Th. 14. 1744. H.² W. 15/2; C.G.
W. 28/3; W. 4/4, F. 20. 1745. James-street T. 4/6; G.F. M. 16/12,
T. 17, S. 28. 1746. D.L. F. 3/1–Th. 9, Th. 23; F. 7/2, Th. 20;
M. 10/3, T. 11; T. 14/10, F. 31; G.F. M. 6/1; N.W. Clerkenwell
M. 22/12. 1747. C.G. S. 19/12. 1748. S. 2/1, S. 9, M. 11; Th.
25/2; Th. 24/3; Th. 28/4; F. 14/10, F. 21, F. 28; M. 7/11, M. 28;
W. 14/12; D.L. W. 6/1, F. 15, M. 25; W. 10/2; F. 15/4; W. 4/5.
1749. C.G. Th. 5/1; Th. 20/4, T. 25, F. 28; M. 1/5; M. 25/9;
W. 4/10; W. 1/11, W. 8.

T.   Papal Tyranny in the Reign of King John (C.G. Feb. 1744/5) 8°
1745; 8° 1745 (Dublin).

1745. C.G. F. 15/2–T. 26; Th. 4/4. 1746. S. 8/2.

Theat. Dial. The Lady's Lecture. A Theatrical Dialogue between Sir
Charles Easy and his Marriageable Daughter 8° 1748.

CIBBER, THEOPHILUS.

T.   An Historical Tragedy of the Civil Wars In the Reign of King
Henry VI. (Being a Sequel to the Tragedy of Humphrey Duke
of Gloucester; And an Introduction to the Tragical History of
King Richard III.) Alter'd from Shakespear, in the Year 1720
(D.L. July 1723) 8° (?1723); 8° 1724 (2nd).

1723. D.L. W. 3/7 (as The Civil Wars between York and Lancaster).

B.O. Patie and Peggie; or, The Fair Foundling (D.L. Nov. 1730) 8° 1730.

　　1730. D.L. W. 25/11, Th. 26, M. 30; W. 2/12. 1731. F. 23/4; M. 31/5. [It is to be observed that the author's preface is dated April 20, 1730. The piece may have been produced before November.]

C. The Lover (D.L. Jan. 1730/1) 8° 1730; 12° 1731 (Dublin, *bis*).

　　1731. D.L. W. 20/1–T. 26, Th. 28, F. 29; M. 5/4.

Pant. The Harlot's Progress; or, The Ridotto al' Fresco: A Grotesque Pantomime Entertainment (D.L. March 1733) 4° 1733.

　　1733. D.L. S. 31/3.

T. Romeo and Juliet, A Tragedy, Revis'd, and Altered from Shakespear...To which is added, A Serio-Comic Apology, For Part of the Life of Mr. Theophilus Cibber...Interspersed with Memoirs and Anecdotes...Concluding with a Copy of Verses, call'd, The Contrite Comedian's Confession (H.² Sept. 1744) 8° (1745).

　　1744. H.² T. 11/9, W. 12, F. 14, M. 17, W. 19, S. 29; T. 2/10, S. 13; Th. 1/11; M. 17/12.

F. The Auction 8° 1757.

CLANCY, Dr MICHAEL.

*T. Tamar, Prince of Nubia (S.A. Dublin *c.* 1739).

T. Hermon Prince of Choroea, or, The Extravagant Zealot (Dublin 1740) 8° 1746. [This play was advertised in *The General Advertiser* for April 14, 1746, as acted in Ireland.]

C. The Sharper (Smock Alley, Dublin, Jan. 1737/8) 8° 1750, in The Memoirs of Dr. Michael Clancy.

COFFEY, CHARLES.

(B.O.) The Beggar's Wedding. A New Opera (Smock Alley, Dublin, March 1729; H.² May 1729) 8° 1729; 8° 1729 (Dublin, 2nd); 8° 1731 (4th); 12° 1733 (5th) 8° 1763.

　　In the following lists I have distinguished The Beggar's Wedding, as announced in the bills, from Phebe, although for some seasons the titles seem to have been interchangeable. 1729. Smock Alley, Dublin 24/3; H.² Th. 29/5–S. 31; T. 3/6–F. 6; T. 1/7 (22nd night); B.F. Reynolds, Aug.; S.F. Reynolds, Sept. and F. 19/9; S.F. Lee and Harper, Sept. 1730. D.L. M. 6/4; T. 14/4, S. 18; T. 13/10; M. 16/11; H.² Th. 30/4 (reduced to one act by the author, probably Phebe); T. 28/7; M. 26/10; M. 14/12. 1731. D.L. W. 22/12. 1732. W. 2/2. 1733. H.² S. 12/5. 1735. G.F. T. 22/4. 1736. D.L. W. 20/10. 1737. S. 5/3. 1738. C.G. T. 18/4, W. 19, F. 28; W. 3/5, Th. 11, T. 16, Th. 18. 1739. M. 23/4; D.L. M. 30/4. 1749. C.G. F. 17/11, S. 18. [On the Irish performances of this and other ballad-operas see W. J. Lawrence *Early Irish Ballad Opera and Comic Opera* in *The Musical Quarterly* July 1922.]

(B.O.) Phebe; or, The Beggars Wedding. An Opera, In One Act 8° 1729. This play is the above reduced to one act.

　　1729. D.L. F. 13/6 (one act), W. 18, T. 24, F. 27; F. 4/7; T. 8/7, F. 11, T. 15, T. 29; S. 27/9; H.² S. 5/7, W. 9, Th. 10, S. 12, W. 16, W. 23, M. 28; W. 6/8, Th. 7, F. 8, W. 13, S. 16; L.² S. 19/7; B.F. Fielding, Aug.; B.F. Reynolds S. 9/8; S.F.

Reynolds, Sept. 1730. D.L. M. 27/4; W. 6/5; G.F. T. 23/6,
F. 26; F. 24/7; W. 14/10, Th. 15, S. 31; M. 2/11; M. 30/11.
1731. S. 16/1, S. 23; M. 20/12–W. 22; D.L. M. 19/4; M. 10/5;
T. 6/7; Tott. Court F. New Theatre, Aug. 1732. G.F. Th. 27/1,
F. 28. 1734. M. 25/3; F. 26/4; F. 17/5. 1746. C.G. M. 24/2,
T. 25, Th. 27; S. 1/3–T. 4, Th. 6, S. 15, M. 17; S. 12/4, T. 29;
Richmond F. 8/8. 1747. C.G. S. 7/3, Th. 19; M. 4/5, W. 6,
T. 12, F. 15, S. 16, T. 19. 1748. M. 18/4. 1749. F. 29/9; M. 2/10,
F. 13.

(B.O.) The Devil upon Two Sticks: Or, The Country Beau. A
Ballad Farce (D.L. April 1729) 8° 1745.

    1729. D.L. W. 16/4. 1730. M. 23/2.

(B.O.) Southwark Fair; or, The Sheep-Shearing (S.F. Reynolds
1729) 8° 1729.

(B.O.) The Female Parson: or, Beau in the Sudds. An Opera (H.²
April 1730) 8° 1730.

    1730. H.² M. 27/4, Th. 30.

(B.O.) The Devil to Pay; or, The Wives Metamorphos'd. An Opera
(D.L. Aug. 1731) 8° 1731 (3 acts); 8° 1732 (1 act; later edns. are
reprints of this); 12° 1732; 4° 1732 (engraved); 8° 1733 (5th);
12° 1736; 8° 1738; 8° 1748 (bis); 8° (1777).

    Mottley and Coffey seem to have been responsible for the
original adaptation; the one act piece was a further alteration by
Theophilus Cibber. This unquestionably proved one of the
most popular of the ballad operas; it was originally produced at
D.L. on F. 6/8/1731, appeared at Lee and Harper's booth at S.F.
in September, at G.F. on W. 8/12 (in the one act form), at C.G.
on F. 13/4/1733, at H.² on W. 26/9 of the same year, at L.² on
T. 20/4/1736, at Richmond on W. 25/8/1736, at James-street on
M. 22/11/1742, at N.W. Clerkenwell on M. 20/10/1746, and at the
Old Theatre Southwark on T. 21/10/1746. From the date of
its original production it was played regularly every year at the
patent houses, securing an average of 25 performances each
year.

*F. A Wife and No Wife 8° 1732.

(B.O.) The Boarding-School: Or, The Sham Captain. An Opera
(D.L. Jan. 1732/3) 8° 1733.

    1733. D.L. M. 29/1 (as The Boarding School Romps), W. 31;
Th. 1/2, F. 2.

(B.O.) The Merry Cobler: or, The Second Part of The Devil to Pay,
A Farcical Opera of One Act (D.L. May 1735) 8° 1735.

    1735. D.L. T. 6/5.

CONCANEN, MATTHEW.
  C. Wexford Wells (Dublin) 8° 1721.

CONGREVE, WILLIAM.
  [For his seventeenth century works see the Hand-list of Plays,
1660–1700.]

  M. The Judgment of Paris (D.G. March 1700/1) 4° 1701.
    No record of first performance. 1702. D.L. T. 29/12. 1705.
L.¹ S. 10/3. 1706. H.¹ M. 11/3. 1740. Cliefdon F. 1/8 (as writ
by Dryden). 1742. D.L. F. 19/3. 1748. W. 20/4 (music by Arne).

  O. Semele 8° 1710 (in The Works).

CONOLLY, —

C.   The Connoisseur: or, Every Man in his Folly (D.L. Feb. 1735/6) 8° 1736 (anon.).

    1736. D.L. F. 20/2.

COOKE, THOMAS.

P. Terentii Afri Comediæ 12° 1734 (Latin and English); Terence's Comedys, translated 12° 1748.

Mr Cooke's Edition and Translation of the Comedys of Plautus 12° 1746 (Latin and English).

M.   Albion; or, The Court of Neptune 8° 1724.

D.O.   Penelope [see MOTTLEY].

Sat.   The Battle of the Poets, or The Contention for the Laurel (H.² Nov. 1730) 8° (1731; in The Bays Miscellany; it is described as "introduced as an intire New Act to the Comical Tragedy of Tom Thumb. Written by Scriblerus Tertius.")

    Attributed. 1730. H.² 30/11. 1731. F. 1/1.

(Past.)   The Triumphs of Love and Honour. A Play...To which are added, Considerations on the Stage, and on the Advantages which arise to a Nation from the Encouragement of Arts (D.L. Aug. 1731) 8° 1731.

    1731. D.L. W. 18/8.

F.   The Eunuch, or, The Darby Captain (D.L. May 1737) 8° (1737).

    1737. D.L. T. 17/5. A play called The Eunuch was also first acted at D.L. on T. 9/7/1717 and repeated on Th. 11. The author does not seem to be known. It was probably Heminges' *The Fatal Contract*, as renamed.

T.   The Mournful Nuptials, or Love the Cure of all Woes...To which is prefixed a Preface, containing some Observations on Satire, and on the Present State of our public Entertainments 8° 1739; altered as Love the Cause and Cure of Grief, or The Innocent Murderer (D.L. Dec. 1743) 8° 1744.

    1743. D.L. M. 19/12.

COOPER, Mrs ELIZABETH.

C.   The Rival Widows: or, Fair Libertine (C.G. Feb. 1734/5) 8° 1735.

    1735. C.G. S. 22/2, T. 25, Th. 27; S. 1/3, T. 4, Th. 6.

*C.   The Nobleman, or the Family Quarrel.

    1736. H.² M. 17/5–W. 19.

CORYE or COREY, JOHN.

C.   A Cure for Jealousie (L.¹ c. Dec. 1699) 4° 1701.

    No records of performance; published May 27, 1701 (*Post Man*).

F.   The Metamorphosis: Or, The Old Lover Out-witted...Written Originally by the Famous Moliere (L.¹ Sept. 1704) 4° 1704.

    1704. L.¹ M. 2/10 (3rd time). 1728. H.² T. 15/10, W. 16. 1729. W. 12/3.

CRAUFORD, DAVID.

C.   Courtship A-la-Mode (D.L. July 1700) 4° 1700.

    1700. D.L. T. 9/7.

C.   Love at First Sight (L.¹ March 1704) 4° (1704).

    1704. L.¹ S. 25/3.

CROSS, RICHARD.

*F.   The Hen-Peck'd Captain; or, The Humours of the Militia.

    1749. D.L. S. 29/4 (probably not performed; see *Biog. Dram.* ii. 290–1).

CROXALL, Dr SAMUEL.
 Dr. Perf. The Fair Circassian...Done from the Original By a Gentleman-Commoner of Oxford 4° 1720; 12° 1721; 12° 1729; 12ᵛ 1751;
   12° 1755; 12° 1756; 12° 1759; 8° 1765.

CUNNINGHAM, JOHN.
 F. Love in a Mist. A Farce. Now Acting at the City-Theatre in
   Dublin, With great Applause (Dublin, April 1747) 12° 1747
   (Dublin).

CUTTS, JOHN.
 T. Rebellion Defeated: or, The Fall of Desmond 4° 1745.

DALTON, Dr JOHN.
 M. Comus, a Mask: (Now adapted to the Stage) As alter'd from
   Milton's Mask at Ludlow-Castle (D.L. March 1737/8) 8° 1738
   (4 edns); 8° 1741 (6th); 8° 1744 (7th).
     1738. D.L. S. 4/3–T. 7, Th. 9, S 11, T. 14, Th. 23; M. 3/4–
   W. 5; Th. 4/5. 1739. W. 28/11–F. 30; S. 1/12–Th. 6. 1740.
   Th. 10/1; T. 8/4; Th. 1/5; W. 10/12, Th. 11, S. 13, W. 17. 1741.
   S. 31/1; T. 10/2; T. 17/3; Th. 16/4; M. 12/10–W. 14; F. 30/10;
   Th. 19/11; W. 30/12. 1742. S. 2/1, F. 15; T. 9/2; Th. 1/4;
   S. 15/5. 1743. F. 11/2, S. 12; T. 8/3; Th. 14/4. 1744. C.G.
   S. 3/3–T. 6. 1745. D.L. M. 14/1, T. 15, Th. 24; Th. 19/12;
   C.G. M. 14/1, W. 16, Th. 17, S. 26; W. 6/2; M. 25/3. 1746.
   D.L. W. 15/1; M. 17/2. 1747. S. 24/1; F. 13/11; C.G. Th. 26/3;
   W. 29/4. 1748. S. 10/12–T. 13, Th. 15, F. 16. 1749. D.L. W.
   11/10, Th. 12, Th. 19.

DANCE, JAMES.
 C. Pamela...As it is Perform'd, Gratis, at the late Theatre in Good-
   mans Fields (G.F. Nov. 1741) 8° 1742 (anon.).
     The character of Jack Smatter is said to have been written by
   GARRICK. 1741. G.F. M. 9/11–S. 21, T. 24, F. 27; F. 4/12,
   M. 14, F. 18. 1742. F. 26/2.

DARCY, JAMES.
 T. Love and Ambition (Smock Alley, Dublin, Dec. 1731) 8° 1732.
 *T. The Orphan of Venice (Dublin 1749).

DAVEY, SAMUEL.
 T. The Treacherous Husband (Dublin ?1737) 8° 1737 (Dublin).
 *O. Whittington and his Cat (Dublin ?1739).

DAVYS, Mrs MARY.
 C. The Northern Heiress: Or, The Humours of York (L.² April
   1716) 8° 1716.
     1716. L.² F. 27/4, S. 28; T. 1/5.
 C. The Self Rival 8° 1725 (in Works).

DELAMAYNE, THOMAS.
 Dr. Poem. Love and Honour...taken from Virgil. In Seven Cantos
   12° 1742.

DENNIS, JOHN.
   [For his seventeenth century works see the Hand-list of Plays,
   1660–1700.]
 T. Iphigenia (L.¹ Dec. 1699) 4° 1700.
     [See the supplementary notes and the Hand-list of Plays, 1660–
   1700.]

C. The Comical Gallant: or, The Amours of Sir John Falstaffe (D.L. 1702) 4° 1702.

T. Liberty Asserted (L.¹ Feb. 1703/4) 4° 1704.
  1704. L.¹ Th. 24/2–S. 26, T. 29; Th. 2/3, S. 4, M. 6, Th. 9, S. 11, Th. 16, M. 27. 1707. H.¹ F. 2/5. 1746. C.G. W. 23/4, F. 25.

C. Gibraltar: Or, The Spanish Adventure (D.L. Feb. 1704/5) 4° 1705.
  1705. D.L. F. 16/2 (deferred from T. 13), T. 20.

M. Orpheus and Eurydice 4° 1707.

T. Appius and Virginia (D.L. Feb. 1708/9) 4° 1709.
  1709. D.L. S. 5/2–W. 9.

T. The Invader of his Country: or, The Fatal Resentment (D.L. Nov. 1719) 4° 1720.
  1719. D.L. W. 11/11 (3 performances, probably Th. 12 and F. 13).

DODSLEY, ROBERT.

Dr. Sat. The Toy-Shop (C.G. Feb. 1734/5) 8° 1735 (3 edns); 12° 1737; 12° 1754; 12° 1767; 12° 1787; also in Trifles 8° 1745.
  1735. C.G. M. 3/2, T. 4, Th. 6–T. 11; Th. 6/3, Th. 13, S. 15, T. 18, M. 24, T. 25, S. 29; Th. 10/4, M. 14, Th. 17, M. 21; Th. 1/5, F. 2, T. 6, M. 12, T. 20; T. 16/9, W. 17; T. 2/12; L.² S. 19/4, W. 30; W. 7/5, W. 14; G.F. W. 30/4; F. 2/5. 1736. C.G. W. 6/10, W. 20. 1737. M. 24/1; S. 12/3, M. 21; M. 2/5; F. 30/9. 1738. T. 24/10; W. 8/11. 1739. T. 6/11; Th. 13/12. 1741. D.L. Th. 9/4. 1743. C.G. Th. 17/3, M. 21; W. 27/4. 1745. Richmond S. 30/8; Twickenham W. 3/9.

Dr. Tale. The King and the Miller of Mansfield (D.L. Jan. 1736/7) 8° 1737; 12° 1737 (Dublin); 8° 1745; 12° (1751); 12° 1764 (Belfast).
  1737. D.L. S. 29/1; T. 1/2–F. 18, T. 22; M. 14/3, Th. 17, M. 21, Th. 24, M. 28, Th. 31; W. 13/4, M. 25; Th. 5/5, M. 16, Th. 19, M. 23; S. 11/6. 1738. T. 17/1–Th. 19, S. 21, M. 23; M. 6/2, T. 21; Th. 16/3, S. 18, S. 25; Th. 13/4; M. 1/5, F. 5, F. 12; F. 26/5, T. 30; Punch M 24/4. 1739. D.L. T. 16/1, W. 17, F. 19, S. 20; Th. 1/2, F. 9; Th. 5/4, S. 7, M. 9, T. 10; Th. 26/4; F. 25/5, S. 26, W. 30, Th. 31. 1740. T. 8/1, Th. 10, F. 11, M. 14; T. 4/3, Th. 6; F. 2/5, M. 5, M. 19, W. 21, F. 30; T. 9/9; M. 20/10, F. 24; S. 22/11; G.F. S. 25/10–T. 28. 1741. D.L. T. 24/2; S. 7/3; S. 4/4; S. 2/5, S. 9, W. 27; Th. 17/9, S. 19; F. 9/10; C.G. M. 9/3, Th. 12, M. 16; W. 8/4, M. 27; F. 1/5, F. 8, M. 11; W. 9/12. 1742. T. 20/4, M. 26; W. 5/5, T. 11, M. 17; D.L. F. 23/4, W. 28, F. 30; S. 1/5–T. 4, S. 8, Th. 13, M. 17, M. 24, T. 25, Th. 27; S. 25/9. 1743. T. 4/1; M. 23/5, T. 24, Th. 26; C.G. M. 2/5. 1744. H.² S. 13/10, T. 16. 1745. New Theatre, Shepherds Mount May Fair Th. 7/2, Th. 28; G.F. S. 30/3; T. 2/4, W. 17; D.L. W. 8/5. 1746. G.F. F. 10/1, M. 13; C.G. M. 13/10, W. 15; S. 8/11, M. 10, T. 18. 1747. D.L. M. 20/4. 1748. M. 2/5, T. 3; T. 18/10, T. 25; W. 9/11, T. 22; W. 7/12, T. 13. 1749. F. 27/1; F. 5/5; T. 26/9; C.G. M. 17/4, S. 22; T. 2/5, W. 3; F. 6/10, W. 11.

(B.O.) Sir John Cockle at Court. Being the Sequel to the King and the Miller (D.L. Feb. 1737/8) 8° 1738; 8° 1745; 12° 1767 (Belfast).
  1738. D.L. Th. 23/2, S. 25, M. 27, T. 28; T. 2/5.

(B.O.) The Blind Beggar of Bethnal Green (D.L. April 1741) 8° 1741;
   12° 1745; 12° 1758 (Glasgow); 8° 1761.
       1741. D.L. F. 3/4.
Pant. Rex & Pontifex, Being an Attempt to introduce upon the Stage
   a new Species of Pantomime, 8° 1745 (in Trifles).
M. The Triumph of Peace (D.L. Feb. 1748/9) 4° 1749.
       1749. D.L. T. 21/2, Th. 23, S. 25, M. 27, T. 28; Th. 2/3, S. 4,
       M. 6.
T. Cleone (C.G. Dec. 1758) 8° 1758; 12° 1759 (Belfast); 8° 1765 (4th);
   8° 1771 (4th); 8° 1781; 8° 1786 (5th).

DORMAN, JOSEPH.
Dr. Ent. Sir Roger de Coverly: or, The Merry Christmas (D.L. Dec.
   1746) 8° 1740.
       1746. D.L. T. 30/12. A benefit performance was given for the
       author on T. 18/11/1740.

DOWER, E.
Dr. Tale. The Salopian Esquire: or, The Joyous Miller…To which are
   added, Poems on his late Grace John Duke of Marlborough…To
   which is annexed by Way of Essay, The Reason for not bringing
   this Dramatick Tale on the Stage, and the Reception the Poem
   on his late Grace John Duke of Marlborough, met with at her
   Grace's House in the Friery, near St. James's 8° 1739.

DOWNES, Capt.
C. All Vows Kept (Smock Alley Dublin ? 1733) 12° 1733 (Dublin,
   anon.); 8° 1733.

DOWNING, GEORGE.
*Pant. The Tricks of Harlequin: or, The Spaniard Out-witted (L.²
   Nov. 1739) 12° 1739 (Derby, anon.). [This, according to the
   Biographia Dramatica, is the comic part of *Perseus and Andromeda,
   or The Cheats of Harlequin.*]

DRAPER, MATTHEW.
C. The Spend-Thrift (H.² Jan. 1730/1) 8° 1731.
       1731. H.² W. 20/1, M. 25, W. 27; F. 5/3.

DRURY, ROBERT.
(B.O.) The Devil of a Duke: or, Trapolin's Vagaries. An Opera
   (D.L. Aug. 1732) 8° 1732 (anon.); 8° 1732 (2nd, with additions).
       1732. D.L. Th. 17/8 (further performances deferred in order
       that the piece might be shortened); S. 23/9, T. 26; Th. 19/10.
(B.O.) The Mad Captain. An Opera (G.F. March 1732/3) 8° 1733
   (anon.).
       1733. G.F. M. 5/3, T. 6, S. 10, T. 13, M. 26; M. 9/4; S. 5/5;
       W. 7/11–F. 9; Th. 27/12. 1734. T. 1/1; S. 27/4.
(B.O.) The Fancy'd Queen. An Opera (C.G. Aug. 1733) 8° 1733
   (anon.).
       1733. C.G. T. 14/8, Th. 16.
(B.O.) The Rival Milliners: or, The Humours of Covent-Garden.
   A Tragi-Comi-Operatic-Pastoral Farce (H.² Jan. 1735/6) 8°
   1737 (*bis*); 12° (1740?, 3rd); 12° 1761 (Dublin, 4th).
       1736. H.² M. 19/1, T. 20; M. 2/2; W. 12/5 (as *The Temple
       Rake or the Rival Milliners*); F. 30/7; L.² T. 23/3. 1737. H.²
       W. 9/2; F. 4/3.

DU BOIS, P. B.
   Past.　Aminta 12° 1726; 8° (1726, Oxford).
DUNCOMBE, WILLIAM.
    T.　Athaliah 8° 1724; 12° 1726; 12° 1746.
    T.　Lucius Junius Brutus (D.L. Nov. 1734) 8° 1735; *12° 1747.
        1734. D.L. M. 25/11–S. 30.
D'URFEY, THOMAS.
    [For his seventeenth century works see the Hand-list of Plays,
    1660–1700.]
    C.　The Bath, or, The Western Lass (D.L. May 1701) 4° 1701.
        See the supplementary notes; published July 22, 1701 (*Post
      Boy*). Whincop seems to be wrong in saying it was acted in 1697.
        1702. D.L. T. 8/12.
    C.　The Old Mode & the New, or, Country Miss with her Furbeloe
      (D.L. March 1702/3) 4° (1703).
        1703. D.L. Th. 11/3, S. 13.
  D.O.　Wonders in the Sun: or, The Kingdom of the Birds (H.¹ April
      1706) 4° 1706.
        1706. H.¹ F. 5/4–W. 10, F. 26 (comic scenes only), T. 30 (do.);
      Th. 2/5 (do.).
    C.　The Modern Prophets: or, New Wit for a Husband (D.L. May
      1709) 4° (1709).
        1709. D.L. T. 3/5–Th. 5.
    New Opera's, with Comical Stories, and Poems, on Several
    Occasions, Never before Printed. Being the remaining Pieces,
    Written by Mr. D'Urfey 8° 1721. [Contains 1. The Two Queens
    of Brentford: or, Bayes no Poetaster: A Musical Farce, or Comical
    Opera. Being The Sequel of the Famous Rehearsal, Written by
    the late Duke of Buckingham. 2. The Grecian Heroine: or, The
    Fate of Tyranny. A Tragedy, Written 1718. 3. Ariadne: or, The
    Triumph of Bacchus. An Opera.]
 Scenario.　The English Stage Italianiz'd, In a New Dramatic Enter-
    tainment, called Dido and Æneas: or, Harlequin, A Butler, a
    Pimp, a Minister of State, Generalissimo, and Lord High Admiral,
    dead and alive again, and at last crown'd King of Carthage, by
    Dido. A Tragi-Comedy, after the Italian Manner; by way of
    Essay, or first Step towards the farther Improvement of the
    English Stage. Written by Thomas D'Urfey, Poet Laureat de Jure 8°
    1727. [This piece is undoubtedly spurious; cf. *supra* p. 257.]
EGLETON, Mrs.
 *B.O.　The Maggot.
      1732. L.² T. 18/4.
ESTCOURT, RICHARD.
    C.　The Fair Example: or The Modish Citizens (D.L. April 1703)
      4° 1706.
        1703. D.L. S. 10/4; F. 26/11. 1717. L.² W. 16/10, Th. 17,
      S. 19; F. 1/11; S. 7/12. 1718. Th. 9/1; M. 17/2; W. 30/4; W.
      15/10.
   Int.　Prunella: An Interlude Perform'd in the Rehearsal...The Sense
    and Musick collected from the most Famous Masters. By Mr.
    Airs, for the Advantage of Mr. Estcourt (D.L. Feb. 1707/8) 4°
    (1708).
        1708. D.L. Th. 12/2 (as *Prunella, Mr. Bayes Practice*).

FABIAN, R.
  C.   Trick for Trick (D.L. May 1735) 8° 1735.
       1735. D.L. S. 10/5. 1741. G.F. F. 2/10, M. 5, W. 7.

FARQUHAR, GEORGE.
       [For his seventeenth century works see the Hand-list of Plays,
       1660–1700.]
  C.   Sir Harry Wildair: Being the Sequel of the Trip to the Jubilee
       (D.L. *c.* April 1701) 4° 1701; 16° 1735.
       No records of first performance; published May 13, 1701 (*Post
       Man*). 1737. L.² T. 1/2–F. 4; T. 15/3.
  C.   The Inconstant: or, The Way to Win Him (D.L. *c.* Feb. 1701/2)
       4° 1702; 12° 1718.
       No records of first performance; published March 13, 1701/2
       (*Post Man*). 1716 L.¹ T. 18/12. 1723. 16/10. 1730. G.F.T. 6/1; M.
       7/12; H.² F. 13/11. 1731. G.F. M. 4/1; M. 1/3; M. 22/11. 1732.
       M. 15/5; S. 14/10. 1733. Th. 25/10. 1734. Th. 28/3; M. 14/10.
       1735. S. 1/2. 1736. H.² Th. 19/2; C.G. T. 6/4; T. 11/5; G.F. Th.
       13/5; L.² Th. 11/11. 1737. Th. 20/1. 1739. D.L. T. 10/4, S. 14.
       1740. G.F. W. 19/11. 1742. M. 22/3; Th. 29/4. 1744. D.L. Th.
       11/10; F. 7/12, F. 21. 1745. M. 18/11.
  C.   The Twin-Rivals (D.L. Dec. 1702) 4° 1703.
       1702. D.L. M. 14/12. 1716. L.¹ S. 3/11–W. 7, F. 16; T. 11/12,
       S. 15. 1717. M. 21/1; Th. 14/3; S. 6/4; Th. 23/5; T. 22/10;
       W. 6/11. 1718. T. 29/4. 1719. M. 27/4; Th. 15/10. 1725. D.L.
       M. 29/11, T. 30; W. 1/12, Th. 2, F. 17. 1726. Th. 20/1; T. 19/4;
       M. 12/12. 1735. H.² Th. 21/8. 1736. D.L. S. 3/1–W. 7, F. 9;
       M. 2/2, T. 3; M. 5/4; T. 25/5; M. 15/11; H.² W. 14/1. 1737.
       W. 9/2; D.L. W. 16/2; S. 2/4; W. 11/5. 1738. M. 17/4; W. 18/10;
       S. 18/11; Th. 21/12. 1739. Th. 9/1; T. 8/5, F. 18; S. 22/9; F.
       21/12; C.G. Th. 12/4, M. 30. 1740. D.L. M. 28/1; Th. 13/11;
       C.G. M. 5/5. 1741. D.L. W. 1/4; W. 21/10; Th. 17/12; C.G.
       F. 1/5. 1743. D.L. F. 28/1; T. 24/5; W. 23/11. 1745. F. 4/1;
       G.F. Th. 28/2; S. 2/3; S. 20/4; M. 11/11. 1746. C.G. Th. 2/1,
       F. 3; D.L. T. 14/1; T. 11/3; W. 5/11; G.F. W. 19/11. 1747.
       C.G. Th. 29/1; Th. 5/2; S. 16/5. 1749. Th. 23/11; M. 11/12.
  (F.C.) The Stage Coach (L.¹ *c.* Jan. 1703/4) 4° 1704 (Dublin); 4° 1705.
       1704. L.¹ W. 2/2 (last new farce). 1705. H.¹ F. 16/11. 1707.
       M. 14/4; M. 26/5. 1709. D.L. T. 17/5, Th. 19, T. 24, T. 31;
       W. 1/6; Th. 8/12; H.¹ S. 1/10, T. 4, S. 8; S. 5/11; M. 5/12, M. 26.
       1710. D.L. Th. 9/2; H.¹ T. 11/4; F. 21/7; Greenwich S. 23/9.
       1711. D.L. T. 26/6. 1712. S. 3/5, T. 13; T. 17/6; T. 5/8; F.
       24/10. 1713. W. 28/1; F. 19/6; M. 7/12. 1714. M. 18/1; T. 19/10.
       1715. L.² Th. 6/1; Th. 3/11, T. 8; Stationers' Hall T. 1/3. 1716.
       D.L. T. 14/8, T. 21; T. 23/10, T. 30. 1717. M. 3/6; F. 16/8,
       F. 23; L.² S. 23/11. 1718. M. 24/2; D.L. T. 13/5; T. 8/7, T. 22;
       F. 29/8; Richmond M. 28/7. 1719. D.L. T. 19/5; T. 28/7; L.²
       T. 19/5. 1720. D.L. F. 29/4; F. 20/5, W. 25; T. 14/6; T. 2/8,
       S. 20. 1721. T. 27/6. 1722. F. 25/5. 1723. H.² Th. 10/1; D.L.
       F. 3/5, W. 29; F. 28/6; T. 9/7. 1724. Th. 6/2; Th. 14/5, W. 20;
       M. 19/10. 1725. F. 14/5, F. 21. 1727. M. 24/4. 1730. Th.
       8/1. 1733. C.G. Th. 29/3, S. 31; F. 20/4, T. 24; W. 2/5. 1734.
       G.F. T. 7/5, M. 20. 1736. L.² Th. 29/4. 1739. C.G. T. 3/4,
       Th. 26; S. 5/5, M. 14, W. 23, T. 29. 1740. M. 24/3; F. 2/5, T. 13.

1745. G.F. W. 2/1–F. 4, T. 15–Th. 17; Th. 7/2, F. 8; Th. 7/11;
D.L. M. 30/12, T. 31. 1746. W. 1/1, M. 13, W. 15, Th. 16,
F. 24, T. 28; S. 8/2, Th. 13; G.F. F. 24/1; W. 19/11–F. 21, M. 24,
T. 25. 1747. D.L. T. 3/3.

C.   The Recruiting Officer (D.L. April 1706) 4° 1706; 4° (1706 2nd);
4° (N.D. 4th); 8° 1711; 12° 1714 (5th); 8° 1723 (10th). 12° 1736.
        1706. D.L. M. 8/4–W. 10, F. 12–W. 17, S. 20; T. 11/6; S.
7/12; Bath. M. 16/9; D.G. Th. 24/10; F. 1/11; H.¹ Th. 14/11, M. 18,
S. 30; S. 28/12. [Later dates given in abstract; in brackets
number of performances each year.] 1707. D.L. Th. 2/1 (12);
H.¹ M. 10/2 (6). 1708. D.L. F. 16/1 (3). 1709. F. 6/5 (4); H.¹
Th. 22/9 (4). 1710. Th. 16/3 (4); Greenwich Th. 27/7. 1711.
D.L. M. 5/2 (2); Greenwich M. 23/7; T. 25/9. 1712. D.L. S.
2/2 (4). 1713. M. 12/1 (2). 1714. M. 4/1 (3); L.² S. 18/12 (3).
1715. D.L. W. 26/1; L.² Th. 24/2 (6). 1716. D.L. W. 11/1;
L.² Th. 2/2 (3). 1717. D.L. W. 2/1 (3); L.² F. 8/2 (4); S. F.
Pinkethman W. 25/9. 1718. L.² T. 27/5 (2); D.L. Th. 29/5 (2).
1719. D.L. F. 2/1 (2). 1720. M. 8/2 (3); L.² T. 10/5 (3). 1721.
D.L. T. 21/3 (2); L.² Th. 12/10 (2). 1722. D.L. Th. 3/5 (2);
L.² T. 8/5 (3); S.F. theatre actors W. 26/9. 1723. L.² F. 15/2 (3);
D.L. M. 18/3; H.² M. 15/4. 1724. L.² F. 17/1 (6); D.L. T. 10/3
(2); Epsom Wells S. 4/7. 1725. L.² M. 25/1 (3); D.L. T. 2/3 (4).
1726. L.² Th. 20/1 (3); D.L. W. 16/2 (2). 1727. L.² F. 3/2 (5);
D.L. W. 8/2. 1728. T. 2/1 (3); L.² W. 8/5. 1729. H.² F. 31/1 (3);
D.L. F. 16/5; S.F. Reynolds T. 23/9; L.² W. 8/10; G.F. F. 31/10.
1730. L.² Th. 22/1 (5); G.F. S. 7/2 (6); S.F. Lee and Harper
Th. 8/10; Richmond T. 27/10; D.L. F. 6/11. 1731. L.² T. 16/2
(3); G.F. S. 20/3 (2); D.L. T. 19/10. 1732. G.F. W. 9/2 (5);
H.² F. 31/3 (2); L.² Th. 27/4 (3); Bowling Green Southwark T.
26/12. 1733. H.² W. 21/2 (3); C.G. W. 11/4 (2); G.F. F. 4/5 (2);
D.L. W. 31/10. 1734. H.² F. 11/1; G.F. S. 2/2 (3); C.G. M. 4/3
(2); L.² S. 12/10; D.L. S. 14/10. 1735. G.F. M. 6/1 (4); C.G. M.
13/10; D.L. Th. 30/10; H.² S. 13/12. 1736. D.L. S. 7/2 (2); G.F.
W. 25/2; C.G. M. 22/3 (3); L.² M. 19/4 (4). 1737. W. 19/1 (2);
D.L. Th. 26/5 (2). 1738. C.G. S. 22/4 (3). 1739. T. 24/4 (3);
D.L. S. 22/12. 1740. F. 11/1 (4); C.G. S. 2/2 (8); G.F. W. 22/10
(2). 1741. C.G. S. 14/2 (5); G.F. Th. 16/4 (2); D.L. T. 8/9
(4). 1742. G.F. F. 1/1 (3); C.G. Th. 14/1 (3); D.L. T. 2/2 (9);
L.² M. 13/12 (5). 1743. D.L. M. 24/1 (7); S.F. W. 30/3. 1744.
D.L. T. 17/1 (6); H.² M. 23/4 (2); May F. New Theatre Beaux-
street F. 8/6; G.F. M. 26/11 (3). 1745. D.L. M. 21/1 (6); G.F.
M. 29/4 (2); C.G. M. 13/5 (2); New theatre Shepherds Market
Th. 11/7. 1746. G.F. Th. 2/1 (4); D.L. Th. 6/2 (3); C.G. T. 6/5
(2); N.W. Clerkenwell M. 20/10. 1747. C.G. W. 28/1 (2); G.F.
T. 3/2; D.L. M. 16/11 (2). 1748. C.G. S. 13/2 (3); N.W. Good-
man's Fields M. 4/4; D.L. T. 1/11. 1749. C.G. T. 3/1 (3).

C.   The Beaux Stratagem (H.¹ March 1706/7) 4° 1707 (9 editions;
the first is undated); 8° 1711; 8° 1730 (7th); 12° 1748 (9th); 16°
1749 (10th); 12° 1752; 12° 1768.
        1707. H.¹ S. 8/3, T. 11, Th. 13, S. 15, M. 17, Th. 20, S. 29,
M. 31; S. 5/4, T. 15, T. 29; Th. 5/6; T. 14/10; M. 10/11; T. 2/12.
[Later dates in abstract only; in brackets number of performances
each year.] 1708. D.L. W. 28/1 (5). 1709. Th. 3/3 (4); H.¹ M.
19/12. 1710. W. 3/5 (1). 1711. D.L. M. 8/1 (5). 1712. M. 28/1

(4). 1713. W. 21/1 (2). 1714. Th. 18/3 (2). 1715. T. 19/4 (3). 1716.
T. 21/2 (3). 1717. M. 7/1 (4). 1718. W. 22/1 (5). 1719. S.
7/2 (4). 1720. W. 10/2 (5). 1721. S. 15/4 (2); H.² F. 14/7
(2); L.² S. 18/11 (4). 1722. W. 17/1 (4); D.L. W. 28/3 (3). 1723.
M. 21/1 (3); H.² Th. 14/3; L.² T. 28/5 (2). 1724. S. 11/1 (7);
D.L. F. 10/4 (2). 1725. L.² T. 2/2 (7); D.L. Th. 11/2 (4). 1726.
L.² T. 1/2 (5); D.L. F. 18/2 (4). 1727. L.² T. 31/1 (4); D.L.
F. 26/5 (4). 1728. Th. 14/3 (5); L.² W. 18/9. 1729. T. 28/1 (4);
D.L. M. 17/2 (2); H.² T. 8/4; G.F. M. 3/11 (2); room next
H.¹ M. 1/12. 1730. L.² S. 24/1 (4); H.² F. 6/2 (2); G.F. M. 2/3
(3); D.L. S. 25/4; S.F. Lee and Harper Th. 24/9. 1731. H.²
S. 16/1 (2); G.F. Th. 11/2 (5); L.² S. 6/3 (4); York buildings
F. 20/8; D.L. S. 6/11. 1732. M. 3/1 (5); L.² W. 5/1 (5); H.²
S. 1/4; G.F. Th. 23/3 (5). 1733. D.L. T. 16/1 (3); C.G. T. 6/2
(2); G.F. T. 13/3 (3); H.² M. 19/3. 1734. C.G. W. 16/1 (4);
G.F. F. 18/1 (4); D.L. Th. 7/2 (3). 1735. G.F. M. 27/1 (ʋ);
C.G. T. 18/3 (3); L.² W. 30/4; D.L. W. 14/5; H.² T. 26/8 (altered,
2). 1736. C.G. S. 28/2 (5); L.² W. 16/6 (2); H.² Th. 29/7; Rich-
mond S. 28/8. 1737. H.² S. 5/3; D.L. T. 12/4 (3); L.² T. 12/4;
C.G. F. 18/11. 1738. W. 1/2 (3); D.L. T. 9/5 (3). 1739. C.G.
W. 3/1 (3); D.L. M. 12/3 (5). 1740. C.G. F. 25/1 (2); D.L.
Th. 8/5 (3); G.F. W. 15/10 (3). 1741. G.F. T. 20/1 (3); C.G.
W. 21/1 (5); D.L. T. 22/9 (2); H.² T. 6/10. 1742. C.G. T. 26/1
(4); G.F. T. 2/2; D.L. W. 3/2 (7). 1743. D.L. W. 12/1 (9);
L.² T. 15/3; James-street Th. 31/3; C.G. M. 31/10. 1744. D.L.
Th. 9/2 (6); H.² W. 16/5; C.G. T. 27/11. 1745. D.L. Th. 3/1
(6); G.F. F. 18/1 (3); New theatre Shepherds Market, May F.
Th. 7/2; C.G. Th. 7/11. 1746. G.F. M. 24/2 (3); D.L. T. 4/3
(4); C.G. S. 5/4 (5); Old theatre Southwark T. 21/10. 1747. D.L.
M. 26/1 (5); C.G. Th. 2/4. 1748. F. 8/1 (4); D.L. M. 25/1
(3); H.² T. 22/11. 1749. D.L. T. 17/1 (5); C.G. F. 28/4 (2).

FENTON, ELIJAH.
T.   Mariamne (L.² Feb. 1722/3) 8° 1723; 12° (1723?); 16° 1726.
        1723. L.² F. 22/2–T. 26, Th. 28; S. 2/3–T. 5, Th. 7, S. 9,
     T. 12, Th. 14, S. 16; M. 1/4, M. 15; Th. 16/5; W. 18/12. 1724.
     W. 29/1; W. 5/2; T. 12/5; Th. 12/11. 1726. Th. 24/3; S. 30/4.
     1727. F. 3/11. 1728. M. 1/4. 1730. W. 6/5. 1733. C.G. F.
     13/4. 1735. Th. 13/3. 1739. T. 13/3; M. 9/4; S. 15/9. 1745.
     M. 11/3, T. 12.

FIELDING, HENRY.
C.   Love in Several Masques (D.L. Feb. 1727/8) 8° 1728; 8° 1728
        (Dublin).
        D.L. F. 16/2, S. 17, M. 19, T. 20.
C.   The Temple Beau (G.F. Jan. 1729/30) 8° 1730; 8° 1730 (Dublin).
        1730. G.F. M. 26/1–Th. 29, S. 31; M. 2/2–Th. 5, T. 10; T.
     3/3; F. 5/6; Th. 9/7. 1731. S. 13/3. 1736. Th. 25/3; T. 27/4.
(Burl.) The Author's Farce; And The Pleasures of the Town (H.²
        March 1729/30) 8° 1730 (by Scriblerus Secundus); 8° 1730 (*bis*);
        8° 1730 (Dublin); The A. F.; with a Puppet-Show, call'd the
        Pleasures of the Town 8° 1750 (3rd; altered text).
        1730. H.² M. 30/3; W. 1/4, F. 3, M. 6, T. 7, M. 13, Th. 16,
     F. 17, M. 20, F. 24, S. 25; F. 1/5, M. 4, W. 6–F. 8, M. 11, W. 13–
     F. 15, M. 18, W. 20–F. 22, M. 25, W. 27–F. 29; M. 1/6, W. 3–

F. 5, M. 8, W. 10–F. 12, T. 16, W. 17, F. 19, S. 20, M. 22; F. 3/7;
W. 21/10, F. 23; W. 18/11; W. 23/12. 1731. M. 4/1, Th. 7, F. 8,
W. 13; W. 3/2, Th. 4, S. 6; F. 19/3, W. 31; F. 2/4, M. 5, W. 7,
F. 9; M. 10/5; F. 18/6. 1732. F. 12/5. 1734. D.L. T. 15/1–M. 21.
1748. C.G. M. 28/3.

(Burl.) Tom Thumb. A Tragedy (H.² April 1730) 8° 1730 (by Scriblerus Secundus); 8° 1730 (Dublin); 8° 1730 (2nd, revised); 8°
1730 (3rd); The Tragedy of Tragedies; or, The Life and Death
of Tom Thumb the Great 8° 1731 (3 impressions, by Scriblerus
Secundus); 8° 1737 (3rd); 8° 1743 (Dublin); 8° 1751 (4th); 8°
1765; 12° 1776 (5th).

  1730. H.² S. 25/4, M. 27; F. 1/5, M. 4, W. 6–F. 8, M. 11,
W. 13–F. 15, M. 18, W. 20–F. 22, M. 25, W. 27–F. 29; M. 1/6,
W. 3–F. 5, M. 8, W. 10–F. 12, T. 16, W. 17, F. 19–M. 22; Th.
2/7, F. 3 (36th performance), F. 17, S. 18, W. 22–F. 24; F. 23/10,
M. 26; F. 4/12, M. 7, M. 14, W. 23, W. 30; B.F. Reynolds, Aug.;
S.F. Pinkethman, Sept. 1731. H.² Th. 14/1, F. 15; G.F. M. 15/3,
S. 20, M. 22, S. 27; M. 26/4. Tragedy of Tragedies. 1731. H.²
W. 24/3, F. 26, M. 29, W. 31; F. 2/4, M. 5, W. 7, F. 9, Th. 22,
F. 23, M. 26, W. 28; M. 10/5, M. 17; F. 18/6; G.F. W. 5/5.
1732. H.² M. 21/2; S. 1/4; D.L. W. 3/5, F. 12, Th. 25; L.² T. 2/5–
Th. 4. M. 22. 1733. D.L. Th. 3/5. 1736. H.² M. 3/5. 1740.
D.L. Th. 17/4, S. 26, M. 28, W. 30; W. 7/5, F. 16, Th. 22,
W. 28; C.G. S. 26/4; S. 3/5, F. 23. 1741. T. 10/3; T. 7/4; G.F.
Th. 2/4, F. 3, Th. 16. 1742. D.L. M. 29/3. 1745. W. 17/4,
Th. 18, M. 22, W. 24, F. 26, M. 29; T. 7/5, F. 10, M. 13, Th. 23;
T. 8/10, Th. 10, T. 15. 1746. W. 29/1; W. 5/2; W. 14/5, M. 19;
W. 11/6. 1747. G.F. M. 6/4. 1748. D.L. S. 29/10.

C. Rape upon Rape; or, The Justice Caught in his Own Trap (H.²
June 1730) 8° 1730 (anon.); The Coffee-House Politician; or, The
Justice Caught in his own Trap 8° 1730.

  1730. H.² T. 23/6, W. 24, F. 26, T. 30; W. 1/7, Th. 2, F. 10;
M. 30/11 (as The C. H. P., with an entire new act); L.² F. 4/12,
S. 5, M. 7, Th. 17.

(B.O.) The Welsh Opera: or, The Grey Mare the Better Horse (H.²
April 1731) 8° (1731 by Scriblerus Secundus); The Genuine
Grub-Street Opera. As it was intended to be Acted at the New
Theatre in the Hay-Market 8° 1731; The Grub-Street Opera. As
it is Acted at the Theatre in the Hay-Market...To which is added,
The Masquerade, A Poem 8° 1731.

  1731. H.² Th. 22/4, F. 23, M. 26, W. 28; M. 17/5, W. 19
(revised), W. 26; T. 1/6, W. 2, F. 4. Advertisement on June 5
that the opera was being lengthened and would be performed
shortly. As The Grub-Street Opera it seems to have come out in
July, although there is no advertisement of it.

F. The Letter-Writers: Or, a New Way to Keep A Wife at Home
(H.² March 1730/1) 8° 1731; 8° 1750.

  1731. H.² W. 24/3, F. 26, M. 29.

(B.O.) The Lottery. A Farce (D.L. Jan. 1731/2) 8° 1732 (three
editions); 8° 1733; 8° 1748 (4th); 12° 1758 (Glasgow); 8° 1759
(Dublin); 8° 1761 (5th).

  1732. D.L. S. 1/1–S. 8, Th. 20–S. 22, T. 25, Th. 27, S. 29; T. 1/2
(altered), Th. 10–S. 12, S. 26; S. 4/3, T. 7, T. 14, S. 18, T. 28;
F. 5/5, S. 6; Th. 28/9; Th. 5/10, Th. 12; Th. 9/11. 1733. W. 4/4,

Th. 5, T. 24. 1734. M. 11/3 (1 act); S. 27/4; T. 29/10; W. 11/12;
L.² Th. 16/5, W. 29; C.G. Th. 5/12; G.F. M. 2/12, T. 3. 1735.
D.L. M. 17/3; Th. 8/5; W. 3/12; C.G. F. 11/4; M. 29/9; G.F. W.
23/4; H.² Th. 12/6. 1736. D.L. M. 15/3, T. 23; G.F. W. 28/4.
1737. L.² W. 27/4; C.G. M. 16/5; D.L. T. 15/11. 1739. Th. 18/1,
W. 24; Th. 12/4; T. 23/10; W. 7/11; C.G. F. 21/12. 1740. D.L.
M. 21/4. 1742. T. 30/3. 1743. C.G. F. 25/11; Th. 1/12, W. 7,
F. 9, M. 12, Th. 15, F. 16, M. 19. 1744. M. 9/4, M. 16; W. 2/5,
F. 4; W. 10/10, M. 15, Th. 18; F. 2/11, F. 9, T. 27–Th. 29;
F. 21/12. 1745. Th. 21/3; W. 11/12; D.L. M. 16/12, F. 20,
M. 23, S. 28. 1746. S. 20/12, F. 26; C.G. S. 20/12, T. 23, T. 30.
1747. M. 11/5; T. 24/11; F. 4/12, M. 7; D.L. F. 27/11, S. 28; T.
1/12. 1748. C.G. T. 16/2, W. 17; F. 7/10, M. 24; D.L. S. 10/9,
S. 17, T. 11/10; T. 1/11; F. 9/12. 1749. S. 11/3; Th. 26/10;
F. 3/11, Th. 30.

C.   The Modern Husband (D.L. Feb. 1731/2) 8° 1732 (*bis*); 8° 1732
(Dublin).

      1732. D.L. M. 14/2–T. 22, Th. 24, S. 26–T. 29; Th. 2/3,
S. 18.

C.   The Old Debauchees (D.L. June 1732) 8° 1732 (by the author of
The Modern Husband); The Debauchees: or, The Jesuit Caught
8° 1745; 8° 1746 (2nd); 8° 1750 (3rd).

      1732. D.L. Th. 1/6, T. 6, F. 23, W. 28; T. 4/7, F. 7. 1733.
H.² T. 27/3. 1738. Punch's theatre S. 6/5. 1745. D.L. Th. 17/10,
S. 19, T. 22, Th. 24, S. 26–Th. 31; F. 1/11–S. 9, T. 12–S. 16,
Th. 21; Th. 19/12, Th. 26; G.F. M. 2/12, T. 3, F. 6, M. 9, T. 10,
F. 13. 1746. T. 14/1, M. 27, T. 28; W. 5/2, T. 11; D.L. M. 1/12,
T. 2, M. 8. 1747. D.L. Th. 29/1. 1748. F. 22/1, S. 23.

(Burl.)   The Covent-Garden Tragedy (D.L. June 1732) 8° 1732 (anon.);
8° 1754.

      1732. D.L. Th. 1/6. 1738. Punch's theatre T. 25/4–S. 29;
M. 1/5, W. 3–F. 5, T. 9. 1742. B.F. Fawkes and Pinchbeck, Aug.
1748. Panton-street, May (puppets).

(B.O.)   The Mock Doctor. Or The Dumb Lady Cur'd. A Comedy.
Done from Moliere (D.L. June 1732) 8° 1732 (anon.); 8° 1732
(2nd, with additions); 8° 1734; 12° 1735 (Dublin); 8° 1742 (3rd);
12° 1752 (Dublin); 4° 1753 (4th).

      1732. D.L. F. 23/6; T. 4/7, F. 7, Th. 28; T. 1/8, F. 11, T. 15,
S. 19; F. 8/9, T. 12, Th. 14, S. 16, T. 19, Th. 21, S. 30; T. 3/10,
S. 7, T. 10, T. 17; Th. 16/11, Th. 30. 1733. T. 23/1; M. 26/3; M.
9/4, W. 18, M. 23, F. 27; W. 9/5; W. 19/12; G.F. T. 13/2 (1 act),
S. 17, Th. 22, S. 24, M. 26, T. 27; Th. 1/3, S. 3; W. 28/3, F. 30,
S. 31; M. 2/4–W. 4, T. 10–Th. 12, T. 17, W. 18; F. 4/5, Th. 10,
M. 14–W. 16; Th. 27/9; W. 3/10, Th. 25; T. 27/11; H.² T. 20/3;
Th. 12/7; Th. 25/10; W. 14/11; Th. 13/12; C.G. Th. 9/8. 1734.
G.F. W. 9/1, S. 19; T. 5/2; M. 11/3, Th. 28; H.² F. 11/1; M. 4/3;
Th. 10/10; D.L. M. 25/3; T. 8/10–Th. 10; C.G. F. 18/10, W. 23,
Th. 24, S. 26; Th. 7/11. 1735. G.F. M. 10/3; Th. 24/4; W. 3/12–
F. 5; D.L. S. 29/3; M. 14/4, T. 22; F. 9/5; T. 1/7, F. 4; S.
27/9; Th. 27/11; W. 17/12; York buildings T. 3/6; L.² M. 16/7;
H.² M. 4/8. 1736. D.L. S. 20/3; M. 12/4; T. 28/9; Th. 28/10;
L.² M. 29/3; M. 19/4; G.F. S. 17/4, T. 27; H.² S. 26/6. 1737.
D.L. S. 19/3, T. 29; W. 20/4, W. 27; W. 25/5; Th. 13/10, W. 19;
Th. 10/11; C.G. T. 31/5; L.² F. 5/8, T. 9. 1738. D.L. F. 27/1;

T. 21/3; T. 11/4; F. 27/10; Punch's theatre M. 3/4–S. 22, T. 25–
S. 29. 1739. D.L. Th. 4/1, S. 6, W. 10, M. 15, W. 31; M. 26/3;
W. 25/4; Th. 17/5, M. 28; Th. 2/8, F. 10; C.G. F. 18/5; T. 21/8;
W. 5/9, M. 17; M. 1/10; Th. 1/11, T. 20, W. 28; S. 15/12, W. 19.
1740. F. 25/1; F. 18/4, F. 25; W. 21/5; M. 22/9, M. 29; W. 8/10;
T. 18/11; D.L.S. 22/3; M. 14/4; F. 23/5, Th. 29; Th. 9/10, S. 18,
W. 22, Th. 23; G.F. Th. 16/10–S. 18, F. 24, F. 31; M. 3/11,
W. 5; W. 10/12, Th. 11. 1741. T. 20/1; M. 6/4, W. 29; W. 23/9;
T. 20/10, W. 21; M. 2/11; C.G. M. 30/3; Th. 23/4; F. 25/9;
D.L. M. 20/4, M. 27; F. 1/5, Th. 14, F. 15, S. 23, M. 25, Th. 28;
S. 5/9. 1742. S. 20/3, M. 22; Th. 1/4, T. 6, T. 27; S. 15/5;
S. 11/9; Th. 4/11; James-street T. 12/10; L.² F. 26/11, M.
29. 1743. D.L. T. 1/3; L.² T. 8/3, T. 15; F. 3/6; C.G. W.
20/4; M. 17/10, W. 19, W. 26, M. 31; M. 14/11; S. 10/12.
1744. D.L. M. 12/3; H.² F. 20/4; Th. 10/5, W. 16; S. 29/9;
C.G. F. 11/5; W. 3/10. 1745. D.L. T. 8/1, F. 11, W. 16; S. 12/10;
James-street M. 14/1; G.F. F. 18/1–S. 26; F. 1/11, M. 4, Th. 21;
C.G. T. 2/4, F. 26, T. 30; M. 7/10; T. 12/11, F. 15; T. 31/12.
1746. G.F. W. 22/1; M. 3/2; T. 18/3; Th. 30/10; Th. 6/11, F. 7;
M. 15/12; C.G. Th. 13/2; W. 7/5; W. 1/10, S. 4–F. 17; T. 4/11;
D.L. F. 6/6, M. 9. 1747. G.F. F. 2/1; C.G. Th. 29/10; W. 25/11;
W. 9/12. 1748. F. 1/1; Th. 14/4; W. 21/9, F. 30; M. 10/10;
D.L. S. 12/11, W. 16, F. 25; F. 16/12. 1749. C.G. T. 3/1; W.
18/10; M. 6/11, T. 14; D.L. S. 16/9.

. The Miser. A Comedy. Taken from Plautus and Moliere (D.L.
Feb. 1732/3) 8° 1733; 8° 1733 (Edinburgh); 8° 1733 (Dublin);
8° 1744 (2nd); 8° 1748 (Glasgow); 8° 1754 (3rd); 12° 1755 (Glasgow); 8° 1761 (4th); 12° 1762 (Dublin).

  1733. D.L. S. 17/2–T. 20, S. 24, T. 27; Th. 1/3, S. 3, T. 6,
T. 13, S. 17, T. 27, F. 30; T. 3/4, Th. 5, F. 6, T. 10, Th. 12,
S. 21, Th. 26; Th. 3/5, F. 4, T. 8, W. 16, Th. 31; W. 24/10,
F. 26, M. 29; F. 16/11; H.² T. 27/11, Th. 29; M. 3/12. 1734.
D.L. M. 14/1; W. 6/2, M. 25; Th. 16/5; T. 8/10; S. 23/11;
T. 31/12; L.² M. 15/4. 1735. D.L. S. 8/2; Th. 2/10; M. 15/12.
1736. S. 31/1; Th. 19/2; Th. 6/5; M. 25/10; T. 30/11; S. 18/12;
G.F. Th. 18/3, S. 20; M. 12/4, Th. 29. 1737. D.L. W. 9/2;
T. 24/5; S. 17/9. 1738. S. 11/2; T. 11/4; F. 12/5; Th. 2/11,
F. 10; S. 23/12. 1739. Th. 8/2; F. 2/3; Th. 26/4; F. 25/5; S. 15/9;
F. 2/11; F. 7/12. 1740. Th. 17/4. 1741. G.F. M. 16/3; W. 15/4;
S. 26/12; D.L. S. 4/4; S. 2/5; Th. 17/9; M. 9/11; C.G. S. 12/12,
T. 15, Th. 31. 1742. D.L. F. 1/1; M. 1/2; S. 1/5, W. 19; S. 25/9;
F. 26/11; M. 27/12; C.G. W. 17/2; T. 25/5; M. 8/11; G.F. T.
18/5; James-street T. 12/10. 1743. L.² M. 4/4; C.G. W. 11/5;
Th. 17/11; W. 7/12, F. 30; D.L. T. 4/10. 1744. W. 25/1; T. 8/5;
C.G. Th. 2/2; T. 17/4, Th. 19; F. 11/5; F. 30/11; S. 15/12;
H.² F. 20/4; Th. 10/5; G.F. W. 12/12. 1745. Th. 3/1; Th. 7/3;
C.G. F. 25/1; Th. 2/5; T. 26/11; D.L. F. 20/12. 1746. S. 11/1;
M. 10/2; Th. 6/3; F. 16/5; T. 30/12; C.G. M. 13/10; G.F. W.
26/11. 1747. C.G. Th. 22/1; D.L. T. 17/3. 1748. W. 3/2. 1749.
W. 25/1; T. 21/2; F. 12/5; T. 24/10; T. 5/12.

*F. Deborah or a Wife for You All.
  1733. D.L. F. 6/4.

(F.) The Intriguing Chambermaid. A Comedy of Two Acts...Taken
from the French of Regnard (D.L. Jan. 1733/4) 8° 1734;

8° 1748 (Dublin); 8° 1750; 12° 1758 (Dublin); 8° 1761; 8° 1765 (Cork).

1734. D.L. T. 15/1–Th. 17, M. 21, W. 23, T. 29, Th. 31; M. 22/4; M. 13/5, Th. 16, T. 21, Th. 23; M. 11/11, W. 13, S. 16; S. 7/12. 1735. S. 22/2; S. 22/3; F. 5/12, Th. 11, F. 19. 1736. Th. 1/1, M. 5; Th. 26/2; S. 2/10, Th. 21; M. 8/11; F. 17/12; C.G. M. 17/5. 1737. D.L. S. 26/3; M. 2/5, W. 11, S. 21, F. 27, T. 31. 1738. Th. 2/3; W. 3/5, M. 15; Th. 21/9; T. 24/10; W. 29/11. 1739. W. 3/1, F. 5, Th. 25; F. 2/2, W. 28. 1740. W. 14/5; T. 11/11; S. 6/12, T. 16. 1741. S. 14/3, T. 17; W. 1/4, T. 7; W. 13/5, Th. 21; T. 15/9; Th. 8/10. 1742. S. 2/10; Th. 9/12. 1743. W. 13/4; W. 11/5. 1745. Th. 28/11, F. 29; W. 4/12, S. 7, T. 10. 1746. Th. 2/1; S. 15/2, T. 18; M. 28/4; Th. 23/10, Th. 30; W. 5/11; G.F. M. 10/2, T. 25. 1747. D.L. S. 4/4; Th. 1/10, Th. 15, F. 30; M. 23/11; S. 19/12. 1748. T. 5/1, Th. 21; M. 14/3, S. 19; S. 2/4, W. 13; T. 4/10, Th. 13, F. 14, S. 22; W. 2/11, T. 8, F. 18, M. 21; S. 3/12, S. 10. 1749. M. 16/1, T. 24, S. 28; W. 1/2; T. 7/3, M. 13; W. 5/4; Th. 18/5; Th. 28/9; F. 13/10, W. 18, M. 23; S. 4/11, W. 8, F. 24.

C. Don Quixote in England (H.[2] April 1734) 8° 1734; 8° 1754; 8° 1760 (Edinburgh).

See the supplementary notes; published April 18, 1734 (*Grub Street Journal*). 1734. L.[2] T. 1/10.

(B.O.) An Old Man Taught Wisdom: Or, The Virgin Unmask'd. A Farce (D.L. Jan. 1734/5) 8° 1735; 8° 1735 (2nd); 8° 1740 (Dublin); 8° 1742 (3rd); 8° 1747 (Dublin); 8° 1749 (4th); 12° 1761 (Glasgow).

1735. D.L. M. 6/1–F. 10, T. 14, F. 17–T. 21, T. 28, W. 29; S. 1/2, M. 17, T. 18; M. 24/3, Th. 27; F. 11/4, W. 16, M. 21, W. 23, T. 29; S. 17/5, Th. 22; T. 3/6; S. 6/9, T. 9, Th. 11, T. 30; S. 22/11, M. 24, S. 29; Th. 18/12, M. 22, T. 30. 1736. T. 6/1; S. 10/4, F. 16, Th. 29; F. 28/5; M. 18/10; M. 1/11, F. 12. 1737. T. 25/1; T. 15/3; F. 15/4, T. 26; F. 6/5, S. 14; F. 20/5, M. 30; Th. 8/9, S. 10, Th. 29; Th. 6/10, F. 21. 1738. M. 20/3; M. 22/5, W. 31; Th. 7/9; W. 6/12. 1739. M. 1/1, T. 23, F. 26; S. 3/3, Th. 8, Th. 22; F. 27/4; F. 11/5, S. 12, T. 15, W. 23; S. 22/9, T. 25; F. 5/10. 1740. W. 6/2; S. 1/3, M. 3, Th. 13, S. 29; Th. 10/4; F. 9/5; S. 27/9; T. 7/10; T. 4/11, F. 7, F. 14, W. 26; M. 8/12, M. 15; G.F. S. 22/11–F. 28; W. 3/12–F. 5, F. 12. 1741. T. 27/1, W. 28; M. 2/2, M. 9, Th. 12, M. 16, Th. 26, S. 28; Th. 9/4, M. 13, F. 17; T. 5/5; M. 14/9, F. 18, F. 25, W. 30; M. 19/10, Th. 22; D.L. S. 21/3; Th. 16/4; M. 1/6; T. 8/9, T. 22. 1742. G.F. W. 13/1, W. 20; M. 1/2, T. 2, F. 12, W. 17; Th. 25/3; Th. 27/5; D.L. M. 8/3, M. 15; Th. 8/4, S. 24; T. 18/5; Th. 16/9, T. 21; T. 26/10; C.G. W. 6/10, F. 8, M. 11, W. 13, Th. 14, M. 18, Th. 21, W. 27; S. 6/11; L.[2] W. 1/12, F. 3, M. 6, W. 8, F. 17, M. 20. 1743. D.L. S. 15/1; M. 14/3, Th. 24; M. 11/4, Th. 21, F. 29; M. 9/5; Th. 13/10; L.[2] M. 14/3, T. 22; M. 11/4; C.G. T. 22/3; T. 3/5, F. 6, W. 11; F. 30/9; M. 3/10; Th. 17/11, S. 19. 1744. S. 7/1; F. 27/4; M. 7/5, W. 9; M. 24/9; D.L. Th. 12/1; Th. 29/3; G.F. M. 26/11, Th. 29; M. 10/12, S. 15, S. 29. 1745. Th. 31/1; F. 1/2, T. 5; S. 23/3, M. 25; Th. 4/4; T. 26/11–F. 29; New theatre May fair M. 18/2, Th. 21; C.G. T. 23/4, S. 27, T. 30; T. 7/5, W. 29; W. 25/9; W. 9/10; W. 6/11; D.L. W. 11/12–F. 13;

Broughton's Amphitheatre M. 24/6. 1746. C.G. F. 24/1; M. 20/10, W. 22, M. 27, F. 31; Th. 6/11; D.L. M. 17/2; M. 17/3; Th. 25/9; T. 7/10; G.F. T. 18/2; M. 10/11, T. 11, W. 26, Th. 27. 1747. Th. 5/2; D.L. Th. 23/4; F. 23/10; F. 6/11; C.G. Th. 7/5, W. 13, F. 22. 1748. D.L. W. 20/1, W. 27; T. 8/3; T. 19/4; W. 23/11, S. 26; M. 5/12, W. 14, S. 17, F. 30; C.G. F. 29/4; T. 3/5, F. 6. 1749. D.L. F. 20/1; F. 3/2; W. 10/5; Th. 21/9; Th. 5/10, T. 17, F. 27; Th. 2/11, Th. 16.

C. The Universal Gallant: or, The Different Husbands (D.L. Feb. 1734/5) 8° 1735.

    1735. D.L. M. 10/2–W. 12 (see *Gentleman's Mag.* for failure).

Dr. Sat. Pasquin. A Dramatick Satire on the Times: Being the Rehearsal of Two Plays, viz. A Comedy call'd, The Election; And a Tragedy call'd, The Life and Death of Common-Sense (H.² March 1735/6) 8° 1736; 8° 1736 (Dublin); 8° 1737 (10th); 8° 1740 (2nd); 8° 1754 (3rd).

    1736. H.² F. 5/3–T. 9, Th. 11–W. 31; Th. 1/4–T. 20 (39th), T. 27, Th. 29, F. 30; S. 1/5, T. 4–S. 15, Th. 20–W. 26; M. 7/6, F. 11, Th. 17; F. 2/7. 1737. L.² M. 24/1, T. 25.

(Burl.) Tumble-Down Dick: or, Phæton in the Suds. A Dramatick Entertainment of Walking, in Serious and Foolish Characters: Interlarded with Burlesque, Grotesque, Comick Interludes, call'd, Harlequin a Pick-Pocket...Being ('tis hop'd) the last Entertainment that will ever be exhibited on any Stage. Invented by the Ingenious Monsieur Sans Esprit. The Musick compos'd by the Harmonious Signior Warblerini. And the Scenes painted by the Prodigious Mynheer Van Bottom-Flat (H.² April 1736) 8° 1736; 8° 1744.

    1736. H.² Th. 29/4, F. 30; S. 1/5, T. 4–T. 11, Th. 13–S. 15, Th. 20–T. 25, Th. 27–S. 29.

F. Eurydice, A Farce: As it was d—mned at the Theatre-Royal in Drury-Lane (D.L. Feb. 1736/7) 8° 1743 (in *Miscellanies* ii. 251–90).

    1737. D.L. S. 19/2 (acted as *E. or the Devil Henpeck'd*).

(Dr. Sat.) The Historical Register, For the Year 1736...To which is added a very merry Tragedy, called, Eurydice Hiss'd, or, A Word to the Wise (1. H.² March 1737; 2. H.² April 1737) 8° (1737, written by author of *Pasquin*); 8° (1737, with alterations); 8° 1737 (Dublin, *bis*); 8° 1741; 8° 1744 (3rd).

    1. 1737. H.² M. 21/3; M. 25/4 (21st)–F. 29; M. 2/5, T. 3, Th. 5.

    2. H.² W. 13/4, M. 25 (11th)–F. 29; M. 2/5, T. 3.

C. Plutus, the God of Riches...Translated from the Original Greek of Aristophanes 8° 1742. [In this Fielding collaborated with Young.]

F. Miss Lucy in Town. A Sequel to the Virgin Unmasqued. A Farce; With Songs (D.L. May 1742) 8° 1742 (anon.); 8° 1756 (2nd); 8° 1764 (3rd).

    1742. D.L. Th. 6/5, F. 7, M. 10, W. 12, F. 14, W. 19, Th. 20, S. 22; S. 30/10; M. 1/11–W. 3, S. 6, F. 12, M. 15, F. 19, T. 30; W. 1/12.

Int. An Interlude between Jupiter, Juno, and Mercury 8° 1743 (in *Miscellanies* vol. i).

C. The Wedding-Day (D.L. Feb. 1742/3) 8° 1743 (in *Miscellanies* vol. ii).

1743. D.L. Th. 17/2, S. 19–T. 22, Th. 24, S. 26.
C.   The Fathers: or, The Good-Natur'd Man 8° 1778.

FINCH, ANNE, *Countess of WINCHELSEA*.
T.   Aristomenes 8° 1713 (in Miscellany Poems, On Several Occasions. Written by a Lady).

FOOTE, SAMUEL.
*Ent.   The Diversions of the Morning [printed in Tate Wilkinson's The Wandering Patentee, 12° 1795].
   1747. H.² W. 22/4 (often repeated).
*F.   The Auction of Pictures.
   1748. H.² M. 18/4 (often repeated).
[For his later works see the Hand-list of Plays, 1750–1800.]

FREEMAN, MARK (*evidently a pseudonym*).
(Pol. B.O.)   The Downfal of Bribery: or, The Honest Men of Taunton. A New Ballad Opera Of Three Acts. As it was lately perform'd by a Company of Players at a certain noted Inn at Taunton in Somersetshire. By Mark Freeman, of the said Town, Freeholder, and Grocer...To which is added, A New Ballad by way of Epilogue 8° (1733).

FROWDE, PHILIP.
T.   The Fall of Saguntum (L.² Jan. 1726/7) 8° 1727; 12° 1727 (Dublin); 12° 1735 (3rd).
   1727. L.² M. 16/1–T. 24, Th. 26–S. 28; Th. 18/5.
T.   Philotas (L.² Feb. 1730/1) 8° 1731; 16° 1735.
   1731. L.² W. 3/2–T. 9.   1732. S. 29/4.

FYFE, ALEXANDER.
D.O.   The Royal Martyr, K. Charles I 4° 1705; 4° 1709.

GARDINER, MATTHEW.
B.O.   The Sharpers (Aungier St. Dublin, Feb. 1739/40) 12° 1740.
*T.   The Parthian Hero, Smock Alley, Dublin, March 1741/2, 8° 1741.

GARRICK, DAVID.
F.   Lethe: or, Esop in the Shades...Written by Mrs Garick (D.L. April 1740) 8° 1745 (surreptitious); Lethe. A Dramatic Satire 8° 1749; 12° 1749 (Dublin); 8° 1757 (5th); 8° 1762 (6th); 8° 1767 (6th).
   1740. D.L. T. 15/4.   1741. G.F. T. 7/4, W. 15, M. 20, F. 24, M. 27, Th. 30; M. 4/5; S. 28/11; T. 22/12, W. 30.   1742. S. 2/1, T. 5–Th. 7, T. 12, M. 18, F. 22, M. 25, T. 26, F. 29; S. 6/2, W. 10, M. 15, Th. 18, S. 20; M. 15/3, M. 29; T. 6/4, Th. 8, M. 26; F. 21/5.   1749. D.L. M. 2/1–W. 4, F. 6–S. 14, W. 18, Th. 26; Th. 13/4, F. 28; Th. 11/5.
C.   The Lying Valet...As it is Performed Gratis, at the Theatre in Goodman's Fields (G.F. Nov. 1741) 12° 1741 (Dublin); 8° 1742; 8° 1743 (2nd); 8° 1743 (3rd); 8° 1756 (6th).
   1741. G.F. M. 30/11–Th. 10/12, S. 12, S. 19.   1742. F. 8/1– M. 11, Th. 14, S. 16, T. 19, Th. 21, S. 23; Th. 11/2, T. 16, S. 27; Th. 1/4, M. 19, S. 24, T. 27, Th. 29; S. 1/5, W. 5, Th. 6, S. 8, M. 17–W. 19, M. 24; James-street Th. 25/11.   1743. Theatrical booth, Southwark F. 18/2; W. 30/3; D.L. Th. 3/3, T. 15, Th. 17, S. 19; M. 25/4–W. 27, S. 30; M. 2/5, W. 4, T. 10, Th. 12, S. 14, M. 16, W. 18–F. 20; S. 17/9, T. 20, Th. 22, T. 27, Th. 29; T. 11/10, T. 18, Th. 20, S. 22, Th. 27, S. 29; T. 1/11, Th. 3, S. 5,

F. 11, T. 15, Th. 17, S. 26; S. 3/12, M. 19; L.² Th. 17/3; M. 4/4; Richmond S. 6/8; C.G. M. 10/10. 1744. D.L. W. 18/1; W. 28/3; T. 10/4, W. 18; W. 9/5, F. 11, W. 23; Th. 20/9; Th. 11/10; T. 18/12; C.G. F. 30/3; W. 25/4; H.² M. 23/4; G.F. F. 30/11; T. 11/12, W. 12, M. 17, F. 21, F. 28. 1745. S. 5/1, M. 14, T. 29; W. 6/2; M. 11; T. 19/3, T. 26, Th. 28; M. 29/4; F. 8/11, M. 11–Th. 14, F. 22; W. 11/12; New theatre, Shepherds' Mount, May F. S. 9/2; D.L. T. 12/2; S. 6/4, S. 20; W. 1/5, Th. 9; M. 18/11, W. 20; James-street F. 8/3. 1746. G.F. Th. 9/1; M. 3/3, Th. 20; T. 9/12, W. 10; D.L. S. 11/1; F. 7/2, T. 25, Th. 27; W. 30/4; S. 11/10, Th. 16, F. 17; W. 12/11, T. 25; C.G. T. 18/3; M. 21/4; Th. 1/5; T. 30/9; W. 8/10; T. 11/11; Richmond F. 25/7. 1747. G.F. F. 9/1, Th. 29; F. 6/2, T. 10, F. 20, M. 23; T. 17/3; D.L. T. 27/1; W. 4/2; T. 31/3; T. 29/9; Th. 26/11; C.G. Th. 26/3; T. 7/4, W. 22, W. 29; W. 20/5. 1748. D.L. S. 2/1, T. 26; T. 2/2, M. 8; T. 1/3; M. 7/3, S. 26, M. 28; M. 25/4; T. 17/5, W. 18; T. 13/9; M. 7/11, Th. 10, Th. 17, Th. 24; F. 2/12, Th. 22, S. 31; H.² M. 29/2; C.G. F. 23/9. 1749. D.L. S. 21/1; Th. 2/2, F. 17; T. 14/3; Th. 6/4; W. 20/9; Th. 12/10, S. 21; M. 6/11; C.G. M. 3/4.

F. Miss in her Teens: or, The Medley of Lovers (C.G. Jan. 1746/7) 8° 1747 (anon.); 8° 1747 (2nd); 8° 1748; 8° 1758.

    1747. C.G. S. 17/1–S. 31; M. 2/2–S. 7; M. 30/3, T. 31; Th. 2/4, S. 4, M. 6, Th. 9, S. 11; T. 21/4, Th. 23, M. 27; F. 29/5; G.F. M. 2/3, M. 9, T. 10, Th. 12, M. 16, Th. 19, M. 23, T. 24, Th. 26, M. 30, T. 31; Th. 2/4, S. 4; T. 7/4, S. 11; B.F. Chettle, Aug.; D.L. S. 24/10–W. 28, S. 31; M. 9/11, Th. 12, T. 24; T. 22/12, W. 30. 1748. F. 1/1, T. 12, Th. 28; T. 9/2; Th. 10/3, T. 15; W. 27/4; F. 13/5; F. 21/10, F. 28; C.G. Th. 14/1, F. 15, T. 19; M. 8/2; Th. 21/4, S. 30; M. 2/5, W. 4, Th. 5; H.² M. 25/1; N.W. Shepherds' Market, May; N.W. Clerkenwell M. 21/11. 1749. D.L. W. 25/1; Th. 16/3; M. 3/4, T. 4, M. 10, F. 14; M. 1/5, F. 12; T. 3/10; C.G. W. 19/4; F. 20/10; Th. 9/11, M. 13, Th. 30.

T. Romeo and Juliet. By Shakespear. With Alterations, and an Additional Scene (D.L. Nov. 1748) 8° 1750 (anon.); 8° 1753 (by D. Garrick).

    1748. D.L. T. 29/11 (see *supra* p. 59). [For his later works see the Hand-list of Plays, 1750–1800.]

GATAKER, THOMAS.

(B.O.) The Jealous Clown: or, The Lucky Mistake. An Opera (Of One Act) (G.F. Dec. 1730) 8° 1730.

    1730. G.F. W. 16/12–F. 18. 1731. W. 13/1, Th. 14.

GAY, JOHN.

T.C.F. The Mohocks. A Tragi-Comical Farce. As it was Acted near the Watch House in Covent-Garden. By Her Majesty's Servants 8° 1712 (anon.).

C. The Wife of Bath (D.L. May 1713) 4° 1713; 8° 1730 (revised by author).

    1713. D.L. F. 15/5. 1730. L.² M. 19/1 (altered)–W. 21.

T.C.P.F. The What D'Ye Call It (D.L. Feb. 1714/5) 8° (1715); 8° (1715, 2nd); 8° 1716 (3rd); 8° 1725 (4th); 12° 1736.

    1715. D.L. W. 23/2–S. 26; T. 1/3, S. 5, M. 14, S. 19, M. 21, S. 26, M. 28; S. 2/4, M. 4; W. 4/5, M. 9; T. 18/10, W. 26;

W. 16/11, W. 30; W. 7/12, S. 10, W. 28. 1716. M. 2/1;
Th. 1/3; W. 18/4, F. 27; M. 21/5, W. 23; Th. 1/11, M. 12, T. 27;
S.F. Pinkethman Sept. 1717. D.L. T. 29/10. 1718. T. 11/3;
T. 1/4, M. 14; W. 4/6; T. 30/12. 1719. T. 14/4, F. 17; Th. 21/5.
1720. S. 23/4; Th. 26/5; F. 14/10. 1722. S. 7/4. 1723. T. 8/1,
S. 19; W. 17/4; F. 31/5; T. 15/10, W. 30. 1724. W. 8/1, Th. 23;
M. 24/2. 1725. F. 30/4. 1727. T. 2/5, F. 19, F. 26. 1728. F. 17/5.
1729. L.² Th. 20/3, T. 25; D.L. S. 19/4; S. 3/5, T. 6, T. 20,
F. 30. 1730. L.² Th. 2/4, F. 24; D.L. T. 20/1; S. 11/4; G.F.
W. 15/4, F. 24, M. 27; F. 15/5; T. 3/11. 1731. D.L. M. 15/3;
Th. 1/4, Th. 29; S. 8/5; W. 11/8; Th. 30/9; G.F. Th. 1/4; L.²
W. 21/4. 1732. M. 7/2; M. 1/5; G.F. F. 14/4, M. 17, M. 24;
Richmond Th. 17/8; D.L. T. 7/11. 1733. S. 3/2; G.F. T. 24/4;
W. 9/5. 1735. C.G. T. 8/4; G.F. Th. 10/4, W. 16. 1736. D.L.
S. 18/9. 1737. F. 4/3; T. 10/5, W. 18, T. 24. 1738. F. 14/4. 1739.
C.G. T. 16/1, F. 19; T. 13/3; D.L. W. 9/5. 1740. C.G. S. 2/2;
Th. 6/11. 1743. D.L. F. 15/4; C.G. W. 16/11, F. 18. 1744. S. 24/11.
1746. Th. 3/4; S. 3/5, T. 6; M. 6/10, F. 10, F. 24; W. 5/11,
Th. 13. 1748. D.L. W. 3/2, Th. 4.

C. Three Hours after Marriage (D.L. Jan. 1716/7) 8° 1717; 8° 1761
(Dublin, with a key).
   This piece seems to have been written by Gay, Pope and
Arbuthnot in collaboration. 1717. D.L. W. 16/1–W. 23. 1737.
L.² F. 5/8, T. 9. 1746. D.L. Th. 13/3, S. 15; Th. 10/4.

Past. Dione 4° 1720 (in Poems vol. ii); 8° 1730 (Dublin).
   See *supra* p. 275.

T. The Captives (D.L. Jan. 1723/4) 8° 1724.
   1724. D.L. W. 15/1–W. 22.

(B.O.) The Beggar's Opera (L.² Jan. 1727/8) 8° 1728 (*bis*); 4° 1729
(3rd); 8° 1733 (3rd); 8° 1735 (4th); 8° 1742 (5th); 8° 1749 (6th);
12° 1745 (7th); 8° 1754 (7th); 12° 1760 (Edinburgh); 8° 1765;
12° 1772 (Glasgow).
   1728. L.² M. 29/1, W. 31; Th. 1/2–Th. 29; F. 1/3–T. 5, Th. 7,
M. 11, T. 12, S. 16, T. 19, S. 23, T. 26, S. 30; T. 2/4 (40th),
M. 8, T. 9, Th. 11, S. 13, Th. 25, S. 27; W. 1/5, S. 4, T. 7, Th. 9,
F. 10, F. 17, T. 21, F. 24, T. 28, F. 31; T. 4/6, F. 7, M. 10,
W. 12, F. 14, W. 19; F. 13/9, F. 20, M. 23, W. 25, F. 27; F.
4/10, T. 8, F. 11, F. 18, F. 25, Th. 31; W. 6/11, Th. 14, F. 15, Th. 21,
Th. 28; W. 11/12, T. 17, S. 21; H.² W. 26/6; W. 3/7, M. 8, W. 10,
M. 15, M. 22, W. 24, M. 29, W. 31; M. 5/8, W. 7, W. 14, F. 16, T. 20,
Th. 22; T. 8/10, Th. 10, Th. 24; Th. 8/11, M. 11, S. 30; M. 23/12,
M. 30; B.F. Fielding and Reynolds, Aug., and S.F. Sept. [Later
years given in abstract only; in brackets number of performances
each year.] 1729. L.² F. 25/4 (6); H.² Th. 1/5 (5); B.F. Rayner
and Pullen, Aug. 1730. L.² S. 31/1 (10); H.² W. 18/3; G.F.
W. 15/7 (10). 1731. L.² F. 22/1 (3); G.F. W. 27/1 (4); C.G. T.
22/4 (2); H.² T. 12/5; York buildings W. 24/9. 1732. L.² S. 22/1
(6); H.² F. 10/3 (5); G.F. W. 3/5 (2); D.L. T. 11/7 (14); C.G.
S. 16/12 (10). 1733. M. 1/1 (14); G.F. W. 24/1 (9); D.L. S.
10/2 (5); H.² W. 14/2 (3). 1734. C.G. T. 8/1 (3); G.F. Th. 7/2 (2);
L.² Th. 4/4 (2); Hampton Court (D.L. Co.) Th. 27/6. 1735.
C.G. F. 3/1 (3); G.F. F. 10/1 (4); L.² T. 20/5 (2); H.² T. 12/8;
York buildings W. 24/9. 1736. C.G. F. 13/2 (9); L.² T. 20/4 (5);
H.² S. 26/6 (2); D L. F. 31/12. 1737. S. 1/1 (16); C.G. Th. 20/1

(4); L.² F. 29/7 (2). 1738. D.L. W. 25/1 (7); C.G. Th. 20/4 (2). 1739. D.L. W. 10/1 (7); C.G. S. 28/4. 1740. D.L. T. 29/1 (13); C.G. M. 28/4; G.F. W. 31/12. 1741. Th. 1/1 (19); D.L. W. 22/4 (10); H.² T. 27/10. 1742. D.L. T. 12/1 (6); G.F. Th. 27/5. 1743. D.L. F. 14/1 (7); L.² M. 14/2 (4); Richmond S. 30/7 (2); C.G. M. 7/11 (7). 1744. S. 28/1 (6); D.L. M. 13/2 (7); G.F. F 14/12 (2). 1745. T. 1/1 (6); C.G. M. 21/1 (9); H.² F. 25/1; D.L. F. 26/4 (7); Richmond W. 28/8; Twickenham T. 10/9. 1746. D.L. M. 13/1 (10); G.F. W. 22/1 (7); C.G. M. 10/2 (8); N.W. Clerkenwell M. 22/12. 1747. G.F. Th. 15/1 (5); D.L. T. 20/1 (5); C.G. M. 9/2 (12); G.F. W. 11/2 (3). 1748. C.G. F. 1/1 (10); D.L. M. 28/3 (3); N.W. Clerkenwell M. 21/11. 1749. C.G. M. 9/1 (9); D.L. F. 27/1 (7).

(B.O.) Polly: An Opera. Being the Second Part of the Beggar's Opera 4° 1729; 8° (1729, pirated); 8° 1729 (pirated); 8° 1729 (Dublin); 12° 1777 (as first acted at the Haymarket with Colman's alterations); 12° 1779 (Dublin).

Past. O. Acis and Galatea: An English Pastoral Opera...Set to Musick by Mr. Handel (L.² March 1731) 8° 1732 (anon.); 8° 1740; 8° 1742; 8° 1747; 8° 1757; 4° 1764; 4° 1768; 8° 1775.
     1731. L.² F. 26/3. 1732. H.² W. 17/5, F. 19; H.¹ S. 10/6, T. 13, S. 17, T. 20; T. 5/12, S. 9, T. 12, S. 16. 1734. T. 7/5. 1736. C.G. W. 24/3, W. 31. 1739. L.² Th. 13/12, Th. 20. 1740. Th. 21/2; F. 28/3. 1741. W. 11/3.

(B.O.) Achilles. An Opera (C.G. Feb. 1732/3) 8° 1733; 12° (1772?); 8° 1779; Achilles in Petticoats. An Opera...Written by Mr. Gay, with alterations 8° 1774.
     1733. C.G. S. 10/2–T. 13, Th. 15, S. 17–T. 20, Th. 22, S. 24– T. 27; Th. 1/3, S. 3–T. 6, Th. 8, S. 10, T. 13; W. 25/4; W. 28/11. 1734. Th. 28/2. 1737. T. 25/1, Th. 27.

C.   The Distress'd Wife (C.G. March 1733/4) 8° **1743**; 8° **1750** (2nd).   1734. C.G. T. 5/3, Th. 7, S. 9, S. 16.

(F.) The Rehearsal at Goatham 8° **1754.**

GAY, JOSEPH (see *BREVAL*).

GIFFARD, WILLIAM.

D.O. Merlin; or, The British Inchanter; and King Arthur, the British Worthy 8° 1736. [The *Biographia Dramatica* says this was acted at G.F.]

GILDON, CHARLES.

[For his seventeenth century works see the Hand-list of Plays, 1660–1700.]

C.   Measure for Measure: Or, Beauty the Best Advocate...Written Originally by Mr. Shakespeare: And now very much Alter'd; With Additions of Several Entertainments of Musick (L.¹ *c.* Feb. 1699/1700) 4° 1700 (anon.).
     The "Entertainments of Musick" include the masque of *Dido and Æneas*, acted by itself at L.¹ S. 29/1 and S. 8/4, 1704. No records of first performance. 1706. H.¹ F. 26/4.

T.   Love's Victim: or, The Queen of Wales (L.¹ *c.* April 1701) 4° 1701 (anon.).
     No records of first performance; published May 20, 1701 (*Post Man*).

T. The Patriot, or the Italian Conspiracy (D.L. *c.* Nov. 1702) 4° 1703 (anon.); reissued the same year as *The Italian Patriot.*

(Burl.) A New Rehearsal; or, Bayes the Younger 12° 1714 (anon.).

GOODALL, WILLIAM.

(B.O.) The False Guardians Outwitted 8° 1740 (in The True English-man's Miscellany).

GORDON, ALEXANDER.

C. Lupone: or, The Inquisitor (H.² March 1731) 8° 1731.
    1731. H.² M. 15/3, T. 16.

GORING, CHARLES.

T. Irene; or, The Fair Greek (D.L. Feb. 1707/8) 4° 1708.
    1708. D.L. M. 9/2–W. 11.

GOULD, ROBERT.

T. Innocence Distress'd. [See the Hand-list of Plays, 1660–1700.]

GRANVILLE, GEORGE, Lord LANSDOWNE.

[For his seventeenth century works see the Hand-list of Plays, 1660–1700.]

C. The Jew of Venice (L.¹ Jan. 1701) 4° 1701 (anon.); 8° 1713.
    No records of first performance; published Jan. 17, 1701 (*Post Man* and *London Gazette*). 1706. H.¹ W. 23/10. 1711. D.L. S. 3/2; Greenwich Th. 23/8; S. 8/9. 1715. L.² M. 28/2; T. 22/3; F. 8/7; F. 18/11. 1716. F. 20/1; F. 20/7. 1717. Th. 16/5. 1718. F. 24/1; S. 26/4. 1719. F. 2/1; S.F. Bullock, Sept. 1720. L.² F. 26/2. 1721. T. 28/3; T. 17/10; F. 10/11. 1722. F. 5/1; F. 16/11. 1723. F. 25/1. 1727. M. 17/4; M. 13/11, Th. 30. 1728. Th. 23/5. 1729. Th. 23/1; T. 16/12. 1730. W. 7/10; S. 21/11. 1731. M. 22/2; W. 20/10. 1732. T. 25/1. 1734. C.G. F. 8/2. 1735. T. 11/2. 1736. Th. 12/2. 1739. T. 23/1. The masque of Peleus and Thetis, included in this comedy, was given at the Swan Tavern W. 29/4, 1747.

D.O. The British Enchanters; or, No Magick like Love (H.¹ Feb. 1705/6) 4° 1706 (anon.); 8° 1721 (in Poems on Several Occasions).
    1706. H.¹ Th. 21/2; S. 9/3, T. 12; F. 3/5. 1707. S. 22/3, T. 25; M. 14/4.

GRIFFIN, BENJAMIN.

T. Injured Virtue: or, The Virgin Martyr...As it was Acted at the Play-House in Richmond, By his Grace the Duke of Southampton and Cleaveland's Servants 12° 1715.
    1714. King's Arms Southwark M. 1/11.

F. Love in a Sack (L.² June 1715) 12° 1715; 12° 1719.
    1715. L.² T. 14/6; T. 5/7, Th. 21; W. 30/8. 1716. M. 16/1.

F. The Humours of Purgatory (L.² April 1716) 12° 1716.
    1716. L.² T. 3/4, W. 4, F. 6. 1745. G.F. M. 18/11–W. 20, M. 25.

F. The Masquerade: or, An Evening's Intrigue (L.² May 1717) 12° 1717.
    1717. L.² Th. 16/5.

C. Whig and Tory (L.² Jan. 1719/20) 8° 1720.
    1720. L.² T. 26/1 (acted about 8 times); S. 17/12, M. 19. 1729. D.L. F. 25/7 (revised by author), T. 29; F. 1/8. 1730. F. 24/4. 1731. W. 6/1.

GRIMES, —

*O. An Opera alluding to the Peace (Cordwainers Hall) 8° 1712.

GRIMSTONE, WILLIAM, Lord Viscount.
  C.   The Lawyer's Fortune: or, Love in a Hollow Tree 4° (1705; anon.); 4° 1705; 12° 1736; 8° 1736.

GWINNET, RICHARD.
  C.   The Country 'Squire: or, A Christmas Gambol (private perform-ance) 8° 1732; The Glo'stershire Squire: or, A Christmas Gambol. A Comedy. As it was Acted At a Gentleman's Seat near that City 8° 1734 (2nd; a reissue with new title-page).

HAMILTON, NEWBURGH.
  F.   The Petticoat-Plotter (D.L. June 1712) 12° 1720.
      1712. D.L. Th. 5/6; F. 4/7, F. 18; T. 12/8. 1715. L.² Th. 17/11 (marked as new), F. 18. 1718. F. 18/4. 1728. H.² M. 19/8.
  C.   The Doating Lovers; or, The Libertine Tam'd (L.² June 1715) 12° 1715.
      1715. L.² Th. 23/6, M. 27, T. 28.

HAMMOND, WILLIAM.
  (B.O.)   The Preceptor; or, The Loves of Abelard and Heloise. A Dramatick Entertainment (Smock Alley, Dublin, Nov. 1739) 8° 1740.

HARPER, SAMUEL.
  C.   The Mock Philosopher. A New, Pleasant, and Diverting Comedy, representing the Humours of the Age 12° 1737.

HARRISON, THOMAS.
  Dr. Poem.   Beltshazzar; or, The Heroick Jew 12° 1727; 12° 1729.

HARRISON, WILLIAM.
  Dr. Ent.   The Pilgrims, or The Happy Converts. A New Dramatick Entertainment 4° 1701.

HATCHETT, WILLIAM.
  T.   The Rival Father: or, The Death of Achilles (H.² April 1730) 8° 1730.
      1730. H.² W. 8/4, Th. 9, W. 22.
  H.T.   The Chinese Orphan...Alter'd from a Specimen of the Chinese Tragedy, in Du Halde's History of China. Interspers'd with Songs, after the Chinese Manner 8° 1741.

HAVARD, WILLIAM.
  T.   Scanderbeg (G.F. March 1732/3) 8° 1733.
      1733. G.F. Th. 15/3, M. 26.
  H.T.   King Charles the First...Written in Imitation of Shakespeare (L.² March 1736/7) 8° 1737; 8° 1765.
      1737. L.² T. 1/3 (no title given; billed as an historical play), Th. 3–T. 8, Th. 10, S. 12, M. 14, Th. 17, S. 19, T. 22; M. 11/4, W. 13, F. 15, T. 19, M. 25; T. 10/5, W. 18. 1740. D.L. F. 9/5.
  T.   Regulus (D.L. Feb. 1743/4) 8° 1744.
      1744. D.L. T. 21/2, Th. 23, S. 25–T. 28; Th. 1/3; W. 18/4.
  F.   The Elopement (D.L. April 1763).

HAWKER, ESSEX.
  (B.O.)   The Wedding. A Tragi-Comi-Pastoral-Farcical Opera...With an Hudibrastick Skimmington (L.² May 1729) 8° 1729 (as at L.²); 8° 1734; The Country-Wedding and Skimmington 8° 1729 (as acted at D.L.).
      1729. L.² T. 6/5; D.L. F. 18/7, T. 22, F. 25; F. 1/8, Th. 7; B.F. Hall and Oates, Aug. 1730. L.² M. 20/4, M. 27, W. 29;

W. 6/5, F. 15, W. 20; D.L. M. 11/5, Th. 14; T. 20/10. 1731.
G.F. S. 23/1 (1 act), M. 25–S. 30; F. 5/2, S. 6, W. 17, Th. 18.
1732. D.L. M. 8/5. 1733. C.G. T. 3/4; Th. 3/5. Another *Country
Wedding* was acted at D.L. on T. 27/7, 1714.

HAWKINS, WILLIAM.
   T. Henry and Rosamond 8° 1749; 8° 1758 (Oxford, in Tracts in
       Divinity vol. ii, which also contains The Siege of Aleppo and
       Cymbeline).

HAWLING, FRANCIS.
  *F. It Should have come Sooner, or the Historic, Satiric Tragi-Comic
       Humours of Exchange Alley.
          1723. D.L. T. 30/7; F. 2/8, F. 9.
   C. The Impertinent Lovers: or, A Coquet at her Wit's End...With
       a Preface, and Remarks upon its Usage. Submitted to Sir Richard
       Steel, and the three Gentlemen concerned with him as Patentees
       (D.L. Aug. 1723) 8° 1723 (anon.).
          1723. D.L. F. 16/8.

HAYWOOD, Mrs ELIZA.
   T. The Fair Captive (L.¹ March 1720/1) 8° 1721.
          1721. L.¹ S. 4/3–T. 7; Th. 16/11.
   C. A Wife to be Lett (D.L. Aug. 1723) 8° 1724 (*bis*); 12° 1735.
          1723. D.L. M. 12/8–W. 14.
   T. Frederick, Duke of Brunswick–Lunenburgh (L.¹ March 1728/9)
       8° 1729 (*bis*).
          1729. L.¹ T. 4/3, Th. 6, S. 8.
(Burl.) The Opera of Operas; or, Tom Thumb the Great. Alter'd
       from the Life and Death of Tom Thumb the Great. And Set to
       Musick after the Italian Manner (H.¹ May 1733) 8° 1733 (anon.;
       probably by Mrs Haywood and William Hatchett; music by
       Arne); 8° 1733 (same title, save that the music is given By Mr.
       Lampe; this text has some alterations).
          1733. H.¹ Th. 31/5; M. 4/6, W. 6, F. 8, M. 11, W. 13; M.
       29/10 (1 act), W. 31; Th. 1/11, S. 3–T. 13, Th. 15–S. 17;
       F. 28/12; D.L. W. 7/11; Th. 13/12. 1734. H.¹ M. 21/1, M. 28.
       1740. C.G. W. 30/4.

HEWITT, JOHN.
   T. The Fair Rivals (Bath, Duke of Grafton's men) 8° 1729 (Bath).
   T. Fatal Falshood: or Distress'd Innocence. A Tragedy In Three
       Acts (D.L. Feb. 1733/4) 8° (1734).
          1734. D.L. M. 11/2, T. 12, Th. 14, F. 15.
   C. A Tutor for the Beaus: or, Love in a Labyrinth (L.¹ Feb. 1736/7)
       8° 1737; 8° 1738.
          1737. L.¹ M. 21/2, T. 22, Th. 24.

HIGGONS, BEVIL.
   T. The Generous Conqueror: or, The Timely Discovery (D.L.
       c. Dec. 1701) 4° 1702.
          No record of first performance; published Jan. 15, 1701/2
       (*Post Man*).

HILL, AARON.
   T. Elfrid: or The Fair Inconstant (D.L. Jan. 1709/10) 4° (1710).
          1710. D.L. T. 3/1, W. 4, Th. 5, M. 9; T. 21/2. 1723. H.¹
       W. 24/7.

F. The Walking Statue; or, The Devil in the Wine Cellar (D.L. Jan. 1709/10) 4° (1710, printed with above).
1710. D.L. M. 9/1 (4th), T. 10, Th. 12, F. 13, M. 16, T. 17, S. 21, S. 28, T. 31; F. 3/2, T. 7, W. 8, S. 18, T. 21; S. 25/3; M. 10/4, W. 12, S. 15; Th. 11/5; Greenwich S. 29/7; M. 7/8, M. 14. 1711. D.L. M. 30/4; Th. 31/5; T. 5/6, T. 12; F. 13/7. 1712. W. 6/2; Th. 15/5, M. 19, T. 20; T. 10/6, Th. 19. 1713. W. 10/6. 1714. M. 19/4. 1715. L.² F. 21/1; Th. 24/2; T. 22/3; W. 28/9. 1716. M. 2/1; T. 24/4; W. 25/7; F. 17/8; F. 30/11. 1717. T. 28/5; F. 28/6. 1719. T. 5/5. 1720. Th. 31/3; W. 4/5, T. 10. 1721. M. 13/2. 1722. W. 2/5, T. 8, M. 21, T. 22. 1723. D.L. F. 26/7, T. 30; F. 2/8. 1729. F. 20/6, T. 24, M. 30. 1731. L.² Th. 1/4. 1737. C.G. T. 15/3. 1745. Richmond S. 17/8. 1746. G.F. M. 17/3.

T. The Fatal Vision: or, The Fall of Siam (L.² Feb. 1715/6) 8° 1716. 1716. L.² T. 7/2, W. 8, Th. 9, S. 11–T. 14; T. 6/3.

T. The Fatal Extravagance (L.² April 1721) 8° 1720; 8° 1721 (Dublin); 8° 1726; 12° 1726 (4th, enlarged to 5 acts); *8° 1729 (Dublin); 8° 1730 (4th, 1 act). [The title-page to the 1720 edition declares the author to be Joseph Mitchell; but it was included in Hill's Works 1760.]
1721. L.² F. 21/4 (not the first performance); W. 22/11. 1722. Th. 11/1; M. 7/5 (2 acts). 1730. S. 21/2, T. 24, Th. 26, S. 28; Th. 5/3, T. 10; T. 21/4; T. 12/5. 1733. C.G. T. 26/6, F. 29; F. 27/7, T. 31. 1734. M. 25/11. 1736. H.² M. 2/2 (2 acts); F. 30/7.

H.T. King Henry the Fifth: or, The Conquest of France, By the English (D.L. Dec. 1723) 8° 1723.
1723. D.L. Th. 5/12–T. 10, Th. 26.

T. Athelwold (D.L. Dec. 1731) 8° 1732; 12° 1732 (Dublin). 1731. D.L. F. 10/12–M. 13.

T. The Tragedy of Zara (D.L. Jan. 1735/6) 8° 1736 (bis); 8° 1752 (3rd). 1736. D.L. M. 12/1–T. 27. Zara had also been performed at York buildings by amateurs in 1735 (Th. 29/5; M. 2/6, F. 6, Th. 12, W. 18).

T. Alzira (L.² June 1736) 8° 1736; 8° 1744 (3rd). 1736. L.² F. 18/6, T. 22, F. 25; Th. 1/7, F. 2, W. 7, W. 14, F. 16, W. 21; Th. 14/10. 1737. Th. 21/4. 1744. D.L. M. 30/4 (from the text of a new edition).

T. Meropé (D.L. April 1749) 8° 1749; 8° 1750 (2nd); 8° 1753; 8° 1758. 1749. D.L. S. 15/4–T. 25; S. 6/5, S. 13.
[For his later works see the *Biographia Dramatica*.]

HILL, Sir JOHN.
O. Orpheus F. 1740.

HIPPISLEY, JOHN.
(B.O.) Flora, An Opera...Made from Hob, or, The Country Wake (L.² April 1729) 8° (1729, Southwark, anon.); Flora; An Opera... Being the Farce of the Country-Wake, alter'd after the Manner of the Beggar's Opera...Written by a Gentleman 8° 1729 (2nd); 8° 1729 (3rd); 8° 1730; 8° 1732 (4th); Flora; or, Hob in the Well... By Mr. Hippisley 12° 1748 (6th); 12° 1768 (7th; by Mr. Hippisley).
1729. L.² F. 18/4, M. 21, W. 23, T. 29, W. 30; Th. 1/5–S. 3, W. 7, Th. 8, M. 12, Th. 15, M. 19, F. 23; F. 19/9, W. 24; M. 6/10,

W. 8, Th. 30; F. 7/11, T. 11; M. 1/12, Th. 18, M. 29; H.² S. 26/7;
T. 19/8; B.F. Bullock, Aug.; S.F. Sept. [Later lists given in
abstract only; in brackets number of performances each year.]
1730. L.² M. 2/2 (12); H.² Th. 12/3; G.F. M. 15/6 (11). 1731.
L.² M. 11/1 (10); G.F. F. 15/1 (10); H.² W. 10/3 (2). 1732. G.F.
T. 25/1 (10); L.² S. 22/4 (7). 1733. C.G. Th. 18/1 (10); G.F.
F. 6/4 (9); H.² W. 26/12. 1734. W. 2/1 (6); G.F. T. 8/1 (5);
C.G. Th. 17/1 (4); D.L. S. 28/9 (2). 1735. C.G. S. 22/3 (2);
G.F. Th. 27/3 (4); D.L. W. 7/5. 1736. C.G. M. 22/3 (7); L.²
F. 2/4; Richmond S. 28/8. 1737. C.G. M. 10/1 (8); L.² F. 25/2.
1738. C.G. M. 13/3 (4). 1739. M. 15/1 (4); D.L. M. 14/5. 1741.
G.F. F. 6/2 (2). 1743. Theatrical booth, Southwark F. 25/2.
1744. C.G. T. 1/5; D.L. W. 16/5. 1745. G.F. T. 30/4 (3); C.G.
W. 1/5 (2). 1746. G.F. Th. 2/1 (8). 1747. S. 24/1 (6); D.L.
T. 10/2 (11). 1748. S. 9/1 (3); C.G. W. 21/12 (2). 1749. G.F.
M. 27/2; C.G. M. 10/4 (2).

(B.O.) A Journey to Bristol: or, The Honest Welchman (Bristol
   1730?; L.² April 1731) 8° (1731).
      1731. L.² F. 23/4. 1733. C.G. M. 2/4, S. 21.
(B.O.) A Sequel to the Opera of Flora (L.² March 1731/2) 8° 1732
   (Written by the author of Flora).
      1732. L.² M. 20/3; M. 10/4, F. 21.

HOADLY, Dr BENJAMIN.
  C. The Suspicious Husband (C.G. Feb. 1746/7) 8° 1747 (3 edns); 12°
      1749 (3rd); 12° 1760 (Dublin, 3rd); 12° 1776 (Dublin).
         1747. C.G. Th. 12/2–W. 25; S. 21/3, T. 24; T. 28/4, Th. 30;
      S. 2/5; W. 18/11–S. 21, W. 25; T. 29/12; D.L. F. 4/12–Th. 10,
      M. 21. 1748. S. 16/1; F. 5/2; S. 12/3; T. 19/4; T. 3/5, T. 17;
      T. 25/10; Th. 29/12; H.² M. 25/1; C.G. M. 8/2; Th. 3/3. 1749.
      D.L. M. 30/1, T. 31; M. 13/3; W. 26/4; Th. 26/10; S. 18/11;
      C.G. M. 23/10, T. 24; T. 7/11, Th. 30.

HOADLY, Dr JOHN.
      *The Contrast [written apparently by Dr. John and Dr Benjamin
      Hoadly].
         1731. L.² F. 30/4; T. 4/5, S. 8.
  (M.) Love's Revenge. A Dramatic Pastoral in Two Interludes. Set
      to Musick by Dr. Greene 8° 1734 (anon.); 4° (1737); 8° 1745.
  (M.) Phoebe. A Pastoral Opera. Set to Music by Dr. Greene 8° 1748
      (anon.).

HOPER, Mrs.
     *T. Edward the Black Prince; or, The Battle of Poictiers (G.F. March
      1746/7).
         1747. G.F. Th. 5/3, S. 14 (as The Battle of Poictiers, or, The
      English Prince).
         *The Cyclopædia.
         1748. H.² Th. 31/3; W. 13/4.
  (Burl.) Queen Tragedy Restor'd: A Dramatick Entertainment (H.²
      Nov. 1749) 8° 1749.
         1749. H.² Th. 9/11, S. 11 (advertised on 17/10 for 19/10 but
      evidently deferred).

HUGHES, JOHN.
  D.O. Calypso and Telemachus (H.¹ May 1712) 8° 1712; 8° 1717 (2nd);
      12° 1735.

1712. H.[1] W. 14/5, S. 17, W. 21, S. 24; W. 25/6. 1717. L.[2] W. 27/2; Th. 7/3, S. 9.

M. Apollo and Daphne (D.L. Jan. 1715/6) 4° 1716.
1716. D.L. Th. 12/1, S. 14, M. 16, S. 21, T. 24.

T. Orestes 8° 1717.

T. The Siege of Damascus (D.L. Feb. 1719/20) 8° 1720; 12° 1721.
1720. D.L. W. 17/2–F. 26; F. 29/4. 1722. Th. 6/12. 1733. C.G. Th. 15/3, S. 17; T. 24/4. 1735. D.L. S. 22/3. 1737. T. 11/1, W. 12, F. 14, S. 15, T. 18, S. 29; T. 26/4; W. 19/10. 1738. S. 28/1; S. 25/3; W. 6/12. 1739. T. 23/1; M. 31/12. 1743. C.G. W. 5/1– S. 15, S. 29; Th. 3/3, Th. 10; T. 5/4, T. 19; M. 23/5. 1744. F. 3/2, M. 27; F. 5/10; M. 26/11. 1745. Th. 3/1. 1747. T. 20/1; T. 10/2. 1749. Th. 23/2.

M. Cupid and Hymen 8° 1735 (in Works, which contains also a translation of one act of L'Avare as The Miser. In The Monthly Amusement 1709 appeared another translation from Molière, The Misanthrope, later included, without indication of authorship, in Ozell's collection).

HUMPHREYS, SAMUEL.
O. Ulysses (L.[2] April 1733) 4° 1733.
1733. L.[2] M. 16/4.

HUNT, WILLIAM.
T. The Fall of Tarquin; or, The Distressed Lovers (York, Merchant Taylor's Hall, Duke of Norfolk's men) 4° 1713 (York); 12° 1713 (York).

HUNTER, JOHN.
*Relig. Dr. Wanderer and Traveller 8° 1733.

HURST, Capt. ROBERT.
T. The Roman Maid (L.[2] Aug. 1724) 8° 1725.
1724. L.[2] T. 11/8, F. 14, T. 18.

HYLAND, WILLIAM.
Dr. Piece The Ship-wreck 8° 1746. [The head title reads The Ship Wreck; or, The Farmer on the Coast.]

JACKSON, ——
T. Ajax 12° 1714. [Apparently in collaboration with Rowe.]

JACOB, GILES.
F. Love in a Wood: or, The Country 'Squire 12° 1714 (by G. J.).

JACOB, Sir HILDEBRAND.
T. The Fatal Constancy (D.L. April 1723) 8° 1723.
1723. D.L. M. 22/4, T. 23, F. 26, M. 29. 1724. W. 12/2, Th. 13.

—. The Nest of Plays; Consisting of three Comedies. viz. The Prodigal Reform'd, The Happy Constancy, and The Tryal of Conjugal Love...Being the first Play licensed by the Lord Chamberlain since the last Act concerning the Stage (C.G. Jan. 1737/8) 8° 1738.
1738. C.G. W. 25/1.

JEFFREYS, GEORGE.
T. Edwin (L.[2] Feb. 1723/4) 8° 1724.
1724. M. 24/2, T. 25; T. 3/3, Th. 5.

T. Merope (L.[2] Feb. 1730/1) 8° 1731.
1731. L.[2] S. 27/2; M. 1/3, T. 2.

O. The Triumph of Truth 4° 1754 (in Miscellanies).

JOHNSON, CHARLES.

C. The Gentleman-Cully (L.¹ *c.* Dec. 1701) 4° 1702 (anon.).
    No records of first performance; published Jan. 15, 1701/2
    (*Flying Post*).

C. Fortune in her Wits 4° 1705 (anon.).

T. Love and Liberty...As it is to be Acted at the Theatre Royal in
    Drury Lane 4° 1709.

T. and F. The Force of Friendship...To which is added a Farce,
    called Love in a Chest (H.¹ April 1710) 4° 1710.
    1710. H.¹ Th. 20/4; M. 1/5.

C. The Generous Husband: or, The Coffee House Politician (D.L.
    Jan. 1710/11) 4° (1711).
    1711. D.L. S. 20/1, M. 22.

C. The Wife's Relief: or, The Husband's Cure (D.L. Nov. 1711)
    4° 1712; 12° 1736.
    1711. D.L. M. 12/11, T. 13, Th. 15–T. 20; S. 1/12, F. 14,
    S. 29. 1712. M. 4/2. 1713. T. 3/11, W. 11. 1715. L.² F. 7/10,
    S. 8, W. 19; F. 25/11. 1717. F. 11/1; T. 26/11. 1718. M. 27/1;
    S. 5/4. 1722. H.² M. 17/12. 1728. L.² F. 19/7. 1736. T. 5/10,
    Th. 7, S. 16; D.L. W. 13/10–M. 18, W. 20; W. 10/11. 1737.
    T. 25/1; L.² F. 11/2; M. 16/5. 1741. G.F. M. 2/2, F. 6. 1742.
    M. 4/1.

Play. The Successful Pyrate (D.L. Nov. 1712) 4° 1713 (*bis*).
    1712. D.L. F. 7/11–T. 11; T. 16/12.

T. The Victim (D.L. Jan. 1713/4) 12° 1714 (*bis*); 12° 1717 (4th).
    1714. D.L. T. 5/1–M. 11.

C. The Country Lasses, or, The Custom of the Manor (D.L. Feb.
    1714/5) 12° 1715; 8° 1753; 12° 1768; 8° 1779.
    1715. D.L. F. 4/2–M. 7, W. 9. 1729. D.L. F. 27/6; F. 4/7,
    T. 8; S. 9/8. 1730. M. 11/5; W. 18/11. 1734. G.F. M. 2/12,
    T. 3, S. 14. 1735. T. 4/3. 1736 M. 29/3; L.² T. 14/12, W. 15,
    W. 22. 1739. C.G. T. 27/3, S. 31; M. 2/4; T. 15/5. 1740. Th. 15/5,
    S. 17, W. 28; S. 15/11; T. 16/12. 1741. T. 5/5. 1745. G.F.
    T. 2/4; F. 3/5. 1746. C.G. T. 22/4. 1747. F. 6/2; S. 19/12,
    S. 26.

F. The Cobler of Preston (D.L. Feb. 1715/6) 8° 1716 (3 edns.); 12°
    1767 (Dublin).
    1716. D.L. F. 3/2–M. 6, W. 8–F. 10, T. 14, Th. 16, S. 18,
    T. 21, Th. 23, S. 25, M. 27; F. 6/4; Th. 25/10.

T. The Sultaness (D.L. Feb. 1716/7) 8° 1717 (*bis*).
    1717. D.L. M. 25/2–Th. 28.

C. The Masquerade (D.L. Jan. 1718/9) 8° (1719, *bis*).
    1719. D.L. F. 16/1–Th. 22, T. 27.

C. Love in a Forest (D.L. Jan. 1722/3) 8° 1723.
    1723. D.L. W. 9/1–T. 15.

C. The Female Fortune-Teller (L.¹ Jan. 1725/6) 8° 1726 (*bis*).
    1726. L.¹ F. 7/1–Th. 13, F. 21.

(B.O.) The Village Opera (D.L. Feb. 1728/9) 8° 1729 (*bis*); 12° 1729
    (Dublin).
    1729. D.L. Th. 6/2–M. 10, Th. 27. 1730. H.² Th. 8/1, F. 9,
    F. 16.

T. The Tragedy of Medæa...With a Preface containing some Re-
    flections on the New Way of Criticism (D.L. Dec. 1730) 8° 1731.
    1730. D.L. F. 11/12–M. 14.

*B.O. The Ephesian Matron.
    1732. D.L. M. 17/4, S. 29.
Play. Cælia: Or, The Perjur'd Lover (D.L. Dec. 1732) 8° 1733.
    1732. D.L. M. 11/12, T. 12

JOHNSON, HENRY.
  T. Romulus 8° 1724.

JOHNSON, SAMUEL (of Cheshire).
  (Burl.) Hurlothrumbo; or, The Super-Natural (H.² March 1729) 8°
    1729 (*bis*); 8° 1729 (Dublin).
    1729. H.² S. 29/3; M. 7/4, W. 9–W. 23, F. 25, S. 26, T. 29, W. 30;
    S. 3/5, M. 5, Th. 8–W. 14, S. 17, M. 19. 1730. Th. 29/1; W. 18/2;
    M. 20/4. 1731. F. 20/8 (evidently dismissed). 1732. M. 1/5. 1741.
    F. 15/5.
*(Burl.) The Cheshire Comics, or, The Amours of Lord Flame.
    1730. H.² M. 23/2, W. 25, F. 27; W. 16/4.
  (Burl.) The Blazing Comet; The Mad Lovers; or, The Beauties of
    the Poets (H.² March 1731/2) 8° 1732.
    1732. H.² Th. 2/3 (called "A Dramatic Everything"), F. 3,
    M. 6, M. 27; W. 19/4 (with a new scene), Th. 20, W. 26.
*"An Opera in a Comedy." All Alive and Merry, or Men in Pursuit
    of Money.
    1737. L.² M. 10/1–M. 17.
*O.C. The Fool Made Wise.
    1741. H.² S. 11/4, M. 13, S. 18.
*F. Sir John Falstaff in Masquerade.
    1741. H.² S. 11/4, M. 13, S. 18.

JOHNSON, Dr SAMUEL.
  T. Irene (D.L. Feb. 1748/9) 8° 1749; 8° 1754 (2nd); 8° 1781.
    1749. D.L. M. 6/2–M. 20 (as *Mahomet and Irene*).
KELLY, JOHN.
  C. The Married Philosopher (L.² March 1732) 8° 1732 (by a gentle
    man of the Temple); 8° 1732.
    1732. L.² S. 25/3, T. 28; S. 1/4, S. 15, Th. 20.
  (B.O.) Timon in Love: or, The Innocent Theft. A Comedy. Taken
    from Timon Misanthrope of Sieur de Lisle (D.L. Dec. 1733) 8°
    1733 (anon.).
    1733. D.L. W. 5/12, Th. 6, S. 8.
  (B.O.) The Plot (D.L. Jan. 1734/5) 8° 1735 (anon.).
    1735. D.L. W. 22/1, F. 24, S. 25.
*(F.) The Fall of Bob; or, The Oracle of Gin. A Tragedy by Timothy
    Scrub, of Rag Fair, Esq. [*Biographia Dramatica* says acted at
    H.² and printed 12° 1736; on Th. 6/1, 1737 *The Battles of Parnassus
    and Fall of Bob* was advertised to be acted on Th. 13 or F. 14;
    for these see the supplementary notes.
  (B.O.) The Levee. A Farce...As it was Offer'd to, and accepted for
    Representation by the Master of the Old-House in Drury-Lane,
    but by the Inspector of Farces denied a Licence 8° 1741; 8° 1744.

KILLIGREW, THOMAS.
  C. Chit-Chat (D.L. Feb. 1718/9) 8° (1719); 12° 1719 (Hague?); 8°
    (1719, 2nd).
    1719. D.L. S. 14/2–T. 17, Th. 19, S. 21–T. 24, Th. 26, S. 28;
    M. 2/3, Th. 19; F. 20/11; Richmond S. 6/6.

KNIPE, CHARLES.
F. The City Ramble; or, The Humours of the Compter (L.² June
    1715) 12° 1715; 12° 1736.
        1715. L.² Th. 2/6, M. 6, T. 7; F. 8/7; M. 17/10; F. 4/11, M.
        28; S. 31/12. 1736. C.G. S. 27/3.

LAMBERT, BARROWDALE.
*Dr. Piece. The Wreckers 8° 1747.

LANGFORD, ABRAHAM.
*Ent. The Judgment of Paris 8° 1730 (appended to Bellaria; or the
    Fair Unfortunate).
B.O. The Lover his own Rival (G.F. Feb. 1735/6) 8° 1736; 8° 1753.
        1736. G.F. T. 10/2–F. 13, M. 16; Th. 18/3, M. 29; Th. 1/4,
        Th. 8, T. 13. 1740. Punch's theatre W. 2/1. 1743. May F. Yeates,
        Warner and Rosoman, May.

LEDIARD, THOMAS.
O. Britannia. An English Opera...With the Representation of a
    Transparent Theatre, Illuminated, and adorn'd with a great
    Number of Emblems, Mottoes, Devices and Inscriptions, and
    embellish'd with Machines, in a Manner entirely New. The
    Musick compos'd after the Italian Manner, By Mr. Lampe (H.²
    Nov. 1732) 4° 1732.
        1732. H.² W. 15/11, M. 20, Th. 23, M. 27.

LEIGH, JOHN.
C. Kensington-Gardens; Or, The Pretenders (L.² Nov. 1719) 8° 1720.
        1719. L.² Th. 26/11 (acted about 7 times).
F. Hob's Wedding. A New Farce of Two Acts. Being the Sequel
    of the Country Wake (L.² Jan. 1719/20) 12° 1720 (anon.).
        1720. L.² M. 11/1 (acted 7 times). 1723. H.² M. 28/1.

LEVERIDGE, RICHARD.
M. The Comick Masque of Pyramus and Thisbe (L.² April 1716) 8°
    1716.
        1716. L.² W. 11/4; F. 26/10, M. 29; W. 21/11, Th. 22; S. 29/12.
        1717. F. 25/1, Th. 31; S. 23/3. 1723. Richmond M. 9/9.

LEWIS, DAVID.
T. Philip of Macedon (L.² April 1727) 8° 1727; 12° 1727 (Dublin).
        1727. L.² S. 29/4; T. 2/5, Th. 11.

LILLO, GEORGE.
(D.O.) Silvia; or, The Country Burial. An Opera (L.² Nov. 1730)
    8° 1730 (Dublin, anon.); 8° 1731 (bis).
        1730. L.² T. 10/11–Th. 12. 1736. C.G. Th. 18/3 (2 acts).
T. The London Merchant: or, The History of George Barnwell
    (D.L. June 1731) 8° 1731; 8° 1731 (2nd); 8° 1731 (3rd); 8° 1740
    (7th); 12° (1750?); 12° 1763 (12th).
        1731. D.L. T. 22/6, F. 25, W. 30; F. 2/7, T. 6, F. 9, T. 13,
        F. 16, T. 20, F. 23, T. 27, F. 30; T. 3/8, W. 11, Th. 13, M. 16,
        F. 20; S. 16/10, S. 23, Th. 28, F. 29; Th. 11/11; Th. 9/12; S.F.
        Great theatrical booth, Sept.; G.F. M. 27/9, W. 29; F. 1/10, M. 4,
        F. 15; W. 10/11, M. 29. 1732. Th. 13/1; T. 15/2; Th. 13/4; M. 16/10;
        Th. 28/12; D.L. Th. 20/1; M. 10/4; W. 17/5, M. 29; M. 21/8;
        Th. 26/10; H.² Th. 1/6. 1733. G.F. S. 6/1; F. 19/10; H.² M.
        26/3; W. 26/12; C.G. T. 7/8, F. 10, F. 17; D.L. W. 10/10. 1735.
        G.F. S. 22/2; W. 8/10; York buildings T. 3/6; W. 1/10; D.L.

T. 1/7, F. 4; F. 26/12; L.² F. 11/7; F. 1/8. 1736. G.F. M. 1/3; H.² M. 26/4; L.² T. 9/11. 1737. T. 8/2; W. 22/6. 1740. C.G. F. 23/5; G.F. W. 29/10; F. 7/11. 1741. G.F. S. 28/2; T. 31/3; F. 2/10; T. 8/12; D.L. M. 1/6. 1742. G.F. T. 23/3; James-street M. 8/11. 1743. D.L. S. 1/10; T. 27/12. 1744. W. 16/5; G.F. T. 11/12. 1745. Th. 17/1; M. 25/11; T. 10/12. 1746. T. 11/2; Th. 13/11. 1747. M. 2/2, Th. 19. 1749. D.L. M. 8/5; F. 22/9, S. 23, S. 30; T. 31/10; T. 26/12; C.G. T. 26/12.

T. The Christian Hero (D.L. Jan. 1734/5) 8° 1735 (bis).
    1735. D.L. M. 13/1–Th. 16.

T. Fatal Curiosity. A True Tragedy of three Acts (H.² May 1736) 8° 1737; 12° 1762 (2nd); 12° 1768; 12° (N.D. 8th); 8° 1780; 8° 1783 (altered by Colman).
    1736. H.² Th. 27/5–M. 31; T. 1/6, W. 2, M. 21. 1737. M. 2/5 (revised). 1741. G.F. S. 14/2, T. 17; T 3/3. 1742. James-street M. 22/11. [Generally acted under the title, Guilt its own Punishment or Fatal Curiosity.]

Play. Marina...Taken from Pericles Prince of Tyre (C.G. Aug. 1738) 8° 1738.
    1738. C.G. T. 1/8, F. 4, T. 8.

T. Elmerick: or, Justice Triumphant (D.L. Feb. 1739/40) 8° 1740.
    1740. D.L. S. 23/2–T. 26, Th. 28; S. 1/3, M. 3.

M. Britannia and Batavia 8° 1740.

T. Arden of Feversham (D.L. July 1759) 12° 1762; 12° 1763 (Dublin).

LOCKMAN, JOHN.
O. Rosalinda, A Musical Drama (Hickford's room Jan. 1739/40) 4° 1740.
    1740. Hickford's room F. 4/1, F. 11, F. 18, F. 25; Th. 27/3; F. 18/4, F. 25.

LYNCH, FRANCIS.
C. The Independent Patriot: or, Musical Folly (L.² Feb. 1736/7) 8° 1737.
    1737. L.² S. 12/2, M. 14, T. 15.

*C. The Man of Honour (see *Biographia Dramatica* iii. 14).

LYON, WILLIAM.
*F. The Wrangling Lovers: or, Like Master like Man 8° 1745 (Edinburgh).

MACKLIN, CHARLES.
H.T. King Henry VII: or, The Popish Impostor (D.L. Jan. 1745/6) 8° 1746.
    1746. D.L. S. 18/1–T. 21.

*F. A Will and No Will, or A Bone for the Lawyers.
    1746. D.L. W. 23/4.

*F. The Suspicious Husband Criticized, or, The Plague of Envy.
    1747. D.L. T. 24/3, Th. 26; Th. 30/4.

F. The Fortune-Hunters....As it was Acted at Mac L—n's Amphi-theatre 8° 1750.
[For the last work see E. A. Parry, *Charles Macklin*, p. 196 where it is cited as the F. H. or The Widow Bewitched. For later works see the Hand-list of Plays, 1750–1800.]

MACSWINY, or SWINY, or SWINEY, OWEN.
C. The Quacks, or, Love's the Physician...As it was Acted (after

being twice forbid) at the Theatre Royal in Drury-Lane (D.L.
March 1704/5) 4° 1705; 8° 1745.

    1705. D.L. Th. 29/3; M. 9/4, T. 10, Th. 19; Th. 28/6; T. 10/7.
1745. S. 30/3.

MADDEN, Dr SAMUEL.

T. Themistocles, the Lover of his Country (L.² Feb. 1728/9) 8°
1729 (anon. 3 edns).

    1729. L.² M. 10/2-T. 18, Th. 20.

MALLET, DAVID.

T. Eurydice (D.L. Feb. 1730/1) 8° 1731 (bis); 12° 1735; 8° 1759;
8° 1780.

    1731. D.L. M. 22/2-S. 27; M. 1/3, T. 2, Th. 4, S. 6, T. 9,
Th. 11, S. 13; M. 26/4.

T. Mustapha (D.L. Feb. 1738/9) 8° 1739; 8° 1760.

    1739. D.L. T. 13/2-Th. 22, S. 24, T. 27, W. 28; Th. 1/3, S. 3.

M. Alfred (Cliefdon Aug. 1740) 8° 1740; as an opera (D.L. March
1744/5) 8° 1745; 8° 1751; Alfred the Great. A Drama for Music
4° 1753; 8° 1754.

    Written in collaboration with JAMES THOMSON. 1740.
Cliefdon F. 1/8. 1745 D.L. W. 20/3; W. 3/4.

M. Britannia (D.L. May 1755) 8° 1755.

T. Elvira (D.L. Jan. 1762/3) 8° 1763.

MANLEY, Mrs MARY DE LA RIVIÈRE.

    [For her seventeenth century works see the Hand-list of Plays,
1660–1700.]

T. Almyna: or, The Arabian Vow (H.¹ Dec. 1706) 4° 1707 (anon.);
4° 1717. 1706. H.¹ M. 16/12-W. 18.

T. Lucius, the First Christian King of Britain (D.L. May 1717) 4°
1717; 4° 1720 (2nd).

    1717. D.L. S. 11/5, M. 13, S. 18. 1720. W. 27/4.

B.O. The Court Legacy. A New Ballad Opera 8° 1733 (by the author
of the New Atlantis).

MANNING, FRANCIS.

C. The Generous Choice (L.¹ c. Feb. 1699/1700) 4° 1700.

    No record of first performance; published March 19, 1699/1700
(Post Boy).

C. All for the Better: Or, The Infallible Cure (D.L. c. Oct. 1702)
4° 1703 (anon.).

MARSH, CHARLES.

T. Amasis King of Egypt (C.G. Aug. 1738) 8° 1738.

    1738. C.G. T. 22/8, W. 30.

    [For his later alterations of Shakespeare see the Hand-list of Plays,
1750–1800.]

MARTYN, BENJAMIN.

T. Timoleon (D.L. Jan. 1728/30) 8° 1730; 8° 1730 (2nd); 8° 1730
(Dublin).

    1730. D.L. M. 26/1-Th. 29, S. 31; M. 2/2-M. 9, M. 16, T. 17;
W. 13/5; T. 17/11. 1733. G.F. T. 20/2, Th. 22, S. 24, T. 27.

MAXWELL, JOHN.

(B.O.) The Tepan: or, Virtue Rewarded 8° 1739 (York, anon.).

(B.O.) The Shepherd's Opera 8° 1739 (York, anon.).

T. The Faithful Pair; or Virtue in Distress 8° 1740 (York).

T.   The Royal Captive 8° 1745 (York).
T.   The Loves of Prince Emilius and Louisa 8° 1755 (York).
T.   A New Tragedy, called The Distressed Virgin 8° 1761 (York).

MENDEZ, MOSES.
(F.) The Double Disappointment: or, The Fortune Hunters. A
    Comedy (D.L. March 1745/6) 8° 1760 (anon.).
        1746. D.L. T. 18/3, S. 22; Th. 3/4, M. 7, F. 11, M. 14, Th. 17,
    T. 22; S. 3/5, W. 7; S. 1/11, T. 4, F. 7–T. 11, S. 15–T. 18, Th. 20,
    S. 22, M. 24, W. 26; S. 6/12, T. 9, S. 27. 1747. T. 20/1, S. 24;
    Th. 5/2; M. 2/3, M. 23; F. 10/4, T. 21, S. 25, T. 28; F. 8/5,
    Th. 14, S. 16; S. 19/9, T. 22; S. 17/10, W. 21; W. 4/11, T. 10;
    T. 15/12, T. 29. 1748. W. 13/1; Th. 3/3; T. 12/4, M. 18, S. 23;
    M. 9/5, W. 25.
Mus. Ent. The Chaplet (D.L. Dec. 1749) 8° 1749; 8° 1750; 12° 1753;
    8° 1756 (2nd); 8° 1759 (3rd).
        1749. D.L. S. 2/12–T. 19, Th. 21, S. 23, Th. 28. The run
    continued into 1750, and the piece was frequently revived.
    [For his later works see the Hand-list of Plays, 1750–1800.]

MESTAYER, HENRY.
T.   The Perfidious Brother 12° 1716; 12° 1720 (2nd).

MICHELBURNE, JOHN.
T.C. Ireland Preserv'd: or The Siege of London-Derry. Together
    with the Troubles of the North. F. 1705 (anon.); F. 1708 (written by
    the then Governour); *8° 1739 (Dublin); 8° 1750 (*bis*); 12° 1774.

MILLER, Rev. JAMES.
C.   The Humours of Oxford (D.L. Jan. 1729/30) 8° 1730 (anon.).
        1730. D.L. F. 9/1–S. 17.
C.   The Mother-in-Law: Or, The Doctor the Disease (H.² Feb.
    1733/4) 8° 1734 (anon.); 8° 1734 (2nd, To which is added A New
    Scene of the Consultation of Physicians).
        1734. H.² T. 12/2–T. 26, Th. 28; S. 2/3, T. 5, Th. 7, S. 9;
    D.L. T. 12/3; M. 1/4; F. 3/5; S. 19/10; F. 1/11, M. 18. 1735.
    S. 4/1; M. 17/3; Th. 23/10. 1736. M. 23/2; W. 2/6; F. 12/11;
    W. 29/12. 1737. W. 25/5; M. 24/10. 1739. S. 28/4. 1740. Th. 7/2.
C.   The Man of Taste (D.L. March 1734/5) 8° 1735 (*bis*); 8° 1744.
        1735. D.L. Th. 6/3 (as The M. of T. or The Guardians), S. 8,
    T. 11, S. 15, T. 18, T. 25, S. 29; M. 7/4–Th. 10, S. 12, T. 15,
    Th. 17, Th. 24, W. 30; S. 3/5, M. 12, Th. 15, F. 16, M. 19,
    W. 21, M. 26, T. 27, W. 28; M. 2/6; T. 9/9; S. 22/11; Th. 4/12,
    M. 22. 1736. Th. 26/2; F. 30/4; S. 22/5. 1737. F. 15/4; F. 20/5.
    1738. S. 13/5. 1739. W. 25/4.
(T.C.) The Universal Passion. A Comedy (D.L. Feb. 1736/7) 8°
    1737 (anon.).
        1737. D.L. M. 28/2; T. 1/3, Th. 3, M. 7, T. 8, M. 14, M. 21,
    Th. 24, M. 28, Th. 31. 1741. S. 14/3; F. 17/4.
Dr. Piece. The Coffee House (D.L. Jan. 1737/8) 8° 1737; 12° 1743;
    8° 1781.
        1738. D.L. Th. 26/1.
C.   Art and Nature (D.L. Feb. 1737/8) 8° 1738.
        1738. D.L. Th. 16/2.
Dr. Fable. An Hospital for Fools (D.L. Nov. 1739) 8° 1739; 8° 1781.
        1739. D.L. Th. 15/11, S. 17.
    The Works of Molière 12° 1739 (translated by Miller and H. Baker).

T. Mahomet the Impostor (D.L. April 1744) 8° 1744; 8° 1745; 8°
1766 (4th, with new improvements); 8° 1776; 8° 1778.
 In this play Miller collaborated with Dr *JOHN HOADLY.*
1744. D.L. W. 25/4–F. 27; S. 24/11.

(B.O.) The Picture: or, The Cuckold in Conceit (D.L. Feb. 1744/5)
8° 1745.
 1745. D.L. M. 11/2.

MITCHELL, JOSEPH.
 [For The Fatal Extravagance, see *AARON HILL.*]

B.O. The Highland Fair; or, Union of the Clans…With the Musick,
which wholly consists of Select Scots Tunes (D.L. March 1730/1)
8° 1731.
 1731. D.L. S. 20/3, T. 23, S. 27; T. 20/4.

MOLLOY, CHARLES.
C. The Perplex'd Couple: Or, Mistake upon Mistake (L.² Feb.
1714/5) 12° 1715 (anon.).
 1715. L.² W. 16/2–F. 18. From the last-mentioned bill it
appears that this comedy was originally called *All Jealous.*

C. The Coquet: Or, The English Chevalier (L.² April 1718) 8° 1718.
 1718. L.² S. 19/4–T. 22.

(F.) The Half-Pay Officers (L.² Jan. 1719/20) 12° 1720 (anon.).
 1720. L.² M. 11/1 (acted 7 times). 1723. H.² M. 28/1. 1730.
H.² Th. 12/3.

MOORE, EDWARD.
C. The Foundling (D.L. Feb. 1747/8) 8° 1748; 8° 1755; 12° 1786.
 1748. D.L. S. 13/2–T. 23, Th. 25, S. 27, M. 29; S. 5/3, Th. 17;
S. 16/4; W. 11/5. 1749. F. 20/1, S. 21; S. 11/3.
 [For his later works see the Hand-list of Plays, 1750–1800.]

MOORE, Sir THOMAS.
T. Mangora, King of the Timbusians. Or, The Faithful Couple
(L.² Dec. 1717) 4° 1717.
 1717. L.² S. 14/12–W. 18.

MORELL, Dr THOMAS.
T. Hecuba, translated from the Greek 8° 1749.

MORRIS, ROBERT.
(Pol.) T. Fatal Necessity; or, Liberty Regain'd 8° 1742.

MOSS, THEOPHILUS.
C. The General Lover 8° 1749.

MOTTEUX, PETER ANTHONY.
 [For his seventeenth century works see the Hand-list of Plays,
1660–1700.]

Int. The Words of a New Interlude, called the Four Seasons, or Love
in Every Age. And of all the Musical Entertainments, in the New
Opera, called The Island Princess (D.L. *c.* Jan. 1698/9) 4° 1699.

Int. Acis and Galatea (D.L. 1701) *4° 1701; 8° 1723.
 No record of first performance. 1702. L.¹ 11/12. 1703. Th. 11/2;
W. 28/4. 1704. S. 12/2; F. 14/7. 1705. S. 31/3. 1706. H.¹ M. 1/4,
F. 26. 1709. S. 12/11, S. 19; Th. 22/12, S. 31. 1710. S. 21/1.
1715. L.² T. 22/11, Th. 24, M. 28; F. 16/12. 1716. F. 13/1;
S. 14/4. 1723. D.L. T. 16/7, F. 19, F. 26, T. 30; T. 6/8, F. 9,
F. 16. 1724. T. 5/5, F. 15, M. 18, M. 25; F. 30/10. 1725. M.
17/5, M. 24. The comic part, renamed *The Country Wedding,* was

acted at D.L. in July 1714 and at C.G. in March 1738/9. See
Roger and Joan under Anonymous Plays.

Int. Britain's Happiness...Perform'd at both the Theatres. Being part
of the Entertainment Subscrib'd for by the Nobility 4° 1704.

C. Farewel Folly: or, The Younger the Wiser...With A Musical
Interlude, call'd The Mountebank: or, The Humours of the Fair
(D.L. Jan. 1704/5) 4° 1707 (anon.).
> 1705. D.L. Th. 18/1–T. 23; W. 7/2.

MOTTLEY, JOHN.

T. The Imperial Captives (L.² Feb. 1719/20) 8° 1720 (3 editions).
> 1720. L.² M. 29/2; Th. 3/3 (3rd).

T. Antiochus (L.² April 1721) 8° 1721 (*bis*).
> 1721. L.² Th. 13/4–S. 15.

(B.O.) Penelope. An English Opera (H.² May 1728) 8° 1728.
> In this Mottley was assisted by Cooke. 1728. H.² W. 8/5,
Th. 9, F. 17.

(B.O.) The Craftsman, or Weekly Journalist. A Farce (H.² Oct. 1728)
8° 1729.
> 1728. H.² T. 15/10, W. 16, S. 19, S. 26, Th. 31; F. 1/11. 1731.
G.F. M. 15/2 (marked as new), T. 16.

C. The Widow Bewitch'd (G.F. June 1730) 8° 1730 (anon.).
> 1730. G.F. M. 8/6–Th. 11, M. 15, M. 22, T. 23; Th. 2/7.

NESBIT, G.

*T. Caledon's Tears; or, Wallace 12° 1733 (Edinburgh).

NEWTON, JAMES.

C. Alexis's Paradise; or, a Trip to the Garden of Love at Vaux-Hall
8° (1722?).

NORRIS, HENRY.

C. The Royal Merchant; or, The Beggar's Bush (D.L. June 1705)
4° 1706 (by H. N.).
> 1705. D.L. T. 12/6, T. 19, S. 30; S. 6/10; S. 1/12, W. 26.
1706. F. 1/2; Th. 14/3; S. 25/5; H.¹ T. 22/10; F. 8/11. 1707.
H.¹ F. 14/2; F. 14/11. 1708. D.L. T. 23/3. 1710. D.L. S. 5/4;
Greenwich S. 12/8; H.¹ F. 17/11. 1712. D.L. F. 25/1. 1713.
W. 10/6; F. 13/11. 1714. F. 17/12. 1715. W. 7/12. 1716. L.²
W. 4/1, M. 9; M. 5/3; S. 21/4; F. 8/6; D.L. T. 24/1. 1717. L.²
T. 15/1; F. 22/11. 1718. W. 19/2; Th. 15/5. 1719. S. 21/2;
T. 5/5; Th. 5/11; M. 28/12. 1720. S. 30/4; M. 23/5; Th. 6/10.
1721. Th. 1/6. 1723. F. 11/1, M. 21; M. 11/3, S. 23; Th. 9/5,
M. 20; S. 26/10; F. 15/11; S. 21/12. 1724. T. 14/1; T. 11/2;
T. 10/3; T. 19/5; W. 7/10; D.L. F. 16/10; T. 1/12. 1725. L.²
M. 15/2; F. 9/4; W. 12/5; W. 29/9; M. 22/11. 1726. Th. 6/1,
T. 25; S. 12/3; M. 23/5; M. 19/9; W. 28/12. 1727. T. 28/2;
M. 9/10. 1728. Th. 16/5. 1729. M. 20/1; T. 18/11. 1730. W. 14/1;
W. 20/5; W. 21/10; T. 1/12; G.F. W. 21/10; W. 9/12. 1731.
M. 11/1; L.² W. 10/2; T. 25/5; F. 15/10; M. 6/12. 1732. Th. 20/1;
M. 13/3; T. 16/5. 1733. C.G. M. 2/4; T. 15/5; M. 17/12. 1734.
T. 29/1. 1735. Th. 13/2; T. 15/4; F. 31/10; G.F. M. 24/3; L.²
W. 14/5. 1736. C.G. T. 3/2; F. 14/5. 1738. F. 6/1; T. 4/4; F.
17/11; T. 26/12. 1739. M. 12/2; M. 21/5; T. 20/11, F. 30;
Th. 27/12. 1740. M. 18/2; F. 9/5; F. 3/10; F. 26/12; D.L. W.
29/10–F. 31. 1741. C.G. Th. 26/11; M. 28/12. 1742. T. 11/5;
T. 21/12, T. 28. 1743. Th. 17/2; M. 18/4; W. 5/10; Th. 15/12.

1744. T. 14/2; M. 30/4; G.F. S. 22/12, S. 29. 1745. F. 1/2;
C.G. W. 16/10; M. 23/12. 1746. G.F. W. 1/1; F. 14/11; C.G.
S. 3/5. 1747. T. 17/3; G.F. Th. 9/4. 1748. C.G. W. 27/1; Th. 25/2;
W. 16/11. 1749. Th. 12/1; Th. 9/11; S. 2/12.
*F. The Deceit (Smock Alley, Dublin) 12° 1723.

ODELL, THOMAS.
C. The Chimæra (L.² Jan. 1720/1) 8° 1721 (anon.).
    1721. L.² Th. 19/1 (as The C. or A Hue and Cry to Change
    Alley; acted 3 times).
(B.O.) The Patron: Or, The Statesman's Opera (H.² May 1729) 8°
    (1729); 8° 1729 (Dublin).
    1729. H.² W. 7/5.
F. The Smugglers (H.² May 1729) 8° 1729; 8° 1729 (Dublin, To
    which is added, The Art of Dancing < by Soame Jenyns >).
    1729. H.² W. 7/5.
C. The Prodigal: Or, Recruits for the Queen of Hungary (H.² Oct.
    1744) 8° 1744.
    1744. H.² Th. 11/10.

ODINGSELLS, GABRIEL.
C. The Bath Unmask'd (L.² Feb. 1724/5) 8° 1725; 12° 1725 (Dublin);
    12° 1735.
    1725. L.² S. 27/2; M. 1/3, T. 2, Th. 4, S. 6–T. 9, T. 16; S. 17/4,
    F. 30; Th. 27/5; T. 26/10. 1728. Th. 21/3.
C. The Capricious Lovers (L.² Dec. 1725) 8° 1726.
    1725. L.² W. 8/12–F. 10.
(B.O.) Bayes's Opera (D.L. March 1730) 8° 1730.
    1730. D.L. M. 30/3, T. 31; W. 1/4. 1731. F. 23/7.

OLDMIXON, JOHN.
Past. Amintas, a Pastoral. Made English out of Italian 4° 1698.
D.O. The Grove, or, Love's Paradice (D.L. c. Feb. 1699/1700) 4° 1700.
    1700. D.L. 19/2. Published March 16, 1699/1700 (Post Man).
T. The Governour of Cyprus (L.¹ 1703) 4° 1703.

OWEN, ROBERT.
T. Hypermnestra, or, Love in Tears 4° 1703; 12° 1722 (2nd).

OZELL, JOHN.
T. The Cid; or, The Heroic Daughter 12° 1714.
    Two Tragedies, viz. Britannicus; and Alexander the Great 12°
    1714.
F. The Litigants 12° 1715.
T. Cato of Utica (L.² May 1716) 12° 1716; 12° 1719.
    1716. L.² M. 14/5–W. 16; F. 21/12.
C. The Fair of Saint-Germain 8° 1718.
T. Manlius Capitolinus...Done from the French of M. de la Fosse
    12° 1719.
C. L'Avare...New done into English 8° 1732.
C. L'Embaras des Richesses...The English Translation by Mr.
    Ozell 12° 1735.
C. The Comedy of the Cheats of Scapin 12° 1792.

PATERSON, JOSEPH.
(B.O.) The Raree Show, or the Fox trap't. An Opera 8° 1739 (York);
    8° 1740 (Chester, 2nd with alterations).

PATERSON, WILLIAM.
T.   Arminius 8° 1740.

PATRICK, SAMUEL.
Terence's Comedies, translated into English Prose 8° 1745; 8°
1750; 8° 1767.

PECK, FRANCIS.
Dr. Piece.   Herod the Great 4° 1740 (in New Memoirs of the Life
and Poetical Works of Mr. John Milton).

PENNECUIK, ALEXANDER.
*Past.   Corydon and Cochrania 1732.

PHILIPS, AMBROSE.
T.   The Distrest Mother (D.L. March 1711/12) 4° 1712 (*bis*); 12° 1718
(4th); 12° (1723? Hague); 8° 1726 (Hague); 12° 1731; 12° 1734
(7th); 12° 1735; 12° 1748; 12° 1751; 8° 1756.
    1712. D.L. M. 17/3, T. 18, Th. 20, S. 22–T. 25, Th. 27, S. 29;
S. 27/9; S. 18/10; T. 25/11; M. 22/12. 1713. T. 10/2; M. 13/4;
S. 24/10. 1714. Th. 1/4. 1715. S. 19/2; M. 7/3; M. 9/5; F. 2/12. 1716.
Th. 16/2; T. 23/10. 1717. T. 15/1. 1718. T. 20/5. 1719. F. 17/4,
S. 25. 1720. S. 23/4. 1721. S. 21/1. 1722. F. 13/4; Th. 18/10.
1723. S. 19/1; S. 30/3; W. 27/11. 1724. M. 27/1; S. 29/2; T.
20/10; S. 5/12. 1725. S. 20/2; T. 26/10. 1726. T. 4/1; S. 19/2;
Th. 14/4. 1727. M. 16/1; M. 13/3; F. 14/4; T. 24/10. 1728.
T. 8/10; S. 16/11, S. 23. 1729. Th. 16/1; T. 4/3; Th. 17/4.
1730. F. 20/11. 1731. W. 3/2; Th. 13/5; G.F. M. 15/2, T. 16,
Th. 25; T. 7/12. 1732. D.L. F. 9/6; T. 7/11. 1733. W. 10/1;
G.F. W. 17/1. 1734. D.L. F. 8/2; G.F. M. 18/2; F. 26/4; Th. 12/12.
1735. C.G. Th. 9/1, F. 10, Th. 16; Th. 13/11; W. 10/12. 1736.
F. 23/1; W. 4/2; F. 15/10; F. 31/12; G.F. F. 20/2; D.L. T. 23/3.
1737. S. 16/4; S. 7/5; C.G. F. 6/5; F. 7/10. 1738. Th. 12/1;
T. 31/10; S. 9/12; D.L. S. 22/4. 1739. C.G. T. 4/12. 1740.
D.L. S. 19/1; S. 15/3; C.G. W. 13/2; G.F. W. 26/11. 1741.
C.G. T. 17/2; D.L. M. 14/12. 1742. F. 5/2; C.G. M. 29/11,
S. 18/12. 1743. S. 26/2; W. 13/4; D.L. F. 29/4. 1744. C.G. Th.
23/2; D.L. W. 17/10; H.² S. 20/10. 1745. D.L. F. 11/1. 1747.
C.G. S. 4/4, T. 7; F. 1/5. 1748. D.L. Th. 10/3, T. 15. 1749.
C.G. S. 28/1, M. 30; W. 1/2, F. 3, W. 8, Th. 9, S. 11, M. 13,
T. 14, Th. 16; Th. 16/11; D.L. W. 5/4.
T.   The Briton (D.L. Feb. 1721/2) 8° 1722.
    1722. D.L. M. 19/2, T. 20, Th. 22, S. 24–T. 27; Th. 1/3;
T. 3/4.
T.   Humfrey, Duke of Gloucester (D.L. Feb. 1722/3) 8° 1723; 8°
1723 (2nd); 8° 1723 (Dublin). [This and the other two plays were
issued in 8° 1725 as Three Tragedies.]
    1723. D.L. F. 15/2–M. 25.

PHILIPS, JOHN.
T.C.F.   The Earl of Mar Marr'd; With the Humours of Jockey, the
Highlander 8° 1715; 8° 1715 (2nd); 8° 1716 (3rd).
T.C.F.   The Pretender's Flight, or, a Mock Coronation, with the
Humours of the Facetious Harry Saint John...being the Sequel
of the Earl of Mar Marr'd 8° 1716; 8° 1716 (Dublin).
F.   The Inquisition...As it was Acted at Child's Coffee-House. And
the King's-Arms Tavern, In St. Paul's Church-Yard. Wherein

The Controversy between the Bishop of Bangor and Dr. Snape, is fairly Stated, and set in a true Light 8° 1717.

PHILLIPS, EDWARD.
 B.O. The Chambermaid (D.L. Feb. 1729/30) 8° 1730 (anon.); 12° 1735.
    1730. D.L. T. 10/2.
 B.O. The Mock Lawyer (C.G. April 1733) *8° 1733; 12° 1737.
    1733. C.G. F. 27/4; Th. 18/10 (marked as new), F. 19; T. 11/12–
    Th. 13, S. 15, M. 17, W. 19, F. 28, M. 31. 1734. F. 4/1, W. 16,
    W. 23; S. 27/4; Th. 2/5, F. 10, M. 13. 1735. Th. 8/5, M. 26.
    1736. M. 15/3 (1 act); M. 5/4. 1737. Th. 10/3; T. 10/5, Th. 12;
    F. 20/5; M. 10/10, W. 12. 1738. M. 8/5; M. 2/10. 1740. D.L.
    Th. 20/3. 1745. Richmond S. 24/8.
 (B.O.) The Livery Rake and Country Lass. An Opera (May 1733)
    8° 1733. [It is certain that the two pieces mentioned in the bills
    are the same, acted under different titles.]
    1733. D.L. S. 5/5 (The L. R. or the Intriguing Servant); M.
    8/10; H.² M. 15/10 (The L. R. Trapped or the Disappointed
    Country Lass). 1734. D.L. T. 8/1–Th. 10, M. 14 (The L. R.).
    1736. T. 25/5.
 (Pant.) A New Dramatic Entertainment called the Royal Chace: or,
    Merlin's Cave (C.G. Jan. 1735/6) 12° 1736.
    1736. C.G. F. 23/1.
 (B.O.) Briton, Strike Home! or, The Sailor's Rehearsal. A Farce
    (D.L. Dec. 1739) 8° 1739; 8° 1758 (Glasgow).
    1739. D.L. M. 31/12. 1740 B.F. Fawkes, Pinchbeck and
    Tuwins, Aug.
PHILLIPS, R.
 T. The Fatal Inconstancy: or, The Unhappy Rescue 4° 1701.
PHILLIPS, THOMAS.
 M. Love and Glory (D.L. March 1733/4) 8° 1734.
    1734. D.L. Th. 21/3; M. 29/4 (reduced, and renamed Britannia).
 *B.O. The Rival Captains; or, The Impostor Unmasked.
    1736. H.² W. 26/5, M. 31; T. 1/6, W. 2, F. 11, Th. 17, M. 21;
    F. 2/7.
PHILLIPS, Capt. WILLIAM.
 C. St. Stephen's Green Or The Generous Lovers (T.R. Dublin) 4°
    1700 (Dublin anon.); 8° 1720.
 T. Hibernia Freed (L.² Feb. 1721/2) 8° 1722 (anon.).
    1722. L.² T. 13/2, Th. 15, S. 17–T. 20, Th. 22; S. 17/3
 T. Belisarius (L.² April 1724) 8° 1724; 8° 1758 (2nd).
    1724. L.² T. 14/4–M. 20; T. 24/11. 1725. Th. 28/1.
PIX, Mrs [MARY GRIFFITH].
    [For her seventeenth century works see the Hand-list of Plays,
    1660–1700.]
 C. The Beau Defeated: Or The Lucky Younger Brother (L.¹ c.
    March 1699/1700) 4° (1700, anon.).
    No records of performance; published April 18, 1700 (Post
    Boy).
 T. The Double Distress (L.¹ c. March 1700/1) 4° 1701.
    No records of performance; published April 3, 1701 (Post Man).
 T. The Czar of Muscovy (L.¹ c. March 1700/1) 4° 1701.
    No records of performance; published April 15, 1701 (Post
    Man).

    C. The Different Widows: or, Intrigue All-A-Mode (L.[1] c. Nov. 1703) 4° (1703, anon.).
        No records of performance; published Dec. 1703 (*Term Catalogues* iii. 371).
    T. The Conquest of Spain (H.[1] May 1705) 4° 1705 (anon.).
        No records of performance; date from Downes.
    C. The Adventures in Madrid (H.[1] c. June 1706) 4° (1706).

POPPLE, WILLIAM.

    C. The Lady's Revenge: Or, The Rover Reclaim'd (C.G. Jan. 1733/4) 8° 1734; 8° 1734 (Dublin).
        1734. C.G. W. 9/1–S. 12.
    C. The Double Deceit, Or, A Cure for Jealousy (C.G. April 1735) 8° 1736.
        1735. C.G. F. 25/4, M. 28. 1736. Th. 26/2.

POTTER, HENRY.

    (B.O.) The Decoy. An Opera (G.F. Feb. 1732/3) 8° 1733.
        1733. G.F. M. 5/2 (as *The D. or the Harlot's Progress*), T. 6, Th. 8, S. 10.

POWELL, MARTIN.

    *Mock O. Venus and Adonis; or, The Triumphs of Love (Punch's theatre March 1712/3) 8° 1713.
        1713. Punch M. 23/3, W. 25; W. 1/4, Th. 2, T. 14; Th. 14/5.

PRITCHARD, ——.

    Pant. The Fall of Phæton (D.L. Feb. 1735/6) 8° 1736. [This includes Harlequin Restor'd, or, Taste a la Mode.]
        1736. D.L. S. 28/2 (called a Dramatick Masque).

RALPH, JAMES.

    (Burl.) The Fashionable Lady; or Harlequin's Opera. In the Manner of a Rehearsal (G.F. April 1730) 8° 1730.
        1730. G.F. T. 2/4–S. 4, M. 13, S. 18, T. 21–Th. 23; Th. 28/5; T. 2/6, W. 17; M. 27/7; W. 11/11; F. 4/12. 1731. T. 4/5.
    T. The Fall of the Earl of Essex...Alter'd from the Unhappy Favourite of Mr. Banks (G.F. Feb. 1730/1) 8° 1731 (anon.).
        1731. G.F. M. 1/2–Th. 4. 1734. T. 16/4. 1745. W. 2/1, T. 29; F. 13/12.
    F. The Lawyer's Feast (D.L. Dec. 1743) 8° 1744.
        1743. D.L. M. 12/12–W. 14, F. 16.
    F. The Cornish Squire (D.L. Jan. 1733/4) 8° 1734 (altered).
        1734. D.L. Th. 3/1, F. 4, T. 8–Th. 10, W. 23.
    C. The Astrologer (D.L. April 1744) 8° 1744.
        1744. D.L. T. 3/4 [billed for Th. 5, but not performed].

RAMSAY, ALLAN.

    M. The Nuptials 8° 1723; 8° 1723 (*Edinburgh*).
    Past. The Gentle Shepherd. A Scots Pastoral Comedy 12° 1725 (Edinburgh); 8° 1727 (Dublin); 12° 1750 (Glasgow, 10th); 12° 1755 (Edinburgh); 12° 1763 (Newcastle); 8° 1754 (Aberdeen); 12° 1758. [This was first acted at the Grammar School, Haddington, in 1729. The first public performance took place at the Canongate Concert Hall, Edinburgh, in Nov. 1747. In 1754 a Scots company played it at H.[2] See W. J. Lawrence, *Reviving 'The Gentle Shepherd,' The Graphic*, Sept. 1, 1923. Theophilus Cibber's version, *Patie and Peggy*, appeared at D.L. in 1730.]

RANDAL, JOHN.
   B.O. The Disappointment...alter'd from a Farce after the Manner of
      the Beggar's Opera (H.² 1732) 8° 1732 (bis).

REED, JOSEPH.
   *F. The Superannuated Gallant 12° 1745 (Newcastle).
   [For his later works see the Hand-list of Plays, 1750–1800.]

ROBE, Mrs J.
   T. The Fatal Legacy (L.² April 1723) 8° 1723 (anon.).
      1723. L.² T. 23/4, W. 24, F. 26.

ROBINSON, WILLIAM.
   Burl. T. The Intriguing Milliners and Attornies Clerks...As it was de-
      sign'd to be Acted at the Theatre-Royal in Drury-Lane. Written
      in Imitation of the Style and Manner of —— 8° 1738; 8° 1740.

ROWE, NICHOLAS.
   T. The Ambitious Step-Mother (L.¹ c. Dec. 1700) 4° 1701; 8°
      (1701?); 4° 1702 (2nd); 12° (1720, Hague); 12° 1760.
         No record of first performance; published Jan. 29, 1700/1
      (Post Man). 1706. H.¹ F. 6/12. 1715. L.² W. 14/12, F. 30. 1722.
      D.L. Th. 25/1, F. 26.
   T. Tamerlane (L.¹ c. Dec. 1701) 4° 1701; 4° 1702; 4° 1703 (2nd);
      12° (1720, Hague); 12° 1750 (Dublin).
         No record of first performance; published Jan. 6, 1701/2
      (Flying Post) or 26 (London Gazette). 1704. L.¹ Th. 6/4. 1705.
      S. 13/1. 1706. H.¹ T. 19/11. 1708. D.L. Th. 15/4. 1710. T. 7/3;
      Greenwich S. 30/9. 1715. L.² F. 13/5, M. 16, Th. 26; S. 15/10.
      1716. D.L. M. 5/11–S. 10, Th. 15; Th. 6/12, Th. 27. 1717.
      S. 16/3; M. 29/4; M. 4/11, T. 5. 1718. W. 29/1; M. 28/4; T. 4/11,
      W. 5; L.² S. 1/2; T. 11/3; W. 8/10; T. 4/11. 1719. D.L. Th. 1/1;
      Th. 12/3; M. 4/5; Th. 5/11. 1720. F. 4/11, S. 5. 1721. S. 11/2;
      S. 4/11, M. 6; L.² S. 25/4; S. 14/10; S. 4/11. 1722. T. 15/5;
      M. 5/11, T. 6; D.L. M. 21/5; M. 5/11, T. 6. 1723. L.² S. 2/2;
      W. 15/5; M. 4/11, T. 5; D.L. M. 4/11, T. 5. 1724. W. 4/11,
      Th. 5; L.² W. 4/11, Th. 5. 1725. D.L. S. 1/5; Th. 4/11, F. 5;
      L.² Th. 4/11, F. 5. 1726. D.L. F. 4/11, S. 5; L.² F. 4/11, S. 5.
      1727. D.L. Th. 16/2; S. 25/3; Th. 11/5; S. 4/11, M. 6; L.² S. 4/11,
      M. 6. 1728. D.L. T. 13/2; T. 28/5, W. 29; S. 14/9; M. 4/11,
      T. 5; L.² M. 4/11. 1729. D.L. T. 4/2; M. 5/5; W. 31/12; H.²
      F. 2/5; L.² T. 4/11, W. 5. 1730. D.L. Th. 7/5; W. 4/11, Th. 5;
      L.² Th. 4/6; W. 4/11, Th. 5; G.F. Th. 5/11, M. 9, S. 21. 1731.
      D.L. T. 19/1; Th. 4/11, F. 5; T. 28/12; G.F. F. 12/2; Th. 25/3;
      Th. 4/11, F. 5; L.² Th. 4/11, F. 5. 1732. G.F. T. 28/3; S. 4/11,
      M. 6, T. 7, S. 11; S. 30/12; D.L. S. 4/11; L.² S. 4/11, M. 6.
      1733. H.² T. 20/2; M. 5/11, T. 6; D.L. M. 5/11; C.G. M. 5/11,
      T. 6. 1734. D.L. M. 4/11, T. 5; C.G. M. 4/11, T. 5, W. 6;
      F. 27/12; G.F. M. 4/11, T. 5. 1735. D.L. T. 21/1; T. 4/3: T. 4/11,
      W. 5; G.F. M. 14/4; T. 4/11–Th. 6, S. 22; C.G. T. 4/11, W. 5.
      1736. D.L. Th. 4/11, F. 5; L.² Th. 4/11; C.G. Th. 4/11, F. 5.
      1737. D.L. F. 4/11, S. 5, M. 7; C.G. F. 4/11, S. 5. 1738. F. 21/7;
      S. 4/11, M. 6; D.L. S. 4/11–T. 7. 1739. D.L. M. 5/11, T. 6;
      C.G. M. 5/11. 1740. D.L. T. 4/11, W. 5; C.G. T. 4/11, W. 5;
      G.F. T. 4/11, W. 5. 1741. W. 4/11; D.L. W. 4/11, Th. 5; C.G.
      W. 4/11, Th. 5. 1742. Th. 4/11, F. 5; D.L. Th. 4/11. 1743.
      F. 4/11, S. 5; C.G. F. 4/11. 1744. M. 5/11, T. 6; D.L. M. 5/11,

S. 10, Th. 22, M. 26, F. 30. 1745. James-street M. 14/1; D.L.
M. 4/11, T. 5, C.G. M. 4/11, T. 5. 1746. T. 4/11, W. 5;
G.F. T. 4/11, W. 5; D.L. T. 4/11. 1747. W. 4/11, Th. 5. 1748.
F. 4/11, S. 5; C.G. F. 4/11, S. 5. 1749. S. 4/11, M. 6; D.L.
S. 4/11, M. 6.

T. The Fair Penitent (L.[1] c. May 1703) 4° 1703; 8° (1703); 12° 1714;
    12° 1718; 12° (1723?, Hague); 8° 1732 (Dublin); 12° 1735; 12°
    1742; 12° 1768; 12° 1759 (Edinburgh).
        No record of first performance. 1703. L.[1] T. 8/6. 1715. L.[2]
    Th. 18/8, T. 23; Th. 3/11. 1716. S. 7/4. 1718. S. 11/1, Th. 16;
    S. 15/3. 1719. D.L. T. 11/8. 1721. F. 2/6. 1723. H.[2] M. 16/12,
    T. 17. 1724. F. 3/1; Th. 12/3. 1725. D.L. F. 12/11–M. 15;
    S. 11/12. 1726. W. 19/1; Th. 8/9. 1727. S. 11/3; T. 11/4; S. 9/12.
    1728. Th. 2/5; T. 22/10; T. 17/12. 1729. T. 11/2. 1730. G.F.
    Th. 15/1, S. 24; W. 27/5; T. 27/10; D.L. Th. 19/2, S. 21; Th.
    19/3; S. 5/12; H.[2] T. 7/7; M. 7/12. 1731. G.F. F. 22/1; Th. 29/4;
    D.L. T. 12/10. 1732. T. 21/3; Th. 14/9. 1733. C.G. T. 17/4;
    H.[2] Th. 12/7. 1734. D.L. S. 30/3; F. 19/4. 1736. C.G. M. 15/3;
    Th. 15/4; G.F. T. 23/3; M. 5/4. 1737. C.G. F. 11/2, Th. 24;
    S. 2/4; T. 15/11. 1738. F. 3/2; S. 18/11; D.L. S. 29/4. 1739.
    C.G. S. 27/1; S. 6/10; D.L. S. 3/11. 1740. Th. 27/3; G.F. Th.
    20/11. 1741. T. 7/4; W. 2/12, Th. 3, S. 12, M. 28. 1742. S. 16/1,
    F. 22; Th. 11/2, M. 22, S. 27; M. 19/4; M. 24/5; C.G. Th. 21/10;
    S. 6/11; F. 10/12. 1743. L.[2] F. 21/1; T. 8/3; C.G. T. 25/1; M.
    14/3; T. 12/4; F. 20/5; D.L. Th. 24/3; M. 18/4; T. 20/12. 1744.
    C.G. T. 7/2; Th. 29/3; F. 28/9; James-street S. 24/3; D.L. S. 21/4;
    S. 20/10, W. 31. 1745. C.G. Th. 24/1; D.L. Th. 7/2; M. 11/3;
    S. 6/4, T. 30; Th. 12/12; James-street F. 8/3. 1746. D.L. W. 29/1;
    C.G. F. 14/11, S. 15, W. 19–S. 22, Th. 27, S. 29; M. 1/12, T. 16;
    G.F. W. 31/12. 1747. C.G. M. 30/3; Th. 7/5, W. 27; G.F. S. 11/4.
    1748. D.L. M. 1/2, T. 2, Th. 4, S. 6; T. 22/3; T. 26/4; S. 22/10;
    C.G. M. 10/10, W. 12. 1749. T. 24/1; M. 27/2; S. 25/11; W. 6/12;
    C.G. M. 6/3.

C. The Biter (L.[1] Dec. 1704) 4° 1705; 12° 1720; 12° 1726.
        1704. L[1].M. 4/12 ("last new Farce").

T. Ulysses (H.[1] Nov. 1705) 4° 1706; 8° 1726 (Dublin).
        1705. H.[1] F. 23/11–W. 28, F. 30; S. 1/12, Th. 6, S. 8, S. 15.

T. The Royal Convert (H.[1] Nov. 1707) 4° 1708; 12° 1738; 8° 1768
    (Edinburgh).
        1707. H.[1] T. 25/11, W. 26, Th. 27–S. 29; M. 1/12. 1708. S. 3/1.
    1724. H.[2] M. 13/1, Th. 16; Th. 20/2; M. 16/3. 1739. C.G. Th. 4/1,
    F. 5, T. 9, Th. 18; Th. 15/3.

T. The Tragedy of Jane Shore, Written in Imitation of Shakespear's
    Style (D.L. Feb. 1713/4) 4° (1714); 12° 1714 (2nd); 12° (1723?,
    Hague?); 8°(1720?, Dublin); 12° 1728; 12° 1735; 8° 1748 (Glasgow).
        1714. D.L. T. 2/2–T. 9, Th. 11, S. 13–T. 16, Th. 18, S. 20,
    T. 23, Th. 25; M. 1/3, Th. 4, T. 16; T. 20/4; S. 25/9; S. 6/11;
    S. 11/12. 1715. W. 23/2; T. 17/5; T. 18/10. 1716. M. 2/1; S. 12/5;
    Th. 1/11, F. 30. 1717. B.F. Leigh and Norris, Aug.; D.L. S. 30/11.
    1718. S. 11/1; Th. 6/3; T. 21/10; T. 30/12. 1719. B.F. Bullock
    and Widow Leigh, Aug.; D.L. S. 5/12. 1720. S. 26/3. 1721.
    S. 1/4; T. 14/11. 1722. H.[2] Th. 28/6. 1723. D.L. T. 8/1; S. 30/11;
    S.F. Pinkethman, Sept. 1724. H.[2] M. 2/3; D.L. Th. 12/3; S.
    25/4; T. 22/12. 1727. Th. 9/2; Th. 16/3; M. 27/11; Th. 28/12;

B.F. Miller, Aug. 1729. G.F. F. 7/11. 1730. M. 13/7; S. 5/12.
1731. D.L. M. 22/3; G.F. Th. 18/11. 1732. D.L. T. 15/8. 1733.
G.F. M. 12/2; D.L. F. 13/4; H.² M. 29/10. 1734. Th. 17/1;
G.F. T. 19/3; M. 11/11. 1735. C.G. S. 25/1, M. 27; F. 7/2;
T. 13/5; W. 3/12, F. 5; G.F. F. 31/1; H.² W. 17/9; York buildings
M. 29/9. 1736. C.G. W. 14/1; T. 9/3; F. 26/11; H.² W. 11/2;
G.F. M. 16/2. 1737. C.G. F. 28/1; Th. 27/10. 1738. S. 28/1;
W. 18/10. 1739. W. 10/1; Th. 22/11; D.L. S. 17/3. 1740. G.F.
M. 3/11. 1741. M. 9/2; S. 2/5; W. 23/9; C.G. Th. 26/2. 1742.
Th. 18/3; S. 3/4. 1743. L.² F. 11/2; D.L. Th. 3/3, T. 15; S. 9/4,
T. 12, T. 19; Th. 24/11; C.G. M. 3/10. 1744. G.F. F. 21/12,
F. 28; C.G. F. 28/12. 1745. May F. Hussey, May; G.F. F. 6/12.
1747. C.G. F. 2/1–T. 6, Th. 8, S. 10, M. 12, F. 16; M. 23/3;
M. 27/4; F. 29/5. 1748. D.L. S. 2/1–T. 5, F. 8–M. 11, F. 29;
M. 14/3; Th. 21/4; W. 2/11; C.G. F. 21/10; S. 3/12, M. 5, M. 19,
W. 28. 1749. T. 7/2; M. 13/3; Th. 2/11; T. 12/12; D.L. Th. 16/3;
T. 4/4.

T. The Tragedy of Lady Jane Gray (D.L. April 1715) 4° 1715; 12°
1718 (Hague?); 12° 1727 (4th).
    1715. D.L. W. 20/4–W. 27, F. 29; M. 2/5, Th. 12. 1716. S. 11/2.
1731. G.F. Th. 30/12, F. 31. 1732. S. 1/1, W. 19; T. 21/3; T.
25/4; Th. 5/10, F. 27; W. 22/11. 1733. W. 19/9. 1734. T. 29/1;
M. 25/2; F. 11/10. 1735. S. 8/2; T. 25/3. 1738. D.L. Th. 12/10,
S. 14; M. 18/12. 1740. G.F. M. 24/11. 1745. D.L. M. 11/11,
T. 12. 1749. C.G. S. 16/12–S. 23.

RYAN, LACY.
(B.O.) The Cobler's Opera (L.² April 1728) 8° 1729.
    1728. L.² F. 26/4. 1729. M. 17/3 (altered); W. 9/4, Th. 10,
Th. 24. 1731. G.F. T. 20/4; D.L. F. 11/6 (as *The Amours of
Billingsgate*), T. 15; F. 2/7; F. 12/11. 1733. G.F. W. 25/4. 1739.
C.G. T. 24/4; Th. 3/5.

SANDFORD, ——.
C. The Female Fop: or, The False One Fitted (H.² Dec. 1723) 8°
1724 (anon.).
    1723. H.² Th. 12/12, F. 13, T. 31.

SAVAGE, JOHN.
T.C. The Life of Guzman de Alfarache...To which is added...Celes-
tina 8° 1708.

SAVAGE, RICHARD.
C. Love in a Veil (D.L. June 1718) 8° 1719.
    1718. D.L. T. 17/6, F. 20, T. 24; T. 22/7.
T. The Tragedy of Sir Thomas Overbury (D.L. June 1723) 8° 1724.
    1723. D.L. W. 12/6, F. 14, W. 19; W. 2/10.

SETTLE, ELKANAH.
    [For his seventeenth century works see the Hand-list of Plays,
1660–1700.]
D.O. The Virgin Prophetess: or, The Fate of Troy (D.L. May 1701)
4° 1701 (anon.); Cassandra, or, The Virgin Prophetesse 4° 1702;
The Musical Entertainments in the Virgin Prophetess 4° 1701.
    1701. D.L. M. 2/5, Th. 15, M. 19, T. 20.
(D.O.) The Siege of Troy. A Drammatick Performance (B.F. and S.F.)
8° 1707.

1707. B.F. Mrs Minns, Aug. 1724. S.F. Lee and Harper, Sept.
1747. B.F. Lee, Yeates and Warner, Aug.; S.F. Sept.

C. The City-Ramble: or, A Play-House Wedding (D.L. Aug. 1711)
4° (1711 anon).

    1711. D.L. F. 17/8, T. 21, T. 28, W. 29.

D.O. The Lady's Triumph. A Comi-Dramatic Opera (L.² March
1717/8) 12° 1718.

    1718. L.² S. 22/3–T. 25, Th. 27; T. 1/4, M. 14, Th. 17; M. 2/6

SEWELL, Dr GEORGE.

T. The Tragedy of Sir Walter Raleigh (L.² Jan. 1718/9) 8° 1719;
8° 1719 (2nd); 8° 1719 (3rd, corrected); 8° 1722 (5th, with a new
scene); 8° 1745 (6th).

    1719. L.² F. 16/1–M. 19, W. 21, F. 23–M. 26, W. 28; M. 2/2,
F. 6; T. 10/3; W. 1/4; S. 31/10. 1720. S. 14/5. 1721. T. 17/1.
1722. S. 21/4. 1729. W. 17/9; F. 19/12. 1739. D.L. M. 24/9–S. 29;
M. 1/10, T. 2; T. 27/11.

T. The Tragedy of Richard the I. King of England 8° 1728.

SHADWELL, CHARLES.

C. The Fair Quaker of Deal, or, The Humours of the Navy (D.L.
Feb. 1709/10) 4° 1710; 12° 1715.

    1710. D.L. S. 25/2–T. 28; Th. 2/3, S. 4, M. 6, M. 13, S. 18,
S. 25; T. 11/4; W. 3/5; F. 2/6; Th. 7/12, F. 8, T. 26; Greenwich W. 12/7, M. 17, M. 24. 1711. D.L. T. 6/2; Th. 31/5; T.
16/10. 1712. M. 10/3; F. 23/5; W. 26/11. 1713. T. 24/2; F. 29/5;
W. 7/10. 1714. M. 1/2; S. 24/4. 1715. L.² F. 7/1, Th. 13; M. 7/2;
S. 21/5; M. 12/12. 1717. T. 21/5; S. 28/12, M. 30. 1718. M. 13/1;
Th. 29/5; F. 3/10, T. 21; D.L. T. 21/1; M. 15/12. 1719. L.² M.
16/3; T. 26/5. 1720. T. 19/4; F. 18/11; D.L. T. 16/8; F. 28/10.
1721. F. 4/8; L.² M. 13/11; T. 5/12, F. 29. 1722. F. 1/6; M. 22/10.
1723. T. 12/11. 1724. T. 7/1, T. 28; T. 2/6; F. 30/11. 1725.
W. 27/1; F. 14/5; F. 12/11. 1726. F. 11/2. 1730. G.F. M. 30/3,
T. 31; F. 19/6; T. 10/11; L.² M. 18/5; M. 12/10; D.L. T. 20/10,
S. 31. 1731. G.F. T. 23/3; F. 14/5; M. 8/11. 1732. L.² W. 26/1;
G.F. F. 28/4; C.G. Th. 14/12. 1737. W. 9/11–F. 11. 1738. M.
2/1; S. 15/4; T. 16/5; F. 22/9; Th. 14/12. 1739. F. 12/1; Th. 15/2,
T. 20; S. 5/5; F. 26/10. 1740. T. 12/2; M. 26/5; W. 12/11. 1741.
F. 2/1; S. 25/4. 1742. Th. 25/2; M. 8/3; M. 19/4; F. 21/5. 1743.
W. 4/5; S. 19/11. 1746. T. 7/1; T. 4/2; G.F. M. 13/1, T. 14,
F. 24; T. 18/3. 1748. C.G. W. 13/4.

C. The Humours of the Army (D.L. Jan. 1712/3) 4° 1713.

    1713. D.L. Th. 29/1, S. 31; M. 2/2–Th. 5. 1746. W. 23/4,
S. 26, W. 30; F. 26/12, W. 31. 1747. Th. 26/2.

•F. The Merry Wives of Broad Street (by the author of The Humours
of the Navy).

    1713. D.L. T. 9/6.

F. The Hasty Wedding; or, The Intriguing Squire (Dublin) 8°
1717.
Five New Plays (Dublin) 12° 1720. [This contains: 1. The Hasty
Wedding; 2. The Sham Prince: or, News from Passau; 3. Ro-
therick O'Connor, King of Connaught: or, The Distress'd Princess;
4. The Plotting Lovers: or, The Dismal Squire; 5. Irish Hospitality: or, Virtue Rewarded.]

SHEFFIELD, JOHN, Duke of BUCKINGHAMSHIRE.
  T. Julius Caesar 4° 1722 [see Love and Folly 4° 1739 under Operas].
  T. Marcus Brutus 4° 1722.

SHERIDAN, THOMAS.
  F. The Brave Irishman (Aungier-street, Dublin, Feb. 1736/7, as *The Honest Irishman*; or, *The Cuckold in Conceit*; G.F. Jan. 1745/6) 12° 1754; 12° 1755; 12° 1756; 8° (1757); The Brave Irishman: or, Captain O'Blunder. Supposed to be written by T....S S....N, Esq; And Revised with Several Corrections and Additions by J....N P....S T....N 8° 1759; 12° 1773 (Belfast).
     1746. G.F. F. 31/1 [acted originally in Dublin 1737].

SHERIDAN, Dr THOMAS.
  T. Philoctetes 8° 1725.

SHIRLEY, WILLIAM.
  T. The Parricide; or, Innocence in Distress (C.G. Jan. 1738/9) 8° 1739.
     1739. C.G. W. 17/1.
  *Burl. O. King Pepin's Campaign (D.L. April 1745) 8° 1755.
     1745. D.L. M. 15/4, T. 16, F. 19.
  T. Edward the Black Prince; or, The Battle of Poictiers: An Historical Tragedy. Attempted after the Manner of Shakespear (D.L. Jan. 1749/50) 8° 1750.
     [For his later works see the Hand-list of Plays, 1750–1800.]

SHUCKBURGH, CHARLES.
  T. Antiochus, A New Tragedy...by a Gentleman of Gloucestershire 8° 1740.

SMART, CHRISTOPHER.
  *C. The Grateful Fair; or, A Trip to Cambridge (Pembroke, Cambridge *c.* 1747; see *The Old Woman's Magazine; Poems* 1791; and see G. C. Moore Smith *College Plays* (1923) p. 72).

SMITH, EDMUND.
  T. Phædra and Hippolitus (H.[1] April 1707) 4° (1707); 8° 1711; 12° 1719 (3rd); 8° (1720, 3rd); 12° 1745; 1751 (Dublin); 12° 1768 (Edinburgh).
     1707. H.[1] M. 21/4 (4th), T. 22, F. 25, S. 26. 1723. L.[2] F. 18/1, S. 19, T. 22; W. 6/2; S. 4/5. 1726. D.L. S. 3/12, M. 5, S. 31. 1745. James-street W. 27/3.

SMOLLETT, TOBIAS GEORGE.
  T. The Regicide: Or, James the First, of Scotland 8° 1749 (by the author of Roderick Random).

SMYTHE, JAMES MOORE.
  C. The Rival Modes (D.L. Jan. 1726/7) 8° 1727.
     1727. D.L. F. 27/1, S. 28, T. 31; W. 1/2, Th. 2, F. 3.

SOMMER, HENRY.
  (Pant.) Orpheus and Eurydice; with the Pantomime Entertainment (L.[2] 1740) 4° 1740.

SOUTHERNE, THOMAS.
     [For his seventeenth century works see the Hand-list of Plays, 1660–1700.]
  T. The Fate of Capua (L.[1] *c.* March 1699/1700) 4° 1700.
     No records of performance; published April 29, 1700 (*London Gazette* and *Post Man*).

T.   The Spartan Dame (D.L. Dec. 1719) 8° 1719 (3 edns.).
     1719. D.L. F. 11/12 (acted about 9 times).
Play. Money the Mistress (L.² Feb. 1725/6) 8° 1726.
     1726. L.² S. 19/2–T. 22.

SPATEMAN, THOMAS.
M.   The School-Boy's Mask 8° 1742.

STEELE, Sir RICHARD.
C.   The Funeral; Or, Grief A-la-mode (D.L. *c.* Dec. 1701) 4° 1702;
     8° 1711; 12° 1721; 12° (1721); 8° 1721; 12° 1721 (Hague?); 12°
     1735; 12° 1768.
        No record of first performance; published Dec. 20, 1701 (*Post
     Boy*). 1702. D.L. S. 24/1. 1703. F. 28/5 (as *The Funeral a la Mode*);
     M. 1/11; W. 15/12. 1705. W. 12/12. 1708. Th. 18/3. 1709. Th.
     31/3. 1710. H.¹ W. 8/2; D.L. Th. 14/12. 1711. F. 9/2; Th. 26/4;
     Th. 8/11. 1712. M. 14/1; F. 30/5; W. 12/11. 1713. W. 8/4;
     M. 11/5; W. 9/12. 1715. T. 22/2; M. 21/11. 1716. Th. 9/2;
     M. 30/4; T. 11/12. 1717. W. 16/10. 1718. W. 12/2; T. 27/5.
     1721. Th. 13/4; F. 26/5; W. 18/10; W. 20/12. 1722. M. 16/4;
     M. 22/10; M. 17/12. 1723. T. 7/5; F. 1/11. 1724. F. 3/1; T. 19/5;
     F. 6/11. 1725. T. 19/1; W. 5/5; F. 15/10; M. 20/12. 1726. F.
     13/5; Th. 22/9; Th. 29/12. 1727. Th. 4/5; F. 20/10. 1728. M.
     26/2; M. 13/5; W. 23/10. 1729. F. 10/1; Th. 8/5. 1730. F. 2/1;
     F. 17/4; W. 25/11. 1731. Th. 4/2; F. 26/11. 1732. M. 24/1;
     Th. 23/3; T. 14/11. 1733. G.F. M. 15/10, T. 16, M. 29–W. 31;
     F. 9/11. 1734. M. 7/1; F. 15/2; W. 22/5; W. 27/11; D.L. M. 25/3;
     T. 16/4. 1735. G.F. M. 10/2; C.G. W. 31/12. 1736. Th. 1/1–S. 3,
     F. 9, Th. 29; Th. 25/3; S. 17/4; M. 31/5; W. 29/9; G.F. Th. 1/4.
     1737. C.G. Th. 10/3; M. 2/5; F. 30/9; S. 12/11; L.² W. 27/4.
     1739. C.G. F. 16/2; Th. 1/3; Th. 26/4; T. 6/11. 1740. Th. 10/1;
     W. 30/4; F. 14/11; D.L. T. 22/4. 1741. C.G. F. 23/1; Th. 23/4;
     Th. 14/5. 1742. S. 2/1, F. 15; M. 8/2; S. 8/5. 1743. W. 19/10.
     1745. T. 1/1; M. 11/11, W. 20. 1746. G.F. M. 27/1, T. 28; S.
     22/3; C.G. T. 4/3. 1747. M. 26/1; G.F. M. 9/3. 1748. C.G.
     F. 29/1. 1749. D.L. F. 13/1, S. 14; S. 25/2; T. 21/11.
C.   The Lying Lover: or, The Ladies Friendship (D.L. Dec. 1703)
     4° 1704; 12° 1712 (2nd); 12° 1717 (3rd); 8° 1752 (Dublin); 12°
     1732 (5th); 12° 1760 (6th).
        1703. D.L. Th. 2/12–W. 8. 1746. F. 4/4, T. 8, S. 19;
     Th. 1/5.
C.   The Tender Husband: Or, The Accomplish'd Fools (D.L. April
     1705) 4° 1705; 12° 1735; 8° 1740 (Dublin).
        1705. D.L. M. 23/4–Th. 26, S. 28; S. 19/5; S. 23/6; W. 24/10;
     Th. 15/11; Th. 20/12. 1706. W. 16/1; T. 26/2; Th. 30/5; Th.
     6/6; H.¹ S. 7/12, M. 9. 1707. T. 25/2; T. 11/11. 1708. D.L. Th.
     5/2; Th. 27/5. 1709. Th. 27/1. 1710. H.¹ Th. 5/1, Th. 26. 1711.
     D.L. Th. 11/1; Th. 10/5; T. 18/12. 1712. M. 3/11. 1714. Th. 28/1;
     F. 19/4. 1715. M. 28/2; Th. 7/4; M. 31/10. 1716. F. 10/2; T.
     15/5, W. 23; T. 27/11. 1717. Th. 7/3. 1718. T. 7/1; W. 23/4;
     Th. 30/10. 1719. S. 31/1; M. 18/5; Th. 15/10. 1720. T. 31/5.
     1721. F. 27/1; T. 17/10. 1722. M. 8/1; M. 9/4; Th. 25/10. 1723.
     F. 18/1; T. 26/3; M. 18/11. 1724. T. 4/2; M. 2/11. 1725. M.
     15/2; S. 17/4; Th. 3/6; Th. 28/10; W. 29/12. 1726. S. 30/4;
     T. 18/10; W. 30/11. 1727. Th. 19/10; M. 11/12. 1728. Th. 4/4;

Th. 24/10. 1729. T. 14/1; S. 8/3; M. 28/4. 1730. M. 19/1; M.
20/4; G.F. F. 6/11, S. 7. 1732. M. 27/3; F. 12/5; D.L. Th. 27/4;
Th. 28/12. 1733. G.F. M. 1/1; Th. 1/3; W. 4/4, M. 30; T. 29/5;
Th. 4/10; D.L. F. 26/1; W. 2/5; H.² M. 15/10; Th. 8/11. 1734.
Th. 24/1; D.L. W. 24/4; W. 8/5; S. 2/11; F. 13/12; G.F. Th.
16/5; Th. 3/10. 1735. D.L. F. 24/1; M. 3/2; G.F. Th. 6/2. 1736.
D.L. M. 12/4; M. 3/5; Th. 16/9; T. 16/11; G.F. S. 17/4; Richmond
M. 26/7. 1738. C.G. M. 20/11, T. 21; D.L. S. 25/11; F. 1/12,
W. 27. 1739. C.G. M. 29/1; M. 23/4; W. 30/5; S. 1/12; D.L.
S. 27/10. 1740. M. 7/1; M. 11/2; T. 28/10; C.G. Th. 21/2; S. 11/10.
1741. D.L. F. 23/10; C.G. F. 27/11. 1742. D.L. F. 29/1; Th.
18/2; Th. 13/5; T. 21/9; W. 29/12; C.G. Th. 11/2; W. 12/5.
1743. D.L. Th. 20/10. 1745. T. 10/12.

C. The Conscious Lovers (D.L. Nov. 1722) 8° 1723 (bis); 12° 1723
(Hague?); 16° 1735; 12° 1745 (Glasgow); 8° 1750 (3rd); 8° 1757
(Dublin); 12° 1760; 8° 1761 (Cork); 12° 1764.

    1722. D.L. W. 7/11–T. 27; M. 10/12, F. 14, T. 18, F. 28. 1723.
T. 26/2; T. 12/3; Th. 4/4, T. 30; S. 14/9. 1724. T. 18/2; W.
22/4; Th. 19/11. 1725. T. 27/4. 1726. M. 3/1; Th. 24/2; Th.
31/3; F. 29/4. 1727. S. 11/2; Th. 2/3; M. 10/4; Th. 21/9. 1730.
G.F. W. 14/1; Th. 16/4; L.² M. 23/11–W. 25; W. 2/12. 1731.
Th. 7/1, S. 23; Th. 11/3; M. 5/4; W. 12/5; M. 20/9; T. 14/12;
Richmond Th. 22/7. 1732. L.² S. 19/2; S. 18/11. 1733. G.F.
Th. 18/1, F. 19; F. 2/2; F. 18/5; D.L. W. 4/4, S. 28; C.G. Th.
17/5. 1734. D.L. F. 26/4; F. 24/5; F. 25/10. 1735. F. 17/1;
M. 24/3; T. 29/4; Th. 5/6; G.F. M. 13/1; Th. 17/4; M. 25/3;
C.G. M. 14/4; F. 23/5; W. 22/10. 1736. T. 6/1; S. 1/5; F. 22/10;
D.L. M. 9/2–M. 16; W. 3/3, M. 15; Th. 26/8, T. 31; W. 15/12;
G.F. F. 16/4, F. 30. 1737. C.G. S. 8/1; Th. 17/3; Th. 12/5; M.
24/10; D.L. T. 1/2; T. 22/3; F. 22/4; T. 13/9; S. 12/11. 1738.
C.G. S. 7/1, M. 16; T. 21/3; W. 3/5; W. 11/10; W. 6/12; D.L.
F. 27/1; M. 27/2. 1739. C.G. M. 8/1; T. 8/5; W. 5/9; Th. 1/11;
D.L. Th. 1/2, F. 2, M. 5. 1740. C.G. F. 4/1, Th. 17; Th. 20/3;
Th. 23/10; T. 18/11; D.L. T. 25/3; S. 19/4; Th. 15/5, S. 20/9;
G.F. M. 10/11. 1741. C.G. M. 9/3; T. 7/4; S. 2/5; F. 11/12;
G.F. Th. 2/4; D.L. W. 8/4. 1742. C.G. T. 5/1; T. 23/2; Th. 11/3;
F. 30/4; W. 29/9; S. 27/11; D.L. M. 5/4; S. 22/5; Th. 16/9; Th.
21/10; F. 17/12. 1743. C.G. W. 26/1; Th. 24/3; M. 25/4; M.
24/10; D.L. M. 25/4; W. 18/5; T. 13/9; M. 12/12. 1744. C.G.
W. 18/1; F. 30/3; T. 24/4; W. 28/11; D.L. Th. 17/5; Th. 27/9;
Th. 25/10; S. 17/11; F. 28/12; H.² Th. 4/10, S. 6, T. 9, Th. 18.
1745. C.G. F. 1/2; T. 30/4; M. 2/12; D.L. T. 5/2; M. 22/4;
S. 5/10; W. 6/11; Twickenham T. 23/7; W. 3/9. 1746. C.G.
Th. 16/1; T. 15/4; M. 17/11; G.F. M. 10/3; Th. 18/12. 1747.
M. 23/2; C.G. S. 28/2; W. 22/4; F. 8/5; D.L. Th. 19/3, T. 31;
T. 7/4; S. 7/11; Th. 3/12, W. 30. 1748. T. 26/1; F. 15/4; W. 4/5;
Th. 6/10, M. 31; C.G. M. 28/11. 1749. D.L. M. 2/1; M. 3/4;
M. 1/5; T. 28/11; M. 4/12, S. 16; C.G. T. 18/4; F. 27/10, S. 28.

STERLING, JAMES.
  T. The Rival Generals (Dublin) 8° 1722.
  T. The Parricide (G.F. Jan. 1735/6) 8° 1736.
      1736. G.F. Th. 29/1, S. 31; M. 2/2, T. 3; W. 3/3 [this play
    seems to have been produced in Ireland about 1726].

STEVENS, Capt. JOHN.
>   C.   The Spanish Libertines...To which is added, a Play, call'd An
>   Evening's Adventures 8° 1707.

STEVENS, JOHN.
>   C.   The Modern Wife; or, The Virgin her own Rival...As it was
>   acted Gratis, at the New Theatre in the Hay-Market, By a Com-
>   pany of Gentlemen for their Diversion (H.² 1744) 8° 1744.
>>   No record of a performance at H.²; put on as a new play at
>>   G.F. 1745, Th. 18/4, F. 19.

STURMY, JOHN.
>   T.   Love and Duty: Or, The Distress'd Bride (L.² Jan. 1721/2) 8° 1722.
>>   1722. L.² M. 22/1–S. 27.
>   C.   The Compromise: or Faults on both Sides (L.² Dec. 1722) 8°
>   1722 (anon.).
>>   1722. L.² S. 15/12–T. 18.
>   T.   Sesostris: or, Royalty in Disguise (L.² Jan. 1727/8) 8° 1728; 12°
>   1728 (Dublin).
>>   1728. L.² W. 17/1–T. 23, F. 26, S. 27.

TATE, NAHUM.
>   [For his seventeenth century works see the Hand-list of Plays,
>   1660–1700.]
>   T.   Injur'd Love: or, The Cruel Husband...design'd to be Acted at
>   the Theatre Royal 4° 1707.

TAVERNER, WILLIAM.
>   Play.   The Faithful Bride of Granada (D.L. *c.* May 1704) 4° 1704 (anon.).
>>   No records of performance; published June 1704 (*Term
>>   Catalogues* iii. 412).
>   C.   The Maid the Mistress (D.L. June 1708) 4° 1708 (anon.); 12°
>   1732 (2nd).
>>   1708. D.L. S. 5/6, T. 8. 1737. L.² M. 21/3.
>   C.   The Female Advocates: Or, The Frantick Stock-Jobber (D.L.
>   Jan. 1712/3) 4° 1713 (anon.).
>>   1713. D.L. T. 6/1.
>   *C.   Every Body Mistaken.
>>   1716. L.² S. 10/3–T. 13. [A masque presented in this play,
>>   called *Presumptuous Love* was printed, 4° (1716).]
>   C.   The Artful Husband (L.² Feb. 1716/7) 4° (1717); 4° (1717, 2nd);
>   12° 1721 (3rd); 8° 1725 (Dublin).
>>   1717. L.² M. 11/2, T. 12, M. 18, T. 19, Th. 21–
>>   S. 23; S. 2/3; M. 1/4, M. 8, W. 24; S. 11/5, F. 17; Th. 24/10.
>>   1718. F. 14/2; S. 8/3; Th. 3/4; W. 4/6. 1721. T. 18/4; F. 5/5.
>>   1747. D.L. T. 3/3, Th. 5, T. 10, Th. 12, Th. 26; M. 4/5.
>   C.   The Artful Wife (L.² Dec. 1717) 8° 1718.
>>   1717. L.² T. 3/12–Th. 5.
>   C.   'Tis Well if it Takes (L.² Feb. 1718/9) 8° 1719.
>>   1719. L.² S. 28/2–T. 3, S. 7; F. 3/4.

THEOBALD, Dr JOHN.
>   T.   Merope 8° 1744.

THEOBALD, LEWIS.
>   T.   The Persian Princess: or, The Royal Villain (D.L. May 1708)
>   12° 1715; 4° 1717.
>>   1708. D.L. M. 31/5; T. 1/6.

T. Electra 12° 1714.

T. Ajax 12° 1714.

T. The Perfidious Brother (L.² Feb. 1715/6) 4° 1715 (*bis*).
    1716. L.² T. 21/2, Th. 23, S. 25, M. 27.

T. Œdipus, King of Thebes 12° 1715.

C. Plutus, or the World's Idol 12° 1715.

C. The Clouds 12° 1715.

O. Pan and Syrinx; an Opera of one Act (L.² Jan. 1717/8) 8° 1718.
    1718. L.² T. 14/1, S. 18, Th. 23, S. 25, T. 28; S. 8/2, S. 15,
    Th. 27; Th. 6/3, M. 17; F. 9/5, Th. 22.

M. The Entertainments, set to Musick, for The Comi-Dramatick
Opera, called, The Lady's Triumph. Written by Mr. Theobald,
and set to Musick by Mr. Galliard 8° 1718 (the masque of Decius
and Paulina is given on pp. 11–27); 12° 1718 (appended to The
Lady's Triumph, see *SETTLE*); Decius and Paulina...to which
are added, The other Musical Entertainments...in the Opera of
Circe 4° 1719. [The text of the 1719 edition is an expanded form
of that of 1718. The masque was produced first at L.² in March
1718, and later was used in a revival of Circe in April 1719.]

T. The Tragedy of Richard the II...Alter'd (L.² Dec. 1719) 8° 1720.
    1719. L.² Th. 10/12 (acted 10 times). 1721. S. 7/1; T. 24/10.

(Pant. O.) A Dramatick Entertainment, call'd Harlequin, a Sorcerer,
With the Loves of Pluto and Proserpine (L.² Jan. 1724/5) 8° 1725
(anon.).
    1725. L.² Th. 21/2.

(Pant. O.) Vocal Parts of an Entertainment called Apollo and Daphne;
or, The Burgo-Master trick'd (L.² Jan. 1725/6) 8° 1726; 8° 1731
(6th); 8° 1734 (5th).
    1726. L.² S. 15/1.

(Pant. O.) The Rape of Proserpine...Set to Musick by Mr. Galliard.
(L.² Feb. 1726/7) 4° 1727; 4° 1727 (4th); 12° 1731 (5th).
    1727. L.² M. 13/2.

Play. Double Falshood; or, The Distrest Lovers. Written Originally by
W. Shakespeare; And now Revised and Adapted to the Stage
By Mr. Theobald (D.L. Dec. 1727) 8° 1728 (*bis*); 8° 1767 (3rd).
    1727. D.L. W. 13/12–F. 22, T. 26. 1728. M. 18/3; M. 1/4;
    W. 1/5. 1729. M. 21/4. 1740. C.G. S. 13/12, M. 15. 1741. F. 15/5.

(Pant. O.) Perseus and Andromeda (L.² Jan. 1729/30) 4° 1730 (anon.);
4° 1730 (2nd, with alterations); 4° 1730 (4th. To which is added
The Sailor's Ballad); 4° 1731 (5th).
    1730. L.² F. 2/1.

D.O. Orestes (L.² April 1731) 8° 1731.
    1731. L.² S. 3/4, T. 6, S. 10, M. 19, T. 20, T. 27.

T. The Fatal Secret (C.G. April 1733) 12° 1735.
    1733. C.G. W. 4/4–F. 6.

(Pant. O.) The Vocal Parts of an Entertainment call'd Merlin; or,
the Devil of Stonehenge (D.L. Dec. 1734) 8° 1734.
    1734. D.L. Th. 12/12.

(Pant. O.) Orpheus and Eurydice (C.G. Feb. 1739/40) 8° 1740
(anon.).

O. The Happy Captive...With an Interlude, In Two Comick Scenes,
Betwixt Signor Capoccio, a Director from the Canary Islands,
and Signora Dorinna, A Virtuosa (H.² April 1741) 8° 1741.
    1741. H.² Th. 16/4, Th. 23. 1742. L.² F. 29/1.

THOMSON, ADAM.
>   B.O.   The Disappointed Gallant: or, Buckram in Armour (New
>   Theatre, Edinburgh) 8° 1738 (Edinburgh, anon.).

THOMSON, JAMES.
>   T.   The Tragedy of Sophonisba (D.L. Feb. 1729/30) 8° 1730; 12°
>   1730; 4° 1730.
>>   1730. D.L. S. 28/2; M. 2/3, T. 3, Th. 5, S. 7–T. 10, Th. 12,
>>   S. 14, T. 17. 1733. C.G. F. 6/7, T. 10.
>   T.   Agamemnon (D.L. April 1738) 8° 1738 (*bis*); 8° 1746 (in English
>   Miscellanies vol. ii).
>>   1738. D.L. Th. 6/4–M. 10, S. 15; T. 18/4–Th. 20, T. 25.
>   T.   Edward and Eleonora...As it was to have been acted at the Theatre-
>   Royal in Covent-Garden 8° 1739; 12° 1739 (Dublin); 12° 1751
>   (Dublin); 8° 1758.
>   T.   Tancred and Sigismunda (D.L. March 1744/5) 8° 1745; 8° 1752;
>   8° 1755; 8° 1766; 12° 1768 (Edinburgh).
>>   1745. D.L. M. 18/3, Th. 21, S. 23–T. 26, Th. 28; M. 1/4, T. 2.
>>   1747. G.F. M. 16/2, W. 18; T. 3/3. 1749. D.L. T. 7/3.
>   T.   Coriolanus (C.G. Jan. 1748/9) 8° 1749; 12° (1749 (Dublin).
>>   1749. C.G. F. 13/1–T. 24.

THURMOND, JOHN.
>   *(Pant.)   The Dumb Farce.
>>   1719. D.L. Th. 12/2.
>   *(Pant.)   A Duke and No Duke.
>>   1720. D.L.
>   *(Pant.)   The Escapes of Harlequin by Sea and Land, or Columbine
>   Made Happy at Last
>>   1722. D.L. W. 4/4.
>   (Pant.)   Harlequin Doctor Faustus: with the Masque of the Deities
>   (D.L. Nov. 1723) 8° 1724.
>>   1723. D.L. T. 26/11.
>   (Pant.)   Harlequin Sheppard. A Night Scene in Grotesque Characters
>   (D.L. Nov. 1724) 8° 1724.
>>   1724. D.L. S. 28/11.
>   (Pant.)   Three Entertainments...viz. 1. Harlequin Doctor Faustus:
>   with the Masque of the Deities; 2. Apollo and Daphne: or,
>   Harlequin's Metamorphoses; 3. Harlequin's Triumph 12° 1727.
>>   1. See above. 2. 1726. D.L. F. 11/2. 3. 1727. D.L.
>   *(Pant.)   Apollo and Daphne, or, Harlequin Mercury 8° 1725.
>>   1723. D.L. M. 12/8.
>   (Pant.)   The Miser; or, Wagner and Abericock: a Grotesque Enter-
>   tainment (D.L. 1727) 8° 1727.

TOLSON, FRANCIS.
>   T.   The Earl of Warwick: or, British Exile (D.L. June 1719) 8°
>   (1719).
>>   1719. D.L. F. 26/6; F. 3/7.

TRACY, JOHN.
>   T.   Periander (L.² Jan. 1730/1) 8° 1731; 8° 1731 (Dublin).
>>   1731. L.³ W. 13/1–S. 16, M. 25.

TRAPP, Dr JOSEPH.
>   T.   Abra-Mule: Or, Love and Empire (L.¹ Jan. 1703/4) 4° 1704; 4°
>   1708 (2nd); 8° 1711 (Hague); 12° 1720 (4th); 8° 1725 (Dublin);
>   12° 1727 (5th); 12° 1728 (6th); 12° 1735; 8° 1743.

1704. L.[1] T. 18/1–T. 25, F. 28; Th. 10/2; M. 20/3; M. 3/4, T. 25; T. 12/12. 1710. D.L. Th. 26/1. 1711. T. 20/3. 1721. L.[2] S. 18/3, M. 20; W. 26/4; Th. 2/11, T. 28. 1722. S. 19/5; S. 27/10; M. 26/11. 1723. F. 17/5. 1726. S. 2/4; M. 9/5. 1735. C.G. S. 15/2, M. 17, T. 18; T. 11/3; F. 18/4. 1736. S. 27/3. 1741. Th. 12/3; M. 13/4. 1744. Th. 8/3.

T. The Tragedy of King Saul. Written by a Deceas'd Person of Honour 4° 1703.

TROTTER, Mrs CATHARINE (afterwards COCKBURN).

[For her seventeenth century works see the Hand-list of Plays, 1660–1700.]

C. Love at a Loss; or, Most Votes carry it (D.L. c. Nov. 1700) 4° 1701.

    1700. D.L S. 23/11. Published May 3, 1701 (Post Boy).

T. The Unhappy Penitent (D.L. c. Feb. 1701) 4° 1701.

    1701. D.L, T. 4/2. Published Aug. 2, 1701 (Post Man).

T. The Revolution of Sweden (H.[1] Feb. 1705/6) 4° 1706.

    1706. H.[1] M. 11/2 (6 performances).

VANBRUGH, Sir JOHN.

[For his seventeenth century works see the Hand-list of Plays, 1660–1700.]

C. The Pilgrim. A Comedy. Written Originally by Mr. Fletcher, and now very much alter'd, with several Additions. Likewise A Prologue, Epilogue, Dialogue and Masque, Written by the late Great Poet Mr. Dryden, Just before his Death, being the last of his Works (D.L. March 1700) 4° 1700 (anon.); 8° 1735.

    Published June 18, 1700 (Post Man and London Gazette; cp. Term Catalogues, Trinity Term, 1700, iii. 199). 1700. D.L. 25/3; 6/7. 1703. S. 3/7; F. 8/10, Th. 14; Th. 11/11; Th. 16/12. 1704. F. 14/1; Th. 23/3; F. 3/11. 1706. T. 29/1; S. 9/2. 1707. H.[1] W. 30/4; T. 20/5, F. 23, F. 30; M. 27/10; F. 21/11. 1708. M. 5/1; D.L. M. 24/5. 1709. T. 15/3; H.[1] M. 31/10. 1710. M. 20/2; T. 11/4; Th. 18/5; F. 10/11. 1711. D.L. M. 5/11. 1712. T. 29/1; F. 31/10. 1713. F. 9/1; T. 29/9. 1714. F. 15/1; F. 24/9. 1715. F. 28/1; L.[2] F. 30/9; S. 5/11. 1716. T. 24/4; D.L. Th. 19/7; Th. 16/8. 1717. F. 15/2. 1718. L.[2] W. 15/1; M. 10/3, Th. 20. 1719. M. 12/1; T. 17/11; D.L. T. 16/6; M. 26/10. 1720. S. 11/6. 1721. L.[2] S. 1/4; F. 19/5. 1722. Th. 29/3; S. 28/4. 1723. F. 1/2, F. 8; W. 1/5; S. 16/11, W. 27; M. 30/12. 1724. W. 15/1, F. 24; Th. 20/2; F. 24/4; F. 6/11. 1725. F. 15/1; M. 12/4; T. 11/5. 1726. T. 3/5; W. 2/11. 1727. M. 8/5; F. 27/10; F. 29/12. 1728. Th. 14/3; M. 20/5. 1729. T. 8/4; F. 9/5; T. 2/12. 1730. G.F. M. 21/12, T. 22, S. 26–T. 29. 1731. F. 8/1; T. 9/2; T. 18/5. 1732. L.[2] T. 18/4. 1733. C.G. M. 3/12, F. 28. 1734. F. 10/5. 1738. T. 25/4; D.L. Th. 30/11; S. 2/12–T. 5, S. 16. 1739. S. 5/5. 1740. Th. 3/1; S. 8/3, M. 10. 1741. T. 6/1; Th. 2/4; C.G. F. 18/12, S. 19, T. 22, S. 26. 1742. W. 20/1; T. 9/2; M. 1/3; M. 10/5; T. 7/12. 1743. F. 6/5. 1744. F. 21/12. 1746. W. 5/2; W. 7/5. 1748. Th. 21/4.

C. The False Friend (D.L. c. Feb. 1701/2) 4° 1702 (anon.).

    No record of first performance; published Feb. 10, 1701/2 (Post Man). 1710. H.[1] S. 4/3, T. 7. 1715. D.L. S. 5/11, M. 7, F. 25. 1724. L.[2] W. 14/10, F. 16, S. 17; S. 21/11. 1725. S. 13/2; M.

15/3; T. 4/5; W. 3/11. 1726. S. 5/2; S. 5/3; W. 11/5; S. 12/11.
1727. W. 11/1; Th. 23/2; S. 14/10; F. 10/11. 1728. T. 16/1. 1729.
S. 8/2, S. 22; S. 29/3; T. 6/5; F. 31/10. 1730. M. 12/1; F. 17/4;
F. 16/10; S. 28/11; Th. 3/12. 1731. S. 20/2; T. 16/3; W. 26/5;
F. 8/10. 1732. T. 18/1; T. 14/3; F. 3/11. 1733. C.G. Th. 8/11.
1734. T. 22/1. 1735. M. 15/12. 1736. M. 2/2, Th. 5; W. 28/4.
1738. S. 18/3; S. 29/4; F. 24/11. 1739. F. 26/1; S. 29/12.

F. The Country House (D.L. Jan. 1698) 8° 1715; 12° 1719; La
Maison Rustique or the Country House 12° 1740.
    1703. D.L. S. 23/1. 1705. S. 16/6, Th. 28. 1715. L.² F. 14/1,
M. 17, T. 18, Th. 20; T. 1/2, Th. 10, F. 11, T. 15; T. 1/3; M.
17/10; M. 28/11; S. 31/12. 1716. W. 14/11. 1721. M. 24/4; W.
22/11; W. 6/12. 1722. Th. 11/1. 1723. M. 18/2; T. 19/3; Th.
2/5; M. 3/6; T. 22/10. 1724. M. 6/4; Th. 4/6; T. 10/11. 1725.
F. 22/10. 1726. W. 19/10. 1727. W. 15/2; T. 21/3; F. 24/11,
S. 25. 1728. M. 6/5; Th. 12/12. 1729. T. 25/3; T. 29/4; M. 19/5,
T. 20. 1730. S. 3/1, M. 5; Th. 19/2. 1731. T. 26/1; F. 19/11.
1732. W. 9/2, T. 15; M. 27/3. 1733. C.G. M. 3/12, M. 10, F. 21,
S. 29. 1734. D.L. S. 30/3; C.G. M. 7/10. 1735. T. 14/1; F. 18/4;
M. 5/5. 1737. M. 28/3; M. 11/4, F. 22. 1739. W. 25/4; M. 7/5,
W. 9; S. 3/11. 1742. T. 7/12. 1746. W. 3/12.

F. Squire Trelooby (L.¹ March 1704) 8° 1734 (see *JAMES RALPH*).
    1704. L.¹ Th. 30/3; T. 23/5; T. 6/6.

C. The Confederacy (H.¹ Oct. 1705) 4° 1705; 12° 1751; 12° 1762.
    Often acted as *The City Wives Confederacy*. 1705. H.¹ T. 30/10,
W. 31; Th. 1/11, F. 2, T. 6; T. 4/12, W. 26. 1706. W. 12/6; W.
11/12. 1709. D.L. S. 17/12, M. 19. 1710. M. 2/1, W. 11; T. 30/5;
Th. 23/11, F. 24; Greenwich M. 11/9. 1711. D.L. F. 2/2. 1712.
F. 19/12. 1713. F. 11/12. 1715. L.² S. 8/1, F. 21; T. 1/2. 1716.
Th. 12/1, T. 24; M. 20/2; M. 7/5; M. 12/11. 1719. Th. 2/4.
1720. M. 28/3. 1725. Th. 16/12–T. 21. 1726. T. 4/1, M. 17;
Th. 17/2; W. 20/4; W. 26/10. 1727. S. 7/1; T. 21/2; W. 5/4;
W. 3/5; F. 9/6; F. 22/9; S. 28/10; F. 1/12. 1728. W. 10/1; M.
25/3; M. 6/5; S. 2/11; M. 30/12. 1729. L.² Th. 24/4; M.
24/11. 1730. W. 28/1; S. 14/2; Th. 30/4; S. 31/10; S. 19/12.
1731. W. 17/2; W. 21/4; F. 28/5; Th. 11/11. 1732. W. 16/2;
Th. 30/3; Th. 11/5; M. 2/10. 1733. C.G. F. 18/5; T. 16/10;
F. 7/12. 1734. W. 20/2; Th. 25/4; D.L. M. 11/3. 1735. C.G.
Th. 15/5. 1736. M. 1/3; L.² T. 23/3; W. 19/5. 1737. C.G. F. 21/1;
D.L. S. 8/10, Th. 13, S. 15, T. 18; F. 18/11. 1738. W. 1/2; M.
29/5; S. 11/11, F. 24. 1739. F. 12/1; S. 8/12, S. 15. 1740. W. 7/5.
1741. M. 9/2; Th. 9/4; M. 4/5. 1742. M. 22/3; S. 3/4. 1743.
L.² M. 14/3; C.G. F. 18/11. 1744. M. 10/12, Th. 20. 1745. T.
14/5; S. 30/11. 1746. S. 4/1; S. 15/2; M. 5/5; D.L. M. 24/2;
Th. 3/4; S. 22/11. 1747. Th. 22/1; M. 23/2; F. 8/5; Th. 1/10.
1748. W. 18/5; Th. 15/9. 1749. Th. 9/11; T. 19/12.

C. The Mistake (H.¹ Dec. 1705) 4° 1706.
    1705. H.¹ Th. 27/12–M. 31. 1706. T. 1/1, W. 2; M. 25/3. **1710.**
D.L. S. 11/2; Th. 9/3, M. 27; Greenwich S. 19/8; F. 1/9. 1715.
L.² W. 5/1, M. 10; W. 2/11. 1726. M. 24/10, F. 28. 1727. F. 13/1;
Th. 9/2, S. 25; Th. 12/10; M. 27/11. 1728. Th. 11/1; T. 30/4;
M. 16/12. 1729. Th. 8/5; F. 14/11. 1730. Th. 8/1; F. 6/2; W. 8/4;
S. 9/5; M. 26/10; T. 22/12. 1731. M. 11/1; S. 13/2; W. 8/4;
M. 31/5; F. 22/10; M. 20/12. 1732. T. 15/2; M. 15/5; T. 17/11.

1733. G.F. F. 14/12, S. 15, W. 19; C.G. M. 31/12. 1734. F. 1/2;
G.F. F. 22/2; F. 13/12. 1735. Th. 23/1, F. 24; C.G. F. 17/10, S.
18. 1736. T. 27/1; M. 8/3; T. 25/5. 1738. T. 31/1; S. 4/3; F. 5/5;
W. 15/11. 1739. Th. 1/2; Th. 24/5; F. 5/10; Th. 29/11. 1740.
F. 15/2, T. 26; W. 15/10. 1741. T. 6/1; Th. 7/5; S. 24/10; S.
5/12. 1742. F. 19/2; Th. 22/4. 1743. F. 14/10. 1744. T. 21/2.
1745. T. 19/11.

*F. The Cuckold in Conceit.
    1707. H.[1] S. 22/3.

C. A Journey to London, being part of a Comedy, written by the
late Sir John Vanbrugh, and printed after his own Copy, which
(since his Decease) has been made an intire Play by Mr. Cibber,
and call'd The Provok'd Husband 8° 1728.

WALKER, T.

F.C. The Wit of a Woman (L.[1] June 1704) 4° 1705 (anon.).
    1704. L.[1] S. 24/6; Th. 17/8.

WALKER, THOMAS.

(B.O.) The Quaker's Opera (S.F. Sept. 1728) 8° 1728 (bis, anon.).
    1728. S.F. Lee, Harper and Spiller, Sept.; H.[2] Th. 31/10; F.
1/11, T. 5, W. 6.

Play. The Fate of Villany (G.F. Feb. 1729/30) 8° 1730 (anon.).
    1730. G.F. T. 24/2, Th. 26, S. 28. [For an Irish revival in
1744 as Love and Loyalty see W. R. Chetwood, General History
of the Stage, p. 247.]

WALKER, WILLIAM.

C. Marry, or Do Worse (L.[1] Nov. 1703) 4° 1704 (anon.).
    1703. L.[1] M. 1/11. 1747. D.L. M. 30/3.

WANDESFORD, OSBORNE SYDNEY.

T. Fatal Love, Or, The Degenerate Brother (H.[2] Jan. 1729/30) 8°1730.
    1730. H.[2] W. 21/1, Th. 22; M. 2/2.

WARD, EDWARD.

T. Honesty in Distress, but reliev'd by no Party; A Tragedy, as it is
basely acted by her Majesty's Subjects upon God's Stage the
World 8° 1708.

WARD, HENRY.

The Works of Mr. Henry Ward, Comedian 8° 1746 (3rd edition).
[Contains: 1. The Happy Lovers; or, The Beau Metamorphos'd,
a ballad farce; 2. The Petticoat-Plotter; or, More Ways than One
for a Wife, a farce; 3. The Widow's Wish; or, An Equipage of
Lovers, a farce. The first was acted at L.[2] on W. 31/3/1736.]

F. The Vintner Trick'd (D.L. April 1746) 8° (1746).
    1746. D.L. W. 9/4, M. 21.

WEDDELL, Mrs.

F. The City Farce 8° 1737 (anon.); 8° 1737 (3rd).
T. Inkle and Yarico 8° 1742 (by the Author of The City Farce).

WEEKES, JAMES EYRE.

*M. Orpheus and Eurydice 12° 1743 (Cork; in Poems on Several
Occasions).

WELSTED, LEONARD.

C. The Dissembled Wanton; or, My Son Get Money (L.[2] Dec. 1726)
8° 1727; 8° 1728 (2nd).
    1726. L.[2] W. 14/12–F. 16, M. 19, W. 21.

WEST, GILBERT.
> Dr. Poem. The Institution of the Order of the Garter 4° 1742.

WEST, RICHARD.
> T. Hecuba (D.L. Feb. 1725/6) 8° 1726 (anon.).
>> 1726. D.L. W. 2/2–F. 4.

WETHERBY, JAMES.
> *F. Paul the Spanish Sharper 8° 1730.

WHINCOP, THOMAS.
> T. Scanderbeg: or, Love and Liberty…To which are added A List of all the Dramatic Authors, with some Account of their Lives; and of all the Dramatic Pieces ever published in the English Language, to the Year 1747 8° 1747.

WHITEHEAD, WILLIAM.
> T. The Roman Father (D.L. Feb. 1749/50) 8° 1750 (*bis*).

WILKINSON, RICHARD.
> C. Vice Reclaim'd; or, The Passionate Mistress (D.L. June 1703) 4° 1703.
>> 1703. D.L. W. 23/6–M. 28. As The Quaker's Wedding, published 12° 1723. 1719. L.² Th. 22/10. 1720. S. 23/1. 1721. W. 10/5, T. 30.

WILLIAMS, JOHN.
> C. Richmond Wells: or, Good Luck at Last (Richmond July 1722) 12° 1723.
>> 1722. Richmond M. 23/7.

WISEMAN, Mrs JANE.
> T. Antiochus the Great: or, The Fatal Relapse (L.¹ 1702) 4° 1702.

WORSDALE, JAMES.
> (B.O.) A Cure for a Scold. A Ballad Farce…Founded upon Shakespeare's Taming of a Shrew (D.L. Feb. 1734/5) 8° (1735); 8° 1738 (Dublin).
>> 1735. D.L. T. 25/2, Th. 27; S. 1/3, Th. 20; M. 5/5.
> Mus. Ent. The Queen of Spain, or, Farinelli in Madrid (H.² Jan. 1743/4) 12° 1741 (Dublin).
>> 1744. H.² Th. 19/1 [produced originally at Aungier Street, Dublin, 16/4, 1741].

YARROW, JOSEPH.
> B.O. Love at First Sight; or, The Wit of a Woman (York) 8° 1742 (York).
> F. Trick upon Trick; or, The Vintner Outwitted 8° 1742 (York). [This is practically the same as The Bilker Bilk'd in The Stroler's Pacquet open'd. See also the pantomime, Trick upon Trick.]
> *Mus. Int. Nancy 8° 1742 (York).

YOUNG, EDWARD.
> T. Busiris, King of Egypt (D.L. March 1718/9) 8° 1719; 12° 1719 (Hague?); 12° 1733; 12° 1735; 12° 1761.
>> 1719. D.L. S. 7/3–T. 10, S. 14, T. 17, S. 21; Th. 2/4, F. 3. 1722. M. 12/2, T. 13. 1736. L.² W. 3/3.
> T. The Revenge (D.L. April 1721) 8° 1721; 8° 1733 (Dublin); 12° 1735; 8° 1752; 12° 1776.
>> 1721. D.L. T. 18/4–M. 24. 1723. H.² F. 20/12, S. 21. 1724. W. 8/1. 1732. W. 24/5. 1736. M. 19/1, T. 20. 1744. C.G. M.

12/11–W. 14, S. 17, T. 20; T. 4/12, T. 18. 1745. Th. 10/1, T. 15,
T. 22; Th. 7/2; T. 19/3. 1746. G.F. M. 27/10; C.G. Th. 13/11.
1748. Th. 1/12. 1749. S. 7/1.
[For his other works see the Hand-list of Plays, 1750–1800.]

UNKNOWN AUTHORS.

*Pant. The Adventures of Harlequin in Spain.
  1741. Tottenham Court F. Middleton, Aug.
*Droll. The Adventures of Robin Hood, Earl of Huntingdon, and his
  Man Little John 1724. S.F. Lee, Sept. This is probably the basis
  of the B.O. Robin Hood and Little John given in 1730 at B.F.
  and S.F. at Lee and Harper's booth; printed 8° 1730.
D.O. Alarbas...By a Gentleman of Quality 4° 1709.
*Ent. of M. Alexis and Dorinda.
  1725. L.² Th. 15/4.
*F. All Puzzled (mentioned in Chetwood, and dated 1702; probably
  fictional).
*Pant. Amadis, or, The Loves of Harlequin and Columbine.
  1718. L.² F. 24/1.
*Pant. The Amorous Adventure, or, The Plague of a Wanton Wife.
  1730. H.² F. 17/7.
*Pant. The Amorous Goddess, or, Harlequin Married.
  1744. D.L. W. 1/2.
C. The Amorous Miser: or, The Younger the Wiser 4° 1705.
*M. The Amorous Sportsman, or, The Death of the Stag.
  1732. G.F. W. 20/12.
*M. of D. The Amours of Mars and Venus.
  1746. N.W., G.F. M. 1/9.
*Droll. Amurath, the Great Emperor of the Turks, containing the
  Distressed Loves of Achmet and Selima, or, The London Prentice's
  Glory.
  1730. S.F. Pinkethman, Sept. 1731. Tottenham Court F. Aug;
  New theatre at Tottenham Court, Sept.
*F. Androboros. A Biographical Farce in Three Acts, viz. The Senate,
  the Consistory, and the Apotheosis, printed at Moropolis, since
  August 4° 170 . [Attributed to Governor Hunter; cf. Biog. Dram.
  ii. 28.]
O. Apollo and Daphne 8° 1734.
C. The Apparition; or, The Sham Wedding (D.L. Nov. 1713) 4°
  1714.
  [Written by a gentleman of Ch. Ch. Oxon.] 1713. D.L. W.
  25/11, Th. 26.
*T. Arden of Feversham.
  1736. H.² W. 21/1 (said in bill to be by Mrs Haywood).
*Droll. Argalus and Parthenia.
  1745. May F. Middleton, May.
(Pol.) The Assembly. A Comedy, Written by a Scots Gentleman 8°
  1722. [Attributed to Pitcairne; see Biographia Britannica and
  Dict. Nat. Biog.]
*Pant. As You Like It, or, Harlequin's Whim.
  1746. N.W. Clerkenwell, Sept.
(M.) Aurora's Nuptials. A Dramatic Performance, occasioned by the
  Nuptials of William, Prince of Orange, and Anne, Princess Royal
  of England (D.L. 1734) 4° 1734. [Music by J. F. Lampe.]

F. The Author's Triumph: or, The Managers Manag'd...By a Lover of the Muses (? acted April 1737) 8° 1737.
>This piece was advertised for Th. 14/4/1737 at L.² On Th. 28/4 appeared a notice that it would be printed as it was to have been performed. The title-page confirms this.

*Ballet. Bacchus and Ariadne.
>1734. C.G. T. 26/2.

*M. Bacchus and Cupid.
>1715. L.² Th. 24/3.

*Ballet. Le Badinage de Provence.
>1735. D.L. Th. 23/10.

*O. The Banished General, or, The Distressed Lovers. With the Comical Humours of Nicodemus Hobble Wallop Esq; and his Man Gudgeon.
>1731. B.F. Miller, Miller and Oates, Aug.; S.F. Lee and Harper, Sept.

*C. The Baronet Bit, or, The Noble Englishman Rewarded.
>1741. B.F. Fawkes and Pinchbeck, Aug; S.F. Sept.

*B.O. The Barren Island, or, Petticoat Government.
>1734. B.F. Ryan, Legar, Chapman and Hall, Aug.

*Droll. The True and Ancient History of Bateman, or, The Unhappy Marriage.
>1703. B.F. Parker and Doggett, Aug. 1728. B.F. Hall and Miller, Aug. 1733. Tottenham Court F. Lee, Harper and Petit, Aug. 1748. Panton-street, March (puppets).

*C. The Bath Intrigues.
>[Ascribed to Mrs Manley.]

F. The Battle of Sedgemoor 8° 1707 (in Buckingham's Works); 8° 1714 (do.).

*Pant. Baucis and Philemon, or, The Wandering Deities. Interspersed with a New Pantomime called Harlequin Mountebank.
>1740. N.W. Lemon-street G.F. M. 7/4.

*F. The Bawdy-House School; or, The Rake Demolish'd 12° 1744.

*Ent. of M. The Beau Demolished.
>1715. L.² W. 9/2.

*Ent. The Beggar's Pantomime, or, The Contending Colombines (L.² Dec. 1736) 12° 1736 (attributed to Henry Woodward).
>1736. L.² T. 7/12.

Moral Drama. Bickerstaff's Unburied Dead (L.² Jan. 1742/3) 8° 1743.
>1743. L.² F. 14/1, M. 17, W. 19, F. 21, M. 24, W. 26; W. 2/2, F. 4. 1748. C.G. W. 27/4 (as *The Drones Demolished, or B. U. D.*).

*Pant. The Birth and Adventures of Harlequin.
>1735. C.G. S. 8/11.

*Ent. of D. The Biter Bit.
>1731. G.F. W. 2/6.

*O. The History of King Bladud, Founder of Bath.
>1711. Punch's Theatre W. 12/12–Th. 20. 1712. T. 5/2, W. 6, F. 22, S. 23.

T. The Bondman; or, Love and Liberty (D.L. June 1719) 8° 1719.
>1719. D.L. T. 9/6, F. 12; Th. 29/10. [Ascribed to Betterton.]

Dr. Ent. The Bravo turn'd Bully; or The Depredators...Founded on Some late Transactions in America 8° 1740.

Ent. Britannia, or, The Royal Lovers.
>1734. G.F. M. 11/2.

Alleg. M. Britannia Rediviva: or, Courage and Liberty 12° 1746.
> 1746. N.W. Clerkenwell.

(Burl.) The British Stage; or, The Exploits of Harlequin: A Farce.
As it is Performed by a Company of Wonderful Comedians at
both Theatres, with Universal Applause; With all its Original
Songs, Scenes, and Machines. Design'd as an After-Entertain-
ment for the Audiences of Harlequin Doctor Faustus, and the
Necromancer 8° 1724.

F. The Broken Stock-Jobbers; or, Work for the Bailiffs. A New
Farce, as it was lately Acted in Exchange Alley 8° 1720.

*F. Bulls and Bears.
> 1715. D.L. F. 2/12–M. 5.

O. Callista...As it was designed to have been perform'd at one of the
Theatres 8° 1731; 8° 1731 (2nd, revised and corrected).

*Droll. The Captive Prince, or, Love and Loyalty. With the Comical
Humours of Sir John Falstaff and Ancient Pistol.
> 1744. May F. Hallam, May.

*T. Caradoc the Great (apparently *The Valiant Welshman*, altered).
> 1727. L.² F. 19/5 (said in the bills to be an alteration of an ancient
> play).

*F. Cartouche; or, The Robbers 8° 1722.
> 1723. L.² M. 18/2–Th. 21 (as *C. or the French Robber*); T. 19/3;
> Th. 2/5; M. 3/6; T. 3/12. 1727. S. 18/3. 1730. M. 2/3.

Cato Major 8° 1725 (see *Biog. Dram.* ii. 89).

Dr. M. Cephalus and Procris...With a Pantomime Interlude, call'd
Harlequin Grand Volgi (D.L. Oct. 1730) 8° 1733.
> 1730. D.L. W. 28/10.

*Ballet. Le Chasseur Royal.
> 1735. D.L. M. 10/11.

*O. Chaste Susanna, or, The Court of Babylon.
> 1711. Punch's Theatre M. 3/12–S. 8.

*Pant. The Cheats of Harlequin.
> 1729. D.L. Th. 8/5.

*Pant. O. The Cheats of Harlequin.
> 1735. C.G. Th. 13/2.

*B.O. The Cheats of Scapin.
> 1736. B.F. Fielding and Hippisley, Aug.

*Pant. The Cheats, or, The Tavern Bilkers.
> 1717. L.² M. 22/4.

Dr. Tale. The Cheshire Huntress and The Old Fox Caught at Last
12° 1740.

*B.O. The Chimney Sweeper.
> 1736. G.F. Th. 29/1, S. 31; M. 2/2, T. 3.

*(B.O.) The Chimney Sweeper's Opera.
> 1728. H.² M. 27/5.

*Pant. The Chinese Triumph.
> 1747. S.W. April.

*(B.O.) Chuck; or, The School-Boy's Opera 8° 1736.
> [This play was acted at Smock Alley, Dublin, 27/1, 1728/9. It
> was erroneously attributed to Cibber in 1736. See W. J. Lawrence
> on *Early Irish Ballad Opera* in *The Musical Quarterly*, July
> 1922.]

*Pant. The Chymical Counterfeits; or, Harlequin Worm Doctor.
> 1734. G.F. M. 9/12.

T.   Cinna's Conspiracy (D.L. Feb. 1712/3) 4° 1713.
    Ascribed to Colley Cibber. 1713. D.L. Th. 19/2–M. **23.**
*C. Int. City Customs (D.L. W. 30/6/1703).
*Past. Cleora, or, The Amorous Old Shepherdess.
    1736. L.² F. 16/4.
*B.O. The Clown's Stratagem, or, A New Way to get a Wife.
    1730. D.L. M. 18/5, Th. 21.
*F. The Club of Fortune Hunters, or, The Widow Bewitch'd.
    1748. D.L. Th. 28/4.
*Ent. The Cobler, or, The Merry Wife Constant.
    1733. C.G. M. 14/5.
(B.O.) The Cobler of Preston. An Opera, As it is Acted at the New
    Booth in Dublin, With Great Applause 12° 1732 (Dublin; head
    title and running title *The Cobler of Preston's Opera*; acted by a
    children's company at Madam Violante's booth, in January 1731/2).
*Pant. Colombina.
    1735. D.L. W. 5/2.
*O. Colonel Split-Tail 8° 1730.
*B.O. The Comical Disappointment, or, The Miser Outwitted.
    1736. H.² W. 14/7.
*Pant. The Comical Distresses of Pierrot.
    1729. D.L.
*B.O. A Comical Revenge, or, A Doctor in Spight of his Teeth.
    1732. D.L. T. 2/5, F. 12.
(Pol.) The Commodity Excis'd; or, The Women in an Uproar. A New
    Ballad Opera. As it will be privately Acted, in the Secret Apart-
    ments of Vintners and Tobacconists. By Timothy Smoke
    8° 1733.
(Pol.) The Congress of the Beasts. Under the Mediation of the Goat,
    for negotiating a Peace between the Fox, the Ass wearing a Lion's
    Skin, the Horse, the Tygress, and other Quadrupedes at War.
    A Farce...now in Rehearsal at a New Grand Theatre in Germany.
    8° 1748.
*Droll. The Consequence of Industry and Idleness: or, The Appren-
    tice's Guide.
    1748 B.F. Yates, Aug.
*Hist. Dr. Piece. The Conspiracy Discovered, or, French Politics
    Defeated (from Henry V).
    1746. D.L. M. 4/8, W. 6, F. 8.
(Pol.) The Conspirators. A Tragi-Comic Opera, as it was Acted in
    England and Ireland without Applause 8° 1749 (Carrickfergus,
    according to title-page; no doubt London).
*Droll. The Constant Lovers; with the Humours of Sir Timothy
    Littlewit and his Man Trip.
    1714. S.F. Pinkethman, Sept.
*Droll. The Constant Lovers, or, The False Friend.
    1719. B.F. Bullock and Widow Leigh, Aug.
*F. The Consultation.
    1705. H.¹ T. 24/4, W. 25.
*M. The Contending Deities.
    1733. G.F. M. 7/5.
*B.O. The Contract, or, The Biter Bit.
    1736. H.² W. 21/1.
F. The Contre Temps; or, Rival Queans. A Small Farce, as it was

lately Acted with great Applause at H—d—r's private Th—re near the H—y M—t 8° 1727; reprinted in Cibber's Works.

*Pant. The Cooper Deceiv'd, or, Harlequin Executed.
    1748. N.W., G.F. May.
    *A Sort of Thing (if you Please, a Comedy) called The Coquet's Surrender, or, the Humorous Punster; printed as The Court Lady, or, The Coquet's Surrender (H.² May 1732) 8° 1730; 8° 1733 (both editions are mentioned in the *Biog. Dram.*; in all probability the first does not exist).
    1732. H.² M. 15/5.

*Ent. of D. La Coquette et les Jaloux.
    1734. D.L. T. 3/12.

*Ent. of M. The Cornish Hero, or, Jack the Giant Killer.
    1725. L.² F. 16/4.

*Pant. The Country Farmer, or, Trick upon Trick.
    1738. S.F. Lee, Sept.

*Ent. of D. The Country Revels.
    1732. D.L. F. 17/11.

(B.O.) The Country Wedding, or, The Cocknies Bit (H.²) 8° 1749.

*Droll. The Country Wedding, or, The Fulham Waterman Defeated.
    1740. Punch's Theatre M. 14/1.

(Sat.) C - - - and Country. A Play of Seven Acts. In which will be reviv'd, the Entertaining Scene of The Blundering Brothers. To which will be Added, The Comical Humours of Punch. The Whole concluding with the Grand Masque, call'd, Downfall of Sejanus. Written by a Masquerader; and Dedicated to those who were present at the last Ball, on Thursday, January 16. F. 1735.

B.O. (Pol.) Court and Country: or, The Changelings 8° 1743.

C. The Court Lady [see The Coquet's Surrender].

B.O. The Court Medley: or, Marriage by Proxy 8° 1733.

T. Courtnay Earl of Devonshire; or, The Troubles of the Princess Elizabeth…Comprehending a great part of the Reign of Queen Mary, with the Death of Jane Gray 4° (1705?).

*F. The Credulous Husband.
    1747. H.² W. 22/4 (from *The Old Batchelour*).

*"Pompous T." The Cruel Uncle, or, The Usurping Monarch.
    1743. B.F. Yeates, Warner and Rosoman, Aug.

*Ent. Cupid and Bacchus.
    1707. D.L. T. 21/1.

Pant. Cupid and Psyche: or, Colombine-Courtezan. A Dramatic Pantomime Entertainment 8° 1734.
    1734. D.L. M. 4/2.

*Pant. Cupid's Triumph, or, The Fatal Enchantment.
    1740. Punch's Theatre W. 2/1 (by actors).

*B.O. A Cure for Covetousness, or, The Cheats of Scapin.
    1733. B.F. Fielding and Hippisley, Aug. (from Molière).

*Play (3 acts). The Cynick, or, The Force of Virtue (probably an alteration of Lyly's *Alexander and Campaspe*; see Genest iii. 319).
    1731. G.F. M. 22/2–W. 24.

*Past. Damon and Daphne.
    1733. D.L. M. 7/5; ascribed to Theophilus Cibber.

*Pant. The Death of Harlequin.
    1716. L.²

*Pant. The Defeat of Apollo, or, Harlequin Triumphant.
    1737. H.² W. 26/1.
(Sat.) The Deposing and Death of Queen Gin...An Heroic Comi-
    Tragical Farce 8° 1736.
*Droll. The Devil of a Duke, or, The Conjurer's Bastard.
    1741. B.F. Fawkes and Pinchbeck, Aug.
*Pant. The Devils in the Wood, or, Harlequin Statue.
    1747. N.W., G.F. M. 22/6.
*Pant. Diana and Actaeon.
    1730. D.L. Th. 23/4. 1746. N.W. Clerkenwell, Sept. (with
    music by Lampe).
*Ent. of D. The Difference of Nations, or, The Dancing Europeans.
    1733. G.F. M. 12/3.
O. Dione (H.² Feb. 1733) 8° 1733.
    Music by Lampe. 1733. H.² F. 23/2; F. 16/3.
*Dr. Ent. The Distressed Beauty, or, The London Prentice.
    1722. Richmond M. 20/8; S.F. Pinkethman, Sept.
T. The History and Fall of Domitian, the Roman Actor (L.¹ June
    1722; an alteration of Massinger) 8° 1722.
    1722. L.¹ W. 13/6, F. 15, W. 20; W. 25/7; Th. 22/11.
*Dr. Ent. Don Carlos, Prince of Spain.
    1734. B.F. Fielding and Oates, Aug.
*Droll. Don John, or, The Libertine Destroyed.
    1734. B.F. Ryan, Legar, Chapman and Hall, Aug.
*Ent. Don Jumpedo.
    1749. C.G. M. 27/3. [This was a skit on the Bottle Conjuror
    hoax, see The London Magazine, 1749, vol. XVIII, p. 34.]
*Droll. Dorastus and Fawnia, or, The Royal Shepherdess.
    1703 B.F. Parker, Aug. 1729. B.F. Bullock, Aug.
*Pant. Double Jealousy.
    1736. D.L. S. 27/3.
(Pol.) The Double Traitor Roasted: A New Scots Opera...Acted by
    a Select Company of Comedians, near Westminster Hall 8° 1748.
*Ent. of D. The Dutch and Scotch Contention, or, Love's Jealousy.
    1729. L.¹ W. 22/10.
*Dr. Piece. The True and Ancient History of the Loves of King
    Edward the Fourth, and his famous Concubine Jane Shore,
    Containing the Reign and Death of King Edward.
    1742. B.F. Turbott and Yeates, Aug. [The B.F. and S.F.
    performances chronicled under Rowe (cp. *supra*, p. 352) may be
    of this droll.]
*Droll. King Egbert, King of Kent and Monarch of England; or, The
    Union of the Seven Kingdoms.
    1719. B.F. Spiller and Leigh, Aug.
C. The Election 12° 1749.
T. Electra 12° 1714.
(M.) England's Glory. A Poem. Performed in a Musical Entertain-
    ment before Her Majesty on her Happy Birthday. F. 1706.
    Music by James Kremberg.
*Droll. The Envious Statesman, or, The Fall of Essex.
    1732. B.F. Fielding and Hippisley, Aug.
*Droll. The Ephesian Duke, or, Blunder upon Blunder, yet all's Right
    at Last (from Shakespeare).
    1743. B.F. Fawkes and Pinchbeck, Aug.

*C. Every Man in his Humour (altered).

    1725. L.² M. 11/1–W. 13.

(Sat.) Exchange Alley; or, The Stock-Jobber turn'd Gentleman; with the Humours of our Modern Projectors. A Tragi-Comical Farce 8° 1720.

*(Sat.) Excise. A Tragi-Comical Ballad Opera 8° 1733.

*Droll. The True and Ancient History of Fair Rosamond.

    1734. B.F. Hippisley, Bullock and Hallam, Aug. 1736. B.F. Hallam and Chapman, Aug. 1741. B.F. Hallam, Aug. 1748. Panton-street, April (puppets).

*O. The Fairy Queen.

    1711. Punch's Theatre M. 14/5.

*Pant. The Fairy Queen; or, Harlequin turn'd Enchanter by Magic Art.

    1730. D.L. F. 15/5.

*Droll. The Faithful Couple, or, The Royal Shepherdess.

    1722. S.F. Miller, Sept.

T. The Faithful General (H.¹ Jan. 1705/6) 4° 1706 (dedication signed M. N.).

    1706. H.¹ Th. 3/1.

*Ballet. The Faithful Shepherd.

    1735. C.G. F. 3/10.

Past. The Faithful Shepherd 8° 1736 (adaptation of Guarini).

*F. The Falling out of Lovers is the Renewing of Love.

    1710. Greenwich W. 30/8.

T. The Fall of Mortimer (H.² May 1731) 8° 1731; 8° 1732; 8° 1763 (attributed to *WILLIAM HATCHETT*).

    1731. H.² W. 12/5–F. 14, F. 21, M. 24, W. 26, F. 28; T. 1/6, W. 2, F. 4, S. 5; M. 7/6, M. 14.

*Pant. The Fall of Phæton.

    1733. B.F. Lee and Harper, Aug.

*O. The False Triumph [or, Paris's Triumph].

    1712. Punch's Theatre M. 17/3, W. 19; M. 7/4, W. 9, F. 11, S. 12; W. 7/5. 1713. T. 14/4.

*F. Fame, or, Queen Elizabeth's Trumpets.

    1737. H.¹ W. 4/5.

*(B.O.) Farewell and Return; or, The Fortune of War. A Ballad Farce 12° (1739?).

*B.O. The Farmer's Son, or, The Maiden's Second Slip.

    1733. H.² W. 14/3, T. 27.

*Ent. The Farrier Nicked, or, The Exalted Cuckold.

    1734. Ryan, Legar, Chapman and Hall, Aug.

C. The Fashionable Lover; or, Wit in Necessity (D.L.? 1706) 4° 1706.

C. The Fate of Corsica: or, The Female Politician...Written by a Lady of Quality 8° 1732.

*T. The Fate of Milan.

    1724. H.¹ M. 24/2.

*Ent. of Music. The Fate of Narcissus. Interspers'd with a Comic Piece, call'd, The Chymical Counterfeits.

    1748. S.W. M. 20/6.

*B.O. Father Girard the Sorcerer, or, The Amours of Harlequin and Miss Cadiere.

    1732. G.F. W. 2/2–W. 9, S. 12–W. 16; T. 21/3.

*O. Faustus Trip to the Jubilee.

    1712. Punch's Theatre W. 12/3; M. 21/4, T. 22.

*F. The Female Enthusiast, or, The Spiritual Mountebank Detected. [Noted in *The General Advertiser* S. 30/6, 1744, to be acted soon at H.²]

*C. Female Innocence; or, A School for a Wife, as it was Acted at Mrs. Lee's Great Booth, on the Bowling Green, Southwark, by Comedians from the Theatre, Southwark 8° (1732).
    1732. S.F. Lee and Harper, Sept.

(B.O.) The Female Rake; or, Modern Fine Lady (H.² April 1736) 8° 1736; The Woman of Taste, or, The Yorkshire Lady 12° 1739 (in *The Curiosity*, a collection of pieces). Attributed to *JOSEPH DORMAN*.
    1736. H.² M. 26/4.

*M. The Festival.
    1733. H.² S. 24/11–T. 27, Th. 29; Th. 6/12, S. 8, M. 10, S. 15–T. 18, Th. 27, S. 29.

Past. The Fickle Shepherdess...Play'd all by Women (L.¹ c. March 1702/3) 4° 1703.

*Past. Flora's Holiday, or, The Shepherd's Welcome to the Spring.
    1736. C.G. Th. 6/5.

*Ent. of D. La Follet.
    1725. D.L. Th. 23/9.

(B.O.) The Footman. An Opera (G.F. March 1731/2) 8° 1732.
    1732. G.F. T. 7/3, Th. 9, S. 11, T. 14, F. 17, S. 18.

*F. The Footman turn'd Gentleman.
    1717. L.² Th. 14/3, M. 18; W. 24/4.

B.O. The Fortunate Prince; or, Marriage at Last 8° 1734. [This piece is almost identical with *The Court Medley* q.v.]

Sat. Fortune's Tricks in Forty Six 8° 1747.

*Pant. The Fortune Tellers.
    1740. D.L. T. 15/1.

*(Pol.) The Fox Uncas'd; or, Robin's Art of Money-Catching 8° 1733.

*Droll. The French Doctor Outwitted, or, The Old One in Danger of being Dissected.
    1743. B.F. Hippisley and Chapman, Aug.

*Pant. The Frolicksome Lasses, or, Harlequin Fortune-Teller.
    1747. B.F. Chettle, Aug.

*Droll. Fryer Bacon and Fryer Bungay, with the Comical Humours of their Man Miles.
    1711. Punch's Theatre T. 20/11, Th. 22–S. 24; F. 21/12, S. 22. 1740. M. 10/3.

*C. The Gardener's Wedding.
    1740. Punch's Theatre T. 25/3. 1744. H.² Th. 18/10, S. 20.

Play. The General Cashier'd. A Play, As Design'd for the Stage 4° 1712.

*B.O. The Gentleman Gardener.
    1749 C.G. W. 29/3 (perhaps the same as James Wilder's play, printed 12° 1751 as acted in Dublin).

*F. George Dandin.
    1747. D.L. W. 25/11.

*Droll. The Glorious Princess, or, Virtue Triumphant.
    1747. B.F. Godwin and Reynolds, Aug.

*Droll. The Glorious Queen of Hungary, or, The British Troops Triumphant.
    1743. B.F. Turbutt and Doves, Aug.

*? The Governor of Barcelona.
    1711. D.L. T. 26/6 (not acted 6 years).
*F. La Guinguette, or, Harlequin turn'd Tapster.
    1716. D.L. W. 11/4, F. 13, F. 20, M. 23, M. 30.
*Droll. Guy, Earl of Warwick, showing what Perils he underwent for
the Fair Phillis, as Killing a Dreadful Dragon and then the Giant
Colbrand 8° 1730.
    1730. S.F Lee and Harper, Sept. 1731. B.F. Lee and Harper,
Aug.
*Dr. Piece. The Happy Hero. Interspers'd with the Humorous
Scenes of All Alive and Merry.
    1746. B.F. Warner and Fawkes, Aug.
C. The Happy Marriage; or, The Turn of Fortune. As it is Acted at
Lincoln's Inn Fields. Written by a Young Gentleman 12° 1727.
*Past. Epithalamion. The Happy Nuptials.
    1733. G.F. M. 12/11–M. 26, W. 28.
*Pant. Harlequin Anna Bullen.
    1727. L.² Dec.
*Pant. Harlequin Captain Flash, or, Colombine in her Teens.
    1747. N.W., G.F. April.
*Pant. Harlequin Collector, or, The Miller Outwitted.
    1748. N.W., G.F. May.
*Pant. Harlequin Englishman, or, The Frenchman Bit.
    1742. G.F. M. 1/3.
*Pant. Harlequin Executed; or, The Farmer Disappointed.
    1716. L.² 26/12.
*Pant. Harlequin Gladiator.
    1725. Figg's New Amphitheatre W. 10/3.
*Pant. Harlequin Happy and Poor Pierot Married.
    1728. D.L. F. 18/10.
*Pant. Harlequin Happy, or, Jack Spaniard Hit.
    1740. Tottenham Court F. Lee and Phillips, Aug.
*Pant. Harlequin Happy, or, The Miller Bit.
    1745. New Theatre Shepherd's Market Th. 11/7.
*Pant. Harlequin Hermit, or, The Arabian Courtezan.
    1739. N.W., G.F. M. 18/6.
Mus. Pant. Harlequin Incendiary: or, Colombine Cameron 8° 1746.
    1746. D.L. M. 3/3.
*Pant. Harlequin in the City, or, Colombine turn'd Elephant.
    1734. G.F. F. 18/10.
*Ent. of Music. Harlequin Invader, or, Colombine Cameron.
    1746. B.F. Lee and Yeates jun., Aug.
*Pant. Harlequin Invisible, or, The Emperor of China's Court.
    1724. L.² W. 8/4.
*Pant. Harlequin Orpheus, or, The Magic Pipe.
    1735. D.L. M. 3/3.
*Pant. Harlequin Restored, or, The Country Revels.
    1732. D.L. Th. 14/12.
*Pant. Harlequin Scapin, or, The Old One Caught in a Trick.
    1740. B.F. Hippisley and Chapman, Aug.
*Pant. Harlequin Sclavonian, or, Monsieurs in the Suds.
    1744. May F. Hallam's theatre T. 1/5.
*Pant. Harlequin's Contrivance, or, The Plague of a Wanton Wife.
    1730. B.F. Reynolds, Aug; S.F. Pinkethman, Sept.

*Pant. Harlequin's Contrivances, or, The Jealous Yeoman Defeated.
    1732. G.F. F. 21/4.
*Pant. Harlequin's Distress, or, The Happiness of Colombine.
    1739. Tottenham Court F. Phillips, Aug.
*Pant. Harlequin Shipwrecked; concluding with the Loves of Paris
    and Œnone.
    1736. G.F. F. 20/2.
*Pant. Harlequin Sorcerer.
    1741. Tottenham Court F. Lee and Woodward, Aug.
Pant. Harlequin Student: or The Fall of Pantomime, with the Restora-
    tion of the Drama; An Entertainment As it is now performing,
    with great Applause, by Persons for their Diversion, between the
    two Parts of the Concert, At the late Theatre in Goodman's
    Fields. With the Scenes of Action and Tricks as they are variously
    introduced. Also, A Description of the Scenes and Machines
    painted by Mr. Devoto, particularly of Shakespear's Monument
    As lately erected in Westminster Abbey: And the Words of the
    Songs and Chorus's, as set to Music, by Mr. Prelleur (G.F.
    March 1740/1) 8° 1741.
    1741. G.F. T. 3/3.
*Pant. Harlequin's Whim, or, A True Touch of the Times.
    1745. May F. Middleton, May.
*Pant. Harlequin the Man in the Moon.
    1741. S.F. Lee and Woodward, Sept.
*Pant. Harlequin turn'd Cook, or, A New Way to Dress an Old
    Dish.
    1746. N.W. Clerkenwell, Sept.
*Pant. Harlequin turn'd Dancing-Master, or, The Highlander Bit.
    1730. G.F. W. 1/4.
*Pant. Harlequin turn'd Judge.
    1717. D.L. Th. 5/12.
*Pant. Harlequin turn'd Philosopher, or, The Country Squire Out-
    witted.
    1739. B.F. Hallam, Aug.
*T. The History of Hengist, Saxon King of Kent.
    1700. D.L. M. 3/6.
*Droll. The History of Henry VIII and Anne Bullen.
    1732. B.F. Mills and Oates, Aug.
Mus. Dr. Henry and Emma (Songs printed 8° 1749).
    1749. C.G. F. 31/3.
*Ent. of M. Hercules and Omphale.
    1746. N.W. Clerkenwell, Sept.
*Droll. Hero and Leander.
    1728. B.F. Lee, Harper and Spiller, Aug.
*Droll. Herod and Mariamne.
    1723. S.F. Bullock, Sept.
*F. The Heroick Footman.
    1736. H.² M. 16/2.
T. Heroick Friendship 4° 1719 (wrongly attributed to Otway).
*O. Heroic Love, or, The Death of Hero and Leander.
    1712. Punch's theatre M. 7/1–S. 12.
M. Hibernia's Triumph (Smock Alley, Dublin, Nov. 1748) 4° 1748.
*Pant. A Hint to the Theatres, or, Merlin in Labour.
    1736. H.² M. 15/11.

*B.O. The Honest Electors; or, The Courtiers sent back with their
        Bribes 8° (1733).
*B.O. Hudibras, or, Trulla's Triumph.
        1730. L.² M. 9/3.
Burl. O. Hudibrasso 8° 1741 (in A Voyage to Lethe by Captain
        Samuel Cock).
*Pant. The Humours of Harlequin, with the Loves of Several Deities.
        1729. H.² T. 25/2.
*F. The Humours of the Compter (L.² Nov. 1717) 12° 1717.
        1717. L.² W. 13/11 (This may be Knipe's *The City Ramble* q.v.).
B.O. The Humours of the Court: or, Modern Gallantry...As it was
        intended to have been Perform'd at one of the Theatres 8° 1732.
*F. The Humours of the Forc'd Physician (from Molière).
        1732. B.F. Fielding and Hippisley, Aug.
C. The Humours of the Road: or, A Ramble to Oxford 8° 1738.
        [Dedication signed William Quaint, Bellman.]
*Pant. The Humours of the Town, or, Pantaloon Deceiv'd.
        1748. N.W., G.F. Th. 4/8.
F. The Humours of Wapping 12° 1703.
Dr. Sat. The Humours of Whist...As it is Acted every Day at White's
        and other Coffee-Houses and Assemblies 8° 1743.
*B.O. The Hunter, or, The Beggar's Wedding (evidently an alteration
        of *Phebe*).
        1729. B.F. Fielding S. 23/8.
*Pant. Hymen's Triumph, or, Trick upon Trick.
        1737. L.² T. 1/2.
*F. The Hypochondriac (an alteration of *The Humours of Purgatory*).
        1718. L.² M. 28/4. 1719. T. 28/4. 1720. S. 9/1; M. 8/2.
C. Ignoramus, or, The English Lawyer (D.L. 1736?) 12° 1736.
*B.O. The Imaginary Cuckold (from Molière).
        1733. D.L. W. 11/4, Th. 19, W. 25; F. 18/5.
*Sat. The Impostor Detected.
*Pant. The Imprisonment of Harlequin.
        1746. S.W., Sept.
*Pant. The Imprisonment, Release, Adventures and Marriage of
        Harlequin.
        1740. G.F. M. 15/12.
F. The Inconsolables; or, The Contented Cuckold 8° 1738.
*T. The Indian Empress, or, The Conquest of Peru.
        1731. H.² W. 17/2, Th. 18.
*Droll. The Industrious Lovers, or, The Yorkshire-Man Bit.
        1749. S.F. Phillips, Sept.
T.C.F. The Informers Outwitted 8° 1738.
*Droll. The Injured General, or, The Blind Beggar of Bethnal Green
        or The Woman Never Vexed.
        1721. B.F. Pinkethman, Miller and Norris, Aug.; S.F. Sept.
        1723 B.F. Pinkethman and Norris, Aug.; Richmond M. 9/9.
        1724. B.F. Pinkethman, Aug. 1725. S.F. Powell jun., Sept.
C. Injur'd Love, or, The Lady's Satisfaction (D.L. April 1711) 4°
        (1711).
        1711. D.L. S. 7/4–T. 10, F. 13–M. 16.
*Pant. The Intriguing Columbine, or, Signior Quaverini in the
        Stocks.
        1747 N.W. Clerkenwell, April.

C. The Intriguing Courtiers; or The Modish Gallants...wherein the Secret Histories of several persons are represented 8° 1732 (*bis*).

*C. The Intriguing Footman, or, The Spaniard Out-witted.
 1742. B.F. Goodwin, Aug.

C. The Intriguing Widow: or, The Honest Wife 4° 1705 (Dedication signed J. B.); 4° 1711.

*Pant. Italian Jealousy, or, French Gallantry.
 1729. L.² T. 8/4.

*Pant. The Italian Shadows.
 1720. L.² M. 18/4.

(Burl.T.) Jack the Gyant Killer: a Comi-tragical Farce of One Act 8° 1730.

*M. of D. Jason and Medæa.
 1747. N.W., G.F. M. 3/8.

*Ent. of D. The Jealous Doctor; or, The Intriguing Dame.
 1717. L.² M. 29/4.

*Pant. The Jealous Farmer Deceiv'd, or, Harlequin a Statue.
 1739. C.G. M. 9/4.

*C. The Jealous Husband.
 1732. G.F. M. 21/2, T. 22, Th. 24.

*Pant. The Jealous Husband Outwitted.
 1732. H.¹ M. 18/9.

*B.O. The Jealous Taylor, or, The Intriguing Valet.
 1731. H.¹ Th. 14/1–M. 18; W. 3/2, Th. 4, S. 6, W. 10, F. 26; F. 5/3, F. 12, F. 19; F. 28/5; S. 5/6, M. 7, M. 14.

*Ent. Jealousy Deceived.
 1730. G.F. W. 7/1.

*Droll. Jephtha's Rash Vow, or, The Virgin's Sacrifice.
 1703. Pinkethman, Bullock and Simpson, Smithfield T. 24/7. 1718. S.F. Pinkethman and Norris, Sept. 1733. B.F. Lee and Harper, Aug.

B.O. The Jew Decoy'd: or, The Progress of a Harlot 8° 1735.

B.O. The Jovial Crew: a Comic Opera 8° 1731; 8° 1732; 8° 1760; 8° 1761; 12° 1766; 8° 1767. [According to the *Biographia Dramatica* this adaptation of Brome's play was made by Roome, Concanen and Sir William Yonge.]
 1731. D.L. M. 8/2–T. 16, Th. 18; M. 5/4, W. 28, F. 30; T. 20/7, F. 30; S. 25/9; T. 9/11, T. 16, Th. 18, M. 22; Th. 16/12. 1732. Th. 16/3, F. 17. 1744. M. 9/4, M. 23. 1746. T. 15/4, F. 18.

*Ent.? The Jubilee.
 1749. C.G. T. 9/5.

M. The Judgment of Hercules 8° 1740.

Past. B.O. The Judgment of Paris, or, The Triumph of Beauty 8° 1731.
 1731. L.² T. 4/5.

*Pant. Jupiter and Europa, or, The Intrigues of Harlequin.
 1723. L.² S. 23/3 (Weaver gives 1721 as the date).

*Ent. Jupiter and Io; with a comic interlude called Mother Shipton's Wish; or, Harlequin's Origin.
 1735. G.F. Th. 23/1.

F. The Juror 8° 1718 (5 edns; by W. B.).

*F. Justice Triumphant, or, The Organ in the Suds 8° 1747.

*C. The Kentish Election 8° 1735 (by L. N.).

*Droll. The Life of King Ahasuerus, or, The Delightful History of Esther.
 1719. Punch's theatre, Easter.

*B.O. A King and No King, or, The Polish Squabble.
    1733. G.F. W. 31/10.

B.O. The Ladies of the Palace; or, The New Court Legacy 8° 1735.

Sat. Lethe Rehears'd; or, A Critical Discussion of the Beauties and
Blemishes of that Performance 8° 1749.

*C. Like to Like; or, A Match Well Made (alteration of Shirley's
The Sisters).
    1701. D.L. S. 15/3. 1723. L.² Th. 28/11, F. 29.

*F. The Little French Lawyer.
    1749. D.L. S. 7/10, T. 10.

B.O. Lord Blunder's Confession; or, Guilt makes a Coward 8° 1733
(by the author of *Vanelia*).

C. The Lottery (H.² Nov. 1728) 8° 1728.
    1728. H.² T. 19/11–W. 21, S. 23; T. 10/12. 1729. Th. 2/1.

*Ent. of M. Love and a Bumper.
    1718. L.² T. 4/3.

*Sat. Love and Friendship; or The Rival Passions 8° 1723 (in To
Diaboloumenon; or, The Proceedings at the Theatre Royal in
Drury Lane).

Ser. Love and Friendship (C.G. March 1744/5) 4° 1744.
    1745. C.G. W. 6/3 (music De Fesch).

Ser. Love and Friendship 8° 1746.
    1746. D.L. T. 8/4.

*Droll. Love and Jealousy, or, The Downfall of Alexander the Great.
    1733. B.F. Fielding and Hippisley, Aug.

B.O. Love and Revenge; or, The Vintner Outwitted: An Opera 8°
1729.
    1730. H.² Th. 12/2; F. 20/3.

*F. Love in a Labyrinth, or, A School for a Wife.
    1746. B.F. Lee and Yeates jun., Aug.

F. Love in All Shapes 8° 1739.

*C. Love is the Doctor (from Molière).
    1734. L.² Th. 4/4.

*Pant. Love Runs all Dangers.
    1733. H.² F. 16/3.

*Ent. of D. The Loves of Mars and Venus.
    1717. D.L. S. 2/3.

*D.O. Love's Triumph, or, The Happy Fair One.
    1718. S.F. Bullock and Leigh, Sept.

T.C. Love the Leveller: or, The Pretty Purchase (D.L. Jan. 1703/4)
4° 1704 (by G. B.).
    1704. D.L. W. 26/1, Th. 27.

C. Love without Interest, or The Man too hard for the Master
(D.L. *c.* March 1698/9) 4° 1699.

*Ent. The Loyal and Generous Free-Mason.
    1731. L.² M. 5/4.

C. The Lucky Prodigal, or, Wit at a Pinch (L.² Oct. 1715) 12° 1715.
    1715. L.² M. 24/10–Th. 27.

C. The Lunatick...Dedicated to the Three Ruling B—S at the New-
House in L.—I.—F. 4° 1705.
    1729. H.² S. 1/3, M. 3, Th. 6. It is not certain that the 1705
and 1729 comedies were identical.

*B.O. Macheath in the Shades, or, Bayes at Parnassus.
    1735. C.G. T. 11/3.

*Ent. The Mad Lovers, or, Sport upon Sport; with the comical Humours of 'Squire Gray Goose and his Man Doodle, Lady Gray Goose and Captain At-all.

> 1738. Tottenham Court F. Fielding and Hallam, Aug.

*Droll. Mad Tom of Bedlam.

> 1730. B.F. Pinkethman and Giffard, Aug. This may be the same as Tom of Bedlam, or, The Distressed Lovers. With the Comical Humours of Squire Mumskull, said in the bill to be written by Doggett, and given at Tottenham Court F. 1730 by the G.F. Company.

*Ent. of D. The Magician, or, Harlequin a Director.

> 1722. L.² Th. 5/4.

*Droll. The Maiden Queen, or, The Rival Generals; Interspers'd with a Diverting Comedy call'd The Fair Hypocrite, or, the Fond Cuckold.

> 1745. May F. Yeates, May.

(Pol. T.) Majesty Misled; or, The Overthrow of Evil Ministers 8° 1734; 8° 1769; 8° 1770 (reissue).

F. Make a Noise Tom (or, the Yorkshire Bonfire). A farce, occasion'd by the lighting of a loyal bonfire with the Brush of Iniquity, Mᵣ B - - - y who was burnt in effigie at the town of Wakefield, in Yorkshire 8° 1718.

*Ent. The Man's Bewitched, or, The Devil to Do about Her.

> 1738. B.F. Pinkethman, Aug.; S.F. Hallam, Sept.

*Theat. Sat. Marforio, being a Comi-tragical Farce call'd The Critick of Taste, or, A Tale of a Tub.

> 1736. C.G. S. 10/4.

*Ent. of D. Mars and Venus; or, The Mouse Trap.

> 1717. L.² F. 22/11.

C. The Match Maker Fitted; or, The Fortune-Hunters rightly served 12° 1718.

*Droll. The True and Ancient History of Maudlin, the Merchant's Daughter of Bristol, with the Comical Humours of Roger, Antonio's Man.

> 1729. B.F. Hall and Oates, Aug. 1734. S.F. Fielding and Oates, Sept.

*Ent. of M. Meleager and Atalanta, or, The Calydonian Chace.

> 1747. S.W. April.

*C. The Mercenary Lover.

*Droll. The Birth of Merlin, the British Enchanter, or, The Child has found his Father; with the Comical Humours of Sir Nicodemus Nothing, Simon Go To'ot and his Sister, Joan.

> 1724. S.F. Norris, Chetwood, Orfew and Oates, Sept. 1731. S.F. Great Theatrical Booth, Sept. 1736. Tottenham Court F. Petty's Old Playhouse, Aug. 1738. S.F. Lee, Sept.

F. The Merry Pranks; or, Windmill Hill 4° 1704.

*F. The Merry Sailors; or, Landlord Bit. 1707.

*B.O. The Merry Throwster.

> 1731. G.F. M. 8/3.

*Pant. The Metamorphoses of Harlequin.

> 1740. C.G. T. 12/2.

*F. The Metamorphosis of the Beggar's Opera.

> 1730. H.² W. 11/3.

(Pol.) The Metamorphosis; or Harlequin Cato. A Comedy 8° 1723.

*Droll. The Miller's Holiday, or, Love in a Furze Bush.
>   1730. Tottenham Court F. Reynolds, Aug.
*Ent. of M. Minerva and Ulysses, or, The Fate of Polypheme.
>   1746. S.W. Sept.
*Burl. The Mirrour. With the Practice of a Dramatick Entertainment,
>   call'd The Defeat of Apollo; or, Harlequin Triumphant, and a
>   farce call'd, The Mob in Despair.
>   1737. H.² W. 26/1.
*T.C. The Miseries of Love.
>   1732. H.² W. 29/11.
(Pol.) The Mission from Rome into Great Britain in the Cause of
>   Popery and the Pretender 4° (?1746).
*F. Mississipi.
>   1720. L.² W. 4/5.
*O. The Mistake, or, The Constant Lover Rewarded.
>   1740. Punch's theatre M. 11/2.
*Pant. The Mistakes.
>   1730. D.L. W. 28/10.
*F. The Mock Countess.
>   1733. D.L. M. 30/4; M. 14/5. 1734. C.G. M. 11/11, T. 12.
>   1735. Th. 15/5, Th. 22. 1737. M. 7/3. 1738. T. 1/8, F. 4, T. 8.
*B.O. The Mock Mason.
>   1733. G.F. F. 13/4 (not marked as new production).
Sat. C. The Mock Preacher.
*B.O. The Modern Pimp, or, The Doctor Deceived.
>   1736. B.F. Hallam and Chapman, Aug. 1741. B.F. Hallam,
>   Aug.
(Sat.) The Modern Poetasters; or, Directors no Conjurors: A Farce
>   8° (1725) "By Isaac Bickerstaff, jun."
C. The Modern Receipt, or, A Cure for Love 12° 1739 (an alteration
>   by J. C. of As You Like It).
(B.O.) Momus turn'd Fabulist: or, Vulcan's Wedding. An Opera.
>   8° 1729 (attributed to Ebeneezer Forrest).
>   1729. L.² W. 3/12–S. 13, Th. 18, M. 22. 1730. T. 3/2–Th. 5;
>   T. 3/3; F. 8/5; F. 12/6; T. 15/12. 1731. F. 12/2; S. 20/3; T. 23/11.
>   1735. C.G. M. 13/10. 1737. Th. 28/4.
*Pantomimical Something. Monstrum Horrendum, or, The Practice
>   of a Modern Comic Entertainment.
>   1732. H.² F. 12/5.
*F. More Ways than One to Win Her.
>   1745. G.F. Th. 7/3; T. 23/4.
*F. The Mountebank, or, Country Lass.
>   1715. L.² W. 21/12, T. 27, W. 28. 1716. T. 10/1, Th. 19;
>   M. 20/2; M. 5/3.
C. Mr. Taste the Poetical Fop: or, The Modes of the Court...By the
>   Author of the Opera of Vanelia, or the Amours of the Great 8°
>   (1732).
*F. The Mutineer, or, Love in Distress.
>   1744. James-street M. 10/12.
*Ent. of D. Myrtillo.
>   1721. L.²
Ent. The Necromancer, or Harlequin Doctor Faustus (L.² Dec. 1723)
>   8° 1723; 8° 1724.
>   1723. L.² F. 20/12.

(Pol.) A New Comedy. Acted by the French King and his Privy
Council. Translated out of the French 4° 1704.

*Droll. The Noble Englishman, or, The History of Darius King of
Persia, and the Destruction of Babylon. With the Pleasant Humours of Captain Fearful and his Man Nine-Pence.
1721. S.F. Lee, Sept. 1741. B.F. Lee and Woodward,
Aug.

*D.O. The Noble Soldier, or, Love in Distress.
1717. S.F. Bullock and Leigh, Sept. 1719. S.F. Bullock and
Widow Leigh, Sept.

C. No Fools Like Wits, or, The Female Vertuosoes (L.² Jan. 1720/1)
8° 1721.
1721. L.³ T. 10/1 (a slightly altered reprint of Wright's seventeenth century comedy).

*F. No Joke like a True Joke.
1732. H.² W. 24/5.

(Pol.) The Northern Election; or Nest of Beasts. A Drama of Six
Acts, Now in Rehearsal near Mittaw, in Courland, under the
Inspection of the Author, a Russian Poet; and serving as a Sequel
to the Congress of Beasts,&c. Done into English, from the Original,
by T.N. and B.W. 8° 1749.

Droll. The Northern Heroes, Or, The Bloody Contest between
Charles the Twelfth, King of Sweden, and Peter the Great, Czar
of Muscovy. With the Loves of Count Gillensternia, a Swedish
General, and the Fair Elmira, a Russian Princess. With a Comic
Interlude, call'd, The Volunteers; or, The Adventures of Roderick
Random, and his Friend Strap (B.F. 1748) 8° 1748.
1748. B.F. Bridges, Cross, Burton and Vaughan, Aug.

*Pant. The Nuns turn'd Libertines, or, The Devil turn'd Humourist.
1730. Mrs Lee's theatrical booth, Dec.

*Dr. Ent. The Nuptial Masque, or, The Triumphs of Cupid and
Hymen (music by Galliard).
1734. C.G. S. 16/3, S. 23, T. 26; T. 2/4.

F. The Oculist 8° 1747.

B.O. The Operator 4° 1740.

C. The Oracle 8° 1741.

*Burletta. Orpheus 8° 1749.

*O. Orpheus and Eurydice.
1712. Punch's theatre Th. 7/2–S. 9.

Pant. The Fable of Orpheus and Eurydice, with A Dramatick Entertainment in Dancing thereupon; Attempted in Imitation of the
Ancient Greeks and Romans 8° 1718.
1718. D.L. Th. 6/3 (arranged by Weaver).

(Sat.) The Oxford Act 8° 1733.

*M. of Music. Pan and Syrinx.
1740. C.G. T. 16/12. This seems to have been Theobald's
masque revived.

*Ent. of Music. The Passion of Sappho.
1718. L.² S. 15/11.

(Pol.) The Patriot: Being A Dramatic History of the Life and Death
of William; the First Prince of Orange...By a Lover of Liberty
4° 1736.

*Droll. The Perjured Prince, or, The Married General; with the

Comical Humours of Squire Calveshead, his Sister Hoyden and his Man Aminadab.
>   1728. B.F. Bullock, Aug.

*Pant. The Perplex'd Husband.
>   1748. C.G. W. 20/4.

*Pant. Perseus and Andromeda. [Besides Theobald's piece, there seem to have been no less than four entertainments of this name, one given at D.L. in 1716, another at D.L. on F. 15/11, 1728, another at L.² on Th. 18/11, 1731, and a fourth at C.G. in November 1749.]

*Droll. The Tragedy of King Philip and Queen Mary.
>   1739. Tennis Court Hay. W. 19/12.

*Ent. of D. The Plots of Harlequin.
>   1724. H.² Th. 20/2.

*Sat. Polite Conversation (from Swift).
>   1740. D.L. W. 23/4. This was acted at Smock Alley and at Aungier Street, Dublin, in the spring of 1738.

*B.O. Politics on Both Sides.
>   1735. L.² W. 23/7, F. 25, W. 30.

(Pol.) Porsenna's Invasion: or, Rome Preserv'd. A Tragedy 8° 1748.

C. The Portsmouth Heiress: or, The Generous Refusal 4° 1704.

M. Presumptuous Love (L.² March 1715/6) 4° 1716.
>   1716. L.² S. 10/3–T. 13.

F. The Prison Breaker; or, The Adventures of John Sheppard 8° 1725.

*D.O. The Prodigal Son, or, The Libertine Reclaimed.
>   1724. B.F. Lee, Aug. 1746. N.W. Mayfair Th. 1/5 (called a comedy).

*Ent. of D. The Professor of Folly.
>   1718. L.² F. 3/1.

C. The Projectors 8° 1737 (by W. H.).

*Ent. of D. Punch's Defeat, or, Harlequin Triumphant.
>   1748. H.² Th. 14/4.

*Operatic Puppetshow. Punch's Oratory, or, The Pleasures of the Town.
>   1730. Tottenham Court F. Reynolds, Aug. (see Fielding's *The Author's Farce*).

*O. Punch's Politics, or, The Nuns' Conclave.
>   1730. Mrs Lee's theatrical booth, Dec.

Mock O. Pyramus and Thisbe (C.G. Jan. 1744/5) 8° 1745 (music by Lampe).
>   1745. C.G. F. 25/1–T. 29, Th. 31; F. 1/2–F. 8; S. 2/3, S. 30; Th. 25/4; F. 27/9; F. 4/10, F. 11, W. 16, Th. 31; F. 8/11, T. 19, Th. 28; F. 20/12. 1746. T. 14/1, S. 18; F. 7/2, T. 18. 1748. W. 13/4.

T. The Rape (L.² Nov. 1729) 8° 1729 (an alteration of Brady's play).
>   1729. L.² T. 25/11–F. 28.

(Pol.) The Rehearsal: A Farce; or, A Second Part of Mrs. Confusion's Travail and Hard Labour...by Mercurius Britannicus 4° 1718.

*Dr. T.C. Sat. The Rehearsal of Kings, or, The Projecting Gingerbread Maker.
>   1737. H.² W. 9/3, M. 14, T. 15, Th. 17.

T.C. The Restauration, or, Right will take Place 8° 1714 (wrongly attributed to Villiers, Duke of Buckingham).

*Pant. The Restoration of Harlequin, or, Mezzetin Outwitted.
>   1746. N.W. G.F. M. 1/9.

*Droll. The Historical Tragedy of King Richard III.
    1743. Tottenham Court F. Yeates, Warner and Rosoman, Aug.
T. The Rival Brothers (L.¹ 1704) 4° 1704 [the running title reads, A Fatal Secret or The Rival Brothers].
*Ent. The Rival Highlanders, or, The Devil of Stonehenge.
    1740. Punch's theatre M. 17/3.
*Droll. The Rival Queens, or, The Death of Alexander the Great. Intermix'd with a Comic call'd A Wife well Manag'd, or, A Cure for Cuckoldom.
    1741. Tottenham Court F. Middleton, Aug.
*Pant. The Robbers, or, Harlequin trapped by Columbine.
    1724. L.² M. 2/3.
*Pant. Robin Goodfellow, or, The Rival Sisters.
    1738. D.L. M. 30/10.
C.M. Roger and Joan; or, The Country Wedding (C.G. March 1738/9) 4° 1739.
    1739. C.G. 20/3.
* — Roger's Wedding.
    1710. H.¹ T. 11/4.
(Pol. B.O.) Rome Excis'd. A New Tragi-comi-ballad-opera 8° 1733.
C. The Roving Husband Reclaim'd...Writ by a Club of Ladies, in Vindication of Virtuous Plays 4° 1706.
T. The Royal Captives (H.² March 1729) 8° 1729.
    1729. H.² Th. 27/3.
*Droll. The Royal Champion, or, St. George for England.
    1728. S.F. Lee, Harper and Spiller, Sept.
*Droll. The Royal Heroe, or, The Lover of his Country.
    1744. May F. Hallam's new theatre T. 1/5.
B.O. The Royal Marriage...by a Gentleman of the University of Oxford 8° 1736 (bis).
*Droll. The Royal Revenge, or, The Princely Shepherd.
    1722. S.F. Walker, Sept.
*Droll. The Rum Duke and the Queer Duke, or, A Medley of Mirth and Sorrow.
    1730. Tottenham Court F. Reynolds, Aug.
*Past. O. Rural Love, or, The Merry Shepherd.
    1732. D.L. F. 4/8.
*Ent. The Rural Sports.
    1740. D.L. M. 27/10.
*B.O. The Sailor's Opera.
    1731. D.L. W. 12/5.
*B.O. The Sailor's Opera; or, An Example of Justice to Present and Future Times.
    1737. H.² T. 3/5, Th. 5.
B.O. The Sailor's Opera; or, A Trip to Jamaica 12° 1745.
*Ent. The Sailor's Progress.
    1748. N.W., G.F. Dec.
*Ent. of Singing and D. The Sailor's Rendezvous at Portsmouth.
    1747. D.L. T. 17/11.
*B.O. The Sailor's Wedding, or, The Humours of Wapping.
    1731. G.F. W. 21/4, T. 27; T. 4/5, M. 10, T. 11, Th. 13, F. 14.
    1732. Th. 4/5 (altered). 1739. B.F. Hallam, Aug. (as The S. W. or The Wapping Landlady).
C. St. James's Park 8° 1733.

*F. The Savage.
　　1727. L.² M. 27/2; M. 6/3.
*Ent. of D. The Savoyard Travellers.
　　1749. D.L. Th. 9/11.
*Droll. Scaramouch Scapin, or, The Old Miser caught in a Sack. With the Comical Tricks, Shifts and Cheats of Scaramouch's Three Companions, Trim the Barker, Sly and Bully Bounceabout.
　　1742. B.F. Hippisley, Aug.
*Ent. The Schemes of Harlequin, or, Monsieur La Saxe's Disappointment.
　　1746. B.F. Hussey, Aug.
*F. A School for Women.
　　1735. C.G. Th. 20/3.
*Ent. of M. Scipio and Africanus (sic).
　　1747. S.W. M. 10/8.
*Droll. Scipio's Triumph, or, the Siege of Carthage; with the Comical Humours of Noodle Stitch Puzzle and Scipio.
　　1730. B.F. Reynolds, Aug.
*Ent. The Scotch Figaries, or, Harlequin Barber.
　　1747. N.W., G.F. M. 3/8.
*C. See if you like it, or, 'Tis all a Mistake (from Plautus and Shakespeare).
　　1734. C.G. W. 9/10, F. 11, M. 14; S. 2/11.
*Droll. The True and Famous History of Semiramis, Queen of Babylon, or, The Woman wears the Breeches. Containing the Distressful Loves of Prince Alexis and the Princess Ulamia; the pleasant Adventures of Sir Solomon Gundy and his Man Spider, and the Comical Humours of Alderman Doodle, his Wife and Daughter Hoyden.
　　1725. B.F. Pinkethman and Norris, Aug.
*F. Sganarelle (This may not be a new piece).
　　1709. D.L. W. 1/6, S. 4.
*M. of speaking and D. The Sham Conjurer.
　　1741. C.G. S. 18/4.
*F. The Sham Doctor.
　　1740. Punch's theatre F. 14/3.
*F. The Sham Pilgrims (from Beaumont and Fletcher).
　　1734. D.L. Th. 3/1.
*Ent. of D. The Shepherd's Holiday.
　　1729. G.F. T. 25/11.
*Ent. of D. The Shepherd's Mount.
　　1735. D.L. T. 29/4.
*Ent. The Ship Launching, or, Harlequin turn'd Fryar.
　　1749. N.W., G.F. M. 28/8.
*Ent. of D. The Shipwreck; or, Perseus and Andromeda (by Weaver).
　　1717. D.L. T. 2/4 [see Perseus and Andromeda].
*Droll. The Siege of Barcelona, or The Soldier's Fortune. With the taking of Fort Mountjouy. Containing the pleasant and comical exploits of that renowned Hero Captain Blunderbuss and his man Squib.
　　1706. B.F. Pinkethman, Aug.
*Droll. The Siege of Bethulia, containing the History of Judith and Holofernes, together with the Humours of Rustego and his Man Terrible.
　　1721. B.F. Lee, Aug. 1729. B.F. Lee and Harper, Aug.; S.F. Sept. 1730. B.F. Aug.

¹*The Siege of Carthagena.

 1741. B.F. Fawkes and Pinchbeck, Aug.; S.F. Sept.

C. Sir Giddy Whim, or, The Lucky Amour 4° 1703.

*Droll. The Comical Humours of Sir John Falstaff.

 1733. S.F. Cibber, Griffin, Bullock and Hallam, Sept.

*F. Sir Peevy Pet.

 1737. H.² Th. 17/3.

*Droll. The True and Ancient History of Sir Richard Whittington, Thrice Lord Mayor of London, and his Cat.

 1711. Punch's theatre M. 10/12, T. 13. 1712. S. 5/1; W. 19/3. 1718. S.F. Pack, Spiller and Hall, Sept. 1723. S.F. Spiller and Hall, Sept. 1731. S.F. Lee and Harper, Sept. 1732. Tottenham Court F. Lee and Harper, Aug. 1748. Panton-street (puppets). May. 1749. S.F. Lee, Yeates and Warner, Sept.

T. Socrates Triumphant; or, The Danger of Being Wise in a Commonwealth of Fools 8° 1716 (in Military and Other Poems).

*F. The Soldier's Fortune (2 acts; from Otway).

 1748. C.G. T. 8/3.

*F. The Soldier's Stratagem.

 1719. Richmond M. 31/8.

*F. The Spanish Curate (from Beaumont and Fletcher).

 1749. D.L. Th. 19/10.

*F. Squire Brainless, or, Trick upon Trick (attributed to Hill).

 1710. D.L. Th. 27/4–S. 29.

*C. Squire Basinghall, or, The Cheapside Beau.

 1735. L.² W. 23/7, F. 25, W. 30; F. 1/8, W. 6, F. 8, F. 22; F. 5/9.

*B.O. The Stage Coach Opera.

 1730. D.L. W. 13/5, W. 27; Th. 19/11; G.F. F. 17/7. 1731. M. 22/2 (marked as new)–W. 24, S. 27; S. 6/3, Th. 11, T. 16, T. 23, M. 29; T. 6/4, M. 19, W. 28. 1732. G.F. Th. 27/4; F. 5/5, Th. 11.

(B.O.) The Stage Mutineers: or, A Play-House to be Lett. A Tragi-Comi-farcical-ballad opera...By a Gentleman late of Trinity College, Cambridge 8° 1733.

 1733. C.G. F. 27/7, T. 31; Th. 2/8, F. 3, T. 7, Th. 9, F. 10, T. 14, Th. 16, F. 17, M. 20.

F. The Stage Pretenders; or, The Actor turn'd Poet 8° 1720.

(Pol.) O. The State Juggler; or, Sir Politick Ribband. A New Excise Opera 8° 1733.

*O. The State of Innocence; or, The Fall of Man.

 1712. Punch's theatre M. 14/1, T. 15, Th. 17–T. 22, Th. 31; F. 1/2, S. 2, W. 13; M. 31/3; W. 2/4, F. 4.

C. The State of Physic 8° 1742.

*Ent. The Stratagem of Harlequin, or, The Miser Tricked.

 1732. S.F. Lee and Harper, Sept.

*Pant. The Stratagems of Harlequin, or, The Peasant Tricked.

 1730. B.F. Lee and Harper, Aug.; S.F. Sept.

Drolls. The Strolers Pacquet open'd. Containing Seven Jovial Drolls or Farces, Calculated for the Meridian of Bartholomew and Southwark Fairs. Representing the Comical Humours of Designing Usurers, Sly Pettifoggers, Cunning Sharpers, Cowardly Bullies, Wild Rakes, Finical Fops, Shrewd Clowns, Testy Masters, Arch Footmen, Forward Widows, Stale Maids, and Melting Lasses 8° 1742. [Contains: 1. The Bilker Bilk'd: or, A Banquet

of Wiles (from Bullock's The Woman's Revenge; cp. The Biter
Bit and Yarrow's Trick for Trick); 2. The Witchcraft of Love: or,
Stratagem on Stratagem (from Centlivre's The Man's Bewitch'd);
3. The Braggadochio: or, His Worship the Cully (from Congreve's
The Old Batchelor); 4. The Feign'd Shipwreck, or, The Imaginary
Heir (from Fletcher's The Scornful Lady); 5. The Guardians over-
reached in their own Humour: or, The Lover Metamorphos'd
(from Centlivre's A Bold Stroke for a Wife); 6. The Sexes Mis-
match'd, or A New Way to get a Husband (from Southerne's
Oroonoko and Fletcher's Monsieur Thomas); 7. The Litigious
Suitor Defeated; or a new Trick to get a Wife (from Bullock's
Woman is a Riddle).

B.O. The Sturdy Beggars. A New Ballad Opera 8° 1733.

*Ent. The Sultan.
 1729. L.² T. 28/10.

*Droll. Tamerlane the Great, with the Fall of Bajazet Emperor of
the Turks.
 1733. B.F. Cibber, Griffin and Hallam, Aug.; S.F. Cibber,
Griffin, Bullock and Hallam, Sept. 1747. B.F. Hussey, Aug.

*Ent. The Tavern Bilkers. Weaver mentions this as acted at D.L. in
1702.

*Ent. The Temple of Apollo.
 1749. N.W., G.F. M. 28/8.

*Ent. The Temple of Jupiter. With the Loves of Venus and Adonis.
 1748. N.W., G.F. March.

*Pant. Thamas Kouli Kan, the Persian Hero; or, The Distressed Princess.
 1741. B.F. Turbott, Aug.; B.F. Yeates, Aug.

*F. The Theatre.
 1720. L.² F. 22/4, S. 23.

*F. The Theatres 8° 1733.

*Past. B.O. Tho' Strange 'Tis True, or, Love's Vagaries.
 1732. L.² Th. 23/3.

*(B.O.?) The Throwster's Opera.
 1731. G.F. W. 2/6.

*Ent. of Music. Tithonus and Aurora; Interspers'd with a New Comic
Piece call'd, Harlequin's Whim.
 1748. S.W. March.

F. Tittle Tattle; or, Taste A-la-Mode. A New Farce. Perform'd
with Universal Applause by a Select Company of Belles and Beaux,
at the Lady Brilliant's Withdrawing Room, Pour tuer le Tems.
By Timothy Fribble, Esq; 8° 1749.

*Ent. The Top of the Tree, or, a Tit Bit for a nice Palate.
 1739. B.F. Hippisley, Chapman and Legar, Aug.

*C. The Town Airs.
 1723. H.² M. 23/9.

*Droll. The Town Rake, or, Punch turn'd Quaker.
 1711. Punch's theatre M. 26–F. 30; S. 1/12. 1712. S. 5/1, W.
23–S. 26; M. 25/2, F. 29; M. 28/4. 1713. F. 20/3, S. 21.

*Ent. Trick upon Trick, or, an Odd Affair between Harlequin, his
Associates and the Vintner of York (see The Stroler's Pacquet
open'd and Yarrow's Trick upon Trick).
 1739. Tottenham Court F. Great Booth, Aug.

*Ent. The Triumphs of Love.
 1735. C.G. F. 17/10.

*B.O. The Trooper's Opera 1736.
*Droll. Twice Married and a Maid Still, or, Bedding Makes the Bargain.
>   1717. S.F. Pinkethman and Pack, Sept.
*C. The Twin Venturers.
>   1710. D.L. W. 17/5.
F. Tyranny Triumphant! and Liberty Lost; the Muses Run Mad; Apollo struck dumb; and all Covent-Garden Confounded...By Patrick Fitz-Crambo, Esq; 8° 1743.
*T. The Tyrant.
>   1722. H.² M. 31/12. 1723. Th. 10/1.
T. The Unfortunate Duchess of Malfy; or, The Unfortunate Brothers (H.¹ July, 1707) 4° 1708.
>   1707. H.¹ T. 22/7, T. 29; F. 8/8.
*Ent. The Union of the Three Sister Arts.
>   1723. L.² F. 22/11.
*F. The Unlucky Lovers, or, The Merry London Cuckolds.
>   1717. D.L. Th. 18/7; F. 9/8.
*O. The Unnatural Brother, or, The Orphan Betrayed.
>   1712. Punch's theatre W. 23/1–T. 29; M. 4/2.
*Droll. The Unnatural Parents, or, The Fair Maid of the West. With the Comical Humours of Trusty, her Father's Man and Dame Strikefire, the Wicked Witch of Cornwall.
>   1727. B.F. Lee and Harper, Aug. 1748. B.F. Lee and Yeates sen. and jun., Aug.
*Pant. The Usurer, or, Harlequin's Last Shift.
>   1733. H.² F. 23/2.
The Usurper Detected.
*O. Valentine and Orson.
>   1713. Punch's theatre M. 16/11.
*Droll. Valentine and Orson, with the comical Whining Humours of Peter Pitiful.
>   1724. S.F. Pinkethman, Sept.
O. Vanelia: or, The Amours of the Great...As it is acted by a Private Company near St. James's 8° 1732 (six editions).
T. Vanella 8° 1736.
*M. Venus Cupid and Hymen.
>   1733. D.L. M. 21/5.
*Ent. of Music. Vertumnus and Pomona.
>   1748. D.L. Th. 27/10.
*O. The Vices of the Age Displayed, or Poor Robin's Dream.
>   1711. Punch's theatre W. 26/12–M. 31. 1712. T. 1/1–F. 4; M. 11/2, T. 12. 1713. M. 23/3, W. 25.
*F. The Vintner in the Suds (this may be Yarrow's Trick upon Trick).
>   1740. D.L. F. 25/4.
*F. Virtue's Escape, or, Good Luck at Last.
>   1733. H.² S. 12/5.
C. Int. The Volunteers: or, The Adventures of Roderick Random, and his Friend Strap (see *The Northern Heroes*).
>   1748. B.F. Bridges, Cross, Burton and Vaughan, Aug.
*Ent. Wagner and Abericot. Mentioned by Weaver as acted at D.L. in 1726.
B.O. The Wanton Countess: or, Ten Thousand Pounds for a Pregnancy 8° 1733.

B.O. The Wanton Jesuit: or, Innocence Seduced 8° **1731.**
>   1732. H.² F. 17/3.

*C. The Wanton Trick'd, or, All Alive and Merry.
>   1743. Tottenham Court F. Yeates, Warner and Rosoman, Aug.

*Ent. The Wapping Landlady, or, Harlequin Statue.
>   1748. N.W., G.F. March.

Droll. Wat Tyler and Jack Straw, being the Representation of that Celebrated Heroic Action of Sir William Walworth, Lord Mayor of London, Performed in the Reign of King Richard the Second (title from bill) 8° 1730 (as W.T. and J.S., or, The Mob Reformers).
>   1730. B.F. Pinkethman and Gifford, Aug.

*B.O. Wat Tyler, or, The State Menders.
>   1733. D.L. F. 19/1.

 B.O. The Wedding; or, The Country Housewife 8° **1734.**

 B.O. The Whim, or, The Merry Cheat.
>   1741. C.G. F. 17/4.

(B.O.) The Whim: or, The Miser's Retreat. A Farce. Alter'd from the French of La Maison Rustique (G.F. 1734?) 8° **1734.**

*Ent. of D. The White Joke.
>   1730. G.F. T. 28/4.

*Ent. The Whitson Holidays.
>   1749. N.W. Clerkenwell F. 28/4.

*F. A Will and No Will, or, A New Case for the Lawyers (from Regnard).
>   1748. D.L. T. 22/3, T. 29, Th. 31; M. 11/4, Th. 21, F. 22.

 B.O. The Woman of Taste, or The Yorkshire Lady 8° **1738.**

*F. A Woman will have her Will.
>   1713. D.L. W. 3/6.

*Ent. The Wrangling Deities, or, Venus upon Earth.
>   1741. B.F. Lee and Woodward, Aug.

*Ent. of D. The Yellow Joke.
>   1730. G.F. M. 29/6.

*C. The Young Coquette.
>   1705. D.L. S. 16/6, Th. 28. 1706. S. 9/3 (2 acts).

 C. The Younger Brother; or, The Sham Marquis (L.² Feb. 1718/9) 8° **1719.**
>   1719. L.² S. 7/2–T. 10.

II. *Italian Operas, Oratorios and Serenatas.*

[In the preparation of this list, the standard histories of music have been referred to, as well as some manuscript collections in the British Museum. The Colman manuscript and the manuscript Catalogue of Opera Librettos compiled by Mr Barclay Squire are of noteworthy value. For the privilege of using the latter I am indebted to the courtesy of Mr Squire and the Museum officials.]

O. Admeto (Admetus), re di Tessaglia (Ital. and Eng.) 8° 1731 (*bis*). Altered from Aurelio Aureli's *L'Antigona delusa da Alceste*; music Händel. 1727. H.¹ T. 31/1; S. 4/2, T. 7, S. 11, T. 14, S. 18, T. 21, S. 25, T. 28; S. 4/3, T. 7, S. 11, T. 14, S. 18, T. 21, S. 25; T. 4/4, S. 15, T. 18; S. 30/9; T. 3/10, S. 7, S. 14, T. 17; S. 4/11.

1728. S. 25/5, T. 28; S. 1/6. 1731. T. 7/12, S. 11, T. 14, S. 18. 1732. T. 4/1, S. 8, T. 11.

O. Adriano in Siria (Adrian in Syria; Ital. and Eng.) 8° 1735; 1750.

Metastasio; dedication signed Angelo Cori; music Veracini. 1735. H.[1] T. 25/11, S. 29; T. 2/12, S. 6, T. 9, S. 13, T. 16, S. 20, S. 27, T. 30. 1736. S. 7/2, T. 10, S. 14, T. 18/5, S. 22, T. 25, S. 29.

O. Alceste (Ital. and Eng.) 8° 1744.

Adaptation by Paolo A. Rolli from Metastasio's *Demetrio*; music Lampugnani. 1744. H.[1] T. 24/4, S. 28; T. 1/5, S. 5, T. 8, F. 11, T. 15, S. 19, S. 26; S. 2/6, T. 5, S. 9, S. 16.

O. Alcina (Ital. and Eng.) 8° 1735.

Originally written by Antonio Marchi; music Händel. 1735. C.G. W. 16/4, S. 19, W. 23, S. 26, W. 30; S. 3/5, W. 7, S. 10, W. 14, S. 17, W. 21, W. 28; W. 4/6, Th. 12, W. 18, W. 25, S. 28; W. 2/7, W. 9. 1736. S. 6/11, W. 10, S. 13. 1737. F. 10/6, T. 21.

O. Alessandro (Alexander; Ital. and Eng.) 8° 1726.

Paolo Rolli; music Händel. 1726. H.[1] Th. 5/5, S. 7, T. 10, Th. 12, S. 14, T. 17, Th. 19, S. 21, T. 24, Th. 26, T. 31; S. 4/6, T. 7. 1727. T. 26/12, S. 30. 1732. S. 25/11, T. 28; S. 2/12, T. 19, T. 26, S. 30.

O. Alessandro in Persia (Ital. and Eng.) 8° 1741.

Francesco Vanneschi; pasticcio by Galuppi. 1741. H.[1] S. 31/10; T. 10/11, S. 14, T. 17, S. 21, T. 24, S. 28; T. 1/12, S. 5. 1742. S. 2/1 (bills missing but acted 6 times); S. 13/11, T. 16, S. 20, T. 23, S. 27.

*O. Alessandro Severo.

Zeno?; pasticcio by Händel. 1738. H.[1] S. 25/2, T. 28; S. 4/3, T. 7, S. 11; T. 30/5.

Orat. Alexander Balus 4° 1748.

Morell; music Händel. 1748. C.G. W. 23/3, F. 25, W. 30.

*O. Alexander the Great.

1715. L.[2] T. 26/4 (what this piece was, I have been unable to discover; it is probably not an Italian opera).

O. Alfonso (Ital. and Engl.) 8° 1744.

Paolo Rolli; music Lampugnani. 1744. H.[1] T. 3/1, S. 7, T. 10, S. 14, T. 17, S. 21, T. 24, S. 28.

Ser. L'Allegro, il Penseroso ed il Moderato 4° 1740 (*bis*); 4° 1741 (Dublin); 8° (1750?).

Music Händel. 1740. L.[2] W. 27/2; Th. 6/3, M. 10; W. 23/4. 1741. S. 31/1; S. 7/2; W. 8/4. 1743. C.G. F. 18/3.

O. Almahide (Ital. and Eng.) 4° 1710.

Music perhaps by Buononcini. 1710. H.[1] T. 10/1, F. 13, T. 17, F. 20, T. 24, F. 27, T. 31; F. 10/2, T. 14, T. 21; T. 14/3, T. 28; T. 25/4; T. 9/5. 1711. S. 14/4, W. 18, S. 21; W. 2/5; W. 14/11, S. 17, W. 28; S. 1/12, S. 29. 1712. M. 14/1.

O. Amadigi di Gaula (Amadis of Gaul; Ital. and Eng.) 8° 1715.

Probably Heidegger; music Händel. 1715. H.[1] W. 25/5; S. 11/6, W. 15, S. 18, T. 28; S. 2/7, S. 9. 1716. Th. 16/2, T. 21, S. 25; S. 3/3, T. 6; W. 20/6; Th. 12/7. 1717. S. 16/2, S. 23; Th. 21/3; Th. 11/4; Th. 30/5.

O. L'Ambleto (Hamlet; Ital. and Eng.) 8° 1712.

Apostolo Zeno; dedication signed by Cav. Nicolius Grimaldi;

music Francesco Gasparini. 1712. H.¹ W. 27/2; S. 1/3, S. 8, T. 11, S. 15, T. 18.

O. Angelica e Medoro (A. and Medorus; Ital. and Eng.) 8° 1739.
Altered from Metastasio's *L'Angelica*; dedication signed by Angelo Cori; music Pescetti. 1739. C.G. S. 10/3, S. 17, S. 24; W. 11/4.

*O. Annibale in Capua.
Pasticcio. 1746. H.¹ T. 4/11, S. 8, T. 18, S. 22, T. 25, S. 29.

*O. Antigone.
Music Galuppi. 1746. H.¹ T. 13/5, T. 20, S. 24, T. 27, S. 31; T. 3/6, S. 7, T. 10, S. 14, T. 17, S. 21, T. 24, S. 28.

O. Antioco (Antiochus; Ital. and Eng.) 8° 1712.
Not by Zeno, as stated by Burney; dedication signed J. J. Heidegger; music possibly by Gasparini. 1711. H.¹ W. 12/12, S. 15, W. 19, S. 22. 1712. W. 2/1, S. 5, W. 9, S. 19; S. 2/2, S. 16; S. 5/4, W. 23, W. 30; W. 14/5; S. 14/6.

O. Aquilio, Consolo (Aquilius; Ital. and Eng.) 8° 1724.
Pasticcio. 1724. H.¹ Th. 21/5, T. 26, S. 30; T. 2/6, S. 13.

*O. Arbace (Arbaces).
1734. H.¹ S. 5/1, T. 8, S. 12, T. 15, S. 19, T. 22; Th. 28/3, S. 30.

O. Ariadne in Crete (Ital. and Eng.) 8° 1733.
Francis Colman; music Händel. 1734. H.¹ S. 26/1, T. 29; S. 2/2, T. 5, S. 9, T. 12, S. 16, T. 19, S. 23, T. 26; S. 2/3, T. 5, S. 9, T. 12, S. 16; T. 16/4, S. 20; W. 27/11, S. 30; W. 4/12, S. 7, W. 11.

O. Ariadne in Naxus (Ital. and Eng.) 8° 1734.
Rolli; music Porpora. 1733. L.² S. 29/12. 1734. T. 1/1, S. 5, T. 8, S. 12, T. 15, S. 19, S. 26, T. 29; S. 2/2, T. 19, S. 23; S. 20/4, T. 23, Th. 25, S. 27, T. 30; S. 4/5, T. 7, F. 31; T. 4/6, S. 8, T. 11, S. 15.

*O. Ariodante.
Originally written by Antonio Salvi; music Händel. 1735. C.G. W. 8/1, W. 15, S. 18, W. 22, W. 29; W. 5/2, W. 12, Th. 20, M. 24; M. 3/3. 1736. W. 5/5, F. 7.

O. Aristodemo, Tiranno di Cuma (Ital. and Eng.) 8° 1744.
Rolli; pasticcio. 1744. H.¹ T. 3/4, S. 7, T. 10, S. 14, T. 17, S. 21.

O. Arminio (Ital. and Eng.) 8° 1714.
Not the *Arminio* of Antonio Salvi. 1714. H.¹ Th. 4/3, S. 6, Th. 11, S. 13, Th. 18, S. 20; S. 10/4; S. 1/5, S. 29; S. 23/10, T. 26; W. 3/11; S. 11/12, W. 15, W. 22. 1715. S. 26/3. Newly set by Händel. 1737. C.G. W. 12/1, S. 15, W. 19, S. 22, W. 26; S. 12/2.

O. Arsace (Ital. and Eng.) 8° 1721.
Rolli; pasticcio. 1721. H.¹ W. 1/2, S. 4, W. 8, S. 11, W. 15, S. 18, Th. 23, T. 28; W. 10/5; W. 1/11, W. 8.

O. Arsaces (Ital. and Eng.) 8° 1737.
Alteration by Rolli from Salvi; pasticcio. 1737. S. 29/10; T. 1/11. 1738. T. 9/5.

O. Arsinoe, Queen of Cyprus 4° 1705; 4° 1707.
Translation by Motteux from Tomaso Stanzani; music Clayton. 1705. D.L. T. 16/1, Th. 25; Th. 1/2; M. 5/3, Th. 8, T. 13, T. 20, T. 27; Th. 12/4, Th. 19; S. 12/5, Th. 31; Th. 7/6, Th. 21;

T. 10/7; S. 27/10; S. 17/11, M. 19, T. 27, F. 30; T. 11/12, T. 18;
St. James' T. 6/2. 1706. D.L. W. 23/1; Th. 14/2, Th. 21, Th. 28;
S. 9/3; F. 14/6, T. 25, F. 28; D.G. T. 9/7; Th. 8/8. 1707. D.L.
T. 18/2, S. 22; S. 1/3.

O. Artamene (Ital. and Eng.) 8° 1746.
Adaptation from Bartolomeo Vitturi; music Gluck. 1746. H.¹
T. 4/3, S. 8, T. 11, S. 15, T. 18, S. 22; T. 8/4, S. 12.

O. Artaserse (Ital. and Eng.) 8° 1724.
Altered from Apostolo Zeno and Pariati; dedication signed
N. Haym; music Ariosti. 1724. L.² T. 1/12, S. 5, W. 9, S. 12,
T. 15, S. 19, T. 22, S. 26, T. 29.

O. Artaserse (Ital. and Eng.) 8° 1734; 8° 1735; 8° 1754.
Metastasio; music Hasse and Riccardo Broschi. 1734. H.¹ T.
29/10; S. 2/11, T. 5, S. 9, T. 12, S. 16, T. 19, S. 23, T. 26; T.
3/12, S. 7, S. 28, T. 31. 1735. T. 7/1, S. 11, T. 14, T. 21, S. 25,
T. 28; S. 15/3, S. 22; T. 22/4, S. 26, T. 29; S. 17/5, F. 23, T. 27;
T. 3/6. 1736. S. 3/1, S. 10, T. 13; S. 27/3, T. 30; S. 3/4; T. 1/6,
S. 5.

*Int. L'Asilo d'Amore (no doubt Metastasio's work).
1739. C.G. W. 11/4.

O. L'Astarto (Ital. and Eng.) 8° 1720.
Adapted by Rolli from the opera of Zeno and Pariati; music
Buononcini. 1720. H.¹ S. 19/11, W. 23, S. 26, W. 30; S. 3/12,
W. 7, S. 10, W. 14, S. 17, W. 21. 1721. S. 7/1, W. 11, S. 14,
W. 18, S. 28; S. 4/3, T. 7, S. 11, T. 14, S. 18; S. 1/4, T. 11; S.
24/6, W. 28; S. 11/11, W. 15, S. 18, W. 22. 1722. W. 6/6, S. 9.
1734. L.² T. 26/2; S. 2/3, T. 5, S. 9; S. 6/4, T. 16.

O. Astianatte (Astyanax; Ital. and Eng.) 8° 1727.
Altered from Antonio Salvi by Haym; music Buononcini. 1727.
S. 6/5, T. 9, S. 13, T. 16, T. 23, S. 27, T. 30; S. 3/6, T. 6.

O. Atalanta (Ital. and Eng.) 8° 1736.
Music Händel. 1736. C.G. W. 12/5, S. 15, W. 19, S. 22, W.
26, S. 29; W. 2/6, W. 9; S. 20/11, S. 27.

Orat. Athalia. An Oratorio or Sacred Drama 4° 1733; 8° 1756.
Humphreys; music Händel. Oxford, July 1733. 1735. C.G.
T. 1/4–Th. 3, W. 9, S. 12.

O. Bellerofonte (Bellerophon; Ital. and Eng.) 8° 1747.
Music Terradellas. 1747. H.¹ T. 24/3, S. 28, T. 31; S. 4/4,
T. 7, S. 11.

*O. Belmira.
Pasticcio. 1734. L.² S. 23/3, S. 30; T. 2/4.

Orat. Belshazzar 4° 1745; 4° 1751.
Music Händel. 1745. H.¹ W. 27/3, F. 29.

*O. Berenice.
Music Händel. 1737. C.G. W. 18/5, S. 21, W. 25; W. 15/6.

*Int. Le Bourgeois Gentilhomme.
1737. H.¹ S. 21/5.

O. Busiri, overo. In Van si fugge l'Amore (Ital. and Eng.) 8° 1740.
Music Pescetti. 1740. H.¹ S. 10/5, T. 13, S. 17, T. 20.

O. La Caduta dei Giganti (Ital. and Eng.) 8° 1745.
Music Gluck. 1746. H.¹ T. 7/1, S. 11, T. 14, S. 18, T. 21, S. 25.

O. Caius Fabricius (Ital. and Eng.) 8° 1733.
Altered from Zeno; pasticcio. 1733. H.¹ T. 4/12, S. 8, S. 15,
S. 22.

O. Caius Marius Coriolanus (Caio Mario Coriolano) 8° 1723.
  Haym; music Attilio Ariosti. 1723. T. 19/2, S. 23, T. 26; S. 2/3,
  T. 5, S. 9, T. 12, S. 16, T. 19, S. 23; T. 23/4; T. 7/5, S. 11.
  1724. T. 17/3; Th. 16/4. 1732. S. 25/3, T. 28; S. 1/4, T. 11, S. 15.
O. Calfurnia (Calphurnia; Ital. and Eng.) 8° 1724.
  Grazio Bracciuoli, altered by Haym; music Buononcini. 1724.
  S. 18/4, T. 21, S. 25, T. 28; S. 2/5, T. 5, S. 9, Th. 14, S. 16;
  S. 6/6, T. 9.
O. Camilla 4° 1706; 4° 1707; 8° 1709; 8° 1717; 8° 1726.
  Silvio Stampiglia (*Il Trionfo di Camilla*); dedication signed
  Owen Swiny; music Buononcini adapted by Haym. 1706. D.L.
  S. 30/3; S. 6/4, Th. 11, T. 23, T. 30; Th. 16/5, Th. 23; T. 4/6;
  F. 5/7; Th. 12/12, S. 14, T. 17, S. 21, S. 28; D.G. Th. 1/8;
  T. 26/11. 1707. D.L. S. 4/1, S. 11, S. 18, S. 25, W. 29; S. 1/2, S.8,
  W.12, S.15, Th.27; S.8/3, Th.13, S.29; Th. 24/4; Th. 15/5, S.24;
  S. 15/11; S. 6/12, T. 9, S. 13. 1708. H.¹ T. 27/1, S. 31; T. 3/2,
  S. 7, T. 10, S. 21; S. 13/3, S. 27; T. 6/4, S. 24. 1709. T. 25/1,
  Th. 27, S. 29; W. 2/2, S. 5, S. 12, W. 16, S. 19; Th. 17/3; T. 5/4,
  W. 27; S. 7/5, S. 21; Th. 20/10; M. 7/11, M. 14; F. 2/12, T. 13.
  1717. L.² W. 2/1, S. 5, W. 9, S. 12, W. 16, S. 19, W. 23, S. 26;
  W. 13/2, S. 16, W. 20; T. 2/4, T. 9; W. 3/7. 1719. T. 24/2;
  M. 9/3, S. 14; Th. 16/4. 1726. S. 19/11, T. 22, Th. 24–S. 26,
  T. 29; Th. 1/12, T. 6, Th. 8, S. 10, S. 17, T. 20, S. 31. 1727.
  T. 3/1, Th. 5, Th. 12; W. 1/2, W. 8; Th. 16/3; Th. 6/4, W. 12,
  M. 24, Th. 27; Th. 2/11, W. 8; Th. 7/12. 1728. S. 16/11; S. 14/12.
O. Catone (Ital. and Eng.) 8° 1732.
  Metastasio; translation into English by Humphreys. 1732.
  H.¹ S. 4/11, T. 7, S. 11, T. 14, S. 18.
*O. Cefalo e Procri.
  1742. H.¹ (bills missing; Burney says acted 3 times iv. 448).
O. (Ciro) L'Odio e l'Amore (Ital. and Eng.) 8° 1721.
  Adaptation by Rolli from Matteo Noris; music Attilio Ariosti.
  1721. H.¹ S. 20/5, W. 24, S. 27, W. 31; S. 3/6, S. 10, S. 17,
  W. 21. 1722. S. 17/11, T. 20, S. 24, T. 27; S. 1/12.
O. Clearte (Ital. and Eng.) 8° 1716.
  1716. H.¹ W. 18/4, S. 21, W. 25, S. 28; S. 5/5, S. 12; W. 6/6,
  W. 13, S. 30; S. 8/12, S. 15, S. 22. 1717. S. 30/3; S. 1/6.
O. Clotilda (Ital. and Eng.) 8° 1709.
  Possibly the same as the *Clotilda* of G. B. Neri; pasticcio. 1709.
  H.¹ W. 2/3, S. 5, S. 12, T. 15, S. 19, Th. 24, S. 26. 1711. W.
  16/5, S. 19, W. 23.
C.O. La Comedia in Comedia (Ital. and Eng.) 8° 1748.
  Altered from the adaptation by Vanneschi of C. A. Pelli's play
  performed at Venice 1741; music Rinaldo da Capua. 1748. H.¹
  T. 8/11, S. 12, T. 15, S. 26. 1749. S. 7/1, T. 10; S. 11/3; S. 3/6.
O. La Conquista del Vello d'Oro (The Conquest of the Golden
  Fleece; Ital. and Eng.) 8° 1738.
  Music Pescetti. 1738. H.¹ S. 28/1, T. 31; S. 4/2, T. 7, S. 11,
  T. 14, S. 18, T. 21, S. 25; T. 23/5.
O. Creseo (Croesus), Rè di Lidia (Ital. and Eng.) 8° 1714.
  Dedication signed N. Haym. 1714. H.¹ W. 27/1, F. 29; W. 3/2,
  T. 9, S. 13, T. 16, S. 20, T. 23, S. 27; W. 31/3; S. 8/5, S. 22.
O. Crispo (Ital. and Eng.) 8° 1721.
  Rolli; music Buononcini. 1722. H.¹ W. 10/1, S. 13, W. 17,

S. 20, W. 24, S. 27, W. 31; S. 3/2, T. 6, S. 10; W. 11/4, S. 14,
W. 18, S. 21; W. 16/5, S. 19; W. 13/6, S. 16; S. 29/12. 1723.
W. 2/1, T. 8.

O.   Il Dario (Ital. and Eng.) 8° 1725.
        Music Attilio Ariosti. 1725. M. 5/4, S. 10, T. 13, S. 17, T. 20,
     S. 24, T. 27.

Orat. David e Bersabea 8° 1734.
        Music Porpora. 1734. L.² W. 20/3, W. 27; W. 3/4, M. 8,
     W. 10. 1735. F. 28/2; T. 1/4, Th. 3.

(Orat.) David's Lamentation over Saul and Jonathan. A Lyrick Poem
     (by Lockman; music Boyce; as performed in the Apollo Society,
     April 16, 1736) 4° 1736; 8° (1740; in *A Miscellany of Lyric Poems*).

Orat. David's Lamentation over Saul and Jonathan 4° 1740 (5 editions)
        Lockman; music Smith. 1740. Hickford's room F. 22/2, F.
     29; F. 7/3, F. 14, F. 21, Th. 27; T. 1/4.

Orat. Deborah 4° 1733; 8° 1749 (Dublin); 4° 1764.
        Humphreys; music Händel. 1733. H.¹ S. 17/3, T. 27, S. 31;
     T. 3/4, S. 7, T. 10. 1734. T. 2/4, S. 6, T. 9. 1735. C.G. W. 26/3,
     M. 31. 1744. H.¹ S. 3/11, S. 24.

*O. Deidamia.
        Music Händel. 1741. L.² S. 10/1, S. 17, S. 24.

O.   Demetrio (Ital. and Eng.) 8° 1737.
        Altered from Metastasio; music Pescetti. 1737. H.¹ S. 12/2,
     T. 15, S. 19, T. 22, S. 26; S. 5/3, T. 8, S. 12, T. 15, S. 19, T. 22,
     S. 26, T. 29; S. 2/4.

*O. Demofoonte.
        1737. H.¹ T. 24/5; T. 7/6, S. 11.

Ser. Diana and Endymion.
        Music Pescetti. 1739. H.² S. 1/12, T. 4, S. 8.

*O. Dido.
        1737. C.G. W. 13/4, W. 20, W. 27; W. 1/6.

O.   Didone (Ital. and Eng.) 8° 1748.
        Altered from Metastasio; music Hasse. 1748. H.¹ S. 26/3;
     S. 2/4, S. 16, S. 23, S. 30.

C.O. Don Calascione (Ital. and Eng.) 8° 1749.
        G. Barlocci; music Gaetano Latille. 1749. H.¹ S. 21/1, T. 24,
     S. 28, T. 31; S. 4/2, S. 25; S. 4/3; S. 22/4; S. 6/5, S. 20.

*O. Dorinda.
        1712. H.¹ W. 10/12, S. 13, W. 17, S. 20, W. 24, W. 31. 1713.
     S. 3/1, S. 31; S. 7/2; S. 21/3; S. 25/4. 1714. S. 9/1, S. 16, S. 23.

O.   Elisa (Ital. and Eng.) 8° 1725.
        Pasticcio, arranged by Haym. 1726. H.¹ S. 15/1, T. 18, S. 22,
     T. 25, S. 29; T. 1/2.

O.   Elpidia, overo Li Rivali Generosi (Ital. and Eng.) 8° 1725.
        Apostolo Zeno; music said to be by Leonardo Vinci. 1725.
     H.¹ T. 11/5, T. 18, S. 22, T. 25, S. 29; T. 1/6, S. 5, T. 8, S. 12,
     T. 15, S. 19; T. 30/11; S. 4/12, T. 7, S. 11, T. 14.

O.   Enea nel Lazio (Æneas in Latium; Ital. and Eng.) 8° 1734.
        Rolli; music Porpora. 1734. L.² S. 11/5, T. 14, S. 18, T. 21,
     S. 25, T. 28; S. 15/6.

O.   Enrico (Ital. and Eng.) 8° 1742.
        Vanneschi; music Galuppi. 1743. H.¹ S. 1/1, T. 4, S. 8, T. 11,
     S. 15, T. 18, S. 22, T. 25, S. 29; T. 1/2, S. 5, T. 8, S. 12, T. 15,
     S. 19; T. 22/3, S. 26.

O. L'Erminia. Favola Boschereccia d'Eulibio Pastore Arcade (Ital. and Eng.) 8° 1723.

Rolli; music Buononcini. 1723. H.[1] S. 30/3; T. 2/4, S. 6, T. 16, S. 20, S. 27, T. 30; S. 4/5.

O. Ernelinda (Ital. and Eng.) 8° 1713; 8° 1715.

Altered from F. Silvani's *La Fede tradita e vendicata*; dedication signed Heidegger; pasticcio. 1713. H.[1] Th. 26/2, S. 28; T. 3/3, S. 7, T. 10, S. 14, S. 28; S. 11/4; S. 2/5, S. 30. 1714. S. 3/4, W. 7, S. 17, S. 24; W. 12/5; S. 5/6, W. 23; T. 16/11, S. 20; S. 4/12, S. 18. 1715. S. 9/4.

*Orat. L'Errore di Solomone.

Music Veracini. 1744. H.[1] T. 20/3, Th. 22.

Orat. Esther 4° 1732; 4° 1733 (4th); 4° 1742 (Dublin); 4° 1756 (Salisbury); 4° 1757; 8° 1761; 4° (1761).

Humphreys; music Händel (originally composed for Duke of Chandos 1720). 1732. H.[1] T. 2/5, S. 6, T. 9, S. 13, T. 16, S. 20. 1733. S. 14/4, T. 17. 1735. C.G. W. 5/3, F. 7, W. 12, F. 14, W. 19, F. 21. 1736. W. 7/4, W. 14. 1737. W. 6/4, Th. 7. 1740. L.[2] W. 26/3.

O. Etearco (Ital. and Eng.) 8° 1711.

Silvio Stampiglia; dedication signed N. Haym; music Buononcini. 1710. H.[1] S. 20/12. 1711. W. 10/1, S. 13, W. 17, S. 20, W. 24, S. 27, W. 31.

O. Ezio (Ital. and Eng.) 8° 1732.

Altered from Metastasio; English translation by Humphreys; music Händel. 1732. H.[1] S. 15/1, T. 18, S. 22, T. 25, S. 29.

O. Faramondo (Pharamond; Ital. and Eng.) 8° 1737.

Altered from Zeno; music Händel. 1738. H.[1] T. 3/1, S. 7, T. 10, S. 14, T. 17, S. 21, T. 24; T. 16/5.

O. Farnace (Pharnaces; Ital. and Eng.) 8° 1723.

Altered from Lorenzo Morari; music Buononcini. 1723. H.[1] W. 27/11, S. 30; W. 4/12, S. 7. 1724. S. 4/1, S. 11.

*[Musical Ent.] The Feast of Hymen (Festa d' Imeneo) 8° 1734.

Music Porpora. 1736. H.[1] T. 4/5, S. 8, T. 11, S. 15.

O. Fernando 8° 1734.

Music Porpora. 1734. L.[2] T. 8/2, S. 9, T. 12, S. 16.

O. Fetonte (Phæton; Ital. and Eng.) 8° 1747.

F. Vanneschi; music Paradies. 1747. H.[1] S. 17/1, S. 24, T. 27, S. 31; T. 3/2, T. 10, S. 14, T. 17, S. 21.

*O. La Finta Frascatana.

1748. H.[1] S. 31/12.

O. Flavio, Re de' Longobardi (Flavius; Ital. and Eng.) 8° 1723.

Haym; music Händel. 1723. H.[1] T. 14/5, S. 18, T. 21, S. 25, M. 27, Th. 30; T. 11/6, S. 15. 1732. T. 18/4, S. 22, T. 25, S. 29.

O. Il Floridante (Ital. and Eng.) 8° 1721.

Rolli; music Händel. 1721. H.[1] S. 9/12, W. 13, S. 16, W. 20, S. 23, W. 27, S. 30. 1722. W. 3/1, F. 5; T. 13/2, T. 20; W. 25/4, S. 28; W. 23/5, S. 26; T. 4/12, S. 8, T. 11, S. 15, T. 18, S. 22, W. 26. 1727. S. 29/4; T. 2/5. 1733. S. 3/3, T. 6, S. 10, T. 13; T. 8/5, T. 15, S. 19.

O. Gianguir 8° 1742.

Apostolo Zeno; music Hasse, Lampugnani, Brivio and Rinaldo da Capua. 1742. H.[1] T. 2/11, S. 6, T. 9.

Comic Int. Il Giocatore (The Gamester; Ital.) 8° 1736.
>   Music G. M. Orlandini. 1737. H.¹ S. 1/1, T. 4, S. 15, T. 18,
>   S. 22; S. 12/2.

C.O. Il Giramondo (Ital. and Eng.) 8° 1749.
>   1749. H.¹ S. 18/2.

O. Giulio Cesare in Egitto (Julius Cæsar; Ital. and Eng.) 8° 1724;
>   8° (1725; 2nd).
>   Haym; music Händel. 1724. H.¹ Th. 20/2, S. 22, T. 25, Th. 27,
>   S. 29; T. 3/3, S. 7, T. 10, S. 14, S. 21, T. 24, S. 28; T. 7/4, S. 11.
>   1725. S. 2/1, T. 5, S. 16, T. 19, S. 23, T. 26; T. 2/2, S. 6, T. 9.
>   1730. S. 17/1, S. 24, T. 27, S. 31; T. 3/2, S. 7, S. 14, T. 17,
>   S. 21; S. 21/3, T. 31. 1732. T. 1/2, S. 5, T. 8, S. 12.

*O. Giustino (Justin).
>   Music Händel. 1737. C.G. W. 16/2, S. 19, T. 22, F. 25; W.
>   2/3, F. 4; W. 4/5, W. 11; W. 8/6.

O. Griselda (Ital. and Eng.) 8° 1721.
>   Adaptation by Rolli from Zeno; music Buononcini. 1722. H.¹
>   Th. 22/2, S. 24, T. 27; S. 3/3, S. 10, T. 13, S. 17, W. 28, S. 31;
>   W. 4/4, S. 7; W. 2/5, S. 5, W. 9, W. 30; S. 2/6. 1733. T. 22/5,
>   S. 26, T. 29; S. 2/6, T. 5, S. 9.

Int. Grullo e Moschetta (Ital. and Eng.) 8° 1737.
>   Music G. M. Orlandini. 1737. H.¹ S. 19/2, T. 22, S. 26; S. 5/3,
>   T. 8, S. 19, T. 22; T. 19/4, S. 23; S. 14/5.

*O. Hercules.
>   Rossi. 1712. H.¹ S. 3/5, W. 7, S. 10; W. 4/6, W. 11.

Mus.O. Hercules 8° 1745.
>   T. Broughton; music Händel. 1745. H.¹ S. 5/1, S. 12.

Orat. Hercules 4° 1749.
>   Music Händel. 1749. C.G. F. 24/2; W. 1/3.

O. L'Idaspe Fedele (Hydaspes; Ital. and Eng.) 4° 1710; 8° 1712.
>   Dedication signed Nicolino Grimaldi; music Francesco
>   Mancini. 1710. H.¹ Th. 23/3, Th. 30; S. 1/4, S. 15, T. 18, F. 21,
>   F. 28; T. 2/5, F. 5, F. 12, T. 23, T. 30; W. 22/11, S. 25, W. 29;
>   S. 2/12, W. 20, F. 22, W. 27, S. 30. 1711. W. 7/2, S. 10, S. 17,
>   T. 20; W. 4/4, S. 7, S. 28; W. 30/5; W. 21/11, S. 24; W. 5/12,
>   S. 8, W. 26. 1712. S. 12/1, Th. 17; W. 20/2; Th. 27/3, S. 29;
>   S. 26/4. 1715. S. 7/5, W. 11, S. 14, S. 21; Th. 2/6; S. 27/8.
>   1716. W. 9/5.

O. Ifigenia in Aulide (Iphigenia; Ital. and Eng.) 8° 1735.
>   Rolli; music Porpora. 1735. H.¹ S. 3/5, T. 6, S. 10, T. 13, T. 20

Operetta. Imeneo (Hymen; Ital. and Eng.) 8° 1742 (Dublin).
>   Music Händel. 1740. L.² S. 22/11; S. 13/12.

Int. L'Impresario (Ital. and Eng.) 8° 1737.
>   Taken from the intermezzi in Metastasio's *Didone Abbandonata*;
>   music Domenico Sani. 1737. H.¹ S. 26/3, T. 29; S. 2/4, S. 16;
>   T. 10/5.

O. L'Incostanza (Ital. and Eng.) 8° 1745.
>   Vanneschi; pasticcio. 1745. H.² S. 9/2, S. 16, S. 23; S. 2/3,
>   S. 9, S. 16, S. 23, S. 30; S. 6/4, S. 20.

Past. O. La Ingratitudine Punita (Ital. and Eng.) 8° 1748.
>   1748. H.² T. 12/1, T. 26; T. 2/2; H.¹ T. 1/3 (altered).

Orat. Israel in Egypt 4° (1740).
>   Music Händel. 1739. H.¹ W. 4/4, W. 11, T. 17. 1740. L.² T. 1/4.

O. Issiphile (Ital. and Eng.) 8° 1735.

Altered from Metastasio; dedication signed Angelo Maria Cori; music Pietro Sandoni. 1735. H.¹ T. 8/4, S. 12, T. 15, S. 19.

Orat. Jephtha (by John Hoadly; music Greene) 8° 1737; 8° (1740; in *A Miscellany of Lyric Poems*).

Orat. Joseph (music de Fesch) 4° 1745.

Orat. Joseph and his Brethren 4° 1744.
James Miller; music Händel. 1744. C.G. F. 2/3, W. 7, F. 9, W. 14. 1745. W. 20/3; W. 3/4; H.¹ F. 15/3, F. 22. 1747. C.G. W. 18/3, F. 20, W. 25.

Orat. Joshua 4° 1748; 4° 1754; 4° 1756.
Morell; music Händel. 1748. C.G. W. 9/3, F. 11, W. 16, F. 18.

Orat. Judas Macchabæus 4° 1748; 8° 1748 (Dublin); 4° 1757; 4° 1762.
Morell; music Händel. 1747. C.G. W. 1/4, F. 3, W. 8, F. 10, M. 13, W. 15. 1748. F. 26/2; T. 1/3, F. 4; F. 1/4, M. 4, Th. 7.

Orat. Judith 8° 1733.
William Huggins; music de Fesch. 1733. L.² F. 16/2. 1740. Hickford's room F. 29/2 (marked as new).

O. Lotario (Lotharius; Ital. and Eng.) 8° 1729.
Altered from the *Adelaide* written by A. Salvi; music Händel. 1729. H.¹ T. 2/12, S. 6, T. 9, S. 13, T. 16, S. 20, T. 23. 1730. S. 3/1, S. 10, T. 13.

Ser. Love and Folly 4° 1739 (this includes as intermezzi the choruses from Buckingham's *Julius Cæsar*).
Music Galliard. 1739. H.¹ S. 14/4. 1740. Hickford's room M. 31/3. 1744. L.² T. 11/12.

O. Love's Triumph 4° 1708.
Motteux, adaptation from Ottoboni's *La Pastorella*; music Cesarini Giovannini del Violone and Francisco Gasparini. 1708. H.¹ Th. 26/2, S. 28; T. 2/3, S. 6, T. 9, S. 20, T. 23; S. 17/4.

O. Lucio Papirio Dittatore (Ital. and Eng.) 8° 1732.
1732. H.¹ T. 23/5, T. 30; S. 3/6, T. 6.

O. Lucio Vero, Imperatore di Roma (Ital. and Eng.) 8° 1715.
Zeno; music anon. 1715. H.¹ S. 26/2; S. 5/3, S. 12, S. 19; S. 2/4, S. 23, S. 30. 1716. W. 1/2, S. 4, S. 11.

O. Lucio Vero, Imperator di Roma (Ital. and Eng.) 8° 1727.
Music Ariosti. 1727. H.¹ S. 7/1, T. 10, S. 14, T. 17, S. 21, T. 24, S. 28.

O. Lucio Vero, Imperator di Roma (Ital. and Eng.) 8° 1747.
Pasticcio, mainly from Händel. 1747. H.¹ S. 14/11, S. 21, S. 28; S. 5/12, S. 19, S. 26. 1748. S. 2/1, S. 9; S. 19/3 (Burney says acted 14 times in 1747 and 8 in 1748).

*C.O. La Maestra.
1749. H.¹ M. 27/2.

O. Mandane (Ital. and Eng.) 8° 1742.
Metastasio's *Artaserse* under a new name; pasticcio. 1742. H.¹ S. 4/12, T. 7, S. 11, T. 14, S. 18, T. 21.

O. Meraspe overo L'Olimpiade (Ital. and Eng.) 8° 1742.
Altered from Metastasio by Rolli; pasticcio. 1742. H.¹ 20/4 (bills missing).

O. Merode e Selinunte overo La maggior Prova dell' Amicizia (Ital. and Eng.) 8° 1740.
Rolli; pasticcio. 1740. H.¹ T. 22/1, S. 26, T. 29; S. 2/2, T. 5, S. 9, T. 12, S. 16, T. 19, S. 23, T. 26; S. 1/3, T. 4, S. 8; S. 24/5, T. 27, S. 31.

O. Merope (Ital. and Eng.) 8° 1736.
    Altered from Zeno. 1737. H.[1] S. 8/1, T. 11, S. 15, T. 18,
    S. 22, T. 25, S. 29.

Orat. The Messiah 4° 1742 (Dublin); 8° 1745 (Dublin); 4° (1755) and
    frequently after.
    1749. C.G. Th. 23/3. Produced originally in Dublin 13/4/1742.

O. Mitridate (Ital. and Eng.) 8° 1746.
    Pasticcio. 1736. H.[1] S. 24/1, T. 27, S. 31; T. 3/2. Vanneschi;
    music Terradellas. 1746. T. 2/12, S. 6, T. 9, S. 13, T. 16, S. 20,
    T. 23, S. 27, T. 30. 1747. S. 3/1, T. 6, S. 10; S. 9/5, S. 16, S. 23,
    S. 30.

O. Il Muzio Scevola (Mutius Scevola; Ital. and Eng.) 8° 1721.
    Rolli; music Mattei, Buononcini and Händel. 1721. H.[1] M. 15/4,
    W. 19, S. 22, W. 26, S. 29; W. 3/5, S. 6, S. 13, W. 17; W. 7/6,
    W. 14. 1722. W. 7/11, S. 10, T. 13.

O. Narciso (Narcissus; Ital. and Eng.) 8° 1720.
    Music Scarlatti, with additional songs by Thomas Roseingrave.
    1720. H.[1] M. 30/5; Th. 2/6, S. 11, W. 15, S. 18.

*O. Il Negligente.
    Music Ciampi. 1749. H.[2] T. 21/11, S. 25, T. 28; S. 2/12, T. 5,
    S. 9, T. 12, S. 16.

O. Numitore (Ital. and Eng.) 8° 1720.
    Rolli; music Giovanni Porta. 1720. H.[1] S. 2/4, T. 5, S. 9,
    T. 19, S. 23; Th. 26/5; S. 25/6.

O. Olimpia in Ebuda (Ital. and Eng.) 8° 1740.
    Rolli; music Hasse. 1740. H.[2] S. 15/3, T. 18, S. 22, T. 25,
    S. 29; T. 8/4, S. 12, T. 15, S. 19, T. 22, S. 26, T. 29; S. 3/5,
    T. 6, Th. 15.

O. Onorio (Honorius; Ital. and Eng.) 8° 1734 (for 1736).
    D. Loeli and G. Boldini; music F. Campi. 1736. H.[1] T. 13/4.

*C.O. L'Opera du Gueux (translation of *The Beggar's Opera*).
    1749. H.[2] M. 1/5, Th. 4, F. 5, T. 9–Th. 11, S. 13.

C.O. Orazio (Ital. and Eng.) 8° 1748 (*bis*).
    Music Pietro Auletta. 1748. H.[1] T. 29/11; S. 3/12, T. 6, S. 10,
    T. 13. 1749. S. 14/1, M. 16; T. 21/2; M. 6/3.

*O. Oreste (Orestes).
    Overture Händel. 1734. C.G. W. 18/12, S. 21, S. 28.

O. Orfeo (Orpheus; Ital. and Eng.) 8° 1735.
    Rolli; pasticcio. 1736. H.[1] T. 2/3, S. 6, T. 9, S. 13, T. 16,
    S. 20, T. 23; T. 6/4, S. 10, S. 17, Th. 29; S. 1/5; T. 8/6, T. 15;
    T. 22.

O. Orlando (Ital. and Eng.) 8° 1732.
    English translation by Humphreys; Italian text, Bracciuoli;
    music Händel. 1733. T. 23/1, S. 27; S. 3/2, T. 6, S. 10, S. 17,
    T. 20; S. 21/4, T. 24, S. 28; T. 1/5, S. 5.

O. Ormisda (Ital. and Eng.) 8° 1730.
    Zeno. 1730. H.[1] S. 4/4, T. 7, S. 11, T. 14, S. 18, T. 21, S. 25,
    T. 28; S. 2/5, T. 5, S. 9, T. 12, Th. 14; T. 9/6; T. 24/11, S. 28;
    T. 1/12, S. 5, T. 8.

O. Ottone, Re di Germania (Otho; Ital. and Eng.) 8° 1723; 8° 1726.
    Haym; music Händel. 1723. H.[1] S. 12/1, T. 15, S. 19, T. 22,
    S. 26, T. 29; S. 2/2, T. 5, S. 9, T. 12, S. 16; T. 26/3; T. 4/6,
    S. 8; W. 11/12, S. 14, W. 18, S. 21, S. 28. 1724. W. 1/1. 1726.
    S. 5/2, T. 8, S. 12, T. 15, S. 19, T. 22, S. 26, M. 28; S. 5/3, T. 8.

1727. T. 11/4, Th. 13. 1733. T. 13/11, S. 17, T. 20, S. 24. 1734.
T. 10/12, S. 14, T. 17, S. 21, M. 23, S. 28, T. 31.

*Ser. Parnasso in Festa, or Apollo and the Muses celebrating the
Nuptials of Thetis and Pallas.
Music Händel. 1734. H.¹ W. 13/3, S. 16, T. 19, S. 23, T. 26.
1737. C.G. W. 9/3, F. 11. 1740. L.² S. 8/11. 1741. H.¹
S. 14/3.

O. Partenio (Parthenius) 8° 1738. [Ital. and Eng.]
Music Veracini. 1738. H.¹ T. 14/3, S. 18, T. 21, S. 25; T. 4/4,
S. 8, T. 11; T. 6/6.

O. Partenope (Ital. and Eng.) 8° 1730.
Silvio Stampiglia; music Händel. 1730. H.¹ T. 24/2, S. 28;
T. 3/3, S. 7, T. 10, S. 14, T. 17; S. 12/12, T. 15, S. 19, T. 29.
1731. S. 2/1, T. 5, S. 9. 1737. C.G. S. 29/1; W. 2/2, S. 5, W. 9.

O. Il Pastor Fido (The Faithful Shepherd; Ital. and Eng.) 8° 1712;
8° 1734 (3rd).
Rossi; music Händel. 1712. H.¹ S. 22/11, W. 26, S. 29; W. 3/12,
S. 6, S. 27. 1713. S. 21/2. 1734. S. 18/5, T. 21, S. 25, T. 28; T. 4/6,
S. 8, T. 11, T. 18, S. 22, T. 25, S. 29; W. 3/7, S. 6; C.G. S. 9/11,
W. 13, S. 16, W. 20, S. 23.

*Ser. Peace in Europe.
1749. H.¹ S. 29/4.

O. Penelope (Ital. and Eng.) 8° 1741.
Rolli; music Galuppi. 1741. H.¹ S. 12/12, T. 15, S. 19, T. 22,
S. 26, T. 29. 1742. F. 19/2, T. 23, S. 27.

*O. Polidoro.
Pasticcio. 1742. H.¹ T. 19/1 (bills missing; ran 17 nights).

O. Polifemo (Ital. and Eng.) 8° 1735.
Rolli; music Porpora. 1735. H.¹ S. 1/2, T. 4, S. 8, T. 11,
S. 15, T. 18, S. 22, T. 25; T. 4/3, S. 8, T. 11, T. 25, S. 29; T.
28/10; S. 1/11, T. 4.

O. Poro, Re dell' Indie (Ital. and Eng.) 8° 1731.
Metastasio's *Alessandro* under a new name; English translation
by Humphreys; music Händel. 1731. H.¹ T. 2/2, S. 6, T. 9,
S. 13, T. 16, S. 20, T. 23, S. 27; T. 2/3, S. 6, T. 9, S. 13, T. 16,
S. 20, T. 23, S. 27; T. 23/11, S. 27, T. 30; S. 4/12. 1736. C.G.
W. 8/12, W. 15, W. 22. 1737. W. 5/1.

Int. Pourceaugnac et Grilletta (Ital.) 8° 1737.
Music G. M. Orlandini. 1737. H.¹ T. 25/1, S. 29; T. 1/2, S. 5,
T. 8; S. 12/3, T. 15.

O. Pyrrhus and Demetrius (Ital. and Eng.) 4° 1709; 4° 1710.
Translation by MacSwiny of the *Pirro e Demetrio* of Adriano
Morselli; music Scarlatti altered by Haym. 1708. H.¹ T. 14/12,
S. 18, T. 21, Th. 23, T. 28, Th. 30. 1709. S. 1/1, W. 5, S. 8,
W. 12, S. 15, T. 18, S. 22; W. 9/2, W. 23, S. 26; T. 8/3, T. 22, T. 29;
S. 2/4, S. 9, T. 12, S. 16, S. 30; W. 4/5, S. 14, T. 17, S. 28;
Th. 27/10; Th. 3/11, Th. 10, T. 21; F. 9/12, W. 13, F. 16, F. 30.
1710. F. 6/1; F. 3/2; T. 11/3; W. 6/12, S. 9, W. 13, S. 16, S. 30.
1711. W. 3/1, S. 6; S. 3/2, T. 13; S. 12/5. 1716. S. 10/3, T. 13,
S. 17, S. 24; W. 4/4, W. 11; W. 2/5, T. 15, S. 26; S. 2/6. 1717.
S. 2/2; S. 2/3.

O. Radamisto (Ital. and Eng.) 8° 1720 (*bis*); 8° 1728.
Alteration by Haym of *L'amor tirannico* of D. Lalli; music
Händel. 1720. H.¹ W. 27/4, S. 30; T. 4/5, S. 7, W. 11, S. 14,

W. 18, S. 21; W. 8/6, W. 22; W. 28/12, S. 31. 1721. W. 4/1,
S. 21, W. 25; T. 21/3, S. 25; S. 25/11, W. 29; S. 2/12,
W. 6.

O. Riccardo primo, Re d' Inghilterra (Ital. and Eng.) 8° 1727.
Rolli; music Händel. 1727. H.¹ S. 11/11, T. 14, S. 18, T. 21,
S. 25, T. 28; S. 2/12, T. 5, S. 9, T. 12, S. 16.

O. Rinaldo (Eng. and Ital.) 8° 1711; 8° 1731 (revised by author;
English transl. by Humphreys).
Italian words by Rossi, English words by Aaron Hill; music
Händel. 1711. H.¹ S. 24/2, T. 27; S. 3/3, T. 6, S. 10, T. 13, S. 17,
T. 20, S. 24; W. 11/4, W. 25; S. 5/5, W. 9, S. 26; S. 2/6. 1712.
W. 23/1, S. 26, T. 29; Th. 7/2, S. 9, W. 13, S. 23; T. 1/4. 1713.
T. 24/3; W. 6/5, S. 9. 1714. Th. 30/12. 1715. T. 4/1, S. 8, S. 15,
S. 22, Th. 27, S. 29; S. 5/2, S. 12, S. 19; S. 25/6. 1717. S. 5/1,
S. 12, S. 19, W. 23, S. 26; S. 9/2; S. 9/3; Th. 2/5, S. 18; W. 5/6.
1731. T. 6/4, S. 10, T. 20, S. 24, T. 27; S. 1/5.

O. Rodelinda 8° 1725.
Haym; music Händel. 1725. H.¹ S. 13/2, T. 16, S. 20, T. 23,
Th. 25, S. 27; T. 2/3, S. 6, T. 9, S. 13, T. 16, S. 20, T. 30; T. 6/4;
S. 18/12, T. 21, Th. 23, T. 28. 1726. S. 1/1, T. 4, S. 8, T. 11.
1731. T. 4/5, S. 8, T. 11, S. 15, T. 18, T. 25, S. 29.

O. Rosalinda (Ital. and Eng.) 8° 1744.
Rolli, adapted from *As You Like It*; music Veracini. 1744.
H.¹ T. 31/1; S. 4/2, T. 7, S. 11, T. 14, S. 18, S. 25, T. 28; S. 3/3,
S. 31.

*O. Roxana (or Alessandro nell' Indie).
Music Lampugnani. 1743. H.¹ T. 15/11 (marked as revival),
S. 19, S. 26, T. 29; S. 3/12, T. 6, S. 10, T. 13, S. 17, T. 20, T. 27,
S. 31; T. 6/3, S. 10, T. 13, S. 17. 1746. T. 15/4, S. 19, T. 22,
S. 26, T. 29; S. 3/5, T. 6, S. 10. 1747. T. 24/2, S. 28; T. 3/3,
S. 7, T. 10, S. 14, T. 17, S. 21. 1748. S. 20/2, S. 27; T. 8/3, S. 12.

O. Sabrina (Ital. and Eng.) 8° 1737.
Rolli. 1737. H.¹ T. 26/4, S. 30; T. 3/5, S. 7, T. 10, S. 14,
T. 17, S. 21, T. 31; T. 7/6, S. 11.

Orat. Samson 4° 1743; 8° 1749; 8° 1751; 4° 1752; 4° 1759; 4° 1760.
Newburgh Hamilton from Milton; music Händel. 1743. C.G.
F. 18/2, W. 23, F. 25; W. 2/3, W. 9, F. 11, W. 16, Th. 31. 1744.
F. 24/2, W. 29. 1745. H.¹ F. 1/3, F. 8. 1749. C.G. F. 3/3, F. 10,
W. 15.

Orat. Saul 4° 1738; 4° 1740; 4° 1750.
Music Händel. 1739. H.¹ T. 16/1, T. 23; S. 3/2, S. 10; T. 27/3;
Th. 19/4. 1740. L.² F. 21/3. 1741. W. 18/3. 1744. C.G. F. 16/3,
W. 21. 1745. H.¹ W. 13/3.

O. Scipione (Ital. and Eng.) 8° 1726; 8° 1730.
Zeno, altered by Rolli; music Händel. 1726. H.¹ S. 12/3, T. 15,
S. 19, T. 22, S. 26, T. 29; S. 2/4, T. 12, S. 16, T. 19, S. 23, T. 26,
S. 30. 1730. T. 3/11, S. 7, T. 10, S. 14, T. 17, S. 21.

O. Scipione in Cartagine (Ital. and Eng.) 8° 1743.
Dedication signed F. Vanneschi; music Buranello or Galuppi?.
1742. H.¹ (bills missing; Burney says ran 9 times in March and
2 in June).

*Orat. Semele 4° 1743.
Alteration from Congreve; music Händel. 1744. C.G. F. 10/2,
W. 15, F. 17, W. 22; H.¹ S. 1/12, S. 8.

*O. Semiramide.
    1733. H.¹ T. 30/10; S. 3/11, T. 6, S. 10.
O.   La Semiramide riconoscuita (Ital. and Eng.) 8° 1748.
    Metastasio; music Hasse. 1748. H.¹ S. 7/5, S. 14.
O.   Sirbace (Ital. and Eng.) 8° 1743.
    Music Galuppi. 1743. H.¹ T. 5/4, S. 9, T. 12, S. 16, S. 23,
    S. 30; S. 7/5, S. 14, T. 17, M. 23.
O.   Siroe, Re di Persia (Ital. and Eng.) 8° 1728.
    Metastasio; music Händel. 1728. H.¹ S. 17/2, T. 20, S. 24,
    T. 27; S. 2/3, S. 9, T. 12, S. 16, T. 19, S. 23, T. 26, S. 30; T. 2/4,
    S. 6, T. 9, S. 13, T. 23, S. 27.
O.   Siroe, Re di Persia (Ital. and Eng.) 8° 1736.
    Metastasio; music Hasse. 1736. H.¹ T. 23/11, S. 27, T. 30;
    S. 4/12, S. 11, T. 14, S. 18, T. 21. 1737. S. 1/1, T. 4; T. 1/2,
    S. 5, T. 8.
Orat. Solomon 4° 1749; 4° 1759 (with additions).
    Morrell; music Händel. 1749. C.G. F. 17/3, M. 20, W. 22.
O.   Sosarme, Re di Media (Ital. and Eng.) 8° 1732.
    Matteo Noris; English translation by Humphreys; music
    Händel. 1732. H.¹ T. 15/2, S. 19, T. 22, S. 26, T. 29; S. 4/3,
    T. 7, S. 11, T. 14, S. 18, T. 21. 1734. S. 27/4, T. 30; S. 4/5.
Orat. Susanna 4° 1749; 4° 1759 (with additions).
    Music Händel. 1749. C.G. F. 10/2, W. 15, F. 17, W. 22.
O.   Tamerlano (Ital. and Eng.) 8° 1724.
    Haym; music Händel. 1724. H.¹ S. 31/10; T. 3/11, S. 7, T. 10,
    S. 14, T. 17, S. 21, T. 24, S. 28. 1725. S. 1/5, T. 4, S. 8. 1731.
    S. 13/11, T. 16, S. 20.
*O. Telemachus.
    Music Scarlatti. 1732. L.² F. 28/4.
O.   Temistocle (Ital. and Eng.) 8° 1742.
    Zeno; music Porpora. 1743. H.¹ T. 22/2; T. 3/3, S. 5 (Burney
says it had a run of 8 nights).
C.O. The Temple of Dulness. With the Humours of Signor Capochio,
    and Signora Dorinna 4° 1745. (See Theobald's *The Happy
    Captive*.)
    Music Arne. 1745. D.L. Th. 17/1–W. 23, T. 29.
Past. O. The Temple of Love 4° 1706.
    Motteux; music Saggione. 1706. H.¹ Th. 7/3, S. 16.
M. The Temple of Peace (acted at Smock Alley, Dublin, Feb. 1748/9)
    8° 1749 (Dublin).
    Introduces songs of Händel, Purcell, Galliard, Arne and Boyce.
    Rest of music by Pasquali.
*Dr. Ent. of Music. Terpsichore.
    Music Händel. 1734. C.G. S. 9/11.
*O. Teseo (Theseus).
    Haym; music Händel. 1713. H.¹ S. 10/1, W. 14, S. 17, W. 21/1,
    S. 24, W. 28; W. 4/2, W. 11, S. 14, T. 17; T. 17/3; W. 15/4,
    S. 18; S. 16/5.
O.   Teuzzone (Ital. and Eng.) 8° 1727.
    Altered from Zeno; music Ariosti. 1727. H.¹ S. 21/10, T. 24,
    S. 28.
O.   Thomyris, Queen of Scythia (partly Eng. partly Ital.) 4° 1707;
    8° 1709; The Royal Amazon 4° 1708; 8° 1719 (4th).
    Motteux; music Scarlatti and Buononcini adapted by Pepusch,

with additions from Agostino Steffani. 1707. D.L. T. 1/4, S. 5,
T. 15, S. 19; S. 3/5, T. 6, T. 20; Th. 18/12. 1708. H.¹ T. 13/1,
S. 17, T. 20, S. 24; S. 14/2, T. 17; S. 10/4, T. 13, T. 20; S. 1/5.
Th. 20. 1709. Th. 17/11, M. 21, Th. 24; T. 6/12, T. 20. 1710.
T. 3/1; T. 7/2, Th. 23. 1717. L.¹ Th. 9/5; S. 1/6. 1718. T. 9/12,
Th. 11, Th. 18, S. 20. 1719. W. 7/1, S. 10; Th. 12/2, S. 14,
Th. 19; Th. 23/4. 1728. S. 9/11, T. 12.

*O. Tito.
>1737. H.¹ T. 12/4, S. 16, T. 19, S. 23.

O. Tito Manlio (Titus Manlius; Ital. and Eng.) 8° 1717.
>1717. H.¹ Th. 4/4, S. 27; S. 4/5, S. 11, S. 25, W. 29.

O. Tolomeo di' Egitto (Ptolomy; Ital. and Eng.) 8° 1728.
>Haym; music Händel. 1728. H.¹ T. 30/4; F. 4/5, T. 7, S. 11,
>T. 14, S. 18, T. 21. 1730. T. 19/5, S. 23, T. 26, S. 30; T. 2/6,
>S. 6, S. 13. 1733. T. 2/1, T. 9, S. 13, T. 16.

C.O. I tre Cicisbei ridicoli (Ital. and Eng.) 8° 1749.
>Music Natale Resta. 1749. H.¹ T. 14/3, S. 18; S. 1/4; Th
>11/5, S. 27.

*(O). Il Trionfo d'Amore (a collection of music).
>1712. H.¹ W. 12/11, S. 15.

O. Il Trionfo della Continenza (Ital. and Eng.) 8° 1745.
>Music Galuppi. 1746. H.¹ T. 28/1; S. 1/2, T. 4, S. 8, T. 11,
>S. 15, T. 18, S. 22, T. 25; S. 1/3.

Orat. Il Trionfo del Tempo e della Verità (The Triumph of Time
and Truth) 4° 1737.
>Morrell; music Händel. 1737. C.G. W. 23/3, F. 25; F. 1/4,
>M. 4. 1739. S. 3/3.

O. (The Triumphs of Love) The Loves of Ergasto...Represented at
the Opening of the Queen's Theatre in the Hay-Market (Ital.
and Eng.) 4° 1705.
>Music Greber. 1705. H.¹ M. 9/4, T. 24.

*O. Venceslao (Wenceslaus).
>1717. H.¹ Th. 14/3, S. 16; M. 13/5.

O. Venceslao (Wenceslaus; Ital. and Eng.) 8° 1731.
>Zeno; English translation by Humphreys. 1731. H.¹ T. 12/1,
>S. 16, T. 19, S. 23.

O. Vespasiano (Ital. and Eng.) 8° 1724.
>Altered from G. C. Corradi; dedication signed N. F. Haym;
>music Händel. 1724. H.¹ T. 14/1, S. 18, T. 21, S. 25, T. 28;
>S. 1/2, S. 8, T. 11, S. 15.

O. Xerxes 8° 1738.
>Music Händel. 1738. H.¹ S. 15/4, T. 18, S. 22, T. 25; T. 2/5.

III. *Repertoire of the French and Italian Comedians, acting chiefly at the Little Theatre in the Hay-market.*

[A few of the performances took place at the Opera House in
the Haymarket and a few at L.I.F. I have indicated in brackets
the writers of those pieces the authorship of which is ascertainable.
The lists of Delandine and of Lévis, as well as Boulmier's *Histoire*

du Théâtre italien and his *Histoire du Théâtre de l'Opéra comique*, in addition to other more specialised works, have for this purpose been consulted. It may not be unfitting here to express my thanks to Professor J. G. Robertson for his invaluable assistance, not only in indicating to me sources of information, but in identifying many of the pieces mentioned. Mr W. J. Lawrence has drawn my attention to the fact that the Italian company was ridiculed in *The Touchstone* (1728) from which it appears that Nicolini Grimaldi, Joe Grimaldi's grandfather, was one of the comedians. For the most part the titles given are from the original advertisements, but I have chosen out of variant forms that which is most correct. Thus Molière's *L'Étourdi* occurs sometimes with the correct spelling, sometimes as *Le Tourdy*. It may be suggested that the "Guerardy" of the bills refers to the collection of plays issued under the name of Gherardi.]

Les Adieux d'Arlequin (1720. T. 21/6).

Agnès de Chaillot (Dominique and Le Grand; 1735. F. 17/1; Th. 10/4).

Alcibiade (Campistron; 1722. M. 9/4).

Les Amans réunis (Beauchamp; 1735. M. 20/1, F. 24. 1749. T. 14/11).

Les Amans trompés (1721. Th. 20/4).

Les Amours de Colombine et de Scaramouch, Pedant Scrupuleux et Pierot Ecolier (1725. M. 29/3).

Les Amours de Nanterre (Sutreau; 1734. Th. 14/11, Th. 21).

Amphitryon (Molière; 1721. M. 11/12, F. 22. 1722. Th. 15/3).

Andromaque (Racine; 1722. Th. 4/1).

Les Animaux raisonnables (Le Grand and Fuzelier; 1720. Th. 17/3, S. 19, S. 26; Th. 9/6. 1721. Th. 23/3. 1725. F. 29/1; M. 22/2. 1734. M. 11/11, F. 15).

Argentina Ortolana (1727. Th. 23/3).

Argentina strega per Amore (1726. S. 12/11, T. 22. 1727. Th. 12/1. Printed in London as Argentina Strega per Amore: or Harlequin Multiply'd by Argentina's Witchcraft, for Love. With their wonderful flights and Apparitions; and the Magick Transformation of Silvio, Cittio and Brighella 8° 1726. Another piece styled Argentina, Or, The Sorceress was printed 8° the same year).

Arlechino Principe in Sogno (1726. W. 14/12. Printed 8° 1726 as Arlechino Prencipe in Sogno, &c. Or, Harlequin Prince in a Dream, German Baron, Flying Phisician, and Pretty Marget).

Arlequin Ambassadeur d'amour (1725. W. 7/4).

Arlequin Avocat (1721. M. 13/2).

Arlequin Balourd (The bills say written in London by P. M. Poscope; published 8° 1719 as Arlequin Balourd, Comedie italienne. 1719. M. 16/2, Th. 19, T. 24, Th. 26. 1720. S. 19/3. 1734. S. 27/12. 1735. F. 14/2; F. 28/3; Th. 15/5).

Arlequin Capite (1726. W. 27/4).

Arlequin Cartouche (Riccoboni; 1722. F. 12/1, T. 16, F. 19, Th. 25; Th. 1/2, F. 2, M. 19; Th. 29/3. 1725. M. 12/4, W. 21, F. 23. 1735. Th. 16/1; W. 5/3).

Arlequin Chevalier errant (1721. T. 7/2).

Arlequin Cuisinier à la Guinguette (1721. Th. 28/12. 1725. W. 27/1).

Arlequin Directeur (1721. M. 27/3).

Arlequin Docteur chinois (see A. Major Ridicule; 1720. Th. 9/6).

Arlequin Docteur Faustus (1725. M. 8/3, M. 15; W. 14/4).

Arlequin Empereur dans la Lune ("ancienne pièce avec de nouvelles scènes par Remy et Chaillot" according to Boulmier; see the Hand-list of Plays, 1660–1700, p. 392; 1719. S. 7/3, T. 10, Th. 12. 1721. T. 2/5, Th. 4. 1725. F. 9/4, W. 28. 1735. M. 27/1, W. 29; S. 1/2, M. 3, Th. 13).

Arlequin et Octave persécutés par les dames inconnues (1725. M. 25/1).

Arlequin et Scaramouch Soldats Deserteurs (1720. M. 7/3, T. 8. 1721. M. 20/2. 1724. W. 30/12. 1725. F. 5/2. 1735. F. 17/1; W. 5/2; Th. 15/5, M. 19).

Arlequin feint Astrologue [Statue, Enfant, Ramoneur, Nègre et Skilett] (Delisle; 1720. Th. 24/3, S. 26; T. 5/4. 1724. M. 28/12. 1725. M. 8/2, Th. 18; F. 16/4. 1734. Th. 7/11, Th. 14; F. 6/12, M. 16. 1735. F. 31/1; Th. 27/2; M. 24/3; M. 28/4; M. 26/5).

Arlequin Femme grosse (1725. M. 3/5).

Arlequin Gardien du Fleuve d'Oubly (1734. M. 4/11; F. 13/12. 1735. F. 11/4).

Arlequin Gazettier comique d'Holande (1725. W. 13/1; F. 30/4).

Arlequin Gentilhomme par hazard (1725. Th. 18/2; Th. 22/4).

Arlequin Homme à bonnes fortunes (1718. F. 26/12. 1720. T. 22/3. 1721. F. 10/2; T. 26/12. 1722. F. 5/1. 1725. F. 1/1 (as A. Petit Maitre a bonne fortune by Guerardy). 1726. W. 20/4. 1749. F. 17/11 (as by Baron)).

Arlequin Hulla (possibly A. H. ou la Femme répudiée by Lesage and d'Orneval; 1722. M. 5/3, Th. 8, M. 12, T. 27, F. 30. 1734. M. 18/11; F. 6/12, Th. 12. 1735. F. 17/1; F. 28/2; M. 24/3; M. 28/4; F. 2/5, F. 23. 1749. W. 22/11).

Arlequin invisible (Lesage; 1721. M. 4/12, F. 15).

Arlequin jouet de la Fortune (Vivières de Saint Bon; 1719. T. 20/1).

Arlequin Laron, Provost et Juge (1718. F. 28/11. 1719. Th. 5/3. 1720. T. 3/5. 1721. F. 13/1).

Arlequin Limonadier (1721. T. 18/4).

Arlequin lui Colombine (1721. S. 25/2; Th. 2/3).

Arlequin Major ridicule (1718. F. 19/12. 1721. Th. 19/1; F. 17/2. 1725. M. 1/3; Th. 1/4. 1726. T. 3/5).

Arlequin Misanthrope (De Barante; 1719. T. 3/3. 1734. F. 22/11).

Arlequin Nouvelliste de Tuileries (1721. Th. 9/2. 1725. M. 10/5).

Arlequin Piroquet (1721. Th. 23/3).

Arlequin poli par l'Amour (Marivaux; 1734. W. 20/11; M. 23/12. 1735. F. 31/1).

Arlequin Prince des Curieux et Colombine Docteur en droit (1725. W. 3/2).

Arlequin cru Prince par Magie (1719. T. 17/3. 1721. T. 3/1. 1725. Th. 18/3. 1726. W. 5/10).

Arlequin Protée (the bill says by "Guerardy"; 1721. F. 28/4. 1725. M. 4/1; Th. 25/2).

Arlequin Sauvage (de l'Isle; 1735. M. 20/1; M. 10/2, Th. 20, W. 26; F. 21/3, W. 26; F. 18/4; M. 2/6, W. 4).

Arlequin son Sergeant ("The Philosophical Lady"; 1735. F. 25/4).

Arlequin Tiresias (1734. W. 4/12. 1735. F. 24/1; F. 18/4).

Arlequin toujours Arlequin (Lelio fils, Dominique and Romagnesi; 1734. Th. 26/12. 1735. Th. 27/2; Th. 20/3; M. 12/5).

Arlequin Valet étourdi (1725. W. 6/1; M. 22/2).

[The following pieces appear with English titles only:

Harlequin an Anchoret (1735. F. 7/3).

Harlequin as Mad Springlet (1735. M. 17/2; Th. 27/3; W. 21/5).

Harlequin Captain of Bandittos (1727. M. 16/1).

Harlequin Dead and Revived (1720. S. 5/3).

Harlequin the French Lawyer or Grapignant (1719. T. 20/1; Th. 5/2).

Harlequin in Constantinople (1720. S. 12/3).

Harlequin's Contrivances (1735. F. 14/3).]

Atrée et Thyeste (Crébillon; 1722. Th. 18/1).

Attendez-moi sous l'orme (Regnard; 1720. F. 6/5, M. 9. 1722. Th. 1/3. 1725. M. 4/1).

L'Auberge d'Arlequin (1725. M. 15/3).

L'Avare (Molière; 1721. F. 3/2; S. 30/12. 1722. M. 1/1; T. 6/2. 1734. S. 2/11. 1735. W. 12/3).

L'Avocat Patelin (Brueys; 1721. F. 15/12).

La Baguette de Vulcain (Regnard and Dufresny; 1721. T. 19/12. 1725. M. 26/4. 1734. W. 13/11).

La Baguette enchantée (1724. F. 18/12).

Les Bains de la Porte de St. Bernard (Boisfranc; 1719. Th. 22/1. 1720. F. 27/5; W. 1/6, T. 21).

Le Baron de la Crasse (Poisson; 1719. T. 27/1. 1720. T. 31/5. 1734. M. 16/12. 1735. F. 3/1; M. 17/3).

Il Baron di Hoffenburgo (1726. S. 10/12).

La Belle Esclave (Claude de L'Estoille; 1725. F. 15/1).

Belphegor (Le Grand; 1735. F. 3/1; F. 11/4).

Blunder upon Blunder (1735. T. 21/1).

Le Bourgeois Gentilhomme (Molière; 1720. F. 29/4; T. 10/5. 1721. M. 27/2; S. 4/3. 1722. M. 26/3. 1735. M. 13/1, W. 15).

Britannicus (Racine; 1722. M. 5/2).

Le Carillon de Maître Gervaise (1720. Th. 16/5. 1734. F. 22/11. 1735. W. 12/2).

Cartouche, ou les Voleurs (Le Grand; 1727. Th. 6/4, described as "quite different to what hath yet been seen on any Stage in Europe," F. 14).

La Chercheuse d'esprit (Favart; 1749. F. 17/11).

Le Chevalier à la Mode (Dancourt; 1722. Th. 5/4).

Le Cid (P. Corneille; 1722. S. 13/1, M. 15).

La Clemenca d'August (1722. Th. 22/2).

Le Coché supposé (Hauteroche; 1722. F. 5/1; M. 26/2; T. 10/4).

Le Cocu battu et content (Poisson; 1721. F. 6/1. 1725. W. 6/1; Th. 4/3).

Le Cocu imaginaire (Molière; 1722. M. 2/4. 1735. F. 9/5).

Collin-Maillard (Dancourt; 1722. M. 9/4).

Colombine (1726. Th. 14/4).

Colombine Avocat pour et contre (De Fatouville; 1718. W. 3/12, F. 5. 1721. Th. 5/1).

Les Comédiens esclaves (Lelio fils, Dominique and Romagnesi; 1734. W. 18/12. 1735. M. 14/4).

A Comedy within a Comedy (perhaps Dancourt's La Comédie des Comédiens; 1727. Th. 2/3).

Il Convitato di Pietra (1726. W. 21/12).

Le Coq du Village (Favart; 1749. T. 14/11, W. 15).

La Coquette sans la sçavoir (Favart and Rousseau de Toulouse; 1749. M. 20/11).

Crispin, Rival de son Maître (Le Sage; 1721. T. 5/12. 1722. T. 23/1; M. 12/3).

La Critique des Comédiens français (1725. Th. 25/2).

La Dama Demonis (1727. S. 8/4).

Dame Alison (1735. W. 12/2).

La Dame invisible (1721. M. 24/4).

De la Carulca Espagnola (1721. Th. 4/5).

Démocrite amoureux (Regnard; 1721. T. 12/12. 1725. M. 1/2).

Le Deuil (Hauteroche or Corneille; 1721. T. 17/1).

Le Deuil comique (1725. M. 1/3).

Les deux Arlequins ("The Mistake"; Le Noble; 1718. W. 10/12, F. 12. 1720. T. 31/5. 1721. Th. 2/2. 1725. F. 7/5, Th. 13. 1734. W. 11/12. 1735. F. 21/3; F. 25/4).

Les deux Octaves (1725. M. 11/1).

Les deux Pierots (1721. M. 20/3).

Diana's Madness (perhaps Diane et l'Amour by Morand; 1726. S. 5/11).

Didone abbandonata da Eneo (Metastasio; published 8° 1726 as Didone abbandonata da Enea. Tragedia Heroi comica. To which is added a Farce, call'd, La Generosità per Forza di Pantalone Economo in Campagna. The only copy of this I have seen (in my own possession) lacks the farce) 1726. S. 17/12).

Le Disgrazie d' Arlechino (published 8° 1726 as Le Disgratie d' Arlechino: (viz.) Harlequin's Misfortunes; or, his Marriage interrupted by Brighella's Cunning. With his comical Circumcision, &c. A Comedy. 1721. T. 18/4. 1726. W. 30/11).

Le Divorce (Regnard, but once billed as *Le D. ou Arlequin fourbe, fourbe et demi*. 1718. T. 30/12. 1719. Th. 15/1; Th. 12/2. 1720. Th. 16/6. 1721. T. 17/1. 1725. W. 21/4. 1734. F. 8/11).

Don Japhet d'Arménie (Scarron; 1721. Th. 21/12).

La Donna più constante dell' Huomo (1727. Th. 9/2).

Don Pasquin d'Avalos (an *intermède* in Montfleury's L'Ambigu comique, ou les Amours de Didon et d'Enée. 1721. M. 18/12. 1725. W. 13/1. 1735. M. 7/4).

La double Inconstance (Marivaux, but once billed as *La d. I. ou Arlequin à la Cour malgré lui*. 1734. M. 11/11. 1735. Th. 23/1; M. 3/2, M. 10, W. 26; W. 23/4).

Le Dragon de Moscovie (1719. M. 16/3. 1720. F. 20/5. 1721. F. 20/1. 1725. W. 14/4; W. 5/5).

L'École des Amans (Lesage and Fuzelier, or Joly; 1720. M. 4/4).

L'École des Femmes (Molière; 1721. F. 28/4. 1735. Th. 20/3; F. 2/5. 1749. W. 15/11).

L'École des Jaloux (Montfleury has a play of this title (c. 1664) but the author of the later piece seems unknown. 1721. Th. 12/1).

L'École des Maris (Molière; 1721. Th. 14/12. 1735. F. 7/3).

L'Embarras des Richesses (Dallainval; 1734. M. 25/11; Th. 26/12. 1735. T. 21/1; F. 28/2; T. 18/3, S. 22; Th. 1/5, M. 12, F. 23. 1738. M. 9/10).

The Enchanted Island of Arcadia (1726. F. 21/10, T. 25).

L'Enfant prodigue (1719. Th. 19/3).

L'Epreuve réciproque (Le Grand; 1722. M. 22/1; T. 6/2; M. 5/3).

L'Esprit de Contradiction (Dufresny; 1722. Th. 1/2).

L'Esprit follet (both D'Ouville and Hauteroche have comedies of this name. 1719. Th. 8/1; Th. 12/2. 1720. T. 17/5. 1721. M. 16/1; M. 13/3. 1725. F. 1/1; M. 1/2. 1734. F. 8/11).

L'Été des Coquettes (Dancourt; 1722. Th. 18/1; M. 19/2).

L'Étourdi (Molière; 1718. F. 21/11, W. 26. 1719. Th. 5/2. 1720. M. 9/5; Th. 9/6. 1734. Th. 12/12. 1735. W. 26/3).

Les Fâcheux (Molière; 1725. M. 18/1).

The Faithful Wife (1726. W. 28/9).

Le Faucon (De l'Isle; 1735. W. 28/5).

La Fausse Coquette (De Barante; 1718. F. 14/11, W. 19. 1720. Th. 12/5; F. 30/12. 1726. M. 25/4. 1734. M. 18/11. 1735. F. 21/2, M. 24; W. 19/3).

La Femme diablesse, ou les Épouvantes d'Arlequin (1725. M. 15/2; M. 12/4).

La Femme jalouse (Joly; 1735. W. 29/1).

La Femme juge (Montfleury; 1721. T. 19/12. 1722. T. 2/1).

La Femme vengée (De Fatouville; 1726. M. 28/3).

Le Festin de Pierre (probably an Italian piece adapted by Letellier; 1721. M. 6/3. 1722. Th. 11/1. 1725. W. 7/4. 1735. M. 17/3).

La Fille à la Mode (see *Le Parisien*).

La Fille Capitaine, ou la Fille sçavante (Montfleury; 1718. W. 17/12. 1720. Th. 17/3; T. 26/4. 1721. T. 10/1. 1725. F. 29/1; M. 19/4. 1734. M. 4/11. 1735. Th. 6/2, Th. 20; F. 25/4).

Les Filles errantes (Regnard has a play of this name, but the bill says by "Guerardy"; 1719. Th. 8/1. 1725. F. 22/1; Th. 22/4. 1735. W. 14/5).

La Foire de St. Germain (Regnard has a play of this name, as have Dancourt and Le Grand; but the bill says by "Guerardy"; 1718. F. 7/11, W. 12. 1720. M. 16/5. 1721. M. 2/1; M. 10/4. 1725. F. 8/1. 1734. W. 13/11, Th. 21).

Les Follies Amoureuses (Regnard; 1719. S. 14/3. 1720. T. 22/3; T. 17/5. 1721. M. 6/2. 1725. W. 27/1; M. 19/4. 1735. Th. 13/3; Th. 17/4; M. 5/5).

Les Fourberies d'Arlequin ("Tissue de scènes de l'ancien théâtre italien" (Boulmier); 1720. Th. 10/3, T. 15. 1721. T. 14/2).

Les français à Londres (Boissy; 1734. F. 29/11; W. 4/12, M. 9. 1735. F. 21/2, M. 24).

The French Cuckold (1735. Th. 6/2, F. 14; M. 3/3; M. 7/4, Th. 17; M. 5/5; M. 2/6, W. 4).

Les Funérailles (Lesage and d'Orneval; 1722. M. 8/1).

Le Furbarie per Vendetta (Printed 8° 1726 as Le Furbarie per Vendetta: or, Brighella's Revenge contrariated by Argentina. With Harlequin's Transformation, viz. A Physician, Master of Musick, Lady Pancake, Swaggerer, Giant, and Grand Bashaw. Together with his comical Agress and Regress to and from the Tower. 1726. S. 19/11; W. 7/12).

George Dandin (Molière; 1719. T. 27/1. 1721. M. 9/1. 1722. T. 27/3. 1725. M. 18/1. 1735. F. 9/5).

La Girlande enchantée (1725. W. 20/1; F. 5/2).

The Greatest Glory of a Prince (1726. T. 1/11).

Le Grondeur (Brueys and Palaprat; 1722. F. 30/3).

Gustavus Vasa (Piron; 1735. W. 5/2).

Les Hauberges d'Arlequin (1720. M. 20/6).

L'heureux Naufrage (Barbier; 1721. M. 23/1. 1726. M. 11/4; F. 6/5. 1734. F. 15/11. 1735. T. 18/2; Th. 27/3).

L'honorata Povertà di Rinaldo (1727. W. 4/1).

Les Horaces (P. Corneille; 1722. M. 2/4).

Inez de Castro (Houdart de la Motte; 1735. Th. 10/4).

L'Inganno fortunato (1727. W. 25/1).

L'Ingrat (Destouches; 1722. S. 17/2).

Les Intrigues d'Arlequin (1725. Th. 25/2. 1726. M. 18/4. 1735. W. 12/3, Th. 13; M. 7/4; W. 28/5).

Iphigénie (Racine; 1722. T. 23/1).

L'Isle des Amazones (Lesage and d'Orneval; 1724. Th. 17/12).

Les Jaloux désabusés (Campistron; 1722. Th. 29/3).

Les Jeux de l'Amour et du Hazard (Marivaux; once as *ou Arlequin Maître et Valet*; 1734. F. 29/11. 1735. M. 3/3; Th. 8/5. 1749. M. 20/11).

Le Joueur (Regnard or perhaps Riccoboni; 1720. M. 4/4; F. 6/5. 1721. M. 16/1; Th. 9/2; Th. 7/12. 1725. M. 11/1, W. 20; F. 23/4. 1734. F. 13/12. 1735. F. 14/3).

Le Legataire universel (the bill says by Regnard; 1721. T. 7/2; M. 18/12. 1725. M. 26/4; M. 10/5).

Lucrezia romana violata (1726. S. 31/12).

Le Malade imaginaire (Molière; 1720. M. 13/6, F. 17. 1734. M. 23/12. 1735. F. 7/2).

Le Mariage forcé (Molière; 1721. Th. 5/1; M. 11/12. 1724. W. 30/12. 1735. F. 7/2, T. 18; W. 19/3. 1736. Th. 8/4).

Il Matrimonio disturbato (1726. S. 26/11).

La Matrone d'Ephèse (Fuzelier; 1725. F. 16/4. 1735. W. 14/5).

Le Médecin malgré lui (Molière; 1725. F. 22/1; F. 7/5. 1734. W. 11/12).

Les Ménechmes (Regnard; 1721. T. 5/12. 1722. T. 9/1).

Le Menteur (P. Corneille; 1722. S. 20/1, M. 22).

Il Mercante prodigo (1726. W. 16/11).

Les Metamorphoses d'Arlequin (1724. Th. 17/12, F. 18. 1725. Th. 4/3; W. 5/5. 1726. W. 13/4).

Le Misanthrope (Molière; 1721. F. 29/12).

Mithridate (Racine; 1722. M. 29/1).

Monsieur de Pourceaugnac (Molière; 1721. Th. 20/4, M. 24).

Monsieur Guinaudin (1721. Th. 9/3).

La Mort de Lucrèce (1726. F. 22/4).

Most Knowing least Understanding (1726. F. 28/10).

Octave étourdi (1726. F. 15/4).

Œdipe (Voltaire; 1722. T. 10/4. This might be the Œdipe travesti of Riccoboni and Dominique).

L'Ombre d'Arlequin et le Diable boiteux (1725. M. 29/3).

L'Opéra de Campagne (Dufresny; 1719. Th. 29/1. 1721. T. 21/2).

Il Padrone servo (Goldoni; 1726. W. 28/12).

Pantaloon (1726. M. 7/11).

Le Parisien duppe dans Londres, ou, la Fille à la Mode (1720. Th. 29/12 as La Fille à la Mode ou le Badeau de Paris). 1721. Th. 9/3. 1725. Th. 13/5. 1726. Th. 24/3, described as a new Italian comedy).

La Parodia del Pastor Fido (1727. T. 25/4, W. 26; W. 10/5).

La Parodie du Cid (1724. M. 21/12).

Pasquin et Marforio, ou Arlequin Genealogiste et les Follies de Colombine (Dufresny and de Barante; 1721. F. 6/1. 1725. Th. 11/3).

Les Pasquinades italiennes, ou, Arlequin Médecin des Mœurs (1719. T. 6/1).

Phèdre et Hippolyte (probably Pradon; 1722. M. 8/1).

Le Phœnix (probably de Castera; 1721. Th. 16/3).

Pierrot grand Vizier (from Le bourgeois Gentilhomme, according to the bills; 1725. Th. 18/3).

Pierrot le furieux (1722. Th. 15/3).

Pierrot Maître Valet (1719. Th. 29/1; T. 3/2).

Le Port de Mer (Boindon; 1720. T. 3/5. 1722. M. 29/1; S. 17/2).

Le Portrait (Saint Foix or Beauchamp; 1734. F. 27/12. 1735. W. 23/4).

La Précaution inutile (Gallet; 1719. S. 14/2; M. 2/3. 1721. Th. 26/1; Th. 23/2).

Les Précieuses ridicules (Molière; 1722. Th. 1/2, M. 12).

Le Prince travesti (Marivaux; 1735. M. 17/2).

Il Proteo Novello (1727. Th. 16/3).

Les quatre Arlequins par Magie (1725. M. 8/3. 1726. M. 9/5).

The Reformed Officer (1735. M. 21/4).

Les Rendezvous interrompus, ou, Arlequin Docteur domestique (1725. Th. 1/4).

Le Retour de la Foire de Bezons (Gherardi; 1721. Th. 12/1).

Le Retour imprévu (Regnard or La Chaussée; 1722. Th. 5/4).

Rhadamiste et Zénobie (Crébillon; 1721. Th. 28/12. 1722. S. 6/1).

Rodogune (P. Corneille; 1722. M. 12/2).

Samson, Judge of Israel (probably Riccoboni; 1734. M. 2/12, M. 9. 1735. W. 12/2).

Scaramouch Pedant scrupuleux, ou, L'Écolier (see Les Amours de Colombine; 1719. S. 14/3).

Scaramouch persecuté par Arlequin faux Diable (1725. M. 3/5).

La Sérénade (Regnard; 1720. F. 20/5. 1721. W. 12/4. 1722. M. 5/2, Th. 22. 1725. F. 15/1; W. 28/4).

Lo Spirito foletto (1726. S. 3/12. 1727. Th. 16/2).

La Surprise d'Amour (Marivaux; 1735. S. 1/2).

La Sylphide (Dominique and Romagnesi; 1735. Th. 23/1; T. 18/3).

Le Tableau de Mariage (1725. M. 15/2).

Tartuffe (Molière; 1719. T. 13/1. 1721. T. 24/1; T. 31/1; M. 4/12. 1725. Th. 11/2; F. 30/4).

The Tender Return (? Le Retour de Tendresse of Fuzelier; 1735. W. 22/1).

La Thèse des Dames (De Barante; 1721. W. 12/4).

Timon le Misanthrope (De l'Isle; but billed once as *T. le M. ou le Vol innocent d'Arlequin*; 1726. W. 11/5. 1734. W. 6/11. 1735. W. 22/1; M. 14/4; W. 21/5).

Le Tombeau de Maître André (De Barante; 1720. M. 20/6. 1721. T. 24/1, T. 31. 1724. M. 21/12. 1725. F. 9/4. 1734. M. 25/11).

Le Traitant de France (1722. Th. 8/2).

Les Trois Frères Rivaux (Lafont; 1722. S. 6/1; Th. 8/2; Th. 8/3).

L'Usurier Gentilhomme (Le Grand; 1722. F. 2/2).

Les Vacances des Procureurs (1725. M. 8/2; Th. 11/3).

Les Vendanges de Luresnis (1721. T. 26/12, S. 30. 1722. F. 2/2, M. 19).

La Vie est un Songe (Boissy; 1735. Th. 16/1; Th. 13/2; W 5/3).

SUPPLEMENTARY TO CHAPTER I

I. *Introductory*

S INCE the original appearance of this volume, a considerable amount of research has been devoted to various aspects of the eighteenth-century drama: references to such books and essays are given in the supplementary notes to the several chapters.

So far, unfortunately, no one has been bold enough to attempt a comprehensive bibliographical survey of dramatic literature during the period, and this remains, consequently, a prime desideratum; but at least the work accomplished by those who have applied themselves to the bibliographies of certain selected authors has shown how perplexing and at the same time how fascinating is the study of these plays in their printed texts. New conditions now began to govern the publication of dramas. The first years of the century saw the gradual change from the familiar aristocratic quarto of the Restoration age to the more bourgeois octavo; soon Tonson's duodecimos became popular, at least for reprints, and engravings of scenes or performers in costume increasingly sought to attract the reading public to the dramas they adorned; the growth of this reading public made piracy a profitable exploit for the less reputable among the printers; whereas practically all earlier plays had been issued from London, English provincial, Scottish and Irish publishers now came to find a lucrative trade in the dissemination of cheap reprints and even of stolen texts.

All of these new conditions, of course, make the bibliography of eighteenth century drama a tangled wilderness compared with which Restoration bibliography may well seem a smooth and well-tended parkland. Perhaps it will prove impossible ever to survey the entire field satisfactorily, but it is to be hoped that at least the studies of the writings of individual dramatists will be so far multiplied as to cover the greater part of this territory. In the meantime, the developing

interest in eighteenth century texts has induced certain booksellers to examine more carefully such copies as come to their
hands, and as a result preliminary work is being accomplished
by demonstrating the extreme rarity of certain editions, by
unearthing others hitherto unrecorded and by listing some
among the thousands of variant issues even in editions rela-
tively well known. It is perhaps not usual in a book of this
kind to mention particular booksellers by name, but it would
be ungracious for any student of the eighteenth-century
theatre not to record his appreciation of the contributions
made to his subject by Ifan Kyrle Fletcher and by Pickering
and Chatto: their investigations have brought to light many
variations hitherto unnoted.

In the process of preparing *A History of Late Eighteenth
Century Drama* (1927) the Larpent collection of dramatic
manuscripts was located in the Henry E. Huntington Library
and references were there made to its holdings from 1750 to
1800; but unfortunately the information concerning the
whereabouts of the collection came too late to be of service
for the volume covering the years 1700 to 1750. Now, a full
catalogue of all the two thousand five hundred plays has been
published[1], and in the supplementary notes to the Hand-list
indication is given, from this source, of the texts available.
Already several researchers have described, and some have
published, manuscript plays preserved in this Larpent series
and it is to be expected that for years to come further treasure-
trove will be unearthed, thus adding to our knowledge of the
dramatic literature of the period.

The drama belongs, of course, partly to literature and partly
to the theatre. Part of the work necessary for its proper
evaluation must be carried out in this area of bibliography
and the analysis of texts; the other part of the work lies within
the field of investigation into stage conditions. Here there
has been much activity of late. A new journal, *Theatre Notebook*, incorporating the bulletin of the Society for Theatre
Research, has provided incentive and opportunity for detailed

[1] Dougald MacMillan, *Catalogue of the Larpent Plays in the Huntington
Library* (1939).

examination of numerous particular questions, and a most valuable introduction to the eighteenth-century stage has been prepared by one of the Society's most active members, Richard Southern[1]. This volume is particularly important for its description of the still extant relics of diverse theatres built during these years or immediately thereafter. Most of these theatrical relics lie outside of London, and the fortunes of the "provincial" stage have, in general, been attracting more attention than they had in the past[2]. To the earlier studies of strolling players[3] have been added many others, each providing fresh material for our understanding of the subject. Frederick T. Wood has brought forward interesting information concerning provincial actors and managers[4], while Sybil Rosenfeld and others have gathered much valuable material from local records[5]. From these further allusions have come to light concerning the activities of those early companies which still followed Elizabethan traditions by travelling under the names of noble patrons. Doggett's troupe, bravely attempting a production of the opera *Dioclesian* at Norwich

---

[1] *The Georgian Playhouse* (1948).

[2] The Society for Theatre Research has published as its first book a bibliography, compiled by Alfred Loewenberg, of *The Theatre of the British Isles* (1950).

[3] Notably Alwin Thaler, "Strolling Players and Provincial Drama after Shakespeare" (*PMLA*, 1922, xxxvii. 243–80), Elbridge Colby, "A Supplement on Strollers" (*PMLA*, 1924, xxxix. 643–54) and Una Ellis-Fermor, "Studies in the Eighteenth Century Stage" (*Philological Quarterly*, 1923, iii. 289–301). A very interesting picture of strolling players appears in Breval's *The Play is the Plot*.

[4] "Strolling Actors in the Eighteenth Century" (*Englische Studien*, 1931/32, lxvi. 16–53) and "Some Aspects of Provincial Drama in the Eighteenth Century" (*English Studies*, 1932, xiv. 65–74).

[5] Sybil Rosenfeld, *Strolling Players and Drama in the Provinces, 1660–1765* (1938). "The Players in Norwich, 1669–1709" (*Review of English Studies*, 1936, xii. 129–38); "The Players in Norwich, 1710–1750" (*id.* 1936, xii. 1–20); "Actors in Bristol, 1741–1748" (*TLS*, Aug. 29, 1936). Most of the special studies devoted to particular theatres are concerned rather with the second half than with the first half of the century, but mention should be made here of: B. S. Penley, *The Bath Stage* (1892); G. T. Watts, *Theatrical Bristol* (1915); M. E. Board, *The Story of the Bristol Stage 1490–1925* (1925); T. L. G. Burley, *Playhouses and Players of East Anglia* (1928); T. Hannam-Clark, *Drama in Gloucestershire* (1928). E. L. Avery discusses "The Summer Theatrical Seasons at Richmond and Twickenham, 1746–1753" (*NQ*, 23 and 30 Oct., 6 Nov. 1937).

in 1700, styled itself the Duke of Norfolk's Servants[1]: this troupe is recorded up to 1718. The Duke of Richmond's men were at Norwich in 1721, and even towards the end of the half century the Duke of Grafton's men were still proudly presenting their patent.

II. *The Audience*

Many contemporaries were fully aware of the changing audience during this time, and innumerable were the allusions to its deteriorating taste[2]. Poetry no longer was truly appreciated; politics and business were interests which submerged an interest in art; rowdy factionism ruled. Again and again we meet with records of disturbance within the theatre's doors and, on the other hand, of the attempts made by worthy moralists to restrain what they styled the "dangerous and growing evil" of a "Publick Nuisance[3]."

One particular feature of this changing audience was the vast increase in the number of self-appointed critics[4]. Just after the turn of the mid-century Fielding ironically stated in *The Covent-Garden Journal*[5] that

By a record of the Censors Office and now in my Custody, it appears, that at a censorial Inquisition, taken *Tricesimo qto. Eliz.* by one of my illustrious Predecessors, no more than 19 Critics were enrolled in the Cities of London and Westminster; whereas at the last Inquisition taken by myself, 25° *Geo. 2di.* the Number of Persons claiming a Right to that Order, appears to amount to 276302.

[1] Alfred Jackson, "Play Notices from the Burney Newspapers 1700–1703" (*PMLA*, 1933, xlviii. 817).

[2] Julian L. Ross, "Dramatist versus Audience in the Early Eighteenth Century" (*Philological Quarterly*, 1933, xii. 73–81).

[3] See the notices from newspapers gathered by Alfred Jackson in "London Playhouses 1700–1705" (*Review of English Studies*, 1932, viii. 291–302) and "The Stage and the Authorities (as revealed in the Newspapers)" (*id.* 1938, xiv. 53–62). This subject is examined by Joseph Wood Krutch in *Comedy and Conscience after the Restoration* (1924) and by Sister Rose Anthony in *The Jeremy Collier Stage Controversy 1698–1726* (1937).

[4] Charles Harold Gray has an important survey of *Theatrical Criticism in London to 1795* (1931), showing the growing attention paid to the theatre in the journals of the time.

[5] Jan. 11, 1752. See Clarence C. Green, *The Neo-classic Theory of Tragedy in England during the Eighteenth Century* (1934), pp. 59–60.

Sometimes, indeed generally, they prowled the theatres as lone wolves; sometimes they hunted in packs. In the early years of the century there was even a "*Kitcat* side" of the auditorium when that club was in its full glory[1]. The fact that so large a proportion of the audience belonged to this "Order" of critics, combined with the very definite codes to which they subscribed, unquestionably played its part in the shaping of the drama's destiny.

A critical tendency, when applied to creative writing, leads towards the development of satire, and satirical productions soon bring thoughts of censorship. In satire the early eighteenth century excelled, and we need feel no surprise at the establishment of the Licensing Act of 1737[2]. Controls were being tightened from the early twenties, particularly after the appointment of Francis Henry Lee as Master of the Revels on May 18, 1725, but, as *The Beggar's Opera* showed, these controls were not sufficiently strong. New theatres were springing up; Fielding's satires cut deeply; and in the early months of 1737 a proposal was made for still another London playhouse. The story of Walpole's chicanery in pressing the Licensing Act through Parliament is well known, and there seems to be no doubt but that William Giffard and John Potter (owner of the Haymarket) were concerned with the cheat[3]. As a result, the Government assumed power over the stage and posterity benefited both by the treasury of manuscript plays deposited in the Lord Chamberlain's office and by the turning of Henry Fielding from the play to the novel.

The success of these new playhouses which so disturbed the authorities was, of course, based on the growing interest of the middle classes in the theatre—and this development was one which found its parallels in numerous countries of

---

[1] Robert J. Allen, "The Kit-Cat Club and the Theatre" (*Review of English Studies*, 1931, vii. 56–61).

[2] On this Act and the circumstances that brought it about, see P. J. Crean, "The Stage Licensing Act of 1737" (*Modern Philology*, 1938, xxxv. 239–55); D. H. Stevens, "Some Immediate Effects of *The Beggar's Opera*" (*Manly Anniversary Studies* (1922), pp. 180–9; and Emmett L. Avery, "Proposals for a New London Theatre in 1737" (*NQ*, May 23, 1942, clxxxii).

[3] See also J. Paul de Castro in *NQ*, June 20, 1942.

continental Europe[1]. The conclusions reached by one who has surveyed this continental field apply equally well to England:

The earlier age was aristocratic, heroic, artistic; the later age, democratic, prosaic, didactic—with a marked trend toward the utilitarian. ...The primary interests of the Age of Enlightenment... were not aesthetic. Artistic standards were subordinated, and "truths" were examined and judged not by their poetic but by their philosophical, sociological and humanitarian values[2].

By these audiences the form of the sentimental drama was being shaped.

III. *The Theatre*

Much new material has recently been unearthed concerning eighteenth-century theatres, and, although most of the available material concerns stages erected after 1750, by indirection at least a great deal of fresh light has been thrown on earlier practice.

Considerable obscurity, however, still surrounds the work of the scenic designers and painters of the period. What was displayed to admiring spectators in "the Paintings made by Mr Robinson"[3] for the operatic *Dioclesian* in 1700 we cannot tell, and except for one man all his companions are in like case. This one man is Thomas Lediard, some of whose efforts have been brought recently to our notice[4]. Concerned for a time (1724–7) with the Hamburg Opera House, Lediard returned to his native country in 1732, and during that year introduced English audiences to "a Transparent Theatre, Illuminated, and adorn'd with a great Number of Emblems, Mottoes, Devices and Inscriptions, and embellish'd with Machines, in a Manner entirely New[5]."

[1] For these parallels see Fred O. Nolte, *The Early Middle Class Drama* (*1696–1774*) (1935).
[2] F. O. Nolte, *op. cit.* pp. 15, 210–11.
[3] *Post Boy*, May 14–16, 1700.
[4] See Richard Southern, "Lediard and Early 18th Century Scene Design" (*Theatre Notebook*, 1948, ii. 49–54); Ifan Kyrle Fletcher, "The Discovery of Thomas Lediard (*id.* pp. 42–5); Sybil Rosenfeld, "The Career of Thomas Lediard" (*id.* pp. 46–8) and Alfred Loewenberg, "Notes on the Hamburg Opera" (*id.* pp. 55–7).
[5] See *supra*, p. 341.

Such efforts clearly anticipate much of the scenic spectacularism so prevalent in the latter part of the century; and alongside these must be placed those other "realistic" tendencies which ultimately established the fourth wall convention[1].

The tentative nature of the attempts made in this period at things new is well shown in the costumes in which the actors clad themselves. There can be no doubt but that "historic" costuming did not really make a real impression until the very last decades of the century, and even then the accomplishments of those years were sufficiently primitive to permit Planché, still a further half-century ahead, to create a revolution by his carefully "correct" designs for *King John*. Yet the phrase "New Dress'd in the Habits of the Times" was one invented before the year 1750[2]. In 1747 Garrick presented *Albumazar* "New Dress'd after the Manner of the Old English Comedy" and in 1750 "the English characters" in *Edward the Black Prince* were "dress'd in the Habit of those Days." Judging from critical strictures, not only then but many years later, the vaunted accuracy in design must have seemed far from the truth and even so must have been applied only to two or three principal performers, but the first tentative steps were being taken along the path which led to Charles Kean and his archaeologically correct productions at the Princess' Theatre in the second half of the nineteenth century.

IV. *The Actors and Actresses*

It has long been recognised, of course, that a new style in acting was set forth by Garrick in the forties, but only of late years have efforts been made to explore the basic theory

[1] Richard C. Boys ("Rural Setting in the Drama: An Early Example," *NQ*, March 21, 1936, clxx) draws attention to the scene in Charles Johnson's *The Country Lasses* (D.L. 1715), which aims at a realistic depiction of rustic surroundings.

[2] Dougald MacMillan, *Drury Lane Calendar 1747–1776* (1938), pp. xxix–xxx, and Donald T. Mackintosh, "New Dress'd in the Habits of the Times" (*TLS*, Aug. 25, 1927).

behind this alteration in style[1]. From Betterton to Booth the old classical, traditional method of delivery and of interpretation prevailed, but when Garrick appeared as Richard III and Macklin as Shylock a fresh standard was set. Fundamentally this was associated with the aesthetic concept of intuitive identification of the actor with his rôle—a concept first fully expressed by Rémond de Sainte-Albine in *Le comédien* (1747) and introduced to England by John Hill in his two works called *The Actor*, in 1750 and 1755. If we call the Garrick-Macklin method realistic-romantic, we realise how closely allied to the other arts was this of acting: in those mid-years of the century the public was awaiting the first flush of the new movement in poetry pointing towards Coleridge and Wordsworth.

SUPPLEMENTARY TO CHAPTER II

I. *Introductory*

It cannot be said that the eighteenth century excelled in the production of tragedy, yet tragedies always played a considerable part in the weekly repertoires and in critical discussions the tragic loomed more important than the comic. Ideas on the subject, of course, varied from person to person, but perhaps we shall best gain orientation by assuming that those fifty years show a struggle between the classically inclined traditionalists on the one hand and, on the other, those who found reason to question older beliefs[2]. The classicists believed in an ordered nature associated with reason in the human being, in an ethical interpretation of

[1] Lily B. Campbell, "The Rise of a Theory of Stage Presentation in England during the Eighteenth Century" (*PMLA*, 1917, xxxii. 163–200); Earl R. Wassermann, "The Sympathetic Imagination in Eighteenth-Century Theories of Acting" (*Journal of English and Germanic Philology*, 1947, xlvi. 264–72) and Alan S. Downer, "Nature to Advantage Dressed: Eighteenth-Century Acting" (*PMLA*, 1943, lviii. 1002–37).

[2] The most thorough study of this theme is that by Clarence C. Green, *The Neo-classic Theory of Tragedy in England during the Eighteenth Century* (1934). See also Earl R. Wasserman, "The Pleasures of Tragedy" (*ELH*, 1947, xiv. 283–307) and Baxter Hathaway, "The Lucretian 'Return upon Ourselves' in Eighteenth-Century Theories of Tragedy" (*PMLA*, 1947, lxii. 672–89).

tragic katharsis, in the application of rules. On the other hand, many forces operated against them, most notably that of Shakespeare[1]. The individuality and vitality of his characters, the fact that he too was a part of nature, the success of his works despite their contravening of the rules made adherence to the stricter critical traditions hazardous, and finally helped to open up a path for the romantically adventuresome. That the preoccupation with critical questions exercised some force in preventing the development of effective tragedies during these fifty years must be regarded as certain, but the fundamental cause of weakness was not this; the age would have liked to produce great tragedy, yet the whole manner of its being, its prime interests and preoccupations, were far removed from the sphere wherein the tragic muse holds her court.

II. *Elizabethan, Restoration and Foreign Models*

The impress made by Shakespeare on this period is well attested, and some recent studies have served to increase our appreciation of its force[2]. Gradually the other Elizabethan playwrights faded in importance as his star ascended[3].

---

[1] David Lovett, "Shakespeare as a Poet of Realism in the Eighteenth Century" (*ELH*, 1935, ii. 267–89).

[2] See particularly James R. Sutherland, "Shakespeare's Imitators in the Eighteenth Century" (*Modern Language Review*, 1933, xxviii. 21–36), and, for the critical attitudes, D. Nichol Smith, *Shakespeare in the Eighteenth Century* (1928). A. H. Scouten lists "Shakespeare's Plays in the Theatrical Repertory when Garrick came to London" (*University of Texas Studies in English*, 1945, pp. 257–70). On the interesting question of "Shakespeare's Ladies," E. L. Avery has some further reference in "Fielding's Last Season with the Haymarket Theatre" (*Modern Philology*, 1939, xxxvi. 283–92). Avery also draws attention, in "The Dramatists in the Theatrical Advertisements, 1700–1709" (*Modern Language Quarterly*, 1947, viii. 448–54), to the fact that Shakespeare's name is mentioned in the bills usually only for his lesser-known works: evidently the others were so well-known they needed no indication of authorship. Charles Washburn Nichols ("A Reverend Alterer of Shakespeare," *Modern Language Notes*, 1929, xliv. 30–2) comments on an interesting letter contributed by "Philo-Shakespeare" to *The Daily Journal*, March 5, 1737; this "Philo-Shakespeare" was an early precursor of the later opponents of "alterations" of the plays.

[3] On Webster see Hazelton Spencer's analysis of *Injur'd Love* ("Tate and *The White Devil*," *ELH*, 1934, iii. 235–49) and B. L. Joseph's dis-

The countering influence of Corneille, Racine[1] and Voltaire[2] was, of course, also strong, but it could not compete with Shakespeare's on the stage, and even among members of the reading public attracted, was operative only upon a comparatively small circle.

II. *The Playwrights*

Numerous scholars have, within the past few years, added considerably to our knowledge of the work of individual authors of these fifty years and of the circumstances relating to the composition and production of their plays[3]. On Johnson's *Irene* an interesting essay has been contributed by David Nicol Smith[4]. Rowe's achievements have been surveyed by J. R. Sutherland[5] and by Alfred Jackson[6]. A specially interesting, although unhappily mediocre author, Charles Johnson, deserves the attention devoted to him by M. Maurice Shudofsky[7] if only because of the wide range and experimental quality of his writings. Aaron Hill has importance because of his relations with Voltaire, and his career is described both

cussion of "Lewis Theobald and Webster" (*Comparative Literature Studies*, 1945, xvii–xviii. 29–31).

[1] See J. Voisine, "Corneille et Racine en Angleterre au xviii⁰ siècle" (*Revue de littérature comparée*, 1948, xxii. 161–75).

[2] To the works mentioned in the text should be added: Georg Baumgärtner, *Voltaire auf der englischen Bühne des 18. Jahrhunderts* (Strasburg, 1913) and Harold Lawton Bruce, *Voltaire on the English Stage* (1918).

[3] Reference should have been made in the text to Richard Foster Jones, *Lewis Theobald* (1919). *Addison's Cato* (Münster, 1936) is studied in a dissertation by A. Zeitvogel, and F. E. Noack examines *Die bürgerlichen Züge in Addison's Cato* (1940).

[4] *Essays and Studies by Members of the English Association*, 1929, xiv. 35–53.

[5] *Three Plays by Nicholas Rowe* (1929).

[6] "Rowe's Historical Tragedies" (*Anglia*, 1930, liv. 307–30). An appreciative study of this dramatist is included by Bonamy Dobrée in his *Restoration Tragedy 1660–1720* (1929), pp. 149–66. For the political elements in his work see Willard Thorp, "A Key to Rowe's *Tamerlane*" (*Journal of English and Germanic Philology*, 1940, xxxix. 124–7).

[7] "Charles Johnson and Eighteenth Century Drama" (*ELH*, 1943, x. 131–58).

by H. Ludwig[1] and Dorothy Brewster[2]. Earl Harlan similarly examines the life and work of Elijah Fenton[3]. An account of the circumstances relating to the first play banned under the Licensing Act of 1737, Henry Brooke's *Gustavus Vasa*, is given by Herbert Wright[4], and full justice has been done by several writers to Lillo's epoch-making *London Merchant* and its fortunes[5].

SUPPLEMENTARY TO CHAPTER III

I. *Introductory*

The comedy of the age is obviously more important than the tragedy, and it is natural that to this theme most modern critical endeavour has been applied. Here, as in the realm of tragedy, aesthetic speculations richly accompanied creative effort[6] and, although tragedy remained on its throne as the

---

[1] *The Life and Works of Aaron Hill* (1911).

[2] *Aaron Hill, Poet, Dramatist, Projector* (1913). Phyllis M. Horsley "Aaron Hill: An English Translator of *Mérope*" (*Comparative Literature Studies*, 1944, xii. 17–23) shows that this translation was completed by 1745 although not acted till 1749, and gives a critical analysis of its style.

[3] *Elijah Fenton 1683–1730* (1937).

[4] *Modern Language Review*, 1919, xiv. 173–82.

[5] George Bush Rodman ("Sentimentalism in Lillo's 'The London Merchant'," *ELH*, 1945, xii. 45–61) discusses the play in the light of Bernbaum's definition of sentimentalism; his views are examined by Raymond D. Havens in a following article (*id.* 1945, xii. 183–7). The strong commercial morality which recommended this drama to contemporary audiences is amusingly illustrated by Claude M. Newlin in "The Theatre and the Apprentices" (*Modern Language Notes*, 1930, xlv. 451–4). G. Lossack has a dissertation on *George Lillo* (Göttingen, 1939). T. V. Benn contributes "Notes sur la fortune du *George Barnwell* de Lillo en France" (*Revue de Litterature Comparée*, 1926, vi. 682–7) and Lawrence M. Price discusses "The Bassewitz Translation of *The London Merchant*, 1752*" (*Journal of English and Germanic Philology*, 1944, xliii, 354–57). The same author describes the fortunes of "George Barnwell on the German Stage" (*Monatshefte für deutschen Unterricht*, 1943, xxxv 205–14).

[6] For a general survey of enquiries into the basic quality of the comic see J. W. Draper, "The Theory of the Comic in Eighteenth-Century England" (*Journal of English and Germanic Philology*, 1938, xxxvii. 207–23).

queen of the stage, many men applied themselves to the task of determining wherein lies the secret of laughter.

Meanwhile, the playwrights proceeded to pour forth their works, some intent only on producing variants of already established successes, others keenly watching contemporary audiences in an effort to catch the fleeting tastes of the time, still others definitely led by conscious theory towards the creation of new forms of drama.

Among the native influences operative on the dramatic work of these years that of Jonson still remained powerful; its force has been well surveyed by Robert Gale Noyes[1]. Increasing attention, too, has been given to the influence of French authors and the indebtedness of many English playwrights to their Parisian colleagues has been more fully examined.[2] In addition to the titles mentioned in the text, it may here be observed that Dancourt's *La Parisienne* (1691) gave Garrick's *Miss in Her Teens* (C.G. 1747) and from his *Le chevalier à la mode* (1687) came Mrs Pix' *The Beau Defeated* (1700). The anonymous *Injur'd Love* (D.L. 1711) has been traced to Montfleury's *La femme juge et partie* (1669), Hewitt's *A Tutor for the Beaus* (L.[2] 1737) to Boissy's *Le François à Londres* (1727) and Vanbrugh's *The False Friend* (D.L. 1702) to Le Sage's *Le traître puni* (1700). From Destouches' *Le curieux impertinent* (1710) came Molloy's *The Coquet* (L.[2] 1718).

The activities of the French and Italian comedians have already been noted, but a few further details may be given of

---

[1] *Ben Jonson on the English Stage, 1660–1776* (1935). In connection with the influence of Shakespeare's plays note may be made of "A Calendar of Performances of *1 Henry IV* and *2 Henry IV* during the First Half of the Eighteenth Century" (*Journal of English and Germanic Philology*, 1944, xliii. 23–41), by A. H. Scouten and Leo Hughes.

[2] Willard Austin Kinne, in *Revivals and Importations of French Comedies in England, 1749–1800* (1939), includes not merely plays written after 1749 but also numerous earlier comedies revived in the later years. John Harrington Smith has notes on "French Sources for Six English Comedies, 1660–1750" (*Journal of English and Germanic Philology*, 1948, xlvii. 390–4): among these comedies are Molloy's *The Coquet*, Hewitt's *A Tutor for the Beaus*, Mrs Pix' *The Beau Defeated* and the anonymous *Injur'd Love*. An analysis of Fielding's indebtedness in *The Intriguing Chambermaid* (D.L. 1734) to Regnard's *Le retour imprévu* is provided by A. E. H. Swaen (*Neophilologus*, 1944, xxix. 117–20). Brief notes on sources are given in the Hand-list of Plays.

their work[1]. The first French company appeared at Lincoln's Inn Fields in 1718, opening with *La foire de St Germain*[2]. In February 1719 they transferred to the Opera House in the Haymarket and presented their repertory for over a month. Another troupe played in the latter theatre from March 5 to June 21, 1720, and the Little Theatre in the Haymarket welcomed the French comedians between December 29, 1720 and May 4, 1721, between November 4, 1721 and April 10, 1722 and between December 17, 1724 and May 13, 1725. Italian players were in this house from March 28 to May 11, 1726; they returned on September 28 and continued there till May 10, 1727. With such extensive seasons, it is natural to suppose that their influence was widespread on the English playwrights, adding materially to what these playwrights gained from their reading of the printed texts.

II. *The Comedies of Manners*

To the last playwrights in the "manners" tradition— Congreve, Farquhar and Vanbrugh—much critical work has been devoted during the past couple of decades, but there is no need to repeat the references already given in the volume devoted to the Restoration drama. It may, however, be noted here that the short paragraph given in the text concerning *The Beaux Stratagem* should be qualified by the observation that this play, while unquestionably inspired by the comic tradition established in Etherege's works, definitely shows in certain scenes the presence of an element alien to the spirit of the comedy of wit. Farquhar has a feeling for benevolence which anticipates much in the sentimental drama to come: there is even a hint in his scenes of the still later melodrama. After this comedy, deems Henry Ten Eyck Perry[3], "moral correctness was to come first and truth to intellectual processes must take a secondary position[4].

[1] On this see Emmett L. Avery, "Foreign Performers in the London Theatres in the Early Eighteenth Century" (*Philological Quarterly*, 1937, xvi. 105–23).

[2] Hence the publication of Ozell's *The Fair of Saint-Germain* that year.

[3] *The Comic Spirit in Restoration Drama* (1925), p. 120.

[4] M. A. Larson has an interesting paper on "The Influence of Milton's Divorce Tracts on Farquhar's *Beaux Stratagem*" (*PMLA*, 1924, xxix. 174–8).

Among the lesser playwrights Mrs Centlivre is one who, like Mrs Behn, has attracted some considerable attention[1]. Fielding's plays, too, have been carefully studied, both critically in connection with his later comic epic[2] and historically in connection with his theatrical ventures[3]. Colley Cibber is another author whose triple activities as writer, actor and manager give him peculiar importance for a study of the drama of this age[4]. An especially noteworthy critical estimate of his plays is provided by F. W. Bateson[5]: in this he likens Cibber to Marivaux, the psychologist rather than the propagandist of sensibility, and emphasises his position in the development of "genteel comedy[6]." Just what particular plays are to be included under this title, of course, may some-

[1] Robert Seibt analyses her plays and discusses their sources in "Die Komödien der Mrs Centlivre" (*Anglia*, 1909, xxii. 434–80 and 1910, xxiii. 77–119). F. T. Wood surveys her work in "The Celebrated Mrs Centlivre" (*Neophilologus*, 1931, xvi. 268–78) and there are chapters on her in F. W. Bateson, *English Comic Drama 1700–1750* (1929), Walter and Clare Jerrold, *Five Queer Women* (1929) and Mona Wilson, *These Were Muses* (1924). Brief notes on her origin appear in J. W. Bowyer, "Susanna Freeman Centlivre" (*Modern Language Notes*, 1928, xliii. 78–80).

[2] W. R. Irwin, "Satire and Comedy in the Works of Henry Fielding" (*ELH*, 1946, xii. 168–88). Winfield H. Rogers ("The Significance of Fielding's *Temple Beau*," *PMLA*, 1940, lv. 440–4) finds in this play "the first manifestation of his mature satiric technique." For the French influence on his work see *L'influence française sur les œuvres de Fielding* (1928) by G. E. Parfitt.

[3] Emmett L. Avery, "Fielding's Last Season with the Haymarket Theatre" (*Modern Philology*, 1939, xxxvi. 283–92) and "Some Notes on Fielding's Plays" (*Research Studies of the State College of Washington*, 1935, iii. 48–50); A. H. Scouten and Leo Hughes, "The New Theatre in the Haymarket, 1734 and 1737" (*NQ*, Jan. 15, 1944, clxxxvi).

[4] F. D. Senior, *The Life and Times of Colley Cibber* (1928) and D. M. E. Habbema, *An Appreciation of Colley Cibber* (1928) tell the story of his life and survey his dramatic works.

[5] *English Comic Drama 1700–1750* (1929), pp. 14–41.

[6] John Harrington Smith, in *The Gay Couple in Restoration Comedy* (1948), pp. 218–19, questions the validity of this term, but it is a useful name for a fairly well-defined type: Smith is, however, right in suggesting that the type first appears in Burnaby's *The Reform'd Wife*, one of the main sources of *The Double Gallant*. F. W. Bateson (*Review of English Studies*, 1925, i. 343–6) notes that only the title of Cibber's play comes from Corneille's *Le galand doublé*, although Mrs Centlivre's *Love at a Venture*, based on this French comedy, was utilised by Cibber. R. H. Griffith ("A 'Wildfrau' Story in a Cibber Play," *Philological Quarterly*, 1933, xii. 298–302) draws attention to the interesting use of a traditional folk-theme in *The Careless Husband*.

times be a question of debate[1], but fundamentally there is to
be recognised a peculiar tone expressed in a number of early
eighteenth-century comedies which links them together and
gives justification for the use of this term.

III. *The Comedies of Sensibility*

Sentimentalism was, of course, one of the most characteristic new moods developed during the eighteenth century,
and various efforts have been made to define its essential
quality and to explore its varied ramifications[2]. Of particular
interest are the conclusions reached by J. Harrington Smith
in his study of the peregrinations of the "gay couple" in
Restoration comedy. As this couple gradually give place to the
man and woman of sense, he notes, the "exemplary comedy"
comes to take the place of the older aristocratic comedy
of amoral wit[3]. While perhaps we cannot accept the term "exemplary" as fully descriptive of the sentimental style, undoubtedly there is justification for thus insisting on the complete
change in orientation towards comedy's heroes and heroines.

In this sphere of dramatic activity several authors have
received individual attention[4]. Steele's work has received
attention[5]; although "he was an essayist first of all, a dramatist

---

[1] For example, M. Maurice Shudofsky (*Modern Language Notes*, 1940,
lv. 396–9) believes that in the reference to *The Gentleman Cully* (*supra*,
p. 169) the text of the present volume does not do justice to the reaction in
this comedy against the Restoration hero-rake. Conversely, J. Harrington
Smith (*op. cit.* p. 218) would not include Mrs Davys' *The Northern Heiress*.

[2] F. T. Wood has two articles, "The Beginnings and Significance of
Sentimental Comedy" (*Anglia*, 1931, lv. 368–92) and "Sentimental
Comedy in the Eighteenth Century" (*Neophilologus*, 1933, xviii. 37–44 and
281–9), which present interesting notes on individual plays but which seem
based on an overwide interpretation of the term: in assessing the quality of
eighteenth-century sentimentalism there is not much value in moving back
to the medieval moralities. On interpretations of the term see also the
several recent studies of *The London Merchant* referred to above, p. 418.

[3] *The Gay Couple in Restoration Comedy* (1948). V. F. Calverton, in
"Social Change and the Sentimental Comedy" (*Modern Quarterly*, 1926,
iii. 169–88) relates the new form to the altering pattern of society. I have
not seen J. E. Cox, *The Rise of Sentimental Comedy* (1927).

[4] For Mrs Haywood, reference should be given to G. F. Whicher's
earlier study, *The Life and Romances of Mrs Eliza Haywood* (1915).

[5] The standard life is that by G. A. Aitken (1889). F. W. Bateson
(*op. cit.* pp. 42–60) has some illuminating pages on his work.

only secondarily," his importance in effecting a change in comic attitude has been clearly appreciated[1]. The relationship between this sentimental comedy and revived interest in Shakespeare's comedies of romance is well exemplified in James Miller's *The Universal Passion*[2]. Another author of prime import in this field is Edward Moore[3], whose *The Foundling* so deeply impressed contemporaries. It has been pointed out[4] that this play has definite connections with Richardson's *Clarissa* and that, at the same time, it may have suggested the sub-title for *Tom Jones*[5].

IV. *Farces*

Many of the farces so popular during these years were intended simply for light entertainment, but several, at least, had satirical intent. Among them perhaps the most interesting, because of its distinguished authorship, is *Three Hours after Marriage*, and of this a full account has been given by George Sherburn[6]. Fielding's use of contemporary events in *The Letter Writers* and *The Modern Husband*, and of political material in *Eurydice Hiss'd*, has also been the subject of analysis[7].

---

[1] As testimony to the impress made on contemporaries by *The Conscious Lovers* note should be made of Paolo Rolli's early Italian translation as *Gli Amanti Interni* (1724).

[2] Powell Stewart has an analytic study of this play in relation to its sources—*Much Ado about Nothing* and *La Princesse d'Élide*—in "An Eighteenth-Century Adaptation of Shakespeare" (*University of Texas Studies in English*, 1932, pp. 98–117).

[3] See John Homer Caskey, *The Life and Works of Edward Moore* (1927).

[4] Ralph L. Collins, "Moore's *The Foundling*—An Intermediary" (*Philological Quarterly*, 1938, xvii. 139–43).

[5] This play was translated by Mme Riccoboni as *L'Enfant Trouvé* in the *Nouveau Théâtre Anglais* (1769), vol. i, and anonymously into German as *Der Fündling* (1778).

[6] "The Fortunes and Misfortunes of *Three Hours after Marriage*" (*Modern Philology*, 1926, xxiv. 91–109).

[7] Charles B. Woods, "Notes on Three of Fielding's Plays" (*PMLA*, 1937, lii. 359–73). Satirical elements in some other among Fielding's farces are dealt with by Charles W. Nichols in "Fielding and the Cibbers" (*Philological Quarterly*, 1922, i. 278–89) and in "Social Satire in Fielding's *Pasquin* and *The Historical Register*" (*ib.* 1924, iii. 309–17).

SUPPLEMENTARY TO CHAPTER IV

I. *Italian and English Operas*

The introduction of Italian opera into England, its early fortunes and the character of the pieces presented have all been more fully explored during recent years[1]. How the critics reacted to the new dramatic species has also been minutely examined[2]. A special study has been devoted to the "little Metastasio" of the Royal Academy of Music—Paolo Rolli[3].

II. *Ballad-Operas*

The ballad-opera now has a separate general volume surveying its entire career[4], and thanks to this and to special essays we can the better assess the value of Gay's truly extraordinary achievement[5].

[1] To earlier studies should be added A. J. Armstrong, *Operatic Performances in England before Handel* (1918). D. I. West surveys *Italian Opera in England* (1938). Francis Colman's "Opera Register, 1712–34" was reproduced in *The Mask*, 1926, xii. 110–14. The contents of this manuscript are discussed by Robert W. Babcock (*Music and Letters*, 1943, xxiv. 155–9). Edward Dent has a study of *Händel in England* (1936). *The Rise of English Opera* (1951) by E. W. White presents a vivid account of the first experiments.

[2] Siegmund A. E. Betz, "The Operatic Criticism of the *Tatler* and *Spectator*" (*Musical Quarterly*, 1945, xxxi. 318–30); Franz Montgomery, "Early Criticism of Italian Opera in England" (*Musical Quarterly*, 1929, xv. 415–25). In connection with the reference, *supra*, p. 226, to the "author" of *A Comparison of the French and Italian Musick and Operas* it may be noted that this work of 1709 was an expanded translation of Lecuf de la Viéville, *Comparison de la Musique italienne et de la Musique française* (Brussels, 1705).

[3] Tarquinio Vallese, *Paolo Rolli in Inghilterra* (Milan, 1938). Among the English authors who tried to rival the Italians on their own ground, most interesting is Henry Carey: F. W. Bateson presents an assessment of his work (*op. cit.* pp. 104–14).

[4] Edmond McAdoo Gagey, *Ballad Opera* (1937).

[5] James R. Sutherland discusses the origin of *The Beggar's Opera* (*T.L.S.* April 25, 1935); J. Loiseau examines its significance ("John Gay et le Beggar's Opera," *Revue Anglo-Américaine*, 1934–5, xii. 3–19); its contribution to comedy is analysed by Bertrand H. Bronson ("The Beggar's Opera," *University of California Publications in English*, 1941, viii. 197–231); Charles W. Hughes outlines the career of "John Christopher Pepusch" (*Musical Quarterly*, 1945, xxxi. 54–70), who was concerned

III. *Pantomimes*

The genesis and essential nature of the English pantomime is another subject to which some considerable research has been devoted. General accounts of the harlequinade and *commedia dell' arte* do not, perhaps, have much fresh light to throw on those earlier years, since their emphasis tends to be placed either on Renaissance Italian or on late Georgian and Victorian English developments[1], but there are as well particular studies of the formative years at the beginning of the eighteenth century.

Emmett L. Avery surveys the course of pantomimic entertainments from the beginnings to 1737[2]. On the whole, he is inclined to accept Weaver's claim for the priority of *The Tavern Bilkers* in 1702; he notes the impetus given to such pieces by the rivalry between Drury Lane and Lincoln's Inn Fields in 1717 and 1723; and he usefully divides the species into three main forms—the "serious" ballet of action, the *commedia dell' arte* type and, the most common, a mixed playlet wherein the harlequinade is bound to a pantomimic narrative[3]. Despite the tremendous popularity of these shows

with its music; Jean B. Kern provides "A Note on *The Beggar's Opera*" (*Philological Quarterly*, 1938, xvii. 411–13), drawing attention to the political satire in the second act; Arthur V. Berger stresses its attack on the Italian opera (" *The Beggar's Opera*, the Burlesque, and Italian Opera," *Music and Letters*, 1936, xvii. 93–105). Notes on the sources of the tunes (by W. H. Flood) are printed in L. Melville, *The Life and Letters of John Gay* (1921); Cäcelie Tolksdorf analyses the relationship between *John Gays "Beggar's Opera" und Bert Brechts "Dreigroschenoper"* (Bonn, 1934). F. W. Bateson (*op. cit.* pp. 78–103, discusses Gay's dramatic work as a whole, and his life is narrated, popularly, by P. F. Gaye (1938) and, with admirable thoroughness, by William Henry Irving (1940). A. E. H. Swaen has followed his essay on the airs of *The Beggar's Opera* with a kindred study of "The Airs and Tunes of John Gay's *Polly*" (*Anglia*, 1936, lx. 403–22).

[1] E.g. the present writer's *Masks, Mimes and Miracles* (1931); Cyril W. Beaumont, *The History of Harlequin* (1927).

[2] "Dancing and Pantomime on the English Stage, 1700–1737" (*Studies in Philology*, 1934, xxxi. 417–52).

[3] Mitchell P. Wells ("Some Notes on the Early Eighteenth-Century Pantomime," *Studies in Philology*, 1935, xxxii. 598–607) comments on the fact that the term "pantomime" was not used at this time for *commedia dell' arte* performances but was applied to motley collections of song, dance and clownery. He discusses particularly Rich's *Necromancer* (1723), Thurmond's *Harlequin Dr Faustus* (1724) and the *Father Girard* of 1724.

and the increasing returns they gave to the managers, the age did not lack an awareness of its shortcomings in the welcome it gave to such trivial entertainments, and Avery has no difficulty in gathering together a weighty array of critical fulminations against Harlequin's intrusion into the English playhouse[1].

In connection with this intrusion, attention may be called to three advertisements of the year 1702. For Saturday, August 22, the *Daily Courant* announces *The Jovial Crew* at Drury Lane, with the promise that "Monsieur Serene and another Person lately arrived in *England*, will perform a Night Scene by a Harlequin and a Scaramouch, after the Italian manner." On Friday, September 18, we are informed, "Mr *Penkethman* acts the part of *Harlequin* without a Masque," while on Tuesday, October 20, there was "a Mimick Night Scene after the Italian manner, by a New Scaramouch and Harlequin." From short pieces like these, no doubt, the later great pantomimic displays took their being.

Fundamentally, of course, the pantomime is an outgrowth of all the diverse "entertainments" which so characterised theatrical productions at the beginning of the century. Already the taste for such shows had been fully evident during the late nineties of the century preceding[2]. "In the space of Ten Years past," says Downes in 1708[3], "Mr *Betterton* to gratify the desires and Fancies of the Nobility and Gentry; procur'd from Abroad the best Dances and Singers," and, although he declares that these, being "Exorbitantly Expensive, produc'd small Profit to him and his Company," we must believe that this astute actor-manager, and his companions, found that these extra-dramatic shows were essential if audiences were to be attracted to the playhouses.

Nor were Downes' "Dances and Singers" all: anything

---

[1] "The Defense and Criticism of Pantomimic Entertainments in the Early Eighteenth Century" (*ELH*, 1938, v. 127–45). Charles Washburn Nichols discusses "Fielding's Satire on Pantomime" (*PMLA*, 1931, xlvi. 1107–12).

[2] See vol. i, p. 340 of this *History*.

[3] *Roscius Anglicanus* (ed. M. Summers, 1929), p. 46.

and everything was included[1]. "Entertainments of singing between the acts"—"a new Entry by the little Boy, being his last time of Dancing before he goes to France"—"several new Comical Dances"—"a new Pastoral Dialogue"—"Entertainments of Italian Singing by the Famous Signiora *Maria Margarita Gallia*, lately arriv'd from Italy"—"the Famous Mr Clynch being now in Town, will for this once, at the desire of several Persons of Quality, perform his Imitation of an *Organ* with 3 Voices, the *Double Curtel*, and the *Bells*, the *Huntsman* with his *Horn* and *Pack of Dogs*; All which he performs with his Mouth on the open Stage, being what no Man besides himself could ever yet attain to"—"Next a Gentleman will perform several Mimick Entertainments on the Ladder, first he stands on the top-round with a Bottle in one hand and a Glass in the other, and drinks a Health; then plays several Tunes on the Violin, with fifteen other surprizing Performances which no Man but himself can do. And will[2]": these and similar announcements in the newspapers amply show how much "music-hall" entertainment was presented at Drury Lane, Lincoln's Inn Fields and the Haymarket at the start of the new century, and how fully the ingredients of pantomime were lying ready for the hands of its first concocters.

Among the concocters, most famous was, of course, John Rich, who acted under the name of "Lun." It seems now proved[3] that this name he took from a French performer, Francisque Moylin or Molin, who acted under Rich's direction in 1716.

---

[1] Emmett L. Avery, "Vaudeville on the London Stage, 1700–1737" (*Research Studies of the State College of Washington*, 1937, v. 65–77), surveys this subject well.

[2] Aline Mackenzie ("Another Note on 'Gulliver's Travels'," *NQ*, Dec. 11, 1948, cxciv) interestingly shows that Swift seems to have been influenced by these popular entertainments when elaborating his political satire.

[3] C. A. C. Davis, "John Rich as 'Lun'" (*NQ*, May 31, 1947, cxcii).

IV. *Burlesques and Rehearsals*

The critical tendency in this period was responsible for its success in the production of burlesque. Here a most valuable survey has been provided by Dane Farnsworth Smith[1]. The sub-title of his volume—"The Self-Conscious Stage and its Burlesque and Satirical Reflections in the Age of Criticism"— in itself summarily describes what was indeed one of the chief characteristics of the playhouse of this time. And it is significant that he closes his account with an examination of the work of Henry Fielding. In those last plays through which the future author of *Tom Jones* turned his motley laughter at the follies of contemporary opera and at the errors to be found in political life we find perhaps the true key to an understanding of the theatre in the early eighteenth century. Fielding himself failed to write any dramatic masterpiece, but he drew audiences to his satirical shows. He "failed in writing drama," says Farnsworth Smith, "and succeeded in writing for the stage." He "was living in a journalistic age" and all these pieces are "hardly more than journalistic offerings...." Even his method of composition was that of the journalist. As Arthur Murphy, writing in 1762, so picturesquely relates:

When he had contracted to bring on a play, or a farce, it is well known by many of his friends now living, that he would go home rather late from a tavern, and would, the next morning, deliver a scene to the players written upon the papers, which had wrapped the tobacco, in which he so much delighted.

[1] *Plays about the Theatre in England from The Rehearsal in 1671 to the Licensing Act of 1737* (1936).

SUPPLEMENTARY TO APPENDIX A

Drury Lane. A general account of the fortunes of this house has been written by W. J. M. Pope (1946), while Dougald MacMillan gives, in *Drury Lane Calendar, 1747–1776* (1938) a complete record of its performances during the mid-years of the century. It should be noted that this theatre was altered in 1742.

Lincoln's Inn Fields (old theatre). In 1705 Christopher Rich leased this house, which in 1714 was rebuilt, under the supervision of the architect Edward Shepherd.

Haymarket (Opera House). Alterations in the structure were carried out in 1709 and 1720.

Lincoln's Inn Fields (new theatre). The architect was Edward Shepherd and the theatre was abandoned in 1732. In 1718 it was under the management of Christopher Bullock. F. T. Wood analyses "The Account-books of Lincoln's Inn Fields Theatre, 1724–1727" (*NQ*, April 1, 15, 22 and 29, 1933, vol. clxiv).

Haymarket (the Little Theatre). Built and owned by J. Potter. Its most important activities were during the period when Fielding's company acted there: see Emmett L. Avery, "Fielding's Last Season with the Haymarket Theatre" (*Modern Philology*, 1939, xxxvi. 283–92). That the building was still owned by Potter in 1738 is shown by J. Paul de Castro (*NQ*, June 20, 1942, vol. clxxxii; cp. article by E. L. Avery, *ib.* May 23, 1942). The later history of the house is told by Cyril Maude in *The Haymarket Theatre* (1903).

Goodman's Fields. For the story of this theatre see F. T. Wood, "Goodman's Fields Theatre" (*Modern Language Review*, 1930, xxv. 443–56) and P. J. Crean, "The Stage Licensing Act of 1737" (*Modern Philology*, 1938, xxxv. 239–55). The first playhouse was set up by Thomas Odell (opened 31/10/1729) with Henry Giffard in the company: the season ended on 19/7/1730 and a second season began on 2/10/1730. Despite an order of 28/4/1730 ordering its closure (see *supra*, p. 284) performances continued till 9/6/1730. Odell tried a third season, opening in September 1730, but apparently in the summer of 1731 he handed over his authority to Henry Giffard, who, after alterations in the building, ran a season from 27/9/1731 and started making preparations for an entirely new building. This, designed by Edward Shepherd, opened on 2/10/1732. The following year Giffard purchased a share in Drury Lane, but he continued to operate Goodman's Fields until 16/5/1736. By the new Licensing Act the theatre was now closed, and in 1738 was advertised for sale. On 15/10/1740, however, Giffard recommenced activities under a subterfuge and had the distinction of introducing Garrick to a London audience (19/10/1741). The theatre closed, evidently finally, on 27/5/1742. There was another entertainment house at New Wells, Goodman's Fields, between 1739 and 1751 (see *Theatre Notebook*, 1946, i. 50).

Covent Garden. A history of this theatre is given by H. S. Wyndham, *Annals of Covent Garden Theatre* (1906). The architect was Edward Shepherd. Note may be taken of the fact that in the Christmas and Easter seasons of 1732-3 John Rich, who had transferred his Lincoln's Inn Fields company to Covent Garden, established a new tradition by attracting holiday customers to both houses, with some actors "doubling" at the two houses (see Leo Hughes and A. H. Scouten, "John Rich and the Holiday Seasons of 1732-3" (*Review of English Studies*, 1945, xxi. 46-52).

Punch's Theatre. Originally Martin Powell's puppets were shown in St Martin's-lane ("Punch's Opera") but they moved to the Little Piazza, Covent Garden, in 1711.

Sadler's Wells. There was a music room here from 1683, but the theatre was not set up until 1740.

Brief accounts of the provincial theatres appear in later volumes of this *History*. Reference should, however, be given here to Alfred Loewenberg's most useful bibliography, *The Theatre of the British Isles, excluding London* (1950), which gives allusions to much source material on this subject.

SUPPLEMENTARY TO APPENDIX C

The supplementary notes to the Hand-list of Plays seek to present additional information concerning dates of performance and publication, many of the new facts being derived from the numerous studies devoted during recent years to various aspects of this subject. For the early years, the "Tentative Calendar of Daily Theatrical Performances in London, 1700-1701 to 1704-1705" (*PMLA*, 1948, lxiii. 114-80), by Emmett L. Avery and A. H. Scouten, is invaluable. This utilises the material presented in the "Morley" list given by Leslie Hotson in *The Commonwealth and Restoration Stage* (1928). Reference should also be made here to two articles by Alfred Jackson, "London Playhouses, 1700-1705" (*Review of English Studies*, 1932, viii. 291-302) and "Play

Notices from the Burney Newspapers, 1700–1703" (*PMLA*, 1933, xlviii. 815–49). Other special articles by E. L. Avery and A. H. Scouten are alluded to elsewhere.

For Drury Lane from 1747 a full record now appears in Dougald MacMillan's *Drury Lane Calendar, 1747–1776* (1938).

As has been noted above, when the present volume was being prepared I had not yet located the Larpent collection of dramatic manuscripts, and references to such plays as fell before 1750 were consequently not included in the original Hand-list. Now, however, Dougald MacMillan has prepared an important *Catalogue of the Larpent Plays in the Huntington Library* (1939) and I have inserted here allusions to all the relevant pieces. It should be observed that, whereas in later volumes of this series, I used the numbering of the old manuscript catalogue, the new references given here follow MacMillan's numbers. [L. 1 thus indicates his catalogue reference for "1. *The Nest of Plays*."]

For fresh information in the opera section I am deeply indebted to Alfred Loewenberg's *Annals of Opera, 1597–1940* (1943).

In the presentation of these supplementary facts use is made of a plus sign (+) to indicate that material is being given which adds to information in the original Hand-list. A + sign before the name of an author or the title of a play means that no such name or title is to be found in the text. Although the scope of the present Hand-list is considerably fuller than that of any of the other volumes in this series, I have left it as it was originally planned, since nowhere else can a student find information concerning the range of performances of new plays within the period 1700–1750. While checking against recent specialised studies has revealed a few dates additional to those in the text, the number of observed errors has, to my gratification, proved negligible. At the same time, it should be emphasised that only such a "new Genest" as is at present being projected can hope to provide a definitive record of productions during these years: until that is finally issued the notes given here may be of at least summary service.

p. 294]   *ADDISON, JOSEPH.*
        Cato [+1729. W. 27/10.].

p. 295]   The Drummer. [Lee W. Heilman (*TLS*, Oct. 1, 1931) shows
        there was a second edition in 1716, and also another
        "second" and a "third" in 1722.]

   +*ARBUTHNOT, JOHN.*
        Three Hours after Marriage (D.L. Jan. 1716/7). See *JOHN
        GAY.*

   ARNE, THOMAS AUGUSTINE.
        +Henry and Emma (C.G. March 1749). See *UNKNOWN
        AUTHORS.*

p. 296]   *AYRE, WILLIAM.*
Amintas. [A translation of Torquato Tasso, *Aminta* (1573).]
Merope. [A translation of F. S. Maffei, *Merope* (1713).]

BAKER, THOMAS.
The Humour of the Age. [+1701. D.L. S. 1/3, Th. 13. 1703. W. 30/6.]
Tunbridge-Walks. [*The Daily Courant*, Jan. 15, 1702/3, announces publication "next week."]

p. 297]   +*BEALING, RICHARD.*
Boadicea or The British Queen. MS. recorded in *TLS*, Aug. 22, 1918.

p. 299]   *BOADENS, CHARLES.*
The Modish Couple. [*HMC, Egmont*, i. 205 and 216, records a news-letter attributing this play to Lord John Hervey and the Prince of Wales—an attribution probably correct. See Charles B. Woods, "Captain B——'s Play" (*Harvard Studies and Notes in Philology and Literature*, 1933, xv. 243–55), and E. M. Gagey, *Ballad Opera* (1937), p. 234.]

BOYER, ABEL.
Achilles. [See the Hand-list of Plays, 1660–1700.]

BOYLE, CHARLES.
As You Find It. [Publication announced in *Post Man*, May 6–10, 1703.]
+Altemira. [See *ROGER BOYLE.*]

BOYLE, ROGER.
[See the Hand-list of Plays, 1660–1700.]
Altemira. [A revised version, executed by *CHARLES BOYLE*, of the earlier play, *The Generall.*]

BRERETON, THOMAS.
Esther. [A translation of Racine, *Esther* (Saint-Cyr, 1689).]

p. 300]   *BREVAL, JOHN DURANT.*
The Strolers. [+1723. T. 23/7.]

p. 301]   *BURNABY, WILLIAM.*
[For this author's works see the edition by F. E. Budd (1931).]
Love Betray'd. [Publication announced in the *Post Man*, Feb. 9–11, 1702/3.]

CAREY, HENRY.
[The *Dramatick Works* 4° 1703 contain all the plays listed except *Hanging and Marriage.*]
The Contrivances. [All the texts after that of 1729 are of the ballad-opera version.]

p. 302]   Betty. [A ballad-opera version of *Hanging and Marriage*. See F. T. Wood, "Henry Carey's *Betty*" (*Review of English Studies*, 1933, ix. 64–6).]
+The Disappointment (H.² 1732). See *JOHN RANDAL.* [F. T. Wood (*Review of English Studies*, 1929, v. 66–9) argues that "Randal" was a pseudonym and that this ballad-opera version of Susannah Centlivre's *A Wife well Manag'd* (D.L. 1715) was by Carey.]
The Honest Yorkshire-Man. [See A. H. Scouten and Leo Hughes, "The First Season of "The Honest Yorkshire-

p. 302]   man'" (*Modern Language Review*, 1945, xl. 8–11). Written
during the summer of 1734, it was given to Fleetwood at
D.L.; this theatre closed before it could be performed, and
Carey gave it to L.², where it was put in rehearsal. Before
production there, it was then passed to H.², where it
appeared on T. 15/7/1735. At G.F. it was presented on
W. 6/8/1735, and towards the end of August B.F. and the
"Welsh Fair" saw further productions under the title of
A Wonder. The pirated 1736 text is recorded in *The Daily
Advertiser*, Dec. 26, 1735; the authorised text was issued in
Jan. 1735/6.]

The Dragon of Wantley. [E. L. Avery ("Fielding's Last
Season with the Haymarket Theatre," *Modern Philology*,
1939, xxxvi. 283–92) shows that this appeared as an
"Oratorio" at H.² on M. 16/5/1737.]

p. 303]   Margery. [+L. 11.]

CENTLIVRE, SUSANNAH.

The Stolen Heiress. [Acted as *The Heiress*, which is the
running title in the 1703 quarto—announced for publication
in the *London Gazette*, Jan. 14–18, 1702/3.]

Love's Contrivance. [Publication announced in the *Daily
Courant*, June 16, 1703.]

The Gamester. [+12° 1725 (Dublin); 12° 1734. Based on
Regnard, *Le joueur* (1696).]

p. 304]   The Busie Body. [+8° [1715]; 12° 1727; 12° 1741; 12° 1747
(Dublin); 8° 1749; 8° 1765. +1749. D.L. T. 3/1.]

p. 305]   The Wonder. [There were two editions in 1714 and also
12° 1725 (Dublin), 12° 1735, with several later reprintings.]

A Wife well Manag'd. [On the Ballad-opera version see
HENRY CAREY and *JOHN RANDAL*.]

A Bold Stroke for a Wife. [+12° 1727 (Dublin); 12° 1733.]

p. 306]   ## CHAVES, A.

The Cares of Love. [+1705. L.¹ W. 1/8, probably F. 3 and
T. 7.]

+CHETWOOD, WILLIAM RUFUS.

The Stage Coach Opera (D.L. May 1730). See *UNKNOWN
AUTHORS*.

CIBBER, COLLEY.

[Slightly variant texts of some of this author's plays appear in
the *Plays* (2 vols., 1721), the *Dramatic Works* (4 vols., 1760)
and the *Dramatic Works* (5 vols., 1777).]

p. 307]   The Tragical History of King Richard III. [See the Hand-list
of Plays, 1660–1700. +12° 1718; 12° 1736. +1704. D.L.
T. 4/4. For revisions in the text see A. C. Sprague, "A New
Scene in Colley Cibber's *Richard III*" (*Modern Language
Notes*, 1927, xlii. 29–33).]

Love Makes a Man. [+1700. M. 9/12, Th. 12, S. 14, W. 18.
1701. W. 15/1; F. 13/6. Publication announced in the *Post
Man*, Jan. 18–21, 1700/1.]

p. 308]   She Wou'd and She Wou'd Not. [+12° 1717. +1748. D.L.
Th. 14/4.]

The Careless Husband. [+8° 1725; 12° 1733; 12° 1734.

p. 308] +1705. S. 27/1. Harry Glicksman has a general survey of "The Stage History of Colley Cibber's *The Careless Husband*" (*PMLA*, 1921, xxxvi. 245–50).]

p. 310] The Comical Lovers. [+12° 1736.]

The Double Gallant. [+12° 1736. +1707. T. 4/11. Indebted to Thomas Corneille, *Le galand doublé* (1660).]

The Lady's Last Stake. [+12° 1732. +1715. D.L. S. 17/12, M. 19. 1723. D.L. S. 9/11, M. 11.]

+Cinna's Conspiracy (D.L. Feb. 1712/13). See *UNKNOWN AUTHORS.*

Hob. [+1724. L.² W. 18/11. An alteration of Doggett, *The Country-Wake* (1696).]

Ximena. [An adaptation of Pierre Corneille, *Le Cid* (1636).]

p. 312] The Non-Juror. [+12° 1736. Based on Molière, *Tartuffe* (1664).]

The Refusal. [+8° 1722; 12° 1735; 12° 1736; 12° 1749 (Dublin). Based on Molière, *Les femmes savantes* (1672).]

The Provok'd Husband. [+8° 1728 (Dublin); 12° 1728 (Dublin); 8° 1730; 12° 1734; 12° 1735; 8° 1741; 8° 1743; 12° 1748 (Dublin). Written in collaboration with SIR JOHN VANBRUGH.]

p. 313] Damon and Phillida. [+8° 1730; 8° 1731; 8° 1733 (Dublin); 12° 1734; 8° 1749. A further ballad-opera version of *Love in a Riddle* (D.L. 1729).]

p, 314] *CIBBER, THEOPHILUS.*

+The Beggar's Wedding (D.L. 1731). See *CHARLES COFFEY.*

The Auction. [This consists of scenes taken from Henry Fielding, *The Historical Register* (H.² 1737).]

COFFEY, CHARLES.

The Beggar's Wedding. [+8° (1730, 3rd, with "musical melodies"). A ballad-opera version of T. Jevon, *The Devil of a Wife* (1686).]

+*COLMAN, FRANCIS.*

Ariadne in Crete (H.¹ Jan. 1733/4). See *ITALIAN OPERAS.*

p. 315] *CONCANEN, MATTHEW.*

+The Jovial Crew (D.L. Feb. 1730/1). See *Sir WILLIAM YONGE.*

CONGREVE, WILLIAM.

The Judgment of Paris. [The first performance may have been on F. 21/3/1700/1: see Lucyle Hook in the *Huntington Library Quarterly*, 1945, viii. 309 and 311. Publication announced in the *Post Man*, March 22–25, 1701.]

p. 316] *COOKE, THOMAS.*

+Penelope (H.² May 1728). See *JOHN MOTTLEY.*

CORYE, JOHN.

[For his earlier works see the Hand-list of Plays, 1660–1700.]

CRAUFORD, DAVID.

Love at First Sight. [Publication announced in the *Post Boy*, July 20–23, 1700.]

CROSS, RICHARD.

The Hen-Peck'd Captain. [+L. 71.]

p. 317]   DALTON, JOHN.
  Comus. [+L. 6.]
 DANCE, JAMES.
  Pamela. [William M. Sale, Jr. ("The First Dramatic Version
p. 317] of *Pamela*," *Yale University Library Gazette*, 1935, ix. 83–8)
  shows that two plays were published anonymously in the
  autumn of 1741: (1) *Pamela; or, Virtue Triumphant*,
  "designed to be acted at Drury Lane," and (2) *Pamela*, as
  acted at G.F. (dated 1742). A second edition of the latter
  appeared in 1742, and two pirated editions were issued, one
  in 8° and one in 12°, with the date 1741. Although attributed
  to Dance, the G.F. version is stated by Garrick to be the
  work of *HENRY GIFFARD*; Dance may have been the
  author of the other text; but the whole question of authorship is obscure.]

 DENNIS, JOHN.
  Iphigenia. [See the Hand-list of Plays, 1660–1700.]
p. 318] The Comical Gallant. [An alteration of *The Merry Wives of
  Windsor*. Publication announced in the *Post Man*, May
  16–19, 1702.]
  The Invader of his Country. [An alteration of *Coriolanus*.]

 DODSLEY, ROBERT.
  The Toy-Shop. [+12° [1739], 8° 1745, 8° 1763.]
  Sir John Cockle at Court. [+L. 5.]
p. 319] The Blind Beggar of Bethnal Green. [+L. 25.]
  The Triumph of Peace. [+L. 76.]

 DORMAN, JOSEPH.
  Sir Roger de Coverly. [+L. 61.]
  +The Female Rake (H.² April 1736). See *UNKNOWN
  AUTHORS*.

p. 320]   DU BOIS, P. B.
  Aminta. [A translation of T. Tasso, *Aminta* (1573).]

 DUNCOMBE, WILLIAM.
  Athaliah. [A translation of J. Racine, *Athalie* (Saint-Cyr),
  5/1/1691).]
  Lucius Junius Brutus. [A translation of Voltaire, *Brutus*
  (Paris, 11/9/1730).]

 D'URFEY, THOMAS.
  The Bath. [+1701. D.L. S. 31/5; M. 9/6.]
  The Old Mode & the New. [Publication announced in the
  Daily Courant, April 13, 1703.]

 ESTCOURT, RICHARD.
  The Fair Example. [Based on F. Dancourt, *Les bourgeoises à
  la mode* (Paris, 15/11/1692).]

p. 321]   FARQUHAR, GEORGE.
  Sir Harry Wildair. [+1701. D.L. F. 2/5, S. 3, W. 28.]
  The Inconstant. [+1716. L.² W. 19/12, M. 31. 1719. D.L.
  T. 6/10. 1723. W. 13/11.]
  The Stage Coach. [The two texts are different: W. J. Law-
  rence ("The Mystery of 'The Stage Coach'," *Modern
  Language Review*, 1932, xxvii. 392–7) suggests that the

p. 321]   Dublin edition is from the original MS., the other from a
          stage version. See also R. Crompton Rhodes (*id.* 1933,
          xxviii. 482–4). The farce is based on Jean de la Chapelle,
          Les carosses d'Orléans (Paris, 2 or 9/8/1680). One song was
          contributed by *P. A. MOTTEUX.*]

p. 322]   The Beaux Stratagem. [+1734. H.² M. 24/6; F. 16/8.]

p. 323]   *FENTON, ELIJAH.*
          Mariamne. [+12° 1729, 12° 1735, 12° 1745, 12° 1750, 12°
          1759 (Dublin), 12° 1760. +1723. L.² 7/12. Based on
          Voltaire, *Marianne* (1724).]

p. 324]   *FIELDING, HENRY.*
          The Lottery. [+1734. H.² F. 7/6, F. 14, W. 19, W. 26;
          M. 1/7, M. 29, W. 31. 1748. D.L. Th. 29/9.]

p. 325]   The Covent-Garden Tragedy. [+1734. H.² W. 17/4, Th. 18,
          F. 19, M. 29; M. 27/5; L.² F. 24/5.]
          The Mock Doctor. [+8° 1732 (4th). +1734. H.² W. 5/6,
          M. 17; M. 5/8. Based on Molière, *Le médecin malgré lui*
          (1666).]

p. 326]   The Miser. [+1734. H.² W. 14/8. Based on Molière, *L'avare*
          (1668). For an undated folio text, claimed by Charles
          Stonehill (*TLS*, Oct. 22, 1925) to be a first printing, see
          Stanley E. Read's note in the *Huntington Library Bulletin*
          May 1931, i. 211–13): the folio is a careless reprint of the
          octavo edition.]
          The Intriguing Chambermaid. [+L. 77 (containing additions
          made for Mrs Clive's benefit on 13/3/1749). Based on
          J. F. Regnard, *Le retour imprévu* (Paris, 11/2/1700).]

p. 327]   Don Quixote in England. [+12° 1734 (Dublin). +1734. H.²
          F. 5/4, M. 8, T. 9, Th. 11, W. 17, Th. 18, F. 19, M. 29;
          revived with additions M. 19/8, W. 21.]
          An Old Man Taught Wisdom. [+1747. D.L. Th. 31/12.
          1749. M. 20/2.]

p. 328]   The Universal Gallant. [E. L. Avery (*Research Studies of the
          State College of Washington*, 1938, vi. 46) shows this play
          was ready a full year before production.]
          Pasquin. [+1737. H.² F. 25/2; S. 19/3; W. 4/5, M. 9.]
          The Historical Register. [The date of the première has been
          established by E. L. Avery ("Fielding's Last Season with
          the Haymarket Theatre," *Modern Philology*, 1939, xxxvi.
          283–9); see also his "An Early Performance of Fielding's
          Historical Register" (*Modern Language Notes*, 1934, xlix.
          407). Here and in an article by A. H. Scouten and Leo
          Hughes ("The New Theatre in the Haymarket, 1734 and
          1737," *NQ*, Jan. 15, 1944, clxxxvi) dates are given of other
          performances. For *Eurydice Hiss'd* +1737. H.² F. 6/5,
          M. 9, W. 11, Th. 12, M. 23.]
          Miss Lucy in Town. [+L. 33.]
          The Wedding-Day. [+L. 39.]

p. 329]   +*FORREST, EBENEEZER.*
          Momus turn'd Fabulist (L.² Dec. 1729). See *UNKNOWN
          AUTHORS.*

p. 329]   *GARDINER, MATTHEW.*
The Sharpers. [A ballad-opera called *The Sharpers; or, The Female Matchmakers* was given at H.¹ on M. 28/2/1737. As this was accompanied by *The Parthian Hero; or, Love in Distress*, it is to be assumed that the two plays are Gardiner's.]

GARRICK, DAVID.
Lethe. [+L. 22, and L. 72 (the latter with additions of 1771–2). +1749. D.L. F. 7/4. Based on J. Miller, *An Hospital for Fools* (D.L. 1739). Additional scenes were provided for performances in 1741, 1749, 1756 and 1772.]
The Lying Valet. [+1748. D.L. W. 11/5. Based on *All without Money*, one of the short plays in P. A. Motteux, *The Novelty* (L.I.F. 1697), itself a translation of *Le souper mal-apprêté* by Noël le Breton, sieur de Hauteroche.]

p. 330]   Miss in her Teens. [+L. 62. Based on F. C. Dancourt, *La Parisienne* (1691).]
+Albumazar (D.L. Oct. 1747).
[This alteration of the play by Thomas Tomkis may be by Garrick. 1747. D.L. S. 3/10, T. 6, Th. 8, S. 10, T. 13; T. 17/11. 1748. W. 13/4.]

GAY, JOHN.
The What D'Ye Call It. [+1748. D.L. M. 21/3.]
p. 332]   Polly. [+8° 1742. See James R. Sutherland, "'Polly' among the Pirates" (*Modern Language Review*, 1942, xxxvii. 291–303).]
Acis and Galatea. [This was first performed, about 1721, at Canons, the seat of the Duke of Chandos. W. H. Irving (*John Gay*, 1940, p. 283) notes three undated editions in the Harvard Library—"probably all earlier than the 1732 edition. One of these is superscribed as 'performed at Oxford'."]
The Distress'd Wife. [Revived April 27, 1771, as *The Modern Wife.*]

+*GIFFARD, HENRY.*
Pamela (G.F. Nov. 1741). See supplementary notes to *JAMES DANCE.*

GILDON, CHARLES.
Measure for Measure. [Publication noted in the *Post Boy*, July 25–27, 1700.]
p. 333]   The Patriot. [Publication noted in the *Post Man*, Dec. 17–19, 1702. An adaptation of Nathaniel Lee, *Lucius Junius Brutus* (D.G. 1680).]

GRANVILLE, GEORGE.
The British Enchanters. [+8° 1710; 12° 1732 (Dublin).]

p. 334]   *HAMILTON, NEWBURGH.*
+Samson (C.G. Feb. 1743). See *ITALIAN OPERAS.*

HARRISON, WILLIAM.
The Pilgrims. [Publication noted in the *Post Boy*, Nov. 7–9, 1700.]

p. 334] *HATCHETT, WILLIAM.*
+The Opera of Operas (H.¹ May 1733). See *ELIZA HAYWOOD.*

HAVARD, WILLIAM.
Regulus. [+L. 36.]

p. 335] *HAWKINS, WILLIAM.*
Henry and Rosamond. [This was acted at Birmingham in 1761.]

HAYWOOD, ELIZA.
A Wife to be Lett. [+8° 1729.]
Frederick, Duke of Brunswick-Lunenburgh. [+12° 1729 (Dublin).]

HEWITT, JOHN.
A Tutor for the Beaus. [An adaptation of Boissy, *Le François à Londres* (1727).]

p. 336] *HILL, AARON.*
+Rinaldo (H.¹ Feb. 1710/11). See *ITALIAN OPERAS.*
+Pastor Fido (H.¹ Nov. 1712). See *ITALIAN OPERAS.*
The Fatal Extravagance. [See Paul S. Dunkin, "The Authorship of *The Fatal Extravagance*" (*Modern Language Notes*, 1945, lxi. 328–30) and P. P. Kies, "The Authorship of *The Fatal Extravagance*" (*Research Studies of the State College of Washington*, 1945, xiii. 155–8): both argue that Hill and Mitchell collaborated in writing this play.]
King Henry the Fifth. [+8° 1765 (3rd).]
Athelwold. [An adaptation of *Elfrid*, above.]
The Tragedy of Zara. [+12° 1737 (Dublin); 8° 1755 (Edinburgh); 8° 1758; 8° 1760. An adaptation of Voltaire, *Zaïre* (1732).]
Alzira. [+12° 1736 (Dublin); 8° 1737; 12° 1760. An adaptation of Voltaire, *Alzire* (1736).]
Meropé. [+12° 1749 (Dublin); 12° 1755 (Edinburgh). An adaptation of Voltaire, *Mérope* (Paris, 20/2, 1743).]
+The Roman Revenge (Bath, *c.* 1753) 8° 1753; 8° 1754; 8° 1759; 8° 1760. [An adaptation of Voltaire, *La mort de César* 1743).]
+The Insolvent: or, Filial Piety....Partly on a Plan of Sir William Davenant's and Mr Massenger's (H.¹ M. 6/3/1758) 8° 1758.
[Hill died in 1749, hence this production is posthumous. For the manuscript play on which the play was founded, *The Guiltless Adultress: or, Judge in His own Cause*, and for the history of the text, see J. Frank Kermode, "A Note on the History of Massinger's 'The Fatal Dowry' in the Eighteenth Century" (*NQ*, May 3, 1947) cxcii,.]
+The Dramatic Works of Aaron Hill 8° 1760 (2 vols.). [This includes, besides the above plays: (1) O. *The Muses in Mourning*; (2) Pant. *Merlin in Love*; (3) Burl. *The Snake in the Grass*; (4) T. *Saul*; (5) O. *Daraxes.*]

HIPPISLEY, JOHN.
Flora. [+12° 1736. There is doubt concerning the authorship of this piece; the same text has been printed under the names both of Hippisley and Cibber. Presumably, how-

p. 336]   ever, the former was responsible for the ballad-opera version, based on the latter's interlude farce of 1711. A similar doubt, and judgment, applies to *A Sequel to the Opera of Flora*.]

p. 337]   HOADLY, BENJAMIN.
+Jephtha (1737). See *ITALIAN OPERAS*.
The Suspicious Husband. [+L. 63, as *The Rake*. +1748. D.L. T. 27/9; S. 26/11.]

+HUGGINS, WILLIAM.
+Judith (L.¹ Feb. 1732/3). See *ITALIAN OPERAS*.

HUGHES, JOHN.
Calypso and Telemachus. [Music Galliard.]

p. 338]   HUMPHREYS, SAMUEL.
+Rinaldo (H.¹ Feb. 1710/11). See *ITALIAN OPERAS*.
+Venceslao (H.¹ Jan. 1730/1). See *ITALIAN OPERAS*.
+Poro (H.¹ Feb. 1730/1). See *ITALIAN OPERAS*.
+Ezio (H.¹ Jan. 1731/2). See *ITALIAN OPERAS*.
+Sosarme (H.¹ Feb. 1731/2). See *ITALIAN OPERAS*.
+Esther (H.¹ May 1732). See *ITALIAN OPERAS*.
+Catone (H.¹ Nov. 1732). See *ITALIAN OPERAS*.
+Orlando (H.¹ Jan. 1732/3). See *ITALIAN OPERAS*.
+Deborah (H.¹ March 1732/3). See *ITALIAN OPERAS*.
+Athalia (C.G. April 1735). See *ITALIAN OPERAS*.

JACKSON, ——.
Ajax. [A translation of Sophocles' play.]

JACOB, Sir HILDEBRAND.
The Nest of Plays. [+L. 1.]

JEFFREYS, GEORGE.
Merope. [An adaptation of F. S. Maffei, *Merope* (1713).]

+JENNENS, CHARLES.
L' Allegro, il Penseroso ed il Moderato. See *ITALIAN OPERAS*.

p. 339]   JOHNSON, CHARLES.
Fortune in her Wits. [A translation of A. Cowley, *Naufragium Joculare*.]
The Force of Friendship. [A manuscript in the Folger Shakespeare Library is noted by Bernard M. Wagner ("A Lost Volume of Plays," *TLS*, July 11, 1935) and Edward Niles Hooker ("Charles Johnson's *The Force of Friendship* and *Love in a Chest*: A Note on Tragicomedy and Licensing," *Studies in Philology*, 1937, xxxiv. 407–11) shows that this manuscript proves that originally the play was a tragicomedy, including the piece later separated and called *Love in a Chest*.]
The Generous Husband. [+1711. D.L. T. 23/1.]
The Victim. [An adaptation of Jean Racine, *Iphigénie in Aulide* (Versailles, 18/8, 1674).]
The Sultaness. [An adaptation of Jean Racine, *Bajazet* (1672).]

p. 340]   JOHNSON, SAMUEL (*of Cheshire*).
A Fool Made Wise. [The Larpent collection has (L. 14)

p. 340]   *Sir John Falstaff in Masquerade*, a farce, with application dated April 26, 1739, and (L. 29) *The Fool Made Wise or Sir John Falstaff in Masquerade*. It seems that an original farce was later made into a comic opera.]

KELLY, JOHN.

The Married Philosopher. [A close adaptation of P. N. Destouches, *Le Philosophe marié* (1727).]

Timon in Love. [A close adaptation of Louis François Delisle de la Drévetière, *Timon le misantrope* (1722).]

The Fall of Bob. [Emmett L. Avery ("Fielding's Last Season with the Haymarket Theatre," *Modern Philology*, 1939, xxxvi. 283–92) notes the production of this burlesque tragedy, as *The Fall of Bob, alias Gin*, at H.¹ on F. 14/1/1737. It was repeated on S. 15, M. 17 and W.19.]

p. 341]   *LEWIS, DAVID.*

Philip of Macedon. [The L.¹ Account Book says the house was dismissed on S. 29/4: see F. T. Wood, "The Account Books of Lincoln's Inn Fields Theatre, 1724–1727," *NQ*, April 29, 1933, clxiv.]

LILLO, GEORGE.

Silvia. [+12° 1731.]

The London Merchant. [See R. H. Griffith, "Early Editions of Lillo's *London Merchant*" (*University of Texas Bulletin*, July 8, 1935, pp. 23–7). He notes: 8° 1733 (5th corrected— a piracy), 12° 1735 (6th—sheets of the legitimate 5th), 12° 1737 (probably a piracy).]

p. 342]   Fatal Curiosity. [A. H. Scouten and Leo Hughes ("The New Theatre in the Haymarket, 1734 and 1737," *NQ*, Jan. 15, 1944, vol. clxxxvi) record a performance on M. 21/3/1737.]

Marina. [+L. 9.]

Elmerick. [+L. 19.]

LOCKMAN, JOHN.

+David's Lamentation (1736). See *ITALIAN OPERAS*.

Rosalinda. [+L. 18.]

MACKLIN, CHARLES.

King Henry VII. [+L. 55, as *The Alternative, Tyranny or Liberty*.]

A Will and No Will. [+L. 58. +1748. D.L. T. 22/3. T. 29, Th. 31; M. 11/4. An adaptation of Regnard, *Le legataire universel* (1708).]

MACSWINY, or SWINY, OWEN.

p. 343]   The Quacks. [+1705. D.L. Th. 31/5.]

+Pyrrhus and Demetrius (H.¹ Dec. 1708). See *ITALIAN OPERAS*.

MALLETT, DAVID.

Alfred. [+L. 27, and, as opera, printed, L. 51.]

MANNING, FRANCIS.

All for the Better. [Publication noted in the *Post Boy*, Nov. 7–10, 1702.]

p. 344]   *MENDEZ, MOSES.*

The Double Disappointment. [+L. 57.]

The Chaplet. [+L. 82. Music Boyce.]

p. 344]   *MILLER, JAMES.*
The Coffee House. [+L. 3. An adaptation of J. B. Rousseau.]
Art and Nature. [+L. 2.]
An Hospital for Fools. [+L. 15.]
+Polite Conversation (D.L. April 1740). See *UNKNOWN AUTHORS.*
+The Camp Visitants. L. 23. [Application dated Dec. 11, 1740; said to be in Miller's hand.]
+Joseph and his Brethren (C.G. March 1744). See *ITALIAN OPERAS.*

p. 345]   Mahomet the Impostor. [+L. 46. An adaptation of Voltaire, *Le fanatisme* (1741).]
The Picture. [+L. 48, printed text with manuscript corrections. An adaptation of Molière, *Sganarelle* (1660).]

MOLLOY, CHARLES.
The Perplex'd Couple. [A close adaptation of Molière, *Le cocu imaginaire* (1660).]
The Coquet. [An adaptation of Destouches, *Le curieux impertinent* (1710).]

MOORE, EDWARD.
The Foundling. [+8° 1748 (2nd); 12° 1759 (Dublin); 8° 1780; 8° 1783; L. 68.]

MORELL, THOMAS.
+Judas Macchabaeus (C.G. April 1747). See *ITALIAN OPERAS.*
+Joshua (C.G. March 1748). See *ITALIAN OPERAS.*
+Alexander Balus (C.G. March 1748). See *ITALIAN OPERAS.*
+Solomon (C.G. March 1749). See *ITALIAN OPERAS.*

MOTTEUX, PETER ANTHONY.
[See R. N. Cunningham, "A Bibliography of Peter Anthony Motteux" (*Oxford Bibliographical Society Proceedings*, 1931–33, iii. 317–37).]
The Four Seasons. [See the Hand-list of Plays, 1660–1700.]
Acis and Galatea. [Performed in the opera, *The Mad Lover*. Publication of songs noted in *Post Boy*, May 20–22, 1701.]

p. 346]   Britain's Happiness. [+1704. D.L. T. 22/2.]
+Arsinoe (D.L. Jan. 1704/5). See *ITALIAN OPERAS.*
Farewell Folly. [F. W. Bateson ("Motteux and *The Amorous Miser*," *Review of English Studies*, 1927, iii. 340–2), taking issue with the discussion of this play, *supra*, pp. 209–10, thinks *Farewel Folly* is a version of *The Amorous Miser*, that the text is that acted at D.L. and that *The Amorous Miser* probably was never performed. See also the comments by R. N. Cunningham, *infra*, under *The Amorous Miser*.]

MOTTLEY, JOHN.
+The Devil to Pay (D.L. Aug. 1731). See *CHARLES COFFEY.*

+*MOUNTFORT, WILLIAM.*
[For his earlier works see the Hand-list of Plays, 1660–1700.]

p. 346]   T. Zelmane, or, The Corinthian Queen (L.¹ Nov. 1704).
4° 1705. 1704. L.¹ M. 13/11, S. 18.
[It is probable that this play has been wrongly fathered on
Mountfort.]

p. 347]   *OLDMIXON, JOHN.*
Amintas. [See the Hand-list of Plays, 1660–1700. A trans-
lation of T. Tasso, *Aminta* (1573).]
The Governour of Cyprus. [Publication noted in *English Post*,
Jan. 11–13, 1702/3.]

OWEN, ROBERT.
Hypermnestra. [Publication noted in *Daily Courant*, May 12,
1703.]

OZELL, JOHN.
The Cid. [A translation of Pierre Corneille, *Le Cid* (1636).]
Britannicus. [A translation of Jean Racine, *Britannicus* (Paris,
13/12, 1669).]

p. 347]   Alexander the Great. [A translation of Jean Racine, *Alexandre
le Grand* (Paris, 4/12/1665).]
The Litigants. [A translation of Jean Racine, *Les plaideurs*
(1668).]
Cato of Utica. [A translation of F.-M.-C. Deschamps, *Caton
d'Utique* (1715).]
The Fair of Saint-Germain. [A translation of Regnard and
Dufresny, *La foire Saint-Germain* (1695).]
Manlius Capitolinus. [A translation of Antoine de la Fosse
d'Aubigny, *Manlius* (1698).]
L'Avare. [A translation from Molière.]
L'Embaras des Richesses. [A translation of the play of this
title by Alainval (1725).]
The Cheats of Scapin. [A translation of *Les fourberies de
Scapin* (1671).]
+Monsieur de Pourceaugnac, 12° 1704. [A translation from
Molière.]

p. 348]   *PATERSON, WILLIAM.*
Arminius. [+L. 17; application dated Jan. 4, 1739/40;
licence refused.]

PHILIPS, AMBROSE.
The Distrest Mother. [An adaptation of Jean Racine, *Andromaque* (1667).]

PHILIPS, JOHN.
The Earl of Mar Marr'd. [This was acted at the King's Arms,
Norwich, on Jan. 16, 1715/6: see Sybil Rosenfeld, "The
Players in Norwich, 1710–1750" (*Review of English Studies*,
1936, xii. 1–20).]

p. 349]   *PHILLIPS, EDWARD.*
Briton's, Strike Home! [+L. 16.]

PHILLIPS, WILLIAM.
[For a possible earlier work see the Hand-list of Plays, 1660–
1700.]

PIX, MRS.
The Beau Defeated. [Based on F. C. Dancourt, *Le chevalier
à la mode* (1687).]

p. 350] +*POPE, ALEXANDER.*
Three Hours after Marriage (D.L. Jan. 1716/7). See *JOHN GAY.*

RALPH, JAMES.
The Cornish Squire. [On the relationship of this text to the *Squire Trelooby* of 1704 (by Congreve, Vanbrugh and Walsh) see John C. Hodges, "The Authorship of *Squire Trelooby*" (*Review of English Studies*, 1928, iv. 404–13).]
The Astrologer. [+L.44. An adaptation of Tomkis' *Albumazar*.]

RAMSAY, ALLAN.
The Gentle Shepherd. [For a brief citation of the numerous printed editions, many issued from Scottish and English provincial towns, see *The Cambridge Bibliography of English Literature* (1941), ii. 970–1).]

p. 351] *RANDAL, JOHN.*
The Disappointment. [See supplementary notes to *HENRY CAREY.*]

p. 351] +*RICH, JOHN* ["LUN"].
Harlequin Executed (L.² Dec. 1716). See *UNKNOWN AUTHORS.*
The Jealous Doctor (L.² April 1717). See *UNKNOWN AUTHORS.*
Amadis (L.² Jan. 1718). See *UNKNOWN AUTHORS.*
The South-Sea Director (? L.² 1720).
Jupiter and Europa (L.² March 1723). See *UNKNOWN AUTHORS.*
The Necromancer (L.² Dec. 1723). See *UNKNOWN AUTHORS.*
The Sorcerer (? L.² 1724).
Daphne and Apollo (? L.² 1726).
The Rape of Proserpine (? L.² 1726). [See also under *L. THEOBALD.*]

ROBE, JANE.
The Fatal Legacy. [An adaptation of Jean Racine, *La Thébaïde* (1664).]

+*ROOME, EDWARD.*
The Jovial Crew (D.L. Feb. 1731). See *Sir WILLIAM YONGE.*

ROWE, NICHOLAS.
The Ambitious Stepmother. [+12° 1720 (3rd).]
Tamerlane. [+12° 1717 (4th); 12° 1720 (5th); 12° 1730 (6th).]

p. 352] The Fair Penitent. [+12° 1730.]
Ulysses. [+12° 1714 (2nd); 12° 1720 (3rd). +1706. H.¹ T. 19/2.]
The Royal Convert. [+12° 1720 (3rd); 12° 1726 (3rd).]
The Tragedy of Jane Shore. [+12° 1720 (3rd).]

p. 353] The Tragedy of Lady Jane Gray. [+12° 1720 (3rd).]

SETTLE, ELKANAH.
The Virgin Prophetess. [Publication noted in the *Post Boy*, Feb. 12–14, 1701/2, as *Cassandra; or, The True Virgin*

p. 353]   *Prophetess.* The play was announced for performance "this day" in the *Post Man*, May 13–15, 1701, but this seems to refer to production on M. 12/5.]

p. 354] *SHADWELL, CHARLES.*

The Humours of the Army. [Based on F. C. Dancourt, *Les curieux de Compiègne* (1698).]

[*The Plotting Lovers* is an adaptation of Molière, *Monsieur de Pourceaugnac* (1669).]

p. 355] *SHERIDAN, THOMAS.*

The Brave Irishman. [W. H. Grattan Flood ("Thomas Sheridan's *Brave Irishman*," *Review of English Studies*, 1926, ii. 346–7) shows that this was performed at the Aungier-street Theatre, Dublin, on M. Feb. 21, 1736/7, as *The Honest Irishman; or, The Cuckold in Conceit.* On June 12, 1742 it appeared at the Smock Alley house as *The Brave Irishman.* Based on Molière, *Monsieur de Pourceaugnac* (1669).]

SHERIDAN, Dr THOMAS.

Philoctetes. [A translation of Sophocles' play.]

p. 355] *SHIRLEY, WILLIAM.*

Edward the Black Prince. [+L. 81.]

SMITH, EDMUND.

Phaedra and Hippolitus. [An adaptation of Jean Racine, *Phèdre* (1677).]

SMOLLETT, TOBIAS GEORGE.

[For *The Absent Man* see Alan Dugald McKillop, "Smollett's First Comedy" (*Modern Language Notes*, 1930, xliv. 396–7) and for his later works see the Hand-list of Plays, 1700–1750.]

p. 356] *STEELE, Sir RICHARD.*

The Lying Lover. [+1703. D.L. W. 15/12.]

The Tender Husband. [From the advertisements in the *Daily Courant* it seems that this play was intended to be called originally *The City Nymph, or, The Accomplish'd Fools.* +8° 1711; 8° 1712; 8° 1717; 12° 1731.]

[For a bibliography of Steele's works see G. A. Aitken, *Richard Steele* (1889), vol. ii, app. 5. The same author, in his edition of the *Dramatic Works* (1894), prints two dramatic fragments, *The School of Action* and *The Gentleman.*]

p. 358] *THEOBALD, Dr. JOHN.*

Merope. [A translation of Voltaire, *Mérope* (1743).]

p. 359] *THEOBALD, LEWIS.*

Electra. [A translation of Sophocles' play.]

Ajax. [A translation of Sophocles' play.]

Œdipus. [A translation of Sophocles' play.]

Plutus. [A translation of Aristophanes' comedy.]

The Clouds. [A translation of Aristophanes' comedy.]

Double Falshood. [John Cadwalader ("Theobald's Alleged Shakespeare Manuscript," *Modern Language Notes*, 1940, lv. 108–9) quotes a letter of 1727 which shows that an original early MS. did actually exist. Eduard Castle

p. 359]   ("Theobalds Double Falsehood," *Archiv für das Studium der neuren Sprachen*, 1936, clxix. 182–99) devotes an essay to an examination of the history of this play.]

Orpheus and Eurydice. [L. 20. Music by J. F. Lampe.]

The Happy Captive. [+L. 47 as *The Temple of Dullness, with the Humours of Sigr. Capochio and Sigra. Dorinna*, dated Jan. 12, 1744/5: this is a further elaboration of Theobald's work. A later *Capochio and Dorinna* appeared with Cibber's name attached to it, but the ascription is certainly wrong and the piece is no more than a shortened version of the original play. See George W. Whiting, "*The Temple of Dulness* and Other Interludes" (*Review of English Studies*, 1934, x. 206–11).]

p. 360]   *THOMSON, JAMES.*

Agamemnon. [+L. 4; 8° 1738 (2nd); 8° 1738 (Dublin).]

Edward and Eleonora. [+L. 12, dated March 26, 1738/9, licence refused. On the various settings of this play and of *Agamemnon*, see John Edwin Wells, "Thomson's *Agamemnon* and *Edward and Eleonora*—First Printings", (*Review of English Studies*, 1942, xviii. 478–86).]

Tancred and Sigismunda. [+L. 50.]

Coriolanus. [+L. 74.]

+Alfred (Cliefdon, Aug. 1740). See *DAVID MALLET*.

p. 361]   *TRAPP, JOSEPH.*

The Tragedy of King Saul. [This was probably the work of Roger Boyle, Earl of Orrery: see the Hand-list of Plays. 1660–1700.]

VANBRUGH, Sir JOHN.

The Pilgrim. [+1700. D.L. 18/6; S. 19/10; T. 19/11.]

The False Friend. [Based on Le Sage, *Le traître puni* (1700) itself founded on Rojas, *La traición—busca el castigo*.]

p. 362]   The Country House. [Originally acted in 1698: see the Hand-list of Plays, 1660–1700. An adaptation of Dancourt, *La maison de campagne* (1688). +1724. W. 11/11.]

Squire Trelooby. [For this adaptation of Molière, *Monsieur de Pourceaugnac*, see under *JAMES RALPH*. A play published as *Monsieur de Pourceaugnac or Squire Trelooby*, 4° 1704, was repudiated by the translators, Vanbrugh, William Congreve and William Walsh. This seems to have been acted also: 1706. H.¹ M. 28/1, T. 29, Th. 31; F. 1/2, M. 4, M. 18.]

The Confederacy. [Based on Dancourt, *Les bourgeoises à la mode* (1692).]

The Mistake. [Based on Molière, *Le dépit amoureux* (1656). +12° 1726 (Dublin); 12° 1735.]

p. 363]   The Cuckold in Conceit. [Obviously based on Molière, *Le cocu imaginaire* (1660).]

WALKER, WILLIAM.

[For an earlier work see the Hand-list of Plays, 1660–1700. Publication noted in the *Post Man*, Nov. 2–4, 1703.]

p. 363]   +*WALSH, WILLIAM.*

Squire Trelooby (L.¹ March 1704). See *Sir JOHN VAN-BRUGH.*

WARD, HENRY.

[*The Happy Lovers,* printed in his *Works,* was separately printed 8° 1736.]

+*WEAVER, JOHN.*

[This author was responsible for several pantomimes, for which see *UNKNOWN AUTHORS—The Tavern Bilkers* (? D.L. 1702), *Perseus and Andromeda* (D.L. 1716), *The Loves of Mars and Venus* (D.L. 1717), *Harlequin turn'd Judge* (D.L. 1717), *Orpheus and Eurydice* (D.L. 1718). He also claims a *Cupid and Bacchus* acted at D.L. in 1719. There is a play of this title at D.L. 1707 and a *Bacchus and Cupid* at L.² 1715, but I cannot trace this particular piece.]

p. 364]   *WHITEHEAD, W.*

The Roman Father. [+L. 84. An adaptation of Pierre Corneille, *Horace* (1640).]

[For his later works see the Hand-list of Plays, 1750–1800.]

WISEMAN, JANE.

Antiochus the Great. [The *Post Man,* Nov. 11–13, 1701, announces publication "next week"; it was then being acted.]

+*WOODWARD, HENRY.*

Int. Tit for Tat; or, A Dish of the Auctioneer's Own Chocolate (S.A. Dublin, April 1748; D.L. S. 18/3/1749).

Pant. Queen Mab....A New Entertainment in Italian Grotesque Characters (S.A. Dublin, F. 5/2/1748, as *Fairy Friendship; or, The Triumph of Hibernia*; D.L. W. 26/12/1750).

[For his later works see the Hand-list of Plays, 1750–1800.]

+*YONGE, Sir WILLIAM.*

C.O. The Jovial Crew (D.L. Feb. 1731) 8° 1731; 8° 1732 8° 1760; 8° 1761.

[A ballad opera version of Brome's comedy, written in collaboration with *EDWARD ROOME* and *MATTHEW CONCANEN.* See under *UNKNOWN AUTHORS.*]

YOUNG, EDWARD.

Busiris. [+8° 1722; 12° 1730 (Dublin); 12° 1733. +1719. D.L. W. 15/4. A manuscript was sold in 1930 (see F. S. Boas in *T.L.S.,* May 22, 1930.]

p. 365]   *UNKNOWN AUTHORS.*

Amadis. [+1724. L.² M. 5/10 (described as a "Dramatick Opera."]

The Amorous Miser. [R. N. Cunningham, "A Bibliography of the Writings of Peter Anthony Motteux" (*Oxford Bibliographical Society, Proceedings and Papers,* 1931–3, iii. 317–37) argues that this is a piracy of Motteux' *Farewell Folly.* This is fundamentally the same view as that of F. W. Bateson: see, *supra,* under *MOTTEUX,* and pp. 209–10.]

p. 367]   +Ent. Britannia Triumphans. 8° 1703.
[Advertisement in *Post Man*, May 15–18, 1703. By "S.P."]
The Cheats. [This is evidently Weaver's pantomime, which
he says was acted at D.L. in 1702: see *infra*, *The Tavern
Bilkers*. +1717. L.² 22/4. 1725. L.² 18/1.]

p. 368]   Cinna's Conspiracy. [An adaptation of Pierre Corneille, *Cinna*
(1640).]
+Pant. Columbine; or, Harlequin turn'd Judge (L.² Dec. 1717).

p. 370]   Electra. [An anonymous translation of Sophocles' play.]

p. 371]   The Faithful General. [+1706. H.¹ F. 4/1, S. 5.]
The Faithful Shepherd. [A translation of G. B. Guarini, *Il
pastor fido* (1590).]
Fame. [The full title is: *Fame: or, Queen Elizabeth's Trumpets; or, Never Plead's Hopes of being a Lord Chancellor;
or, The Lover turn'd Philosopher; or, The Miser's Resolve
upon the Lowering of Interest.*]

p. 372]   +The Friendly Impertinents. [Announced in the *Daily
Advertiser* for S. 27/4/1734, but no evidence of actual performance.]
George Dandin. [Obviously a version of Molière's play, but
no information available.]

p. 374]   Harlequin Sorcerer. [This may be *Harlequin, a Sorcerer* (L.²
Jan. 1724/5) by Lewis Theobald.]
Henry and Emma. [+L. 79, with sub-title, *or, The Nut-brown
Maid*. The songs are by T. A. Arne.]

p. 375]   The Hypochondriac. [For *The Humours of Purgatory*, on
which this is based, see *BENJAMIN GRIFFIN*.]
The Imaginary Cuckold. [It is possible that this version of
Molière's *Le cocu imaginaire* may be by *CATHERINE
CLIVE*.]
Injur'd Love. [An adaptation of Montfleury, *La femme juge
et partie* (1669).]

p. 377]   +The King and Titi; or, The Medlars (announced in the
Daily Advertiser, May 30, 1737).
The Little French Lawyer. [An adaptation of Beaumont and
Fletcher's play.]
+F. The Lordly Husband. [H.² F. 16/5, 1737.]
Love and Friendship. [+L. 53, printed text.]
Love is the Doctor. [There is no information concerning this
adaptation of Molière's *L'amour médecin*.]

p. 378]   +B.O. Macheath turn'd Pyrate; or, Polly in India (H.²
W. 30/5, 1737).
[Based on *Polly* (1729) by *JOHN GAY*.]
+D.O. The Mad Lover. [For this perplexing work see
A. C. Sprague, *Beaumont and Fletcher on the Restoration
Stage* (1926), pp. 271–3. It may have been an operatic
version of the Beaumont and Fletcher play, but nothing
save some songs, "ayres" and Motteux' masque of *Acis
and Galatea* have come down to us.]
+Methodism Display'd: a Farce of One Act. As it was
intended to be Perform'd at the Moot-Hall in Newcastle,
Nov. 4, 1743. Alter'd and Publish'd by Mr. Este, From
a Farce, call'd Trick upon Trick; or, the Vintner in the

p. 378]   Suds 8° [1744]. [See Leo Hughes, in *University of Texas Studies in English*, 1950. xxix. 151–61.]

p. 379]   Momus turn'd Fabulist. [An adaptation of Louis Fuzelier, *Momus fabuliste, ou, les noces de Vulcain* (1719).]

p. 380]   The Northern Heroes. [See Howard Buck, "A *Roderick Random* Play" (*Modern Language Notes*, 1928, xliii. 111–12).]
+ C. Pamela; or, Virtue Triumphant 8° 1741. [See supplementary notes to *JAMES DANCE*.]

p. 381]   + Sat. The Plotters, A Satire. 8° 1722.
Polite Conversation. [+ L. 21. Probably by *JAMES MILLER*.]

p. 382]   Robin Goodfellow. [+ L. 10.]
+ O. Robin Hood....As it is perform'd at Lee's and Harper's Great Theatrical Booth in Bartholomew Fair. 8° 1730.
+ T. The Roman Actor...revived with Alterations. 8° 1722. [Attributed to *THOMAS BETTERTON*.]

p. 384]   Sir Giddy Whim. [Publication noted in the *Post Man*, Sept. 23–25, 1703.]
The Stage Coach Opera. [See W. J. Lawrence, "The Mystery of 'The Stage Coach'" (*Modern Language Review*, 1932, xxvii. 392–7) and E. M. Gagey, *Ballad Opera* (1937), pp. 106–7. This was presented at S.A. Dublin, 2/4, 1730, and was printed in a Dublin edition of Farquhar's *Works*. Lawrence attributes it to W. R. Chetwood (but see R. C. Rhodes in the *Modern Language Review*, 1933, xxviii. 482–4).]
The State of Innocence. [See R. D. Havens, "An Adaptation of One of Dryden's Plays" (*Review of English Studies*, 1928, iv. 88).]

p. 385]   The Tavern Bilkers. [See, *supra*, The Cheats.]

p. 386]   The Unfortunate Duchess of Malfy. [An adaptation of Webster's tragedy.]
Vanelia. [This may be by *JAMES MILLER*.]

p. 387]   + The Wedding Night; or, Tamer Tam'd. [L. 24; application dated 13/12/1740 for D.L. An alteration of Fletcher's *The Woman's Prize*.]
The Whim, or, The Merry Cheat. [+ L. 28.]
The Young Coquette. [From the advertisement it seems that this is a play—or probably a shortened version of a play—belonging to the nineties of the preceding century.]

II. *Italian Operas.*

Admeto. [+8° 1727.)

p. 388]   Alessandro in Persia. [+L. 30, printed text.]

Alexander Balus. [+L. 70.]

Alfonso. [+L. 42, printed text.]

L'Allegro, il Penseroso ed il Moderato. [+L. 26. Words adapted from Milton by Charles Jennens.]

p. 389]   Antigone. [+L. 60, printed text.]

Aristodemo. [+L. 45.]

Arminio. [The *Arminio* of 1737 has the libretto of A. Salvi.]

Arsinoe. [Published Jan. 17, 1704/5 (*Daily Courant*).]

p. 390]   Artamene. [Adaptation executed by F. Vanneschi.]

Bellerofonte. [Libretto by F. Vanneschi.]

Belshazzar. [+L. 52.]

Berenice. [Libretto by A. Salvi.]

p. 390]   Busiri. [Libretto by P. Rolli.]

La Caduta dei Giganti. [Libretto by F. Vanneschi.]

Clotilda. [Adapted by J. J. Heidegger.]

La Comedia in Comedia. [+L. 73, printed text.]

p. 392]   Deidamia. [Libretto by P. Rolli.]

p. 393]   The Feast of Hymen. [Libretto by P. Rolli.]

Fernando. [Libretto by P. Rolli.]

Gianguir. [+L. 35, printed text.]

p. 394]   Il Giocatore. [This is the operatic version of *The Gamester*, libretto by A. Salvi, originally called *Il marito giogatore e la moglie bacchettona* (Venice, 1718).]

Giustino. [Libretto adapted by N. Beregani.]

L'Idaspe Fedele. [Libretto probably by G. F. Candi.]

La Ingratitudine Punita. [+L. 67.]

p. 395]   Joshua. [+L. 69.]

Judas Macchabæus. [+L. 65.]

+The Loves of Ergasto (H.¹ April 1705). See *The Triumph of Love.*

Love's Triumph. [Reissued 8° 1713 as *The Triumph of Love*).]

p. 396]   Narciso. [The dedication is signed by P. Rolli, who no doubt was concerned with the preparation of the text.]

+L' Odio e l' Amore (H.¹ May 1721). See *Ciro.*

Orazio. [+L. 75.]

p. 397]   Partenio. [Libretto by P. Rolli. +L. 7, printed text.]

Penelope. [+L. 32, printed text.]

p. 398]   Rodelinda. [Libretto by A. Salvi, altered by N. Haym.]

Roxana. [+L. 41. This is Händel's *Alessandro* (H.¹ May 1726) under a new name).]

Samson. [+L. 38.]

Scipione in Cartagine. [+L. 34, printed text.]

Semele. [+L. 43.]

p. 399]   +La Serse. [Altered by N. Miniato; music Händel.]

Solomon. [+L. 78.]

Tamerlano. [Libretto by A. Piovene, altered by N. Haym.]

p. 400]   Il Trionfo della Continenza. [+L. 56, printed text.]

Xerxes. [+L. 8, printed text.]

III. *Repertoire of the French and Italian Comedians.*

p. 402] Arlequin et Scaramouche Soldats Deserteurs. [+1726. M. 2/5.]

Arlequin feint Astrologue. [+1726. Th. 31/4.]

Arlequin Gentilhomme. [+1725. Th. 7/1.]

Arlequin jouet de la Fortune. [+1721. Th. 16/2.]

Arlequin Major ridicule. [Although a performance was announced, the company did not act on May 3, 1726.]

Arlequin Nouvelliste de Tuileries. [With sub-title, *ou, le Retour de la Foire de Bezons*: see p. 406, *infra*.]

Arlequin poli par l'Amour. [+1735. M. 5/5.]

Harlequin as Mad Springlet. [Also listed as *Arlequin Esprit Folet* and *Harlequin a Mad Spright*. See *L'Esprit follet*, p. 404, *infra*.]

p. 403] Attendez-moi sous l'orme. [+1721. F. 20/1; F. 29/12.]

La Baguette de Vulcain. [+1721. F. 6/1.]

Le Carillon de Maître Gervaise. [+1719. Th. 15/1.]

Le cocu imaginaire. [+1721. Th. 2/3; F. 22/12. 1722. Th. 4/1.]

Le Deuil. [+1721. Th. 21/12.]

p. 404] Les deux Arlequins. [+8° 1718, as *The Two Harlequins*.]

L'École des Femmes. [+1721. M. 3/3.]

L'École des Maris. [+1722. T. 16/1.]

The Enchanted Island of Arcadia. [+8° 1726, as *The Inchanted Island of Arcadia; or The Magician Doctor. With Harlequin King of the Woods*.]

+La Fausse Turque, ou, l'École des Jaloux (1721. M. 13/2). [This may be the same as *l'École des Jaloux, supra*.]

p. 405] Les Filles errantes. [+1735. S. 27/3, with sub-title, *ou, Arlequin Aubergiste; or The Wandering Ladies and Harlequin an Innkeeper*.]

Les Follies Amoureuses. [+1720. S. 25/2. 1722. F. 12/1.]

George Dandin. [+1721. Th. 14/12.]

Le Joueur. [+1722. Th. 1/3.]

p. 406] Le Mariage forcé. [+1721. F. 17/2; Th. 16/3. 1722. T. 2/1. 1725. M. 25/1. 1726. F. 15/4; M. 18/4.]

p. 406] Le Médecin malgré lui. [+1721. Th. 19/1; F. 10/2. 1725. Th. 7/1.]

Le Parisien duppe dans Londres. [+1719. Th. 1/1.]

Les quatre Arlequins. [+1721. M. 20/3.]

Scaramouch Pedant scrupuleux. [+1721. Th. 16/2.]

p. 407] La Sylphide. [+1735. Th. 1/5.]

Tartuffe. [+1735. M. 21/4; M. 19/5.]

L'Usurier Gentilhomme. [+1722. M. 15/1.]

Les Vacances. [+1721. Th. 16/1; Th. 23/2. 1722. T. 9/1 as *Les Vacances, ou, les Frères Fumeux*).]

IV. *Plays at the Fairs.*

[The following titles, some of which are likely to represent playlets recorded in the Hand-list under different headings, are included here, for the sake of completeness, from notes generously provided by Miss Sybil Rosenfeld]

The Adventures and Marriage of Harlequin in Turkey (Welsh Fair (Queen Elizabeth's Wells), 1742).

All Alive and Merry, or the Happy Miller just arriv'd (Tottenham Court, Yeates, 1740).

Amorous Parley, or the Lady's Conquest (B.F., Norwich Comedians, ?1740).

The Amours of Harlequin; or The Bottle Conjuror Out-done. With the Escape of Harlequin into a Quart-Bottle (B.F., Yeates, 1749).

Constant Lovers with the comical humours of Monsieur Ragout (B.F., Fielding and Oates, 1734).

The Constant Quaker, or the Humours of Wapping (B.F., Hussey, 1748; S.F., Hussey, 1748).

Crispin and Crispianus, or a Shoemaker a Prince. With the comical humours of Barra(   )y, and the Shoemaker's Wife (May F., Miller, 1702).

Cupid and Psyche (S.F. 1714).

The Descent of the Heathen Gods. With the Loves of Jupiter and Alcmena; or Cuckoldom No Scandal (B.F., Yeates, 1749).

The Dutchman Outwitted; or Harlequin Happy (May F., Phillips and Hussey, 1746).

Every Thing in Season, or Harlequin at Ease (B.F., Norwich Comedians, ?1740).

The Fair Hypocrite; or The Fond Cuckold (May, F., Yeates, 1745).

The Fair Lunatick; Or, The Generous Sailor...Interspers'd with interlude The Jovial Jack Tars; Or, All Well Match'd (B.F., 1749).

The False Friend. With the comical humours of Sir Timothy Timberhead and his sister Jezebel (Hounslow, F., Bullock and Pack, 1720).

Harlequin Disaffected, or the Biter Bit (B.F. Turbutt and Dove, 1743).

Harlequin Fortune Teller (May Fair Wells, 1748).

Harlequin Grand Vol-Gi (Tottenham Court F., Yeates, 1740) [See *Cephalus and Procris, supra* p. 367].

Harlequin's Frolics, or the Rambles of Covent Garden (B.F. and S.F., Hussey, 1748; given the same year at Stourbridge F. with sub-title, *or Jack Spaniard caught in a Trap*).

The Harlot's Progress (Bow F., 1730; S.F., Yates, 1733; also, 1733, Leo and Harper).

[This, described as a ballad opera, cannot be Theophilus Cibber's pantomime of 1733; see *supra*, p. 314].

The History of the famous Friar Bacon. With the comical humours of Justice Wantbrains, Hopper the Miller and his son Ralph (S.F., John Leigh and Hall, 1720).

The History of Orpheus and the Death of Eurydice (B.F. and S.F., Yeates, 1740; Welsh F., Yeates, 1740).

The Impostor; or the Biter Bit (B.F., Hippisley, Bullock and Hallam, 1734).

The Indian Merchant; or, the Happy Pair. Interspers'd with the Comical Humour of the Intriguing Chambermaid, Sir John Oldcastle, and the

Drunken Colonel (B.F., Phillips and Yeates, 1742; S.F., Phillips and Lee, 1748).

Injured Love; or the Virgin Martyr (S.F., Nov. 1714).

The Intriguing Harlequin; or Any Wife Better than None (S.F., 1734).

King William's Happy Deliverance and Glorious Triumph over His Enemies, or the Consultation of the Pope, Devil, French King and the Grand Turk, with the whole form of the Siege of Namur (May F., Miller, date unknown).

The Life and Death of King John. Interspers'd with comic piece The Adventures of Sir Lubberly Lackbrains and His Man Blunderbuss (B.F., Cushing, 1749).

The Loves of Harlequin and Columbine (B.F., Lee, 1724).

The Miser Bit; or Harlequin Reveller (B.F., Phillips and Yeates, 1742; S.F., Phillips and Lee, 1748).

The Persian Hero; or the Noble Englishman. With the comical humours of Toby and Dorcas Guzzle of Preston (Welsh F. 1741).

[This seems to be the same as *Thamas Kouli Kan, the Persian Hero, supra*, p. 385. It also appeared as *The King of Persia or the Noble Englishman. With the comical humours of Sir Andrew Ague-cheek at the Siege of Babylon*, B.F., Lee and Woodward, 1741. Probably the same as *The Noble Englishman* (1722), *supra*, p. 380.]

The Schemes of Harlequin or Monsr. La Saxe's Disappointment (B.F., Hussey, 1746).

The Tempest: or, the Distressed Lovers, With the English Hero and the Island Princess, with the comical humours of the Inchanted Scotchman: or Jockey and the Three Witches (B.F., Miller, date unknown).

The Tipplers, or the dumb Philosopher or the Escapes of Harlequin (B.F. Pinkethman and W. Giffard, 1730).

The Universal Monarch Defeated: Or, The Queen of Hungary Triumphant (B.F., Fawkes and Pinchbeck, 1742).

[See *The Glorious Queen of Hungary*, *supra*, p. 372.]

[Miss Rosenfeld has contributed an informative article on "Shepherd's Market Theatre and May Fair Wells" to *Theatre Notebook*, 1951, v. 89–92, and this article has been followed by a complete survey of *The Theatre of the London Fairs in the 18th Century* (Cambridge, 1960), providing additional material both on plays presented in the booths and on the staging of these pieces.]

INDEX

OF PERSONS AND SUBJECTS

[A final volume in this series will present a general comprehensive index of all the English plays catalogued in this and the other Handlists. Consequently the present index is concerned only with persons and subjects.]

Abbe, L', dancer, 46, 278
Achilles Dissected, 241
Actors and actresses, 49–50, 414–15
Adams, Davenport, 244
Adams, G., 294
Addison, J., 19, 51, 96, 182, 192, 257, 294; plays of, 1, 3, 11, 17, 27, 30–1, 33, 39, 51, 55, 57–8, 62, 64, 73, 85, 87–8, 93, 135, 183, 198–9, 223, 228, 233, 235, 264, 294–5, 417, 431
Æschylus, influence of, 90, 93
Aitken, G. A., 193, 199, 422, 444
Alainval, 442
Allen, R. J., 412
Andrieux, F. G. J. S., 101
Anne, Queen, 33, 87, 100, 125, 150, 269
Anonymous plays, number of, 8
Apron stage, 25–6
Arabian Nights, The, 79
Arbuthnot, J., 213, 286, 431; *see* Gay
Arcadianism, 260
Argyle, Earl of, 185, 188
Ariosti, A., 390, 391, 392, 395
Aristophanes, 143, 328, 444
Aristotle, 51
Armstrong, instrumentalist, 279
Armstrong, A. J., 424
Arne, T. A., 236, 248, 265, 294–5, 299, 335, 399, 431
Arthur, J., 53, 295
Ashton, R., 262, 295
Aston, A., 4, 224–5, 229, 295–6; *A Brief Supplement to Colley Cibber*, 175
Aston, W., 22–3, 237, 247, 296
Aubert, Mrs, 33, 133, 296
Aubin, Mrs, 296
Audiences, poorness of, 5; characteristics of, 8–12, 411–12
Augustan Tragedy, 61, 96–114
Auletta, P., 396

Aureli, A., 387
Authentic Memoirs (of Wilks), 41
Avery, E. L., 410, 412, 416, 420, 421, 425, 427, 429, 430, 433, 436, 440
Axon, W. E. A., 199
Aylworth, instrumentalist, 279
Ayre, W., 73, 95, 224, 296, 432
Ayres, J., 44, 233, 237, 247, 296

Babcock, R. W., 424
Babel, musician, 278, 285
Baillie, J., 165, 296
Baily, actor, 276
Baker, Mrs, 278, 279
Baker, Mrs Catharine, 286, 289
Baker, R., 296
Baker, T., 21, 22, 60, 126, 129, 130, 135, 143, 159, 174–6, 181, 216, 231, 296–7, 432
Baldwin, Mary, 291
Ballad Opera, 25, 126, 218, 237–51, 424–5; popularity of, 10
Ballantyne, A., 73
Banister, singer, 278, 285
Banks, John, 24, 48, 50, 55–8, 60, 117, 198, 264; influence of on Rowe, 99, 101
Barante, Brugière de la, 94, 402, 404, 406, 407
Barbier, Mrs, 254, 285
Barford, R., 39, 75, 5, 91, 297
Barlocci, G., 392   8
Baroness, The, 279, 288–9
Barry, J., 40, 114
Barry, Mrs A., 45, 210, 276, 278, 288; acts in *Fair Penitent*, 100
Bassewitz, H. A. B., 120
Bateson, F. W., 421, 422, 424, 425, 441, 445
Bath, theatre in, 4, 55, 410
Baumgärtner, G., 417
Bealing, R., 432
Beauchamp, 401, 406

Beaumont, C. W., 425
Beaumont, F. and Fletcher, J., 29, 57, 128–36, 162, 168, 266, 383, 384, 447
Beckingham, C., 27–8, 38, 52, 89–90, 297
Behn, Aphra, 37, 113, 126, 128–34, 165–7, 171, 178, 195, 197, 421
Bellamy, D., 143, 224, 235, 247, 261, 297
Bellers, F., 70, 84, 297
Benn, T. V., 418
Bennet, P., 215, 297
Benôit XIV, Pope, 72
Bentley, R., 264
Beregani, N., 449
Berger, A. V., 425
Bernbaum, E., 115–6, 118–22, 127, 182–4, 189, 195–6, 199–200, 202
Betterton, Mrs, 276
Betterton, T., 25, 36, 45, 60, 166, 209–10, 222, 237, 271, 278, 292, 415, 426; acts in the Fair Penitent, 100; plays of, 131–6, 141, 211, 276, 297–8
Betz, S. A. E., 424
Bickerstaffe, I., 242, 292
Bicknell, Mrs, 213, 278, 289
Biddle E., 298
Biographia Dramatica, 23, 82–3, 93, 99, 113, 120, 151–2, 167, 173, 199, 206, 209–10, 243, 245–6, 293, 295–6, 355
Björnson, B., 2, 123
Blake, W., 161, 224
Blanch, J., 261, 299
Boadens, C., 14, 201, 299, 432
Board, M. E., 410
Boccaccio, 74, 81
Bogusławski, S., 168
Bois, P. B. du, 224, 320
Boisfranc, 403
Boissy, L. de, 405, 407, 419, 438
Boldini, G., 396
Bond, W., 299
Booth, B., 40, 80, 166, 271, 275, 276, 283, 288, 292, 299, 415
Bourgeois drama, 2, 5, 114–24
Boursault, E., 72
Bowen, W., 278, 279, 286, 289
Bowman, actor, 276, 278
Bowman, Mrs, 276
Bowyer, J. W., 421
Boyce, W., 260, 392, 399
Boyd, Mrs E., 67, 246–7, 299
Boyer, A., 72, 75, 85, 299, 432

Boyle, Charles, 154, 231–2, 299, 432
Boyle, Roger, Earl of Orrery, 20, 70–1, 83, 299, 432, 445; influence of on Shirley, 113; on Rowe, 98; Parthenissa, 102
Boys, R. C., 414
Bracciuoli, G., 391, 396
Bracegirdle, Mrs A., 40, 45, 50, 167, 209–10, 224, 259, 276, 288; acts in Fair Penitent, 100
Bradshaw, Mrs, 49
Brereton, T., 299, 432
Brett, Capt., 271
Breval, J. D., 49, 134, 213, 238, 266, 299–300, 410, 432
Brewster, Dorothy, 418
Bright, actor, 278
Bristol, performances at, 410
British Journal, The, 193
British Theatre, The, 100
Briton, The, 234
Brome, R., 47, 128–31, 142, 247, 446
Brömel, W. H., 121
Bronson, B. H., 424
Brooke, H., 23, 61, 65, 112, 206–7, 300, 418
Brooke, Lord, 6
Brooke, R., 121
Broschi, R., 390
Broughton, T., 260, 394
Brown, A., 123, 300
Brown, J., 90
Brown, T., 262, 300
Browne, M., 68, 84, 215, 300
Bruce, H. L., 72, 417
Bruère, C. de la, 88
Brueys, D. A. de, 403, 405
Buck, H., 447
Budd, F. E., 153, 432
Budgell, E., 87
Bullock, C., 40–1, 126, 140, 278, 279; plays of, 16, 48, 133, 135, 140–1, 146, 160, 172, 211–12, 216, 300–1, 429
Bullock, W., 287
Buononcini, G. B., 227–9, 388, 390, 391, 393, 394, 396, 399
Burlesques, 126, 262–9, 428–9
Burley, T. L. G., 410
Burnaby, W., 126, 156, 159; plays of, 27, 47, 50, 140, 142, 153–4, 162, 195, 301, 421, 432
Burney, C., 225, 227
Burton's Coffee House, 157
Bury, J. B., 107

Cadet, musician, 278, 285
Cadwalader, J., 444
Calmus, G., 240
Calverton, F. V., 422
Campbell, Lily B., 415
Campi, F., 396
Campistron, J. G., 401, 405
Candi, G. F., 449
Capua, R. da, 391, 393
Carey, H., 10, 30–3, 42–3, 52, 211, 233, 235–8, 241, 246, 248, 252, 266–7, 301–3, 424, 432–3; *Of Stage Tyrants*, 43, 252
Carlell, L., 142, 221
Caskey, J. H., 423
Castle, E., 444
Cat-calls, 14
Cato Examin'd, 88
Cavendish, W., Duke of Newcastle, 238
Censorship, 21–2
Centlivre, Mrs S., 4, 8–9, 20, 22, 34, 52, 61, 74, 80–1, 126, 129–38, 142, 144–6, 155–7, 159, 162, 166–8, 172–4, 178, 183, 186, 195–6, 210–11, 220, 241, 303–6, 421, 432, 433
Cervantes, 146, 169, 214, 225
Cesarini, Giovannini del Violone, 229
Chapelle, J. de la, 145, 148, 436
Charke, Mrs C., 23, 261, 272, 306; *Narrative of*, 4
Charles I, King, 39
Charles II, King, 7, 31, 36, 37, 39, 127, 146
Chateauneuf, Madame, 12
Chaves, A., 171, 209, 306, 433
Cherrier, dancer, 47, 278, 279
Chetwood, W. R., 44, 176; plays of, 214, 237, 241, 262, 306, 433; *History of the Stage*, 4, 363
Chodkiewicz, A., 88
Chollet, influence of, 146, 204
Ciampi, L. V., 396
Cibber, C., 5, 8–11, 14–16, 24, 27, 31, 35–40, 42–3, 45, 47–8, 50–1, 53, 55, 57, 66, 70–1, 73, 77–8, 87, 93, 100–4, 125–6, 128–38, 142, 144–5, 150, 152–3, 155, 158–9, 161–4, 167–9, 180, 182–92, 200, 202, 207–9, 212–14, 231–3, 243, 249, 250, 259, 261, 263, 266, 271, 275–6, 278, 283–5, 306–13, 363, 421, 433–4, 438, 445; *Apology*, 5, 16, 22, 25, 40, 60, 191, 213, 227, 252

Cibber, Jenny, 160
Cibber, Mrs, 261; acts in *Agamemnon*, 93
Cibber, T., 7, 28, 69, 164, 184, 198, 200, 237, 244, 250, 254, 261, 271, 313–15, 434; *Lives of the most eminent Actors*, 252; *Epistle to Garrick*, 252
Clancy, M., 112, 314
Clark, printer, 43
Claxton, dancer, 47
Clayton, T., 226, 228, 294, 389
Clément, P., 120
Clive, Mrs, 40, 160, 261, 436; *see* Raftor
Clodio, instrumentalist, 279
Clynch, of Barnet, vocalist, 47
Codrington, Col., 18
Coffey, C., 4, 142, 237, 243–4, 247, 314–15, 434
Cokain, Sir A., 142, 247
Colby, E., 273, 410
Collier, J., 125, 148, 150, 155, 161, 262
Collier, W., theatrical patentee, 271, 276, 283–5, 292
Collins, J. C., 73
Collins, R. L., 423
Colman, F., MS. of, 226, 424; opera by, 389, 434
Comédies à ariettes, 238
Comedy of humours, 174–9
Comedy of intrigue, 165–74
Comedy of manners, 8, 25, 147–65, 420–1
Comedy of sensibility, 25, 179–208, 422–3
Comic epilogue to tragedy, 64–6
Commedia dell' arte, 2, 42, 218, 249, 253–4, 425
Companion to the Play-House, The, 15, 62, 81, 155, 172, 175, 206
Comparison between...Horace and The Roman Father, 95
Comparison of the French and Italian Music, 226–9, 424
Compleat Key to the Beggar's Opera, 211
Compleat Key...to the What D'Ye Call It, 198
Complete Key to Three Hours After Marriage, 215
Concanen, M., 315, 434
Congreve, W., 1–2, 8, 37, 42, 57, 125–6, 128–38, 147–54, 156–7, 159, 161–2, 165, 169, 176, 178, 184, 194–5, 226, 228, 235,

Congreve, W., (*cont.*)
  237, 257, 271, 275, 288–9,
  295, 315, 398, 420, 434, 443,
  445
Conolly, 159–60, 316
Cook, musician, 277
Cooke, printer, 43
Cooke, T., 115, 123, 142–3, 205,
  215, 223, 260, 316, 434
Cooper, Mrs E., 205, 316
Corbet, instrumentalist, 279
Cori, A., 388, 389, 395
Corinna, *Critical Remarks*, 6, 27,
  157, 188
Corneille, P., 403, 405, 406, 421,
  434, 442, 446, 447
Corneille, T., 71–3, 95, 103, 113,
  145, 167, 186, 192, 417, 434
Corradi, G. C., 400
Cory, J., 141, 145, 155, 208, 231, 316
Corye, J., 434
Costume, theatrical, 414
Cottin, dancer, 47
Court and drama, 3
Covent Garden, theatre, 272, 430
Cowley, A., 261, 439
Coxeter, 169
Craftsman, The, 299
Craig, instrumentalist, 279
Crauford, D., 27–8, 154, 316, 434
Crean, P. J., 412, 429
Crébillon, P. J., 403, 406
Critical Remarks on Ulysses, 100
Critical Specimen, A, 16
Critics, in the theatre, 411–12
Cross, actor, 279
Cross, Mrs, 278
Cross, R., 316, 434
Cross, W. L., 158, 245
Crouch, 285
Crowne, J., 47, 71–2, 83, 128–38
Croxall, S., 317
Cumberland, R., 207
Cunningham, J., 216, 317
Cunningham, R. N., 441, 446
Curll, E., *Life of Mrs Oldfield*, 11;
  Life of Wilks, 5, 10
Curtain, in eighteenth century
  theatres, 28, 79
Cutts, J., 317

Daily Courant, The, 6, 11, 33, 36,
  55, 106, 175, 296
Daily Gazeteer, The, 12
Daily Journal, The, 4, 12, 34, 104,
  193
Daily Post, The, 296

Dallainval, 404
Dalton, J., 37, 138, 260, 317, 435
Dampmartin, Vicomte A. H. de,
  88
Dance, J., 183–4, 206, 317, 435
Dancers, in the theatre, 67
Dancourt, F., 145, 151–2, 176, 194,
  216, 403, 404, 405, 419, 435,
  437, 442, 444, 445
Dante, 233
Darcy, J., 81, 317
Davain, instrumentalist, 279
Davenant, Sir W., 70–1, 84, 133,
  214, 220
Davencourt, dancer, 46
Davey, S., 317
Davis, C. A. C., 427
Davys, Mrs M., 163–4, 317, 422
Deaths, on the stage, 53–4
De Castro, P., 412, 429
De Fatouville, N., 403, 404
De Fesch, 395
Dekker, T., 70
Delamayne, T., 317
Delisle, L. F., 145, 146, 203, 249,
  340, 402, 404, 407, 440
Dennis, J., 24, 51, 64, 78, 82, 143,
  214, 264; plays of, 8, 16, 18,
  20, 31–2, 43, 48, 56, 74, 76, 80,
  85–6, 129, 210, 317–8, 435;
  prologue by, 5; thunder in-
  vented by, 36; praises *Cato*,
  88; aim of in tragedy, 63; life
  of, 18
  Character of Sir John Edgar, 17
  Defence of Sir Fopling Flutter, A,
  193
  Essay on the Opera's, An, 227
  Original Letters, 88, 157, 222
  Remarks on the Conscious Lovers
  17, 43, 182–3
  Remarks upon Cato, 88
Dent, E., 424
Desabeye, 278, 285
Deschamps, F. M. C., 88, 442
Destouches, P. N., 145, 199, 202,
  440, 441
Deutsche Schaubühne, Die, 121, 191
Dialogues, in plays, 160
Dibdin, C., 86
Diderot, D., influenced by English
  writers, 2; praises Lillo, 120
Dieupart, C., 226, 279, 285, 290
Digby, G., Earl of Bristol, influence
  of, 142
Disturbances, in the theatre, 11–17,
  411

Divoto, scene painter, 34, 258
Dobrée, B., 417
Dodsley, R., 141, 181–2, 204–6, 232, 238, 249, 318–9, 435
Doggett, T., 40, 276, 278, 283, 288–9, 410; plays of, 131, 134, 250, 278, 434
Domestic plays, 61, 114–24
Dorman, J., 206, 319, 435
D'Orneval, 405
Dorset Garden theatre, 271
Doughty, O., edition of *Polly*, 240
Dower, E., 44, 215, 319
Downer, A. S., 415
Downes, Capt., 319
Downes, J., *Roscius Anglicanus*, 85, 97–8, 100, 104, 222, 227, 233, 291, 426
Downing, G., 319
Draghi musician, 233
Dramas of Italian Operas (MS.), 226
Drame, French, 2, 73, 145–6
Draper, J. W., 418
Draper, M., 178, 319
Drolls, 4, 216
Drunkenness, in theatre, 11
Drury, R., 237–8, 319
Drury Lane theatre, 271, 429
Dryden, J., 1, 7, 60–1, 67, 75, 77, 79, 80, 101, 170, 189, 198, 220, 236, 247, 257, 264–5; influence of on Darcy, 81; on C. Johnson, 81; on Martyn, 81; audience in the time of, 9; plays of, 46, 56–9, 70, 74, 84, 92, 103, 128–38, 142, 151, 158, 167, 186, 264
Du Bois, P. B., 435
Dublin theatres in, 4
Dubost, 88
Duc, P. F. du, 72
Duels in theatre, 11–12
Duffet, J., 46
Dufresny, C. R., 403, 404, 406, 442
Duncombe, W., 63, 71–2, 94, 320, 435
Dunkin, P. S., 438
D'Urfey, T., 6, 8, 22, 32, 128–32, 142, 176, 194, 212, 233, 234, 236, 244, 257, 267, 320, 435
Duscazeau, 199

East, W., 291
Ebbsworth, J., 194
Eccles, musician, 233, 278, 289
Egleton, Mrs, 320
Elford, Mrs, dancer, 46, 278

Elizabeth, Queen, drama in age of, 66–70, 102, 127, 139–42
Ellis-Fermor, Una, 410
Elrington, T., 81
Elwart, musician, 285
Epilogues, spoken by actresses, 49–50
Epine, Mdlle de l', 233
Epsom Wells, theatre at, 4
Essay on the Theatre, An, 34
Essex, J., 292
Estcourt, R., 41, 195, 271, plays of, 133, 145, 183, 194, 278, 320, 435
Etherege, Sir G., 8, 128–32, 135, 137, 139, 143, 154, 157–9, 173, 238, 420
Euripides, 63, 72, 85, 89, 120
Evans, vaulter, 47
Evans, Miss, dancer, 278
Examen of the New Comedy, An, 207

Fabian, R., 321
Faction in judging plays, 14–17
Fairs, plays at, 273, 450–1
Fanshawe, Sir R., 224
Farce, 51, 423
Farinelli, opera singer, 233
Farmer, J., 222
Farquhar, G., 4, 10, 20, 21, 37, 40–1, 126–39, 140, 145–52, 154, 155, 157, 166, 170, 183–4, 321–3, 420, 435; *Essay on Comedy*, 51
Fassini, S., on opera, 226
Fate in tragedy, 64
Faustina, opera singer, 266
Favart, C. S., 403
Fenton, E., 6, 43, 58, 72, 110, 264, 323, 418, 436
Fielding, Mr, duel of, 11
Fielding, H., 7, 8, 10, 14, 18, 23, 28, 34, 41, 45, 65, 67–8, 104, 126, 135, 137, 144–6, 158–60, 165, 166, 173, 174, 177–8, 179, 181, 200–2, 207, 215, 232, 237–8, 245–7, 255–6, 261, 263–5, 272, 323–9, 411, 412, 419, 421, 428, 429, 434, 436; sentimentalism in the works of, 158; support of for domestic tragedy, 124; prologue to *Fatal Curiosity*, 121; *Joseph Andrews* and *Tom Jones*, 3
Figg's New Amphitheatre, 272
Filmer, E., 118

Finch, Anne, Countess of Winchelsea, 329
Firbank, dancer, 287
First nights, disturbances at and packed, 12–15, 17–19
Fitzgerald, P., 11–12, 271
Fleetwood, manager of D.L., 12, 23–4, 44–5, 261, 433
Fletcher, Ifan K., 409, 413
Fletcher, J. (see also Beaumont and Fletcher), 45, 70, 103, 105, 126, 136, 139–40, 148, 150, 158, 165, 168, 199, 223, 235–6, 242, 264, 361
Flickinger, R. C., 27
Flood, W. H. G., 425, 444
Flying Post, The, 301
Foote, S., 329; Roman and English Comedy Consider'd, 207
Ford, J., 1
Forrest, E., 436
Fowell, F. and Palmer, F., 22–3
Franceschini, P., 226
Francisco, musician, 285
Francisco, G., 229
Freeholder's Journal, The, 193
Freeman, M., 237, 251, 329
French actors, 170, 419–20, 449–50
— influence on comedy, 143, 418–9
   on tragedy, 71–3, 417
— rope dancers, 5
— sentimental movement, 202
— singers in opera, 225
Frowde, P., 21, 28–9, 31, 34, 70, 75, 92, 329
Fuzelier, L., influence of, 145, 244, 401, 404, 406, 407, 447
Fyfe, A., 78, 90, 329

Gagey, E. M., 424, 432, 448
Gagging, on the eighteenth century stage, 42
Gaiffe, F., 237
Gallet, 406
Gallia, Maria, 227, 427
Galliard, 260, 359, 380, 395, 399
Galuppi, B., 388, 389, 392, 397, 398, 399, 400
Gardiner, M., 329, 437
Garrick, D., 29, 36, 40, 59–60, 206, 216, 271–2, 329–30, 414, 415, 419, 430, 437; acts in Edward the Black Prince, 113; in Regulus, 83
Gasparini, F., 47, 388, 389, 395
Gataker, T., 26, 237, 245, 330

Gay, J., 2–3, 10, 13, 22, 25, 28–9, 31–2, 36, 42, 111, 122, 126, 132, 134–6, 138, 144, 146–8, 157–8, 182, 198, 211, 213–4, 218, 225, 233, 236–7, 239–43, 245–6, 249–51, 264, 269, 275, 330–2, 423, 424, 425, 437
Gay, Joseph, 190, 213; see Breval
Gaye, P. F., 425
General Advertiser, The, 314
Genest, J., 1, 12, 24, 55, 86, 92, 97, 112, 148, 153, 154, 155, 164, 169–70, 176–7, 187, 201, 208–9, 214, 220, 223, 237, 243, 252
Gentleman's Magazine, The, 328
George, Prince, of Denmark, 176
Gibbon, J., 107
Giffard, H., 437
Giffard, W., 206, 272, 332, 412, 429
Gildon, C., 22, 28, 30–1, 51, 67, 71, 75–6, 78, 82, 86, 98, 101, 116, 125, 134, 220, 332–3, 437; Life of Betterton, 125
Gilliver, printer, 43
Girardeau, Mdlle, singer, 279
Glicksman, H., 434
Gluck, C. W., 390
Goethe, praises Lillo, 120
Goldoni, C., 406
Goldsmith, O., 269
Gollancz, Sir I., 216
Golt, G., 88
Goodall, W., 291, 333
Goodman's Fields, theatres, 272, 429–30
Goodyer, "Beau", duel of, 11
Gordon, A., 333
Goring, C., 80, 333
Gottsched, J. C., 88, 199
Gottsched, L. A. V., 88, 199
Gould, R., 95, 333
Grafton, Duke of, his actors, 4, 304, 335, 411
Granger, Mrs, 279
Granville, G., Lord Lansdowne, 132, 134, 140, 234, 238, 333, 437
Graves, T. S., 42, 273
Gray, C. H., 411
Greber, G., 400
Greek stage, 27
Green, C. C., 411, 415
Greene, Dr., 337, 395
Greg, Sir W. W., 60
Griffin, B., 31, 36, 70, 133, 140, 142, 198, 212, 234, 276, 333
Griffith, R. H., 296, 421

Grimaldi, N., 388, 394, 401
Grimes, 333
Grimstone, William, Lord, 334
Gröber, F., 195
Grub Street Journal, The, 327
Guarini, G. B., 297, 371, 447
Guillemard, G., 88
Guthry, 241
Gwinnet, R., 178, 334
Gwynn, Nell, 65

Habbema, D. M. E., 421
Hallam, killed in theatre, 12
Hamilton, N., 334, 398, 437
Hammond, W., 334
Händel, F., 230, 260, 266, 271,
    285–6, 332, 387, 388, 389, 390,
    392, 393, 394, 395, 396, 397,
    398, 399, 400, 449
Hannam-Clark, T., 410
Harlan, E., 418
Harlequin, 68
Harmonicon, 229
Harper, S., 334, 363
Harris, 272
Harrison, T., 334
Harrison, W., 334, 437
Harvey, scene painter, 34
Hasse, J. A., 390, 392, 393, 396, 399
Hatchett, W., 95, 112, 265, 334,
    371, 438
Hathaway, B., 415
Hauteroche, N. L., 145, 403, 404,
    437
Havard, W., 16–17, 21, 25, 70, 71,
    74–5, 83–4, 113, 138, 232, 334,
    438
Havens, R. D., 418, 448
Hawker, E., 237, 242, 334–5
Hawkins, Sir J., 225
Hawkins, W., 335, 438
Hawling, F., 44, 173, 335
Haym, N., 226, 228, 274, 279,
    288–9, 390, 391, 392, 393, 394,
    396, 397, 398, 399, 400, 449
Hayman, scene painter, 34
Haymarket theatres, 271, 272, 429
Haywood, Mrs E., 17, 26, 31, 50,
    58, 71, 74, 83, 104, 188, 265,
    335, 422, 438
Hazlitt, W., 150
Hegnauer, A. G., 88
Heidegger, J. J., 266, 285, 388, 389,
    393, 449
Heilman, L. W., 431
Heminges, J., 316
Henslowe's Diary, 55

Heroic drama, 60, 74–85
Heroic exclamations, 74–5
Hervey, Lord John, 432
Hewitt, J., 26, 115, 122, 335, 419,
    438
Heywood, T., 101, 116
Higgons, B., 335
Hill, A., 29–30, 39, 50, 53, 59, 65,
    70, 72–3, 81, 83, 93, 108–10,
    115, 116, 118–19, 121, 122–3,
    254, 292, 335–6, 384, 398, 417,
    438
Hill, Sir J., 336, 415
Hippisley, J., 135, 250, 336–7, 438
Hoadly, B., 137, 190, 206–8, 337,
    439
Hoadly, J., 260, 337, 395
Hodges, J. C., 152, 443
Hoffman, L., 120
Hogarth, W., 36, 252
Hook, Lucyle, 434
Hooke, Mrs M., 289
Hooker, E. N., 439
Hoper, Mrs, 67, 267, 337
Hopkins, C., 264
Horsley, Phyllis M., 418
Hotson, L., 430
Howard, Sir R., 47, 128–33, 135–6
Hudson, Mrs, singer, 278
Hudson, W. O., 120
Huggins, W., 395, 439
Hughes, C. W., 424
Hughes, H. S., 263
Hughes, J., 58–9, 107, 144, 235–6,
    237–8, 260, 275, 439
Hughes, L., 421, 430, 432, 436
Humphreys, S., 338, 390, 391, 392,
    393, 396, 397, 398, 399, 400,
    439   ,
Hunt, W., 338
Hunter, J., 338
Hurst, R., 26, 31, 74, 83–4, 338
Husband, B., 279, 287, 289
Hyland, W., 338

Ibsen, H., 2, 123
Immorality, in the eighteenth
    century, 49, 160, 200
Inchbald, Mrs E., 100, 193, 202, 207
Irving, W. H., 425, 437
Irwin, W. R., 421
Italian comedy, 146
— influence on tragedy, 73–4
— singers in opera, 5

Jackson, 338, 439
Jackson, A., 411, 417, 430–1

Jacob, G., play of, 338; *Poetical Register*, 22, 24, 52, 63, 81, 87-8, 97, 107, 118, 147-8, 157, 162, 167, 169, 171, 175, 185, 192, 195, 197-8, 210, 211, 213, 228, 259-60
Jacob, Sir H., 16-17, 53, 91, 184, 205, 338, 439
Jacobites, 15
Jeffreys, G., 31, 48, 62, 65, 95, 116, 338, 439
Jennens, C., 439, 448
Jerrold, W. and Clare, 421
Jevon, T., 133, 142, 434
Johnson, B., 287, 289, 419
Johnson, C., 16, 21, 39, 45, 49, 51, 53, 63, 67, 70, 72-3, 81, 85, 89, 104-5, 115-7, 122, 124, 126, 131-2, 134, 136, 139, 140-2, 144, 146, 156-7, 169, 174-6, 183-4, 187, 196, 211-2, 221, 242, 246, 249, 264, 339-40, 414, 417, 439
Johnson, H., 340
Johnson, S., of Cheshire, 58, 268, 272, 340, 439-40
Johnson, Dr S., 59, 94-5, 340, 417; *Complete Vindication of the Licensers*, 23
Jones, Miss, actress, 160
Jones, R. F., 417
Jonson, B., 128-37, 141-2, 159, 174, 177-9, 194, 238, 252, 257, 261; criticised by Gildon, 125
Joseph, B. L., 416-7

Kean, C., 414
Keen, T., actor, 292
Kelly, J., 23, 50, 126, 145, 184, 202, 215, 237, 249, 256, 340, 440
Kermode, J. F., 438
Kern, Jean B., 93, 425
Kies, P. P., 153, 438
Killigrew, C., 282
Killigrew, T., 18, 132, 157, 187, 340
Kinne, W. A., 419
Knipe, C., 341
Kotzebue, 2
Kremberg, J., 370
Krutch, J. W., 411
Kytes, instrumentalist, 279

La Chaussée, N. de, 406
La Font, J. de, 407
Laforest, dancer, 47
Lafosse, A. de, 347
Lalli, D., 397

Lambert, scene painter, 34
Lampe, J. F., 141, 235-6, 260, 265-6, 302, 335, 341, 370, 445
Lampugnani, G. B., 388, 393, 398
Langford, A., 341
Larpent Collection, 409, 431
Larson, M. A., 420
Lash for the Laureat, A., 190
Latille, G., 392
Latour, instrumentalist, 279
Laureat, The, 43
Lavin, dancer, 47
Lawrence, musician, 278
Lawrence, W. J., 25, 271, 300, 314, 401, 435, 448
Lediard, T., 236, 341, 413
Lee, F. H., 412
Lee, Mrs, 276
Lee, N., 22, 37, 56-9, 60-1, 71, 75-6, 83, 92, 264, 292, 437
Lee, booth holder, 354, 363
Le Grand, M. A., 401, 403, 404, 405
Leigh, J., 6, 46, 53, 177, 278, 341
Lemercier, 101
Lesage, A. R., 402, 403, 405, 419, 445
Lessing, G. E., influenced by English theatre, 2, 120
Letters by Several Eminent Persons, 108
Letter to a Noble Lord, A, 246
Letter to Mr Gay, A, 213
Letter to the Town, A, 12
Leveridge, R., 141, 254, 277-8, 341
Lewis, D., 64, 91, 341, 440
Liadières, P. C., 101
Licensing Act, The, 16, 21, 23, 412, 430
Life and Character of Cato, The, 88
Life and Character of Jane Shore, The, 101
Life of George Castriot, The, 84
Lillo, G., 2, 7, 26, 41, 50, 59, 61, 64, 70-1, 75, 83-4, 97, 111, 115-6, 119-24, 141, 219, 223, 237, 248, 269, 341-2, 418, 440
Lincolns Inn Fields actors, subscription for, 6
Lincoln's Inn Fields, theatres, 271, 272, 429
Lindsey, Mrs, singer, 278
Livy, 89
Lockman, J., 236, 342, 392, 440
Loeli, D., 396
Loewenberg, A., 410, 413, 430, 431
Loiseau, J., 424

London Daily Post, The, 12, 69
London Gazette, The, 301, 317, 355, 361
Lord Chamberlain, The, 21
Lossack, G., 418
Louis XIV, 19, 98
Lounsbury, T. R., 73
Love in tragedy, 62–4
Lovett, D., 416
Lowe, R. W., 12, 16, 22, 40
Lucas, Mrs, dancer, 47
Ludwig, H., 418
Lully, J. B., musician, 233, 279, 285
Lumian, instrumentalist, 279
Lun (i.e. Rich), 10, 427
Lynch, F., 68, 205, 233, 342
Lyon, W., 342

Machines, on the eighteenth century stage, 35
Mackintosh, D. T., 414
Mackenzie, Aline, 427
Macklin, C., 12, 40, 207, 342, 415, 440
MacMillan, D., 409, 414, 429, 431
Macswiny, O. See O. Swiny
Madden, S., 58, 343
Maffei, F. S., 73, 95, 432, 439
Mallet, D., 27, 49, 58, 65, 70, 82–3, 264, 343, 440
Malone, E., 222
Mancini, F., 34, 229, 394
Man in the Bottle Conjurer, 12
Manley, Mrs M., 28, 31, 50, 79, 104, 116, 343
Manning, F., 50, 140, 160, 169–70, 343, 440
Manwayring, said to have aided Cibber, 185
Marchi, A., 388
Margarita (i.e. de l'Épine), 278, 285
Maria, Joanna, 275
Marivaux, P. C., 402, 405, 406, 407
Marks, J., 223, 260
Marmontel, J. F., 120
Marsh, C., 39, 58, 71, 111, 343
Marston, J., 141
Martyn, B., 31, 63, 68, 81, 233, 343
Masques, 224, 258–62
Massinger, P., 70, 99, 137, 222, 438
Mattei, F., 396
Maude, C., 429
Mauprié, Marquis de, 100
Maxwell, J., 343–4
Mayers, Mrs, dancer, 278
Mayne, de la, 223

McKillop, A. D., 444
Mears, catalogue of plays, 176
Medbourne, M., 189
Medley, Mat., 296; see Aston, A.
Medici, Cosimo de', 22
Melville, L., 425
Memoirs of...Jane Shore, 101
Mendez, M., 237, 260, 344, 440
Mestayer, H., 344
Metastasio, P., 236, 388, 389, 390, 391, 392, 393, 394, 395, 397, 399, 421
Metcalfe, J., 291
Michelburne, J., 344
Middle classes in the theatre, 3, 24–5, 412–13
Middlemore, R., 291
Middleton, T., 139, 170–1, 197, 211
Miles, D. H., 190
Miller, J., 13, 14, 65–6, 72, 111, 126, 135, 141, 144–6, 164–5, 177–9, 181–2, 203, 233, 237, 252, 256–8, 344–5, 395, 423, 437, 441
Miller, booth holder, 353
Mills, J., 276, 278, 287
Mills, Mrs, 279
Milton, J., 260, 317, 398, 420, 448
Milward, J., 93
Miniato, N., 449
Minns, Mrs, booth holder, 285, 354
Minor, J., 121
Mins, actor, 289
Mr. Addison turn'd Tory, 88
Mist's Weekly Journal, 39
Mitchell, J., 53, 70, 119, 250, 438; see Hill, A.
Modest Apology, A, 12
Modesty of playwrights, 61
Molière, 22, 141, 143–5, 151–2, 156–8, 163, 165–6, 178, 189, 203, 208–9, 216, 245, 248, 316, 325, 326, 338, 344, 377, 401, 403, 404, 406, 407, 434, 436, 441, 442, 444, 445, 447
Molin, F., 427
Molloy, C., 48, 142, 145, 146, 157, 173, 214, 345, 419, 441
Monmouth, Duchess of, 214
Montfleury, A. J., 404, 405, 419, 447
Montgomery, F., 424
Moore, E., 61, 137, 184, 206, 269, 345, 423, 441
Moore, Sir T., 49, 106, 345
Morand, E., 404

Morari, L., 393
Morel, L., 93
Morell, T., 345, 388, 395, 399, 400, 441
Morris, R., 345
Morselli, A., 229, 397
Moss, T., 345
Motte, Houdard de la, 405
Motteux, P. A., 38, 44, 58, 129, 149, 209–10, 226–9, 259–60, 274, 315, 345–6, 389, 395, 399, 437, 441, 446, 447
Mottley, J., 110, 160, 188, 243, 346, 441
Mottley, J., 110, 160, 188, 243, 346, 441
Mountford, N., 62, 78, 128–30, 132, 442
Mountfort, Mrs, 276
Murphy, A., 428
Muses' Mercury, The, 5
Myers, C. L., 226

Nabbes, T., 141, 177
Nash, Madam de la, 273
Neri, G. B., 229, 391
Nesbit, G., 346
Nettleton, G. H., 1
Newlin, C. M., 418
New Theatrical Dictionary, The, 266
Newton, J., 346
New Wells, theatre, 272
Nichols, C. W., 416, 423, 426
Nicolini (Nicolino Grimaldi), 278
Noack, F. E., 417
Noble savage, the, in drama, 182, 240
Noisy, Mdlle, 46
Nolte, F. O., 413
Norfolk, Duke of, his actors, 411
Noris, M., 391, 399
Norris, H., 132, 134, 278, 346–7
Northman, 228, 274
Norwich, theatre, in, 4, 410, 411
Nouvelles Littéraires, 88
Noyes, R. G., 419

O'Bryan, 40
Odell, G. C. D., 26–30, 34, 37–9, 68, 94, 106, 195, 211, 220, 223, 280
Odell, T., 142, 160–1, 179, 215, 243, 347, 429
Odingsells, G., 178, 347
Oldfield, Mrs, 40, 49–51, 80, 149, 161–2, 167–8, 190, 193, 213, 276, 278, 283, 286; influence on Cibber, 185

Oldmixon, J., 26, 30, 53, 105, 160, 233, 347, 442
Old Woman's Magazine, The, 355
Opera, Italian and English, 1–2, 51, 73, 208, 225–37, 424–5
Orlandini, G. M., 394, 397
Ottoboni, Cardinal, 229, 395
Otway, T., 1, 8, 55–9, 60, 61, 67, 71, 97–8, 105, 111, 115–8, 120, 123–4, 129–30, 131, 198, 247, 257, 264
Ovid, 236
Owen, E., 275–6
Owen, R., 347, 442
Ozell, J., 71, 144, 152, 347, 420, 442

Pack, actor, 166, 278
Paisible, instrumentalist, 47, 279, 285
Palaprat, J., 405
Palmer, C., 150
Pantomimes, 1–2, 25, 51, 208, 251–8, 425
Paradies, P. D., 393
Parallel betwixt...Cato and...Cato of Utica, A, 88
Parfitt, G. E., 421
Pariati, 390
Parry, E. A., 12
Pasquali, G., 399
Paterson, J., 347
Paterson, W., 23, 112, 348, 442
Pathos, popularity of, 60
Patrick, S., 348
Patriotism, in drama, 20
Peck, F., 348
Pelli, C. A., 391
Penley, B. S., 410
Pennecuick, A., 348
Pepusch, J. C., 228, 242, 259–60, 279, 299, 399, 424
Perry, H. T. E., 420
Pescetti, O., 389, 390, 391, 392
Philips, A., 54, 57–9, 72, 86, 95, 106–7, 116, 198, 262, 348, 442
Philips, J., 348–9, 442
Phillips, E., 247, 349
Phillips, R., 349
Phillips, T., 349
Phillips, W., 26, 64, 107, 176, 349, 442
Pickering & Chatto, 409
Pietro, musician, 278
Pilotta, Signorina, opera singer, 285

Pinkethman, actor, 4, 38, 41, 47, 155, 278, 279, 287, 426
Piovene, A., 449
Piron, A., 405
Pix, Mrs M. G., 31, 50, 70, 74, 96–7, 104, 160, 171–2, 181, 349–50, 419, 442
Planché, J. R., 414
Plautus, 140, 143, 158, 178, 316, 326, 383
Players turn'd Academicks, The, 5
Poisson, R., 403
Politics in the theatre, 83, 86, 98, 239, 241, 251
Pope, A., 182, 213, 236, 269, 286, 443; edits Shakespeare, 67; advice of, regarding Cato, 87; supports Lillo, 120; prologue by, 233; attitude to theatre, 3 Dunciad, The, 3, 213–14, 230, 252
Epistle to Dr Arbuthnot, An, 91
Pope, W. J. M., 429
Popple, W., 13, 144, 184, 200–1, 350
Porpora, N., 389, 392, 393, 394, 396, 397, 399
Porta, G., 396
Porter, Mrs M., 160, 276, 278, 283, 286, 291
Post Boy, The, 193, 301, 303, 320
Post Man, The, 296, 301, 303, 316, 321
Potter, H., 350
Potter, J., 23, 412, 429
Potter, Mrs, actress, 93
Powell, G., 11, 100, 276, 282, 287, 289, 292
Powell, M., 272, 350, 430
Powell, Mrs, 278
Price, L. M., 418
Prince, Mrs, 276
Pritchard, 350
Prologues, immoral, 160
Prompter, The, 39
Proposal for the Better Regulation of the Stage, A, 7, 43
Proscenium doors, 25
Provincial theatres, 410–11
Pseudo-classicism, influence of, 5, 24, 27, 51–66, 85–96
Punch's Theatre, 272, 430
Puppet theatre, 273
Purcell, D., 170, 225, 233, 238, 399

Queensberry, Duchess of, 240
Quin, J., 12, 40–1, 65, 91, 93, 123

Racine, influence of, 62, 72–3, 75, 80–1, 86, 95, 117, 120, 129, 136, 401, 403, 405, 406, 417, 432, 435, 439, 442, 443, 444
Rafter, Miss, 15, 244
Ralph, J., 140, 152, 267, 350, 443; Case of our Present Theatrical Disputes, The, 68; Taste of the Town, The, 39; Touch Stone, The, 263
Ramondon, musician, 278
Ramsay, A., 250, 350, 443
Randal, J., 351, 443
Randolph, T., 141, 204, 224
Ravenscroft, T., 9, 55, 128–31, 134, 136–8, 157, 216
Read, S. E., 436
Reed, J., 351
Reflections on the...Provok'd Husband, 190
Regnard, J. F., influence of, 145, 195, 403, 404, 405, 406, 407, 419, 433, 436, 440, 442
Remarks on Lady Jane Gray, 102
Remarks on...the Conscious Lovers, 193
Remarks on the...Roman Father, 95
Remarks on the Tragedy of Eurydice, 83
Remarks on the Tragedy of Timoleon, 81
Rennel, G., 6
Repertoires of the theatres, 55–7, 128–39
Resta, N., 400
Rhodes, R. C., 436
Ricci, M., scene painter, 34
Riccoboni, M. J., 401, 405, 406
Riccoboni, Mme., 423
Rich, C., 274, 287, 291, 429
Rich, J., 30, 34, 68, 83, 252, 271–2, 282, 289, 290–2, 425, 427, 430, 443; revives Hamlet for Shakespeare's monument, 69
Richardson, S., 122, 179, 206, 246, 423
Richmond, Duke of, 4, 411
Richmond, theatres at, 4, 70, 410
Riots, in theatres, 12
Robe, Mrs J., 351, 443
Roberts, instrumentalist, 279
Robertson, J. G., 401
Robins, Mrs, 279
Robins, Gertrude, 121
Robinson, scene painter, 413
Robinson, Miss, 49, 160

Robinson, W., 351
Rodman, G. B., 418
Roger, actor, 285
Rogers, musician, 278
Rogers, W. H., 421
Rogers, Mrs, 276
Rolli, P. A., 388, 389, 390, 391,
    392, 393, 394, 395, 396, 397,
    398, 423, 424, 449
Roome, E., 443
Rose Anthony, Sister, 411
Roseingrave, T., 396
Rosenfeld, Sybil, 410, 413, 442
Ross, J. L., 411
Rossi, 224, 394, 397, 398
Rousseau, J. J., influence of, 145–6,
    182, 203, 441; praises Lillo,
    120
Rowe, N., 18–19, 24, 28, 31, 35,
    50–1, 57–9, 60–2, 70, 74, 81,
    98–102, 111, 114, 116–7, 198,
    209, 252, 257, 264, 338, 351–3,
    417, 443
Rowley, S., 70, 97
Ruel, du, dancer, 278, 289, 292
Ryan, L., 279, 353

S. H., Cursory Remarks on the Non-
    juror, 190
Sack, Le, musician, 285
Sadler's Wells, theatre, 272, 430
Saggione, G., 227, 279, 399
St Foix, G. F. P., 206, 406
St James's Evening Post, 4
Sainte-Albine, R. de, 415
Sale, W. M., 435
Salvi, A., 389, 390, 395, 448,
    449
Salvini, A. M., 88
Salvioli, R., 229
Sandford, 353
Sandoni, P., 395
Sani, D., 394
Sarrazin, G., 240
Saunders, Mrs, 278
Savage, J., 353
Savage, R., 53, 172, 353
Scarlatti, A., 228, 396, 397, 399
Scarron, P., 404, 413–14
Scenery, 30–3
Scenes, entrance to, 11
Schicksalstragödie, 118–9
Schiller, J. C. F., 2, 120
Schlegel, J. H., 94
Schulz, W. E., 240
Scotland, theatres in, 4
Scott, Sir W., 93

Scouten, A. H., 416, 421, 430, 432,
    436
Seibt, R., on Mrs Centlivre, 168,
    421
Seneca, influence of, 89, 93
Senesino, 266, 286
Senior, F. D., 421
Sentimentalism, 1–2, 128, 179–220,
    243, 246, 248
Servandoni, scene painter, 34
Settle, E., 6, 8, 31, 33, 56, 60, 74,
    78, 80, 82, 84, 98, 233–4, 266,
    353–4, 359, 443–4
Sewell, G., 6, 20, 43, 61, 106, 157,
    190, 262, 354
Sewell, W., Vindication of the
    English Stage, A, 88
Shadwell, C., 9, 42, 53, 126, 132–3,
    136, 145, 176, 183, 354, 444
Shadwell, T., 6, 55–7, 125, 128,
    130–3, 137, 142, 174–7, 179,
    206, 223
Shakespeare, W., 10–11, 24, 26, 35,
    46, 48, 52, 55–9, 60–3, 67–9,
    70, 72, 75, 104, 106, 114,
    128–38, 140–2, 144, 162, 170,
    174, 191, 195, 198, 203, 211,
    214, 220, 222, 223, 238, 247,
    252, 256–7, 267, 332, 333,
    355, 359, 370, 383, 423; adap-
    tations of, 44, 111, 157; come-
    dies of criticised by Gildon,
    125; ghost of in epilogues, 67;
    influence of on tragedy, 66–8,
    96, 416; on Havard, 113; on
    Hill, 109; on Rowe, 101; on
    Young, 113; monument of, 69,
    258; revivals of, 67–9, roman-
    tic comedy of, 126
'Shakespeare's Ladies', 416
Sheffield, John, Duke of Bucking-
    hamshire, 355
Shepherd, E., 429, 430
Shepherd's Market, theatre, 273
Sherburn, G., 423
Sheridan, R. B., 218
Sheridan, T., 41, 144, 215, 269, 355,
    444
Sheridan, Dr T., 355, 444
Shirley, J., 141, 156, 187, 205, 222,
    301
Shirley, W., 58, 70–1, 113, 355, 444
Shuckburgh, C., 355
Shudofsky, M. M., 417, 422
Silvani, F., 393
Simpson, instrumentalist, 279
Singer, H. W., 115

Skepwith, Sir T., 271, 291
Smart, C., 355
Smith, actor, 287
Smith, instrumentalist, 279
Smith, E., 72, 80, 232, 355, 444
Smith, D. F., 428
Smith, D. N., 416, 417
Smith, J. C., 236
Smith, J. H., 419, 421, 422
Smollett, T. G., 114, 355, 444
Smythe, J. M., 10, 19, 164, 232, 355
Sommer, H., 355
Sonneck, O. G. T., 31
Sophocles, influence of, 63, 120, 444, 447
Southampton, Duke of, 70, 333
Southern, R., 410, 413
Southerne, T., 8, 37, 47, 55–9, 60–2, 71, 114, 116, 120, 142, 173, 355–6
Southwark, theatre in, 273
Soyan, musician, 278, 285
Spanish drama, influence of, 146
Sparks, actor, 41
Spateman, T., 356
Spectator, The, 36–7, 39, 80, 87, 192–3, 229, 239
Spectatoriaale Schouwburg, 120
Spence, J., 87, 240
Spencer, H., 416
Spiller, actor, 363
Spiller, Mrs, 49
Sprague, A. C., 433, 447
Stage's Glory, The, 252
Stampiglio, S., 227, 391, 393, 397
Stanley, Sir J., 289, 292
Stanning, Sir A., killed in play-house, 11
Stanzani, T., 226, 389
Starr, H. W., 83
Steele, Sir R., 1–3, 10, 19, 29, 34–8, 44–5, 128–32, 134–8, 140, 143–4, 155, 157, 159, 180, 182–3, 188, 191, 193–6, 199–200, 207, 219, 230, 261, 271, 276, 283, 295, 356–7, 422–3, 444; attacked by Dennis, 17; prologue by, 87; pamphlet on, 193
Mr Steele's Apology, 192
Tatler, The, 9, 11, 30, 35–6, 41–2, 62
Steffani, A., 228, 400
Sterling, J., 58, 357
Sterne, L., 121, 179
Stevens, D. H., 412
Stevens, O. H., 240

Stevens, John, 358
Stevens, John, 216, 266, 358
Stewart, P., 423
Stonehill, C., 436
Story on which...the Roman Father is founded, The, 95
Straus, R., 204
Strindberg, A., 2
Stroler's Pacquet Open'd, 4, 216
Strolling actors, 4, 410–11
Sturmy, J., 90, 178, 358
Sutherland, J. R., 416, 417, 424
Sutreau, 401, 437
Swaen, A. E. H., 240, 419, 425
Swift, J., 19, 182, 239; on tragedy, 59; suggestion to Gay, 3; Gulliver's Travels, 233; Thoughts on Various Subjects, 24; adaptation of, 267
Swiny O. (see Macswiny), 22, 32, 36, 58, 79, 129, 144, 208–9, 229, 270, 271, 276, 283–7, 291, 342–3, 391, 397, 440

Tasso, T., 74, 77, 224, 432, 435, 442
Tate, N., 8, 216, 264, 358
Taverner, W., 79, 126, 133, 140–1, 157, 170, 171, 174, 197, 232, 358
Templers, objection of, to Miller, 13
Terence, influence of, 143, 192, 215, 261, 316, 348
Terradellas, D., 390, 396
Thaler, A., 280, 410
Théâtre anglois, Le, 88
Théâtre Italien, Le, 144
Theatre Royal turn'd into a Mountebank's Stage, 190
Theatres, rise of new, 4
Theobald, J., 358, 444
Theobald, L., 6, 31, 57, 67, 71, 78–9, 118, 222, 235, 254, 259, 264, 358–9, 380, 381, 399, 417, 444–5, 447; prologue by, 62
Thomas, W., 113
Thomson, A., 360
Thomson, J., 3, 23, 27, 59, 63, 92–4, 96, 264, 360, 445
Thorp, W., 417
Thurmond, J., 253, 279, 360
Tickell, T., 19, 64
Tofts, Mrs C., 278, 290
Tolksdorf, C., 425
Tolson, F., 360
Tomkis, T., 208, 437

Tories, 16
Tosti, Italian singer, 226
Tour, Madame La, 285
Tracy, J., 82, 111, 360
Tragedy, popularity of, 55–66, 415–6
Tragi-comedy, 220–6
Trapp, J., 20, 79–80, 360–1, 445
Trotter, Mrs C., 104, 176, 361
Trout, actor, 278
Tunbridge Wells, theatre at, 4
Turner, W., 260
Twickenham, performances at, 410

Underhill, C., 42, 278
Unfortunate General, The, 88
Unities, in drama, 52–3

Vadé, J. J., influence of, 145
Valentini (Valentino Urbani), 38, 229, 278, 285
Valeriano, 285
Vanburgh, Sir J., 15, 22, 35, 46, 128–39, 144–5, 147, 148, 150–3, 190, 208, 221, 226, 252, 271, 275, 284–5, 288–9, 291, 361–3, 419, 420, 443, 445
Vanneschi, F., 388, 391, 392, 393, 394, 396, 398, 448, 449
Vasse, influence of, 193
Veracini, F. M., 388, 393, 397, 398
Verbruggen, actor, 276
Victor, B., *History of the Theatres*, 109, 112; *Epistle to Sir R. Steele*, 193
Viéville, L. de la, 424
Villiers, J., Duke of Buckingham, 42, 126, 128–33, 159, 218, 269, 395
Vinci, L., 392
Virgil, 223
Vitturi, B., 390
Voisine, J., 417
Voltaire, 71–3, 88, 90, 94, 108–11, 417, 435, 436, 438, 441, 444; praises *Cato*, 88

Wagner, B. M., 439
Wales, Prince of, 15
Walker, T., 209, 363
Walker, Thomas, 222, 244, 363
Walker, W., 171, 363, 445
Walpole, Sir R., 95, 412
Walsh, W., share in *Squire Trelooby* 152, 443, 445, 446

Walter, instrumentalist, 279
Wandesford, O. S., 19, 71, 363
Ward, Sir A. W., 1, 97–8, 102, 115, 120, 191, 199, 209
Ward, E., 363
Ward, H., 363, 446
Warner, booth holder, 354
Wassermann, E. R., 415
Waterson, O., 183
Watts, G. T., 410
Weaver, J., 48, 252, 380, 383, 385, 386, 425, 446, 447
Webster, B., *The Stage*, 36
Webster, J., 416, 448
Weddell, Mrs, 363
Weekes, J. E., 363
Wells, J. W., 445
Wells, M. P., 425
Welsted, L., 10, 173–4, 233, 363–4
Werner, Z., 121
West, D. I., 424
West, G., 364
West, R., 12, 90, 364
Wetherby, J., 364
Whigs, 16
Whincop, T., 6, 10, 13, 15–16, 18, 22, 24, 81, 83–6, 90–4, 97, 102, 104, 106–7, 109–12, 119, 123, 147–9, 156–7, 159, 165, 167, 169, 172, 175–7, 188, 192, 194, 202, 206, 208, 210–15, 233, 235, 237, 242–4, 246, 248, 260, 263, 364
Whitehead, W., 72, 95, 180, 364, 446
Whiting, G. W., 445
Wilkinson, R., 171, 364
Wilkinson, T., 329
Wilks, R., 30, 39–40, 41, 87, 166–7, 233, 271, 276–8, 283–4
William III, King, 19, 98–9
Williams, J., 364
Willis, Mrs E., 276, 279, 286
Willis, Mrs M., 279, 286
Willis, R., 286
Wilson, Mona, 421
Winchelsea, Countess of, 214
Wiseman, Mrs J., 104, 160, 364, 446
Women as men, in plays, 39–40
Wood, F. T., 410, 421, 422, 429, 432, 440
Woods, C. B., 423, 432
Woodward, H., 446
Woodward, J., 213
Worsdale, J., 364
Wright, H., 418

Wycherley, W., 128–37, 139, 142–3, 150, 153–4, 159–61, 165, 257
Wyndham, H. S., 31, 430

Yarrow, J., 364, 385
Yeats, actor, 272, 354
Yonge, Sir William, 446

Young, E., 3, 26, 50, 57, 59, 70–2, 88, 113, 157, 364–5, 446; letter of, 19
Young, Miss, 279

Zeitvogel, A., 417
Zeno, A., 388, 390, 392, 393, 394, 395, 396, 398, 399, 400